Concepts and Theories of Human Development

SECOND EDITION

Concepts and Theories of Human Development

SECOND EDITION

Richard M. Lerner
The Pennsylvania State University

LEA LAWRENCE ERLBAUM ASSOCIATES, PUBLISHERS
Mahwah, New Jersey

To Sam Goldfarb, Sam Korn, and Sam Karson

Copyright acknowledgments will be found on page 521.

Originally published 1986.

Lawrence Erlbaum Associates, Inc., Publishers
10 Industrial Avenue
Mahwah, New Jersey 07430

LC Card Number: 85-28127

ISBN 0-8058-2682-3

Books published by Lawrence Erlbaum Associates are printed
on acid-free paper, and their bindings are chosen
for strength and durability.

Printed in the United States of America

10 9 8 7 6 5 4 3 2 1

Deaign: Glen M. Edelstein
Cover Design: Naomi Osnos
Cover Art: Detail of Michelangelo sketch (Casa Buonarroti, Florence)

PREFACE to the Second Edition

Ten years have passed since the publication of the first edition of *Concepts and Theories of Human Development*. During that time there has been considerable activity among developmentalists in regard to the philosophical, conceptual, and theoretical issues pertinent to human development. Although the basic organization and orientation of the second edition of *Concepts and Theories of Human Development* remain consistent with those found in the first edition, the revision has profited immensely from the literature of the last decade.

The goals of the book remain the same: to discuss the philosophical and historical bases of the key ideas found in the study of human development; to indicate how these bases relate to the core conceptual issues of development—the nature–nurture controversy, the continuity–discontinuity issue, and the issue of stability–instability in development; to discuss how these issues influence the formulation of different theories of development; to present overviews of instances of the major types of developmental theories, in order to indicate the links among philosophy, concepts, theory, and research; to evaluate research associated with different theories of development in order to appraise the usefulness of a given theory and the soundness of its stance on core issues of development; and to discuss the implications of philosophy, concepts, and theory for the research methods and research designs employed in the study of human development.

Moreover, my orientation toward these presentations remains the same. In both editions it is clear that I favor an approach to development which in the first edition was labeled organismic-interactional, or probabilistic-epigenetic, and which in the second

edition is additionally denoted by such terms as organismic-contextual and developmental-contextual.

The introduction of these new terms may suggest that my thinking has evolved. I hope that it has, and that the changes are evident in the second edition.

In the ten years since the publication of the first edition I have spent considerable time thinking and writing: about the usefulness of a contextual philosophy for developmental theory; about the nature of developmental processes across the lifespan; and about the usefulness of the life-span view of human development as a general orientation in trying to understand the character of developmental processes and the relations between individuals and contexts that may underlie these processes. These interests are reflected throughout the second edition, and have led to broadened discussions of:

- the philosophical and historical bases of the study of human development (Chapters 1 and 2);
- the nature–nurture controversy (Chapter 3), its manifestation in the debate about the heritability of intelligence and of racial differences in IQ (Chapter 4), and its possible "resolution" in regard to developmental theory through the adoption of a probabilistic-epigenetic, or developmental-contextual, orientation (Chapter 5);
- the continuity–discontinuity issue, its relationship to the issue of stability-instability in development, and the issue of the nature of plasticity across the life span (Chapter 6);
- the character of the different theoretical

approaches to development, and their relationship to the key conceptual issues of development (Chapter 7);

- major instances of stage theories (Chapter 8), of differential approaches (Chapter 9), of ipsative approaches (Chapter 10), and of empirical- or theoretical-behavioristic approaches (Chapter 11), and an evaluation of empirical literatures associated with each; and
- the implications of philosophy, concepts, and theory for developmental research methodology and design, and some of the key features, problems, and potentials of developmental research methods (Chapter 12).

The useful expansions of and changes in my thinking that are reflected in the second edition derive from the contributions to the literature made by many colleagues. Their writings and their discussions with me not only have helped me grow intellectually but also have set a standard of excellence to which I can only aspire. Thus, I am deeply grateful to: Margaret M. Baltes, Paul B. Baltes, Albert Bandura, Jack Block, Sandor B. Brent, Orville G. Brim, Jr., Urie Bronfenbrenner, Jeanne Brooks-Gunn, Nancy Busch-Rossnagel, Stella Chess, Anne Colby, W. Edward Craighead, Roger A. Dixon, Sanford Dornbusch, Judith Dunn, Glen H. Elder, Jr., David L. Featherman, Nancy L. Galambos, Arthur S. Goldberger, Eugene Gollin, Gilbert Gottlieb, William T. Greenough, Ruth T. Gross, Norma G. Haan, Beatrix A. Hamburg, Sara Harkness, Willard W. Hartup, Christopher Hertzog, E. Mavis Hetherington, Jerry Hirsch, Karen Hooker, David F. Hultsch, Saburo Iwawaki, Jerome Kagan, Bernard Kaplan, Philip C. Kendall, John R. Knapp, Sam J. Korn, Gisela Labouvie-Vief, Michael E. Lamb, P. Herbert Leiderman, Jacqueline V. Lerner, Michael Lewis, Lynn S. Liben, Gardner Lindzey, Lewis P. Lipsitt, David Magnusson, Gerald E. McClearn, Harry McGurk, Susan M. McHale, John A. Meacham, John W. Meyer, Dale T. Miller, Walter Mischel, Paul H. Mussen, John R. Nesselroade, Willis F. Overton, David S. Palermo, Ross D. Parke, Marion Perlmutter, Anne C. Petersen, Robert Plomin, Hayne W. Reese, M. Bernadette Reidy, Klaus F. Riegel, Matilda W. Riley, Carol D. Ryff, Sandra Scarr, K. Warner Schaie, Ellin K. Scholnick, Martin E. P. Seligman, Virginia S. Sexton, Lonnie Sherrod, Alexander W. Siegel, Ellen Skinner, M. Brewster Smith, Gwendolyn T. Sorell, Graham B. Spanier, Laurence D. Steinberg, Charles Super, Alexander Thomas, Ethel Tobach, Fred W. Vondracek, Alexander von Eye, Franz E. Weinert, Sheldon H. White, Sherry Willis, Michael Windle, and Joachim Wohlwill.

I also wish to thank my excellent graduate students, who were always ready to read and discuss my drafts and always capable of pointing out places where my writing—and my thinking—could be improved. I thank for all their help: Athena Droogas, Patricia L. East, Wendy Gamble, Marjorie B. Kauffman, Joseph S. Kucher, and Kathleen Lenerz. I am grateful to Joy Barger, Teresa Charmbury, and Kathleen Hooven for their expert and professional secretarial assistance. I thank Colleen Kearns and Leslie Parkes for their help in compiling the references and indices.

Finally, during the long gestation period for this second edition I have been fortunate to receive the support of several institutions. I began planning and writing the second edition while I was a 1980–1981 Fellow at the Center for Advanced Study in the Behavioral Sciences. I am grateful for financial support provided by National Institute of Mental Health Grant #5-T32-MH14581-05 and by the John D. and Catherine T. MacArthur Foundation, and for the assistance of the center's staff. Since leaving the center and through this writing, my work has been funded in part by grants from the John D. and Catherine T. MacArthur Foundation and from the William T. Grant Foundation, and I am grateful for this support. I completed the writing of the second edition during the 1983–1984 academic year, which I began as a Visiting Scientist at the Max-Planck Institute for Human Development and Education in Berlin, and which I ended by being once again in residence, throughout the summer, at the Center for Advanced Study in the Behavioral Sciences. I appreciate greatly the support for my work provided by both institutions.

Finally, the institution to which I owe my greatest debt is my family. From Jacqueline Lerner and our children, Justin and Blair, I received all the emotional support and the diversions I needed to keep returning to my task until it was completed.

R.M.L.

University Park, Pennsylvania
September 1985

PREFACE to the First Edition

In this text I have attempted to provide the student with a general introduction to core concepts and major theories in developmental psychology. An integration is made of such concepts and theories, along with their philosophical bases, within a framework that presents divergent points of view about these ideas. However, the Organismic, Interactionist developmental viewpoint is clearly given major emphasis. While discussions of the views and research of learning-oriented developmentalists, for example, are presented and evaluated, as is the work of particular ethological writers, these positions are contrasted with the Organismic developmental notions of such theorists as Piaget, Werner, Schneirla, Kohlberg, and Thomas. The work of these latter theorists is representative of an orientation to developmental psychology which is viewed as being the most tenable and useful conceptual synthesis currently available. In essence then, the text attempts to integrate and evaluate core concepts, major theories, and research in developmental psychology from an Organismic, Interactionist perspective.

The format of this text stands in contrast to most other human development texts which primarily emphasize research findings. Of course, I believe that such "facts" are necessary for students. But the meaning of such information, and indeed what we actually consider to be factual, is constantly altered in the face of empirical advances and new theoretical integrations. Hence, I believe that students will appreciate and assimilate the facts of development if they are acquainted with the "meanings" attached to these facts by developmental psychologists. For this reason, and because of historical trends within the field which have now come to stress the primacy of theoretical integra-

tion, I have written this book to emphasize such integrations. Students are still given "facts," but first they are given some bases for interpreting the possible "meanings" of these facts.

Three interrelated bases for understanding human development are offered. First, the Mechanistic and the Organismic philosophies of science are shown to provide both contrasting views of "humans" and alternative approaches to the major conceptual issues of psychological development. Second, various ways of formulating these issues (the nature-nurture and the continuity-discontinuity controversies) are discussed, and recent empirical research and debate about them are evaluated. For instance, the relevance of the nature-nurture controversy to concerns about the sources of racial differences in IQ scores is indicated. Similarly, the relation between the continuity-discontinuity issue and debates about the ontogenetic (and phylogenetic) generalizability of laws of learning and of life-span changes in intellectual functioning is discussed. Finally, ways are described in which the core conceptual issues of development may provide a basis for understanding the formulation of the major types of theoretical points of view in developmental psychology. The Stage, Differential, Ipsative, and Learning approaches are discussed, and major theories and research within each approach are introduced. Thus the Stage approaches of Piaget, Kohlberg, and Freud, the Differential theoretical formulations of Erikson, the differential empirical work of Kagan and Moss, and the life-span, multivariate, sequential research approaches of Schaie, Baltes, and Nesselroade are presented. In addition, the Ipsative research, involved in the New York Longitudinal Study, of

Thomas, Chess, Birch, Hertzig, and Korn, and the Learning-oriented work of Bijou and Baer and of Mischel is evaluated. Finally, the interrelation of developmental theory and research is presented along with a discussion of its social relevance.

While it is of course possible to provide the student with an integration of theory and fact by combining numerous readings and lecture materials, such a combination would not provide the student with what I consider to be a major asset of this book, which is the organization and integration of this material within what I hope is a convincing and useful framework from which to understand human development. This Organismic, Interactionist point of view, interrelated with its conceptual alternatives, permits an introduction to the study of developmental psychology that is, in my opinion, both pedagogically appropriate and more closely aligned with current emphases in the discipline than is any other single treatment.

During the course of writing the text, my ideas have been challenged and honed by the numerous colleagues with whom I have discussed the material and who have read various portions of several drafts of the book. Specifically, I would like to thank John Knapp, Joseph Fitzgerald, Samuel Karson, Henry Orloff, and Stuart Karabenick, all of Eastern Michigan University, and the many reviewers provided by the publisher. In addition, I am in great debt to the people who provided my training: Harry Beilin, Samuel Messick, Joseph Church, Elizabeth Gellert, and of course, Sam Korn. The diverse contributions of these people have sharpened my ideas, strengthened my arguments, and improved my presentation. Any limitations that remain stem totally from me. I am also grateful to Cathy Gendron for her excellent drawings of psychologists. I am also indebted to the hundreds of students who have listened semester after semester to lectures that attempted to present the material contained in this book and who have read and used various drafts of this book as their course text. Here I would especially like to thank Michael Karson for his thorough work and useful criticisms. My students' enthusiasm, comments, and interactions with me—and likewise the lack of these things—have led to substantial alterations in the format and style of presentation of various text sections.

Ypsilanti, Michigan
January 1976

R.M.L.

CONTENTS

6   The Continuity–Discontinuity Issue   183

10   The Ipsative Approach   360

11   Theoretical- and Empirical-Behaviorism Approaches   406

12   Implications for Research   441

1 | *Human Development: Facts or Theory?*

STUDENTS AND BASIC COURSES IN SCIENCES: FACTS VERSUS THEORY

"Well, I've learned a lot of facts, but what do they all *mean?*"

A typical comment from a college student? I believe so. Many undergraduates feel that college courses are often concerned only with the memorization of facts. It is generally believed by students and professors alike that facts (perhaps crammed into one's head the night before an exam) are usually soon forgotten. On the other hand, general concepts are retained for a much longer time. Still, many basic college courses ask the student to deal with a lot of facts.

Certainly, with today's explosion of scientific research, there are more facts to know than ever before. Thus, to get an overview of a field like child or developmental psychology, a student must become acquainted with such information. Yet as more and more data are collected each year, rapid clarifications, refinements, and advancements are made in factual knowledge (see Ghiselli 1974).

For example, before the work of Fantz and his colleagues (e.g., Fantz 1958; Fantz, Ordy, and Udelf 1962), it was believed that a newborn infant's visual world is comprised of blurry images, either because of incomplete maturation of the visual system or

because of too few appropriate visual experiences. Forever, Fantz was able to demonstrate that even in the first few weeks of life infants are capable of accommodating to nearby visual stimulation and also of seeing patterns. Thus the "fact" that infants can see only diffuse light-and-dark stimulation and not patterns was found not to be a fact at all. Through use of the methods he devised, Fantz was able to clarify, refine, and advance our factual knowledge of infants' visual perception.

Similarly, other such "facts" of psychological development have fallen by the wayside in the face of new research findings. For instance, for many decades a basic belief about intellectual development concerned the decreases in functions that were assumed to characterize the later years of life. It was held that as people progressed through adulthood to old age there was an accelerating decline in their mental functioning (e.g., see Horn 1970; Schaie, Labouvie, and Buech 1973). These decrements were supposed to represent a certain "fact" of psychological development and functioning across the life span as shown by the data in Figure 1.1. Yet, through the work of K. Warner Schaie, Paul B. Baltes, and their colleagues (e.g., Baltes, Dittmann-Kohli, and Dixon 1984; Baltes and Schaie 1974; Nesselroade, Schaie and Baltes 1972; Schaie 1965; Schaie, Labouvie, and Buech 1973; Schaie and Strother 1968), new techniques for the measurement of age

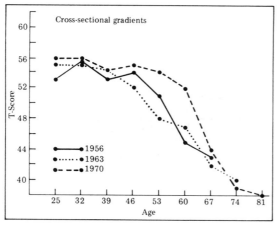

FIGURE 1.1

Age changes in intellectual ability, as revealed by conventional, cross-sectional research techniques. Note the *decreases* in intellectual ability that occur with increases in age.

Source: Schaie, K. W., G. B. Labouvie, and B. U. Buech (1973), Generational and cohort-specific differences in adult cognitive funtioning: A fourteen-year study of independent samples, *Developmental Psychology* 9. Copyright 1973 by the American Psychological Association. Reprinted by permission.

changes in intellectual development and functioning across the life span have been devised. The application of these techniques in several studies has indicated that there may not be a general decline in intellectual functioning throughout the later years after all. Rather, the results of some of these studies (e.g., Schaie, Labouvie, and Buech 1973) indicate that for *some* measures of intellectual functioning there is no age-associated decrease. In fact, for some measures there seems to be an increase!

To illustrate, in 1956 Schaie (Baltes and Schaie 1974; Schaie 1965; Schaie and Strother 1968) began to study 500 people ranging in age from twenty-one (young adulthood) to seventy (the aged years). He administered two tests of cognitive ability, the Thurstone and Thurstone Primary Mental Abilities Test and Schaie's Test of Behavioral Rigidity. Seven years later 301 of the people were retested with the same instruments. Using such statistical techniques

as factor analysis, Schaie and his colleagues found that four different types of cognitive abilities were being assessed by these tests:

1. *Crystallized intelligence,* which measures knowledge attained through education and socialization (for example, verbal comprehension and number skills). This is the type of intelligence measured by most traditional IQ tests (Baltes and Schaie 1974).

2. *Cognitive flexibility,* which measures the ability to shift from one way of thinking to another.

3. *Visual-motor flexibility,* which measures a similar shifting ability, but in tasks requiring a coordination between vision and muscle movements.

4. *Visualization,* which measures the ability to organize and process visual information.

Schaie found that, depending on how his data were analyzed, differential support was found for the presence of intellectual decline. Specifically, when he analyzed his data in accordance with the requirements of a specific type of research design, less evidence was found for decline.

To explain this finding we should note that there are two frequently used ways to design research pertinent to the measurement of development. Cross-sectional studies measure different age groups of people (e.g., five-, ten-, and fifteen-year-olds) at one point in time (e.g., in 1985). In longitudinal studies, in turn, a group of people all born at one point in time (e.g., in 1965) are measured at different points in time (e.g., in 1970, 1975, and 1980, when they are five, ten, and fifteen years old respectively). Thus, both techniques give information about how people of a particular age perform at a given point in time; but in cross-sectional studies people from groups born in different years (i.e., from different birth "cohorts") are studied, while in longitudinal studies people from the same birth cohort (people born in the same year) are studied.

A third type of design for developmental research has been developed by Schaie, Baltes, and John R. Nesselroade (Baltes 1968; Nesselroade and Baltes 1974; Nesselroade, Schaie, and Baltes 1972; Schaie 1965; Schaie and Strother 1968). This type of design is termed *sequential,* and it combines both cross-sectional and longitudinal components. For example, in one instance of a sequential design—a longitudinal sequential one—a cross section of people (i.e., people from different birth cohorts) is longitudinally (repeatedly) studied over the course of several times of measurement.

When Schaie and his colleagues analyzed their data cross-sectionally, they saw the adolescent-to-adulthood decline typically seen in such studies. However, when they looked at the longitudinal data within each of the birth cohort groups in their sequential design, they found a decline on only one of the four measures (visual-motor flexibility). In

fact, for the most important abilities—those involved in crystallized intelligence (Baltes and Schaie 1974) and visualization—a systematic *increase* in scores for all age groups was seen. Even those people over seventy years of age improved from the first testing to the second. Thus, as seen in Figure 1.2, older people scored lower than younger ones on the four measures of intelligence in both 1956 and 1963. However, for both crystallized intelligence and visualization, scores increased between these two times of testing, even for the older groups.

Similarly, data from a study by Schaie, Labouvie, and Buech (1973) show that when members of the same cohort are tested at succeeding times, there are many scores that increase. Yet if these within-cohort curves are not analyzed, and just cross-sectional curves are considered, the typical adolescent-to-adult decline is seen. The graphs in Figure 1.3 illustrate these findings.

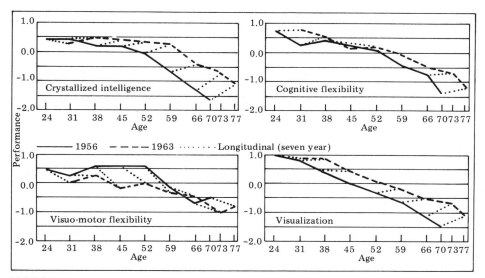

FIGURE 1.2

Age, time, and cohort components of change for four types of cognitive abilities: The solid lines slope downward, indicating that in both 1956 and 1963 older people scored lower than younger ones on various dimensions of intelligence. However, the dashed lines, which show how a given age group's performance changed from the first test to the second, reveal that in older groups crystallized intelligence and visualization go up, not down.

Source: Adapted from Baltes and Schaie (1974).

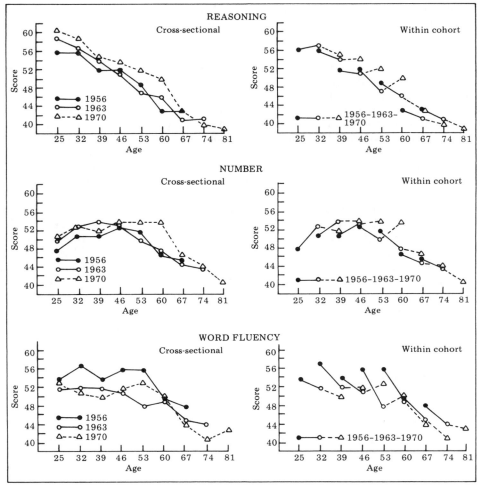

FIGURE 1.3

Cross-sectional (*left*) and within-cohort sequential (*right*) curves for scores on ability tests for reasoning, number, and word fluency, respectively.

Source: Adapted from Schaie, Labouvie, and Buech (1973).

Clearly then, the course of intellectual change from young adulthood onward is not just an age-related phenomenon. The above data indicate that differences in scores and patterns of change in scores from one time of measurement to another are associated mainly with membership in different birth cohort groups. In other words, how well a person performed at any one time, and whether that performance was stable or not, was associated more with cohort differences than with chronological age. It also appears that as far as the absolute level of ability scores are concerned, the measured intelligence of the general population is increasing across history. Perhaps because of better educational techniques, more geared to those cognitive attributes being measured in current tests, members of younger birth cohorts are more likely to achieve higher absolute scores than are members of older birth cohorts.

As such, not only do today's young adults have a higher level of cognitive ability—as measured by tests such as those used by Schaie, Baltes, Nesselroade, Labouvie, and their colleagues—than do members of older birth cohorts, but as is the case with members of *all* cohorts, they are likely to maintain much of this level of functioning across their life span. On the basis of findings from sequential studies, one may expect, then, that many of the levels and types of ability present in earlier life will be maintained or enhanced in the adult and aged years. In short, through the application of new measurement designs, Schaie and his associates were able to demonstrate that a long-held "fact" about cognitive development across the human life span was not a fact after all. Moreover, research by Baltes and Willis (1982) further indicates that even if intellectual decline *is* seen in the aged, it does not represent a necessarily unchangeable feature of their functioning. Baltes and Willis devised several training techniques intended to enhance the intellectual functioning of aged people (i.e., people in their seventh and eighth decades of life). These techniques were successful in increasing the performance on intelligence tests of the aged people, both immediately and in relatively long-term (several months) follow-up tests.

Numerous other examples to illustrate the impermanence of "facts" might be offered. For instance, the idea that adolescence is a developmental period invariably characterized by storm and stress is found both in scientific accounts of the period (Davis 1944; A. Freud 1969; Hall 1904; McCandless 1970) and in the popular media. Many writers have romanticized or dramatized the adolescent experience in novels, short stories, or news articles. Indeed, it is commonplace to survey a newsstand and find a magazine article describing the "stormy years" of adolescence, the new crazes or fads of youth, or the "explosion" of problems with teenagers—for instance, regarding crime or sexuality.

Yet, over the course of the last fifteen or so years, when medical, biological, and social scientists began to study the adolescent period intensively, there began to accumulate sound scientific information that countered these romantic literary characterizations of adolescence. For instance, many people hold a stereotype about adolescence (Anthony 1969) that suggests that because of the supposed rebelliousness and close contact of adolescents with their friends, parents must be more controlling and restrictive of their children during this time. In contrast, Bandura (1964) observed that by adolescence most children had so thoroughly adopted parental values and standards that parental restrictions actually were reduced. In addition, Bandura noted that although the storm-and-stress idea of adolescence implies a struggle by youth to free themselves of dependence on parents, parents begin to train their children in childhood to be *independent*. Finally, Bandura found that adolescents' choice of friends was not a major source of friction between adolescents and parents. Adolescents tended to form friendships with those who shared similar values. As such, the peers tended to support those standards of the parents that already had been adopted by the adolescents.

Bandura pointed out, however, that these observations do not mean that adolescence is a stressless, problemless period of life. He was careful to note that *no* period of life is free of crisis or adjustment problems, and that any period of life may present particular adjustment problems for some people and not for others. Thus one has to be careful about generalizing problems seen in one group of adolescents to all adolescents. To illustrate, in a portion of his study Bandura observed a sample of antisocial boys. Their excessive aggression did lead to their adolescence being associated with storm and stress. However, Bandura found that one could not appropriately view their problems as resulting just from adolescence. Their problem behaviors had been present throughout their childhood as well. However, when the boys were physically smaller, their parents were able to control their aggressive behavior better than they could during adolescence.

From Bandura's study it may be concluded that (1) even when storm and stress is seen in adolescence, it is not necessarily the result of events in adolescence but instead may be associated with developments prior to adolescence; and (2) storm and stress is not necessarily characteristic of the adolescent period—many possible types of adolescent development can occur. The existence of such different paths through adolescence is supported by the results of other studies.

Offer (1969) found three major routes through the adolescent period. He noted that there is a *continuous-growth* type of development involving smooth changes in behavior. Adolescents showing such development were not in any major conflict with their parents, and did not feel that parental rearing practices were inappropriate or that they themselves did not share parental values. Most adolescents fell into this category. Such a pattern is like the one we have seen Bandura describe. A second type of pattern is *surgent growth,* with development involving here an abrupt change but not necessarily the turmoil associated with storm and stress. Finally, however, Offer identified a *tumultuous-growth* type of adolescent development. Here crisis, stress, and problems characterize the period, and for such adolescents, "storm and stress" aptly characterizes the nature of their change.

Thus, only for some people is the adolescent period one of storm and stress. Indeed, based on the Bandura and Offer studies, it may be assumed that such a tumultuous period is involved for only a minority of adolescents. This conclusion is bolstered by the data of Douvan and Adelson (1966). In their study, as in the previously noted studies, most adolescents shared the basic values of their parents and were satisfied with their family life and the style of treatment by their parents. We may see, then, that available data are inconsistent with the stereotype that adolescence is a *generally* stressful and stormy period.

Such data allow us to recognize the point

that in an active science such as developmental psychology, the status of our knowledge will rapidly and continually be altered. It is possible—perhaps even likely—that what is a "fact" when a particular student begins a basic course may no longer be one by the end of it.

I do not intend simply to be irreverent about the role of facts in science. Facts are of course absolutely essential in any active scientific enterprise. But, to paraphrase Ludwig von Bertalanffy (1933), a biologist noted for his important theoretical contributions to that science, a collection of data no more makes a science than does a heap of bricks make a house!

What, then, builds the bricks of a science into a house? I believe it is the conceptual and theoretical issues of a science. An illustration will clarify my position. Certainly the listings in a telephone directory are facts. But a knowledge of the names in the phone book would certainly be, to quote singer-songwriter Bob Dylan, "useless and pointless knowledge." However, if one could relate such data to some conceptual framework, then perhaps some meaning could be provided. Let us suppose that I have a hypothesis, perhaps derived from some theory in social psychology, which predicts that a person with a particular ethnic background would tend to live in a neighborhood with other people having that same ethnic background. To test my hypothesis I spread out a large street map of the city and cut out each name and address in the phone book and place it on the appropriate place on the map. After a while a pattern begins to emerge. People with Italian-sounding names seem to cluster in one area, people with Irish-sounding names in another area, and people with Jewish-sounding names in yet another. This example not only supports a hypothesis but illustrates the important point that a conceptual orientation provides a way of organizing a seemingly meaningless or obscure body of data into a meaningful and perhaps important body of factual knowledge.

We see, then, a major function of theory—

to integrate existing facts, to organize them in such a way as to give them meaning. Developmental psychologists may often have numerous facts available to them—for example, facts relating to children's thinking at various ages in their lives. The results of empirical studies might indicate that young children tend to use relatively general, global, and concrete categories to organize their thinking, while older children use more differentiated, specific, and abstract categories. For instance, the younger children might label all furry, four-legged creatures as "doggies," while the older child might have different labels (e.g., "dogs," "cats," and "horses"), might have a shared, superordinate label ("animals"), and might in addition recognize that all these creatures share the common but abstract quality of "life." While such facts are interesting in and of themselves, their meaning is not obvious; and certainly the implications of such facts for more general psychological development and functioning are not clear. Thus, when a scientist such as Jean Piaget (1950, 1970) offers a theory of the development of thought that allows such facts to be integrated and understood, and moreover specifies the empirically testable implications of such theoretical integrations for other areas of psychological development, the importance is obvious. Such theories are useful to developmental psychology because they integrate existing factual knowledge as well as further advancing our knowledge.

The point is, then, that while facts are important, they alone do not make a science. The development of science, I would argue, relies in addition on the advancement of theory. As a survey of the history of developmental psychology bears witness (Looft 1972), the scientific study of human development has itself evolved through an increasing emphasis on theory and conceptual integration. By turning now to a brief review of the history of the study of human development, we will be able to see not only the changing role of theory; in addition, and importantly, we will be able to introduce many of the key concepts of current develop-

mental psychology—concepts we shall discuss repeatedly in this book. These concepts have had a long history of influence on thinking about human development. As we move historically from the prescientific, philosophical discussions of development to today's current discussions—for instance, of the ways in which the concept of development and developmental psychology's theories and methods are influenced by philosophy—we shall see that issues pertinent to a few key concepts continue to be central.

HISTORICAL ROOTS OF THE STUDY OF HUMAN DEVELOPMENT

Have people always believed that humans develop? Have people always said that infants are different from children and that both are different from adolescents? Indeed, have "special" portions of the life span, such as adolescence or the aged years, always been held to exist? In fact, have people always believed that there is such a phenomenon as human development, and if not, when and why did such a belief arise?

Many of the central questions and controversies about human development are quite old, with roots in ancient Greece and the traditions of Western philosophy. Indeed, in both the 2,000 years of philosophy and about 100 years of pertinent science, the ideas advanced to explain development revolve around the same few issues. These issues represent the core concepts in any discussion of development, and differences among philosophers and scientists can be understood by looking at the stances they take in regard to such basic conceptual issues. These issues pertain most directly to one issue: the *nature-nurture controversy*. Although definable in several ways, this controversy relates to the relative roles of inborn characteristics and experiential influences in human development. Thus, in order to organize and understand the evolution involved in the history of ideas of development, it is necessary first to introduce briefly some definition of the nature-nurture issue.

The Historical Role of the Nature-Nurture Issue

The very first idea ever elaborated about human development involved what is still the most basic issue in development today: the *nature-nurture issue.* This pertains to the source of human behavior and development. Simply, a question is raised about where behavior and development come from. As soon as the very first ideas were formulated about what human behavior was and where it came from, a stance was taken in regard to this issue.

In its most extreme form the issue pertains to whether behavior and development derive from *nature* (or in modern terms, *heredity, maturation,* or *genes*) or, at the other extreme, whether behavior and development derive from *nurture* (or in more modern terms, *environment, experience,* or *learning*). However, whatever terms are used, the issue raises questions about how inborn, intrinsic, native, or in short, nature characteristics (for example, genes) may contribute to development and/or, in turn, how acquired, socialized, environmental, experienced, or in short, nurture characteristics (for example, stimulus-response connections) may play a role in development. Table 1.1 lists some terms used in this and later chapters that pertain to nature and nurture contributions, respectively. This table will be useful to refer to in much of the presentation that follows.

As this chapter proceeds, it will be seen that philosophers and scientists advanced ideas about development that pertain to nature, to nurture, *or* to some combination of the two (and hence they often use terms other than those listed in Table 1.1). It will be argued that all ideas about development relate to this issue and, in turn, that all other issues of development derive from the nature-nurture one. Although a fuller discussion of the relation of the nature-nurture issue to these other core issues of development will be reserved for later chapters, the

TABLE 1.1
Terms Associated with Nature or Nurture Conceptions of Development

Nature Terms	Nurture Terms
Genetic	Acquired
Heredity	Education
Inborn	Empiricism
Innate	Environment
Instinct	Experience
Intrinsic	Learning
Maturation	Socialization
Nativism	
Preformed	

present discussion of the history of philosophical and scientific concern with development can begin with this prominence of the nature-nurture issue in mind. In fact, one can regard this historical review as involving the swinging of a pendulum, a pendulum moving from conceptions of human development stressing nature to conceptions stressing nurture. However, it will be argued that a conception stressing either extreme is not appropriate.

Philosophical Roots

The beginnings of concern with the phenomena in the world around us can be traced to the first philosophers. Attempts to speculate about the elements in the world constitute philosophical statements, and this first occurred more than 2,000 years ago. It is estimated that in about 600 B.C., a Greek named Thales of Miletus (640–546 B.C.) became the first philosopher through his attempts to speculate about the nature of the universe in order to predict a solar eclipse (Clark 1957).

This event indicates that when humans first turned their attention to the nature of phenomena in their world, they were concerned with the characteristics of the universe and not the characteristics of humans themselves. Philosophical concerns about the character of the universe pertain to *cosmology,* and this topic remained the predominant focus of thinkers for several hundred years.

Thus ideas about the nature of humans, not to mention human development, were not historically the first ideas considered by philosophers. In fact, it was about 200 years later that the first major philosophical statement pertinent to the nature of humans was presented. Plato made this presentation.

PLATO (427–347 B.C.)

From Plato's ideas one can derive statements relevant to human development. Yet many of these derivations are indirect. Plato's writings, and those of philosophers for centuries following him, do not reflect a primary concern with human development, although ideas about human change across life were apparent. The portion of Plato's writing from which one can derive his major ideas relevant to development deals essentially with the mind-body problem.

This problem—a major concern to philosophers for over 2,000 years—inquires into the relation between the physical, spatial, and temporal body and the nonphysical, nonspatial, and nontemporal mind (or in Plato's term, "soul"). How does something that does not take up matter, space, or time (a soul) relate to something that does (a body)?

Plato reasoned that souls are eternal. He philosophized that there is a "realm of ideas," a spiritual place where souls reside. At birth, however, the body "traps" a particular soul. The soul remains in the body for the life of the person and returns to the realm of ideas when the person dies. Since the soul resides in the realm of ideas, it enters the body with these ideas at birth. That is, the person is born with *innate ideas,* with preexisting, preformed knowledge.

Thus Plato's idea about the relation between mind and body not only represents the first major statement about what humans are like but also represents a stance in regard to the nature-nurture issue. Humans are not the way they are primarily because of experience or education. They do not have to learn their knowledge. Rather, their knowledge is built into them; it is innate. Hence this first major statement about human behavior is a nature one. In short, Plato said humans are the way they are (that is, having their innate ideas) because they have a soul, and this soul is a nature-based phenomenon.

Additionally, Plato believed that the soul was divided into three layers, and these layers also have implications for a view of human development. The lowest layer of the soul involves humans' desires and appetites. Here passions, emotions, lusts, and physical needs are found (Muuss 1975a). A parallel can be seen between this layer of the soul and what another man, more than 2,000 years later, would call a structure of the personality: Plato's first layer corresponds to the construct of the id in Sigmund Freud's (1949) theory.

Plato labels the second layer of the soul the spirit. Here courage, endurance, and aggressiveness originate (Muuss 1975a). Although humans and animals both have the first and second layers, only humans have the third layer. This is the true, or real, soul. It is, Plato said, reason. It is immortal and, as already noted, only resides temporarily in the body.

What makes this layer idea relevant to a conception of development is that Plato did not believe that the attributes of each layer of the soul were immediately seen from birth. That is, people exercise the attributes of each layer successively, and Plato noted that although reason is certainly present in all humans, the exercise of reason is not achieved by all people (Muuss 1975a). Humans have to be trained in order to have their reasoning abilities drawn from them, and such training is what is involved, of course, in the Socratic method of education. This is the method where existing knowledge is drawn from the person on the basis of questions by the teacher.

In sum, Plato's ideas provided the first major statement relevant to human development. This first conception of human development placed the basis of human functioning in the nature conceptual "camp." Moreover, many of Plato's ideas are compatible with ideas expressed in theories of human development devised thousands of years later (for example, Freud 1949). Furthermore, although not an explicit theory of development, Plato's ideas of the layers of the soul did directly suggest that people differ across their lives in the attributes they manifest. And Plato's ideas about the soul indirectly influenced others to speculate about the makeup of the soul and how its attributes showed themselves. One whose ideas were so influenced by Plato was his most famous student—Aristotle. Stimulated by his teacher's thinking, Aristotle revised Plato's ideas about the soul and about its relation to the body and, most important to us, devised ideas explicitly relevant to understanding development.

ARISTOTLE (384–322 B.C.)

Aristotle was also interested in the mind-body problem. His position differed from Plato's, however. Aristotle proposed the *hylomorphic doctrine,* which said that spirit (*hylo*) and matter (*morph*) were inseparable although distinct. The soul was present in all living organisms and gave life to matter. Aristotle philosophized that this occurred because there was a nonphysical, nonspatial, nontemporal "force" that "breathed life" into matter. He called this force an *entelechy.* In short, Aristotle proposed the idea of *vitalism:* There is a nonempirical entity present in any living organism that imparts life to that organism and directs its functioning.

Although an entelechy is present in all organisms, not all organisms have the same sort of entelechy. Like Plato, Aristotle postulated that layers of the soul existed. But in anticipation of Charles Darwin (1859), who wrote more than 2,000 years later, Aristotle conceived of these levels in a biological-evolutionary manner (Muuss 1975a). Aristotle also believed there were three layers of the soul, but he identified them as a plantlike layer, an animallike layer, and a humanlike layer. The plant layer was associated with life functions related to reproduction and nourishment. Although animals and humans had this layer as part of their souls, plants had only this layer. Animals had their additional second layer, which was associated with functions such as locomotion, sensation, and perception; but animals did not have the third layer of the soul.

This additional layer was found only in humans, who of course had the other two as well. The human layer was associated with thinking and reasoning, and it was the possession of these attributes that Aristotle believed set humans apart from animals and plants. In essence then, Aristotle believed that humans innately possess functions relating to three layers of the soul, and that the layer-related functions pertain to characteristics of life throughout the biological world. Accordingly, while Aristotle's postulation is a notion of development, it is a notion of *phylogeny,* not of *ontogeny.* Ontogeny is concerned with the development of a species from its conception to its death. Phylogeny is also concerned with development, but here the concern is with how a particular species came to exist in the first place, or how it came to have the characteristics we see it possessing today. It is a concern with the so-called evolutionary scale (Hodos and Campbell 1969), or the *phylogenetic* (or *phyletic*) scale. In short, one may talk about either ontogeny or phylogeny and still be concerned with development. When one talks about the latter, however, one speaks of the history of the development of one or more species from their simpler to their more complex forms.

Thus Aristotle's idea of the layers of the soul was related to the idea of phylogenetic development. It considered human attributes vis-à-vis the attributes of other (presumably less elaborate) forms of life. Later in this chapter it will be argued that in fact there are important distinctions between Aristotle's position and a view of phyletic development based on current scientific understanding. Nevertheless, given this important qualification, one may recognize Aristotle's ideas as the first statement directly pertinent to development, albeit less to ontogenetic development than to phyletic development.

However, Aristotle *did* offer ideas about ontogeny as well. First, like Plato, Aristotle believed that the functions associated with each layer of the soul emerged in a sequence from lower to higher. Aristotle was more explicit than Plato about this progression, and divided the maturation of the human being into three stages of seven years each.

The first seven years were labeled infancy, and Aristotle saw humans of this age and animals as alike. Both were ruled by their desires and emotions. Thus, in this first period, Aristotle saw phyletic consistency between humans and animals. The next period of development Aristotle labeled boyhood, while the last period of development was termed young manhood. After the end of this last stage was reached, development was presumably complete. The person of twenty-one was a mature adult.

One measure of Aristotle's continuing influence through history is that his belief that maturity was reached at age twenty-one carried over to modern society. (Until relatively recently the age of majority in the United States was twenty-one. This arbitrary number was influenced by Aristotle's writings.) However, Aristotle's influence was even greater than this. Because his philosophy regarding the mind-body problem was adopted by Saint Thomas Aquinas (1225–74), and then subsequently by the Catholic church, Aristotle's views became almost canonized. They became the only acceptable dogma of the church (Misiak and Sexton 1966; Misiak and Staudt 1954).

Until the Protestant Reformation, begun in the sixteenth century by Martin Luther (1483–1546), Aristotle's philosophy remained unchallenged. Because the Catholic church was, during these several centuries, a truly catholic (that is, universal) institution—and because of the prominence of religion in the lives of people during this period—challenging the dogma of the church was a dangerous act. Challenge could lead to excommunication, and if expelled from the

church there was no place else to go. Accordingly, because any one part of Aristotle's philosophy might be seen as related to another, no part was challenged until the Protestant Reformation provided an alternative to Catholicism. Until the sixteenth century then, no view of development other than Aristotle's, regarding either ontogeny or phylogeny, was put forth. At this time, however, another idea relevant to development was advanced.

THE MEDIEVAL CHRISTIAN ERA

As exemplified by John Calvin (1509–64) and the American Puritans (e.g., the Pilgrims of the ship *Mayflower*), the medieval Christians had a religious philosophy that stressed the innate characteristics of humans. Based on portions of the Book of Genesis, this philosophy stressed the idea of original sin. Humans were said to be born with sin in them, or born basically evil. A second belief was that humans were basically depraved, and that their innate sin would be compounded by the inborn tendency to continue to commit sinful acts. In short, the medieval Christian view of human development was, like the others we have thus far encountered, a nature one.

The nature orientation of this position is best illustrated by the reason given for the presence of innate sin and innate tendencies toward continued badness. Medieval Christianity believed in the *homunculus* idea of creation. The reason for innate sin was that a homunculus—a full-grown but miniature adult—was present from birth in the newborn's head. Instantly created with the child, this homunculus contained the sin and the basic depravity.

Of course, from this view, parents could apply harsh rules and stern punishments to their children. The children—having a preformed adult in them—were only different from other adults in terms of size. Hence when children were bad it was not because they did not know better—any adult knew how to act—it was because the "devil," the homunculus, made them do it.

While this medieval Christian view does represent a conception of development different from Aristotle's, it still represents a nature view. In fact, in this concept children do not have to develop at all (except in size), since they have preformed adults within them. Thus the ideas of Plato, Aristotle, and the medieval Christians do not give us a concept of human development that stresses real change. Furthermore, insofar as the medieval Christian view is concerned, there is no need for a theory of development. However, a philosophical position relevant to a concept of development did arise, and in the span of another 150 years led to a scientific view of development. To reach this philosophical position it is useful first to consider the impact of another view.

RENÉ DESCARTES (1596–1650)

Theological changes resulted in the loss of universal acceptance of Aristotelian philosophy and allowed philosophers to return to issues that had remained unaddressed for hundreds of years. A Frenchman, René Descartes, led this movement. He reconsidered the mind-body problem, and his work marks the beginning of the era of modern philosophy.

In trying to formulate a proof for the existence of God, Descartes found it necessary to raise once again the issue of the relation between the physical body and spiritual soul. He saw the two as separate, as dual, entities. He proposed that they exist as two separate "lines" that cross at a particular location in the body. He said these separate lines cross at the site of the pineal gland (a small gland near the pituitary gland). Descartes termed this dualistic view of mind and body *interactionism.*

Moreover, in a manner similar to Plato's, Descartes said that when the soul interacts with the body at the pineal gland, it gives the body knowledge. Thus, like Plato, Descartes believed in innate ideas. As such, although he was the first modern philosopher—by virtue of readdressing long-unconsidered issues—Descartes returned to a nativistic (nature) conception of human functioning first put forth by Plato. However, Descartes's ideas stimulated other philosophers to reconsider these "old" issues. Other views of the mind-body issue arose. While accepting his dualism, other philosophers rejected his idea of interactionism (Misiak and Sexton 1966).

One major reason for this rejection was Descartes's attempt to "prove" statements about the mind on the basis of assertions that stressed innate characteristics—characteristics that were said to be "just there," that is, independent of any *empirical* (observable) proof. A group of philosophers who rejected Descartes's nativism argued that the only way to explain the existence of a phenomenon—of the mind, for example—was through the formulation of ideas based on empirical events. Together, these philosophers formed a school of thought that evolved in Great Britain in the seventeenth century. One may understand the views of this group, and how they led to a concept of development, by focusing on the contributions of one leading thinker in this British school of empiricism.

JOHN LOCKE (1632–1704)

Several British philosophers held similar ideas about the need to use empirical proof (for example, Thomas Hobbes, James Mill, John Stuart Mill, David Hume, David Hartley, Alexander Bain, and John Locke). We focus on Locke's ideas as an example of the British school's position, and also because of the continuing influence of his ideas on later scientific thinking.

Locke rejected the idea that the mind is composed of innate ideas. Instead he said that at birth the mind is like a blank slate, or to use his (Latin) term, a *tabula rasa.* Any knowledge that the mind obtains is derived from experience. And experience makes its impression on the mind—it writes on the blank slate—by entering the body through the senses. Thus, because we experience, or sense, certain observable events—for example, visual, auditory, and tactile stimulation—our mind changes from having no ideas to having knowledge.

Accordingly, here we finally have a philosophical statement that stresses a concept of ontogenetic development. Moreover, it does so by emphasizing, for the first time, nurture. Experiences from the environment provide the basis of development. The newborn is different from the adult because the newborn has no knowledge and the adult does. Thus there is development—change in knowledge in this case—and the development is based on nurture.

In stressing the role of nurture variables such as sensory stimulation in shaping behavior (or knowledge), Locke provides a philosophical view quite consistent with a major theory in psychology: the behavioristic, learning approach to development. People like Skinner (1938), Bijou (1976), and Bijou and Baer (1961) stress that behavioral changes can be understood in terms of environmentally based stimulus-response relations. In this regard modern learning theorists are quite like Locke. (These more modern views will be discussed later in the chapter.)

However, Locke's influence extended beyond providing a philosophical and historical basis of learning theory. In fact, his ideas had two more general impacts. First, Locke's stress on the environment caused other philosophers to begin to consider the potential role of the environment. One major figure so influenced was Jean Jacques Rousseau (1712–78). Rousseau combined both nativistic and environmental ideas in his philosophy—one quite pertinent to a notion of development—and in so doing became the first philosopher explicitly to take the view that a nature-nurture interaction provided the basis of human development. Rousseau said that all children are born innately good (a nature statement); however, in interaction with civilization (their experience, or nurture) they become corrupted. Hence he argued for a "return to nature" in order to avoid the unfavorable effects of civilized experience.

Thus Locke's emphasis on the environment did influence other philosophers to consider nurture, with the fortunate additional result of leading them to devise other ideas of ontogenetic development. However, Locke's ideas had a second (more indirect but nevertheless more important) influence. A concern with empiricism, with observation, promotes a concern with science. The most basic characteristic of science is observation. Accordingly, in promoting interest in empirical concerns among intellectuals, Locke was—albeit indirectly—promoting interest in scientific concerns among these people.

During this time, the intellectuals in society were also the leaders of society (that is, the ones with the resources and power to get an education). Moreover, developments in such intellectual areas as philosophy, literature, and science were common and popular topics of social conversation. Knowledge of such developments was a mark of the status of being an educated and (usually) a rich and powerful person. As such, Locke's influence promoted a general concern with science among the educated. Accordingly, when new events in science took place, news of them would not only reach other scientists but would also be likely to get the attention of all educated people. Such information, then, if important enough, could not only influence scientists but could have implications for all areas of intellectual concern.

By the middle of the century following Locke's death, an event occurred in science that had such impact. It influenced not only the area of science it pertained to, but all areas of science and of intellectual concern (for example, education, theology, law, and medicine). The event was the publication of a book by a then relatively unknown British naturalist. The book—representing a theory derived from observations made while the author was on a trip to the Galápagos Islands (which are in the Pacific, on the equator)—was *The Origin of Species by Means of Natural Selection,* and the author was Charles Darwin. Published in 1859, it represents the transition from philosophical to scientific concern with the idea of development.

Scientific Roots of Development

Locke's empiricism promoted the influence of science, and as such, provided one basis for the impact of Darwin's ideas. Yet there is a historical irony. Locke's ideas stressed a nurture view of ontogenetic development. However, the scientific view of development that Darwin devised stressed a nature view of phylogenetic development. Accordingly, with the transition from philosophy to science, we see the nature-nurture pendulum swinging back to nature. However, as in philosophy, the pendulum will not stay there. A consideration of Darwin's work is useful to see these swings in science.

CHARLES DARWIN (1809–82)

There are several key ideas in Darwin's theory of evolution. The environment in which a type of animal (a species) exists places demands on that animal. If the only food for an animal in a given environment is the leaves of tall trees, then the animal must be able to reach the leaves in order to survive. The environment "demands" that the animal possess some characteristic that will allow it to reach the high leaves. If the animal has that characteristic, it will fit in with its environment, get food, and survive. If not, it will die.

Imagine, for example, that there were two species of giraffe—one with a long neck (as is the case) and the other with a short one. Because the long-neck giraffe has the characteristics that fit in with the demands of the particular environment, it would survive; the short-neck giraffe would not. Of course, if the setting changed—if, for example, only food very low on the ground were available—the characteristics of the short-neck giraffe would best fit the environment and the outcome would be reversed. The point Darwin stressed is that the characteristics of the natural setting determine which organism characteristics will lead to survival and

Charles Darwin

which ones will not. Thus it is the natural environment that selects organisms for survival. This is termed *natural selection.*

Hence Darwin proposes the idea of *survival of the fittest.* Organisms that possess characteristics that fit the survival requirements for a particular environmental setting will survive. In other words, certain characteristics in certain settings have *fundamental biological significance*—they allow the organism to survive (and hence to have the opportunity to reproduce and pass on the characteristics to offspring). Characteristics shaped by natural selection that meet the demands of the environment (and hence allow survival) are *adaptive* characteristics.

The giraffe example stresses that various

physical characteristics of an organism may be *functional*. In an evolutionary sense, something is functional if it is adaptive, if it aids survival. Thus the *structure* of an organism (its physical makeup, its constitution, its morphological or bodily characteristics) may be functional. However, while Darwin in 1859 emphasized the function of physical structures of species, he later (1872) pointed out that behavior, too, had survival value. Showing fear when a dangerous bear approaches and being able to learn to avoid certain stimuli (snakes) and to approach others (food) are examples of behaviors that are adaptive; they aid our survival.

Thus behavior also has a function. The function of behavior became the focus of much social scientific concern. This concern was reflected not only in the ideas of those interested in the phylogeny of behavior. Additionally, the idea was promoted that the behavioral changes characterizing ontogeny could be understood on the basis of adaptation. Thus the adaptive role of behavior became a concern providing a basis for *all* of American psychology (White 1968) and plays a major part in the ideas of theorists as diverse as Hall (1904), Freud (1949), Piaget (1950), Erikson (1959), and Skinner (1938, 1950). However, before the role of ontogenetic changes in adaptation—and hence in survival—can be completely discussed, it is useful to return to Darwin's ideas about survival and see how they reflect a concern not with ontogeny but with phylogeny.

Not all species survive. There are several reasons why this might happen. The natural environment might change, putting different demands on species. Species members that have adaptive characteristics will pass them on to their offspring and therefore the species will continue. Other species, lacking adaptive characteristics, will no longer be fit to survive and they will die out. Another reason one species might survive instead of another is that some change in the genetic material (for example, through mutation or cross-breeding) might give rise to new characteristics that favor survival. In either of these illustrations, however, evolution would

proceed on the basis of the transmission of adaptive characteristics from parents to offspring. Species would evolve—change with history—as a consequence of the continual interplay between natural selection and survival of the fittest.

The basis of an organism's survival, then, depends not primarily on what it acquires over the course of its ontogeny that may be adaptive. Rather, its potential for adaptive functioning is transmitted to it by the parents. Accordingly, adaptation is a hereditary, or nature, phenomenon. On the basis of evolution—the history of changes in a species, its phylogenetic development—a member of a species either will or will not be born with adaptive characteristics. Thus Darwin presents a nature theory of phylogenetic development.

In summary, based on his observations, Darwin presents the first major scientific theory of development. As noted, this evolutionary view of species development had profound effects on areas of concern other than science. But it is possible to remain within the scientific realm in order to gauge the impact of Darwin's ideas on those concerned not just with nature, phylogenetic issues, but also with issues pertinent to ontogeny and finally, specifically to human development as well. Darwin's ideas were a major influence on the person who both founded the field of developmental psychology and devised the first scientific theory of human development. This man was G. Stanley Hall, and a consideration of his work will bring our discussion—after more than 2,000 years—to a scientific concern with human ontogenetic development.

G. STANLEY HALL (1844–1924)

G. Stanley Hall, who organized the American Psychological Association and became its first president, also started the first American journal of psychology (aptly titled *The American Journal of Psychology*) and the first scientific journal devoted to human development (first titled *Pedagogical Seminary* and then given its present name, *The*

Journal of Genetic Psychology). It was also Hall who wrote the first text on adolescence (a two-volume work titled *Adolescence,* 1904).

On the basis of these and other accomplishments of similar distinction, Hall was one of the most influential and prominent psychologists at the turn of this century (Misiak and Sexton 1966). As such, he did much to shape the nature and direction of the relatively new science of psychology. (The birthday of modern psychology is dated in 1879, with the opening of the first psychological laboratory in Leipzig, Germany, by Wilhelm Wundt.)

Hall's most specific influence was in shaping developmental psychology. As implied by the title of the journal he founded—*The Journal of Genetic Psychology*—Hall saw development from a nature point of view. Although not many people (including his students) adopted his specific nature-based theory of development, they did follow his general nature orientation. Consequently, Hall's influence was to direct scientific concern to human development from a predominantly nature perspective.

In devising his nature viewpoint, Hall was profoundly influenced by Darwin. In fact, Hall fancied himself as the "Darwin of the mind." Hall attempted to translate Darwin's phylogenetic evolutionary principles into conceptions relevant to ontogeny. The ideas by which he believed he could connect phylogeny to ontogeny were derived from those of yet another scientist who was influenced by Darwin, Ernst Haeckel.

The Contribution of Haeckel
Ernst Haeckel was a nineteenth-century scientist who specialized in the then relatively new area of biology called *embryology.* When the sperm of the father organism fertilizes the egg (ovum) of the mother, the basis of a new life is formed. The new life will develop in the now-pregnant mother for a period of time until birth. The period of time from fertilization until birth is called *gestation,* and different species have gestation pe-

G. Stanley Hall

riods of different lengths (in the human it is about nine months).

There are various phases of development during gestation. The period from fertilization to when the fertilized egg (the *zygote*) implants itself in the wall of the uterus is called the *period of the ovum* or the *period of the zygote* (about ten to fourteen days in the human). The next period (from the second week of life through about the eighth to tenth week of life in the human) is termed the *period of the embryo.* In this period all organ systems of the organism emerge. This is the period of development before birth that Haeckel studied. There is a third period of gestation, however. In the human this third period—the *period of the fetus*—ranges from the third through the ninth month of gestation (that is, until birth). In this period there is continued growth of the organ systems developed in the embryonic period. Additionally, functional (behavioral) characteristics of these organ structures begin to appear. The fetus shows body movement (for example, it kicks and thumb sucking can occur).

In studying development in the embryonic period, Haeckel was concerned with the progressive formation of all organ systems present in the organism. He was concerned with these developments in all species of organisms, but particularly in mammals, and this led him to compare embryos of different species. Haeckel looked at the progressive series of changes that the human embryo went through during about a ten-week-long period, and he compared what the embryo looked like at these successive times to the embryos of other species. He saw that the human embryo went through changes that made it look like, first, the fully developed fish embryo; then, the frog embryo; then a bit later, the rat embryo; then still later, the monkey embryo; and finally, the ape embryo.

Haeckel reasoned that this was an ontogenetic progression that mirrored the phylogenetic history, the evolution, of the human species. Humans were, he suggested, first fishlike, then amphibianlike, and so on until they were apelike. Thus, when one looks at the changes characterizing an individual member of a species as it progresses across its ontogeny (here, during its embryological period), one will see a *recapitulation* (a repeating, a mirroring) of the evolutionary changes the species went through. In short, Haeckel said that *ontogeny recapitulates phylogeny.*

Haeckel thought that with this idea he had applied Darwinian evolutionary thinking to the study of ontogeny. In translating Haeckel's ideas about embryological structural ontogeny into ideas pertinent to *postnatal* (after birth) human behavioral ontogeny, Hall thought he was doing the same thing. Yet Hall's and Haeckel's translations were incorrect for several reasons. Let us examine why.

Hall's Recapitulationist Theory
Hall believed that the changes characterizing the human life cycle are a repetition

of the sequence of changes our ancestors went through during their evolution. Thus Hall applied to postnatal life the recapitulationist idea Haeckel used for prenatal, embryological development. However, although arguing that during the years from birth to sexual maturity the person was repeating the history of the species—as had been done prenatally—Hall believed that the postnatal recapitulation was more limited (Gallatin 1975). In fact, according to Gallatin, Hall believed that:

> Rather than reflecting the entire sweep of evolution, childhood was supposed to proceed in stages, each of which mirrored a primitive stage of the human species. Very early childhood might correspond, Hall speculated, to a monkey-like ancestor of the human race that had reached sexual maturity around the age of six. The years between eight and twelve allegedly represented a reenactment of a more advanced, but still prehistoric form of mankind, possibly a species that had managed to survive by hunting and fishing. (Pp. 26–27)

Furthermore, Hall believed that adolescence represented a specific period in ontogeny after childhood. As such, not only was he the first person, within a scientific theory of development, to conceive of adolescence as a distinct portion of the life span (the term had, however, first appeared in the first half of the fifteenth century; Muuss 1975a), but he did so in a manner consistent with a view of development as a lifelong (life-span) process. That is, Hall saw the capacities and changes of childhood continuing into adolescence, *but* at a more rapid and heightened pace. Additionally, he saw adolescence as a period of transition between childhood and adulthood. That is, the stages of life before adolescence stressed the innate characteristics of humans held "in common with the animals" (Hall 1904, I:39). However, the stage of life following adolescence was said to raise a human "above them and make him most distinctively human" (Hall 1904, I:39). In short, adolescence was a period of transition from being essentially beastlike to being essentially humanlike (that is, civilized and mature). This ontogenetic transition mirrored the evolutionary change involved when humans moved, Hall thought, from being essentially like the apes to becoming civilized.

Thus Hall saw adolescence as a period during which a person changed to become civilized. Human evolution, Hall believed, moved the person through this ontogenetic period, putting him or her in the position of being able to contribute to humans' highest level of evolutionary attainment: civilization. Hence, Hall (1904, II:71) said, "Early adolescence is . . . the infancy of man's higher nature, when he receives from the great all-mother his last capital of energy and evolutionary momentum." However, because of the acceleration and heightening capacities in adolescence, and also because of the difficulty of casting off the characteristics of animallike behavior and at the same time acquiring the characteristics of civilization, the adolescent period was a stressful, difficult one. In short, because adolescence was an ontogenetically and evolutionarily crucial "betwixt and between" (Gallatin 1975) phase of human development, it was necessarily, to Hall, a period of storm and stress.

Criticisms of the Recapitulationist Idea

It has been mentioned that Hall's theory of ontogenetic development was not generally accepted. This was because the recapitulationist ideas of both Haeckel and Hall met criticism that severely diminished their usefulness.

First, in regard to Haeckel's ideas, it may be noted that his observation that the human embryo was at times the same as that of the fish or the ape was faulty. Although to the naked eye the similarity may be striking, technological advances with such devices as the electron microscope have enabled us to enlarge the view of these respective embryos considerably. When this is done, one sees that the structures within the cells of each type of embryo are substantially different at *all* times during their respective growth. For instance, from conception through the rest of life, the embryos

of each species have their own specific number of chromosomes (forty-six in the human). As such, apparent similarities among embryos are not real.

A second criticism of both Haeckel's and Hall's recapitulationist applications of Darwinian evolutionary ideas may be mentioned. This is that their applications were based on a totally incorrect understanding of the meaning of evolution. Darwin's theory of evolution states that humans did not always exist. Rather, previous forms of being existed, and through natural selection some forms were adaptive, at least for a time, and continued to evolve until the human species as it is now known came to exist. However, this evolutionary process occurs for all animals, not just humans. Thus, if another animal exists today, it, too, has had an evolutionary history. It, too, is as currently adaptive as the human—albeit to its own environmental setting (or, in evolutionary terms, to its own *ecological milieu*).

Thus, a rat or a monkey or an ape cannot be an ancestor of a human because all of them exist today. All are equal in evolutionary status. All are equally as evolved and as adaptive. This is not to say that there are not differences among the species. There are, of course, differences (for example, in level of complexity). However, that is not the point.

The point is that no human had a rat or a monkey as an ancestor; and when one looks at a monkey embryo or at monkey behavior, one is not therefore looking at humans as they existed in a former, lower evolutionary status (Hodos and Campbell 1969). Although humans and monkeys may have had—millions of years ago—a common ancestor, that creature is long extinct. It no longer exists because it was not fit to survive. Although other forms evolved from it—and *some could* have led to present-day monkeys while *others could* have led to present-day humans—whatever exists today is by definition fit to survive and thus adaptive (Hodos and Campbell 1969). Thus Haeckel and Hall did not appropriately understand the evolutionary process. Humans were never monkeylike in their embryos or in their behavior, since both species have their own evolutionary history and are currently alive and well. Human ontogeny cannot therefore repeat a phase of its evolutionary history if that phase simply never occurred.

Second, even as an analogy, a recapitulationist description of human ontogeny is inappropriate. As initially pointed out by Thorndike (1904), and reemphasized by Gallatin (1975), by two or three years of age a human child has already exceeded the capacities of monkeys, apes, and prehistoric humanlike organisms (for example, the Neanderthals). Sensorimotor, verbal, and social behavior, for example, are all more advanced in the human three-year-old than in "adults" of any of these other species. Additionally, there is no evidence whatsoever that the events in adolescence are a mirror of the history of civilization.

In summary, then, Hall's theory that ontogeny recapitulates phylogeny was simply untenable. Thus, although his work was historically quite important in that it was the first scientific theory of human ontogenetic development, it did not lead many to adopt it specifically. However, his ideas were clearly nature ones (human developmental events arise out of the hereditary transmission of past evolutionary occurrences). And, because of his influence and position in American psychology, his general nature orientation to ontogeny *was* followed even though his specific nature theory was dropped. Thus Hall influenced his students to use a nature orientation in their work in human development. Since two of his students—Lewis Terman and Arnold Gesell—were among the most important developmentalists in the first third of this century, Hall's influence was to start the scientific study of human development on a nature theoretical basis.

The Contributions of Terman and Gesell

Hall's most prominent students were Terman and Gesell. Their contributions illustrate much of the interest in ontogenetic development through the first three decades of this century. Terman was interested in mental measurement. The first intelligence test was constructed by Binet (Binet and Simon 1905a, 1905b) in Paris. Terman was one of the first to translate this test into English (H. H. Goddard in 1910 was the first). Terman, a professor at Stanford University, published the test as the Stanford-Binet (1916) and adopted the intelligence quotient (IQ), suggested by the German psychologist William Stern, to express people's performance on the test (IQ = mental age divided by chronological age, multiplied by 100 to remove the fraction).

Terman's interest in measuring intellectual ability was only in part based on a concern with describing how people differ (that is, individual differences). His interest was also a theoretical one. He believed that intelligence was mostly (if not exclusively) a nature characteristic. Accordingly, not only did he develop an instrument to describe individual differences in intelligence but he also carried out research to try to determine the genetic component of intelligence. One such study was his *Genetic Studies of Genius,* a longitudinal study of intellectually gifted children from 1921 onward (Terman 1925; Terman and Oden 1959). (As noted earlier, a longitudinal study is one in which the same persons are repeatedly measured over time, and Terman's was one of the first begun in this country; Sears 1975.)

Although it did not prove that intelligence is genetically determined (for reasons we shall explore in later chapters), Terman's work, involving nearly fifty years of study and reported in five published volumes over this span (see Terman and Oden 1959), was quite important for several reasons. First, it encouraged several other longitudinal studies of human development. These provided data relevant to changes in development across the life span. Second, Terman's findings did much to dispel myths about the psychological and social characteristics of intellectually gifted people. Although such people were sometimes stereotyped as weak, sickly, maladjusted, or socially inept, Terman provided data showing them to be healthy, physically fit, athletic, and personally and socially adjusted.

Third, Terman's work did much to make developmental psychology a descriptive, normative discipline. His work with the IQ test and his descriptions of the development of gifted people involved making *normative* statements. (A *norm* is an average, typical, or modal characteristic for a particular group.) If nature is the source of human development and environment plays no primary role, then all one need do to be dealing with information pertinent to the inevitable (because of its biological, nature basis) pattern of ontogeny is describe the typical development of people. We shall see in later chapters that there are serious problems with this reasoning. However, Hall's other prominent student, Arnold Gesell, based his work even more explicitly on this reasoning than did Terman, and accordingly did even more to make developmental psychology a normative, descriptive field.

Gesell proposed a theory that can be understood by his term *maturational readiness.* This nature-based theory said that maturational changes are independent of learning (Gesell's conception of what nurture amounted to). Sensorimotor behavior and even many cognitive abilities (for example, vocabulary development) were under the *primary* control of maturation. This means that their pattern of development was maturationally determined. Thus an organism would develop when it was maturationally ready to, and attempts to teach a child before this time could not be helpful.

Hence, in his writing and research (Gesell 1929, 1931, 1934, 1946, 1954), Gesell stressed the need for the careful and systematic cataloging of growth norms. His work provided science with much useful knowledge about the expected sequence and times of emergence of numerous physical and mental developments of children of particular demographic backgrounds. These descriptions would allow people to know, he believed, the nature-based sequence and timing of development and, as such, the point at which a person was maturationally ready for learning. While this belief will be evaluated in a succeeding chapter, the present point is that Gesell's theory and research did much to make developmental psychology not only a nature-based discipline but also one whose major, if not exclusive, focus was descriptive. However, a nurture-based theory of behavior arose to counteract the predominant nature focus.

BEHAVIORISM AND LEARNING THEORY

Just as the pendulum swung between nature and nurture in philosophy, one may argue that it moved similarly in science. In the second decade of this century and continuing through the 1950s, American psychology as well as other areas of social science (e.g., sociology; Homans 1961) came to be quite strongly influenced by a particular conceptual-theoretical movement: a behavioristic, learning-theory view of behavior. Although this movement was not developed from a *primary* concern with children or human development, it was extensively applied to human development. In fact, no learning theory has ever been devised on the basis of information derived primarily from children (White 1970). Philosophically consistent with Locke's empiricist views, this movement stressed that in order for psychology to be an objective science, ideas about behavior had to be derived from empirically verifiable sources.

John B. Watson, emphasizing this orientation, developed his point of view under the label *behaviorism* (Watson 1913, 1918). He stressed that stimuli and responses combined under certain lawful, empirical conditions—the laws of *classical and operant conditioning*—types of learning that will be discussed in later chapters. By focusing on how environmental stimuli gained control over the behavior of organisms, one could know how behavior was acquired and, by implication, developed. That is, development was seen as the cumulative acquisition of objective and empirical stimulus-response relations, and all one had to understand to deal with human development was the way behavior was controlled by the laws of conditioning. Watson applied these ideas to

John B. Watson

children, both in his research (Watson and Raynor 1920) and in his prescriptions for child care (Watson 1928).

The nurture view of behaviorism gave psychologists a position that allowed them to be viewed as objective scientists, like their colleagues in the natural sciences. As such, behaviorism and its variants and extensions (Hull 1929; Skinner 1938) became the predominant conceptual focus in American psychology. As with Watson's work, applications of ideas and principles derived not primarily from humans but from other organisms—usually rats (Beach 1950; Herrnstein 1977)—were made to humans, and ideas pertinent to human development arose. Thus ideas about how humans acquire behavior consistent with the rules of society—that is, how they are *socialized*—were formulated. Such *social-learning* theories were not only pertinent to a nurture view of development but also, at times, involved some attempt to reinterpret nature conceptions of development (e.g., those of

Freud 1949) in nurture terms (Dollard, Doob, Miller, Mowrer, and Sears 1939; Miller and Dollard 1941).

However, in its major impact this nurture view of development was quite distinct from *integration* with nature concerns about development. In fact, through the early 1940s, there was little integration of efforts by nature-oriented and nurture-oriented workers. The learning-oriented workers were doing *manipulative* studies—that is, varying stimuli to ascertain the effect on responses—and their work tended to concentrate on readily observable aspects of behavioral development (e.g., aggressive behaviors). This work constituted an elaborate and fairly precise compendium of how variations in given stimulus characteristics were related to variations in the responses of certain groups of children—basically white, middle-class children of highly educated parents.

Thus, through the 1940s, proponents within the nature *or* nurture camps continued to work, but usually with little concern for integration with each other's endeavors. A major historical event served to alter this and to move developmental science from a primarily descriptive to a primarily theoretical, explanatory-oriented field. The event was World War II.

WORLD WAR II

The events surrounding World War II irrevocably altered the nature of American social science. First, the effects of events in Europe were felt even before the United States entered the war in December 1941. Nazi persecution led many Jewish intellectuals to flee Europe, and many sought refuge and a new start for their careers in the United States. Great pains were taken to find positions in American universities and associated institutions for the refugees, despite the fact that many of them held ideas counter to those predominating in the American academic scene (i.e., behaviorism and learning theory).

For instance, although Freud himself settled in London (and died there in 1939), many psychoanalytically oriented people—

some trained by Freud and/or his daughter Anna—came to this country. Some of them, for example, Peter Blos and most notably Erik Erikson, brought with them psychoanalytic ideas about human development.

In addition, once America entered the war and numerous soldiers had to be treated for psychological as well as physical trauma, the federal government gave universities large amounts of money to train clinical psychologists. This opened the door for many professionals with psychoanalytic orientations to become faculty members at universities previously dominated by behaviorists (Misiak and Sexton 1966). These people had the backgrounds appropriate for teaching clinical skills to the large new groups of future clinicians that were needed.

Thus one impact of World War II was to encourage psychoanalytic thinking in many psychology departments. This orientation represented the introduction of nature-based thinking into departments where behaviorists previously resided in total control of the intellectual domain (Gengerelli 1976). Additionally, it represented just *one* of many different theoretical accounts of human functioning—accounts that stressed either nature or both nature and nurture as sources of behavior and development—that were making inroads into American thinking.

As such, nativistic ideas about perception and learning—introduced by psychologists who believed in what were termed the holistic aspects of behavior—were juxtaposed with the learning ideas of the behaviorists. The *gestalt* (meaning "totality") views represented by these Europeans (people like Max Wertheimer, Kurt Koffka, Wolfgang Köhler, and Kurt Lewin) were shown also to be pertinent to areas of concern such as brain function, group dynamics, and social problems (Sears 1975). Ideas explicitly relevant to development were also introduced. For example, Heinz Werner (1948) presented to Americans a view of development involving continual nature-nurture interactions.

The outcome of these changes in the complexion of intellectual ideas about development, fostered by events relating to World War II, was a pluralism of ideas about development. Now there were numerous interpretations of behavior and development—interpretations that were based on substantially different conceptions of the sources of human behavior and development. Any given behavior, then, could be interpreted according to quite different alternatives, and these alternatives were advanced by respected advocates often working in the same academic contexts. The simultaneous presentation of diverse interpretations promoted a move away from a focus on mere description and toward a primary concern with theoretical interpretations of development. This focus on explanation was heightened in the post–World War II era, in the late 1950s and 1960s.

THE 1950s AND 1960s

Because of the pluralism of perspectives promoted by the events surrounding World War II, developmentalists became less concerned with just collecting descriptive data. Rather, they focused more on the interpretation—the meaning—of development. As such, they became primarily concerned with the comparative use and evaluation of various theories in putting the facts of development together into an understandable whole. One index of this change of focus was the rediscovery of the theory of Jean Piaget.

Piaget's theory of the development of cognition was known in America in the 1920s (Piaget 1923). Yet because of the "clinical" nature of his research methods, his nonstatistical style of data analysis, and the abstract constructs he was concerned with—all of which ran counter to predominant trends in the United States—his theory and research were not given much attention until the late 1950s. At that time, however, due to postwar European intellectual influences, Americans were turning greater attention to the intellectual resources in Europe. Thus the Swiss scientist Piaget was rediscovered, and it can fairly be said that concern with the abstract and conceptual ideas of his theory came to dominate American developmental psychology throughout the 1960s. In fact, his influence continues to this writing, both as a result of further substantiation of his ideas and by promoting discussions of alternative theoretical conceptualizations (Brainerd 1978; Liben 1983; Siegel and Brainerd 1977).

Interest in adult development and aging also began to grow rapidly in the 1960s. As explained by Baltes (1979a), this interest provided a major impetus to the current concern with development across the life span because studies of adult development and aging moved scientific interest beyond the childhood and adolescent years. Major research and theoretical contributions to the study of adult development and aging were provided by Bernice Neugarten and Robert Havighurst at the University of Chicago, in their longitudinal research beginning in the 1950s.

However, as Havighurst (1973) himself pointed out, this work had an intellectual debt to some earlier work done in the 1930s and 1940s. Except for one early work—an article by Sanford (in the *American Journal of Psychology,* 1902) called "Mental Growth and Decay"—interest in life-span changes and in researching the nature of life-span development did not really exist at all before the 1920s. In fact, except for Hall's (1922) text *Senescence* and that by H. L. Hollingworth (1927), it was the 1930s that saw the growth of interests related to development across the entire life span. At this time Else Frenkel-Brunswik began a series of studies at the University of California (Berkeley) on the basis of an interest in life-span development; the work of Charlotte Bühler (1933) in Germany was published and began to become well known; and a book by Pressey, Janney, and Kuhlen (1939) was published. However, the scientists involved in these respective endeavors worked largely in isolation from one another, often unaware of (or at least not making reference to) the contributions of the others (see Baltes 1979a).

Thus it was not until the 1950s, when the work of Neugarten and Havighurst really began, and the intellectual climate in the United States favored conceptual integration and pluralism, that these seeds of life-span interest really took hold. It was the fostering of research and theory in adult development and aging at that time that laid another portion of the foundation for the trends in human development seen in the decades following the 1950s and 1960s. Nevertheless, even before that period there was a long historical tradition behind the perspective that is today labeled the life span view of human development (Baltes 1979a, 1979b; Baltes, Reese, and Lipsitt 1980).

Thus, by the 1960s, concern with development involved a focus on various theories of development, an interest in development into the adult and aged years, *and* a concern with phenomena of development (e.g., the cognitive, or thinking, changes studied by Piaget) that were not only overt, behavioral ones. Bronfenbrenner (1963), in a review of the history of developmental science, similarly notes that from the 1930s to the early

Bernice L. Neugarten

Robert J. Havighurst

1960s there was a continuing shift from studies involving the mere collection of data toward research concerned with abstract processes and constructs. Accordingly, in depicting the status of the field in 1963, Bronfenbrenner said that "first and foremost, the gathering of data for data's sake seems to have lost favor. The major concern in today's developmental research is clearly with inferred processes and constructs" (p. 257).

Similarly, in a review a decade later, Looft (1972) found a continuation of the trends noted by Bronfenbrenner. Looft's review, like Bronfenbrenner's, was based on an analysis of major handbooks of developmental psychology published from the 1930s through the time of the review. Each handbook represented a reflection of the current content, emphasis, and concerns of the field. Looft found that in the first handbook (Murchison, 1931) developmental psychology was largely descriptive. Consistent with our analysis and with Bronfenbrenner's conclusions, Looft saw workers devoting their time essentially to the collection of norms. However, a shift toward more general integrative concerns was seen by 1946, and this trend continued through 1963 (Bronfenbrenner 1963) to 1972 (Looft 1972). Indeed, as a case in point, we may note that the editor of a 1970 handbook (Mussen 1970) pointed out

that "the major contemporary empirical and theoretical emphases in the field of developmental psychology . . . seem to be on *explanations* of the psychological changes that occur, the mechanisms and processes accounting for growth and development" (Mussen 1970, vii).

In sum, it may be seen that a multiplicity of theories, and a concern with the explanation of the processes of development, came to be predominant foci by the beginning of the 1970s. Such concerns lead to the recognition that there is not just one way (one theory) to follow in attempting to put together the facts (the descriptions) of development. Rather, a pluralistic approach to such integration is needed. When followed, it may indicate that more descriptions are necessary. Thus, although observation (*empiricism*) is the basic feature of the *scientific method,* theoretical concerns guide descriptive endeavors. One gathers facts because one knows they will have a meaning within a particular theory. Moreover, since such theory-based research may proceed from any theoretical base, the data generated must be evaluated in terms of their use in advancing understanding of developmental change processes.

THE 1970s THROUGH TODAY

The prominence of theory, the evaluation of theories by criteria of their usefulness in integrating the facts of development, and findings that developmental changes take many different forms at different points in time (and that such changes need to be understood from a diverse array of explanatory stances) led in the 1970s to an increasingly abstract concern with understanding the character of development.

The Role of Philosophical Models
Reese and Overton (1970; Overton and Reese 1973), among others (e.g., Lerner 1976, 1978; Riegel 1973, 1975), pointed out that just as the facts and methods of science are to be understood as shaped by theory, scien-

tific theories, in turn, are shaped by super-ordinate philosophies.

Throughout the 1970s repeated discussions occurred about how two major philosophical positions—what we shall learn in Chapter 2 are termed the mechanistic and the organismic models—shaped developmental theories (e.g., Lerner 1976, 1978, 1979; Overton 1973; Overton and Reese 1973; Reese and Overton 1970; Riegel 1975, 1976a, 1976b; Sameroff 1975). Each of these philosophical positions led to a different set, or "family," of theories. For example, many mechanistic-type theories (as we shall see) stress that even quite complex levels of human behavior can be reduced to rather simple elements: basic stimulus-response (S-R) connections acquired through the "laws," or principles, of classical and operant conditioning (Baer 1970, 1980; Bijou 1976; Bijou and Baer 1961; Skinner 1938, 1950). In turn, many organismic-type theories (as we shall also see) stress that as people develop, they pass through a universal and unchangeable sequence of qualitatively different phases, levels, or "stages," of development (e.g., Erikson 1959, 1963, 1968; Freud 1949, 1954; Piaget 1950, 1970). Since each stage of development is different in kind from all others, organismically oriented developmental psychologists would disagree with mechanistically oriented ones about the appropriateness of reducing one level (or stage) of development to the same terms (the same elements) as another.

Thus the discussions about the influence of the organismic and the mechanistic models led developmental psychologists to recognize that the stances scientists took in regard to key issues of human development—such as whether, because of the appropriateness of reducing all behavior to common elements, there is a sameness, or continuity, across life *or* whether, because of the existence of new stages, there is change, or discontinuity, across life—depended ultimately on philosophical positions. That is, developmentalists recognized that a main (if not the ultimate) reason scientists had different positions regarding concepts and theories of development was that they were committed to different philosophies. In other words, differences about these issues were underlain by nonempirical, philosophical differences and could not therefore be readily decided on the basis of data. Indeed, Reese and Overton (1970; Overton and Reese 1973) pointed out that developmentalists working from different philosophical positions would have different truth criteria for establishing the "facts" of development; that is, because what is a fact to one scientist may not be accepted as a legitimate or relevant fact by another—because of basic philosophical disagreements—disputes *across* philosophical positions could not be settled by facts.

The Dialectical Model

The interest that arose in the 1970s in the philosophical bases of theories of development also led many developmentalists to explore the potential use of philosophies other than the organismic and the mechanistic. For example, during the 1970s Klaus Riegel (1973, 1975, 1976a, 1976b) proposed that dialectical philosophy could be used to devise a unique theory of development, one that focused not just on the organism (and, for instance, its internally guided progression through stages) or just on the environment (as, for instance, the source of the stimulation that provided the basis of S-R connections); instead Riegel (1975, 1976a, 1976b) hoped to forge a dialectical psychology that focused on the *relations* between developing organisms and their changing environments.

Riegel emphasized that such relations involved continual conflicts among variables from several levels of "being" (or levels of organization of life phenomena); for example, the inner-biological, the individual-psychological, the physical-environmental, and the sociocultural levels of analysis. Riegel assumed that constant changes among these multiple reciprocally related levels of analysis were involved in development (Overton 1978). Thus, at least in this respect, his dia-

Klaus F. Riegel

lectical model can be seen as compatible with another model that attracted increasing interest during the 1970s—the one that Pepper (1942) labeled *contextualism* (Hultsch and Hickey 1978; Lerner, Skinner, and Sorell 1980).

The Contextual Model
In contextualism, developmental changes occur as a consequence of reciprocal (bidirectional) relations between the active organism and the active context. Just as the context changes the individual, the individual changes the context. As such, by acting to change a source of their own development—by being both products and producers of their contexts—individuals affect their own development (Bell 1968; Bell and Harper 1977; Lerner 1982; Lerner and Busch-Rossnagel 1981; Lewis and Rosenblum 1974; Schneirla 1957).

Contextualism found many adherents among developmental psychologists during

the 1970s (Lerner, Hultsch, and Dixon 1983). Indeed, two major approaches within developmental psychology that were consistent with contextualism were the ecological view of human development (Bronfenbrenner 1977, 1979) and the life-span developmental psychology perspective (Baltes et al. 1980).

BRONFENBRENNER'S ECOLOGY OF HUMAN DEVELOPMENT

The leading formulator of the ecological approach to human development was Urie Bronfenbrenner (1977, 1979, 1983; Bronfenbrenner and Crouter 1983). Bronfenbrenner argued that much of developmental research involved studying children under artificial "experimental" conditions. Thus, he argued, "Much of contemporary developmental psychology is the science of the strange behavior of children in strange situations with strange adults for the briefest possible periods of time" (1977, 513). Accordingly, Bronfenbrenner asserted that only "experiments created as real are real in their consequences" (1977, 529), and he stressed that research should begin to focus on how children develop in settings representative of their actual world (i.e., in *ecologically valid* settings). For instance, instead of studying children only in the laboratory, one should study them in their homes, schools, and playgrounds.

Bronfenbrenner also argued that developmental psychologists needed a much more precise and differentiated view of the actual ecology of human development; it would not suffice just to view all features of a person's context as representing merely the "stimulus environment." The context of human development was composed of different levels, or systems, of organization; although the systems were interrelated, often in a reciprocal manner (Belsky and Tolan 1981), they were nevertheless sufficiently distinct to necessitate discrimination among them.

Bronfenbrenner proposed four systems within the ecology of human development. The first system he labeled the *microsystem*,

Urie Bronfenbrenner

and he noted that this portion of the context is composed of "the complex of relations between the developing person and environment in an immediate setting containing the person" (Bronfenbrenner 1977, 515). For example, the family is one major microsystem for infant and child development (Belsky 1982; Belsky and Tolan 1981); it involves interactions between the child, his or her parents, and any siblings that are present in the home. Other microsystems of early life include the day-care, nursery, or school setting, involving both child-teacher and child-peer interactions; and the playground, most often involving child-peer interactions.

A child's microsystems may be interrelated. What occurs in the school may affect what happens in the family, and vice versa. Bronfenbrenner noted that such microsystem interrelations constitute a second ecological system. He termed this the *mesosystem,* and he defined it as "the interrelations among major settings containing the developing person at a particular point in his or her life" (Bronfenbrenner 1977, 515).

Often, what happens in a microsystem (e.g., in an interaction between a child and a parent within the family context) may be influenced by events that occur in systems in which the child takes no part. For example, an adult who is a parent also has other social roles, for instance, as a worker. The child is probably not part of his or parents' workplace interactions, but events that affect the parents at work can influence how they treat the child. For instance, if a parent has a particularly bad or tiring day at work, he or she may punish the child more severely than usual for some disapproved act. Thus, because the people with whom the child lives interact in—and are affected by—contexts other than those containing the child, the child may be affected by settings in which he or she plays no direct role. Bronfenbrenner sees such influences as constituting a third system within the ecology of human development. He labels this system the *exosystem,* and he defines it as "an extension of the mesosystem embracing . . . specific social structures, both formal and informal, that do not themselves contain the developing person but impinge upon or encompass the immediate settings in which the person is found, and thereby delimit, influence, or even determine what goes on there" (Bronfenbrenner 1977, 515).

Finally, Bronfenbrenner notes that there exists a *macrosystem* within the ecology of human development. This system is composed of historical events (e.g., wars, floods, famines) that may affect the other ecological systems, as well as cultural values and beliefs that influence the other ecological systems. Natural disasters may destroy the homes, schools, or other microsystems of a person or a group of developing people, and/or they may make certain necessities of life (e.g., food, fresh water) less available. Cultural values can influence the developing child in many ways. For example, cultural beliefs about the appropriateness of breast-feeding and about when weaning from the breast should occur can affect not only the nutritional status of the child but, because mother's milk may make some children less likely to develop allergies later in life, it can also affect their health status. Values about child rearing, and indeed the value or role of children in society, can affect the behaviors developed by a child (e.g., see Baumrind 1971, 1972) *and* can even have implications for whether the child survives.

A particularly dramatic example of how cultural values about the importance of children can affect a child's survival may be taken from information about the culture that existed in the ancient Near East in Carthage:

> Carthaginian society (fl. 800–150 B.C.) attached particular importance to the small child— though the manifestation of this importance was gruesome, indeed horrendous. Punic religious beliefs demanded the sacrifice of the children of the nobility to the gods ... the ancient Carthaginians believed they were handing over to the gods their precious possessions. One has only to spend an hour or so in one of the two infant Necropolises excavated in Carthage and to consider the thousands of tiny grave stelae that mark the sacrifice of each child to sense the potency of the forces that drove the Carthaginians to kill their children, many of whom were as much as three years old when they were delivered up to the gods. (French 1977, 7–8)

THE LIFE-SPAN DEVELOPMENTAL PSYCHOLOGY PERSPECTIVE

A second major instance of a contextually oriented perspective that arose during the 1970s has been labeled (as noted earlier) life-span developmental psychology or the life-span view of human development (Baltes 1979b; Baltes, Reese, and Lipsitt 1980; Lerner, Hultsch, and Dixon 1983). The major formulators of this perspective were Paul B. Baltes, K. Warner Schaie, John R. Nesselroade, Hayne W. Reese, and Orville G. Brim, Jr. As will be discussed more fully in later chapters, this perspective empha-

sizes the potential for systematic change across life and sees this potential as deriving from reciprocal influences, of people on their contexts as well as of contexts on people.

As Baltes (1979b, 2) has indicated, there are two rationales for this contextual emphasis:

> One is, of course, evident also in current child development work. As development unfolds, it becomes more and more apparent that individuals act on the environment and produce novel behavior outcomes, thereby making the active and selective nature of human beings of paramount importance. Furthermore, the recognition of the interplay between age-graded, history-graded, and nonnormative life events suggests a contextualistic and dialectical conception of development. This dialectic is further accentuated by the fact that individual development is the reflection of multiple forces that are not always in synergism, or convergence, nor do they always permit the delineation of a specific set of endstates.

In short, the growth of life-span developmental psychology in the 1970s led to a view of human development that suggested that individual changes across life are both products and producers of the multiple contextual levels in which a person is embedded.

OTHER INSTANCES OF THE INFLUENCE OF CONTEXTUALISM IN THE 1970s

In addition to the ecological and the life-span perspectives, which were of most importance to developmental psychologists, other quite important instances of the influence of contextualism arose in the 1970s. Coming from a remarkably diverse array of intellectual traditions, these instances suggested that contextualism both offered a conceptual framework for asking ecologically meaningful questions and suggested methodological strategies for doing new and potentially more useful empirical research.

For example, in 1974 James J. Jenkins rejected the mechanistic model he had used to guide his associationistic view of memory. He suggested that instead of this traditionally American approach to the study of memory, a contextual approach be adopted

(Jenkins 1974). He argued that "what memory is depends on context" (Jenkins 1974, 789) and defended this view by presenting the results of several empirical studies that demonstrate that:

> What is remembered in a given situation depends on the physical and the psychological context in which the event was experienced, the knowledge and skills that the subject brings to the context, the situation in which we ask for evidence for remembering, and the relation of what the subject remembers to what the experimenter demands. (Jenkins 1974, 793)

Jenkins (1974, 787) noted that to deal adequately with all these sources of variation means that "being a psychologist is going to be much more difficult than we used to think it to be." In part, this difficulty arises because there is no one mode of analysis, or methodological strategy, that suggests itself as always useful for assessment of all the levels of analysis involved in the memory process at all historical moments. Thus not only is methodological pluralism promoted from this contextual perspective, but the criterion of usefulness must also be employed when deciding if a particular methodological strategy is appropriate. That is, one must decide: "What kind of an analysis of memory will be useful to you in the kinds of problems you are facing? What kinds of events concern you?" (Jenkins 1974, 794). In other words, Jenkins (1974, 794) believes that:

> The important thing is to pick the right kinds of events for your purposes. And it *is* true in this view that a whole theory of an experiment can be elaborated without contributing in an important way to the science because the situation is artificial and nonrepresentative in just the senses that determine its peculiar phenomena. In short, contextualism stresses relating one's laboratory problems to the ecologically valid problems of everyday life.

Thus Jenkins (1974) reaches a conclusion quite compatible with the one Bronfenbrenner (1977) stressed.

In turn, a model of psychological functioning with marked similarity to Riegel's (1975, 1976a, 1976b) dialectical one, as well as to

features of the life-span perspective, is Sarbin's (1977) dramaturgical model. This is a technique that, through use of the notion of emplotment, attempts to capture the sequence of reciprocal events between individuals and their changing social contexts. Sarbin (1977) applies his contextualist model to the analysis of data sets pertinent to the genesis of schizophrenia, to the nature of hypnosis, and to the characteristics of imagination, in order to illustrate the integrative utility of contextually derived ideas. His presentation serves to illustrate that contextual ideas can be useful in understanding an array of psychological processes, ranging from those associated with cognition and affect to those traditionally labeled as personality and social ones. Moreover, Sarbin stresses that the interrelation among processes cannot only be integrated by contextual thinking but, in fact, needs to be appreciated if both adaptive and nonadaptive outcomes of person-context relations are to be understood. For example, Sarbin suggests that in the understanding of the bases of schizophrenia the contextualist will, as opposed to the mechanist, take

> as his unit, not schizophrenia, not improper conduct, not the rules of society, but as much of the total context as he can assimilate. His minimal unit of study would be the man who acted as if he believed he could travel unaided through space *and* the person or persons who passed judgment on such claims. (Sarbin 1977, 25)

Thus, as in Riegel's (1976a) model of crises being generated by conflicts among different developmental levels, Sarbin (1977) searches for the bases of adaptive and maladaptive functioning *not* within the realm of individual ("personological") functioning, but rather within the domain of the conflicts and crises created by the degrees of "goodness of fit" (Thomas and Chess 1977) a person experiences in his or her relations with the social context. Sarbin also sees the relevance of his ideas to those put forth in other calls for contextualist thinking. In fact, he sees Jenkins (1974) as well as Cronbach (1975) and

Gergen (1973) as making consonant appeals.

Indeed, these latter two papers are not the only instances of appeal for contextualism in the 1970s; other prominent examples may be cited. The *American Psychologist* is the journal of the American Psychological Association, designed to publish articles of current and broad interest to psychologists. The already-discussed papers by Jenkins (1974), Bronfenbrenner (1977), and Riegel (1977) were published in the *American Psychologist,* and in the last three years of the 1970s three additional papers appeared in the *American Psychologist* that, in different ways, made an appeal for contextualism. Walter Mischel (1977), arguing for considering the role of context in understanding personality, suggested that unless one considered the changing—and bidirectional—relations between people and their worlds, an adequate understanding of consistency and change in the person could not be attained. Leon Petrinovich (1979) promoted "probabilistic functionalism"—an idea drawn from Egon Brunswik's notion of ecological validity—which called for an array of methodological strategies not dissimilar in intent to those suggested in calls for methodological pluralism put forth by contextual thinkers such as Bronfenbrenner (1977) and Jenkins (1974), among others (e.g., Lerner, Skinner, and Sorell 1980). Most interestingly, Albert Bandura (1978) reconceptualized his social-learning theory as involving causal processes that are based on reciprocal determinism. That is, consistent with key emphases in contextualism, Bandura asserted that, "from this perspective, psychological functioning involves a continuous reciprocal interaction between behavioral, cognitive, and environmental influences" (Bandura 1978, 344).

Conclusions

I need not expand here on these last three instances of the promotion of contextual thinking to make the point that there was indeed a set of scholars, previously associated with a diverse array of conceptual ori-

entations within psychology, who saw in the 1970s various theoretical, methodological, and empirical uses for contextually derived ideas. In addition, we have seen that contextualism was associated with two major approaches to the study of human development—the ecological and the life-span—that became prominent during the 1970s.

It is important to reemphasize, however, that this interest in developmental psychology in a contextual model of human functioning was but an instance of the more general concern within this decade with the philosophical bases of the theories and methods used in developmental psychology (Overton and Reese 1973, 1981; Reese and Overton 1970). As we have seen in our historical survey, this interest in philosophy arose as a consequence of the increasingly abstract concern with development that occurred in this century and that took the form of a progression from descriptive and normative research to theoretically based, explanatory research to a concern with philosophical bases. This progression suggests that, in order to understand the issues and concerns of contemporary developmental psychology, one must understand both philosophy and theory and especially the interrelations between them. That is, while facts alone have their place, an understanding of the meanings and implications of facts cannot be achieved without theory, which in turn cannot be adequately dealt with unless its basis in philosophy is appreciated. Moreover, since facts will inevitably change and be modified in the face of new empirical advances, an understanding of the potential meanings and implications of any facts—through the understanding of theory—becomes of enhanced importance.

Yet, while the scientific status of theory per se and the need for and roles of theory remain essentially invariant, we cannot ignore research. If there were no research, then of course theories would be useless exercises. If there were no way to test a given theoretical integration, the formulation would be scientifically useless. Although we will discuss the role of research in developmental psychology at length in Chapter 12, as well as at other points throughout the book, it is appropriate to indicate here some of the important interrelations that exist between research and theory.

Research is often done in order to try to answer the questions raised by science. Such issue-based research results in data, as does all research. A theory may exist or be devised to integrate the facts of a science—the first role of a theory—and to lead to the generation of new facts—the second role of a theory. Someone, however, may think that these same facts can be integrated in another way—that is, with another theory. From such differences theoretical arguments come about. Yet because each different theory attaches different meanings to the same facts, research is done in order to clarify the differing theoretical interpretations. And even if such theoretical differences did not exist, research would be done in order to see if ideas (i.e., hypotheses) derived from the theory could be shown to be empirically supported. In either case research is needed to show the integrative usefulness of a theory or its usefulness in leading to new facts.

Thus, in the abstract, theory and research are inextricably bound; nevertheless some concrete interrelational problems exist. Because of the complexity and abstractness of many of the controversies of a science, the interrelation of research and theoretical issues is not often evident or unequivocal. A common complaint of many people working in science is that there seems to be a widening gap between theory and research. Although there is some truth in this statement, I suggest that if one looks at the relation between research and theory at another, more basic level, an interrelation may be seen.

PHILOSOPHY, THEORY, AND RESEARCH

Everything a scientist does rests upon

1. *assumptions* about the nature of the subject matter;

2. preferences for the *topic* of study within the subject matter; and

3. preferences for the *methods* of study.

Many psychologists are interested in studying how human behavior develops. If I assume, for purposes of illustration, that all behavioral development can be regarded as the acquisition of a series of responses, then I would look for the stimuli in a person's environment that evoke these responses. Consistent with point 1, I would assume that even complex adult behaviors could be understood on the basis of these stimulation-producing-responding relationships, and my job as a scientist would be to tease out the basic stimulus-response relations. Accordingly, and in terms of point 2, the topics that my work would bear upon could perhaps best be subsumed by the terms *learning* or *conditioning*. Moreover, as suggested by point 3, the methods I employed would be those involved with, for instance, classical or operant conditioning. I would probably prefer not to study topics such as "alterations in the balance among the id, ego, and superego in determining changes in the development of people's object relations" or "the need for the development of a sense of trust in the first year of life in order for healthy personality development to proceed." Accordingly, the methods used to study these topics (e.g., clinical interviews, retrospective verbal reports) would not rank very high on my method preference list.

If someone asked me how my work related to general issues in psychological development, I would point out that all scientific research, no matter what topic it bears on, is underlain by a particular philosophy of science or of *human beings*. Continuing with the above illustration, one could ask where my assumption—that behavioral development can be viewed as the cumulative acquisition of responses—came from. Could not other assumptions be made, for example that there is something inborn (innate) in human beings that serves to shape their behavioral development? The answer is yes.

The point here is that the particular assumptions I make are determined by the philosophical view I hold toward the nature of human development.

These assertions lead to a second response to the question of how my work is related to general conceptual issues in development. We have seen how research is underlain by theory and, more primarily, by a philosophy of science or of humanity. Therefore my work *would* be related to general conceptual issues in that it would lead to a determination of the tenability (the defensibility) of my position. As I continued to work from a particular point of view, I would eventually be able to see how well this viewpoint accounted for the phenomena of behavioral development. I would be able to see if my research, based as it is on an underlying philosophical premise, continued to account for these phenomena. Ultimately I would learn whether the variables I was studying were capable of explaining behavioral development or whether other variables necessarily entered into the picture. For example, I would learn whether the exclusive study of the functioning of environmentally based variables—stimuli and responses—can explain behavioral development. If I found this not to be the case—if I found, for example, that hereditary mechanisms seem to play a crucial role—I would be forced either to give up my initial philosophical-theoretical position and adopt another one or to revise my position so that it could account for the functioning of these other variables in terms consistent with my original philosophical-theoretical position.

In a third way, too, the outcome of my research can be seen to have general theoretical relevancy. This third way, however, can be indirect, and its relevancy to general issues or theory may not even be intended. For example, someone else might by chance be able to use the facts that another researcher has found. To explain this third way more completely, let us consider some of the reasons a scientist might conduct a research study.

Some Reasons for Doing Research

The reason why particular psychologists conduct particular studies may be very idiosyncratic and, in general, quite diverse. However, three reasons illustrate the ways in which the outcomes of research can have conceptual relevancy.

First, a person may be interested in illuminating some theoretical controversy. For instance, as already discussed, there may be an observed phenomenon that is accounted for by two different theoretical positions. In adolescent development, for example, it is typically found that there is a marked increase in the importance (saliency) of the peer group. Why does this occur? Both Anna Freud (1969) and Erik Erikson (1968) have devised theories. Consistent with the work of her father, Anna Freud takes what is termed a *psychosexual* position and ties this occurrence primarily to a biological change in the person (i.e., the emergence of a genital drive). Erikson, however, diverges somewhat from strict psychoanalytic (i.e., Freudian) theory and explains it in what he terms a *psychosocial* position, by specifying some possible relations between the developing person and his or her society.

Which theory can best account for the empirical facts? This question constantly arises in the course of scientific inquiry. A clever researcher may be able to devise a study that would put the two different interpretations to a so-called *critical,* or *crucial, test*—a study whose results would provide support for one theoretical position and nonsupport for the other. If the results came out one way, theory A would be supported; if they came out in another way, theory B would be supported.

It is important to note, however, that whether a scientist can perform a crucial test of two theories or only of specific competing hypotheses derived from these theories is *itself* a controversial issue. According to Hempel (1966), a philosopher of science, two hypotheses derived from two different theories can neither be proved nor disproved in any absolute sense. Hempel argues that this is true even if many tests of these two hypotheses are performed by the most sophisticated researchers using the most careful and extensive methods available to them, and even if all test outcomes result in completely favorable results for one hypothesis and completely unfavorable results for the other. Such results would not establish any absolute, conclusive validity for one hypothesis, but rather only relatively strong support for it. It is always possible that future tests of the two hypotheses would result in favorable outcomes for the previously unfavored hypothesis and in unfavorable outcomes for the previously favored one. In addition, it is also possible that if other hypotheses were derived from the two different theories, that tests of these two new competing hypotheses would result in favorable outcomes for the theory that was not supported when the first set of derived hypotheses was tested. Thus, as Hempel argues, in an absolutely strict sense a crucial test is impossible in science.

But the results of testing two competing theoretical positions may be "crucial" (and extremely useful) in a less strict sense. Results of tests of two rival positions can indicate that one theory is relatively untenable, while the other position is relatively tenable. Because tests of the latter theory have resulted in favorable outcomes, making it appear more tenable, it may be considered more *useful*. That is, the theory appears best able to account for existing facts. Because of the theory's demonstrated usefulness, it might play a more prominent role in any further work in the field. Even construing crucial tests in a relatively unstrict way, they are few and far between in psychology. Still, they remain an important and potentially extremely useful impetus for research.

A second reason for doing research is to test ideas—hypotheses—derived from a theory. Such deductions are made in order to see if they can be empirically supported through research. A researcher would start by saying that if his or her theory is making appropriate statements, then certain things should necessarily also be the case. Let us

say, for example, that my theory is that as children develop, the conceptual categories they can actively use to designate certain classes of things in their environment become more differentiated. For instance, returning to an earlier-used example, I might suspect that no matter what animal I showed a two-year-old, the child would respond by saying "doggie" (or some equivalent term, such as "woof-woof"). I might also suspect that if I looked at a somewhat older child, say a four- to five-year-old, I would see the ability not only to classify correctly different animals (dogs, cats, elephants) but also the ability to classify correctly different types of dogs (collies, German shepherds, poodles). Thus, in accordance with my theory, I might hypothesize (predict) that as the children I study increase in age, their ability to classify correctly different animals will also increase. If my theory is defensible, my hypothesis, deduced from my theory, should be supported by the results of my study.

By testing deductions, a researcher can provide support or refutation for his or her theory. Research based on such *deductive reasoning* is an important component of scientific thinking, and it will be discussed in further detail below.

However, I have said that there is a third way in which research can be found relevant to theory. Sometimes a researcher may conduct a study just to find out what exists. A person may have no theoretical issue in mind but may be interested only in describing the characteristics of a certain phenomenon or aspect of behavioral development, or in seeing what will be the behavioral result of a certain manipulation. For example, let us say that a person wants to know what reasons five-year-olds and fifteen-year-olds might give to explain why a person should not steal from friends. He or she might then ask groups of five- and fifteen-year-olds to give their reasons for not stealing from friends. The results might be that five-year-olds' reasons seem to be rather concrete, reflecting a fear of punishment and an orientation toward obedience. A five-year-old might say you should not steal because your friend will hit you or your mother will punish you for doing something she says is wrong. The fifteen-year-olds' reasons might be more abstract and reflect the notion that stealing from a friend violates implicit rules of mutual trust and respect, or that as a member of society one implicitly has to respect the rights of others. The researcher reports the information and thus adds additional facts to the literature of the science.

Although the researcher may not intend to relate his or her facts to any theories, the theoretical relevancy of the facts can be found after the research is done. In attempting to ascertain the validity of a particular theory, someone may be able to use the facts as a means to support that theory. Thus the facts reported in the above example could, after their communication, be seen to fit into a theoretical formulation. In fact, Lawrence Kohlberg (1963a) formulated a theory of moral development (discussed in Chapter 8) that could incorporate the hypothesized findings.

In sum, although a fact may now be "loose"—not related to a theory—this does not exclude the possibility that at some later time it may be seen as related to or consistent with a general concept. Many facts not initially intended to be directly related to a theory *do* find their way into one. This takes place through another major type of scientific thinking process: *inductive reasoning.* In this process a scientist will start with sets of facts and then try to find some conceptual formulation to organize and perhaps explain them. Thus a scientist using such reasoning proceeds from observed facts to integrative concepts or theories. We will discuss inductive reasoning again below.

In the various ways outlined above, the outcome of *all* research does bear on the general conceptual and theoretical issues of a science. Although a researcher's reasons for undertaking the study of a topic may not relate to these general considerations, it is important to be aware of this perspective if only to gain an appreciation of the cumulative and dynamic aspects of a science such as developmental psychology. From this per-spective a student will be able to see several things:

1.   Why some people study one topic while others investigate another. Differences in underlying philosophies of science and/or humanity lead to differences in the assumptions a scientist makes about the nature of the subject matter. As we have seen, this leads scientists to look at different aspects of development and hence to investigate different topics.

2.   Why abstract theoretical debates occur. When scientists assume a particular philosophical or theoretical point of view, they become committed to it; they attempt to defend it, to show its tenability. They will attempt to justify their positions through logic and empirical research. Hence, because of commitments to different theoretical points of view, one scientist may interpret a given fact one way, while another scientist interprets it another way.

3.   Why an understanding of these theoretical concepts is crucial for an adequate understanding and appreciation of the research, data, and facts of a science. In sum, if students are given this conceptual perspective, they will know not only some implications of the results of one or more research studies but also the meaning and relevancy of research as it bears on the general concepts of a science.

The Trouble with Textbooks

Unfortunately, it seems that many students do not develop this orientation and appreciation in many basic science courses. Some students report that studying the textbooks for such courses is like studying the telephone directory. Why is this often the case?

Numerous child psychology textbooks capably and clearly describe the dimensions and characteristics of a child's development. They also do a good job of acquainting the reader with the presumed or known processes underlying development. Thus the authors of these texts present to the readers summaries of both the appropriate empirical research and the relevant theoretical notions of child development (for example those of Piaget, Erikson, Freud, Bijou, and Baer). However, these theoretical accounts are necessarily somewhat limited. Full explications of any of these theorists' ideas would fill (and have filled) books of their own. Nevertheless, for the reasons discussed in the preceding section, I believe that a greater emphasis needs to be put on theory and concepts.

The main purpose of most survey texts is not the communication either of theory by itself or, more primarily, of theory joined with the core conceptual issues involved in the study of human development. Rather, these texts emphasize research and empirical generalizations based on these findings. The point here is one of emphasis; most texts certainly do not exclude discussions of theories, but neither do they spend most of their time on them. While most current texts do an outstanding job of presenting empirical results and trends in these findings, such presentations do not directly provide students with an integrative conceptual framework from which to view the field. Since the instructor often does not have the time to supply this framework, many students, after reading such a text, feel that they have interacted with a large mass of complex and often disjointed information, and many of them struggle to understand what it all means.

Because of this, I believe that many incipient developmental psychologists are lost. Never realizing the intellectual excitement that the instructor feels—because he or she is well aware both of empirical trends and the conceptual implications of the research findings—the student may be "turned off" by a delineation of the details of particular studies. Thus, in failing to see the whole picture, the student does not understand the overall importance of the things he or she does learn about the subject.

This Text's Approach

How do I think this book represents a significant departure from the typical text that you might read in an introductory science course?

First and foremost, I must admit that I am biased. I have certain beliefs about how best to teach and to try to understand a science. I believe that a science should be approached from a conceptual, theoretical, and deductively oriented point of view.

As suggested above, there are two major ways to go about studying the phenomena of a science: inductively or deductively. The characteristics and uses of these processes are complex, and although a full explication of these topics is beyond the goals of the present discussion, a brief overview will suffice for our purposes. A more detailed but still introductory presentation of these topics can be found in Hempel (1966).

If one follows the inductive method, one starts with facts. A scientist will first look at some set of data. Then, in an attempt to integrate these facts, he or she will try to devise some general principles. In other words, one first focuses on facts and then tries to formulate a concept that will integrate them. Although the inductive approach is certainly a valid, important, and useful way of studying the phenomena of a science, it has been argued that this approach can lead to the compiling of a "heap of bricks" rather than a "house." This approach can lead to much data being collected without any clear a priori reason; that is, without any preceding, explicitly articulated and considered theoretical rationale. Many facts might be gathered, but their general significance might be unknown or difficult to ascertain. As an alternative I elect to take a deductive approach. I prefer to begin my own scientific research from the theoretical end of the data-theory continuum.

As implied earlier, a theory can be defined as a group of statements (for example, concepts, principles) that integrate existing facts and lead to the generation of new ones. Similarly, Hempel (1966) suggests that a theory explains empirical uniformities that have been previously discovered and usually also predicts new regularities of similar kinds. To be consistent with this definition, then, I would use theory in the following way within the deductive approach:

1.   In order to be considered sound and tenable, my theory should be able to integrate existing facts. That is, it should be able to account for established empirical findings that bear on the content of my theory.

2.   Moreover, based on my theory, I should be able to devise some statements that—if found to be borne out by research— would provide support for my theory (and if found false would refute it). Put in more formal terms, I should be able to generate testable *hypotheses* from my theory. My hypotheses will usually take the form of "if . . . then . . ." propositions; that is, "if my theory is appropriate in saying so and so, then such and such should be the case." In essence, I would be reasoning that if my theory were useful, my deduction from it should be supported by the outcome of my research.

3.   I would then put my deduction to an *empirical test,* for example by doing an experiment or a correlational study. If the results yield the predicted findings, then this new fact, arrived at through deductive reasoning, will be appropriately placed within my theoretical system. This fact will be a brick added to my house rather than piled onto my heap.

In sum, by emphasizing a deductive theoretical perspective I can see how well my facts fit together as a cohesive, understandable whole. Moreover, I can see what sort of information is needed to fill in gaps in my theory or to clarify or refine it. The facts I derive from my deductive approach will not be useless or random. Rather, they will contribute to my theoretical edifice. My deductively arrived-at facts will support, clarify, or refute my theoretical position.

Cattell's Inductive-Hypothetico-Deductive Model

Of course, as a scientist functions in his or her day-in-day-out endeavors, such idealized deductive theoretical reasonings may not occur, and in fact such sharp textbook divisions between inductive and deductive reasoning are typically not maintained (Cattell 1966). Rather, as the scientist attempts to establish "general laws which can be empirically tested and which lead to deductions extending our theoretical understanding and practical control" (Cattell 1966, 11), and thus tries to fulfill the function of science, both inductive and deductive reasoning may typically be used. As indicated above, there may be several reasons for doing a particular research study, and at different times the same scientist may do a particular study for any of these reasons. Thus, as pointed out by Raymond B. Cattell—one of the leading psychologists to contribute to the science—research as it occurs in the real world may have as its starting point other than deductively derived hypotheses. Rather, its initial impetus may be the observation of a curious empirical phenomenon or regularity.

Thus we have drawn a distinction between induction and deduction in order to emphasize the point of view that science best advances when facts are gathered with at least an eye toward eventual integration with theory, yet this distinction may not necessarily characterize the scientific reasoning of the real-life practicing research psychologist. As Cattell argues, all scientists should work toward formulating general principles from which testable deductions are derived. However, this endeavor does not necessarily have to begin with a hypothesis. As we have seen, it may begin just with interesting observations of empirical reality obtained while the scientist is working in the general theoretical atmosphere. From this empirical observation the researcher might induce that this fact is representative of some more general regularity, and as a consequence formulate a hypothesis about the validity of this induction. Then he or she might deduce what empirical consequences would have to be obtained in order for the hypothesis to be confirmed and accordingly make another, higher-order empirical observation, and the whole process would start anew.

Raymond B. Cattell

ity the practicing research scientist often uses both techniques. Yet it still remains the case that *inevitably* deductions from general organizing principles must eventually be drawn and tested in order for theory, and hence understanding, to be advanced. It is for this ultimate reason that I prefer and emphasize the deductive approach to science. Thus the first way in which this book will depart from others (aside from having an *admittedly* biased author) is that the primary orientation will be conceptual and theoretical.

To this end, I will first acquaint you with the basic philosophies of science underlying the conceptual issues of developmental psychology. We will then turn our attention to the conceptual issues themselves—the nature-nurture issue, the subordinate problems of instinct and the critical-periods hypothesis, and the continuity-discontinuity issue along with the interrelated problem of sta-

What we see, then, is that in actuality the method that perhaps best characterizes the reasoning of the practicing scientist is neither purely deductive nor purely inductive. Rather, it may be what Cattell terms *inductive-hypothetico-deductive* in nature. As illustrated in Figure 1.4, this method begins with some empirical observation, which in turn serves as the basis for the induction of some empirical regularity. This induction needs to be subjected to empirical verification, however, in order to ascertain its validity; accordingly, a hypothesis is derived from the induction, and the empirical consequences of this hypothesis are deduced and tested. The result of this test is, of course, another empirical observation, which is seen to continue the inductive-hypothetico-deductive spiral again.

In sum, then, although the conceptual distinction between the inductive and the deductive methods of scientific reasoning is a valid one, we must recognize that in actual-

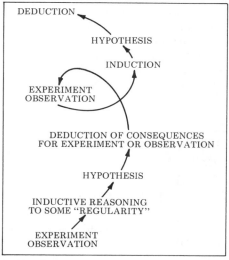

FIGURE 1.4

Cattell's notion of the inductive-hypothetico-deductive spiral.

Source: R. B. Cattell, ed. (1966), *Handbook of multivariate experimental psychology,* Diagram 1.1, p. 16. Copyright © 1966 by Rand McNally & Company, Chicago. Reprinted by permission of Rand McNally College Publishing Company.

bility-instability. After this we will consider three general theoretical approaches to child development—the stage, the differential, and the ipsative—which are inclusive of the general approaches to developmental theory. We will interrelate the core conceptual issues with these three developmental theoretical approaches and another theoretical approach—which involves empirical and theoretical behavioristic orientations—and see how the former bear on the latter. We will then summarize major theoretical positions within each approach. For example, when presenting the stage-theory approach to developmental psychology, we will consider the work of Piaget, of Kohlberg, and of Freud.

Throughout these presentations the major emphasis will be on concepts and theory. However, this does not mean that research studies will be ignored. Research will be integrated into these conceptual discussions throughout the book, and Chapter 12 will be devoted to a presentation of the research and social implications of concepts and theories of human development. However, rather than attempt to review all the research literature bearing on a particular issue, we will discuss a key study or two that illustrate, clarify, or refine the issues.

THE DEVELOPMENTAL CONTEXTUAL (OR ORGANISMIC CONTEXTUAL) POSITION

It will become clear to the reader that I have a preferred theoretical orientation toward human development. This position combines features of organicism and of contextualism. It has been labeled in many ways: probabilistic epigenesis (Gottlieb 1970, 1983), organismic contextualism (Overton 1983), or simply, developmental contextualism (Lerner and Kauffman in press). In Chapter 2 I shall discuss this view more fully. Here, however, let me note that I believe that this point of view presents a useful theoretical integration of important ideas of psychological development. Although, as noted already, extended presentations of this viewpoint will be offered throughout this book, a brief overview of the developmental contextual position is appropriate here.

What is a person? What sort of changes characterize a person as he or she develops? Where do these changes come from? How do they relate to human development? Questions such as these are inevitably involved in any theoretical consideration of psychological development and the developmental contextual theoretical perspective has its own specific answers. Essentially, it asserts that human beings are active rather than passive, and that among the changes characterizing human development are those involving the quality of psychological functioning. It is clear that in a general sense the only sources of behavior are a person's genetic inheritance (nature) and environmental experience and contextual influences (nurture), and thus another component of this organismic position is that human behavioral development is derived from interactions between these two sources.

The specific basic components of the developmental contextual position can be summarized as follows:

1.   Development is characterized by both *quantitative and qualitative* changes in the processes underlying development. For instance, processes involved with a person's perceptual, motivational, or cognitive development undergo changes in kind, or type (quality), and in addition in amount, frequency, magnitude, or duration (quantity). This point of view does not deny that there are some aspects of a person that remain the same across life; rather, it asserts that human development is a synthesis between changes and processes and variables that remain constant (Brim and Kagan 1980; Lerner 1985).

2.   The *laws* that govern the functioning of both constancy and change are related

both to an organism's heredity and to its environment. Hempel (1966) defines a law as a statement asserting some invariant characteristics about a phenomenon or process; we will also grant the status of law to statements that hold only approximately, with certain qualifications or only under certain specifiable conditions, or with a given level of probability.

3. These two sets of factors (heredity and environment) *interact* to account for behavioral development. Logically, there are several possible ways that heredity and environment can be related to each other (Overton 1973; Lerner 1985). First, it is possible that either heredity or environment might act alone as a source of behavioral development; second, it may be the case that the contribution of heredity is added to the contribution of the environment; third, heredity and environment may be related to each other in a multiplicative, or interactionist, manner. In turn, many different types of interaction may occur. Lerner and Spanier (1980) and Lerner (1985) have identified three such types, labeling them weak, moderate, and strong. This last possibility is the one that adherents of the developmental contextual position adopt. Chapters 2 and 3 will include more complete accounts of the varieties of interaction that may exist. Suffice it to say here, however, that strong interactions involve the reciprocal (bidirectional) influences between people and their contexts that we have seen emphasized by Riegel (e.g., 1975) and by adherents of the life-span perspective (e.g., Baltes 1979b).

4. The mode of interaction between heredity and environmental variables thus involves the action of the environment on the organism's characteristics (e.g., a person's unfolding maturational processes, body build, temperament), and the action of the organism on aspects of its environment (for example, parents or teachers). Thus, a crucial and central component of the developmental contextual position is that people themselves play an active, contributory role in their own development. The person does not merely wait while the environment acts

to govern his or her development. Rather, in addition to being shaped by the environment, people act to shape their own world, to play an active, contributory role in their own development. Contrary to the position espoused by such theorists as Skinner (1956), Bijou (1976), Baer (1970), and Bijou and Baer (1961)—who maintain that behavioral development is controlled essentially by the environment—developmental contextually oriented developmentalists consider the role of the person's own activity as a central source of development. Hence, just as much as the environment and its agents (e.g., parents) influence the child, the child's own characteristics influence these environmental agents (see Bell 1968; Lerner 1982; Lerner and Busch-Rosnagel 1981; Schneirla 1957; Thomas et al. 1963).

A major goal of this book will be to expand and clarify the developmental contextual position and to detail how it provides a conceptual framework from which to view psychological development. We shall see too how this point of view allows an interrelation and understanding of the nature-nurture, continuity-discontinuity, and critical-periods issues.

However, as suggested above, there is a major theoretical approach to human development that is philosophically distinct from those derived from either the organismic and/or the contextual perspectives. This point of view is the mechanistic one. To see the manner in which the distinct philosophical positions provide contrasting approaches to the study of human development, let us consider how formulating a definition of a key concept in developmental psychology is complicated by the contrasting philosophical orientations of developmental psychologists. The concept we will consider is that of *development*. My discussion of the issues involved in defining this term will lead, in Chapter 2, to a presentation of the major philosophical models of human development. There we shall see how the philosophical bases of these orientations differ.

In sum, I shall proceed from the philosophy of science to concepts, theories, and eventually to research-derived facts about child development.

DEFINING THE CONCEPT OF DEVELOPMENT

The meaning of the term "development" has engaged, and continues to engage, psychologists and sociologists in philosophical and theoretical debate (Collins 1982; Featherman 1985; Harris 1957; Kaplan 1966, 1983; Lerner 1976, 1985; Overton and Reese 1973; Reese and Overton 1970). The existence of the debate is itself indicative of a key feature of the meaning of the term. That is, development is not an empirical concept. If it were, inspection of a set of data would similarly indicate to any observer whether development was present.

However, different scientists can look at a data set and disagree about whether development has occurred. This is because development is a theoretical concept. It is, as Kaplan (1966, 1983) put it, a concept of postulation. One begins one's study of development with some implicit or explicit concept of what development is. Then, when one inspects a given set of data, one can determine whether the features of the data match, or fit with, one's concept.

In other words, a given scientist's concept of development serves as a conceptual template. The scientist uses this template when he or she looks at data. Observations that coincide with the structure of the template are labeled developmental ones; observations that do not match the template are judged nondevelopmental.

Debates among scientists about the meaning of development arise because different scientists have different templates. Simply put, different scientists have different conceptions of the meaning of the term. These conceptual differences exist because different scientists are committed to distinct philosophical and theoretical beliefs about the nature of the world and of human life. For instance, some scientists find it useful to view the world as a machine and to study humans in terms of the energies needed to set the parts of the machine in motion. Other scientists do not find it useful to see humans as machines made up of discrete parts. Instead, they conceive of humans as integrated wholes, and they study how the structure or the organization of this whole changes over time.

Despite the philosophical and theoretical differences that exist among scientists in their conception of development, there is some agreement about the minimal features of any concept of development. In its most general sense, development refers to change. But clearly, "change" and "development" are not equivalent terms. If they were, there would hardly be a need for the more abstract term "development," and there would seem to be little reason for the philosophical and theoretical debates about the meaning of the term. Thus, although whenever development occurs there is change, not all changes are developmental ones.

For example, the ups and downs of one's checkbook balance involve changes, but few if any scientists would label such changes as development. In addition, random, chaotic, completely disorganized, or totally dispersive changes cannot readily be construed as developmental ones. Changes must have a systematic, organized character in order for them to be labeled as developmental.

But systematicity, or organization, does not suffice to define development. An office organized by one head secretary may run by one system, while another office, organized by another head secretary, may run by a completely different system. If the first secretary leaves his or her job and is replaced by the second secretary, the latter may change the former's system into the one he or she prefers. A system, or an organization, exists during the tenure of the first secretary and then during the tenure of the second. Yet the second system is not an outgrowth of the first; there is no necessary connection between the two. In fact, if the first secretary returns to his or her job, the first system can be reinstated, and in such a case there would again be no necessary connection between the two organizations. Thus, although change occurred, and although at the two points in time across which change was observed a system existed, there was no connection between the two systems. The character of the first system in no way influenced the character of the second. Accordingly, the change in the office was not a developmental one, although it did involve an organized systematic structure.

For organized, or systematic, changes to be developmental ones, they have to have a *successive* character. The idea of successive changes indicates that the changes seen at a later time are at least in part influenced by the changes that occurred at an earlier time, if only to the extent that the range of changes probable at the later time is limited by earlier occurrences. In short, in a most general sense, the concept of development implies systematic and successive changes over time in an organization.

Virtually without exception, however, developmental psychologists go considerably beyond this minimum definition. For instance, historically the concept of development is a biological one (Harris 1957). As such, the unit of concern (or analysis) for most psychologists is typically an individual organism. Furthermore, because the intellectual roots of the concept of development lie in biology, developmental changes are held to be only those systematic, successive changes over time in the organization of an organism *that are thought to serve an adaptive function,* i.e., to enhance survival (Schneirla 1957).

However, as another instance, other developmental psychologists postulate that or-

ganized, successive changes must have a specific form in order for one to say that a *developmental progression* exists. In other words, only when the structure of an organization changes in a particular sequence is development said to occur. For example, Werner (1948, 1957), Werner and Kaplan (1956), and Kaplan (1983) postulate that development exists when a system changes from being organized in a very general or global way (wherein few, if any, differentiated parts exist) to having differentiated parts that are organized into an integrated hierarchy. Werner and Kaplan label this concept of development the *orthogenetic principle,* and indicate that only those structural changes that coincide with this sequence of globality to differentiated and integrated parts fulfill the requirements for a developmental progression (Werner and Kaplan 1956, 1963).

The point to be drawn from the above examples is that despite a relatively high degree of consensus about the point that development is a theoretical concept that, at the least, connotes systematic and successive change in an organization, there is a good deal of disagreement among developmental psychologists about what particular ideas need to be added in order to define the term adequately. As indicated above, these differences in definitions are associated with philosophical and theoretical differences that also divide scientists. The theoretical differences among scientists are ultimately based on their commitments to different philosophical positions (Kuhn 1970; Pepper 1942). As a consequence, it is useful to discuss the different philosophical positions that influence developmental psychologists. We do this in Chapter 2.

2 | *Philosophical Models of Development*

Scientists do not initiate their research without implicit and explicit assumptions. Often these assumptions take the form of theories that guide the selection of hypotheses, methods, data analysis procedures, and so on. Scientists use a specific set of rules to determine reality. Through making observations—the fundamental task of scientists—they measure phenomena objectively under particular conditions. Then scientists attempt to identify regularities among observations. Such regular, predictable relationships among variables are called *laws.* Finally a *theory*—a set of propositions consisting of defined and interrelated constructs integrating these laws—is developed. Besides integrating knowledge, a theory serves the function of guiding further research.

Even though we can determine reality by relying upon an empirical approach to knowledge and can delineate what steps—observations, laws, and theory—are involved, a glance at the scientific literature shows that scientists do not agree about their observations, laws, and theories. This is the case primarily because they make different philosophical assumptions about the nature of the world. Thus, in addition to the relatively empirical facts of science, scientists also hold *preempirical beliefs,* i.e., beliefs not open to empirical test. These assumptions may also be explicit or implicit (Watson 1977); they may take the form of a presupposition about the nature of a specific feature of life—for example, that there is an inevitable connection between early experi-

ence and behavior in later life (Kagan 1980, 1983). In addition, these beliefs may take the form of a more general "paradigm" (Kuhn 1962, 1970), "model" (Overton and Reese 1973; Reese and Overton 1970), "world view" (Kuhn 1962, 1970), or "world hypothesis" (Pepper 1942); that is, a philosophical system of ideas that serves to organize a set, or a "family" (Reese and Overton 1970), of scientific theories and associated scientific methods.

Thus these philosophical models of the world have quite a pervasive effect on the scientific positions they influence: They specify the basic characteristics of humans, and of reality itself, and thus function either to include or exclude particular features of humans and/or of the world's events in the realm of scientific discourse. Thus science is relative rather than absolute. Facts are not viewed as naturally occurring events awaiting discovery. According to Kuhn (1962), science

> seems an attempt to force nature into [a] preformed and relatively inflexible box. . . . No part of the aim of normal science is to call forth new sorts of . . . phenomena; indeed those that will not fit the box are often not seen at all. Nor do scientists normally aim to invent new theories, and they are often intolerant of those invented by others. (p. 24)

Accordingly, an adequate understanding of human development cannot be obtained from any one theory or methodology, nor can it be obtained from a cataloging of empirical "facts." In my view, then, theory and research only have meaning as they are developed and interpreted within the context of a given philosophical perspective. Thus we need to understand the different philosophical assumptions on which the study of development can be based. We need to examine the models, or world views, that are used today in the study of human development.

Since the early 1970s Hayne W. Reese and Willis F. Overton have written a series of essays (Overton 1984; Overton and Reese 1973, 1981; Reese 1982; Reese and Overton, 1970) that explain the ways in which two world views—the mechanistic and the organismic—have shaped theories of development. The work of Reese and Overton was seminal in promoting among other developmental psychologists an interest in exploring the potential role of other world hypotheses

Willis F. Overton

Hayne W. Reese

in shaping theories of development. For instance, as noted in Chapter 1, Riegel (1975, 1977a, 1977b) discussed the potential use of a "dialectical" model of development, and Lerner (1984, 1985; Lerner, Hultsch, and Dixon 1983) as well as Reese and Overton themselves (Reese 1982; Overton 1984; Overton and Reese 1981) discussed the ways in which a "contextual" world hypothesis (Pepper 1942) could be used to devise a theory of development. As I noted in Chapter 1, the dialectical model emphasizes syntheses among the conflicts arising from the interactions among variables from different levels of analysis, e.g., the inner-biological, individual-psychological, physical-environmental, and sociocultural (Riegel 1975, 1976a, 1976b). In turn, we saw in Chapter 1 that contextualism stresses the continually changing context of life, the bidirectional interactions among individuals and the context, and that the timing of these interactions shapes the direction and outcome of development (Pepper 1942). As Overton (1984) has recently made clear, however, these latter models (i.e., the dialectical and the contextual ones) do not readily provide a useful set of ideas for the derivation of scientifically adequate theories of development *unless* they are integrated into mechanistic or organismic conceptions. That is, Overton (1984) maintains that the mechanistic and the organismic models are superordinate in providing a basis for developmental theories; any other model alone will not suffice to provide such a basis, and as such any other model, e.g., contextualism, will have to be integrated with either mechanism or organicism to provide such a basis. I shall argue for a somewhat similar position; however, I make the additional points that the mechanistic view has too many conceptual limitations for use as a model for development, and that in turn, just as contextualism needs organicism to enhance its use, so does organicism need contextualism. To begin to develop this argument we turn to a presentation of the mechanistic, the organismic, and the contextual models.

THE MECHANISTIC MODEL

As explained by Reese and Overton (1970), the mechanistic model

> represents the universe as a machine, composed of discrete pieces operating in a spatio-temporal field. The pieces—elementary particles in motion—and their relations form the basic reality to which all other more complex phenomena are ultimately reducible. In the operation of the machine, forces are applied and there results a discrete chain-like sequence of events. These forces are the only efficient or immediate causes; purpose is seen as a mediate or derived cause. Given this, it is only a short trip to the recognition that complete prediction is *in principle* possible, since complete knowledge of the state of the machine at one point in time allows inference of the state at the next, given a knowledge of the forces to be applied. (p. 131)

In turn, as summarized by Anderson, this philosophical position states that "the workings of our minds and bodies, and of all the animate or inanimate matter of which we have any detailed knowledge, are assumed to be controlled by the same set of fundamental laws, which except under certain extreme conditions we feel we know pretty well" (1972, 393). Simply, a key assumption of the mechanistic position is that the events of all sciences can be uniformly understood by the same set of laws.

For instance, proponents of this viewpoint often hold that physics and chemistry are the basic natural sciences; they thus often believe that the laws of these two disciplines are the one set of fundamental laws alluded to by Anderson (1972). That is, although several different meanings of the term *mechanism* have been used by philosophers and scientists, one major version of the mechanistic position is an interpretation of biological (or psychological) phenomena in physical and chemical terms (Bertalanffy 1933). This interpretation provides an apt illustration for our discussion, and we shall focus on it to explain the position.

In this interpretation it is the laws of chemistry and physics—the rules that depict the mechanisms by which atoms and molecules function—that are the fundamental laws of the real world. Everything involves atoms and molecules; nothing exists in the natural world that is not basically made up of these things. If one understands the mechanisms by which atoms and molecules combine and function, then one understands the laws basic to everything. The mechanics of chemistry and physics then become the ultimate laws of all events.

Thus these basic laws that govern all natural events and phenomena, whether organic or inorganic, are held to apply to all levels of phenomenal analysis. Consistent with Nagel (1957), we define a *level* as a state of organization of matter, or life, phenomena. For example, chemistry, with its particular set of concepts and principles, represents one level of organization, while psychology, with its own set of terms, represents another. One can describe behavior at its own level or in terms of the principles of another level. We can study how children at various age levels develop the ability to perform in certain situations (e.g., on classroom tests) by attempting to discern the psychological factors involved in such behavior; alternatively, these very same behaviors may be described and studied at another level. The children's performance certainly involves the functioning of their physiological systems, a lower level (in the sense of underlying the behavioral level) of analysis. Ultimately, of course, the functioning of their physiological systems involves the functioning of the atoms and molecules that form the basic matter of living, organic material.

We can thus seek to understand psychological functioning by reference to the mechanisms of physics and chemistry. These mechanisms represent the most fundamental level of analysis that can be reached, and since this level is invariably involved in any other level, we can certainly seek to understand psychology by reference to chemistry and physics. These basic physical laws are just as applicable to psychology as they are to physiology, or for that matter to any other event or phenomenon in the natural world. Everything—living or nonliving—is made up of atoms and molecules. Ultimately, then, if we understand the rules by which atoms and molecules function, we can understand the components of all things in the natural world. All we must do to understand biology, psychology, sociology, or the movement of the stars is to bring each down to its most basic constituent elements, to the most fundamental level of analysis: the physical-chemical level. The events and phenomena of all sciences—of everything in the natural world—may be uniformly understood through the mechanisms involved in atoms and molecules.

Hence proponents of the mechanistic philosophical viewpoint would not seek to explain the phenomena of psychology per se; this is not the appropriate level of analysis. Rather, they would attempt to reduce these phenomena of psychological functioning to the fundamental level of analysis—the laws of chemistry and physics. The basic point of this mechanistic position, then, is *reductionism:* reducing the phenomena of a given (higher) level to the elemental, fundamental (lower, or molecular) units that comprise it. It is believed that there is nothing special about the complex pattern of events we call psychological functioning. In the final analysis these events involve the functioning of the very same atoms and molecules that are involved in the workings of a liver, a kidney, or a shooting star. Thus, like everything else, psychological phenomena are governed by the laws of chemistry and physics and, upon appropriate reduction, may be understood in terms of those laws. From this standpoint, then, if we knew enough about chemistry and physics we could eliminate the science of psychology completely. As pointed out by Bolles, this reductionistic assumption involves "the doctrine that all natural events have physical causes, and that if we knew enough about physical and mechanical systems we would then be able to explain, at least in principle, all natural phenomena" (1967, 5).

Reductionism directly implies a *continuity* position. No new laws are needed to explain the phenomena of a given level of study; rather, the same exact laws apply at all levels. Since natural phenomena at any and all levels can be reduced to the phenomena of the fundamental physical-chemical level, these same laws are continuously applicable to all levels of phenomena. Since no new, additional, or different laws are needed to account for or to understand the phenomena that may be thought to characterize any particular level, continuity by definition exists. As we have seen, psychology may be reduced to the level of chemistry and physics *because* the latter level is invariably present in anything that exists.

What this means, then, is that the "real" laws governing any and all events in the world are really the laws of chemistry and physics. In essence, the mechanistic position holds that in the final analysis one must inevitably deal with certain fundamental laws in order to completely, accurately, and ultimately understand any and all living and nonliving matter in the natural world. And, as Anderson has commented, once this concept is accepted:

> It seems inevitable to go on uncritically to what appears at first sight to be an obvious corollary of reductionism: that if everything obeys the same fundamental laws, then the only scientists who are studying anything really fundamental are those who are working on those laws. In practice, that amounts to some astrophysicists, some elementary particle physicists, some logicians and other mathematicians, and few others. (1972, 393)

Because of the belief that reductionism will lead to fundamental knowledge, and because of the associated postulation of continuity in the laws and mechanisms that are involved in an appropriate consideration of natural phenomena, two events may ultimately occur. First, the phenomena in the world labeled psychological would no longer be a focus of scientific concern; these phenomena are not fundamental—they must be reduced to be appropriately understood. Second, the people in the world labeled psychologists would no longer be necessary; these people are not studying fundamental phenomena of the natural world.

What would replace psychology, and in fact all sciences other than the "fundamental" ones, would be a consideration of the basic mechanisms of the physical-chemical level of analysis. To understand every event and phenomenon in the natural world one must understand the mechanisms of physics and chemistry. This statement highlights another major attribute of the mechanistic position. Adherents of this position conceptualize the functioning of the components (the atoms and molecules) of the most fundamental level of analysis within the framework of a machine. As we have seen, according to this model, biological or psychological phenomena are only seemingly complicated constellations of physical and chemical processes. In principle, once we

know the mechanisms of physical and chemical functioning, we know all we have to know about the world. In other words, because the fundamental level of analysis functions mechanistically, all the world is seen as functioning mechanistically.

Since physics and chemistry are machine-like sciences, all that must be done in order to move from one level of analysis to another is to specify the mechanism by which the basic elements of physics and chemistry combine. Since the molecular (physical-chemical) laws apply at the higher (psychological) level, it is necessary only to discern the mechanisms by which these molecular elements are quantitatively added. In other words, to go to a higher level, all one must do is add these elements to what was present at the lower level. If, for example, a rat is made up of ten oranges, all that would be necessary for moving up to the human level would be to add, for instance, another sixteen oranges. Thus the only difference between levels is a quantitative one, a difference in amount, size, magnitude, and so on.

The mechanistic position is diagrammatically illustrated in Figure 2.1. Two levels of analysis are represented; level 1, for example, could be the biological level and level 2 the psychological level. Both are comprised of the same basic thing, in this case oranges. To move from one level to another all one must do is add more oranges. Thus between the two levels there is a continuity in the basic elements that make up each level; put another way, each level can be reduced to the same basic elements.

In summary, adherents of the mechanistic model would view psychology as a branch of natural science (e.g., see Bijou 1976; Bijou and Baer 1961). They seek to reduce the phenomena of psychology to basic mechanical laws (e.g., of physics and chemistry) because of their belief that these laws continuously apply to all phenomenal levels. Hence, in this view, the phenomena of psychology are not unique in nature but are, rather, controlled by the laws that govern all events and phenomena in the natural world.

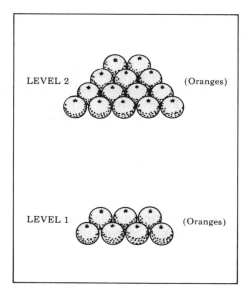

FIGURE 2.1
Mechanistic position: Each level is comprised of the same basic elements.

The position thus holds that there are basic and common laws that govern all things in the universe. Neither biology, psychology, sociology, nor any science (other than physics or chemistry), for that matter, really has its own special laws; rather, in a basic sense, all sciences—and more important, all events and phenomena in the real world—are controlled by a common set of principles. It is believed that the phenomena, or events, that all sciences study can be uniformly subsumed (unified) and understood by one common set of natural-science principles (see Harris 1957).

Thus the basic characteristics of the mechanistic position are as follows:

1. It is a *natural-science* viewpoint.

2. It is a *reductionist* viewpoint.

3. It is a *continuity* viewpoint.

4. It is a *unity-of-science* viewpoint.

5. It is a *quantitative* viewpoint.

6. It is an *additive* viewpoint.

Translating the Mechanistic Model into a Theory of Development

When the mechanistic model is transformed, or translated, into a set of ideas pertinent to psychological development, a reactive, passive, or "empty-organism" model of humans results (Reese and Overton 1970). From this perspective, the human is inherently passive; his or her activity results from the action of external forces; for example, in one behavioristic instance of this mechanistic position, stimuli evoke a response from a passive organism. The works of Skinner (1938), Bijou (1976), Baer (1982), Bijou and Baer (1961), and Gewirtz (1961) are representative of this position. These authors try to formulate the determining mechanisms of human behavioral development according to a natural-science model (Bijou and Baer 1961). They attempt to discern the empirical (observable) and quantifiable parameters of environmental stimulation that fit this model (Gewirtz and Stingle 1968). Viewing behavior as a quantitative addition of discrete elements that combine, analogously, in the mechanical manner of chemistry and physics, such theorists appropriately look to the environment for the source of human behavior/personality development. A machine is passive until extrinsic energy activates it. Human beings, viewed as machines, are also passive until environmental stimulation causes them to act. Their behavioral development becomes just the historical, "mechanical mirror" (Langer 1969) of environmental stimulation. Moreover, as Reese and Overton (1970) explain, *changes* in the "products of the machine," that is, changes over time in the behavior of organisms, do not result from phenomena intrinsic to organisms but rather, again, from alterations in the stimuli impinging on them.

Thus those committed to such a mechanistic position would, in their psychological theorizing, try to explain behavioral development in terms of the principles of classical and operant conditioning (e.g., Baer 1982; Bijou 1976; Bijou and Baer 1961; Gewirtz and Stingle 1968). If human beings are passive, they must await stimulation from the environment in order to act, or more accurately, to *respond*. How does such stimulation bring human behavior under control? Many mechanistic-behavioristic theorists would suggest that the principles of classical (respondent) conditioning and of operant (instrumental) conditioning can explain it. The former set of principles can account for stimulation-produced responding (S → R), while the latter can account for response-produced stimulation (R → S). Given the broad applicability of these types of conditioning in the natural world, they should be able to account for the acquisition of the responses of organisms (Bijou 1976; Bijou and Baer 1961). Such mechanistic-behavioristic theorists deal, then, with the generic human being—the general case of humanity. The laws of conditioning are ubiquitous in their applicability to all human behavior and, for that matter, to the behavior of all organisms (see Skinner 1938). Thus external stimulation provides the material and efficient cause of behavior and development.

Thus, from a mechanistic, behavioristic perspective, organisms differ across their life span only in the quantitative presence of qualitatively identical behavioral units, i.e., elements of the behavioral repertoire acquired by the causally efficient laws of conditioning (e.g., Bijou 1976; Bijou and Baer 1961). As such, the organism is seen as a host (Baer 1976) of these elements, and even the most complex human behavior is believed reducible to these identically constituted units (Bijou 1976). The only constraint on behavioral change in a "consequent" period of life is imposed by past (i.e., antecedent) reinforcement history; that is, the repertoire of behaviors present in the organisms at any point in time may moderate the efficiency by which current stimuli can extinguish or otherwise modify any particular behavior in the repertoire. As will be explained below, however, the meaning of "past reinforcement history" may be such as to preclude any strong view of the potential for developmental change beyond the earliest periods of life.

Indeed, from the mechanistic, behavioral perspective no strong (i.e., idealized) view of development is present. Instead, the concept of development is reduced to a concept of change in the elements of the behavioral repertoire; therefore, the processes by which change is brought about are by addition to or subtraction from the behavioral repertoire via conditioning. Consequently, change at any point in life becomes largely a technological matter always occurring with regard to past reinforcement history, and pertaining to such issues as management of stimulus contingencies and of reinforcement schedules (e.g., in regard to building up, reducing, or rearranging a behavioral chain). Moreover, interindividual differences in response to a stimulus or interindividual differences in intraindividual change may become particularly problematic from this perspective. The only way in which such differences may be accounted for is by reference to differences in past reinforcement history, a history that may be typically uncharted among humans. Indeed, two organisms exposed to the same stimulus history who nevertheless react differently to the same immediate stimulus would present a formidable interpretative problem for this perspective (since an internal organizing structure independent of past stimulus history is not part of this model). Thus, since humans even from quite similar backgrounds (e.g., identical twins reared together) do not behave in exactly the same way, psychologists functioning from this perspective are forced to account for such differences by postulating some unseen but efficiently causal difference in stimulus history or by arguing that such behavioral differences arise merely as a consequence of errors of measurement. Alternatively, such differences may be ignored.

That is, given the belief in the continuous and exclusive applicability of, and *only* of, functional (which in this perspective means efficient, and in some cases material; Skinner 1966) stimulus-behavior relations, only the most simplistic view of the context is found in this perspective (e.g, Bijou 1976). I do not use the term "simplistic" in any pejorative sense; rather, it serves to indicate that in the behavioristic tradition one can use only those features of the context—i.e., the stimulus environment in the terms of this perspective—that can be translated into stimulus-response units. Features of the context that cannot be translated (i.e., reduced) into such units are invisible in this approach. For instance, sociopolitical historical events or emergent qualitative changes in social structures must either be reduced to elementaristic, behavioral terms or ignored.

Moreover, because of a necessarily unequivocal commitment to reduce to efficiently causal antecedents, a strict mechanistic-behavioral position (e.g., the functional-analysis position of Baer 1982) must be committed to the views (1) that early (indeed the earliest) stimulus-response experience is prepotent in shaping the rest of life; and (2) that therefore there can be no true novelty or qualitative change in life. That is, taken literally, a belief that any current behavior or event can be explained by or reduced to an antecedent efficient cause—or a stimulus, in behavioral terms—means that all of life must ultimately be explainable by the earliest experience of such antecedent-consequent relations; that is, any portions of "later" life must be explained by efficiently causal prior events. Thus nothing new or qualitatively distinct can in actuality emerge consequent to these initial events. Zukav (1979) explains this feature of mechanistic thinking (in regard to Newtonian physics) by noting that:

If the laws of nature determine the future of an event, then, given enough information, we could have predicted our present at some time in the past. That time in the past also could have been predicted at a time still earlier. In short, if we are to accept the mechanistic determination of Newtonian physics—if the universe really is a great machine—then from the moment that the universe was created and set in motion, everything that was to happen in it already was determined,

According to this philosophy, we may seem to have a will of our own and the ability to alter the course of events in our lives, but we do not. Everything, from the beginning of time, has been predetermined, including our illusion of having a free will. The universe is a prerecorded tape playing itself out in the only way it can. (Zukav 1979, 26)

In short, the mechanistic-behavioral position represents a "translation" into psychological theory of the natural-science, efficiently causal philosophy that Zukav (1979) describes in regard to Newtonian physics; that is, the first physical antecedent-consequent relation is transformed into the first, or at least quite an early, stimulus-response connection. And, although it is not currently emphasized in many current discussions of mechanistic-behavioral views, for example the functional-analysis perspective (Baer 1982; Reese 1982), the early proponents of this view were quite clear in their belief that early experience was prepotent in shaping all of life (see Kagan 1983). For instance, John Watson (1928) argued that "at three years of age the child's whole emotional life plan has been laid down, his emotional disposition set" (p. 45). Similarly, Edward Thorndike (1905, 330–31) contended that:

Though we seem to forget what we learn, each mental acquisition really leaves its mark and makes future judgment more sagacious ... nothing of good or evil is ever lost; we may forget and forgive, but the neurones never forget or forgive. ... It is certain that every worthy deed represents a modification of the neurones of which nothing can ever rob us. Every event of a man's mental life is written indelibly in the brain's archives, to be counted for or against him.

Such views constitute a belief that the potential changes able to be induced in the person by later experience are quite limited, and that the potential for plasticity in later childhood, adolescence, and in the adult and aged years is markedly constrained by "early experience," by "past reinforcement history."

In sum, the point of the present discussion is to make clear the general nature of the translation of the mechanistic, reductionistic philosophical position into the psychological theoretical position of such mechanistic-behavioristic psychologists as Bijou (1976), Bijou and Baer (1961), and Baer (1982). To such psychologists all behavioral functioning is a consequence of stimulation. To understand behavior at any and all points in development, all one must do is understand the laws by which a person's responses come to be under the control of environmental stimulation. As we have seen, psychologists functioning from this viewpoint often contend that there are two sets of laws that describe and explain how responses come under environmental stimulation: those of classical and operant conditioning. Since all behavior is ultimately controlled by the stimulus world, and since this world exerts its control through the functioning of a fundamental set of laws of conditioning, then all behavior may be understood by reducing it to these same basic laws of stimulus-response relations. All behavior—whether of two different species of animals (rats and humans) or of two different age-groups of children (five- and fifteen-year-olds)—is composed of the same basic stimulus-response elements, and these same basic elements are also always associated on the basis of the same laws. Hence seemingly complex behavior may be understood by reducing it to the same basic constituent elements that make up any and all behavior. And since all behavior may be so reduced, the same laws must therefore be applicable to explain behavior at any (animal or age) level at which it occurs. Continuity in the laws of conditioning, in the rules that account for behavioral functioning, is another aspect of this approach.

Thus all that one must know in order to completely understand behavioral functioning and development is the mechanisms by which stimuli in a person's world come to control that person's behavior at all points in the life span. Once these mechanisms are known, one can reduce behavior at different points in life to common constituent elements. In turn, since the same elements comprise behavior at each level, one can account for any differences in behavior between points in the life span merely by

reference to the quantitative difference in the stimulus-response relations in the person's behavior repertoire. If behavior is composed totally of the stimulus-response relations a person has acquired over the course of life as a function of conditioning, then the difference between behavior at any two points in life could only be a quantitative one in the number of associations acquired. One could move from lower to higher levels of behavior analysis simply by adding on the similarly acquired stimulus-response associations.

By this point, then, the way in which the mechanistic model becomes translated into a theoretical view of psychological development should be clear. Although the mechanistic position is an abstract philosophical view of the nature of the real world, the position is not without its influence in science in general and psychology in particular. In fact, in providing the philosophical basis of the empirical behavioristic or the functional-analysis (Baer 1982; Bijou 1976; Reese 1982) approach to psychology, the mechanistic position presents us with what we will see to be an influential philosophical/psychological view of the nature of humanity. Of course, the position has had important criticisms leveled at it. In fact, one may view the organismic position as a culmination of the objections raised about the assumptions and assertions of the mechanistic position (Bertalanffy 1933). Hence, as a means of transition to our discussion of the organismic position, let us first consider some of the important problems of the mechanistic position.

Problems of the Mechanistic Model

We have seen that the core conceptual basis of the mechanistic model is reductionism. We have also seen that the belief in reductionism is predicated on the assertion that since all matter is made up of basic (e.g., physical-chemical) components, the only appropriate, necessary, and sufficient approach to investigating the fundamental laws of the natural world is to study these basic components. Hence, the adherent of the mechanistic model asserts that to understand any and all levels of phenomena in the real world, these higher levels must be reduced to the laws of the fundamental constituent level. However, Anderson, in describing the reductionistic component of the mechanistic position, also sees the viewpoint as advancing an argument containing a logical error:

> The main fallacy in this kind of thinking is that the reductionist hypothesis does not by any means imply a "constructionist" one: The ability to reduce everything to simple fundamental laws does not imply the ability to start from those laws and reconstruct the universe. In fact, the more the elementary particle physicists tell us about the nature of the fundamental laws, the less relevance they seem to have to the very real problems of the rest of science, much less to those of society (1972, 393).

But why does the ability to reduce from a higher, seemingly more complex, level of analysis to the lower level not necessarily imply the reverse? Why does such reductionistic ability not imply that one can move from the lower to the higher levels—and thereby construct the universe—by simply adding more of the same constituent elements onto what already exists at a lower level? Why, when we attempt to do this, and when we concomitantly learn more and more about the fundamental level, do we seem to be missing an understanding of the important problems and phenomena of the higher levels? Why does the reductionist fail when attempting to also be a constructionist? Again we may turn to Anderson.

> The constructionist hypothesis breaks down when confronted with the twin difficulties of scale and complexity. The behavior of large and complex aggregates of elementary particles, it turns out, is not to be understood in terms of a simple extrapolation of the properties of a few particles. Instead, *at each level of complexity entirely new properties appear,* and the understanding of the new behaviors requires research which I think is as fundamental in its nature as any other. That is, it

seems to me that one may array the sciences roughly linearly in a hierarchy, according to the idea: The elementary entities of science X obey the laws of science Y.

X	Y
Solid-state or many-body physics	Elementary particle physics
Chemistry	Many-body physics
Molecular biology	Chemistry
Cell biology	Molecular biology
.	.
.	.
.	.
Psychology	Physiology
Social sciences	Psychology

But this hierarchy does not imply that science X is "just applied Y." *At each stage entirely new laws, concepts, and generalizations are necessary,* requiring inspiration and creativity to just as great a degree as in the previous one. Psychology is not applied biology, nor is biology applied chemistry. (Anderson 1972, 393, italics added)

What Anderson is saying, therefore, is that the constructionist hypothesis fails because, simply, "more is different." In other words, as one studies levels of higher and higher complexity, one concomitantly sees that new, qualitatively different characteristics come about—or emerge—at each of these levels. The new characteristics are not present at the lower, fundamental level and are therefore not understandable by reduction to it. One cannot move from higher to lower levels (and back again) merely by adding or subtracting more of the same, because as one combines more of the same into a higher level of complexity, this combination has a quality that is not present in the less complex constituent elements as they exist in isolation. Thus the reductionist, mechanistic position fails because reductionism does not mean constructionism, and in turn, constructionism fails because of the presence of qualitatively new properties emerging and characterizing each higher level of analysis.

However, reductionism fails for other reasons as well. Reductionism is predicated on the belief that reference to the constituent elements comprising all matter can suffice in accounting for the nature of phenomena at all levels of analysis. However, we have seen that this continuity assumption is weak. If new, qualitatively different phenomena characterize each higher level of analysis, then by definition continuity does not exist. If something new does exist, this clearly means that *just* the same thing as existed before does not exist. One may not explain all natural phenomena by reference to one common set of continuously applicable fundamental laws. In other words, the shortcomings of the reductionistic, mechanistic position also include the inadequacy of its continuity assumption, and thus this philosophical position is unable to explain all natural phenomena through reduction to one set of fundamental laws. Reductionism cannot be used to explain successfully all levels of phenomena in the natural world because

> this conception appears to ignore the additional fact that once the behavior has been explained physiologically, the physiology still remains to be explained (cf. Skinner, 1950). Furthermore, if physiology in turn is to be explained by biochemistry and it by physics, how physics is to be explained poses an enduring problem because there are no sciences left. In short, this type of explanation leads to a finite regression with one science left unexplained— unless, of course, it is self-explanatory; no one is likely to admit that of physics. (Eacker 1972, 559)

We see, then, that there are many problems with the mechanistic model. It fails to suffice in accounting for the nature of the phenomena present at all levels of analysis because at each level of analysis there exist qualitatively new, and hence discontinuous, phenomena. Hence one should perhaps resort to a point of view that emphasizes these phenomena. What is being alluded to, then, is the fact that the very objections raised about the mechanistic position seem, in their explication, to suggest the necessary characteristics for a point of view that would successfully counter the position. Specifically,

mechanistic constructionism fails because new phenomena emerge to characterize higher levels of analysis; therefore the first component of a successful alternative position would be one positing emergence and qualitative discontinuity as characterizing developmental changes. The notion of emergence would be introduced to counter the problems of reductionism, while the idea of qualitative discontinuity would be raised to address the inability of a mechanistic constructionist position to account for all phenomena present at all levels. In essence, a developing organism would be viewed as a creature passing through qualitatively different levels, or stages, of development— stages made different because of the presence of new (and hence lawfully distinct) phenomena emerging to characterize that portion of the life span.

These alternative views of the nature of differences between levels of analysis, or between portions of the ontogeny of an organism, are represented in the organismic philosophy of science. Let us consider, then, the ways in which this second position offers a viable opposing view of the nature of the world.

THE ORGANISMIC MODEL

As explained by Reese and Overton (1970), the organismic model has as its basic metaphor "the organism, the living, organized system presented to experience in multiple forms" (p. 132). Moreover, they go on to note that

> the essence of substance is activity rather than the static elementary particle proposed by the mechanistic model. . . . In this representation, then, the *whole* is organic rather than mechanical in nature. The nature of the whole, rather than being the sum of its parts, is presupposed by the parts and the whole constitutes the condition of the meaning and existence of the parts . . . the important point here is that efficient cause is replaced by formal cause (i.e., cause by the essential nature of a form). (Reese and Overton 1970, 133)

Adherents of the organismic philosophy of science (e.g., Bertalanffy 1933; Schneirla 1957; Tobach 1981) reject the reductionism of mechanism and maintain that at each new level of phenomenal organization there is an *emergence* of new phenomena that cannot be reduced to lower levels of organization. They hold that one cannot appropriately make a quantitative reduction to a lower organizational level and hope to understand all phenomena at the higher organizational level. This inability to reduce occurs because at each higher organizational level something new comes about, or emerges (Novikoff 1945a, 1945b). Thus a change in quality and not merely in quantity characterizes the differences between one level of analysis and another. If one reduces to the lower level, one eliminates the opportunity of dealing with the new characteristic (which is actually the essential characteristic) of the higher level, the attribute that defines the difference between the lower and higher levels.

For example, going from one animal level to another, or from one stage of human life to another, would be analogous to changing from an orange into a motorcycle. How many oranges comprise a motorcycle? Obviously this is a ludicrous question, because here we have a change in kind, type, or quality, rather than merely in amount, magnitude, or quantity.

The above argument—the irreducibility of a later form to an earlier one—is the essence of the *epigenetic viewpoint*. One cannot reduce a qualitative change, something new, to a precursory form. Epigenesis denotes that at each higher level of complexity there emerges a new characteristic, one that simply was not present at the lower organizational level and thus whose presence is what establishes a new level as just that—a stage of organization qualitatively different from a preceding one. Thus, according to Gottlieb (1970, 111), epigenesis connotes that patterns of behavioral activity and sensitivity are not immediately evidenced in the initial stages of development. Since development is characterized by these qualitative emer-

gences, then by definition the various new behavioral capacities that develop are not actually present until they do in fact emerge.

The doctrine of epigenesis thus asserts that development is characterized by qualitative emergences. New things come about in development. Newness means just that—something not present before, either in smaller or even in precursory form. Simply, then, epigenesis asserts that development is represented by the emergence of characteristics at each new stage of development that were not present in any precursory form before their emergence.

Hence, as indicated above, the presence of qualitatively new characteristics at each higher stage indicates that reduction to lower levels is inappropriate—if full understanding of the new stage is sought. A one-year-old's behavior may perhaps be understood by reference to relatively simple stimulus-response, reflexlike associations; yet when the child reaches about two years of age there may emerge a new symbolic function—language (as an example of the ability to represent physical reality through use of nonphysical symbols). Thus, as one consequence of this representational ability, the child may now show behaviors (e.g., being able to imitate some person or event long after the time of actual viewing) that can best be understood by reference to this emergent symbolic ability; trying to reduce this two-year-old's behavior to the functioning shown at one year of age would be inappropriate because the representational ability that enables one to account for the two-year-old's behavior was simply not present at the earlier age.

Thus an antireductionist view is maintained because the qualitative change that depicts a higher stage of development cannot be understood, since it does not exist, at the lower level. Because the nature of what exists changes from stage to stage, and thus because there is qualitative change from stage to stage, there cannot be complete continuity between stages. New things—variables, processes, and/or laws—represent the differences between stages; hence such qualitative change means that discontinuity (at least in part) characterizes differences between stages. Such differences are in *what* exists and not just in *how much exists.* Thus, to the organismic thinker, laws of the psychological level of analysis are unique in nature—they are not merely reducible to the laws of physics and chemistry. Similarly, each different phyletic or ontogenetic level is viewed as having features qualitatively discontinuous from every other.

This aspect of the organismic position is represented in Figure 2.2, which shows qualitative discontinuity between the two levels represented. Because something new has emerged at the higher level, one cannot reduce one level to another. Although level 1 is comprised of oranges, level 2 is a motorcycle. One cannot hope to understand the functioning of a motorcycle even through an intensive study of oranges!

We have not yet seen on what basis the organismic viewpoint asserts that qualitative discontinuity characterizes development. How do organismic thinkers explain their assertion that epigenesis—qualitative discontinuity—represents differences between levels?

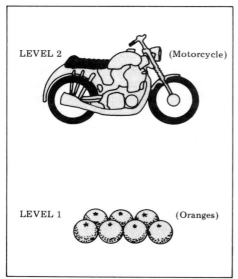

FIGURE 2.2
Organismic position: Qualitative discontinuity exists between levels.

Organismic thinkers would be in agreement with an idea borrowed from Gestalt psychology that the whole (the organism) is more than the sum of its parts. That is, a human organism is more than a liver added to two kidneys, added to one spinal cord, and to one brain, and to one heart, and so on. They would reject the additive assumption underlying the mechanistic position and instead maintain that a multiplicative type of combination would be more accurate. They would argue that organisms as organized systems show in the relations among their constituent elements (their parts) properties that cannot be reduced to physical and chemical terms. One may reach a physical and chemical understanding of a kidney, a brain, and a liver. However, properties will be seen in the organism considered as a whole that derive not from the separate organ systems per se but from their relations with each other. When parts combine they produce a property that did not exist in the parts in isolation. The parts do not merely add up (e.g., $2 + 3 = 5$) but multiplicatively interact (e.g., $2 \times 3 = 6$; hence one more unit is present here than with the additive combination), and this interaction brings about the emergence of a new property.

In essence, the organismic viewpoint asserts that the basis of the epigenetic (qualitatively discontinuous) emergences that characterize development lies in the multiplicative interactions of the constituent parts of the organism. When the parts combine they produce a new complexity, a characteristic existing only as a product of the interaction of these parts. This new property does not exist in any of the constituent parts—or in any of the lower organizational levels—even in precursory form.

Ludwig von Bertalanffy (1933), a leading formulator of the organismic viewpoint, suggests that nothing can be learned about the organism as such from a study of its parts in isolation. This inability exists because an organism in its natural state, viewed as a whole being (and not just as a bunch of constituent parts), shows phenomena that are so different from physical, mechanistic ones that entirely new concepts are needed to understand them. That is, if one accepts the epigenetic, organismic point of view, a mechanistic, reductionistic view of organisms is entirely inappropriate. The characteristics of a whole living organism have nothing in common with the characteristics or structures of a machine. This is so because the characteristics—or parts—of a machine can be separated without a change in their basic properties. For instance, a car's carburetor will still be a carburetor, still have the same properties, whether or not it is attached to a car. But according to the organismic position, this is not the case with living organisms. With living organisms, at each new level of analysis an emergence takes place; with every step building up to the whole living organism, from an atom to a molecule to a cell to a tissue to an organ, new phenomena occur that cannot be derived from the lower, subordinate levels.

Thus knowledge of the functioning of the various subsystems that make up an organism does not lead to an understanding of the whole organism. For example, water has an emergent quality (its liquidness) that cannot be understood by reducing water to its constituent (and gaseous) elements (hydrogen and oxygen). Similarly, human beings have unique characteristics (or qualities)—such as being able to love, being governed by abstract principles of moral and ethical conduct, showing high levels of need achievement—that emerge as phylogenetically distinct (qualitatively discontinuous) features and cannot be understood by mere reduction to underlying neural, hormonal, and muscular processes. And, as I have already noted, a basis for this position, which is put forward by organismic theorists, is a belief in epigenetic processes—that is, a belief that at each new level of behavioral organization there emerge qualitatively new (discontinuous) phenomena that cannot be reduced to lower levels.

In summary, the basic characteristics of the organismic position are:

1. It is an *epigenetic* viewpoint.
2. It is an *antireductionist* viewpoint.
3. It is a *qualitative* viewpoint.
4. It is a *discontinuity* viewpoint.
5. It is a *multiplicative, interactionist* viewpoint.

Translating the Organismic Model into a Theory of Development

When the organismic model is translated into a set of ideas pertinent to psychological development, an active organism model of humans results. From this perspective the human is inherently active; that is, it is the human who provides a source of its behaviors in the world, rather than the world providing the source of the human's behaviors. Humans, by virtue of their structure, give meaning to their behavior; that is, they provide it with organization—with form—by virtue of integrating any given behavior into the whole. Thus humans, by virtue of their activity and their organization, are *constructors* of their world rather than passive responders to it. Moreover, as a consequence of the inherent activity of humans, change, or development, is accepted as given (Reese and Overton 1970). In other words, change may not be reduced to efficient or material causes, although such causes may impede or facilitate change. Rather, formal cause is basic in the organismic perspective (Reese and Overton 1970).

From the organismic perspective, development of a given process (e.g., cognition) is an idealized and goal-directed intraorganism phenomenon. As explained by Pepper (1942):

With organicism, no ordinary common-sense term offers a safe reference to the root metaphor of the theory. The common term "organism" is too much loaded with biological connotations, too static and cellular, and "integration" is only a little better. Yet there are no preferable terms. With a warning we shall accordingly adopt these [p. 280].... The categories of organicism consist, on the one hand, in noting the steps involved in the organic process, and, on the other hand, in noting the principal features in the organic structure ultimately achieved or realized. The structure achieved or realized is always the ideal aimed at by the progressive steps of the process [p. 281].... The pivotal point in the system ... is the goal and final stage of the progressive categories and it is the field for the specification of the ideal categories. (p. 283)

Qualitative change, forged by the inevitable synthesis of contradictions—as for example represented by emergent structural reorganization (e.g., Piaget 1970) or focal reorientation in the mode of dealing with the world or with gratifying one's emotions (e.g., Erikson 1959; Freud 1954)—is seen as the key feature of development. Thus the organismic approach is a holistic one, one wherein formal cause, and in its "purest" philosophical formulation also final (teleological) cause (Nagel 1957; Pepper 1942), provides the basis of developmental explanation. However, given this explanatory orientation, especially when it is cast within an idealized view of developmental progression, material and efficient causative agents—for instance, as derived from the context enveloping the organism—are seen as irrelevant to the sequence of development and as such to the form the organism takes at any point in this sequence. The context can inhibit or facilitate (i.e., speed up or slow down) developmental progression, but it cannot alter the quality of the process or its sequential universality. If a contextual variable does alter the quality or sequence of an organism's progression, then by definition that feature of functioning was not a component of development.

Gottlieb (1970) has labeled this version of organicism as *predetermined epigenesis.* Victor Hamburger's organismic position epitomizes this view:

> The architecture of the nervous system and the concomitant behavior patterns result from self-generating growth and maturation processes that are determined entirely by inherited, intrinsic factors, to the exclusion of functional adjustment, exercise, or anything else akin to learning. (Hamburger 1957, 56)

There is an alternative view of epigenesis, however. It is labeled *probabilistic epigenesis* (Gottlieb 1970, 1983). Its features will be discussed below, in the context of a discussion of how ideas associated with the mechanistic and the organismic models pertain to

several key issues of development. The rationale for this organization is that, as was the case with the mechanistic position, there are several problems we may identify with the organismic position. These problems come to the fore when comparing the mechanistic and the organismic models' positions in regard to the developmental issues we shall discuss. However, I shall argue that many of these problems can be usefully addressed by adopting a probabilistic-epigenetic, rather than a predetermined-epigenetic, view of organicism. But, as I shall argue too, such an adoption in actuality constitutes a divorce from "pure" organicism; instead, what such an adoption does is to create a "marriage" (an integration) between organicism and another model useful in devising an approach to development: that is, a contextual model. As I shall point out in various portions of the next section, organicism and contextualism are often intimately related philosophically (Overton 1984; Pepper 1942), and thus the "marriage" I propose is one between quite compatible models. Thus, by introducing some of the compatibilities between organicism and contextualism in the next section, and also by developing the argument for the usefulness of probabilistic epigenesis in the context of a comparative discussion of mechanism and organicism, and of the uses and problems with each, I shall be setting the stage for both a direct treatment of the contextual model and a discussion of its uses and limitations; therefore, I shall be preparing us for my proposal about an integration of the organismic and the contextual models—an integration that I labeled in Chapter 1 as developmental contextualism.

MECHANISTIC AND ORGANISMIC MODELS AND ISSUES OF DEVELOPMENT

It is useful to begin this section by reiterating some of the key features of the mechanistic and organismic models. The mechanistic model stresses the continuous applicability of a common set of laws or principles. Continuity exists because even quite complex behavior may be reduced to common elements (e.g., stimulus-response connections in S-R, behavioristic theories), elements whose linkage is controlled by forces external to the essentially passive, reactive organism. Thus the task of developmental psychologists, from this perspective, is to identify the efficient antecedents (e.g., the stimuli) controlling consequent behaviors.

The organismic model stresses the integrated structural features of the organism. If the parts making up the whole become reorganized as a consequence of the organism's active construction of its own functioning, the structure of the organism may take on new meaning; thus qualitatively distinct principles may be involved in human functioning at different points in life. These distinct, or new, levels of organization are termed *stages* in this perspective (Lerner 1976; Reese and Overton 1970). From this perspective, the task of developmental psychologists is to assess the different functions of the organism that are associated over time with its changing structure.

From these general distinctions between the two models, there arise several other issues pertinent to understanding development. Reese and Overton (1970; Overton and Reese 1973) and Lerner (1978, 1985) have identified several of these. These issues serve to highlight the distinctions we have drawn already. In addition, their discussion will lead us to a presentation of a third model, contextualism.

Elementarism Versus Holism

The mechanistic model is an elementaristic one. Human functioning is reduced to its core constituent elements (e.g., S-R connections) and, in turn, the laws that govern the functioning of these elements are applicable continuously across life. As a consequence there is no true qualitative discontinuity— no newness, no emergence, no epigenesis—

within this perspective. Only quantitative differences may exist.

The organismic model is a holistic one. As Reese and Overton (1970) explain:

> The assumption of holism derives from the active organism model. More particularly, it derives from the representation of the organism as an *organized* totality, a system of parts in interaction with each other, such that the part derives its meaning from the whole. (p. 136)

Reese and Overton note also that the idea of holism within organicism has been most clearly articulated by Werner and Kaplan (1963), who indicate that the idea

> maintains that any local organ or activity is dependent upon the context, field or whole of which it is a constitutive part: its properties and functional significance [meaning] are, in larger measure, determined by the larger whole or context. (Werner and Kaplan 1963, 3)

As will become clear below when we discuss the world hypothesis of "contextualism" (Pepper 1942), a similar emphasis is placed on the role of the context in providing meaning for the parts that make it up. Thus, as we have already implied and as Pepper (1942) and Overton (1984) have explained, there is considerable similarity between the organismic and the contextual models. However, as we will argue below, the two models are distinct in significant ways, ways which lead us to find contextualism attractive given some of the limitations that exist in an organismic model. These limitations will be explained as we discuss further some of the issues that divide organicism and mechanism. To anticipate, however, these discussions will lead us toward an integration of organicism and contextualism as a means to formulate a concept of development which adequately remedies problems found in exclusively organismic or mechanistic (or contextualistic, for that matter) views.

Antecedent-Consequent Versus Structure-Function Relations

The mechanistic model stresses efficient (and material) causes and, as we have already explained, is thereby concerned with identifying the necessary and sufficient antecedents of a behavior. Behavior is reduced, then, to an analysis of a qualitatively unchanging, continuous, and unbroken chain of cause-effect (e.g., S-R) relations. In organicism, however, the emphasis is on determining the functions associated with the actively constructed structures of the organism. Qualitative changes in structures can occur as the active organism constructs—or better, reconstructs—its organization. Thus novelty, newness, qualitative discontinuity, or epigenesis occurs as a consequence of changing structure-function relations.

But if structure leads to function, what accounts for structure? One answer is simply function. That is, the active organism shapes its structure—which in turn influences the organism's function, and so on, in a continuous and bidirectional (reciprocal) manner (e.g., Gottlieb 1976a, 1976b, 1983; Kuo 1967; Tobach 1981). However, this answer is only one of several possible replies and is in fact quite controversial. Kohlberg (1968), Reese and Overton (1970), Overton (1973), Gottlieb (1976a, 1976b), and Lerner (1976) have noted that there exist several formulations about the *source* of an organism's structure. These formulations divide on the basis of their relative emphases on nature-based processes (e.g., nativistic, preformed, innate variables) and nurture-based processes (e.g., conditioning, the physical ecology of one's context, the events of one's context) in accounting for structure. As such, these formulations divide in respect to what I have suggested (in Chapter 1) is perhaps the key issue of human development—the nature-nurture issue, or the controversy surrounding the source of any facet of human behavioral development.

Mechanistically derived formulations about the nature of psychological structure have tended to emphasize the role of nurture processes (e.g., the laws of classical and operant conditioning) in building up a response repertoire (and/or mediation processes) within the organism (e.g., Bijou 1976; Bijou and Baer 1961). Thus, from this perspective, structure is imposed from outside the organism.

There exist several formulations associated with the organismic model. Several nature-based views stress the role of nativistic variables and indicate that such variables exert a predetermined influence on an organism's structure—an influence independent of any role of nurture variables. Examples here are Chomsky (1965, 1966) and McNeill (1966), who maintain that psychological (linguistic) structures are completely present at birth, and Hamburger (1957), who was cited earlier as maintaining that in the genetic structure lies the basis for the architecture of the nervous system, which in turn directly determines various behavioral functions. Given, then, that the character of, and course of changes in, such structures is believed to be so thoroughly shaped by nativistic variables, it may be apparent why Gottlieb (1970) has labeled such views predetermined-epigenetic.

Some formulations associated with the organismic view emphasize that an *interaction* between nature and nurture variables provides the basis of structure. However, as will be discussed again below, the concept of interaction is itself a complex, controversial one. Indeed, one's concept of interaction—the components one sees as interacting within the organismic whole—determines whether one remains committed to an exclusively organismic model or to a position that integrates organicism and contextualism (Lerner 1985; Lerner and Kauffman in press). For instance, Piaget (1968, 1970) maintained that while there existed an innate (congenital) structure, or organization, structures consequently develop through an interaction between the innate organization and the ongoing activity of the person (Reese and Overton 1970). Note, however, that this concept of interaction sees the focal point, the locus, of interaction *within* the organism. The interaction is between the existing internal organization and the active organism's constructionist functions on or with that organization. While this organismic, internal version of interaction stands as the converse of the mechanistic, more extrinsic notion of interaction (as a relation between past reinforcement history and present stimulus conditions), the Piagetian (1968, 1970) notion of interaction is distinct from those we shall discuss as being associated with the contextual model. That is, to preview that discussion, a *strong* concept of organism-environment interaction (Lerner and Spanier 1978, 1980; Overton 1973), transaction (Sameroff 1975), or dynamic interaction (Lerner 1978, 1979, 1985) is associated with a contextual perspective. This concept stresses that organism and context are always embedded each in the other (Lerner, Hultsch, and Dixon 1983); that the context is composed of multiple levels changing interdependently across time (i.e., historically); and that because organisms influence the context that influences them, they are efficacious in playing an active role in their own development (Lerner and Busch-Rossnagel 1981).

But, as also emphasized in organicism (Werner and Kaplan 1963), because of the mutual embeddedness of organism and context, a given organismic attribute will have different implications for developmental outcomes in the milieu of different contextual conditions; this is the case because the organismic attribute is only given its functional meaning by virtue of its relation to a specific context. If the context changes, as it may over time, the same organismic attribute will have a different import for development. In turn, the same contextual condition will lead to alternative developments in that different organisms interact with it. Thus, to draw quite a subtle distinction in somewhat strong terms, in the type of interactions stressed in contextualism, a given organismic attribute only has meaning for psychological development by virtue of its timing of interaction—that is, its relation to a particular set of time-bound contextual conditions. In turn, the import of any set of contextual conditions for psychosocial behavior and development can only be understood by specifying relations of the context to the specific, developmental features of the organisms within it. This central role of the timing of organism-context interactions in the determination of the nature and outcomes of development provides, as we shall see, a

probabilistic component of epigenesis (Gottlieb 1970; Scarr 1982; Scarr and McCartney 1983). In short, a distinctive feature of a contextual approach is its treatment of the concepts of time and timing.

But, while this perspective gains its potential for providing an approach to developmental theory distinct from organicism from issues associated with the contextual treatment of the concepts of time and timing, it can only do so by building on organicism. This relation is highlighted in the next developmental issue we will discuss.

Behavioral Versus Structural Change

What is it that develops, that changes, with development? Does this development have any necessary direction? As Reese and Overton (1970) explain, the answers to these questions provide developmental psychology with perhaps the most important distinctions between the mechanistic and the organismic (and, we may note here too, the contextual) positions.

Within the mechanistic model qualitatively identical, elements may be added to or subtracted from the machine. For instance, in the behavioralistic translation of the model, lawfully identical S-R connections may be added to or subtracted from the response repertoire. Development is thus a matter of quantitative constancy or change, with elements being added to or subtracted from the organism's repertoire in accordance with, for instance, the laws of conditioning (Bijou and Baer 1961).

With decreases or increases possible in the number of S-R connections in the repertoire, development may be said to be multidirectional within this perspective. In short, in this exemplar of the mechanistic model in developmental psychology, what changes in development is the number of S-R connections in the organism's repertoire, and there is no a priori necessary direction to such change.

Quite a different set of ideas exists within the organismic model. Reese and Overton (1970) note that this model emphasizes changes in structures and functions, and they stress that these changes are specified a priori to move toward a final goal or end state. That is, development is *teleological* within this view; it is goal-directed. Indeed, Reese and Overton (1970) indicate that within the organismic model the definition of development is "changes in the form, structure, or organization of a system, such changes being directed towards end states or goals" (p. 139).

Reese and Overton (1970) explain that development within this view is an a priori concept; that is, the general function of development—the end state or goal (e.g., "maturity," "ego integrity," "genital sexuality," or "formal operations")—is postulated in advance and acts as a principle for ordering change. In short in the organismic perspective, structure-function relations develop and these changes are, in a final sense, unidirectional—they move toward a final end state.

But, although development is thus seen to be an a priori, idealized ordering of structure-function relations, and development is therefore continuous in the sense of always being directed by the final end state, there may be—and typically are—qualitative changes in structure-function relations over the course of development. The possibility of structure-function changes of a qualitative character raises two other key developmental issues on which the models provide divergent perspectives.

Continuity Versus Discontinuity

Continuity means constancy or a lack of change in some feature of development. For example, a given personality trait (e.g., dependency) may be continuously present within a person across his or her life, or a child's growth rate (e.g., two inches a year) may remain constant across the childhood years. Discontinuity means change. Dependency may be altered or transformed into independence, and with puberty and the adolescent growth spurt, a child's growth rate may increase dramatically.

Both the mechanistic and the organismic models speak of continuity and discontinuity. In mechanism, the number of S-R connections (elements) in the response repertoire may be continuous; and in organicism, a given structure-function relation may be continuous for a specific period of the person's life. Thus ideas of continuity may be derived from both models.

However, the models divide clearly when the issue of discontinuity is raised. As we have already implied, only quantitative discontinuity is possible within the translations of mechanism present in developmental psychology. However, within organicism, the active organism may construct—or better, revise—its structure, and in so doing a *new* structure-function relation will exist. Thus qualitative discontinuity is possible within organicism. Such a change constitutes not just more of a previously or already existing structure; rather, it constitutes something new, something that cannot be reduced to a prior state or status of the organism. As noted earlier, such changes are said to be emergent ones, and such qualitative discontinuity is termed epigenesis.

The possibility that life is characterized by qualitatively distinct phases of structure-function relations raises another key developmental issue. This is the issue of stages.

Stages of Development

Like many of the other concepts we have been discussing, the concept of stage is a complex and controversial one (e.g., Brainerd 1978; Flavell 1980; Kessen 1962; Lerner 1980; McHale and Lerner, 1985; Overton and Reese 1973; Reese and Overton 1970; Wohlwill 1973). Here we need to note only that the models clearly divide on the basis of the way the term *stage* is used as a theoretical construct. In mechanistically-derived, behavioristic positions (e.g., Bijou 1976), a stage summarizes the presence of some set, some quantity, of S-R connections. However, there is nothing qualitatively different about organisms at one or another stage of life.

In organismically derived theories, however, a stage denotes a qualitatively distinct level of organization (e.g., Reese and Overton 1970; Schneirla 1957), that is, an organizational structure qualitatively discontinuous with those of prior or later periods. As Reese and Overton (1970) explain:

> Within the active organism model, change is in structure-function relationships or in organization. As organization changes to the extent that new system properties emerge (new structures and functions) and become operational, we speak of a new level of organization which exhibits a basic discontinuity with the previous level. (p. 143)

Sources of Development

The mechanistic position, when translated into a psychological theory, will typically take the form of either a nature or nurture position. Resting on an additive and a mechanistic assumption, the mechanistic position tries to explain behavioral development in terms of a single set of source determinants. Because they are committed to a continuity position, mechanistic thinkers would by definition be committed to the view that the same set of laws can always account for behavior. If continuity is asserted, it is then most difficult to draw one's explanations of behavioral development from different sources of development. (Of course, it may be possible to argue that nature and nurture laws may be reduced to the same laws and are thus not different sources after all; but this type of appeal really begs the question, since once again we are back to one common set of laws.)

As we have seen, mechanistic-behavioristic theorists view the environment (nurture) as the source of the determinants of behavior. Human beings are seen as machines; they are energized to respond by stimulation that derives solely from the environment. Hence humans are seen as essentially passive. They must await energizing stimulation that evokes behavior. Thus human behavior is seen as amorphous, as having no (initial) shape or form. Since all human behavior is derived from the stimulus-environment—in-

dependent of human beings—it has no original form; it is shaped completely by the environment and hence processes or variables not involved with such environmental stimulation really do not contribute at all to the shaping of behavior. Thus heredity (nature) is really never systematically incorporated into these theorists' ideas, and the environment is considered the source of the shaping of human behavior.

It is possible, however, to have a mechanistic-nature theory. Such approaches would also view behavioral development as deriving from a single source, but in this case the source would be nature. Behavioral development would thus be the continuous unfolding of preformed genetic givens. The major thrust of William Sheldon's (1940, 1942) constitutional psychology position can be viewed as consistent with a mechanistic-nature formulation, as can some of the work of some of the European animal behaviorists (ethologists such as Lorenz 1965). Sheldon views body type as the essential determinant of personality or temperament. He maintains that body type—whether essentially fat, muscular, or thin—is primarily genetically determined; hence he views personality as derived essentially from a single source—genetic inheritance. Lorenz (1965) may similarly be viewed as a mechanistic-nature theorist. As we shall discuss in greater detail in Chapter 3, he believes that in some animals there exist behavior patterns called instincts, entities whose structures are totally formed at conception—when one inherits one's genes from one's parents. Hence such instincts are totally unavailable to any environmental influence. The validity of ideas such as those of Sheldon and specifically of Lorenz will be evaluated in Chapters 3 through 5.

The present point is that mechanistic theorists typically emphasize either a nature or nurture viewpoint. Although some (if not most) mechanist-nurture theorists do explicitly admit, for example, that nature may provide an important contributory source of behavior (for instance, see Bijou and Baer 1961), this admission never seems to lead to any systematic consideration of the role of this other source. Because changes in behavior are held to be continuous and additive instead of multiplicative, neither nature nor nurture is systematically taken into account. Such interactionism occurs, however, as one of the predominant points of view within the organismic philosophy of science.

Although all organismic-epigenetic positions have the basic characteristics listed earlier, the precise basis of the determinants of epigenesis is itself a controversial issue among organismic thinkers. What determines when and how the constituent parts comprising the whole organism interact to produce qualitative discontinuity? The basic issue involved in this question is the nature-nurture problem, and relates to the concept of interaction discussed earlier. The question becomes simply, Does the source of epigenesis lie in nature, nurture, or a combination of the two? On the one hand, there are those thinkers who maintain that epigenesis is predetermined through genetic inheritance. Environment is held to play no role in the qualitative emergences that define epigenesis. Although development is seen as going through qualitative changes, some epigenetic thinkers argue that these changes are completely determined by genes; the environment in which these genes exist is seen to play no role in producing the qualitative changes that characterize development (in this regard such epigenetic thinkers are indistinguishable from the mechanistic-nature theorists such as Lorenz). Thus these epigenetic changes are predetermined by invariantly ordered maturational factors such as growth and tissue differentiation, which are held simply to unfold in a fixed sequence—a sequence that arises independent of any experiential context. As noted earlier, this *predetermined-epigenetic* viewpoint is well illustrated by the views of Victor Hamburger (1957). Thus, according to Gottlieb (1970), this version of epigenesis, as it is expressed in the views of Hamburger (1957) and others, means that

> the development of behavior in larvae, embryos, fetuses, and neonates can be explained entirely in terms of neuromotor and neurosensory maturation (i.e., in terms of proliferation, migration, differentiation, and growth of neurons and their axonal and dendritic processes). In this view, factors such as the use or exercise of muscles, sensory stimulation, mechanical agitation, environmental heat, gravity, and so on, play only a passive role in the development of the nervous system. Thus, according to predetermined epigenesis, the nervous system matures in an encapsulated fashion so that a sufficiently comprehensive account of the maturation of the nervous system will suffice for an explanation of embryonic and neonatal behavior, the key idea being that structural maturation determines function, and not vice versa. (Gottlieb 1983, 11)

As will become evident in Chapters 3 and 4, this nature-epigenetic viewpoint has rather severe conceptual limitations (akin to those involved in the type of view represented by Lorenz). In my view, the alternative conception of the source of epigenesis—*probabilistic epigenesis*—appropriately deals with the conceptual issues inherent in a consideration of psychological development. Moreover, this view represents, in opposition to both the mechanistic and the predetermined-epigenetic views, the notion that developmental changes are determined by a multiplicative interaction of two sources of development, nature and nurture. Since the probabilistic-epigenetic position views development as qualitatively discontinuous and further views this discontinuity as arising from an interaction, it is understandable that two different sources of development (hereditary and environmental sources) can be seen to provide the basis of the multiplicative interaction that defines and brings about the qualitative discontinuity.

Schneirla (1957) argues that no behavior is predetermined or preformed. The role of the environment must always be taken into account in trying to understand the qualitative changes that characterize epigenesis—specifically, one must consider the experience of various stimulative events acting on the organism throughout the course of its life span. These stimulative events may occur in the environment outside the organism (exogenous stimulation) or in the environment within the organism's own body (endogenous stimulation). No matter where they occur, however, the influence of patterns of environmental stimulation upon the contribution that genes make toward behavior must always be considered.

Genes must exist in an environment. They do not just float in nothingness. Changes in the environment may help or hinder the unfolding (better, the contribution) of the genes. In other words, the experiences that take place in the environment will play a role in what contribution genes can make. If x-rays invade the environment of the genes, or if oxygen is lacking, or if poisonous chemicals enter this environment, then the role of the genes in contributing to behavior will certainly be different from their role if such environmental stimulative events did not occur.

To illustrate the interaction of genes and external environment (i.e., the environment outside the organism), it is useful to consider the results of experiments testing how exposure to enriched, as opposed to impoverished, environments alters the most basic chemical constituent of genes: DNA. Uphouse and Bonner (1975) assessed the transcription to DNA by RNA from the brains or livers of rats exposed to high environmental enrichment (i.e., living in a cage with eleven other rats and having "toys" and mazes available for exploration), low environmental enrichment (i.e., living in a cage with one other rat but no exploration materials), or isolation (i.e., living in a cage alone and with no exploration materials). The RNA from the brains of the environmentally enriched rats showed a level of transcription of DNA significantly greater than that of the other groups. No significant differences were found with liver RNA. Grouse et al. (1978) also found significant differences between the brain RNA of rats reared in environmentally rich versus environmentally impoverished contexts. In addition, Grouse, Schrier, and Nelson (1979) found that the total complexity of brain RNA was greater

for normally sighted kittens than for kittens who had both eyelids sutured at birth. However, the RNAs from the nonvisual cortices and from subcortical structures were not different for the two groups. Grouse, Schrier, and Nelson conclude that the normal development of the visual cortex, which is dependent on visual experience, involves a greater amount of genetic expression than occurs in the absence of visual experience. Given such findings about the contextual modifiability of genetic material, it is possible to assert that genes are appropriate targets of environmental influence.

Moreover, one cannot say with total certainty what type of environmental stimulative influences will always occur or whether the environment will interact with genes to help or hinder development. Rather, one may say only that certain types of environmental influences will *probably* occur (as they do with the average organism of a certain species) and/or that a given emergence will *probably* take place *if* the gene-experience interaction proceeds as it usually does.

Thus, in order for development to proceed normally (that is, in the appropriate sequence typical for the species), environmental stimulative events must operate on (interact with) the maturing organism at specific times in the organism's development. That is, since epigenesis is determined by both genetic (maturational) and experiential sources, experience must interact with maturation at certain times in the organism's development in order for specific emergences to occur. If the emergence of a particular behavioral development is determined by a maturation-experience interaction, and if for a particular species this interaction usually occurs at a certain time in the life span (e.g., at about six months of age), then if the particular experience involved in this interaction occurs either earlier or later for a given member of the species, there will be a change in the emergent behavioral capacity. Thus the species-typical timing of maturational-experiential interactions is essential in order for the emergences that characterize development to occur normatively.

However, the timing of these interactions is not invariant. One can never expect with complete certainty that these interactions will occur at their typical times for all members of a species. As suggested above, some animals may undergo these interactions earlier than others, while others may undergo them at a later-than-average time. These alterations may or may not lead to significantly different, or substantially altered, characteristics in the resulting behavioral capacity. The point is that although emergent behavioral developments find their source in the interaction between maturation and experience, one cannot expect the time of these interactions always to be the same for all animals in a species. Alterations in the timing of these interactions, if extreme enough, could lead to changes in the behavioral characteristics that developed as a consequence of the interactions. Thus, one can say that certain emergences will probably occur, given fairly typical timing of maturation-experience interactions.

Hence, the probabilistic-epigenetic position recognizes the following:

1. Both experience and maturation are invariably involved in determining the qualitative changes that characterize development.

2. The timing of the interactions between maturation and experience is a factor of critical importance in the determination of behavioral development.

3. Since these interactions cannot be expected to occur at exactly the same time for every organism within a given species, one can say with a given level of confidence only that certain emergences will probably occur.

The probabilistic formulation of epigenesis should appear more complicated than its predeterministic counterpart because it is! Development is an exceedingly complex phenomenon and any accurate conceptual-

ization of it would have to take this complexity into account. Thus Schneirla (1957), recognizing both the complexity of behavioral development and the failure of predetermined-developmental notions to acknowledge that complexity, illustrates the probabilistic-epigenetic viewpoint by stating:

> The critical problem of behavioral development should be stated as follows: (1) to study the organization of behavior in terms of its properties at each stage from the time of egg formation and fertilization through individual life history; and (2) to work out the changing relationships of the organic mechanisms underlying behavior; (3) always in terms of the contributions of earlier stages in the developmental sequence; (4) and in consideration of the properties of the prevailing developmental context at each stage. (1957, 80)

As I have indicated, I believe that this probabilistic-epigenetic viewpoint offers the most appropriate conceptualization of development. Accordingly, this viewpoint will be discussed again.

Conclusions

The mechanistic model stresses a passive organism in an active world; it emphasizes reductionism, continuity of laws governing development, only quantitative behavioral change across life, potential multidirectionality of change, elementarism, and antecedent-consequent relations; and it eschews the idea of stages as qualitatively distinct periods of life. The organismic model stresses an active organism in a relatively passive world, and it emphasizes emergence; qualitative change in structure-function relations across life; unidirectional, teleological, goal-directed change; holism; and the appropriateness of the idea of stages as qualitatively distinct levels of organization.

Each of these two models has led to a set of theories—what Reese and Overton (1970) term a "family of theories"—of use in the study of all or part of the life span. For instance, the behavioristically oriented, functional-analysis approach of Bijou and Baer

(1961; Bijou 1976) exemplifies the translation of the mechanistic model into a theory of development. However, other family members include the social-learning theories of Miller and Dollard (1941), Davis (1944), and McCandless (1970). The theories of Werner (1948), Piaget (1950, 1968, 1970), Freud (1954), and Erikson (1959, 1963, 1968) exemplify the translation of the organismic model into developmental theories.

Both mechanistically and organismically derived orientations encounter problems when attempting to formulate a useful concept of development. Mechanistically derived conceptions cannot, as we have noted, deal directly with novelty or with qualitatively distinct levels of being. In the former case, novelty must be interpreted as reducible to common constituent elements; in the latter case, the influence of cultural, sociological, and physical ecological variables, for instance, must also be reduced to common (e.g., behavioristic) principles in order for their influence to have a place in the continuity perspective of mechanism. Often such reduction is quite forced and/or artificial and, as such, variables from distinct levels of analysis may end up being ignored. Moreover, despite the possibility of multidirectionality in development, we have seen that, in practice, mechanistically derived conceptions often adopt a position involving the continuous applicability of early experience to later life (e.g., Thorndike 1905; Watson 1928). Indeed, we have noted that Zukav (1979) argues that the view of antecedent-consequent relations held by mechanists logically requires such a proscription against discontinuity or change in later life. Finally, there is mechanism's insistence on a passive, empty organism model. Such a conception, especially when translated into a theory of psychological development, is unable to account for the evidence that organisms have characteristics that as much shape their world as their world shapes them (Bell 1968; Bell and Harper 1977; Lerner 1982; Lerner and Busch-Rossnagel 1981; Lewis and Rosenblum 1974), and that these organismic characteristics cannot be adequately interpreted as merely derivative of the organism's conditioning history (Schneirla 1957; Tobach 1981; Tobach and Schneirla 1968).

For these reasons, we are oriented more to formulating an organismically derived concept of development than a mechanistically derived one. However, as we have also implied, there are major conceptual problems with organicism that diminish its usefulness for derivation of a concept of development. Among these are:

1.   The need in organicism to "deal mainly with historic processes even while it consistently explains time away" (Pepper 1942, 280);
2.   The fact that "organicism takes time lightly or disparagingly" (Pepper 1942, 281; and as an instance see Kaplan 1983); and
3.   The teleological features of organicism, wherein for the "fragments" of an organic whole there is "inevitability of connections among fragments ... [an] implication of wholeness contained in them" (Pepper 1942, 292), "an internal drive toward the integrations which complete them" (Pepper 1942, 291), and where, although the particular path to a goal is not predetermined it is nevertheless the case that "the goal was predetermined in the structure of the facts" (Pepper 1942, 295).

These key features of "pure" organicism fail to deal with the point that the timing of interaction of causal developmental variables is probabilistic (Gollin 1981; Gottlieb 1970, 1976a, 1976b; Scarr 1982; Scarr and McCartney 1983; Schneirla 1956, 1957; Tobach 1981; Tobach and Schneirla 1968). As a consequence, there is a lack of concern with the implication that such differences in time may mean that, while the process of development may remain invariant across history (e.g., while an orthogenetic progression in structure-function relations may exist), the ongoing features of developmental trajectories may show considerable interindividual variability, *and* there may be no universally inevitable end state for a developmental progression. In other words, there may be a probabilistic, rather than a predetermined, pattern to epigenetic change.

Moreover, as with mechanistically derived conceptions, the use of "pure" organismic conceptions of development is diminished in light of several sets of findings for which extant organismic views cannot devise adequate interpretations. That is, as opposed to mechanistic conceptions, which encountered difficulty as a consequence of failures to treat adequately organismic features of the person, organismic conceptions have encountered difficulty as a consequence of not being able to test effects on the person ultimately associated with variables derived from the context enveloping the person. Attempts to use a biological model of growth, one based on an organismic conception of development (e.g., Cumming and Henry 1961), to account for data sets pertinent to the adult and aged years were not completely successful (Baltes, Reese, and Lipsitt 1980; Baltes and Schaie, 1973). Viewed from the perspective of this organismic conception, the adult and aged years were necessarily seen as periods of decline (Cumming and Henry 1961). However, all data sets pertinent to age changes, e.g., in regard to intellectual performance, during these periods were not consistent with such a unidirectional-format of change. For example, as noted in Chapter 1, increasingly greater between-people differences in within-person change were evident in such data sets (Baltes 1983; Baltes and Schaie 1974, 1976; Schaie, Labouvie, and Buech 1973). Simply put, as people developed into the adult and aged years, differences between them increased.

On the basis of such data Brim and Kagan (1980, 13) conclude that "growth is more individualistic than was thought, and it is difficult to find general patterns." Factors associated with the historical time within which people were born (i.e., with membership in particular birth cohorts) and/or with events occurring at particular historical times appeared to account for more of these changes, particularly with respect to adult intellectual development, than did age-associated influences (Baltes, Reese, and Lipsitt

1980). Data sets pertinent to the child (Baltes, Baltes, and Reinert 1970) and the adolescent (Nesselroade and Baltes 1974) that considered these birth-cohort and time-of-measurement effects also supported their saliency in developmental change. These findings led scientists to induce conceptualizations useful for understanding the role of these non-age-related variables in development (e.g., Baltes, Cornelius, and Nesselroade 1977; Brim and Ryff 1980), and these conceptualizations have been interpreted as being consistent with a contextual view of development (Baltes 1979b; Lerner 1982; Lerner, Hultsch, and Dixon 1983).

Brim and Kagan (1980, 1) have summarized the character of this developmental-contextual view by noting that this

> conception of human development . . . differs from most Western contemporary thought on the subject. The view that emerges . . . is that humans have a capacity for change across the entire life span. It questions the traditional idea that the experiences of the early years, which have a demonstrated contemporaneous effect, necessarily constrain the characteristics of adolescence and adulthood . . . there are important growth changes across the life span from birth to death, many individuals retain a great capacity for change, and the consequences of the events of early childhood are continually transformed by later experiences, making the course of human development more open than many have believed.

Given the interest in and importance attached to contextualism in the work summarized by Orville G. Brim, Jr., and Jerome Kagan (1980), it is appropriate to evaluate the usefulness of this model for the derivation of an adequate concept of development. While we shall argue that contextualism does have many attractive conceptual features, we shall also point out that—as do mechanism and organicism—it has important problems. Indeed, these problems are of sufficient scope to obviate the use of "pure" contextualism in deriving an adequate concept of development. However, contextual views may be combined with organismic ones. I shall argue that such a synthesis provides a quite useful basis for deriving a concept of development, one that eliminates many of the problems found in the two models taken separately.

THE CONTEXTUAL MODEL

According to Pepper (1942), the main metaphor of contextualism is neither the machine nor the whole organism. It is the historic event. "The real historic event, the event in its actuality, is when it's going on *now*, the dynamic dramatic active event" (Pepper 1942, 232). In contextualism every behavior and incident in the world is a historic event, and thus change and novelty are accepted as fundamental. A contextual model assumes (1) *constant change* of all levels of analysis; and (2) *embeddedness* of each level with all others—that changes in one promote changes in all. The assumption of constant change denotes that there is no complete uniformity or constancy. Rather than change being a phenomenon to be explained, a perturbation in a stable system, change is a given (Overton 1978); thus the task of the scientist is to describe, explain, and optimize the parameters and trajectories of processes (i.e., variables that show time-related changes in their quantity and/or quality).

The second assumption of contextualism is thus raised. It stresses the interrelation of all levels of analysis. Because phenomena are not seen as static but rather as change processes, and because any change process occurs within a similarly (i.e., constantly) changing world (of processes), any target change must be conceptualized in the context of the other changes within which it is embedded. Thus change will constantly continue as a consequence of this embeddedness.

There is an organism in the contextual perspective, but it is conceived of as an "organism in relation" (Looft 1973), or an "organism in transaction" (Dewey and Bentley 1948; Pervin 1968; Sameroff 1975) with its context; these relations are the focus of developmental analysis. The timing of the interaction between organism and context is critical in contextualism. Indeed, as implied earlier, the fact that the timing of interaction plays a central role in contextualism serves to provide a key distinction between it and organicism. As Pepper (1942) explains:

> Organicism takes time lightly or disparagingly; contextualism takes it seriously.... The root metaphor of organicism always does appear as a process, but it is the *integration* appearing in the process that the organicist works from and not the *duration* of the process. When the root metaphor reaches its ultimate refinement the organicist believes the temporal factor disappears. (p. 281)

Although emphasizing that the transaction or "dynamic interaction" (Lerner 1978, 1979, 1980) between organism and context is what develops in development, it is important to note that because of its admittance of multiple causative "agents" (formal, efficient, material, but not final) into developmental explanation, contextually derived perspectives do not exclude features associated with organismic developmental theories. A major example is the use made by contextually oriented theorists (e.g., Lerner and Busch-Rossnagel 1981) of the orthogenetic principle (Werner 1957) to describe the nature of change in the relations between individuals and their contexts; in fact, this principle has been used in even broader contextually related analyses; that is, those pertinent to the relations among large-scale systems in the universe (Prigogine 1978, 1980).

In short, a contextual perspective need not, should not, and typically *does* not (Lerner 1984, 1985) avoid the use of universalistic and thus constantly applicable principles of development. Instead the emphasis in such approaches is on the *relation* between the structural and functional characteristics of the organism and the features (e.g., the demands or presses) of the organism's context. Indeed, particular attention is paid to the mutual constraints and opportunities provided by both elements in the relation—organism and context (Lerner 1984). Thus, rather than seeing ideas such as "orthogenesis," which have traditionally been used primarily to depict intraorganism development (e.g., see Siegel, Bisanz, and Bisanz 1983), in reference to the individual-psychological level of analysis alone, the use of such ideas is made in reference to a "unit of analysis"—the "organism in transaction"—linking individual and context.

However, it is at this point that major problems arise with the use of contextualism as a paradigm from which to derive a concept of development. Contextualism is at its core (Overton 1984) a dispersive paradigm; in other words, a purely contextual approach sees the components of life as completely dispersive (Pepper 1942). Indeed, Pepper (1942) believes that it is the dispersive character of contextualism that is the key idea making it a world view distinct from the organismic one, a world view in turn marked, according to Pepper (1942), by integration. As I argued in Chapter 1, if the term *development* is to have meaning beyond that of mere change it must imply, at the very least, systematic and successive changes in the organization of an organism or, more generally, a system. Thus a world view that stressed only the dispersive, chaotic, and disorganized character of life would not readily lend itself to the derivation of a theory of development.

But, while contextualism may not suffice in and of itself as a model from which an adequate concept of development may be derived, there is a way to combine features of this model with organicism—with which we have seen it is closely aligned (Pepper 1942)—to forge such a concept. As I suggested earlier, this "marriage" is possible by reference to the ideas associated with the probabilistic-epigenetic view of organicism.

Contextualism and Probabilistic Epigenesis

A major point of contrast between organicism and contextualism arises because the contextual perspective excludes any notion of final cause (e.g., see Nagel 1957; Pepper 1942), and thus leads to a belief in the potential plasticity of the organism across life. That is, contextual formulations emphasize

not the intrinsically preformed or inevitable timetables and outcomes of development; instead, such formulations stress that the influence of the changing context on development is to make the trajectory of development less certain with respect to the applicability of norms to the individual (Gottlieb 1970). Thus developmental-contextual conceptions emphasize the probabilistic character of development and in so doing admit of more plasticity in development than do predetermined-epigenetic conceptions. In other words, the contextual view of development, at least as I (Lerner 1976, 1978, 1979, 1980, 1981, 1985; Lerner and Kauffman in press) and other contributors to the conceptual literature of developmental psychology (e.g., Baltes 1979b, 1983; Brim and Kagan 1980) construe it, is akin to the position labeled "probabilistic epigenetic organismic" by Gottlieb (1970), and developed by him (Gottlieb 1976a, 1976b) and earlier by Schneirla (1956, 1957) and Tobach and Schneirla (1968). Overton (1984) has labeled this conception as organismic-contextual.

The term "probabilistic epigenesis" was used by Gilbert Gottlieb (1970)

> to designate the view that the behavioral development of individuals within a species does not follow an invariant or inevitable course, and, more specifically, that the sequence or outcome of individual behavioral development is probable (with respect to norms) rather than certain. (Gottlieb 1970, 123)

Moreover, he explains that this probable, and not certain, character of individual development arises because

> probabilistic epigenesis necessitates a bidirectional structure-function hypothesis. The conventional version of the structure-function hypothesis is unidirectional in the sense that structure is supposed to determine function in an essentially nonreciprocal relationship. The unidirectionality of the structure-function relationship is one of the main assumptions of predetermined epigenesis. The bidirectional version of the structure-function relationship is a logical consequence of the view that the course and outcome of behavioral epigenesis is probabilistic: it entails the assumption of reciprocal effects in the relationship between

structure and function whereby function (exposure to stimulation and/or movement of musculoskeletal activity) can significantly modify the development of the peripheral and central structures that are involved in these events. (Gottlieb 1970, 123)

In sum, as compared to predetermined epigenesis, where the key assumption

holds that there is a unidirectional relationship between structure and function whereby structural maturation determines function (structural maturation → function) but not the reverse, probabilistic epigenesis assumes a bidirectional or reciprocal relationship between structural maturation and function, whereby structural maturation determines function and function alters structural maturation (structural maturation ↔ function). (Gottlieb 1983, 12)

But are the changes depicted in this probabilistic-epigenetic formulation of development completely dispersive? I think not. As does Overton (1984), I believe that when features of organicism, particularly its orthogenetic one (Siegel, Bisanz, and Bisanz 1983), are synthesized with the probabilistic nature of contextual change, a useful *developmental contextual* paradigm is created.

Developmental Contextualism and the Issue of Dispersion

As noted, Pepper (1942) emphasizes that the dispersive nature of contextualism is the feature that is the key to its being a world view distinct from organicism. He argues that:

The historic event which is the root metaphor of contextualism is a nearer approximation to the refined root metaphor of organicism than any common-sense term. This is so true that it is tempting to regard these two theories as species of the same theory, one being dispersive and the other integrative. It has occasionally been said that pragmatism is simply idealism with the absolute left out, which in our terms would be to say that contextualism is simply dispersive organicism. But, the insistence on integration which is characteristic of organicism makes so great a difference that it is wiser to consider them as two theories. (Pepper 1942, 280)

Accordingly, and as explained above, in being completely dispersive, a "pure" contextualism would not be suitable for use as a philosophical model from which to derive a concept of development. However, as I have explained too, a "pure" organicism would also be limited as a paradigm from which to derive a useful concept of development.

In turn, mechanism cannot be used as an alternative to either of these two paradigms because, as I have argued, there is really no concept of developmental change, of qualitative discontinuity, or even of newness or novelty, that can be derived from this paradigm. Thus, either some new paradigm must be adopted or, as Overton (1984) has suggested, it may be possible and useful to merge contextualism and organicism. He terms this merger contextual organicism. My own preference is for the term suggested by Gottlieb (1970): probabilistic epigenesis. In turn, the term developmental contextualism may be used *if* sight is not lost of the fact that one is still referring to an organismic, epigenetic process. That is, it is not just that the context produces alterations in development. Instead, since the context is influenced as well as constrained by the organism's characteristics, we must keep in mind the need to define development in terms of organism-context reciprocal, or dynamic-interactional (Lerner 1978, 1979, 1982, 1984), relations. In short, in contextualism the concept of development is really one of probabilistic epigenesis, of a synthesis between organismic processes and changes and contextual ones. Let us consider more fully the nature and implications of this concept of development.

THE CONCEPT OF DEVELOPMENT IN DEVELOPMENTAL CONTEXTUALISM

Gollin (1981) explains that probabilistic developmental change is not dispersive because the living system—the organism—has organization and internal coherence, and these features constrain the potentials of the *developmental context* to affect the system. He says:

> The determination of the successive qualities of living systems, given the web of relationships involved, is probabilistic. This is so because the number of factors operating conjointly in living systems is very great. Additionally, each factor and subsystem is capable of a greater or lesser degree of variability. Hence, the influence subsystems have upon each other, and upon the system as a whole, varies as a function of the varying states of the several concurrently operating subsystems. Thus, the very nature of living systems, both individual and collective, and of environments, assure the presumptive character of organic change.
>
> Living systems are organized systems with internal coherence. The properties of the parts are essentially dependent on relations between the parts and the whole (Waddington, 1957). The quality of the organization provides opportunities for change as well as constraints upon the extent and direction of change. Thus, while the determination of change is probabilistic, it is not chaotic. (Gollin 1981, 232)

Gollin's position illustrates that one needs to understand that development occurs in a multilevel context, and that the nature of the changes in this context leads to the probabilistic character of development; but one needs to appreciate, too, that the organism shapes the context as much as the context shapes it.

Recent essays by Tobach (1981) and by Scarr and her associates (Scarr 1982; Scarr and McCartney 1983) make similar points. For example, Tobach indicates that

> three processes (contradictions) intercept in time to bring about qualitative changes in the individual (development, which includes growth and maturation): (a) the inner contradiction of the organism; (b) the inner contradiction of the environment; and (c) the outer contradiction between the organism and the environment. Some of the inner contradictions would be the metabolic cycle, and neurohormonal cycles; these have characteristics of negative and positive feedback that bring about continuous change with more or less

stability in the organism. The environment expresses its own contradictions in diurnal and seasonal variations, faunal and floral interrelations, and so on. Given different lighting conditions (environmental contradictions), the effects on the hormonal function (intraorganismic contradictions) bring about changes in the organism's activity that bring it into changing relationships with the abiota and biota, and particularly with conspecifics (contradiction between organism and environment). The intersect of these three processes (contradictions) brings about developmental change in the organism. The organism may act on the environment (the social aspect), resulting in copulation, bringing about a new developmental stage. (Tobach 1981, 60–61)

Scarr (1982) notes:

> Two big questions have occupied developmental theorists from antiquity to the present day. . . . First, is the course of human development directed primarily by structures in the environment that are external to the person, or is development guided principally by the genetic program within? Second, is development primarily continuous or discontinuous? (Scarr 1982, 852)

Answering the first question bears on the idea of probabilistic epigenesis; answering the second relates to the concept of plasticity. In regard to the first issue, Scarr explains:

> Answers to the first question have shifted in recent years from the . . . empiricist position to the . . . nativist view. Neonativist arguments, however, do not assume the extreme preformism of the early century. Development does not merely emerge from the precoded information in the genes. Rather, development is a *probabilistic* result of indeterminate combinations of genes and environments. Development is genetically guided but variable and probabilistic because influential events in the life of every person can be neither predicted nor explained by general laws. Development, in this view, is guided primarily by the genetic program through its multilevel transactions with environments that range from cellular to social. The genetic program for the human species has both its overwhelming commonalities and its individual variability because each

of us is both human and uniquely human. (Scarr 1982, 852–53)

In regard to the second question, Scarr suggests that as a consequence of an organism's biological contributions *and* the probabilistic transactions this biology has with its multilevel context, neither complete consistency nor complete change characterizes the human condition. Instead:

> Human beings are made neither of glass that breaks in the slightest ill wind nor of steel that stands defiantly in the face of devastating hurricanes. Rather, in this view, humans are made of the newer plastics—they bend with environmental pressures, resume their shapes when the pressures are relieved, and are unlikely to be permanently misshapen by transient experiences. When bad environments are improved, people's adaptations improve. Human beings are resilient and responsive to the advantages their environments provide. Even adults are capable of improved adaptations through learning, although any individual's improvement depends on that person's responsiveness to learning opportunities. (Scarr 1982, 853)

In other words, there exists:

> A *probabilistic* connection between a person and the environment. It is more likely that people with certain genotypes will receive certain kinds of parenting, evoke certain responses from others, and select certain aspects from the available environments; but nothing is rigidly determined. The idea of genetic differences, on the other hand, has seemed to imply to many that the person's developmental fate was preordained without regard to experience. This is absurd. By involving the idea of genotype → environment effects, we hope to emphasize a probabilistic connection between genotypes and their environments. (Scarr and McCartney 1983, 428)

Similarly, Gollin (1981) notes that:

> The relationships between organisms and environments are not interactionist, as interaction implies that organism and environment are separate entities that come together at an interface. Organism and environment constitute a single life process. . . . For analytic convenience, we may treat various aspects

of a living system and various external environmental and biological features as independently definable properties. Analytical excursions are an essential aspect of scientific inquiry, but they are hazardous if they are primarily reductive. An account of the *collective behavior* of the parts as an organized entity is a necessary complement to a reductive analytic program, and serves to restore the information content lost in the course of the reductive excursion. . . . In any event, the relationships that contain the sources of change are those between organized systems and environments, not between heredity and environment (Gollin 1981, 231–32).

Similarly, Tobach (1981, 50) notes:

> Gene function is expressed in enzymes and proteins that are fundamental and ubiquitous to all aspects of molecular function and derivatively in physiological integration. However, the preeminence of societal factors in human development in determining the significance of these biochemical processes is also never lost. If the child is discovered to have an enzyme deficiency that is corrected through dietary supplementation, the outcome will depend on whether the child is in a society in which such knowledge is not available, or if the knowledge is available, whether the treatment is available to the individual child. Extremes in chromosomal structures and function such as trisomy-21, despite their demonstrated molecular base, are also variably vulnerable to societal processes.

A final point about the contextual-probabilistic-epigenetic view needs to be highlighted. Although both contextual and mechanistic-behavioral perspectives make use of the context enveloping an organism in attempts to explain development, it is clear that they do so in distinctly different ways. Contextually oriented theorists do not adopt a reflexively reductionistic approach to conceptualizing the impact of the context. Instead, because of a focus on organism-context transactions, and thus a commitment to using an interlevel, or relational, unit of analysis (Lerner, Skinner, and Sorell 1980), the context may be conceptualized as composed of multiple, qualitatively different levels, e.g., the inner-biological, the individual-psychological, the outer-physical, and the sociocultural (Riegel 1975, 1976a, 1976b). Moreover, although both the mechanistic and the contextual perspectives hold that changes in the context become part of the organism's intraindividually changing constitution, the concept of "organism" found in the two perspectives is also quite distinct. In contextualism the organism is not merely the host of the elements of a simplistic environment. Instead the organism is itself a qualitatively distinct level within the multiple dynamically interacting levels forming the context of life. As such, the organism has a distinct influence on that multilevel context that is influencing the organism. As a consequence the organism is, in short, not a host of S–R connections but an active contributor to its own development (Lerner 1982; Lerner and Busch-Rossnagel 1981).

How may such organism-context interactions occur? In other words, how may an organism make an active contribution to its own development? One answer to this question is found in the "goodness of fit" model of person-context relations (e.g., Lerner and Lerner 1983). Just as a person brings his or her characteristics of physical, emotional, and behavioral individuality to a particular social setting, there are demands placed on the person by virtue of the social and physical components of the setting. These demands may take the form of (1) attitudes, values, or stereotypes held by others regarding the person's attributes; (2) the attributes (usually behavioral) of others with whom the person must coordinate, or fit, for adaptive interactions to exist; or (3) the physical characteristics of a setting (e.g., the presence or absence of access ramps for the handicapped) that require the person to possess certain attributes (again, usually behavioral) for the occurrence of efficient interaction.

The person's characteristics of individuality, in differentially meeting these demands, provide a basis for the feedback he or she gets from the socializing environment. For example, considering the second type of contextual demands that exist—those that

arise as a consequence of the behavioral characteristics of others in the setting—problems of fit might occur when a child who is highly irregular in his biological functions (e.g., eating, sleep-wake cycles, toileting behaviors) interacts in a family setting composed of highly regular and behaviorally scheduled parents and siblings.

Lerner and Lerner (1983) and Thomas and Chess (1977) believe that adaptive psychological and social functioning do not derive directly from either the nature of a person's characteristics of individuality per se or the nature of the demands of the contexts within which the person functions. Rather, if a person's characteristics of individuality match (or "fit") the demands of a particular setting, adaptive outcome in that setting will accrue. Those people whose characteristics match most of the settings within which they exist should receive supportive or positive feedback from the contexts and should show evidence of the most adaptive behavioral development. In turn, of course, mismatched people, whose characteristics are incongruent with one or most settings, should show alternative developmental outcomes.

In sum, the present point is that to probabilistic-epigenetic theorists behavioral development becomes, at least in part, a matter of self-activated generation. These theorists view development as arising essentially from the multiplicative interaction of two qualitatively different sources—heredity and environment. Hence it is a logical next step to focus on the meeting place of those factors lying primarily within the organism (hereditary) and those lying primarily outside (environmental). This meeting place is of course the organism itself. By focusing on the contributions that the organism's own characteristics (e.g., its type of behavioral style, its physical appearance) make toward its own further development, developmental-contextual theorists are essentially studying the continual accumulations of the interacting contributions of nature and nurture. This focus brings about a concern with what role various aspects of the organism itself play in shaping its own behavior. A fuller explication of this aspect of the probabilistic-epigenetic viewpoint is made in Chapter 4.

Developmental Contextualism as a "Compromise" Between Mechanism and Organicism

Overton (1984) has suggested that organicism may be integrated with either contextualism or mechanism in order to formulate a synthetic position which capitalizes on the useful features of the mechanistic and the organismic positions. While I have argued that mechanism in and of itself is not useful for forging a true developmental theory, following Overton (1984), I suggest that within developmental contextualism there exists at least two ways of synthesizing some of the potentially useful features of mechanism and, of course, organicism.

The Levels-of-Organization Hypothesis

The first of these means of synthesis has been implied in much of what we have discussed above. It is termed the *levels-of-organization hypothesis* and is illustrated by the work of Schneirla (1957). The compromise notes that there are different levels of organic and/or phenomenal organization and that the laws of the lower levels (e.g., physics and chemistry) are implied in the laws of the higher (e.g., the psychological) level. Yet the laws of the higher level cannot be reduced to or predicted from the laws of the lower level. This is true because such reduction will not lead to an understanding of the emergent quality of the higher level. The reader should recognize that this assertion has been presented as a basic part of the organismic-epigenetic viewpoint. The water example on page 55 is an illustration of this compromise. Another illustration is that although certain neural, hormonal, and muscular processes certainly underlie (are implied in) a person's being in love, reduction of love to these lower levels—or to the still-lower levels of chemistry and physics—is unlikely to result in an understanding of this phenomenon.

An example of the application of the levels-of-organization compromise may be seen by reference to some of the phenomena reported in the literature on children's problem-solving behavior. Kendler and Kendler (1962) devised a way to study problem-solving behavior in various species of organisms (e.g., rats and humans), as well as in humans of various ages (e.g., nursery-school children and college students). In the procedure they devised, subjects are presented first with two large squares and two small squares. One of each type of square is painted black and one of each type is painted white. Thus there are a large black and a large white square, and a small white and a small black square. The subject's task is to learn to respond either to the color dimension (thus ignoring the size) or to the size dimension (thus ignoring the color). For example, a subject may be presented with a large black and a small white square on one trial and then perhaps a large white square and a small black square on another. Now, if size is the aspect of the stimuli that should be responded to and, further, a response toward the bigger of the two squares will always lead to a reward, the subject should choose the large stimulus in each trial, no matter what the color. In other words, the subject first learns that size is the relevant aspect of the stimuli; therefore the subject learns to respond to the difference in size and to ignore (not respond to) differences in color of the squares.

Rats, nursery-school children, and college students can all learn this first problem-solving task. The interesting thing about this type of problem solving is what happens when the rules about the relevant aspect of the stimuli are changed. In the first problem-solving task, size was the relevant dimension (the big squares were rewarded and the small squares were not). Without directly cueing the subject that this rule has changed, it is possible still to keep the size of the stimuli as the relevant dimension (and the color as the nonrelevant), but to make choice of the *small* squares the response that will be rewarded. Thus the same dimension of the stimuli (size) is still relevant, but there has been a reversal as to which *aspect* of the size (from large to small) will lead to a reward. Kendler and Kendler call this type of alteration a *reversal shift;* the same stimulus dimension is still related to reward, but which of the two stimuli within this same dimension is positive and which is negative is reversed. A second type of shift may occur, however, in the second problem-solving task. Instead of size being the reward-relevant dimension, color can be. Now response to the black squares (regardless of their size) will lead to a reward, and response to the white squares (regardless of their size) will not. This type of change involves a shift to the other dimension of the stimuli and is not within the same dimension. Hence the Kendlers term this second type of possible change a *nonreversal shift.* Figure 2.3 illustrates the reversal and the nonreversal shifts. In all cases the stimuli toward which a response will lead to a reward are marked +,

while the stimuli toward which a response will not be rewarded are marked −.

Kendler and Kendler (1962) review the studies of reversal and nonreversal problem solving done with rats, nursery-school children, and college students. After learning the first problem (for example, after making ten correct responses to the large-size stimuli), would it then be easier to learn a reversal shift or a nonreversal shift (again using the learning criterion of ten consecutive correct responses)? The Kendlers' review indicates that rats learn a nonreversal shift more easily than a reversal shift. Moreover, so do most nursery-school children. As do rats, these human children reach the criterion for making a nonreversal shift faster than they reach the criterion for making a reversal shift. However, somewhat older children, as well as college students, find a reversal shift easier.

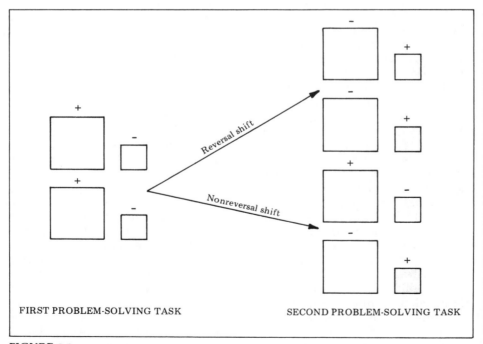

FIRST PROBLEM-SOLVING TASK   SECOND PROBLEM-SOLVING TASK

FIGURE 2.3
Examples of a reversal shift and a nonreversal shift.
Source: H. H. Kendler and T. S. Kendler (1962), Vertical and horizontal processes in problem solving, *Psychological Review* 69. Copyright © 1962 by the American Psychological Association. Reprinted by permission.

The Kendlers interpret these age changes by suggesting that in development there emerges a new mental process in children such that they move from ratlike responses to college-student-like responses; this new mental process, not present at earlier ages (e.g., efficient language processes), alters children's problem-solving behavior so that a reversal shift becomes easier than a nonreversal shift. Hence, while children's problem-solving behavior at the nursery-school level can be accounted for by reference to processes apparently also identifiable in rats, their later behavior may be explained by the emergence of a new mental process. Certainly the processes present in the nursery-school children provided a developmental basis for the processes seen among the older children. That is, it would be unlikely to find older children who now functioned like college students but never functioned like younger children (or rats, too, in this case). Yet these former processes are not sufficient to account for the behavior of the older children. The type of problem-solving behavior changes, and this alteration appears related to the emergence of a new mental function. Any attempt to reduce the laws of the later level to those of the earlier level will avoid dealing with the important emergent processes that apparently characterize the older age level. Thus, although other interpretations of these findings have been offered (see Esposito 1975), the present point is that the work reported by the Kendlers (1962) illustrates the level-of-organization compromise. The laws of the lower level may be involved in those of the higher one, but because those of the higher involve emergent qualities, the former laws will not suffice to account for the phenomena of the higher level if any attempt at reduction is made.

The levels-of-organization compromise is presented diagrammatically in Figure 2.4. Here we see that at level 1 two gases, hydrogen and oxygen, are present; at level 2, however, the two gases combine to produce a substance (water) that has a property (liquidness) that did not exist in either of the level-1 elements in isolation. Although the presence of the lower level's phenomena is

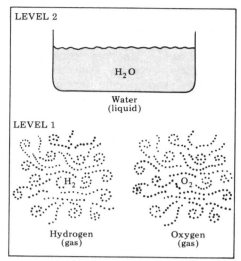

FIGURE 2.4
Levels-of-organization compromise between the mechanistic and the organismic positions.

certainly implied in the phenomena of the higher level, the latter level still has phenomena (e.g., liquidness) that cannot be understood through reduction to those of the lower level.

The General-and-Specific-Laws Compromise
The second compromise between the mechanistic and the organismic positions maintains that there are general and specific laws that govern development: Certain general laws apply to any and all levels of psychological functioning, yet each specific level of psychological development is also governed by specific laws. Such a compromise is often found in the work of organismic theorists, for example Heinz Werner and Jean Piaget (see Chapters 6 and 8). Like other organismic developmental theorists who stress the concepts of stage in their ideas, Piaget views development as involving two processes: first, a general, continuous process that is present at all levels, and in fact is used to account for the continual development of children through the various stages of cognitive development; and second, specific qualitatively distinct phenomena, which

actually serve as the definitional basis of the various stages of development at which they occur.

Sigmund Freud, also an organismic theorist, similarly made use of a compromise between general and specific laws of development. Freud viewed sexual functioning as passing through various "psychosexual stages of development" (1949). However, he saw this development as being energized by a finite amount of mental energy present in every individual at birth. This mental energy passed through the body of a person in a prescribed sequence, and became concentrated at particular locations of the body at specific periods of the person's life. Although this same mental energy was seen as always being involved in sexual functioning at all times in a person's life—and as such represents a general law of development—the manner in which sexual functioning was expressed was dependent on exactly where the mental energy was centered. Thus, to Freud, sexual functioning involved the combined contribution of a continuously applicable mental energy and a specific area (or zone) of the body where this mental energy happened to be located at a certain time in development; this specific characteristic of sexual functioning determined the mode of expression of one's sexuality. Hence Freud's view of psychosexual development, which we will deal with again in Chapter 8, is an example of how organismic developmentalists may utilize the general-and-specific-laws compromise in their theories.

The general-and-specific-laws compromise is represented in Figure 2.5. At both level 1 and level 2 we see that a general law, G, exists. However, at level 1 there is also present a specific law, S_1, while at level 2 there is present a different specific law, S_2.

If at each new developmental level of organization there is an emergence of new phenomena that cannot be reduced to lower organizational levels, how may the laws governing—or the variables involved in—these new phenomena be understood? Typical of other organismic theorists, Schneirla (1957) maintains that to understand this emergence

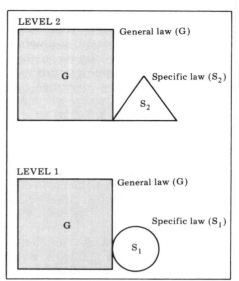

FIGURE 2.5
General-and-specific-laws compromise between the mechanistic and the organismic positions.

one must look at the specific contribution of that developmental level's genetic inheritance (nature) and its environment or experience (nurture). The sources of behavior must lie within these two domains, and one must look at how each level's nature and nurture interact to produce the qualitatively new phenomena that characterize it. This interactive view of the process of development has many uses, several of which will be focused on in succeeding chapters. Here, however, I should note that, as with organicism, mechanism, and contextualism, the developmental-contextual integration I propose also has problems and limitations. Let us consider some of the key ones.

LIMITS AND PROBLEMS OF A DEVELOPMENTAL-CONTEXTUAL PERSPECTIVE

The concepts of organism, of context, and of the relations between the two found in a probabilistic-epigenetic, developmental-contextual perspective are, as a set, quite distinct from those associated with organismic and mechanistic conceptions. As we have argued, such a contextual perspective leads to a multilevel concept of development, one in which the focus of inquiry is the organism-environment transaction. Further, such a contextual orientation places an emphasis on the potential for intraindividual change in structure and function—for plasticity—across the life span. Yet several conceptual and derivative methodological problems must be confronted in order (1) to move such a contextual orientation from merely being a "perspective" to being useful for the derivation of theory (Baltes 1979b), and (2) in turn to use developmental contextualism as a framework within which to study individual-context transactions.

First, substantively, we must recognize that despite the great amount of evidence that exists for human plasticity (Lerner 1984), we still cannot answer several fundamental questions about the contextual dynamically interactive parameters of plasticity. Are different levels of analysis and/or different targets within levels differentially plastic? For example, it may be the case that selected features of our genotype (e.g., the number of chromosomes we possess) cannot be altered (without, at least, severely damaging our organismic integrity) no matter what the nature of our organism-context relations may be. On the other hand, more molar, behavioral features of functioning may not be subject to such restrictions. For instance, are there limits to the number of languages a person can learn to speak or to the number of people's names a person may remember? No current evidence indicates that such limits exist.

In addition to not fully knowing the limits of plasticity that currently characterize levels of analysis, we do not know what further substantive and technological advances may imply for the future character of these limits. If we take the idea of probabilistic epigenesis seriously, and if we recognize that

science and technology represent natural parts of the human ecology, then we cannot anticipate where future scientific advances may lead. Thus current limits of plasticity are not necessarily future ones. These limits are themselves plastic and are likely to change in a direction that, for some of us, lies beyond our imagination.

But recognition that the limits of plasticity can change over time raises a developmental issue. The actualization of plasticity of course involves change, and change can only be identified over time. Numerous questions exist about the rates of change of plastic processes at the several levels of analysis that transact to provide the bases of behavior. First, it is clear that there is a "non-equivalent temporal metric" across the various levels of analysis (Lerner, Skinner, and Sorell 1980) involved in person-context transactions. That is, all levels of the context change over time, but time may not have an identical meaning at all the levels. One way to understand this is to note that the smallest meaningful division of time to detect change differs among levels. If time is one's X axis, with the Y axis reflecting levels of one's target process, then sensible X-axis divisions to detect infant neuromuscular changes may be as small as weeks. However, the smallest sensible division to detect social institutional change may be a year. In addition, even within a given level, time may not have an equivalent meaning at different points in development. For example, on the level of the individual, a one-year separation between birthdays may seem a vast length of time to a five-year-old; to someone experiencing his or her thirty-ninth birthday the one-year period until the fortieth birthday may seem quite short; and to an eighty-five-year-old, a one-year wait for some important event may again seem quite long.

The import of the non-equivalent temporal metric is that it may be difficult to detect the influence of changes promoted on one level on another; for example, a change on the biological level (e.g., promoted through better nutritional programs for children) may be difficult to detect on the societal level. Indeed, if an attempt is made to verify the existence of such an influence, it may be that a long-term, perhaps intergenerational, perspective needs to be taken; or in a within-cohort analysis, it may be that only interindividual differences in intraindividual change, and not intraindividual change itself, can be assessed.

Complicating this issue is that even though the effects of a biological intervention on society may take a long time to detect, there is not necessarily symmetry of influence. That is, "upper level" societal alteration and social change may impact quite visibly and relatively rapidly on "lower level" individual and biological processes. For example, changes in federal government funding programs for school lunch programs for the poor, for aid to dependent mothers, or for Medicare and Medicaid for the elderly can impact relatively quickly on an individual's health, cognitive, and familial functioning variables.

The issues of the non-equivalent temporal metric, and of the asymmetry of interlevel influences, can be seen to lead to other ones. First, given the rates of change of different levels, one needs to know how processes at different levels connect to one another: How do interlevel influences occur? One answer to this question may be to explore the use of a "goodness of fit" model of person-context relations (e.g., Lerner and Lerner 1983), discussed earlier; that is, here individual behavioral characteristics that are congruent with pertinent behavioral presses are studied for their import for adaptive person-immediate-social context (e.g., peer group) exchanges.

Of course, the goodness-of-fit model is not the only conception of person-context relations that may be derived from a developmental-contextual orientation. Indeed, an infinity of interlevel relations may perhaps occur, and there exists a potentially similarly large array of ways to model them. At this writing, we simply have not devoted enough thought and empirical energies to their investigation.

Issues for Intervention

Interventions represent attempts to eliminate, ameliorate, or enhance or optimize an individual's or a group's behavior or social situation in the direction of some desired or valued end (e.g., better health, improved self-concept). A developmental-contextual view of person-context relations, and of plasticity, raises several issues pertinent to intervention. First, the issue of asymmetry of interlevel influences raises largely unaddressed concerns about efficiency and about cost-benefit ratios. For instance, with an intervention targeted at the cognitive-behavioral level, for example the modification of academic achievement, is it more efficient to institute a "bottom-up strategy" (e.g., intervening at the biological level), a "parallel-level strategy" (e.g., intervening by cognitive-behavioral means) or a "top-down" strategy (intervening by instituting or changing social programs)? Which strategy leads to the most benefits, relative to economic, social, and personal costs? We simply do not know the answers to these questions for many of the potential targets of intervention.

Moreover, a decision about the level of analysis on which to focus one's intervention efforts is complicated by the fact that all levels of analysis are developing or changing over time. While this feature of the human condition permits both *concurrent* (same-time, immediate) and *historical* (long-term, delayed) interventions, it again raises questions of efficiency and cost-benefit ratios. For example, when during the life span is it best to intervene to optimize a particular target process (and, of course, on what level is it best to focus one's efforts)? Are periods of developmental transition (e.g., puberty, retirement), or are periods of *relatively* more stability, better times within which to focus one's efforts? Moreover, do some intervention goals, for example the elimination of fetal alcohol syndrome, or FAS (Streissguth et al. 1980), require an intergenerational-developmental rather than an ontogenetic-developmental approach? In the case of

FAS, for instance, might it be of more benefit to intervene with women who are at risk for excessive alcohol use during pregnancy *before* they become pregnant? Again, for most potential targets, intervention issues such as these have remained relatively unaddressed.

A final relatively unaddressed issue that may usefully be raised here relates to the issues of direct and indirect intervention effects and of planned and unplanned effects. If an individual's plasticity both derives from and contributes to the other levels of analysis within which he or she transacts, one must anticipate that actualizing the potential for plasticity at any one level of analysis will influence changes among other variables, both at that level and at others. From this perspective, one should always expect that any direct and/or intended effect of intervention will have indirect and often unintended consequences (Willems 1973).

This recognition leads to two points. First, interventions should not be initiated without some conceptual or theoretical analysis of potential indirect and unintended consequences. For instance, changing a spouse's assertiveness may be the direct intended effect of a cognitive-behavior therapist's efforts. However, the changed assertiveness might lead to a diminution of marital quality and, in addition, to a divorce. Such indirect effects might have been unintended by the therapist and undesired by either therapist or client. Thus my view is that one must think quite seriously about the broader, contextual effects of one's intervention efforts. Clearly, a developmental-contextual perspective would be of use in this regard. It would sensitize one to the general possibility, and perhaps some specific instances, of the indirect effects of one's intervention efforts. Such reflection will be useful in several ways, a major instance of which is that undesirable indirect effects may be anticipated. If so, the issue of cost-benefit ratios can be addressed before intervention begins.

Of course, the fact that undesired effects may arise from intervention efforts raises the point that plasticity is a double-edged sword: A system open to enhancement is also open to deterioration. That is, plasticity permits interventions to be planned in order to improve the human condition, but indirect effects may also cause a deterioration in a target person's life condition and/or the condition of his or her context. Moreover, this problem is complicated by recognizing that as a consequence of people being transactionally related to their multilevel contexts, a failure to intervene, to alter the context of life, is *itself* an intervention; that is, it keeps the context on a trajectory from which it might have been shifted if one had acted. Thus one must assess the cost-benefit ratio not only of one's actions but also of one's failure to act.

Conclusions

I have pointed to some of the key conceptual and methodological issues that remain to be resolved if a developmental-contextual perspective is to be successfully used not only to study individual-context relations but also to intervene to enhance such relations. Pessimism because of the presence of these problems is unwarranted, however. Every approach to human development has limitations, as I hope I have made clear in this chapter. Thus that there are problems to be resolved about developmental contextualism does not single it out from other developmental paradigms. Indeed, given that it was only in the 1970s that this view of contextualism came to the fore, the clarity with which the problems have been articulated, the methodological advances that have already been made (e.g., see Nesselroade and Baltes 1979), and the several data sets that speak to the empirical use of this contextual perspective (Baltes, Reese and Lipsitt 1980; Brim and Kagan 1980) are reasons for great optimism for the future.

Developmental contextualism has influenced and will continue to influence scientific activity. Indeed, all the models we have considered in this chapter have such an influence. Let us conclude this chapter, then, with a brief discussion of the implications of the models for scientific activity.

IMPLICATIONS OF PHILOSOPHICAL MODELS OF DEVELOPMENT FOR SCIENTIFIC ACTIVITY

Philosophical models are not capable of being evaluated in terms of whether or not they are correct (Reese and Overton 1970). Nevertheless, they shape the theories that scientists use to interpret the facts they derive from their studies of the "real" world. Moreover, in shaping theories, world views shape the very questions scientists ask in their study of the real world. The questions that follow from different theories are likely to be quite different, and in turn, the data generated to answer these contrasting questions are unlikely to provide comparable answers.

For instance, a mechanistic theorist who derives a theory of human development may try to reduce behavior to learning principles common to people of all ages. Thus he or she might seek to discover those environmental-behavioral reactions that remain identical from infancy through adolescence and adulthood. Alternatively, an organismically oriented theorist would attempt to find those phenomena that are unique to and representative of particular age periods. In turn, a contextualist would look at the relation of an event to others at earlier times in the life cycle, as well as to current cultural, environmental, and long-term historical influences. Moreover, the reciprocal nature of these interactions would be considered.

The point is that scientific activity derived from alternative world views asks different questions about development. Consequently, scientists committed to alternative world views may collect data on different topics. One scientist is not necessarily functioning correctly and another incorrectly. The issue is *not* one of deciding which theory is best, or which leads to truth and which does not. Theories from different world views ask different questions because the very nature of reality is conceived of differently. Thus what is a true depiction of reality for one world view may be irrelevant for another.

One major implication of the nature of this philosophy-science relationship is that a criterion other than truth must be used to evaluate interpretations of development. Moreover, since one theory is not held to be intrinsically better than another, all theories may be said to have an equal opportunity to advance our understanding of human development. Accordingly, it may be suggested that theories should be evaluated on the basis of their usefulness for *description,* for how well they help scientists *explain* development, and for their use in devising ways to *optimize* human behavior. In this chapter, I have indicated that a developmental-contextual perspective may be particularly useful in these ways. In Chapter 5 the features of a specific set of ideas derived from this perspective will be presented. I label these ideas dynamic interactionism. In addition, the life-span view of human development, with which this dynamic-interactional perspective is associated, will be presented. However, these presentations rest on a discussion of the nature-nurture controversy and on an indication of my specific views about this key issue of psychological development.

3 | The Nature-Nurture Controversy: Implications of the Question, How?

A child is born, and may seem to have few distinguishable capabilities. Soon, however, rather well coordinated sensorimotor behaviors begin to be elaborated. Later, other, more complicated motor patterns emerge. Still later, the child's vocalizations turn to words.

A baby goose (a gosling), moments after it breaks through its shell, begins to walk after its mother. From then on, the goose will attach itself to other geese in all its social behaviors.

Rats that are deprived throughout their early development of stimulus cues for depth are individually placed on a platform that lies between an apparently deep drop-off and a shallow one. Almost all of the rats descend off the platform's shallow side.

Newborn human babies, just a few hours after their birth, suck on a non-nutritive nipple more when the sucking is followed by a recording of their mother's voice than when the sucking is followed by a recording of a female voice that is not their mother's.

What is the source of these diverse behaviors? In fact, what is the source of any behavioral development? Some psychologists have interpreted the emergence of behaviors such as those described above in a way that

suggests that experience seems to play a minimal role, if any, and that innate, maturational, or hereditary factors seem to account for their appearance. Yet other psychologists claim just the opposite. Observing the same behaviors, they offer interpretations emphasizing environmental factors. Still other psychologists (myself included) attempt to interpret such behaviors in a way that takes into account both the contributions of intrinsic and experiential factors.

Where does the truth lie? Perhaps all positions have elements of truth in them, but the arguments about where the sources of behavior lie are by no means resolved. From our discussions in Chapters 1 and 2, it may be seen that the basic issue in developmental psychology is the nature-nurture controversy. Indeed, this controversy has been and remains very much an issue.

For example, as indicated in Chapter 1, some psychologists interested in the study of perceptual processes (the Gestalt school) claim that nativistic factors are most important in determining a person's perception, while others (e.g., Hebb 1949) take an empiricist point of view. In the area of personality, some (e.g., Sheldon 1940, 1942) stress what they claim to be innate sources of a person's temperamental-behavioral functioning, while others (e.g., McCandless 1967, 1970) maintain that acquired, socially learned responses are the source of such functions. In looking at certain types of animal behavior, some writers (e.g., Lorenz 1965) postulate preformed, innate mechanisms to account for observed patterns, while others (e.g., Gottlieb 1970, 1983; Kuo 1967; Lehrman 1953; Schneirla 1957) take a probabilistic-epigenetic approach. Some researchers interested in verbal development stress the primacy of maturation (Gesell and Thompson 1941), while others viewing the same sort of behaviors offer interpretations that stress learning (Gagné 1968). Finally, some psychologists interested in intelligence suggest hypotheses that stress the primacy of heredity factors (e.g., Jensen 1969, 1974, 1980), while others apparently opt to emphasize the role of the environment (Kagan 1969) and/or gene-environment interaction (Lewontin 1976).

Indeed, and in respect to the last instance of the continuing concern with the nature-nurture issue, the renewal of controversy about the nature and nurture of intelligence seemingly opened up a Pandora's box regarding the relative contributions of nature and nurture to such topics as sexism, militarism, social Darwinism, racism (Tobach et al. 1974), educability (Jensen 1973), and sex differences in personality (e.g., Carlson 1972), to name just some of the areas of concern. In fact, as evidenced by recent contributions to the literatures of several disciplines (e.g., Feldman and Lewontin 1975; Loehlin, Lindzey, and Spuhler 1975; Lewontin 1976; Wilson 1975), not only has the debate regarding the contributions of nature and nurture to human functioning not been resolved to date, but instead it has evolved as a concern of multidisciplinary relevance.

Perhaps the best example of the multidisciplinary dimensions of this debate arose in 1975 with the publication of E. O. Wilson's *Sociobiology: The New Synthesis*. Sociobiology, as promoted by Wilson (1975) and others (e.g., Trivers 1971), attempts to integrate through biological reductionism not only the biological sciences but the social sciences and the humanities as well. As noted by the philosopher Caplan (1978, 2), this approach is "the latest and most strident of a series of efforts in the biological sciences to direct scientific and humanistic attention toward the question of what is, fundamentally, the nature of human nature." Consistent with the metatheoretical assumptions we have seen in Chapter 2 associated with those adopting a predetermined-epigenetic position, many sociobiologists construe nature as making a predetermined, immutable contribution to behavior. That is, whatever the proportion of variance in human social behavior with a genetic basis, it is that proportion that is genetically constrained and generally unavailable to contextual influence.

The criticisms of sociobiology have come from the several disciplinary quarters that sociobiologists seek to digest (e.g., see Caplan 1978). Within the biological and social sciences the criticisms have generally been associated with conceptualizations stressing that sociobiologists do not appreciate the plasticity of genes, organisms, or contexts; and that just as genes influence their contexts, the reverse is also the case (e.g., see Grouse et al. 1978, 1979; Uphouse and Bonner 1975).

Thus, in this debate about the usefulness of sociobiological thinking, a key influence on the differences of opinion expressed by participants is the philosophical differences among them. Those who favor sociobiological thinking are essentially arguing from a predetermined-epigenetic viewpoint (see Gottlieb 1983). In turn, those who reject this conceptualization (e.g., Gould 1976) argue from a metatheoretical stance that stresses strong, or dynamic, interactions between heredity and environment (e.g., Lerner 1976, 1978; Lewontin 1976; Overton 1973), and thus a viewpoint consonant with the developmental-contextual position discussed in Chapter 2. Again, then, philosophical division characterizes this instance of the nature-nurture debate.

The details of each of the above controversies need not be specified here in order to make the point that psychology in no way takes a place behind philosophy in the intensity of its debate about the nature-nurture issue, and that in all cases the essence of each debate is always the same—the relative contributions of nature and nurture variables in providing a source of behavior.

TOWARD A RESOLUTION OF THE NATURE-NURTURE CONTROVERSY

By this time you are probably wondering how a controversy that has engaged so many bright men and women for so many years can still remain unresolved. Cannot the issues be detailed in such a way as to somehow diminish the seemingly endless confusion? I think they can. Rather than discuss all the details of the above controversies—which often led to what I feel were conceptual dead ends—let me turn to a review of various psychologists' formulations that were offered in an attempt to resolve the nature-nurture controversy; I will begin my analysis with a review of the seminal ideas of a famous psychologist, a former president of the American Psychological Association, Anne Anastasi. I will then use Anatasi's formulations as a general framework within which to begin to consider the issues necessary for my reconceptualization of the nature-nurture controversy. To illustrate the application of this conceptualization, in Chapter 4 I will consider as a sample case the nature-nurture issue as it has occurred, and continues to exist, in the study of intelligence.

The Position of Anne Anastasi

Anne Anastasi's classic paper, which first appeared in *Psychological Review* in 1958, represents a most lucid and well-considered treatment of the nature-nurture controversy. The essential problem in appropri- ately conceptualizing the nature-nurture controversy, as Anastasi saw it, is that psychologists were asking the wrong questions; therefore, they obviously could not get the right answers. Anastasi attempted to show why previous inquiries led to dead ends, and what the appropriate question is.

As we have seen in Chapter 1, the first way that philosophers as well as psychologists inquired into this problem was to ask, "Which one?" Does heredity or environment, nature or nurture, provide the determining source of behavior? Those who posed the issue in this way were assuming that the independent, isolated action of one or the other provided a source of a behavior. However, we should reject this way of posing the problem, because it is basically illogical. To explain, let us use the terms focused on by Anastasi; that is, nature is *heredity* and nurture is *environment*. The "which one?" question assumes that nature and nurture are independent, separable sources of influence, and as such, that one can exert an influence in isolation from the other. But Anastasi pointed out that such an assumption is illogical. This is because there would be no one *in* an environment without heredity, and there would be no place to see the effects of heredity without environment. Genes do not exist in a vacuum. They exert their influence on behavior in an environment. At the same time, however, if there were no genes (and consequently no heredity), the environment would not have an organism in it to influence. Accordingly, nature and nurture are inextricably tied together. In life they never exist independent of the other. As such, Anastasi argued that *any* theory of development, in order to be logical and accurately to reflect life situations (that is, to have *ecological validity*), must stress that nature and nurture are always involved in all behavior, and it is simply not appropriate to ask "which one?" because they are *both* completely necessary for any organism's existence or for the existence of any behavior.

Some psychologists (e.g., Hebb 1949; Lehrman 1953; Schneirla 1956, 1957), however, had recognized the inappropriateness of the "which one?" question even before Anastasi's (1958) paper was published. Yet others had asked another question that Anastasi maintained was also inappropriate, because it, too, led to a conceptual dead end. They put the issue this way: Granted that nature and nurture are always involved in any behavior, that both of them are always needed, *how much* of each is needed for a given behavior? For intelligence do you need 90 percent heredity and 10 percent environment, or is intelligence perhaps only two parts heredity and eight parts environment? Or some might ask: For personality can it be 50 percent of each, while for perception it is seven parts of one, three parts of the other? In essence, then, psychologists asking this question would attempt to ascertain how much of each source was needed for a given type of behavior.

But this question also leads to a fruitless end, because it—like the "which one?" question—is based on an inappropriate underlying assumption. In the case of the "how much?" question, the assumption may be termed the independent, additive-action assumption. It suggests that the way in which nature and nurture are related to each other is that the contribution of one source is added to the contribution of the other to provide the behavior. We can see that this solution puts the formula into the terms of a recipe: Add one part of X to some part of Y; add some unknown part of nature to an unknown part of nurture to get behavior.

However, such a question raises many others. For example, for the 80 percent of intelligence that might be thought to be nature, one may ask where that 80 percent exerts its influence if not in an environment. And for the 20 percent of intelligence thought to be nurture, how is that 20 percent acted on if an organism does not first have inherited genes? Does not nature play a role with the nurture part? If not, then what can that one part of nurture possibly contribute to? And what of the (unknown) contributory part of nature? Can it contribute to behavior without any environmental support? Where does it contribute if not in an environment? Thus the "how much?" question soon leads to separating out the independent, isolated effects of nature and nurture, a conceptual route we have just taken by means of the "which one?" question. We rejected this route, with its notions of either heredity or environment, because we saw that nature and nurture are always inextricably bound. Thus we must also reject the "how much?" route because it really does not take us well beyond the "which one?" path. In fact, the "which one?" question can be seen to be just a special case of the "how much?" question. That is, the former question implies a 100 percent/0 percent split between nature and nurture, while the latter implies some percentage split less than that.

Thus we see that a conceptualization of the independent action of either source (in either an isolated or an additive manner) will lead us to a conceptually vacuous dead end. We should conclude, then, that two assertions follow directly from our above argument. First, nature and nurture are always completely involved in all behavior. Put another way, 100 percent of nature and 100 percent of nurture always make their contributions to all behavior. Any method of inquiry into the source of behavioral development that does not take cognizance of this statement and seeks to make artificial distinctions between nature and nurture can lead only to conceptual confusion and an empirical blind alley. Second, since independent-action conceptualizations of the contributions of nature and nurture similarly lead to conceptual dead ends, an alternative conceptualization of their contributions, that of *interactive action*, seems more appropriate.

This alternative, which seems useful from our above considerations, is one that indicates that both nature and nurture interact to provide a source of behavioral development. Since both sources have been seen to be necessarily completely present, and since we have seen that it is inappropriate to speak of their contributions as adding to each other, then it seems that we should ask: *How* do nature and nurture interact to produce behavioral development? *How* do the effects of each multiply to provide a source of development? Thus the organismic notion of a multiplicative interaction between nature and nurture as providing the basis of development is necessarily derived.

This third question, the question of "how?", would seem to lead to the appropriate route of investigation into the contributions of nature and nurture. This, Anastasi argued, is the appropriate way to formulate the issue, because it takes cognizance of the logical necessities. It is based on what we may term the interactive, multiplicative-action assumption, which implies (1) that nature and nurture are both fully involved in providing a source of any behavioral development; (2) that they cannot therefore function in isolation from one another but must always interact in their contributions; and (3) that interaction (which, as we have seen, cannot be appropriately construed to mean addition) can be conceptualized as a multiplicative type of interrelation—that is, a type of relation in which the full presence of each source is completely intertwined with the other. In other words, from this view heredity and environment do not add together to contribute to behavior, but rather development is seen as a *product* of nature-nurture interaction.

An analogy will help illustrate this. The area of a rectangle is determined by a formula that multiplies the length by the width (area = length × width). To know the area of a given rectangle, then, one has to look at the product of a multiplicative relation. It is simply incorrect to ask which one, length or width, determines the area, because a rectangle would not exist unless it had both length and width. Similarly, it is incorrect to ask how much of each is necessary to have area, because the two dimensions cannot merely be added; they must be multiplied in order to produce a rectangle.

Of course, although length and width must always be completely present in order to have a rectangle, different values of each will lead to different products (or areas). Thus, in determining a particular product (a given

area) of a length × width interaction, one must ask *how* a specific value of length in interaction (in multiplication) with a specific value of width produces a rectangle of a given area. More generally, then, one must recognize that the same width would lead to different areas in interaction with varying lengths and, in turn, the same length would lead to different areas in interaction with varying widths.

By moving from this analogy back to the question "how?" in regard to the nature-nurture issue, it may be seen that comparable statements may be made. There would be no product—no behavioral development—if nature and nurture were not 100 percent present. Thus the assumptions underlying the "which one?" and "how much of each?" questions are rejected, and it is recognized that any behavioral development is the result of a multiplicative, interactive relation between specific hereditary and environmental influences. Moreover, it should be noted that this means that the same hereditary influence will lead to different behavioral products in interaction with varying environments; furthermore, the same environment will lead to varying behavioral outcomes in interaction with different hereditary influences.

This means that heredity and environment *never* function independently of each other. Nature (for example, genes) never affects behavior directly; it always acts in the context of environment. Environment (for example, social stimulation) never directly produces behavior either; it will show variation in its effects depending on the heredity-related characteristics of the organism on which it acts.

These statements about the reciprocal interdependence of nature and nurture are not just casual matters. Indeed, in Chapter 1 we saw that major philosophers and scientists have tried to conceptualize behavior and development in terms that are inconsistent with the view reflected by the interactive-action conception. Indeed, succeeding chapters will consider theorists who emphasize that various components of development (for example, cognition or personality) can be understood by ideas that stress *either* nature or nurture (that is, the "which one?" question). Thus it is important to point out that others do not necessarily agree that the formulation I favor is the best or most useful one. Nevertheless, I believe that the question "how?" leads the psychologist to a consideration of the interactive effects of nature and nurture in providing a source of development. It seems that only this question casts aside fruitless polemics and allows the psychologist to begin to unravel the decidedly complex interactions of nature and nurture.

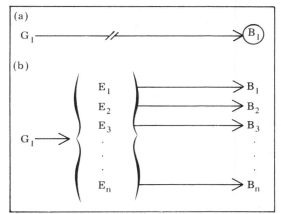

FIGURE 3.1

(a) Heredity (G) does not directly lead to behavior (B). (b) Rather, the effects of heredity on behavior will be different under different environmental (E) conditions.

HEREDITY-ENVIRONMENT INTERACTIONS

Assuredly, if Anastasi had ended her paper after making some of the above points, her contribution to the conceptual clarification of the nature-nurture controversy would have been considered substantial. Anastasi's paper provided additional information, however. After indicating that the appropriate way to conceptualize the nature-nurture controversy is in terms of how these two sets of sources interact, Anastasi proceeded to attempt to specify *how* each source—heredity and environment—may provide a basis of behavioral development.

Nature: The Continuum of Indirectness

Let us focus first on hereditary factors. Anastasi argues that the effects of heredity on behavior are diverse and always indirect. That is, no psychological function is ever inherited as such; heredity always relates to behavior in an indirect way. At the very least, any hereditary influence on behavior must be mediated by—must occur in the context of—a supportive, facilitative environment. This assertion is derived from the rationale that was used to object to the "which one?" question: You need the environment to see the effects of heredity;

there would be no place to see the contribution of nature if there were no environmental context. Accordingly, the specific contribution of heredity to behavior will depend on the specific environment in which that contribution occurs. Consistent with the probabilistic-epigenetic position discussed in Chapter 2, we may assert that any hereditary contribution must occur in an environmental context, and the particular expression of the hereditary contribution that will eventually be seen will depend on the specific characteristics of the environment in which it occurs.

To illustrate, let us represent hereditary contributions by the letter G (for genes), environmental contributions by the letter E, and behavioral outcomes by the letter B. As shown in Figure 3.1, it is possible to conceptualize the contribution of heredity to behavior as being direct. Hence, in this formulation, a particular combination of genes (G_1) will invariably lead to a particular behavioral outcome (B_1). However, it has been argued that this conceptualization is not appropriate. As such, an interactive idea of nature and nurture, illustrated in Figure 3.1, has been advanced. Here the same hereditary contribution (G_1) can be associated with an infinity of behavioral outcomes (B_1 to B_n) as a consequence of interaction in the infinity of environments (E_1 to E_n) that could exist.

Consider as an example the case of a child born with Down's syndrome. The genetic material—the DNA—of genes is arranged on stringlike structures present in the nucleus of each cell. These structures are chromosomes. The typical cells of the human body have forty-six chromosomes, divided into twenty-three pairs. The only cells in the body that do not have forty-six chromosomes are the gametes—the sex cells (sperm in males, ova in females). These cells carry only twenty-three chromosomes, one of each pair. This arrangement assures that when a sperm fertilizes an ovum to form a zygote, the new human so created will have the number of chromosome pairs appropriate for the species. However, in a child born with Down's syndrome, a genetic anomaly exists. There is an extra chromosome in the twenty-first pair—three chromosomes instead of two.

Thus children with Down's syndrome have a specific genetic inheritance. The complement of genes transmitted to people at conception by the union of the sperm and ovum is termed the *genotype*. This is what constitutes our genetic inheritance. At least insofar as the extra chromosome is concerned, the Down's syndrome child has a specific genotype. Yet even though the genotype remains the same for any such child, the behavioral outcomes associated with this genotype differ.

As recently as thirty years ago, Down's syndrome children, who are typically recognized by certain physical (particularly facial) characteristics, were expected to have life spans of no more than about twelve years. They were also expected to have quite low IQ scores. They were typically classified into a group of people who, because of low intelligence, required custodial (usually institutional) care. Today, however, Down's syndrome children often live well beyond adolescence. Additionally, they lead more self-reliant lives. Their IQs are now typically

higher, often falling in the range allowing for education, training, and sometimes even employment.

How did these vast differences come about? Certainly the genotype did not change. Rather, what changed was the environment of these children. Instead of invariably being put into institutions, different and more advanced special education techniques were provided, often on an outpatient basis. These contrasts in environment led to variation in behavioral outcomes despite the same heredity, that is, despite *genotypic invariancy.*

That heredity always exerts its effects indirectly through environment in the development of physical as well as behavioral characteristics may also be illustrated. First, consider the disease *phenylketonuria* (PKU). This disorder, involving an inability to metabolize fatty substances because of the absence of a particular digestive enzyme, led to the development of distorted physical features and severe mental retardation in children. It was discovered that the lack of the necessary enzyme resulted from the absence of a particular gene, and as such, PKU is another instance of a disease associated with a specific genoytpe.

Today, however, many people—perhaps even some college students reading this book—may have the PKU genotype without having either the physical or the behavioral deficits formerly associated with the disease. It was discovered that if the missing enzyme is put into the diets of newborns identified as having the disease, *all* negative effects can be avoided. Again, change in the environment has changed the outcome. In fact, it was found that at about one year of age the PKU child no longer needs the added enzyme since the body either no longer needs it to metabolize fat or produces the enzyme in another way. Here again it may be seen that the same genotype will lead to alternative outcomes, both physical and behavioral, when it interacts in contrasting environmental settings.

Another example illustrates this still further and, more important, provides a basis for specifying the variety of environmental characteristics within which hereditary contributions are embedded. First, imagine that an experiment (improbable for ethical and technological reasons) were done. Say a mother was pregnant with *monozygotic* (identical) twins. These are twins who develop from the same fertilized egg—the same zygote—which splits after conception. Hence the two zygotes have the same genotype. But, importantly, because the zygotes implant on somewhat different parts of the wall of the uterus, there exist somewhat different environments. Imagine further that it was possible immediately after the zygote split into two to take one of them and implant it in another woman who would carry the organism through to birth. Finally, imagine that the first woman, mother A, has lived for the last several years on a diet of chocolate bars, potato chips, and soda pop, smoked two packs of cigarettes a day, and consumed a pint of alcohol each evening. On the other hand, say the second woman, mother B, has had a well-balanced diet and neither smoked nor drank. In all other respects the women are alike.

Here is a situation wherein two genotypically identical organisms are developing in quite different uterine environments. Such differences are known to relate to *prenatal, perinatal* (birth), and *postnatal* behavior on the part of the offspring, and even to have implications for the mother. Thus, despite the genotype identity, the offspring of mother A would be more likely to be born anemic (because of the mother's poor diet) and to be smaller, less alert, and more hyperactive (because of smoking and alcohol intake) than the offspring of mother B.

Although the above study with mother A and mother B is imaginary, the influence of the uterine environment on the offspring is not at all fanciful. The imaginary example was used to illustrate that variations in the environment will cause significant physical and behavioral changes in an offspring despite the genotype. Even physical characteristics such as eye or skin color may be influenced by environmental variations (al-

beit extreme ones) no matter what genes are inherited. If mothers are exposed to extreme radiation or dangerous chemicals (as in the case of mothers in the 1950s who took the tranquilizer *thalidomide*), pigmentation of the eyes or the skin can be radically altered and/or limbs can be severely deformed.

In sum, then, I believe that in order to understand the contributions of heredity to development one needs to recognize that genes influence physical and behavioral characteristics indirectly, by acting in a specific environment. If the same genetic contribution were to be expressed in an environment having other specific characteristics, the same genes might be associated with an alternative behavioral outcome. Accordingly, in order to specify completely the interactions of nature with nurture, one should know all the ways in which the environment can vary (and, as will be argued below, the reverse is also the case).

However, there is an infinity of possible environmental variations; and today one cannot even begin to identify all the chemical, nutritional, psychological, and social variables that may vary in the environment, much less identify the ways in which they provide a significant context for development. One may note at this point, though, that the environment may be thought of as existing at many levels. One can look at the environment in molecular terms—and talk of chemicals in the body of the mother. Or one can use molar terms—and talk of noise and pollution levels in particular settings (for example, urban ones). Consequently, it is useful to specify levels of the environment because it will (1) allow discussion about where the variables that provide the context for nature interactions may lie; and (2) allow for a consideration of nurture interactions. As such, we will now consider levels of environmental variation.

Levels of the Environment

An organism does not exist independent of an environment, and as much as the organism is shaped *by* the environment, the organism *shapes* the environment (Lerner 1982; Lerner and Busch-Rossnagel 1981). As a consequence of this interdependency, both organism and environment may continually change, and it has been suggested that this change involves multiple levels of analysis. These levels—the inner-biological, individual-psychological, physical-environmental, and sociocultural-historical (Riegel 1975, 1976a)—denote the types of nurture-related variables that may provide the context for nature interactions.

The Inner-Biological Level

The genotype is first expressed in utero, in the mother's body. Hence the chemical and physical makeup of the mother can affect the offspring. Chemicals in the mother's bloodstream can enter that offspring through the umbilical cord, the attachment between mother and offspring. As already noted, poor nutrition, excessive smoking or alcohol intake, and other drug intake can affect the unborn child. Additionally, diseases (for example, rubella) can lead to malformations of the heart and limbs and can affect the development and function of sensory organs (the eyes or ears).

The Individual-Psychological Level

Independent of her diet, smoking or drinking habits, and physical health status, the psychological functioning of the mother can affect the unborn child. Excessive maternal stress (for example, "nervousness" about the pregnancy) can affect the offspring. Mothers who have excessive stress in about the third month of pregnancy are more likely to have children with certain birth defects (such as cleft palate, harelip) than are mothers not so stressed (Sutton-Smith 1973). To illustrate the interrelation between all the levels of the environment, it may be suggested that the way maternal stress exerts an influence on the unborn child is by altering the chemicals (for example, adrenalin) in the blood—at the inner-biological level—at a time in the embryological period when specific organs are being formed.

In addition, previous child-rearing experiences can play a part on the individual-psychological level. Experienced parents (those who already have had a child) are not the same people they were before they had a child. (Firstborns thus, in this sense, have different parents than latter-borns, even though the parents involved may be biologically the same.) Thus a mother may be less likely to be stressed by a second pregnancy. Not only might this affect the chemicals in her bloodstream but also, in being less "nervous," she might be less likely to engage in "nervous" behaviors, for example smoking.

Of course, as more information about prenatal care becomes available in society, and as cultural values change, effects on maternal stress and "nervous" behaviors will change. Thus one level of environment is related to another, the individual-psychological to the sociocultural-historical. Before turning to the latter level, however, let us consider the physical-environmental level.

The Physical-Environmental Level

Physical settings differ in such variables as air quality, water purity, noise levels, population density, and general pollution of the environment. Such variables can affect the inner-biological functioning of a person by producing variations in the likelihood of contracting certain diseases (Willems 1973), and can affect the individual-psychological level as well, by producing various levels of stress (Gump 1975). In turn, the quality of the physical setting may be seen as both a product of the values and behaviors of the culture of a society and a producer of changes in the sociocultural setting across time. If values regarding industrialization in the United States had not existed as they did in the early 1960s, and if high levels of industrial waste had not polluted air, land, water, and wildlife, there would have been no basis for the general emergence of countervailing values in the late 1960s and 1970s regarding environmentalism, ecology, and the reduction of pollution. The physical-environmental level is not independent of the sociocultural-historical one.

The Sociocultural-Historical Level

It has been argued that attitudes toward smoking, knowledge about prenatal health care, and values about pollution may change across time to influence the unborn child. Thus, with advances in education (remember the case of children with Down's syndrome), medicine, and science (remember the case of children with PKU), and changes in attitudes, values, and behaviors (regarding smoking, drinking, drug use, and pollution of the environment, for example), the outcome of any given hereditary contribution to development will be altered.

In sum, it may be seen that a variety of behavioral outcomes may result from nature interactions with a multilevel environment. Development is thus an outcome of hereditary contributions "dynamically interacting" with changes in the environmental setting (Lerner 1978, 1979). Thus a genotype is not a blueprint for a final behavioral outcome. There is no one-to-one relation between genotype (our genetic inheritance) and *phenotype* (the observed outcome of development—the outcome of a specific genotype-environment interrelation). Rather, numerous phenotypes can result from the same genotype. The range of potential outcomes that could result from a given genotype's potentially infinite interactions with environments is termed the *norm of reaction* (Hirsch 1970), a concept to which we shall turn later in this chapter.

Here we should note that the indirectness of hereditary effects means that we cannot a priori specify what behavioral effect a particular hereditary contribution will have. Hereditary contributions can express themselves only within the context of their interaction with a mediating environment, and without knowing how this environment will mediate the hereditary effects, we can make no before-the-fact statement about what specific behaviors will result from a particu-

lar hereditary contribution. (This is a particularly essential point; and in Chapter 5 it will be seen as an important feature of the probabilistic-epigenetic view of the nature-nurture controversy.)

Thus there can be no preformed, direct, or invariant hereditary contribution to behavior. As I indicated in Chapter 2, in our discussion of the probabilistic-epigenetic viewpoint, the most accurate way of conceptualizing the contribution of nature factors to behavioral development is (1) to recognize the necessary and crucial role that nurture factors play in providing an interactive context for nature factors; and (2) to recognize that the time at which these factors interact will play an important role in shaping development; that is, the interactive contribution of one factor to the other will not be the same at different points in development. Since the characteristics of nature and nurture factors as well as their time of interaction cannot be expected to occur at exactly the same time or in exactly the same way for every organism, before the fact one can say only that certain things will probably occur. Because of our recognition of points 1 and 2, the best we can do is take a guess, with some degree of confidence in our chances of being correct (i.e., we can make a probabilistic statement), about what sort of specific behavioral development will eventually result from a particular hereditary contribution.

Thus any statement that in effect says that a given hereditary contribution will invariably (in all environmental contexts) result in a certain specific behavior is simply incorrect. Therefore, because it is necessary to adopt an interactionist position, we can make several statements about the indirect effects of heredity on behavior. First, the following points should be clear:

1. The same hereditary influence can be expected to have a different behavioral effect in different environmental conditions; and

2. Alternatively, the reverse may also be true—different hereditary influences can lead to the same behavioral devel-

opment in varying environmental situations.

To be complete, we should also point out that

3. The same environmental effect may be expected to lead to different behavioral outcomes under differing hereditary contributions; and

4. Different environments can lead to the same outcome in the context of varying hereditary contributions.

The point of all this is that the sources of behavior interact with each other in complex ways. And any analysis of behavioral development that attempts to be appropriate in its recognition of this complexity must always attempt to understand the varying status of the interactions of both nature and nurture factors.

Nature: The Continuum of Indirectness

Given heredity's indirect contribution to behavior, Anastasi conceptualizes the contributions of heredity to behavior as varying along a "continuum of indirectness," a hypothetical line whose end points are "least indirect" and "most direct." Such a hypothetical continuum is represented in Figure 3.2. The left end represents those hereditary contributions to a person that are *least indirect* (or most direct) in their influence. One may speculate that such effects may be represented by such physical characteristics as eye color or eventual shape of the nose. But be careful to remember that even these least indirect hereditary effects need, at the very least, the supportive, facilitative influence of the environment. The right end of the continuum represents those hereditary contributions to a person that are *most indirect*. Here the possible number or types of interrelations with the environment increases and, accordingly, resulting behavioral outcomes are much more numerous. Thus, as hereditary influences become more indirect, the range of possible behavioral outcomes of the interaction between heredity and environment similarly increases.

What are some possible illustrations of the range of indirect hereditary contributions to

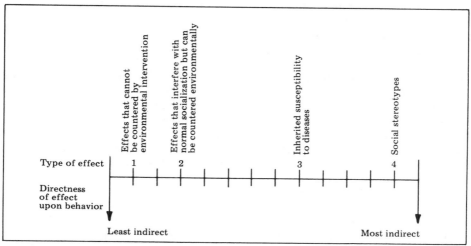

FIGURE 3.2
Contributions of heredity to behavioral development vary along a continuum of indirectness. Numbers 1 through 4 refer to some points along this continuum.
Source: Adapted from comments by Anastasi (1958).

behavior? Anastasi suggests four points along the continuum of indirectness to illustrate this range of effects. These four hypothetical points are ordinal in nature; that is, they are ordered consecutively from "least indirect" effect through "most indirect" effect, although no exact specification of the location of these points can be made. Thus, although we may be sure that these effects are ordered appropriately, we are sure neither of their exact locations along the continuum nor of the relative distances between them. Despite these limitations, Anastasi's specification of these points serves well to illustrate the range of heredity's indirect effects on behavior.

Hereditary effects that in no way can be countered through environmental intervention. Hereditary contributions to behavior that cannot be ameliorated through the use of any known intervention or environmental manipulation are considered to make up the class of hereditary effects that are least indirect in relation to behavior. Although these effects need a supportive, facilitative environment in which to exert their contribution, once they make their contribution to behavior there is nothing that one can now do, through changing the environment, to change that contribution. For example, let us consider again the inheritance of a chromosome trisomy; that is, the inheritance that is associated with Down's syndrome. As noted earlier, such a child has rather distinctive physical (particularly facial) characteristics, and has moderate-to-severe mental retardation. Thus, after the inheritance of such a chromosomal anomaly, there is nothing we can do through environmental intervention, with our current state of knowledge, to avert the inevitability of the child's mental retardation. Although we can certainly attempt to train the child to maximize his or her potential, we cannot now raise that potential to the level it might have reached had the child not inherited a trisomy of chromosome pair 21; we cannot bring the child's intelligence into the nonretarded range. This inheritance thus represents the least indirect contribution of heredity to behavior, a contribution that cannot be

Anne Anastasi

countered through environmental manipulation.

Of course, future scientific advances, for instance in recombinant DNA technology (Berg 1981), may result in knowledge allowing antenatal repair of a flawed human genome (McKusick 1981). Thus, as we saw with PKU, the effect of a given genetic deficit on behavior can be altered, given appropriate scientific advances. As such, an effect currently classified as "least indirect" may not remain so for all time.

Hereditary deficits that interfere with normal socialization but can be countered through environmental intervention. Moving a little further along on the continuum of indirectness brings us to a second class of indirect hereditary effects. These are more indirect in their contribution to behavior because their contribution can be somewhat ameliorated by changes in the environment. Thus, although effects of this second class may interfere with the process by which a child acquires the behaviors that society may define as being necessary and appropriate, such interference may be somewhat counteracted by appropriate environmental modifications.

For example, let us say that because of a genetic anomaly a child is born blind or deaf. Certainly such a handicap would retard the development of the child's communication skills and in this way interfere with normal socialization. Because the child cannot see or hear, the process by which the child develops the behaviors that society designates as necessary or appropriate will not be as efficient as it will be for a child who is not disabled. However, having such an unfortunate inheritance interfere with the development of your communication skills and your socialization in general does not mean that these developments are lost to you forever. As dramatically illustrated in the play *The Miracle Worker,* the story of Helen Keller and her teacher, the handicaps of blindness and deafness can be counteracted. Thus, although a hereditary effect can interfere with socialization, certain environmental modifications can be instituted to modify or possibly even eliminate the effects of that hereditary contribution to behavior.

Inherited susceptibility to disease. A third, still more indirect hereditary contribution to behavior is that type of inheritance that may predispose you to contracting certain diseases. Let us say that as part of your inherited physical characteristics you develop relatively weak musculature in one chamber of your heart. This hereditary contribution may or may not exert any influence on your behavior. But certain environmentally based characteristics you may possess (e.g., you are overweight, lack regular exercise, have a poor diet, and are middle-aged) may interact with your constitution and make you very likely to have a heart attack. Yet in another person not similarly predisposed but having the same environmentally-based characteristics, heart disease may never develop.

Similarly, consider hay fever. If we argue that this disease is hereditarily based, then we can see that our inherited susceptibility may or may not lead to a behavioral effect, depending on the specific environment we live in. If we live in an area where the pollen count is extremely low, our susceptibility to this disease may never affect our behavior. In fact, because there would be little if any pollen to precipitate an attack, we might never even know that we have the disease. But if we live in an area in which the pollen count varies seasonally, then at certain times of the year our behavior will certainly be affected. We will sneeze, our eyes will water, and we will try to seek the comfort and release provided by antihistamines and air-conditioned rooms. Our behavior might be affected even at times of the year when no pollen is present in the air. We might, for example, find ourselves going to a physician all winter to get weekly injections that will diminish the effects of pollen during the late summer. This third point along the continuum of indirectness well illustrates a point made earlier: The same hereditary contribution will have a different effect on behavior under different environmental conditions.

Social stereotypes. A final point along the hereditary continuum of indirectness, certainly representing the *most* indirect effect, may be termed social stereotypes. This may seem somewhat paradoxical; how can social stereotypes be a hereditary effect, albeit the most indirect one, on behavior? Let us follow the reasoning underlying this classification carefully, not only to demonstrate its tenability but also to illustrate the complex interactions between heredity and environment that provide the source of behavioral development.

As we noted above, physical characteristics may be among the least indirect hereditary contributions to a person. Thus certain physical characteristics such as sex, eye color, or skin pigmentation are to a great extent very directly hereditarily determined. The range of variation in these characteristics, despite environmental differences, is not as great as that of other types of characteristics.

How may such physical characteristics lead to social stereotypes? In attempting to function efficiently, people find ways to reduce the complexity of the situations around them. In the real world we are literally bombarded by stimulation coming from numerous, diverse sources. Obviously we cannot respond to all these stimuli simultaneously or even successively. If we did so we would never get anything done, and this certainly would not make us very adaptive organisms. So we attend to some stimuli in our environment and disregard others, depending in part on what information we need or want at that time and in that situation. In this way we can be economical in our social interactions.

A person is one type of stimulus object we encounter in our environment. But a person is also a complex stimulus having many dimensions (sex, age, race, style of dress, apparent status, etc.), and we cannot respond to all characteristics of a person at once if we are to be efficient and economical. So, in order to be economical, we are likely to attend to as few dimensions of a person as possible. Depending in part, for example, on the type of information we need in order to function efficiently at that moment, we attend only to certain stimulus attributes, or cues. On the basis of these cues we place people in certain categories; that is, we associate people's specific stimulus attributes with specific categories of information, behavioral characteristics, or social attributes. By doing this, we need only respond to a certain few dimensions and still be able to function efficiently and economically.

This process of categorization is a very basic one, permeating all our interactions. For example, if we were lost in a big city it might be a successful, but relatively inefficient, strategy to stop and ask various people how to get to a certain location. But if we perceive a person wearing a uniform and a badge standing by an intersection, we might respond by placing that person in the category of police officer. We would then attribute to that person the possession of certain information (e.g., knowledge of directions); we would ask for this information and then be on our way. Thus we see that whenever

we perceive other people (1) we respond to certain stimulus attributes, or cues, they possess (in order to maintain economical interpersonal relations); (2) on the basis of these cues we place these people in certain categories; and (3) on the basis of this categorization we attribute to these persons the possession of certain information or characteristics of behavior.

Now, Anastasi suggests—and from much accumulated evidence (for example, see Lerner and Korn 1972; Secord and Backman 1964) it seems clear—that one major type of cue that people readily use in organizing their interpersonal perceptions and interactions is physical characteristics that are least indirectly hereditarily determined. Thus it is probable that in some societies (and here I am intentionally understating my argument) people are categorized on the basis of certain inherited physical characteristics. If this occurs, we will probably make certain invariant personality attributions and maintain certain invariant behavioral expectancies for all people placed in that category. We will do this because, after all, the reason that we categorize in the first place is to tell us efficiently what to expect about that class of people-stimuli. It would defeat the purpose of economical categorization processes to admit exceptions to our attributions.

What may be the effects of categorizing people on the basis of inherited physical characteristics? In answering this question we will see how such inherited characteristics provide the most indirect hereditary source of behavior: social stereotypes. To address this question, though, let us offer a not-too-imaginary example.

Suppose that there is a society that has as a most salient cue for the categorization of people a certain inherited physical characteristic: skin color. Now, for argument's sake, let us further imagine that one of the two skin-color groups in this society is categorized unfavorably. That is, people in that group, when put into this physically cued category, receive negative behavioral expectations and personality attributions—for example, they are thought of as lazy and shiftless and unable to profit very much from educational experiences. Certainly at least some people in this imaginary category could probably profit from education and are not lazy, but it is likely that such categorizations would be maintained despite experience of such exceptions. If this is the case—that our categorization involves an overgeneralized belief or attitude—then we may term such a categorization a *stereotype*. Thus it is possible that in response to a physical attribute we place a person in a category and in so doing maintain stereotyped expectations about that person.

If a skin-color group were stereotyped as uneducable and lazy, it would not make sense to put much effort into attempting to educate people of that group. Because we would not expect them to learn too much, we would not spend much money on their schooling. In fact, such a group might have a history of going to inferior schools where there were inadequate facilities and poorly qualified teachers. Thus, because of the stereotype, this skin-color group would experience inadequate, inferior, or substandard educational opportunities.

Finally, years later, someone might come along and decide to see if the categorization of these people involves an overgeneralization. He or she finds that this group does not seem to be doing very well educationally— that many people in this group do not score high scholastically, do not seem to have intellectual aptitudes as high as those of members of the other skin-color group, often do not go on to higher education, and accordingly do not often enter into the higher-prestige, higher-salary, higher-socioeconomic-status professions. Thus the person doing this study might conclude that the facts show that this skin-color group cannot profit to any great degree from educational experiences. And many of those in this imaginary society, who may often have made such an attribution about those in this category, might say that they "knew it all along."

But our analysis of the situation is certainly different. What occurred with this stereotyped skin-color group was as follows:

1. On the basis of their relatively direct inheritance of a physical characteristic—their skin color—people in this group were placed in a specific unfavorable category.

2. In turn, on the basis of this categorization, specific negative behavioral expectations were invariably attributed to members of this category (we might suggest here that a basis of both the initial categorization and the concomitant attributions and expectations might lie in the social and economic history of this group).

3. These attributions were associated with differential experiences and opportunities (different when compared to the society's other skin-color group).

4. These differential situations delimited the range of possible behaviors that this group could develop. In other words, the group was channeled into a selected, limited number of behavioral alternatives—the very same behaviors they were stereotypically held to have.

5. Finally, many members of the group developed these behaviors because of the above channeling. That is, the end result of the physically cued social stereotype was a *self-fulfilling prophecy*.

In sum, we see that on the basis of a physically cued categorization we may make a stereotypic attribution and, accordingly, channel the people of that category into certain behavioral patterns by creating social situations within which they cannot do other than develop along the lines of the social stereotype. Our social stereotypes about relatively directly inherited physical cues may have a very profound effect on behavior. They may result in self-fulfilling prophecies.

Unfortunately, of course, the example that we have just considered is not imaginary at all. Although this social-stereotype effect on behavior can obviously function either favorably or unfavorably for the categorized people, the illustration above is probably the most pernicious example of the effect of social stereotypes. From our analysis we can see that a strong argument can be made that the black people of our country have perhaps experienced the most unfortunate effects of this most indirect type of hereditary contribution to behavior—social stereotypes. Thus it seems that black Americans may for many years have been involved in an educational and intellectual self-fulfilling prophecy in our country. This possibility will be important to remember below when we consider in detail in Chapter 4 recent controversy (e.g., Gould 1980, 1981; Hebb 1970; Herrnstein 1971; Jensen 1969, 1973, 1980; Layzer 1974) about the nature and nurture of black-white differences in intelligence and educability.

At this point, however, suffice it to say that social stereotypes certainly seem to represent a potent source of behavioral development. Although this is the most indirect hereditary contribution to behavior, it does nonetheless appear to play a ubiquitous role in our behavioral development. We have used the example of skin color to illustrate the effects of physically cued social stereotypes, but others, more subtle or more obvious, could be mentioned—for example, hair texture, shape of nose, breast size in women, or body build and physical attractiveness. In fact, the effects of social stereotypes about body build and physical attractiveness are a topic to which I have addressed much research (e.g., Lerner 1969, 1972, 1973, 1979, 1982; Lerner and Brackney 1978; Lerner and Gellert 1969; Lerner et al. 1980; Lerner and Karabenick 1974; Lerner, Karabenick, and Meisels 1975a, 1975b; Lerner, Karabenick, and Stuart 1973; Lerner, Knapp, and Pool 1974; Lerner and Korn 1972; Lerner, Orlos, and Knapp 1976; Lerner and Schroeder 1971a, 1971b; Lerner, Sorell, and Brackney 1981; Padin, Lerner, and Spiro 1981), and the interested reader may consult these references to see that the processes involved in the social stereotyping of body build and attractiveness appear to be the same as those involved in the social stereotyping of skin color. With both types of cues, people seem to be channeled into a self-fulfilling prophecy by their society (see, too, Langlois and Stephan 1981; Sorell and Nowak 1981).

Up to this point we have considered the implications of Anastasi's suggested four points along her theoretical continuum of indirectness, the continuum along which heredity contributes to behavior. But the major implication of the question "how?" is that nature interacts with nurture to affect all behavior. We must, then, consider the ways in which the environment contributes to behavioral development. In so doing we can continue to use Anastasi's (1958) paper as a model. Thus we will now look at another continuum—the environmental continuum, or as Anastasi conceptualizes it, the "continuum of breadth."

Nurture: The Continuum of Breadth

Let us now turn our attention to environmental factors. Just as the effects of heredity on behavior can best be understood in relation to environment, the effects of the environment on behavior can best be understood in relation to the nature of the organism. Anastasi conceives of the environment as making its contribution to behavioral development along a continuum of breadth. In other words, environmental factors vary in terms of their pervasiveness of effect on behavior. Some environmental factors, then, may be seen to have very broad, pervasive effects on a person, relating to many dimensions of functioning and enduring in their contributions for relatively long periods of time. Alternatively, other environmental factors may have narrow, minimal effects, making their contributions only to small or limited segments of a person's behavior and exerting their influence for relatively short, transitory periods. Such a continuum of breadth is illustrated in Figure 3.3. Those environmental effects that are derived from the left end of the continuum exert narrow,

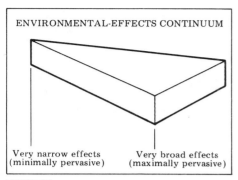

FIGURE 3.3
The contributions of environment to behavioral development vary along a continuum of breadth.

Source: Adapted from comments by Anastasi (1958).

minimally pervasive effects on behavior, while those at the right end are broad and maximally pervasive in nature.

But what are examples of environmental effects? Just what sort of variables are there in the environment that contribute to behavioral development along such a continuum of breadth? Anastasi suggests two general categories of environmental effects.

Organic Effects

The first category of environmental effects may be labeled organic. There are some environmental occurrences that lead to changes in the makeup of the organism; they affect what the organism has and how it functions. In short, these factors change the constitution of one's physical and/or physiological processes.

Typically, one may adventitiously encounter environmental variables that affect the organic makeup of one's body either through contracting a disease or having an accident. However, the eventual behavioral outcomes of such organic changes may, in turn, be either broad or narrow in nature. For example, losing half one's cerebral cortex in an auto crash, or an arm or a leg, or having permanent facial scars after a fire may

all be considered environmentally mediated changes in a person's organic makeup that will have obviously pervasive, enduring effects on behavior. Alternatively, loss of a single finger or toe, while being an organic change, would probably not have as great an effect. Moreover, accidents such as stubbing one's toe certainly affect behavior, but in an obviously more trivial, narrow, and transitory way.

Disease may also be broad or narrow in its behavioral contributions. Contracting a disease such as polio, sickle cell anemia, or muscular dystrophy would certainly have a very pervasive effect on a child's behavioral development and functioning. The range of behaviors that children with such disorders could engage in would differ greatly from those in which children not so affected could engage. On the other hand, some diseases, although affecting the makeup of the organism, do so only in limited or short-term ways. Thus catching a cold or contracting a childhood disease such as chicken pox would affect behavior, but only for a minimal amount of time and probably in not-too-pervasive ways.

Of course, the environment can contribute to behavioral development through organic changes in ways that do not have to be construed as negative. Environmentally based organic changes that facilitate or improve behavioral functioning, rather than deteriorating it, can be induced. Thus such factors as changes in diet, climate, physical regimen, or medical treatments can result in changes in organic makeup that may have facilitative effects on behavioral functioning and development.

Stimulative Effects

The second category of environmental effects on behavior may be termed stimulative. These are environmental events that act as direct stimulative influences on behavioral responses. Here, too, such variables may be broad or narrow in their contributions to behavior. One of the broadest stimulative environmental variables is social class.

Differences among social classes in modes of living, values, presence of material goods, and availability of cultural and educational opportunities represent variations in the types of stimuli to which children of different social classes are exposed. For example, a black child growing up in an urban ghetto is exposed to vastly different stimuli than is a white middle-class child living in a suburban area. These differential stimulus sources, permeating all aspects of the developing child's world, serve to shape varying response repertoires.

A somewhat narrower, less pervasive stimulative influence may be, for example, the college experience. Events in this specific environment certainly evoke intellectual, attitudinal, and behavioral repertoires among students, and such cognitive and behavioral repertoires are, in turn, probably different in nature from those found among young people not exposed to the college experience. Finally, some stimulative influences are exceedingly narrow, trivial, and of short duration in their contributions to behavior. Such minimally pervasive effects are numerous, occurring daily in our interactions in the real world. Thus having a particularly rude, discourteous cabdriver or salesperson may affect us momentarily, but probably not to any great, enduring extent.

In sum, then, Anastasi has suggested that the effects of the environment on our behavioral development vary in their pervasiveness. Whether these effects are organic or stimulative in type, they present a range of environmental influences that will interact with indirect hereditary contributions to provide the source of our development. But, as was the case with hereditary influences on behavior, such environmental effects do not have direct impact on development. Rather, just as the effects of nature on behavior are influenced by nurture, environmental contributions to behavior are influenced by the nature of the organism. From this view, the same environmental event (for example, contraction of a disease, exposure to a particular stimulus) or group of events (for example, those associated with middle-class as opposed to upper-class membership) will lead to different behavioral outcomes depending on the nature of the organism. Using the same symbols as in Figure 3.1, one may see this view illustrated in Figure 3.4. As shown in Figure 3.4a, it is possible to conceptualize the contribution of environment to behavior as being direct. Thus a particular environmental event or set of events (E_1) is seen as directly leading to a particular behavioral outcome (B_1). However, as with the former argument regarding nature contributions, this view is not tenable. We have argued for a dynamic-interactive view of nature and nurture, and the environmental-contribution component of this view is illustrated in Figure 3.4b. Here the same environmental contribution (E_1) can be associated with an array of behavioral outcomes (B_1 to B_n) as a consequence of interaction with organisms having different natures (G_1 to G_n). A basis of *plasticity* (the potential for systematic change) in development is thus promoted, and this may be illustrated in several ways.

First, consider a very general set of experiential events associated with being a child of upper-middle-class parents. Imagine that such parents had two children who were *dizygotic twins*, also termed *fraternal twins*.

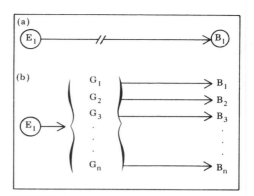

FIGURE 3.4

(a) Environment (E) does not directly lead to behavior (B). (b) Rather, the effects of environment on behavior (B) will be different in interaction with organisms having different heredities (G).

Such siblings are born of the same pregnancy but are from two separate ova that are fertilized at the same time. Thus, although born together, these siblings have different genotypes (unlike monozygotic twins). If one of these twins was born with the genetic anomaly discussed earlier (Down's syndrome) while the other was born with a normal complement of genes, a situation would result wherein children born of the same parents at the same time would potentially be exposed to the same environmental events.

However, whatever the experiences encountered by the Down's syndrome twin, the effects of those experiences could not be expected to result in behaviors falling within a range identical to that of the sibling. Despite advances in special education noted earlier, one still cannot expect a Down's syndrome child to have an IQ score within the normal range (that is, between 85 and 115), and one would not expect the child to attain a high-status vocation. Such expectations could, though, be appropriately maintained in regard to the sibling born with the normal genotype. Thus the hereditary nature of the organism imposes limits on the possible contributions of environment.

Other illustrations of this interaction may be drawn from the information presented above about the prenatal maternal environment. It was noted that if the mother contracted rubella during pregnancy, adverse physical and functional outcomes for the infant might follow. However, this same experience (contraction of rubella) may or may not lead to these outcomes depending on the maturational level of the organism. If the experience occurs during the embryological period, these negative effects are likely to occur; if it happens in the late fetal period, they are not likely to happen. Similarly, excessive maternal stress will or will not be more likely to lead to certain physical deformities (like cleft palate) depending on the maturational level of the organism. Thus, here again, the nature of the organism moderates the influence of experience on development.

It may be concluded, then, that even if one is talking about very narrow sorts of environmental experiences (such as encountering a specific stimulus in a specific transitory situation) or very broad types of experiences (such those associated with membership in one culture versus another), the effects of these environmental influences would not be the same if they interacted with hereditarily (genotypically) different organisms. Nor would the effects be the same even if it were possible to ensure that the different organisms had identical experiences. As long as the nature of the organism is different, the contributions of experience will vary.

It is important to note, then, that all humans are genotypically unique. A conservative estimate is that there are over 70 *trillion* potential genotypes (Hirsch 1970, 73; McClearn 1981)! This means that no two living humans share the same genotype, with the possible exception of identical twins. However, even for these people, the differences in experience they encounter—differences that begin as soon as their respective zygotes implant at different points on the mother's uterine wall—contribute to their diversity, too.

This argument is highlighted by noting that a genotype immediately becomes a phenotype at the moment of conception. The genotype is expressed in one and *only* one environment. Hence, although a norm of reaction exists for the genotype, once it is expressed in one particular context, all the other alternative phenotypes it *could* have resulted in are excluded. Thus even identical twins become (at least slightly) phenotypically different from each other at the moment of implantation.

Conclusions

Because of genotypic uniqueness, all individuals will interact with their environments (be they the same or different) in unique, specific ways. Thus the environment always contributes to behavior, but the precise direction and outcome of this influence can only be completely understood in the context of an appreciation of the genetic individuality of the person. In turn, individual differences in genetic makeup do not in and of themselves directly shape behavior. Interaction with an environment, itself having a host of distinctly individual features, has to be taken into account. In other words, heredity and environment, nature and nurture, are always present and always involved in providing a source of our development. The specific indirect contribution of nature can be understood only in the context of the particular broad-to-narrow contribution of nurture with which it is interacting and, in turn, an exact understanding of how a certain environmental contribution affects behavior can be reached only by understanding how it interrelates with the organism's nature. Thus, in trying to conceptualize how nature and nurture interact, Anastasi relied—as have we—on the *norm-of-reaction* concept as a useful one in conceptualizing the interacting influences of nature and nurture. Let us consider this concept in greater detail.

THE NORM OF REACTION

The concept of norm of reaction has been a popular and useful one for geneticists since it was introduced in the early part of the twentieth century by Woltereck (Dunn 1965). To understand the concept we must first recall that what we inherit from our parents, what they transmit to us when fertilization occurs, is a particular set of genes. This genetic endowment, or genotype (Hirsch 1963), represents the hereditary developmental potential for all our eventual physical, physiological, and behavioral characteristics. However, there is not a one-to-one relation, an *isomorphism,* between our genotype and the eventual characteristics we do develop. That is, our genotype does not represent a genetic blueprint; we cannot specify how a particular genetic contribution will manifest itself behaviorally merely by knowledge of the genotype. As we have

pointed out above, no psychological trait is ever directly inherited. So, the eventual manifestation of our genotype—how the genotype will express itself when behavior develops—depends on the interaction of that genotype with the environment. And of course, this expression will vary under different environmental conditions.

Thus what we see in the developed or developing person is the product of the interaction of the environment with the person's genotype. As noted already, what we see is the phenotype. Therefore, because phenotypes can be expected to be different in varying environmental conditions, despite genotypic invariancy, what our genetic inheritance actually represents is not a predetermined, inevitable blueprint of our eventual characteristics; our phenotype is neither a mere replica of our genotype nor is it isomorphic with it. Rather, our genetic inheritance represents a *range of potential outcomes,* and the developmental outcome that eventually manifests itself will occur due to the interaction of the environment within this range of genetic potential.

This, then, is the norm-of-reaction concept: "The same genotype can give rise to a wide array of phenotypes depending upon the environment in which it develops" (Hirsch 1970, 73). In other words, our genotype—our heredity—gives us a range, or sets the limits, for the development of our characteristics; but the environment, interacting within these limits, plays an essential role in determining what will eventually be developed, or what our phenotype will be. In sum, the norm-of-reaction concept asserts that our genetic inheritance sets the broad limits—the upper and lower boundaries—for our behavioral development, but the eventual behavioral outcome (our phenotype) will depend on the specificities of the environment interacting within our hereditary limits.

Before assessing some of the implications of this concept, let us use an example to illustrate its meaning. We have suggested that the genotype may be conceived of as a range of potential behavioral outcomes, as the hereditary upper and lower limits for the development of a particular psychological characteristic. Now let us suppose that a given child's genotype for intelligence has a range from a low of 40 to a high of 160 IQ points. What will the child's IQ be? In other words, what will the phenotypic IQ be? This will depend, of course, on the specificities of the environment in which the child is reared.

If we reared the child for the first twelve years of his or her life in a clothes closet and then measured the child's IQ, we might suppose that the phenotypic IQ would fall near the lower limit set by the child's genotype, most likely near 40. However, we would expect a different phenotypic IQ if we took another child with the same exact genotype and reared him or her in a more stimulating environment, say in the home of a professional couple who provided facilitative general learning tools and excellent language models and who fostered high achievement motivation (see Bloom 1964). A child reared in such an environment would be likely to have a measured IQ near the upper limit of his or her norm of reaction. Thus, although both children in our example had the same exact genotypic intelligence, their phenotypic intelligence would be quite different because of their markedly varied rearing environments.

In sum, then, we see that the phenotype for any observed psychological characteristic does not depend solely on the person's genotype, or genetic endowment; rather, the phenotype is the end result of a complex interaction of the environment within the genotypic range of potentials represented by that person's norm of reaction.

Psychologists other than Anastasi (e.g., Hirsch 1963, 1970; Schneirla 1957) recognized the utility of the norm-of-reaction concept in conceptualizing the nature of heredity-environment interactions. Hebb (1949), for instance, offered a conceptualization of intelligence consistent with the notions implicit in the norm-of-reaction concept. He suggested that humans are endowed with a range of intellectual potential, a genotypic intelligence. He termed this inherited range of intellectual potential intelligence A. However, psychology has not devised a means of assessing intelligence A; that is, there is no existing technique to appraise a person's genotypic intelligence. Rather, what can be measured is what Hebb termed intelligence B—the outcome of an individual's history of environmental interactions within the context of the person's norm of reaction. Thus, this phenotypic intelligence, intelligence B, is a measurement of the result of an interaction between environment and hereditary endowment.

To the extent, then, that Hebb's (1949) notions are tenable, the norm-of-reaction concept as it applies to this conceptualization of intelligence suggests the following:

1. We are all born with a genotypic intelligence (intelligence A), which represents a range of potential intellectual developments.

2. However, psychologists do not measure intelligence A when administering an IQ test; no means exist to measure this hypothetical construct (see Layzer 1974).

3. Another type of intelligence exists, which is the product of an interaction between the person's environmental history and genotypic intelligence. This second type of intelligence (intelligence B) represents the phenotypic intelligence of the person.

4. This phenotypic intelligence is what is measured by IQ tests.

5. However, the genotype-phenotype intelligence correlation remains unknown; that is, if the genotype represents a range of possible intellectual outcomes, then whether the phenotype represents a low, middle, or high point within this range remains unknown. The person has been endowed with a specific genotype, and through environmental interaction this genotype has provided a basis for the person's phenotype; however,

whether this environmental interaction led to a phenotype that is expressive of the high or low part of the person's genotype cannot be assessed (again, see Layzer 1974 for detailed mathematical reasons).

6. Finally, all this suggests that given another environmental history, the same genotype could be expected to have led to a different phenotype. Still, however, the portion of the norm of reaction to which this new phenotype related would remain unknown.

These points illustrate how one psychologist has used the norm-of-reaction concept in relation to a specific psychological construct: intelligence. In the next chapter, we shall review in greater detail the implications of this concept for the topic of intelligence, but for the moment let us continue our analysis of the norm-of-reaction concept.

The last implication of Hebb's ideas about intelligences A and B (point 6 above) is that although we may expect the same genotype to lead to different phenotypes in different environments, what portion of the genotype is reflected by a specific phenotype remains unknown. This suggests that the norm-of-reaction concept has limitations, and it is important that these limitations be made clear.

Limitations of the Norm-of-Reaction Concept

The relation between genetic endowment and behavior has been a continuing research and theoretical concern of Jerry Hirsch. In several papers (e.g., Hirsch 1970, 1981), he argues that although there is a norm of reaction associated with the observable outcomes of an individual's ontogenetic development (i.e., a person's phenotype), this range is not predictable in advance. In other words, before the person has developed, it is impossible to say that because of his or her genotype, given certain environmental manipulations one type of phenotype will de-

velop, while given other environmental circumstances another phenotype will result. In essence, at the human level there is really no way directly to assess the expected range of phenotypes that can be associated with a given genotype. At best, we can only make statements about particular genotype-environment interactions *after* they have occurred.

In fact, at any level of life organization, the norm of reaction remains largely unknown in most cases (Hirsch 1970). This is so because in order to be able to specify exactly the norm of reaction for any living animal (or plant, for that matter), one must be able to reproduce exactly an individual, specific genotype many times. In effect, one must be able to reproduce several genetically identical organisms. These replicated genotypes must then be exposed to as diverse an array of environments as possible. The range of phenotypes that develop from these exposures would give an estimate of the norm of reaction for that specific genotype. Ideally this exposure should be totally inclusive of all possible environmental conditions to which the genotype might be exposed. Of course, in reality such an infinite exposure could only at best be approximated, so the most that can be done is to offer an approximation of the norm of reaction for any one genotype.

We can agree, then, with Hirsch's conclusion:

> Even in the most favorable materials only an approximate estimate can be obtained for the norm of reaction, when, as in plants and some animals, an individual genotype can be replicated many times and its development studied over a range of environmental conditions. The more varied the conditions, the more diverse might be the phenotypes developed from any one genotype. (Hirsch 1970, 69–70)

Further clarifications of the norm-of-reaction concept need to be made. Hirsch points out that different genotypes should not be expected to have the same norm of reaction. The norm of reaction associated with each individual genotype can be expected to be differentially unique—that is, differentially broad or narrow. Therefore the range of phenotypes that would develop from a specific genotype under varying environmental conditions can be expected to differ from individual to individual. The point here is that each and every person who walks this earth (possibly, but not assuredly, with the exception of identical—monozygotic—twins) has his or her own individual norm of reaction.

To illustrate how our genetic endowment provides a basis of the uniqueness of each human life and provides substance for the claim that all humans have a unique heredity-environment interactive history (Hirsch 1970; Lerner 1978, 1979; McClearn 1981), consider that estimates of the number of gene pairs in humans typically range between 10,000 and 100,000 (Bodmer and Cavalli-Sforza 1976; Stern 1973). If one considers how much genotypic variability can be produced by the reshuffling process of meiosis occurring with 100,000 gene pairs, then the potential for variability is so enormous that "it is next to impossible that there have ever been two individuals with the same combination of genes" (McClearn 1981, 19).

Indeed, we have noted already the estimate by Hirsch (1970) that there are over 70 trillion potential human genotypes, and Bodmer and Cavalli-Sforza (1976) provide further information about the genetic uniqueness of each human by putting forward the estimate that each human has the capacity to generate 10^{3000} different eggs or sperm. In comparison, they estimate that the number of sperm of all men who have ever lived is *only* 10^{24}, and that given these estimates:

> If we consider 10^{3000} possible eggs being generated by an individual woman and 10^{3000} possible sperms being generated by an individual man, the likelihood of anyone ever—in the past, present, or future—having the same genotype as anyone else (excepting multiple identical births, of course) becomes dismissably small. (McClearn 1981, 19)

Moreover, human genetic individuality is enhanced if we recognize that "genetic" does not mean "congenital"; that is, that the "total genome is not functioning at fertilization, or at birth, or at any other time of life" (McClearn 1981, 26); the expression of any individual human genotype is a developmental phenomenon, influenced in regard to the turning on and/or off of genes by the endogenous and exogenous components of the individual's genotype-environment interaction history (Jacob and Monod 1961; McClearn 1970, 1981; Schaie et al. 1975). For instance, McClearn (1981, 26) notes:

> Different genes are decoded and come into play at various times during the lifetime of a particular organism. One illustration of this phenomenon is the differential production of certain kinds of hemoglobin during various phases of development. For example, production of the beta chain accelerates at the time of birth and peaks after a few months, whereas production of the alpha chain rises prenatally and maintains a high level.

As Hirsch (1970, 70) has simply put it, "We must expect norms of reaction to show genotypic uniqueness," and given the evidence we have just reviewed, even if one simplifies the situation enormously in order to make an estimate, we can assume, then, that no two living people (except identical twins) share the same genotype (Hirsch 1970, 73; Jensen 1973, 8).

Because of this uniqueness, all individuals will interact with their environments in unique, specific ways. This assertion points to the necessity of trying to determine individual laws of human behavior—laws that account for the individual's unique pattern of development within his or her environment. Alternatively, Hirsch's argument suggests the futility of attempting to specify general "laws of environmental influence" or of attempting to account for all the variations in human behavior merely by recourse to invariant, overt environmental stimuli and responses.

These implications—first, that each individual is genotypically unique and will interact differently in a given environment than other, genotypically unique people and, therefore, second, that a complete focus on the environment in an attempt to account for all behavioral variation is both misguided and incorrect—are important. They will apply to our discussions of the organismic and the mechanistic-behavioristic theories in subsequent chapters, as well as to our analysis of the ipsative theoretical approach to developmental psychology. Thus our considerations lead us to stress the inescapable fact of human uniqueness; this fact is derived from an appropriate understanding of the genetic basis (or contribution) of individuality.

At this point, though, we can summarize our discussion of the norm-of-reaction concept by stating what it does and does not tell us about how nature and nurture interact to produce behavioral development.

1.   Heredity alone does not determine behavior. An isomorphism does not exist between a genotype and a phenotype.

2.   Rather, what our genotype represents is a range of possible outcomes of development. These outcomes will result from the varying specificities of the interactions of the environment with the genotype, and different phenotypes can be expected to result from different interactions.

3.   However, the norm of reaction can neither be predicted in advance nor, on the human level, even be well estimated or approximated.

4.   Therefore (and this is a crucial point), in actuality, those limits set by our hereditary endowment, by our genotype, can never be specified (Hirsch 1979, 70). We cannot reproduce individual human genotypes and expose them to all possible environmental situations. Because of this fact, we cannot know any given individual's range of genetic potential.

5.   But what we *can* do is recognize that the norm of reaction is unique with each individual and, therefore, since it can be expected to vary from one individual to another, individuals will interact differently with their environments. This process will result in basic phenotypic uniqueness among people.

Thus the norm-of-reaction concept highlights the necessity of focusing on the interaction of nature and nurture in order to understand behavioral development. This concept's implications illustrate that "extreme environmentalists were wrong to hope that one law or set of laws described universal features of modifiability. Extreme hereditarians were wrong to ignore the norm of reaction" (Hirsch 1970, 70).

In sum, in this chapter we have considered general concepts in the nature-nurture controversy and dealt with some of their rather broad implications. At the beginning of this chapter, however, I indicated that the nature-nurture issue is very much alive today and still "rears its head" in many currently researched and debated content areas of psychology. In order to illustrate how these general concepts may be appropriately applied to a specific topic, we shall turn to a discussion of the nature-nurture controversy as it bears on a topic of continuing scientific and public concern: intelligence. More specifically, in Chapter 4 we will consider the nature and nurture of the intellectual differences between black and white Americans.

4 | The Nature-Nurture Controversy: The Sample Case of Intelligence

In the late 1960s the different average group scores of black and white American children on IQ (intelligence) tests became a point of major public concern. The mean (i.e., the arithmetic average) difference between these two groups is often reported to be as high as fifteen IQ points (e.g., Jensen 1980; Scarr-Salapatek 1971a, 1971b) in favor of the white children. That is, on standardized intelligence tests, white children as a group typically score higher than do black children as a group. However, this does not mean that blacks always do worse on IQ tests than do whites. In fact, as Jensen points out:

> Although the average IQ of the Negro population of the United States, for example, is about one standard deviation (i.e., 15 IQ points) below that of the white population, because of the disproportionate sizes of the Negro and white populations, there are more whites with IQs below the Negro average than there are Negroes. (1973, 16)

Until the late 1960s psychologists in the United States interpreted these racial differences in IQ as environmentally based. That is, stress was placed on the cultural disadvantages of black Americans; and the leading hypothesis was that a complex of environmental factors associated with poverty—a complex as yet largely undefined—prevents a child from achieving optimum development (Scarr-Salapatek 1971a, 1971b). Such environmental disadvantage, it was argued, accounts for the inferior performance of black children on standardized IQ tests. In essence it was hypothesized that it is not black children but their environments that are deficient.

Assuredly, no one could argue against the point that black Americans as a group have experienced a history of inferior and possibly even pernicious environmental circumstances. In fact, in our discussion of social stereotypes in Chapter 3 we saw how environmentally based social attitudes may have a destructive effect on blacks' intellectual development. Accordingly, psychologists working with the "environmental differences" hypothesis have attempted to determine the nature of the environmental variables that led black children to inferior performance on IQ tests. They have also contributed to social projects designed to ameliorate blacks' environmental disadvantages (e.g., Project Head Start).

THE GENETIC-DIFFERENCES HYPOTHESIS

What brought the IQ difference between blacks and whites to the general public's attention was that an alternative hypothesis suggested by Arthur R. Jensen (1969) was offered for investigation. Writing in the *Harvard Educational Review,* Jensen (1969) proposed a genetic-differences hypothesis as an alternative to the above environmental-differences explanation of the black-white IQ differences. Jensen suggested that if behavior and characteristics of behavioral functioning (such as intellectual behavior, as indexed by IQ) can be measured and found to have a genetic component, then such behavior can be regarded as no different from other human characteristics, at least insofar as a genetic viewpoint is concerned. Moreover, he asserted that "there seems to be little question that racial differences in genetically conditioned behavioral characteristics, such as mental abilities, should exist, just as physical differences" (Jensen 1969, 80). Accordingly, after reviewing several lines of evidence bearing on the general idea of race differences in intelligence and their possible sources, Jensen advanced

> a not unreasonable hypothesis that genetic factors are strongly implicated in the average Negro-white intelligence difference. The preponderance of the evidence is, in my opinion, less consistent with a strictly environmental hypothesis than with a genetic hypothesis, which, of course, does not exclude the influence of environment or its interaction with genetic factors. (1969, 82)

Thus Jensen proposed what we shall term a "hereditarian" argument, that is, that the black-white differences in mean IQ are not due largely to differences in environmental opportunity but to differences in the gene distributions for these groups (Scarr-Salapatek 1971a). In his attempt to support this hypothesis, Jensen presented empirical data bearing on the racial difference in IQ scores and interrelated these findings with data bearing on another concept in this area of research: the concept of heritability.

Heritability refers to the proportion of a group's individual differences in a trait (e.g., a psychological characteristic such as intelligence) that is due to the individual genetic differences in that group. If a group of people is given a test, not everyone in the group will get the same score; there will be differences between people. In a simple sense, heritability is a concept that indicates the percentage (or proportion) of these differences that can be attributed to (accounted for by) genetic differences between these people.

Jensen argued that IQ is a very highly heritable trait—that is, that individual differences (variation *among* people) in IQ scores within a group are mostly due (e.g., 80 percent) to the genetic variation in that group. In other words, he pointed out that about 80 percent of the differences between the people in certain groups are attributable to genetic differences among these people. Therefore, because of these relations, it might seem tenable to argue that since heritability appears to be a genetic concept, the IQ differences between blacks and whites are in turn genetically based. Of course, Jensen recognized that most of the studies done to assess the heritability of intelligence have been done on white subjects; such estimates—of how much of the differences in IQ scores between members of specific populations can be attributed to genetic differences between these people—cannot be appropriately applied to other populations. Thus, he pointed out:

> Although one cannot formally generalize from *within*-group heritability to *between*-groups heritability, the evidence from studies of within-group heritability does, in fact, impose severe constraints on some of the most popular environmental theories of the existing racial and social class differences in educational performance. (Jensen 1973, 1)

Thus, although Jensen recognized that it is not perfectly legitimate to attempt to apply heritability findings derived within groups of whites to an analysis between these white groups and black groups, he still felt that the findings with whites were impressive enough to cast doubt on the environmental-differences hypothesis.

Thus Jensen offered for consideration a hereditarian, genetic-differences hypothesis. He proposed this hypothesis in an attempt to explain why major educational intervention programs such as Head Start were apparently failing in the attempt to raise the IQs of both black and white lower-class children. Let us follow Hirsch's (1970) analysis of the reasoning used in formulating this hypothesis, and thus of the implication that black Americans are genetically inferior to white Americans in intellectual capacity.

1. First, a trait (such as intelligence) is defined.

2. A means of measuring this trait is devised; a psychological test, designed to measure the trait (intelligence), is constructed. Needless to say, if another definition of the trait were offered, and if other tests of the trait were constructed and used, the empirical expression of the trait could be expected to be different. The possibility that the use of different intelligence tests could lead to different findings in terms of black-white differences in intelligence is important. Intelligence tests do not correlate with each other perfectly; that is, the scores for the same individual on two different intelligence tests are often not exactly equivalent. Therefore, if other tests are given to black and white populations—tests not standardized exclusively on white, middle-class populations, for example, but rather tests that take into account the specificities of the black cultural milieu—then the status of racial differences in IQ might be different. Holding the tenability of this point in abeyance, however, let us assume for argument's sake that the same test is used to measure the trait expression in people.

3. Through a series of studies of test scores for this trait done on populations comprised of people of various degrees of kinship (relationship), the heritability of this trait is estimated.

4. Black and white racial populations are then tested, and their performances on this test of the trait are compared.

5. If the racial populations differ on the test, then because the heritability of the trait measured by the test is now known (and in the case of intelligence has been found to

be high), the racial population with the lower mean score is considered to be genetically inferior. (Hirsch 1970, 69)

On the basis of his formulation of the genetic-differences hypothesis, Jensen (1969) thus suggested that the failure of early intervention programs was due to the high heritability of IQ (see also Scarr-Salapatek 1971a, 1971b). Moreover, since to some reviewers of Jensen's ideas (cf. Jensen 1973), high heritability of a trait indicates that the trait is minimally available to environmental influence, it follows that (1) since IQ is a highly heritable trait, the environment can have little influence in affecting the expression of that trait; and (2) therefore programs such as Head Start that attempt to present alternative environmental influences to some children have little effect because the target of influence is IQ.

The hereditarian, genetic-differences hypothesis is both complex and important; its evaluation will be the major burden of the rest of this chapter. To evaluate it we will have to discuss both the concept of heritability and the usefulness of mathematical models used to estimate it. In addition, we will have to appraise the scientific use of the data modeled by these mathematical estimates of heritability.

That is, how does one find data pertinent to the inheritance of a human characteristic such as intelligence? Intelligence, if it is inherited, is not believed by *any* scholar to derive from the inheritance of a single pair of genes. That is, neither nature- nor nurture-oriented scholars contend that a child inherits his or her intelligence by the pairing of just two *alleles* at conception (an allele is a particular form of a gene; the presence of different alleles is responsible for genetic variation), one from the mother and one from the father. Rather, if intelligence is inherited it is a *polygenic* (many-gene) type of inheritance. In addition intelligence is quite a *plastic* human characteristic; plasticity here refers to the fact that intelligence can take many values (it is a continuous variable), and as such it is distinct from such human characteristics as sex, which of course takes only two basic values (male and female; that is, sex is a discrete variable).

Moreover, study of this polygenic and plastic human characteristic is complicated by the fact that for obvious ethical (and less obvious but important technological) reasons one cannot do true experimental studies of the relative effects of genes and environment on human intelligence. Such a true experiment might involve holding genes constant and seeing if environmental variation led to changes in IQ scores. If it did, then support for a nurture view would be obtained; if it did not—if despite environmental variability a particular set of genes was invariantly related to a particular IQ score—then support for a hereditarian, nature position would be found. In turn, one could vary genes, or actually genetic similarity among people, and see if, in comparable environments, any differences obtained in IQ scores. If such variation did lead to IQ differences, then support for a nature view would be obtained; if such genetic variation did not lead to IQ differences—if despite differences in genes people in comparable environments had corresponding IQ scores—then support for a nurture position would be found.

But, as I have noted, such manipulations cannot be done for ethical and technological reasons (e.g., how could one hold all potentially significant features of the human environment constant?). However, variations may naturally occur that present conditions comparable to a true experiment. For example, some children are born as monozygotic (MZ) twins; that is, as noted earlier, after the ovum is fertilized by the sperm, the one zygote that is formed splits into two genetically identical zygotes. Now, typically, not only do such MZ twins have identical genotypes but, in addition, they have quite similar environments; that is, they are typically also reared in the same home by the same parents. Thus for most MZs there is a gene-environment correlation. Imagine, however, that one could locate a group of MZs who were immediately separated after birth (e.g., because of maternal death or because of financial

stresses on the family) and placed in two radically different environments. If, despite the twins' rearing in separate and distinct environments, their IQs were quite similar, this would be evidence in support of the hereditarian position. Similarly, if one assessed the naturally occurring resemblance among all types of genetically related people—for instance, MZs, dizygotic twins (that is, twins born of the same pregnancy but developed from two different fertilized eggs), cousins, and unrelated people—and found that as genetic resemblance decreased (as it does in the above ordering) IQ resemblance also decreased, then this would seem to lend additional support to the hereditarian position.

While data from true experiments of the role of genes and environment in human intelligence do not exist, "natural experiments" pertinent to family genetic and IQ score resemblance do exist. In the main, these data were the ones most relied on by Jensen (1969). These data provided the key information from which he derived the heritability estimate of .8 for human intelligence. As such, before we discuss the concept of heritability itself and the models used to estimate it, let us evaluate the data used by Jensen and others (e.g., Eysenck, in Eysenck and Kamin 1981a) in these heritability estimates.

Although Jensen relied on many data sets pertinent to family resemblance in genes and in IQ scores, he relied most centrally on the information reported by Sir Cyril Burt (1883–1971), who during his lifetime was one of the world's most famous and celebrated psychologists. Burt was for twenty years the official psychologist of the London County Council, where his responsibilities included administration and interpretation of mental tests in the London schools (Gould 1981). After this, from 1932 to 1950, he held the most influential professorial chair in psychology in Great Britain, the one in University College, London. For his accomplishments in science and service he was knighted and then, in 1971, given the prestigious Edward Lee Thorndike Award of the

American Psychological Association. During his long career Burt published numerous papers reporting his research on family resemblance and IQ (e.g., Burt 1955, 1966). In particular, Burt's work involved reports of assessments of a relatively large sample (i.e., large considering their seeming rarity) of MZs reared apart (e.g., Burt 1955, 1958, 1966; Conway 1958). The findings that Burt reported from this research were such as to lend strong support to the hereditarian position.

Thus, not only because of his positive scientific reputation but because of the scope of his research and the nature of his findings, Burt's reports were heavily relied on by Jensen (1969). As such, in order to begin our evaluation of the scientific data base used in support of the heritability of IQ, and of the genetic-differences hypothesis, let us turn our attention first to the work of Cyril Burt.

THE WORK OF SIR CYRIL BURT

Why were the Burt data of such importance to Jensen's (1969) argument, and indeed to any assertion that most of the variance in intelligence is associated with one's genotype? The evolutionary biologist Stephen Gould (1981, 234–35), in his typically engaging style, answers these questions by noting:

> If I had any desire to lead a life of indolent ease, I would wish to be an identical twin, separated at birth from my brother and raised in a different social class. We could hire ourselves out to a host of social scientists and practically name our fee. For we would be exceedingly rare representatives of the only really adequate natural experiment for separating genetic from environmental effects in humans—genetically identical individuals raised in disparate environments.
>
> Studies of identical twins raised apart should therefore hold pride of place in literature on the inheritance of IQ. And so it would be but for one problem—the extreme rarity of the animal itself. Few investigations have been able to rustle up more than twenty pairs of twins. Yet, amidst this paltriness, one study

seemed to stand out: that of Sir Cyril Burt (1883–1971).

During his long retirement, Sir Cyril published several papers that buttressed the hereditarian claim by citing very high correlation between IQ scores of identical twins raised apart. Burt's study stood out among all others because he had found fifty-three pairs, more than twice the total of any previous attempt. It is scarcely surprising that Arthur Jensen used Sir Cyril's figures as the most important datum in his notorious article (1969) on supposedly inherited and ineradicable differences in intelligence between whites and blacks in America.

The story of Burt's undoing is now more than a twice-told tale. Princeton psychologist Leon Kamin first noted that, while Burt had increased his sample of twins from fewer than twenty to more than fifty in a series of publications, the average correlation between pairs for IQ remained unchanged to the third decimal place—a statistical situation so unlikely that it matches our vernacular definition of impossible.

It is useful to review the information that Kamin (1974) found as he reviewed Burt's (1955, 1958, 1966; Conway 1958) publications. This information reveals so many major problems with Burt's work that a close and fair scrutiny of it will indicate that "the apparent evidence for I.Q. heritability will evaporate to nothing" (Kamin 1974, 35).

Kamin (1974) notes that the Burt study would seem to be impressive and important in several ways. Not only did it purport to study more twin pairs than any of the other three similar studies for which quantitative evidence was available when Kamin did his review (i.e., the studies by Juel-Nielsen 1965; Newman, Freeman, and Holzinger 1937; Shields 1962), but in addition the Burt study reported the largest correlation between the separated MZ twins. These two features of the Burt study (its larger sample and the higher correlation found) are displayed in Table 4.1, which also presents the corresponding information for the other three studies reviewed by Kamin (1974). Kamin notes too that the most important—and a unique—feature of Burt's (1955, 1958, 1966) study is that it claims to provide quantita-

TABLE 4.1
IQ Correlations in Four Studies of Separated MZ Twins

Study	Test	Correlation	Number of pairs
Burt (1955, 1958, 1966)	"Individual Test"	.86	53
Shields (1962)	Dominos + 2 × Mill Hill	.77	37
Newman, Freeman, and Holzinger (1937)	Stanford-Binet	.67	19
Juel-Nielsen (1965)	Wechsler	.62	12

Source: *Adapted from Kamin (1974, 35).*

tive evidence that the environments in which the separated twins were reared were not at all correlated.

If the environments of the separated twins were correlated, one might be able to attribute any similarity in their IQ scores to the experience of being reared in comparable settings; however, if there was no similarity between their environments, then it is argued that only their genetic similarity could account for any correspondence in their IQs. It should be noted here, too, that for the hereditarian position to be supported it is also important that genotype not *interact* with environment. If such interactions occurred they would diminish the impact of genes alone in the determination of IQ scores. Later in this chapter we shall return to the issue of whether it is possible to determine—*in studies of human intelligence*—whether genotype and environment are uncorrelated, or whether they do not interact. If one cannot empirically demonstrate these two points *or* if one cannot legitimately assume the two points to be the case, then it would not be possible to assert unequivocally that it was primarily genetic similarity that provided the basis for correspondences in IQ scores. Here, however, we should reemphasize the point that Burt's study was unique in offering quantitative evidence that the environments of the separated MZ twins were uncorrelated. In short, there seemed to be several quite distinct and important attributes of Burt's (1955, 1958, 1966) study, and because of these it is clear why Burt's study provided such a central role in Jensen's (1969) argument.

But what of the scientific adequacy of Burt's "data"? Kamin (1974) notes that Burt's study of separated MZ twins was part of a larger research effort aimed at accumulating IQ data for several categories of biological relationships (e.g., parent-child, uncle-nephew). Over the years, as the sample size for each category of biological relationship grew, the correlations were reported in a series of publications. But here is where the purported scientific importance of Burt's data begins to unravel. Kamin indicates that the series of publications by Burt

> contain virtually no information about the methods employed in testing I.Q., but the correlations were usually reported to three decimal places. They were astonishingly stable, seeming scarcely to fluctuate as the sample size was changed. Two forms of such stability are illustrated in Table 4.2., which reproduces data contained in Burt's 1955 and 1966 reports.

The intelligence correlations were reported in three forms: for "group test," for "individual test," and for "final assessment." There is, as we shall see, much ambiguity concerning what these terms mean.

This remarkable stability also characterized the unknown "group test" of intelligence which Burt administered to his separated MZ twins. Table 4.3 reproduces the correlations reported by Burt on that test for MZ twins reared apart, and for MZ twins reared together. The table includes data from a 1958 paper by Burt and a 1958 paper by Conway, as well as from the 1955 and 1966 papers. The sample sizes increased over time by 32 pairs for MZs reared apart, and 12 pairs for MZs reared together. There is a minor perturbation which simultaneously afflicted both correla-

TABLE 4.2
Correlations Reported by Burt

	Siblings reared apart		DZs reared together	
	1955 (N = 131)	1966 (N = 151)	1955 (N = 172)	1966 (N = 127)
Intelligence				
Group test	.441	.412	.542	.552
Individual test	.463	.423	.526	.527
Final assessment	.517	.438	.551	.453
School attainment				
Reading, spelling	.490	.490	.915	.919
Arithmetic	.563	.563	.748	.748
General	.526	.526	.831	.831
Physical				
Height	.536	.536	.472	.472
Weight	.427	.427	.586	.586

Note: N refers to number of pairs, as reported by Burt.
Source: *Kamin (1974, 37).*

TABLE 4.3
Correlations for MZ Twins, "Group Test" of Intelligence

Source	Twins reared apart	Twins reared together
Burt, 1955	.771 (N = 21)	.944 (N = 83)
Burt, 1958	.771 (N = "over 30")	.944 (N = ?)
Conway, 1958	.778 (N = 42)	.936 (N = ?)
Burt, 1966	.771 (N = 53)	.944 (N = 95)

Source: *Kamin (1974, 38).*

tions in late 1958, but a benign Providence appears to have smiled upon Professor Burt's labors. When he concluded his work in 1966, his three decimal place correlations were back to where they had been in the beginning. The 1943 paper had contained his first reference to separated MZs. Then, for 15 pairs, the correlation had been reported as .77.

Burt, often without specific acknowledgment, employed "adjusted assessments" of I.Q. rather than raw test scores. The reader must be sharp-eyed to detect this on occasion. The 1956 Burt and Howard paper reported correlations for "assessments of intelligence" for 963 parent-child pairs, 321 grandparent-grandchild pairs, 375 uncle-nephew pairs,

etc. The term "assessments" was not defined, and the description of procedure is characteristic of Burt. "The sources for the latter [assessments], the procedures employed, and the results obtained have already been described in previous publications (Burt, 1955, and refs.)." The Burt and Howard paper, which has been very widely read and cited, goes on to fit a mathematical-genetic model of inheritance to the reported correlations. The fit is excellent.

The reader who troubles to refer to the 1955 paper will discover that many of the 1956 results were not reported there, and he will also discover that the entire description of procedure is contained in a footnote. The footnote includes the following sentence: "For the assessments of the parents we relied chiefly on personal interviews; but in doubtful or borderline cases an open or a camouflaged test was employed." That sentence bears pondering. The scores of children, on the other hand, were "based primarily on verbal and non-verbal tests of intelligence . . . transformed into standard scores . . . for each age . . . converted to terms of an I.Q. scale. . . ." Whatever ambiguity exists in the case of children, clearly the intelligence of adults was simply guessed at in the course of a personal interview. The spectacle of Professor Burt administering a camouflaged test of intelligence to a London grandparent has considerable comic merit, but it does not inspire scientific confidence. The only reported I.Q. correlation between uncle and nephew in the entire scientific literature appears to be Burt's, obtained in this survey in this way.

The same survey was cited by Burt and Howard in 1957, who in reply to a critic stressed that "in each of our surveys, assessments were individually obtained for a representative sample of parents, checked, for purposes of standardization, by tests of the usual type." The 1955 footnote is cited. There is some ambiguity in the meaning of "for purposes of standardization"; but it is entirely clear that over two years Professor Burt's memory had magically transmuted "doubtful or borderline cases" to "a representative sample of parents." The "open or a camouflaged test" of 1955 had become by 1957 "tests of the usual type." Professor Burt, we may conclude, was not always precise in his use of language. The procedural ambiguities are no less marked in the case of Burt's 53 pairs of separated MZ twins. These cases had been gradually accumulated over a period of some 45 years. The most explicit and extended discussion of the twin data was given in Burt's 1966 paper. That paper indicates that all the twins had been separated before the age of 6 months, but it contains no information about the extent or duration of separation. There is no information about the sexes of the twin pairs, nor is their age at testing indicated. They were all, however, "children," and except in three cases "the tests were applied in school." Three very early cases had been dropped from the sample because of a relatively late age of separation. There were, "in the initial survey," some children outside London "originally tested by the local teacher or school doctor; but these have all been since retested by Miss Conway." We are not told whether Miss Conway's test results corresponded to the teachers', nor whether discrepancies were averaged, or handled in some other way. (Kamin 1974, 37–40)

Because of these egregious scientific deficits in Burt's (1955, 1958, 1966) study, Kamin (1974, 41) summarizes simply by indicating that "we do not know what was correlated with what in order to produce the coefficient of .77" between MZ twins reared apart (as shown in Table 4.3). In sum, I agree with Kamin's (1974, 47) overall appraisal that

the conclusion seems not to require further documentation, which exists in abundance. The absence of procedural description in Burt's reports vitiates their scientific utility. The frequent arithmetical inconsistencies and mutually contradictory descriptions cast doubt upon the entire body of his later work. The marvelous consistency of his data supporting the hereditarian position often taxes credibility; and on analysis, the data are found to contain implausible effects consistent with an effort to prove the hereditarian case. The conclusion cannot be avoided: The numbers left behind by Professor Burt are simply not worthy of our current scientific attention.

Reactions to Kamin's (1974) Analysis and Subsequent Developments

Many of Burt's supporters and/or advocates of the hereditarian position in regard to this issue reacted unfavorably to Kamin's (1974) work (see Hirsch 1981 for a detailed history of this reaction). For example, some of those sympathetic to Burt's position denigrated Kamin's competence and claimed that his motives in writing his critique were purely political. For example, Hans J. Eysenck, whose own work in this area we shall consider shortly, wrote to Burt's sister and said that

I think the whole affair is just a determined effort on the part of some very left-wing environmentalists determined to play a political game with scientific facts. I am sure the future will uphold the honor and integrity of Sir Cyril without any question. (quoted in Gould 1981, 234)

In turn, some of Burt's defenders acknowledged that Burt's work and publications may have included some errors, but attributed this to the poor memory and unfortunate carelessness of an aging and infirm scholar (e.g., Jensen 1974; see also Gould 1981 and Hirsch 1981 for a discussion of this reaction).

But on October 24, 1976, Oliver Gillie, medical correspondent of the London *Sunday Times,* wrote a front-page story with the headline "Pioneer of IQ Faked His Research Findings," and which presented information that, as Gould (1981, 235) puts it,

> elevated the charge from inexcusable carelessness to conscious fakery. Gillie discovered, among many other things, that Burt's two "collaborators," a Margaret Howard and a J. Conway, the women who supposedly collected and processed his data, either never existed at all, or at least could not have been in contact with Burt while he wrote the papers bearing their names. These charges led to further reassessments of Burt's "evidence" for his rigid hereditarian position. Indeed, other crucial studies were equally fraudulent, particularly his IQ correlations between close relatives (suspiciously too good to be true and apparently constructed from ideal statistical distributions, rather than measured in nature—Dorfman, 1978), and his data for declining levels of intelligence in Britain.

The Burt issue may be resolved by the findings made and conclusions drawn in a biography of him written by L. S. Hearnshaw (1979) and authorized by Burt's sister before the "scandal" about Burt began to appear. As summarized by Goldberger (1980, 62), prior to beginning work on the biography Hearnshaw's assessment of Burt was

> almost wholly favourable. But as he worked through the large collection of Burt's writings, correspondence, memoranda, diaries, lecture notes, and other material made available to him, Hearnshaw "became convinced that the charges against Burt were, in their essentials, valid."

Herewith some specifics. First, on the separated identical twins, "no data were collected between 1955 and 1966," the period during which Burt claimed to have increased his sample size from 21 pairs to 53 pairs. (On my reading, there is no evidence that the first 21 pairs were any more real.) Second, on the mystery women: "of the more than forty 'persons' who contributed reviews, notes and letters to the journal during the period of Burt's editorship, well over half are unidentifiable, and judging from the style and content of their contributions were pseudonyms for Burt. Howard and Conway were members of a large family of characters invented."

Third, and most intriguing, on the list of individual IQ scores and social class for the 53 pairs of separated identical twins: Christopher Jencks, having seen the summary statistics from this sample in Burt's publications, wrote in December 1968 to ask for the individual figures in order to undertake some regression analysis for his book in progress, *Inequality.* (Jensen, who had many visits and discussions with Burt, never attained that advanced level of curiosity.) Seven weeks later, Burt sent the list with a covering letter which began, "I apologize for not replying more promptly; but I was away for the Christmas vacation, and college (where the data are stored) was closed until the opening of term."

But Hearnshaw reports, "As a matter of fact Burt had not been away for Christmas; his data were not stored at college; and the college had only been closed for a week. . . . According to his diary Burt spent the whole week from 2 January 1969 onwards 'calculating data on twins for Jencks.' . . . Had the I.Q. scores and social class gradings been available they could have been copied out in half an hour at the most. So quite clearly the table of I.Q. scores and social class gradings was an elaborately constructed piece of work." (I confess to some sympathy with Burt at this point: at the age of 86, he was faced with the task of making up 53 pairs of numbers consistent with the mean, standard deviation, and correlation coefficient which he had previously published.)

On the cross-tabulation of fathers' and sons' IQs by social class, Hearnshaw reviews the evidence and finds that "there is no doubt that Burt's reporting of his sources and methods was grossly inadequate, and little doubt that the data he possessed had been subjected to a good deal of 'adjustment.' " (Here Hearnshaw left one avenue of investigation unexplored. In *Science* [29 September 1978], D. D. Dorfman gave a persuasive demonstration that the source of Burt's table was the formula for the bivariate normal distribution function rather than a representative sample of British men.)

Hearnshaw's study of Burt's private papers thus documents what would have been apparent to any thoughtful reader of Burt's public papers: while his figures may have been numbers, they were surely not data. It is remarkable that they passed as data—indeed as crucial data—for so many years.

Indeed, Goldberger's (1980) last point is also raised by Gould (1981) in his own comments about the Hearnshaw (1979) biography. Gould notes that the discovery of such seemingly obviously flawed data "does not touch the deeper issue of why such patently manufactured data went unchallenged for so long, and what this will to believe implies about the basis of our hereditarian presuppositions" (Gould 1981, 236).

One point that is obviously implied is that the power of this presupposition may lead those holding it to misrepresent and distort information. As a case in point, Hirsch (1981, 31) notes that the "balance sheet on Burt" published by the British Psychological Society (Gillie 1980, 12)

> documents the following "falsehoods" propounded by . . . Jensen in the attempt to "cover-up" the Burt scandal:
>
> (1) Jensen said that Professor Hearnshaw had "located some of the identical twins reared apart, tested by Burt and Margaret Howard." This is quite untrue.
>
> (2) Jensen suggested that I was related in some way to Professor William Stephenson, a student of Burt who had quarrelled with him. This is untrue.
>
> (3) Jensen said that Margaret Howard was a faculty member of the Mathematics Department of the University of London yet there is absolutely no evidence for this.
>
> (4) Finally, Jensen attributed political motives to all Burt's detractors, whether or not he had met them, saying that "anyone who has had any contact with them,

or even lunch with them knows this . . . in the first 15 minutes." However, Jensen had never met the Clarkes nor me. And if he could tell me my own political position after 15 minutes I would be grateful because I am not clear what it is myself.

> Earlier, in his discussion of "Burt's Missing Ladies" in *Science,* Gillie (1979, 1036) had documented another Jensen fabrication. "Conway's case is . . . curious. No one . . . knows anything . . . about her . . . Jensen has given her the name Jane . . . but I can find no documentary evidence for this forename." (Hirsch 1981, 31)

But, in summary, despite the directions in which people's hereditarian presuppositions may push them, we may conclude that the events following Kamin's (1974) presentations about Burt's study did nothing to diminish the appropriateness of Kamin's conclusions. In fact, Gillie's reports (1976, 1979, 1980) and Hearnshaw's biography (1979) buttressed Kamin's (1974) view that Burt's "evidence" was no evidence at all. Indeed, although we will not treat the other three studies that Kamin (1974) reviewed (Juel-Nielsen 1965; Newman, Freeman, and Holzinger 1937; Shields 1962) in any detail here, the data they provide—while not faked—do not provide any better evidence for high IQ heritability. Thus Kamin (1974) closes his review of these studies with a position with which I must agree:

> The four separated MZ twin studies reviewed in this chapter led Professor Jensen (1970, p. 146) to conclude: "The overall intraclass correlation . . . 824 . . . may be interpreted as an upper-bound estimate of the heritability of I.Q. in the English, Danish, and North American Caucasian populations sampled in these studies." The conclusion of our own review is vastly different. We have seen that Burt's data, reporting by far the strongest hereditarian effects, are riddled with arithmetical inconsistencies and verbal contradictions. The few descriptions of how the data were collected are mutually inconsistent, as are the descriptions of the "tests" employed. The "assessments" of I.Q. are tainted with subjectivity. The utter failure to provide information about procedural detail can only be described

as cavalier. There can be no science that accepts such data as its base.

To the degree that the case for a genetic influence on I.Q. scores rests on the celebrated studies of separated twins, we can justifiably conclude that there is no reason to reject the hypothesis that I.Q. is simply not heritable. (Kamin 1974, 66–67)

OTHER DATA IN SUPPORT OF THE HEREDITARIAN POSITION

Data from MZ twins reared apart may be the best, but they are not the only, evidence that may be used to support the hereditarian position. These less direct potential bases of support have been reviewed by Goldberger (1980), Gould (1981), Kamin (1974, 1980), and Layzer (1974). These reviewers do not lead us to alter our position regarding the apparently minimal level of support for the hereditarian position. Nevertheless, it is useful to bolster this conclusion by discussing briefly two recent lines of work purporting to provide evidence for the hereditarian position.

Correlations Between IQ and Amplitude and Latency of Evoked Cortical Potentials

Hans J. Eysenck (1979, 1980), whose views about the Burt "case" we noted earlier, has been a strong advocate of the hereditarian position. In his 1979 book, *The Structure and Measurement of Intelligence,* Eysenck makes the claim that culture-bound intelligence tests are appropriate for selection/admission of students into schools because "we are often justified in assuming considerable unformity in cultural background among candidates" (1979, 23). However, Eysenck (1979) provides no support for this belief in cultural uniformity.

What he does do is describe evidence that a feature of brain functioning that, he believes, is not influenced by cultural variables is highly related to scores on culture-bound tests. The feature of brain functioning on

which he focuses is "evoked cortical potentials," an index of the brain's activity in response to stimulation. Eysenck claims that evoked cortical potentials with higher amplitude and shorter latencies indicate greater or more efficient processing of stimulus input. Thus, for instance, he would expect a high negative correlation between latency of response and IQ score, a finding that would indicate that people with higher IQs processed information more rapidly. Such is the nature of the findings that Eysenck indeed reports.

However, Dorfman (1980, 643) notes:

The figures that he displays in support of a strong correlation are taken from Ertl's early work which even Eysenck admits "suffered from technical and methodological deficiencies" (p. 50). He then asserts that Shucard and Horn have also obtained "quite sizable correlations between AEP's [averaged evoked potentials] and IQ" (p. 50). In fact, those investigators reported a correlation of only + 0.24 for fluid intelligence and an absence of correlation for crystallized intelligence in the article cited by Eysenck. He also presents data from "our own laboratories" collected in about 1973. No details are given and no reference is made to any relevant publications in scholarly journals.

In 1980 Eysenck again misrepresented the character of the literature pertaining to the correlation between IQ and evoked cortical potentials. Gould (1980) had written a review of a book of Jensen's (*Bias in Mental Testing,* 1980), wherein Gould criticized the evidence in support of a strong biologically based general factor of intelligence. Commenting on Gould's (1980) review, Eysenck (1980, 52) asserts:

One line of evidence which has become very important in recent years, and which supports the hypothesis of the strong general factor of intelligence, is work with non-cognitive tests, such as measures of reaction time, speed and sensory discrimination, and in particular EEG evoked potentials. None of these are tainted by cultural factors, and all are reactions to simple sensory stimuli, yet they all correlate highly with IQ as measured by traditional tests. In our own recent work EEG evoked potentials show correlations with Wechsler IQ as high as does the Wechsler IQ with, say, the Binet IQ. In other words, non-cognitive tests of this kind, which aim to disclose the biological basis of intelligence, correlate as highly with IQ tests as these correlate with each other.

Eysenck (1980) does not cite any specific scientific literature that supports these claims. Fortunately, however, although Eysenck (1980, 52) characterizes Gould as "little more than an amateur in this field" and notes that to review books on psychology adequately requires "a degree of knowledge and expertise which outsiders simply do not possess," it is Gould who cites the relevant studies and, as such, lets the data "speak for itself." Gould indicates that Eysenck (1980) contends

that IQ would be affirmed as a measure of "intelligence" if it correlates strongly with basic, neurological reactions of the brain that cannot (so he claims) be attributed to cultural or environmental differences. These include: (1) reaction time (in which an experimenter measures how long it takes a subject to react to a stimulus—time from seeing a flashing light to pushing a button, for example); and (2) EEG evoked potentials (in which an experimenter attaches electrodes to a subject's head and records the timing and intensity of electrical responses within his brain to various stimuli). Eysenck then makes a specific claim about such studies—that they correlate as highly with IQ tests as various IQ tests correlate with each other. Ignoramus that I am, I dare not venture into this area of psychological professionalism. So let me, instead, simply cite the contrary opinions of an expert—namely, Arthur Jensen. In *Bias in Mental Testing,* the book that I reviewed, Jensen summarizes [p. 314] many studies on the correlation of Wechsler IQ with Binet IQ, the two tests that Eysenck chooses as his standard. Average correlation is 0.77 for Binet with the Wechsler adult scale (WAIS) and 0.80 for Binet with WISC (Wechsler intelligence scale for children). These high correlations are scarcely surprising since all these tests use similar material, and are constructed with the same end in mind.

On the correlation of IQ with reaction time (an area of Jensen's primary research), Jensen

writes [p. 691]: "Neither I nor anyone else, to my knowledge, has been able to get correlations larger than about −0.4 to −0.5 between choice RT [reaction time] and IQ, with typical correlations in the −0.3 to −0.4 range, using reasonable-sized samples." (The correlations are appropriately negative because *short* reaction time is supposed to accompany *more* intelligence. But they are much lower than the Wechsler-Binet correlation, not equal to it as Eysenck claims. The correlation coefficient, by the way, is a peculiar statistic with a highly asymmetrical distribution that compresses differences at the upper end and magnifies them at the lower end. Thus, a correlation of 0.4 is not "half as good" as one of 0.8, but substantially less intense.)

Jensen is even more dubious about the literature on evoked potential, for he writes [p. 709]: "The AEP average evoked potential and IQ research picture soon becomes a thicket of seemingly inconsistent and confusing findings, confounded variables, methodological differences, statistically questionable conclusions, unbridled theoretical speculation, and, not surprisingly, considerable controversy." The only correlations he cites between IQ tests and evoked potentials average −0.28 with none higher than −0.35 (again, appropriately negative since *less* time between a stimulus and responding brain waves supposedly records *more* intelligence—but again vastly less than the Wechsler-Binet correlation, not equal to it). The −0.28 may be statistically "significant," but vernacular and statistical meanings of the word "significant" are quite unrelated. A statistically "significant" correlation is not necessarily a strong one, but only one that can be adequately discriminated from a value of zero, or no correlation.

The relevant measure, in this case, is the coefficient of determination, or r^2 (the correlation coefficient times itself). An r of −0.28 means that variation in evoked potential accounts for a whopping 8 percent (−0.28 × −0.28, or 0.0784) of the variation in measured IQ! Jensen then casts further doubt upon the literature of evoked potentials [p. 709]: "Visual and auditory AEPs seem to yield quite different, even contrary results, visual latencies usually being negatively correlated with IQ, and auditory latencies being positively correlated. The directions of correlations also seem to flip-flop according to whether the IQs of the sample involved in the study are distributed mostly in the below-average range or mostly in the above-average range of IQs."

But even if the correlations were as high as Eysenck claimed, what would it mean? It wouldn't validate a notion of inborn general intelligence. Who can say that childhood nutrition (both gastronomical and educational) does not affect the growing brain and induce variation equally recorded by reaction time and performance on mental tests? (Gould 1980, 52–53)

In sum, the contention that some measure of cortical activity provides an index of biological functioning "untainted" by cultural factors is not a sound one. In turn, the purported evidence that measures of evoked cortical potentials are highly correlated with measures of IQ is as illusory as Burt's data about IQ resemblance among MZ twins reared apart. Neither Burt's study (1955, 1958, 1966; Conway, 1958) nor Eysenck's assertions (1979, 1980) provide adequate scientific data supporting the hereditarian position.

Reviews of Familial Studies of Intelligence After the Burt "Scandal"

Both before and after the Burt "scandal" surfaced, several summaries were published of the world literature on IQ correlations between relatives. For instance Erlenmeyer-Kimling and Jarvik (1963) published such a review that unfortunately included Burt's reports on MZ twins reared apart as well as his reports on the correlations found for people of other types of relationship (e.g., uncle-nephew correlations). More recent reviews have been published by Roubertoux and Carlier (1978), by Plomin and DeFries (1980), and by Bouchard and McGue (1981). Since the last-noted review is the most recent and comprehensive (at this writing) we will consider the evidence it provides for the genetic determination of intelligence.

The results of the Bouchard and McGue (1981) review are summarized in Table 4.4. The table summarizes their analysis of 111 studies that reported family resemblances in intelligence. Across these studies there were

526 familial correlations based on 113,942 pairings. Table 4.4 summarizes these correlations between both biological and adoptive relatives by using a vertical bar to indicate the median correlation for each type of relationship (e.g., MZ twins reared together, MZ twins reared apart, etc.). In addition, a small arrow is used to indicate the correlation by a simple genetic model of no dominance, no assortative mating, and no environmental effects. The reason Bouchard and McGue (1981, 1055) displayed the predictions derived from such a model is that such a model "provides a noncontroversial pattern against which to compare the results of various familial groupings. Different investigators will undoubtedly fit different models to the data."

The issue of modeling these data is a key one, and later in this chapter I will discuss whether it is possible adequately to model genetic effects on human intelligence using family resemblance data and, if so, whether such a model has ever been used. Here, however, note that the reason it is important to present a model of the inheritance of intelligence is that without the use of a model one cannot appraise the extent to which a given set of correlations supports a hereditarian view of intelligence. In other words, the model here serves as a template; it specifies the nature of the family correlations that would occur if genetic similarity alone accounted for any observed correlations. Obtained correlations are then compared to what is predicted in the model, and to the extent that the model is useful the empirical findings will match the predictions made by the model. Thus, to support a hereditarian position, it is crucial that the model be a conceptually and technically (i.e., mathematically) appropriate means to portray the role of genes in human intelligence.

To anticipate our forthcoming discussion, the inadequacy of such models is the fatal flaw with using family resemblance data, such as in Table 4.4. However, we should note here that Bouchard and McGue (1981) interpret the pattern of average correlations displayed in Table 4.4 as consistent with

TABLE 4.4
Familial Correlations for IQ

	0.0 0.10 0.20 0.30 0.40 0.50 0.60 0.70 0.80 0.90 1.00	NO. OF CORREL- ATIONS	NO. OF PAIRINGS	MEDIAN CORREL- ATION	WEIGHT- ED AVER- AGE	X² (d.f.)	X² d.
MONOZYGOTIC TWINS REARED TOGETHER		34	4,672	.85	.86	81.29 (33)	2.4
MONOZYGOTIC TWINS REARED APART		3	65	.67	.72	0.92 (2)	0.4
MIDPARENT-MIDOFFSPRING REARED TOGETHER		3	410	.73	.72	2.66 (2)	1.3
MIDPARENT-OFFSPRING REARED TOGETHER		8	992	.475	.50	8.11 (7)	1.1
DIZYGOTIC TWINS REARED TOGETHER		41	5,546	.58	.60	94.5 (40)	2.3
SIBLINGS REARED TOGETHER		69	26,473	.45	.47	403.6 (64)	6.3
SIBLINGS REARED APART		2	203	.24	.24	.02 (1)	.0
SINGLE PARENT-OFFSPRING REARED TOGETHER		32	8,433	.385	.42	211.0 (31)	6.8
SINGLE PARENT-OFFSPRING REARED APART		4	814	.22	.22	9.61 (3)	3.2
HALF-SIBLINGS		2	200	.35	.31	1.55 (1)	1.5
COUSINS		4	1,176	.145	.15	1.02 (2)	0.5
NON-BIOLOGICAL SIBLING PAIRS (ADOPTED/ NATURAL PAIRINGS)		5	345	.29	.29	1.93 (4)	0.4
NON-BIOLOGICAL SIBLING PAIRS (ADOPTED/ ADOPTED PAIRINGS)		6	369	.31	.34	10.5 (5)	2.1
ADOPTING MIDPARENT- OFFSPRING		6	758	.19	.24	6.8 (5)	1.3
ADOPTING PARENT- OFFSPRING		6	1,397	.18	.19	6.64 (5)	1.3
ASSORTATIVE MATING		16	3,817	.365	.33	96.1 (15)	6.4

0.0   0.10   0.20   0.30   0.40   0.50   0.60   0.70   0.80   0.90   1.00

Note: The vertical bar in each distribution indicates the median correlation; the arrow, the correlation predicted by a simple polygenic model.
Source: Bouchard and McGue 1981, 1056.

what would be predicted with a model of "polygenic inheritance. That is, the higher the proportion of genes two family members have in common the higher the average correlation between their IQ's" (p. 1055). But, as Bouchard and McGue (1981) go on to point out and as we too shall see, there are many features of the information presented in Table 4.4 that diminish the strength of their interpretation. First, "the individual data points are quite heterogeneous" (p. 1055) within any category of family resemblance. This means that for a group of relatives of a common type of relationship (e.g., MZs reared together or MZs reared apart), their invariant degree of genetic resemblance is not invariantly related to a given degree of IQ resemblance! While some of this

variability may be produced by differences across studies in the tests used to assess intelligence, Bouchard and McGue (1981, 1056) report, "We do not have sufficient data to determine whether the magnitude of the familial correlation is moderated by the specific test used." Thus, it remains quite plausible that within a given category of genetic resemblance environmental interactions moderate levels of IQ resemblance. In addition, we should note that the heterogeneity of "within-genetic resemblance-category family member" correlations presents a formidable problem for those who seek to model genetic influences on human intelligence through the use of such data (Goldberger 1979). We shall return to this point below.

Here we should emphasize that there are additional features of the information in Table 4.4 that mitigate the power of a genetic model and that, in turn, implicate the role of the environment. For instance, Bouchard and McGue (1981) point out that DZ twins of the same sex have more similar IQs than do DZ twins of the opposite sex, and they see this as possibly reflecting a social effect wherein same-sex DZ twins are treated more similarly by their parents than are opposite-sex DZ twins.

In addition, Bouchard and McGue (1981) note that the weighted average correlation for thirty-four correlations reported on 4,672 MZs *reared together* was .86, and that 79 percent of the thirty-four correlations were above .80. They conclude that such a finding "convincingly demonstrates the remarkable similarity of monozygotic twins" (Bouchard and McGue 1981, 1057); but we must expand this conclusion to emphasize that these findings are for MZs reared in the same environment. Not only do these twins share the same genotype but they are also of the same sex (and recall that DZs of the same sex have higher IQ resemblances than do opposite-sex DZs) and are born at the same time. Moreover, the weighted average correlation for MZs reared apart is .72 and Bouchard and McGue (1981, 1056) recognize that this value "is much less than that found for the monozygotic twins reared together, the differences suggesting the importance of between-family environmental differences." However, Bouchard and McGue (1981, 1056) go on to say that "at the same time, the magnitude of this correlation would be difficult to explain on the basis of any strictly environmental hypothesis."

While I would not dispute the uselessness of a *strictly* environmental hypothesis, just as I would suspect that even the most ardent supporter of the hereditarian position would not dispute the uselessness of a *strictly* genetic hypothesis, I must disagree with Bouchard and McGue's (1981) implication that the weighted average of .72 for IQ resemblance among separated MZs provides good support for the hereditarian position. There are two reasons for my disagreement. First, Bouchard and McGue (1981) obtained the weighted correlation of .72 from the reports of three separate investigations. That is, Burt's "data" were deleted and they were left with test results from three other studies on sixty-five pairs of MZs reared apart. Were these the three studies summarized by Kamin (1974) and noted in Table 4.1 of this chapter? Bouchard and McGue (1981) do not indicate in their review the particular three studies they used to identify the sixty-five cases and obtain the weighted correlation of .72. The three studies (other than Burt's) noted in Table 4.1 of this chapter (Juel-Nielsen 1965; Newman, Freeman, and Holzinger 1937; Shields 1962) have a combined sample of sixty-eight. It may be that all or some of the data from one or all of these three studies were part of the data of the unknown three studies summarized by Bouchard and McGue (1981). Unfortunately, we cannot tell from their review if this is the case. Given the inadequate scientific characteristics (Kamin 1974) of the studies by Juel-Nielsen (1965), by Newman, Freeman, and Holzinger (1937), and by Shields (1962), however, we can have no confidence in the accuracy of the weighted correlation of .72 *if* these studies in any way contributed to the weighted correlation. In turn, given the methodological problems of studies of MZs reared apart (Kamin 1974), we should in any event be particularly cautious about relying on such studies unless all their research procedures are fairly and openly evaluated; such evaluation was not part of the report by Bouchard and McGue (1981; for example, see Footnote 8, 1058–59).[1]

---

1. On October 18, 1983, I wrote Professor Bouchard about the three studies of MZ twins reared apart summarized in his article with McGue. My request for information read:
   I am writing in regard to your paper with Matthew McGue in *Science* (1981, Volume 212, pages 1055–1059), 'Familial studies of intelligence: A review.' On page 1056 (column 2, paragraph 2) you note that, 'After deleting the Burt data we are left with test results on but 65 pairs of monozygotic twins reared apart, as reported in three separate investigations.' I would appreciate learning of the references for these three studies and of the numbers of MZ pairs assessed in each study.

Indeed, the particular methodological problems of studies of MZ twins reared apart are my second reason for my disagreement with Bouchard and McGue (1981). These problems have been, of course, discussed by Kamin (1974) and, more recently, by Farber (1981; see also Gruber 1981), who did a reanalysis of all the major studies of MZs reared apart, excluded the doubtful cases (e.g., those of Burt) according to clear and objective criteria, and then attempted to evaluate the information provided by the remaining sample of ninety-five MZs reared apart. Farber (1981) notes that across the several studies she reviewed, about 90 percent of the twin pairs were *selected for inclusion in the study on the basis of known similarities between them*. In other words, MZs who were not similar (along dimensions of interest to the researcher) were systematically and intentionally excluded from the study. Farber estimates that currently there are about 600 pairs of MZ twins being reared apart in the United States alone. Thus the technique of a priori systematic exclusion of dissimilar separated MZs is not only incongruent with an unbiased and objective

scientific analysis, but also, the sample so obtained cannot be representative of the larger population of separated MZs that seems to exist. That is, the group that has been studied is probably only a small proportion of the population of separated MZs that exists (i.e., those who were sufficiently similar); the level of correspondence seen with these inappropriately sampled (and, typically, inappropriately assessed; Kamin 1974) pairs *overestimates* any actual similarity that exists in this population in general. Simply put, researchers seeking similarity excluded those pairs who did not have it and then, when assessing the remaining pairs for similarity, they (claim they) "discovered" it.

It is interesting that Bouchard and McGue (1981) seem to recognize this problem with twin research, but *only* for DZ twins. They note, "The greater similarity of dizygotic twins than of other siblings is most often interpreted as a reflection of greater environmental similarity. It is also likely that bias in the recruitment of dizygotic twins for study is in the direction of increasing psychological similarity" (Bouchard and McGue 1981,

---

Thank you very much for your help in this matter. . . .

About a month later my original letter was returned to me. On the bottom of it someone—I assume Professor Bouchard—had handwritten the following message: See Book reviewed in attached paper—also Taylor, H. The IQ Myth, Ruter 1980. Poor book. I have a critique which will appear in *Intelligence.*

There was no signature. However, reprints of four papers were enclosed: (1) the Bouchard and McGue (1981) paper, about which I had inquired in my October 18 letter to Professor Bouchard; (2) a book review by Duncan (1982) of the Eysenck and Kamin (1981) book, *The Intelligence Controversy;* the review did not identify the three studies by Bouchard and McGue (1981), although Kamin's (1974) reanalysis of the Juel-Nielsen (1965) data was critiqued; (3) a book review by Bouchard (1982) of the Farber (1981) book, *Identical twins reared apart: A reanalysis;* this review also did not identify the three studies cited by Bouchard and McGue (1981), although Farber's (and Kamin's 1974) reanalyses of the Newman, Freeman, and Holzinger (1937) and the Shields (1962) data are critiqued; and (4) an article by David T. Lykken (1982), wherein Lykken identifies (Table 1, 362) "the four major studies of monozygotic twins reared apart." One of these studies is the Minnesota Study (1981), of which Professor Bouchard is the principal investigator. The other three studies are the ones identified by Kamin: that is, Newman, Freeman, and Holzinger (1937), Shields (1962), and Juel-Nielsen (1965). However, the numbers of MZ pairs noted by Lykken as being in these studies are nineteen, forty-four, and twelve, respectively; this results in a total number of seventy-five pairs, which is ten pairs *more* than the number cited for the three studies summarized in Bouchard and McGue, and seven pairs *more* than the number cited by Kamin (1974) for these same three studies.

Although none of the above four articles sent to me explicitly identifies the three articles summarized in the Bouchard and McGue (1981) paper, we may presume they are indeed the ones also reviewed by Kamin (1974). In fact, Professor Robert Plomin, one of the world's leading behavioral geneticists, indicated to me (personal communication, January 1984) that this was the case.

1056). However, a similar recruitment bias may occur with MZs reared apart, and may account for the resemblance in their IQ scores. Bouchard and McGue (1981) fail to indicate this possibility, despite the evidence that exists in support of it (Farber 1981).

Farber (1981) also reports that even with the separated MZs studied there is evidence for the ubiquitous role of environmental influences. She notes that greater separation between the MZs tended to be linearly related to greater disparities in their IQ scores. In turn, most separated MZs come from lower-class and lower-middle-class families and are quite often adopted by families of similar socioeconomic standing or by relatives; thus, although separated, the MZs have similar environments. As a consequence, "The range of environments in which the twins develop is thus reduced, and as the great geneticist Theodosius Dobzhansky pointed out, reducing the variability of the environment increases estimates of heritability" (Gruber 1981, 22). Thus, as Kamin (in Eysenck and Kamin, 1981b) points out, in such a case of comparable rearing environments, the increased estimate of the inheritance of intelligence is an artifact and the IQ score resemblance could be determined as much by environment as by genes. The problems with the determination of estimates of the degree to which the variance in IQ scores is due to variance in genes—that is, the problems with estimating heritability—will be important to focus on below. Here we should note simply that the confidence one may place in the weighted correlation of .72 reported by Bouchard and McGue (1981) as being an accurate estimate of the IQ resemblance of separated MZ twins is not at all great. That this correlation provides useful scientific support for the hereditarian position is far from certain.

Indeed, other information found in Table 4.4 mitigates the hereditarian position. For instance, Bouchard and McGue (1981) note that DZs are more similar than other biological siblings; this suggests not only that the DZs' common birth puts them into a socializing environment at the same time, but it suggests also that this context may treat them similarly. Bouchard and McGue point out too that the IQs of adoptive parents were also consistently related to the IQs of the adopted children; this relation suggests that environmental similarity can lead to IQ resemblance between people. Thus Bouchard and McGue (1981) conclude that "the data clearly suggest the operation of environmental effects" (p. 1058).

In addition, they conclude that it is "indisputable" that "the data support the influence of partial genetic determination for IQ" (Bouchard and McGue 1981, 1058). I certainly would not dispute the broad claim that genes are involved in providing some material basis for such human functioning; indeed, in our discussion of Anastasi's (1958) position I have argued that all human behavior derives from (the interaction of) genes and environment. However, I have argued that the data reviewed by Bouchard and McGue (1981) provide far less scientifically useful and/or certain support for a strong hereditarian view of the bases of IQ than may be taken from initial inspection of Table 4.4. Indeed, the last statements made by Bouchard and McGue (1981) seem to support my conclusion. First, they note that it is "dubious" (p. 1058) whether the data are informative about the precise strengths of the genetic effect. Second, they point out that "the large amount of unexplained variability within degrees of relationship, while not precluding attempts to model the data, suggests that such models should be interpreted cautiously" (Bouchard and McGue 1981, 1058).

That is, as I noted earlier, in order to use data such as those presented in Table 4.4 to determine the extent to which variation in IQ scores is accounted for by variation in genes, some mathematical model of the role of genes and of environment has to be formulated. The result of the application of such a model with a given set of data (e.g., those in Table 4.4) will be the determination of a *heritability* coefficient, which (as noted) is an estimate of the extent to which the variability in some trait distribution (e.g., a distribution of IQ scores) is attributable to genetic variability. Not only do data such as those reviewed by Bouchard and McGue (1981) present problems in attempts to devise models to determine heritability but, in addition, there are major conceptual and technical (mathematical) problems with both the concept of heritability itself and with the models used to estimate heritability. We turn now to a treatment of these issues.

HERITABILITY: CONCEPTS AND MODELS

Since the publication of Jensen's (1969) article in the *Harvard Educational Review,* there have been repeated discussions in the literature about the concept of heritability, about the applicability of the concept to assessments of the genetic contribution to human intelligence, and about the scientific usefulness of the mathematical models used to estimate heritability (e.g., Eysenck and Kamin 1981a, 1981b; Feldman and Lewontin 1975, 1976; Frankel 1976; Goldberger 1979; Gould 1980, 1981; Havender 1976; Hirsch 1970, 1981; Jensen 1973, 1976, 1980; Kamin 1974; Layzer 1974; Morton 1976; Plomin and DeFries 1976; Scarr-Salapatek 1971a, 1971b). These discussions have highlighted the points that the concept of heritability is a complex one and that estimates of heritability are not always formulated appropriately, especially in regard to human intelligence.

Uses and Misuses of the Concept of Heritability

If psychologists are interested in measuring a certain psychological construct or characteristic of people, such as intelligence, they will often formulate a test to measure this characteristic or trait. Now, if a group of people is given such an intelligence test, it is very unlikely that they will all get the exact same score. Rather, some will score low,

some high, and some intermediate. The scores of the group will form a distribution, ranging from high to low. (This is similar to what happens when we, as students, take several tests in a course over a semester and our test scores distribute themselves from high to low.)

If we are interested in representing the way the group functioned on the test in general (or if we want to know how we are doing overall in the course), the first thing we might opt to do is find the mean (the average) score of the distribution. To do this we would simply add up all the individual scores in the distribution and divide this total by the number of scores in the distribution.

Second, we might want to know about the distribution of scores per se. In other words, not everyone in our group got the same score. Rather, within the group there was *variation.* Many people scored near the group mean, a few scored way above it, and a few scored way below it. Statistical analysis would allow us to represent the amount of variation in a distribution through the use of the term *variance* (σ^2). The magnitude of the variance would indicate how much or how little variation in test scores occurred in the distribution.

For our purposes, the important question is not how much variation was present but rather what its source was. For our consideration of the concept of heritability, we would want to know how much of the variation in the test scores making up the distribution was due to variation in the gene distribution of the people tested and how much was due to variation in their environments.

Since we have a distribution of scores, this means that there are differences among the people in our population in their test scores. We may ask several questions—all similar in purpose—about these differences. Why do these people differ? Why do they vary? What is the source of the variation between them? How much of this variation may be attributed to genetic differences between them? How much to environmental differences between them? What percentage of these differences between these people—

what proportion of this variance—involves genetic differences between them? What percentage of these differences between people may be attributed to the corresponding gene differences—the corresponding gene distribution? Note that we are here asking what proportion of the test differences between people corresponds to the *gene differences* between people; we are *not* asking about how much of a given single person's test score is determined by his or her genes. (It should be clear that these are two different questions.) We should keep this distinction in mind and see that since these are two different questions, we can in no way answer the second question by coming to an answer for the first.

However, whenever we answer questions such as the first one—when we try to find out how much of the variation between people is due to gene differences between them—we are addressing questions that will lead us toward the calculation of heritability. Such questions inquire about what proportion of variation in a group of people (a population that has been measured for a particular psychological characteristic) is related to the gene variation among these people. Therefore, consistent with our brief definition of *heritability* above, we may now define this conception as the proportion of trait variation in a population that is attributable to genetic variation in that population, and we may symbolize heritability by the term h^2.

Now, if all the variation in a trait (such as intelligence) could be attributed to the concomitant variation within the gene distribution of the population under study, then no variation whatsoever in the trait would be due to environmental variation. Thus, in such a case, the value for environmental variation in the population would be zero and, accordingly, h^2 would equal one, or +1.0. Alternatively, if no trait variation could be attributed to genetic variation, all the trait variation in the population would have to be a function of environmental variation in the population. Therefore, in this case, h^2 would equal zero, or 0.0. Thus,

we see that h^2 values can range anywhere from zero to plus one, increasing in proportion to the extent that the population's genetic variation accounts for the trait variation. Typically, however, the heritability of a trait falls somewhere within this zero-to-plus-one range.

A heritability score can be calculated in several ways. Basically, however, the main thrust of all calculation methods is to determine the degree to which a specific population of organisms has responded to being bred for the expression (the degree of presence) of some trait (Hirsch 1970). For example, let us say that a particular population of organisms (a specific population of fruit flies, *Drosophila,* for instance) can be distributed in terms of a particular trait (e.g., the tendency to fly toward light). If the distribution of this trait in this population remains the same despite any changes in the genetic similarity of the parents of these flies, then heritability would equal zero. That is, if the genes transmitted to the offspring making up our fly population could be varied and this transmission did not differentially affect the population's trait distribution, then heritability would equal zero. This would be the case because if changes in the genetic similarities or differences among the parents do not lead to any variation in the population's trait distribution, then genetic variation within the population does not contribute to the variation in this population's trait distribution, and h^2 would equal zero.

However, if in another population of *Drosophila* similarly distributed in terms of a particular trait, the genes transmitted by the parents do lead to a change in the population's trait distribution, then, obviously, genetic variation within the population does account for some of this variation; therefore, in this case, the heritability value would be greater than zero. The exact numerical value of heritability would thus be determined by calculating the magnitude of the relationship (the correlation) between the parents and their offspring comprising the population under study.

From these illustrations we should recognize an essential point. Heritability values for the same trait vary in relation to the particular populations under study. That is, the heritability for the same exact trait may be plus one in one population, zero in another, and somewhere between these two scores in still another population. Therefore it should be clear *that heritability is a property of populations and not of traits* (Hirsch 1963). Thus, a trait in an individual cannot be appropriately spoken of as of being heritable; *one cannot correctly speak of the trait intelligence as being heritable.* Rather, all that heritability refers to is the extent to which genetic variation among the members of a specific population of organisms accounts for the trait *distribution* in that population. Jensen (1969) makes the same point. In discussing the appropriateness of applying the concept of heritability to a population of people and the inappropriateness of such application to any individual within that population, Jensen states:

> Heritability is a population statistic, describing the relative magnitude of the genetic component (or set of genetic components) in the population variance of the characteristic in question. It has no sensible meaning with reference to a measurement or characteristic in an individual. A single measurement, by definition, has no variance (1969, 42).

Hence, heritability describes something about a group and not anything about an individual. Heritability relates to the source of differences among people in a population; it says nothing about a given psychological trait within any person in that population.

Therefore, we can see that heritability is a far less meaningful, more limited piece of information than most people seem to realize (Hirsch 1970, 72). As we will discuss in greater detail below, *heritability does not mean genetically determined.* Nor, as the genetic-differences hypothesis implies, does heritability mean unavailable for influence by the environment. Implicit in all we have said about heritability up to this point has been the assumption that the environments of the populations under study have been constant and unvarying. Of course, except

under specially and artifically designed conditions, possible to achieve with *Drosophila* but not with humans, environmental conditions can be expected to vary. Thus it is possible that h^2 might equal one for a population reared under a given set of environmental circumstances and might equal zero for that same population reared under a different set of environmental circumstances. If this is the case, then h^2 values are obviously affected by environment, and one can in no way speak of h^2 as telling anything about genetic determination. Thus, as Hirsch (1970) has cautioned, heritability is only an estimate of the proportion of phenotypic variation of a trait that can be attributed to genetic variation in some *particular generation of a specific population under one set of environmental conditions.* Similarly, Jensen (1969, 43) states that heritability estimates "are specific to the population sampled, the point in time, how the measurements were made, and the particular test used to obtain the measurements."

The above, then, is the only bit of information that a heritability estimate conveys. Thus we should now recognize that this limited information has little potential generalizability due to the facts that a particular heritability estimate can be used only in reference to one particular generation of a particular population that is reared in a specific, invariant environment. In addition, Hirsch (1970) reports that when a heritability estimate is made on a population more than once—that is, when repeated measurements of h^2 are taken—some studies report that h^2 increases, others report that it decreases, and still others report that h^2 varies randomly. Thus, in addition to its other limitations, h^2 seems to fluctuate in a largely unpredictable manner from one time of measurement to the next. In psychological parlance, this is termed *unreliability.* This is a devastating, seemingly fatal, flaw. If a measurement does not come out to be the same value from one time of testing to the next (which means that the measurement is not reliable), what confidence can we place in that measurement? If we cannot even measure a concept reliably, of what use is it? And if a concept cannot be measured reliably, can we justifiably make any social or educational policies on the basis of such measurement? I think the answer to these questions is no. Thus a heritability estimate is not what it may *seem* to be. In addition, we shall now consider information that will suggest that heritability may not even be a good measurement of what it is *supposed* to be. This discussion will provide support for Hirsch's view (1970, 74) that in regard to human intelligence, "the plain facts are that in the study of man a heritability estimate turns out to be a piece of 'knowledge' that is both deceptive and trivial."

Problems in Determining the Heritability of Human Intelligence

Our preceding discussion of heritability was a necessarily general overview of what is a conceptually and technically complicated concept. While this overview may suffice to introduce the character of the issues involved with the concept, we need to recognize that problems with the concept—especially when applied to the topic of determining the extent to which genetic variation accounts for variation in human intelligence—require exceedingly more detailed analyses.

Feldman and Lewontin (1975) point out, for instance, that one must remember to distinguish between *two distinct forms of the heritability concept*—what is termed *broad heritability* and what is termed *narrow heritability*. That is, they indicate that heritability in the broad sense (h^2_B) is the term used for the proportion of all variance that is partitioned into the genetic variance in an analysis of variance of genetic and environmental sources. In effect, in our preceding discussion we have been speaking of h^2_B. However, the genetic variance represented by the term h^2_B can itself be further partitioned into several other components. For instance, there is a contribution that is made by individual alleles (and this is termed *ad-*

ditive variance), a contribution that is made by pairs of homologous (similar) alleles at a given locus (location) of the genome (and this is termed *dominance variance*); and a contribution that is made by combinations of nonhomologous loci (termed *epistatic variance*). Heritability in the narrow sense (h^2_N) is the proportion of the phenotype variance that is additive genetic variance (Feldman and Lewontin 1975).

Feldman and Lewontin (1975) argue, however, that this variance analysis cannot be used in the study of problems of human population genetics. They indicate:

> In problems concerning the population genetics of human behavioral traits, the existence of a variance contribution from genotype-environment interaction and a genotype-environment correlation have long been recognized as major difficulties. On the one hand, the obvious problems these cause for estimation of h^2_N have led to the use of the h^2_B in discussion of such characters. On the other hand, as was implied by Falconer (1960) and emphasized by Moran (1973) and Layzer (1974), the very existence of genotype-environment correlation precludes the valid statistical estimation of the genotypic, environmental, and interaction contributions to the phenotypic variance. That is because correlation makes it impossible to know how much of the phenotype similarity arises from similarity of genotype and how much from similarity of the environment. Thus in human population studies, where experimental controls are either impossible or unethical, statistical inference about the heritability of traits that are phenotypically plastic is invalid. (Feldman and Lewontin 1975, 1164)

The Problem of Genotype-Environment Correlation

It is instructive here to focus on the problem presented for calculation of heritability by genotype-environment correlations. As noted by Feldman and Lewontin (1975), one of those scientists who has dealt with this point has been Layzer (1974). Layzer indicates that

> nearly all the published discussions that I am aware of take it for granted that some meaningful estimate of IQ heritability—high or low,

rough or accurate—can be extracted from the reams of published statistics and that refinements of current techniques for gathering and analyzing test data may be counted on to yield increasingly reliable estimates. These propositions are by no means self-evident, however, and one of my purposes here is to demonstrate that they are actually false.

This conclusion rests upon two arguments: One concerns the limitations of conventional heritability analysis, the other the validity of IQ scores as phenotypic measurements. Contrary to widely held beliefs, (i) heritability analysis does not require the genotype-environment interaction to be small, and (ii) a high phenotypic correlation between separated monozygotic twins does not, in general, imply that the genotype-environment interaction is small. If genotype-environment interaction does contribute substantially to the phenotypic value of a trait (as there are strong biological reasons for supposing in the case of phenotypically plastic traits), then a necessary and sufficient condition for the applicability of heritability analysis is the absence of genotype-environment correlation. This condition is rarely, if ever, met for behavioral traits in human populations. The second argument is that IQ scores contain uncontrollable, systematic errors of unknown magnitude. (Layzer 1974, 1259)

While we shall have reason to refer later to Layzer's analysis of the errors of measurement found in IQ scores, let us focus here on his treatment of the genotype-environment correlation problem. Using the label G for genotype and E for environment, Layzer argues:

> that G and E can be unambiguously defined if, and only if, genotype-environment correlations are absent. Even then, however, a certain practical ambiguity persists. Genetic differences may influence the development of a trait in qualitatively distinct ways. For example, the curves labeled x_1, x_2, and x_3 in Figure 4.1 have different thresholds, different slopes, and different final values. Heritability estimates do not take such qualitative distinctions into account. Thus, if the environmental variable y is distributed in a narrow range about the value y^1, as illustrated in Figure 4.1, h^2 is close to unity. Yet in these circumstances the phenotypic variable could reasonably be considered

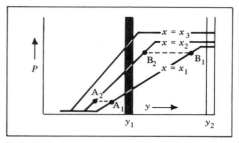

FIGURE 4.1
Phenotypic value (P) of a hypothetical metric trait as a function of an environmental variable (x) for three values of a genotypic variable (y). A_1 and A_2 (also B_1 and B_2) indicate individuals with a common phenotypic value but distinct genotypes x_1 and x_2, respectively.
Source: Layzer, 1974, 1260.

to be largely environmental in origin since it is much greater than the phenotypic variance that would be measured in an environment ($y = y_2$) that permitted maximum development of the trait, consistent with genetic endowment. (Layzer 1974, 1260)

Layzer (1974) then notes that plant and animal geneticists *can* minimize genotype-environment correlation—*by randomizing environments;* thus such researchers can take a step that he argues is *indispensable* for the application of heritability analysis, since without such randomization there is just no means to disentangle genetic and environmental contributions to phenotypic variances. But this step is not done in IQ heritability research. He explains:

> The applicability of heritability analysis does not, as is commonly assumed, hinge on the smallness of the interaction term (R) relative to the terms G and E in Fisher's decomposition of the phenotypic value. In fact, one may reasonably assume on biological grounds that genotype-environment interaction makes a substantial contribution to the phenotypic value of every phenotypically plastic trait, except in populations where the ranges of genetic and environmental variation are severely restricted. Even so, heritability analysis can be applied to phenotypically plastic traits, pro-

vided that the relevant genetic and environmental variables are statistically uncorrelated. When this condition is not satisfied, the contributions of interaction to phenotypic variances and covariances cannot, in general, be separated from the contributions of genotype and environment, and heritability analysis cannot, therefore, be applied meaningfully.

In adult subpopulations, IQ and environment are well known to be more or less strongly correlated. Since differences in IQ are undeniably related to genetic differences (although not, perhaps, in a very simple way), one may safely assume that genotype-environment correlation is significant in adult subpopulations and in subpopulations composed of children reared by their biological parents or by close relatives. Hence, no valid estimate of IQ heritability can be based on data that refer to such subpopulations.

Yet data of precisely this kind make up the bulk of the available material, and many published heritability estimates have been based on them. Burt (1966), Jensen (1969), and Herrnstein (1971) for example, all cite kinship correlation data as evidence for a high value of h^2. (Layzer 1974, 1263)

In sum, the existence of genotype-environment correlation presents a seemingly insurmountable problem in studies of the heritability of human intelligence. Analyses of the heritability of human intelligence that rely on data sets wherein such correlations exist therefore result in flawed estimates. However, the problem of genotype-environment correlation is not the only one precluding a scientifically useful analysis of the heritability of human intelligence. Another major problem is presented by the arrays (sets) of genotypes and environments that are sampled in studies of the heritability of human intelligence.

Problems of Genotype and Environment Sampling

Feldman and Lewontin (1975) make the obvious point that in quantitative human characteristics such as IQ scores, differences in phenotypes can be caused by both genotypes and environments. However, the not-so-obvious point for which they argue is that these two causes of variation cannot be separated by an analysis of variance and its summary statistic—heritability. They indicate that this situation occurs because the variance analysis and the calculation of heritability are done in regard to a particular set of genotypes and environments in a specific population, and are studied at a specific point in time. They argue that this set is usually a biased sample of the full range of genotypes and environments that exist (Feldman and Lewontin 1975).

To illustrate this point they offer the diagram presented in Figure 4.2. This figure illustrates a norm of reaction wherein the phenotype (P) is represented as a function of two genotypes (G_1 and G_2). Feldman and Lewontin (1975, 1166–67) explain:

Obviously, both genotype and environment influence the phenotype in this example. However, if the environments are symmetrically distributed around E_1 [Figure 4.2], there will appear to be no average effect of genotype, while if the population is weighted toward an excess of G_1, the average phenotype across environments will be constant, as is shown by the dashed line. Thus the environmental variance depends on the genotypic distribution, and the

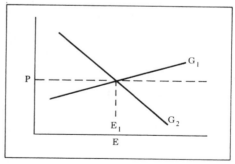

FIGURE 4.2
Phenotype P plotted against an environmental variable E. If the environments are symmetrically distributed around E_1 there is no average effect of genotype. If there is an excess of G_1 in the population the average phenotype will be constant, as represented by the horizontal dashed line.

Source: Feldman and Lewontin 1975, 1166.

genotypic variance depends on the environmental variance. This very important interdependence means that for a character like IQ, where the norm of reaction, the present genotype distribution, and the present environmental distribution are not known, we cannot predict whether an environmental change will change the total variation. Lewontin (1970) gives an extreme example of the latter difficulty where all the variation between two populations is environmental, despite a heritability of 1.0 within each.

Hebb (1970) in addition to Lewontin (1970) and Feldman and Lewontin (1975), has made a similar point. He explains:

> The conception of "heritability" is a misleading one in this context, and some of the geneticists who use it are as confused as the social scientists, so its origin in genetics does not guarantee logical use by psychologists. In a 1953 paper, I showed that the amount of variance attributable to heredity (or to environment) cannot show how important heredity (or environment) is in determining an aspect of behavior. . . . I give here a new example. . . .
> Mark Twain once proposed that boys should be raised in barrels to the age of 12 and fed through the bung-hole. Suppose we have 100 boys reared this way, with a practically identical environment. Jensen agrees that environment has *some* importance (20% worth?), so we must expect that the boys on emerging from the barrels will have a mean IQ well below 100. However, the variance attributable to the environment is practically zero, so on the "analysis of variance" argument, the environment is not a factor in the low level of IQ, which is nonsense. (1970, 568)

Hence, in Hebb's example, environment had no differential effect on the boys' IQs; presumably in all boys it had the same (severely limiting) effect. In having this same effect, environment could contribute nothing to differences between the boys. There was no difference—or variation—in the environment, and so it could not be said to contribute anything to differences between the people. Yet it is also obvious that the environment had a major influence on the boys' IQ scores. It is clear that even with IQ heritability equal to +1.0, the intelligence of

each of the boys would have been different had he developed in an environment other than a pickle barrel. Even if the heritability of IQ for American blacks were +1.0, then alterations in their environmental experiences could still favorably alter the distribution of their IQ scores. *Hence, high h^2 does not mean developmental fixity.* A high h^2 estimate means that environment does not contribute very much to differences among people in their expression of a trait; yet environment may still provide an important (although invariant) source of the expression of that trait.

Thus, consistent with Hebb's (1970) example, Jensen asserts:

> First of all, the fact that learning ability has high heritability surely does *not* mean that individuals cannot learn much. Even if learning ability had 100 percent heritability it would not mean that individuals cannot learn, and therefore the demonstration of learning or the improvement of performance, with or without specific instruction or intervention by a teacher, says absolutely nothing about heritability. But knowing that learning ability has high heritability does tell us this: if a number of individuals are all given equal opportunity—the same background, the same conditions, and the same amount of time—for learning something, they will still differ from one another in their rates of learning and consequently in the amount they learn per unit of time spent in learning. That is the meaning of heritability. It does not say the individuals cannot learn or improve with instruction and practice. It says that given equal conditions, individuals will differ from one another, not because of differences in the external conditions but because of differences in the internal environment which is conditioned by genetic factors. (1973, 56–57)

Hence, in both Hebb's and Jensen's statements we see the view that although heritability may be high, the characteristics in question may still be influenced by environment. In turn, we also see that even when conditions are "equal"—*and in actuality this probably could never occur*—and the differences that people will still assuredly manifest are attributable to genetic factors, this genetic influence is still not absolute, not environment-independent. Even when differences are due to internal differences, such sources are only conditioned by genetic factors; that is, such genetic factors only contribute to this internal environmental source. Clearly, then, when environment contributes nothing to the *differences* between people in population, their gene distribution accounts for these differences; but this again does not mean that the population characteristic is fixed by heredity or that it is unavailable to environmental influence. As both Hebb and Jensen well point out, while contributing nothing to differences between people, environment can still be a uniformly potent source of behavior development and functioning within each of the people in a group.

A point consistent with the ones above has been made by Lehrman (1970), a former student of Schneirla's. Lehrman points out that when a geneticist speaks of a trait as being heritable, all he means is that he is able to predict the trait distribution in the offspring population on the basis of knowing the trait distribution in the parent population. We can predict the distribution of eye color in the offspring generation merely by knowing the distribution of eye color among the parents. Thus, while the geneticist may use the terms *hereditary* or *inherited* as interchangeable with the term *heritable,* he is not, by such interchangeable usage, making any statements about the *process* involved in the development of this trait. In other words, the geneticist is not saying anything at all about the way that nature and nurture provide a source of a heritable trait. Thus the geneticist is not saying anything about the extent to which the expression of the trait may change in response to environmental modification. In short, a geneticist would not say that a highly heritable trait cannot be influenced by the environment. Rather, the geneticist would probably recognize, as we now must, that even if the heritability of a trait is +1.0, an almost infinite number of phenotypic expressions of that trait may be expected to develop as a result

of an interaction with the almost infinite number of environments to which any one genotype may be exposed. The norm of reaction is a biological reality that cannot be ignored.

Accordingly, people who equate heritability with genetic determination assume that as the magnitude of h^2 increases from zero to +1.0, less and less can be done through environmental modifications to alter the expression of the trait. Of course, they alternatively assume that if the value of h^2 is low, this leaves more room for altering the trait through environmental manipulation.

This argument is fallacious. As noted by Jensen, those espousing this position believe

> that there is an inverse relationship between heritability magnitude and the individual's improvability by training and teaching; this is to say, if heritability is high, little room is left for improvement by environmental modification, and conversely, if heritability is low, much more improvement is possible. Hirsch is quite correct in noting a possible fallacy that may be implicit in this interpretation of heritability. . . . (Jensen 1973, 55–56)

Similarly, Scarr-Salapatek (1971a) notes:

> The most common misunderstanding of the concept "heritability" relates to the myth of fixed intelligence: if h^2 is high, this reasoning goes, then intelligence is genetically fixed and unchangeable at the phenotypic level. This misconception ignores the fact that h^2 is a population statistic, bound to a given set of environmental conditions at a given point in time. Neither intelligence nor h^2 estimates are fixed. (p. 1228)

In short, there seems to be some consensus with the view of Feldman and Lewontin (1975) that despite the level that is reached by an estimate of heritability, environmental variation may be a (or the) key causative factor; in addition there seems to be general consensus with a key implication of their view that high heritability does not mean developmental fixity. Moreover, there are other implications of the Feldman and Lewontin (1975, 1976) position. One other important one, which may also be derived from Figure 4.2, is that holding either the environment or the genotype constant does not lead necessarily to a decrease in the total variance. To illustrate they note that

> fixing genotype G_2 (and thus eliminating the genetic variance) increases the total variance because G_2 is more susceptible to environmental change. It is also easy to construct graphs like Figure 4.2 in which environmental change improves the phenotype of both G_1 and G_2 but decreases the proportion of the variance that is genetic.
>
> Figure 4.3 is a case such that, if the environments are weighted to the left, analysis of variance shows a strong genotypic effect. If the environments are weighted toward the right, thus producing improvement in both phenotypes, the proportion of variation that is genetic is reduced. This situation is ignored by both Jensen (1969) and Herrnstein (1971), whose discussion does not take account of this possible form of genotype-environment interaction. (Feldman and Lewontin 1975, 1166)

In short, Feldman and Lewontin (1975) argue that an estimate of heritability does not necessarily accurately portray the character of environmental and genotypic variation causally involved in IQ score differences. Furthermore, they indicate that there are other key problems with using the concept of heritability. One major instance is in attempting to generalize heritability estimates from one group to another. Because this problem was a central flaw in Jensen's (1969) work, we turn now to a discussion of it.

Problems of Generalizing Heritability Estimates

After the publication of Jensen's (1969) article, several reviewers identified a problem of inappropriate generalization in Jensen's analysis (e.g., Gould 1980; Hirsch 1970; Feldman and Lewontin 1975; Lewontin 1976). That is, they made the point that

> *the value of heritability within either the white or the black population carries no implication whatever about the causes for different average values of IQ between the two populations.* (A group of very short people may have heritabilities for height well above 0.9, but still owe their relative stature entirely to poor nutrition.) *Within and between group variation are entirely different phenomena;* this is a lesson taught early in any basic genetics course. Jensen's conflation of these two concepts marked his fundamental error. (Gould 1980, 38; italics added)

Similarly, Feldman and Lewontin (1975, 1167) note that

> we are unable to make any inferences from between-group differences and within-group statistics about the degree of genetic determination of the between-group differences. In other words, the concept of heritability is of no value for the study of differences in meaures of human behavioral characters between groups.

Moreover, when Lewontin (1973) calculated the genetic diversity within populations, within races between populations, and between races, he found that 85 percent of human genetic diversity is accounted for by variation between people within populations. Only about 6 percent of human genetic diversity was found to be attributable to variation between races (Lewontin 1973).

In addition to inappropriate attempts to generalize a within-group heritability estimate between groups, there is an additional

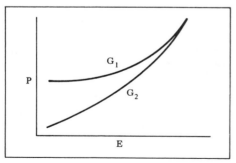

FIGURE 4.3
Phenotype P plotted against an environmental variable E. If the environments are weighted to the left, there is a strong genotypic effect. If the environments are weighted to the right, the genetic variation is reduced.
Source: Feldman and Lewontin 1975, 1166.

instance of inappropriate generalization. This has been explained by Hirsch (1970).

People who attempted to use h^2 as an indication of genetic determinancy appear to be involved in asking and attempting to answer the question "how much?" This is one of the two questions that we have seen Anastasi (1958) reject as illogical. In essence, they ask, "How much heredity and how much environment go into the determination of intelligence?" Or, "Which of the two is more important in determining intelligence?" However, as we know, answering this question is both logically impossible and inappropriate.

As detailed by Hirsch (1970), people working from this orientation typically test a population on the intelligence trait at a single time in their development. In then making a heritability estimate, all that is being done is a determination of the relative proportions of the variation between the individuals in the population that can be assigned to genetic and environmental variation. That is, the reason that a distribution exists is that, as we have seen, by definition individuals differ from each other in their scores on the test for that trait. All that h^2 does, then, is provide an estimate of how much of these *between-individual differences* is due to genetic variation and how much is due to environmental variation.

But people mistakenly use these values to estimate how much of the expression of the tested trait *within a single individual* of that population is determined by heredity and environment. Between-individual data are applied to purported within-individual phenomena. Thus not only is an attempt to ask "How much of each?" illogical, but the collected data can in no way be used appropriately to begin to address the question. As Hirsch emphasized, people taking this approach "want to know how instinctive is intelligence *(with)*in the development of a certain individual, but instead they measure differences between large numbers of fully, or partially, developed individuals" (1970, 77; italics added).

The apparent confusion of those people

taking this approach is further complicated. We have seen that the norm-of-reaction concept leads us to recognize that all individuals in the world, no matter to what race they belong, can be expected to have a unique, individual genotype. In addition, we recognize the impossibility of ever determining with any degree of exactness a human's norm of reaction (or as Hebb, 1949, would term it, intelligence A). Moreover, because of genotypic uniqueness, members of the same racial group cannot be appropriately equated in order to attempt to assess a racial group's norm of reaction. In fact, such a concept makes no sense. Even if it did, however, an exposure of each population genotype to the range of possible environments with which it could interact in order to assess phenotypic variability would remain a theoretical and practical impossibility. There is, then, absolutely no empirical or theoretical basis for any general statement assigning fixed proportions to the contributions of nature and nurture to the intellectual development of a single individual (Hirsch 1970), *much less within every individual in an entire group of people!* Indeed, Jensen stresses, "There is no way of partitioning a given individual's IQ into hereditary and environmental components, as if a person inherited, say, 80 points of IQ and acquired 20 additional points from his environment. This is, of course, nonsense" (1969, 42).

Thus, heritability estimates may not be generalized between populations and, as significantly, they are meaningless and irrelevant for determining the roles of heredity and environment within a given individual. There is one final and very important, albeit quite technical, problem with heritability estimates. That is, you will recall Bouchard and McGue's (1981) warning that the family resemblance data they reviewed (which are summarized in Table 4.4, above) presented formidable problems for devising useful mathematical procedures (models) to appraise the heritability of human intelligence. These problems may be even more severe than Bouchard and McGue (1981) indicate.

Problems With Modeling Heritability

Perhaps the most penetrating analysis of the problems encountered when attempting to devise models with which to estimate heritability from a set of family resemblance data has been presented by Goldberger (1979). He takes up these problems by noting:

> About 1970, a consensus had developed among experts that the genetic component of IQ variance was very high, about 80 percent. In part the consensus was based upon common sense. As one correspondent, the geneticist C. O. Carter, later put it, "[I]t is I think evident to any experienced and unprejudiced observer that the major part of the variation in intellectual ability in school children in Britain is genetic" (*The Times,* 3 November 1976). In greater part, however, the consensus was based on the fitting of statistical models to sets of IQ kinship correlations.
>
> I will be concerned with model fitting rather than with common sense. (Goldberger 1979, 327)

To begin to address the issue of model fitting Goldberger (1979) devised a table wherein each column gave a set of IQ kinship correlations that arose when various pairs of relatives were given IQ tests and their scores were then correlated. Table 4.5 presents this information. In this table it may be seen that the IQ correlation decreases as the biological and/or social "distances" increase.

Model Fitting

As we have discussed above (in regard to the views of Feldman and Lewontin 1975, 1976), in order to partition the variance in IQ scores into genetic and environmental components from data such as those in Table 4.5, one uses some statistical model. The genetic and environmental variance components appear as unknown *parameters* (statistical portions of the model), and these parameters are adjusted to best fit the data. Table 4.6, which is also taken from Goldberger (1979), presents the estimates of the modeled environmental and genetic variance components that have been derived from the major attempts at such work. The column numbers in Table 4.6 correspond to those of Table 4.5.

Goldberger (1979) notes that the column headed "Jinks and Fulker (1970) UK" refers to modeling work done in the United Kingdom that uses seven of Cyril Burt's kinship correlations (and that finds h^2_B to be .83). Of course, these figures were recognized by Goldberger (1979) to be inadmissible and scientifically useless, given the errors and dishonesty associated with them. But Goldberger (1979) notes that both Eysenck and Jensen claimed that even after Burt's "data" were discarded, modeling using other data would confirm the estimates derived from Burt's study. For instance, Goldberger (1979, 329) notes that Eysenck wrote:

> [I]t is noteworthy that many different approaches have resulted in very similar estimates [of IQ heritability] usually centering around the 80 percent mark, although the range of uncertainty gives a lower bound of something like 60 percent and an upper one of 90 percent or thereabouts. [*The Times,* 12 November 1976]

and

> There is ample evidence for the genetic determination of intelligence.... [The] studies are remarkably congruent in the conclusions they allow us to come to. It is typical that opponents are vocal mainly in the pages of newspapers, in the letter columns of population magazines, or in other non-technical places.... [C]ritics seem to fight shy of the technical literature, or the essential examination of the totality of the evidence. [*The Times,* 8 November 1976]

On various subsequent occasions, Eysenck restated his scholarly concern in such distinguished "technical" journals as *New Society* (11 November 1976), *New Scientist* (25 November 1976), *Encounter* (January 1977), and *The Bulletin of the British Psychological Society* (1977).

Eysneck placed particular weight on the contributions of the Birmingham school of biometrical genetics, represented by J. L. Jinks, D. W. Fulker, and L. J. Eaves. Jensen, on the other hand, placed particular weight on the contributions of the Honolulu school, represented by N. E. Morton and D. C. Rao, writing:

TABLE 4.5
IQ Kinship Correlation Sets Used in Various Studies

Type of Relationship	Jinks and Fulker (1970) UK	Eaves (1975) UK	Eaves (1975) US	Eaves (1977) US	Jencks (1972) US	Rao, Morton, and Yee (1976) US	Rao and Morton (1978) US
	(1)	(2)	(3)	(4)	(5)	(6)	(7)
Identical twins reared together	0.92	0.92	0.97	—	0.91	0.89	0.84
Identical twins reared apart	0.87	0.87	0.75	—	0.67	0.69	0.68
Siblings reared together	0.53	0.53	0.59	0.38	0.53	0.52	0.52
Siblings reared apart	0.44	0.44	—	—	—	—	0.25
Parent & biological child reared together	—	0.49	0.55	—	0.48	0.48	0.48
Parent & biological child reared apart	—	—	0.45	—	0.41	—	0.41
Adoptive siblings	0.27	0.27	0.38	—	0.36	0.25	0.32
Adoptive parents	—	0.19	0.28	—	0.23	0.23	0.23
Grandparents	—	0.33	—	—	—	—	—
Uncles	—	0.34	—	—	—	—	—
First cousins	—	0.28	—	0.14	—	—	—
Second cousins	—	0.16	—	0.07	—	—	—
Third cousins	—	—	—	0.03	—	—	—
Spouses	0.39	0.39	0.57	0.46	0.50	0.50	0.51

Notes: Several kinships that were distinguished in the studies are combined here for simplicity: "Sibling" includes fraternal twins along with ordinary siblings; "Adoptive sibling" includes adoptive-adoptive pairs along with adoptive-natural pairs.
In column (4) the entries were calculated by Goldberger from the ANOVA tables in Eaves (1977).
In column (5) the entries were assembled by Goldberger from various pages in Jencks (1972).
Source: *Goldberger 1979, 328.*

TABLE 4.6
Components of IQ Variance as Estimated in Various Studies

| | Jinks and Fulker (1970) UK | Eaves (1975) UK | Eaves (1975) US | Eaves (1977) US | Jencks (1972) US | Rao, Morton, and Yee (1976) US | | Rao and Morton (1978) US | | Eaves Model fitted to Rao and Morton data US |
| | (1) | (2) | (3) | (4) | (5) | (6) | | (7) | | (8) |
						Children	Adults	Children	Adults	
Genetic	83	85	68	60	45	67	21	69	30	58
Additive	62	65	35	60	32	67	21	69	30	31
Nonadditive	21	20	33	0	13	0	0	0	0	27
Environmental	17	15	32	40	35	19	66	31	70	42
Common	9	7	29	0	—	9	51	16	55	26
Specific	8	8	3	40	—	10	15	15	15	16
Covariance	0	0	0	0	20	14	13	0	0	0
Total	100	100	100	100	100	100	100	100	100	100
Kinships	7	14	9	4	No formal fitting	11		16		10
Parameters	4	4	4	2		8		9		4
X²/d.f.	2.1	1.4	1.5	0.6		0.9		4.4		1.0

Source: *Goldberger 1979, 330.*

It is noteworthy that a leading American geneticist, Professor Newton Morton, has made a detailed statistical comparison of British kinship correlations (most all of them from Burt's studies) with those of all the parallel studies done by American investigators, and he finds the differences between the two sets of results to be statistically nonsignificant.... Morton writes: "Whatever errors may have crept into his (i.e., Burt's) material, they do not appear to be systematic".... The scientific weight of all the massive and newer evidence and modern quantitative genetic analyses, in numerous studies by independent investigators using somewhat different methods, now far surpass that of Burt's own pioneer research. Yet the evidence *sans* Burt leads *in toto* to essentially the same general conclusions:... in accounting for individual differences in IQ, genetic factors considerably outweigh the existing environmental influences. [*The Times,* 9 December 1976]

But, despite Eysenck's claims, Goldberger (1979) shows, in Table 4.6, that when Burt's "data" are discarded, a picture quite different from the one portrayed by Eysenck emerges. Indeed, the picture is quite blurred (Goldberger 1979). First, he notes that in the data sets presented in Table 4.5 "the entry for a kinship is not a correlation observed in a single sample, but rather an average across several samples taken at various times and places. For example, in Column 3 the entry of 0.38 for adoptive siblings is actually an average of the figures found in seven adoption studies, the original correlations having ranged from 0.06 to 0.65" (Goldberger 1979, 333). We have seen also in Table 4.4 that the family resemblance data reviewed by Bouchard and McGue (1981) had similar evidence for considerable within-category heterogeneity. Given this heterogeneity, the clarity of any of the models' estimates becomes quite dim. Indeed, Goldberger (1979, 336) summarizes the usefulness of the modeling attempts represented in Tables 4.5 and 4.6 by indicating that

> enough of the structure has been exposed that we can assess the plausibility of the models. Ignorance of genetics need not deter us, because the models involve as much social science theorizing as genetic theorizing. How

marriages take place, how adoption agencies operate, how parents raise their children, how brothers and sisters educate one another—all those processes are reflected in the biometrical-genetic models.

I call attention to two such pieces of theorizing that are incorporated in the Birmingham and Honolulu models. (1) Identical twins share just as much IQ-relevant experience as ordinary siblings do, no more. That happens despite the fact that identical twins are of the same age and sex, while ordinary siblings may differ in age and sex. (2) Adoption agencies place children in families randomly drawn from the population at large. That happens even though every adoption study shows that adoptive parents rank high on virtually every socioeconomic and psychological measure.

If those pieces of theorizing are unbelievable, then the parameter estimates provided by Birmingham and Honolulu (and by me in column (8) of Table 4.6) should not be believed either. For the assumptions are critical rather than incidental ones. If ordinary siblings share less IQ-relevant experience than identical twins do, then the difference between the IQ correlations for those two kinships is partly attributable to environment. If adoptive families span a reduced range of environments, then the IQ correlations among adoptive kin understate the common environment variance in the population at large. Both pieces of theorizing tilt the estimated balance from environment to genes. To explain the persistent use of such assumptions, we need only recognize that without them the models would be indeterminate. If less restrictive, and hence more plausible, specifications were made, the number of unknown parameters would approach and soon exceed the number of observations. Implausible assumptions are needed to identify the parameters and produce the estimates, and thus to keep the model-fitters happy. But estimates produced in that manner do not merit the attention of the rest of us.

CONCLUSIONS

Heritability research, particularly as it has been done in relation to IQ, has involved advancement of fallacious arguments and misapplication of data (see Layzer 1974). At best, heritability is a concept of extremely narrow utility. If misunderstood and misapplied, it leads to the assumption that high heritability means developmental fixity— that the expression of a highly heritable trait cannot be altered through environmental changes—that the trait is simply innate and unavailable to environmental influence (Lehrman 1970). However, in this and the previous chapter we have indicated that no psychological trait is preorganized in the genes and unavailable to environmental influence. Our assessment of the implications of the question "how?" makes such an assertion simply implausible.

Thus any alleged genetic difference (or "inferiority") of black Americans based on the high heritability of intelligence would seem to be an attribution built on a misunderstanding of concepts basic to an appropriate conceptualization of the nature-nurture controversy. An appreciation of the interactive interrelation of heredity and environment, of the parameters of how they in fact interact, of the norm-of-reaction concept, and of the meaning, implications, and limitations of the concept of heritability should lead us to an important conclusion. *All our considerations strongly suggest that the genetic-differences hypothesis of racial differences in IQ makes little compelling scientific sense.* The heritability (in the sense of developmental fixity) of intelligence, or of any other psychological trait for that matter, must be recognized as a psychological unreality. Such terms have, at best, so little scientific utility as to make them functionally worthless (see Layzer 1974).

Hence, in his review of the scientific and mathematical status and bases of the calculation of heritability analyses of IQ, Layzer (1974) argues that there are significant cultural differences between blacks and whites in today's society that speak *against* any attempt to evaluate race differences in IQ scores (even with so-called culture-free tests). He states:

> The definition of IQ has no theoretical context or substratum. Tests of IQ measure what they measure. They are precisely analogous to physical readings made with a black box—a

device whose internal working is unknown. Because we do not know what an IQ test or a black box is supposed to measure or how it works, we cannot know to what extent measurements carried out on different subjects are comparable or to what extent they are influenced by extraneous factors. Thus IQ scores contain uncontrollable, systematic errors of unknown magnitude.

> This helps to explain why different investigators frequently report such widely differing estimates of the same IQ correlation. For example, reported estimates of the parent-child correlation range from .2 to .8, while estimates of the correlation between same-sex dizygotic twins range from .4 to .9 (Erlenmeyer-Kimling and Jarvik, 1963). According to Jensen (1973) there are no objective criteria (other than sample size) for weighting discrepant estimates of the same correlations.

> Because the definition of IQ is purely instrumental, it fails to confer the most essential attribute of a scientific measurement—objectivity. To measure a subject's Stanford-Binet IQ, one must administer a specific test in a specific way under specific conditions. By contrast, a well-equipped physics laboratory does not need to have replicas of the standard meter and the standard kilogram to measure length and mass, and the physicist or biologist is free to devise his own techniques for measuring such quantities. Systematic discrepancies between measurements of the same quantity are never ignored in the physical and biological sciences, because they signal the presence of unsuspected systematic errors or of defects in the theory underlying the measurements.

> IQ scores also differ from conventional measurements in that they have no strict quantitative meaning. The IQ is an index of rank order on a standard test, expressed according to a convenient but essentially arbitrary convention (Stevens, 1946). In effect, the intervals of the IQ scale are chosen in such a way as to make the frequency distribution of test scores in a reference population approximately normal, but other methods of defining the scale could claim equal prior justification.

> These considerations show that IQ scores are not phenotypic measurements in the usual sense. (Layzer 1974, 1262)

These general problems with IQ tests complicate the issues involved in making any valid statements about the genetic basis of IQ differences between the races. Given, then, the additional problems with the calculation of heritability estimates that we have reviewed, it is clear why Layzer believes that "the only data that might yield meaningful estimates of narrow heritability are phenotypic correlations between half-sibs reared in statistically independent environments. No useful data of this kind are available" (Layzer 1974, 1265). It is possible to conclude:

> Under prevailing social conditions, no valid inferences can be drawn from IQ data concerning systematic genetic differences among races or socioeconomic groups. Research along present lines directed toward this end—whatever its ethical status—is scientically worthless.
>
> Since there are no suitable data for estimating the narrow heritability of IQ, it seems pointless to speculate about the prospects for a hereditary meritocracy based on IQ. (Layzer 1974, 1266)

Both Hirsch (1981), and Feldman and Lewontin (1975) reach congruent conclusions. Hirsch (1981, 33) notes:

> Failure conceptually to appreciate and to integrate three fundamentals of biology—individuality, interaction and norm of reaction throughout ontogeny—underlies the confusion. Individuality is a consequence of the fact that members of diploid, bisexual, cross-fertilizing species are genotypically unique. Moreover, although it is a platitude to say that heredity and environment *interact* to produce the phenotype, it is that interaction of unique genotypes with environments which thwarts a simple systems approach.... Not only do genotypes differ in response to a common environment, but one genotype varies in response to different environments. The latter property is called norm of reaction. Interaction and norm of reaction describe aspects of the complex genotype-phenotype relationship. The latter focuses on the developmental outcomes of a single genotype replicated in different environments. The former includes the latter and considers at one time many genotypes and many environments. For an array of genotypes replicated in various sets of environmental conditions, it calls attention to how, out of the variety of possible distributions of phenotypic outcomes, the particular

one obtained will depend on which genotype develops under which conditions.

The key to "establishing the relative roles of heredity and environment" has been believed erroneously to be the heritability estimate. But heritability estimates cannot be made for human intelligence measurements, because the heritability coefficient is undefined in the presence of either correlation or interaction between genotype and environment, both of which occur for human intelligence. When correlation exists, either (1) between genetic and environmental contributions to trait expression, or (2) between environmental contributions to trait expression in both members of a parent-child or sib pair, heritability is not defined. Furthermore, when heritability can be defined, for example in well-controlled plant and animal breeding experiments, it has *no* relevance to measured differences in averaging values of trait expression between different populations: heritability estimates throw no light upon intergroup comparisons! Also, heritability estimates provide no information about ontogeny and are thus irrelevant to the formulation of public policy on education and social conditions.

None of the statements about proportional contributions of heredity and environment to the determination of level of "intelligence" or of many other human traits can be either substantiated or disproven by any conceivable observations.

Finally, Feldman and Lewontin (1975, 1167–68) indicate:

> The problem we have been examining is the degree to which statistical structures can reveal the underlying biological structure of causation in problems of human quantitative genetics. We must distinguish those problems which are by their nature numerical and statistical from those in which numerical manipulation is a mere methodology. Thus, the breeding structure of human populations, the intensities of natural selection, the correlations between mates, the correlations between genotypes and environments, are all by their nature statistical constructs and can be described and studied, in the end, only by statistical techniques. It is the numbers themselves that are the proper objects of study. It is the numbers themselves that we need for understanding and prediction.
>
> Conversely, relations between genotype, en-

vironment, and phenotype are at base mechanical questions of enzyme activity, protein synthesis, developmental movements, and paths of nerve conduction. We wish, both for the sake of understanding and prediction, to draw up the blueprints of this machinery and make tables of its operating characteristics with different inputs and in different milieus. For these problems, statistical descriptions, especially one-dimensional descriptions like heritability, can only be poor and, worse, misleading substitutes for pictures of the machinery. There is a vast loss of information in going from a complex machine to a few descriptive parameters. Therefore, there is immense indeterminancy in trying to infer the structure of the machine from those few descriptive variables, themselves subject to error. It is rather like trying to infer the structure of a clock by listening to it tick and watching the hands. At present, no statistical methodology exists that will enable us to predict the range of phenotypic possibilities that are inherent in any genotype, nor can any technique of statistical estimation provide a convincing argument for a genetic mechanism more complicated than one or two Mendelian loci with low and constant penetrance. Certainly the simple estimate of heritability, either in the broad or narrow sense, but most especially in the broad sense, is nearly equivalent to no information at all for any serious problem of human genetics.

It is perhaps appropriate to end our presentation of the controversy over the nature and nurture of intelligence with the summary statement about this topic offered by Hirsch (1970), since his ideas have been quite important in the clarification of the issues:

> The relationship between heredity and behavior has turned out to be one of neither isomorphism nor independence. Isomorphism might justify an approach like naive reductionism, independence a naive behaviorism. Neither one turns out to be adequate. I believe that in order to study behavior, we must understand genetics quite thoroughly. Then, and only then, can we as psychologists forget about it intelligently. (1970, 81)

In this and the previous chapter we have defined our terms, and in so doing we have been introduced to the problems involved in appropriately conceptualizing the nature-nurture issue. In the next chapter we will see how the general considerations dealt with in Chapters 3 and 4 will allow us to deal with a specific theoretical formulation of psychological development. This formulation takes a probabilistic-epigenetic view of psychological development. As we shall see, the person providing the seminal impetus to the ideas to be expressed in the following chapter is T. C. Schneirla. Thus we will interrelate the issues involved in the nature-nurture controversy discussed in this and the previous chapter with the specific issues raised in Schneirla's interactionist theory.

5 | *The Nature-Nurture Controversy: Dynamic Interactional Perspectives*

In Chapter 3 I argued that the most fundamental issues in the study of human development pertain to the nature-nurture controversy (Lerner 1976, 1978; Overton 1973)—that is, to an inquiry into the source of development. I noted that there is a relationship between a theorist's stance on these issues and his or her response to questions such as, What is development? and What are the processes by which development occurs? Historically, there have been instances in which theorists have emphasized the independent, isolated action of either hereditary mechanisms (e.g., Sheldon 1940, 1942) or environmental mechanisms (e.g., Skinner 1938; Watson 1913, 1918) for some selected subset of an organism's behavioral repertoire (cf. Gould 1981). However, due to the impact of essays by Anastasi (1958), Lehrman (1953), and Schneirla (1956, 1957), today most developmentalists acknowledge that processes or variables from both nature and nurture sources contribute to development.

Nevertheless, I indicated that differences of opinion exist about modes of contribution among variables derived from each of these sources; about the meaning and constitution of the contributing sources; and about how these differences are related to the alterna-

tive philosophical models to which developmental psychologists may be committed. Indeed, as we shall now see, although the concept of interaction is invoked by many theorists to indicate how variables providing the source of development relate to each other, the concept is itself highly controversial. How one defines the concept depends, too, on one's philosophical and concomitant theoretical orientation.

THE CONCEPT OF INTERACTION

Let us consider first the concept of interaction in the mechanistic-behavioral view. Psychologists such as Bijou (1976), for example, argue that a person's development derives from an interaction between past reinforcement history and the current reinforcement context. Since the organism is the "host" (Baer 1976), or locus, of the past reinforcement history, Bijou construes his concept of interaction as pertaining to *organism*-environment relations. Nevertheless, Bijou's (1976) view is that the organism is a largely passive component in the swirl of past and present reinforcements surrounding it. The organism plays no primary role in shaping the context that influences it. Since the entities that interact (past and present stimulus-contingencies) are not qualitatively distinct, and because of the restricted role delegated to the organism in this form of organism-environment interaction, some reviewers (Lerner 1978, 1985; Overton 1973) have characterized the type of interaction illustrated by Bijou's (1976) position as a *weak* interaction.

The type of interaction found in many organismic stage theories may, as with the mechanistic-behavioristic tradition, be characterized as being of the weak variety. This is somewhat ironic because organismic developmental theory has been termed a *strong* developmental position (Overton and Reese 1973; Reese and Overton 1970). Here, although variables associated with both organism and context are said to be involved in the interactions associated with developmental (i.e., stage) progression, environmental (contextual) variables are only seen to facilitate or inhibit trajectories of primarily intrinsic (i.e., maturational) origin (Emmerich 1968); contextual variables cannot alter the direction, sequence, or quality of developmental change.

Moreover, in the predetermined epigenetic version of the organismic perspective, the maturational timetable (Erikson 1959) or other biological phenomena (Freud 1954), which are believed to control the nature of developmental progressions, are all construed to be impervious to environmental influence—insofar as their impact on the quality of development is concerned. The organism is no more an influence on such biological variables than it is a determinant of the array of genes it receives at its conception. Thus, although the prime locus of developmental change lies within the organism, the organism is no more of an active agent in the interaction of this internal basis of development with the external environment than it is in mechanistic-behavioral theories such as those of Bijou (1976; Bijou and Baer 1961).

For reasons of intellectual completeness, it may be noted that another concept of interaction is found in the developmental literature; it can be labeled as *moderate* (Lerner and Spanier 1978, 1980). Here both organism and environment are conceptually equally weighted as influences on developmental outcomes. But the nature of these sources' relation while interacting may be conceptualized as analogous to the interaction term in the analysis of variance. Although organism-associated and environment-associated variables combine (in an additive manner, one describable by the general linear model) to influence developmental outcomes, each is construed to exist independent of (uninfluenced by) the other before (and presumably after) their interaction, and to be unchanged by the other during their interaction.

The concept of moderate interaction is not typically articulated as a feature of a particular theory of human development. Instead, it is found in the perspective to studying behavior that Gollin (1965) labeled the child psychology approach. This perspective is characterized by an ahistorical subjects × tasks approach to the analysis of behavior, and it is contrasted by Gollin (1965) with the historical subjects × tasks-levels approach characteristic of what he terms the child development perspective. In the child psychology approach the goal is to determine the empirical contribution to variation in a dependent variable of organism-related variables (often vaguely represented by using age or sex as a factor), and environment-related variables (typically represented operationally by a specific task or manipulation), separately and in additive combination (i.e., "interactively") with organism-related variables. In other words, the concept of moderate interaction is typically expressed as a methodological component of what is also termed the experimental child psychology approach (Reese and Lipsitt 1970). It views the treatment of subject and task, or of organism and environment (or of heredity and environment, in the analogous analysis of variance approach to determining heritability) as necessarily separate, independent factors whose interaction effect or contribution is a linear, additive one. The interaction effect itself may combine two sources in a nonlinear, multiplicative way. That effect, however, adds linearly to the total variability.

Finally, a *strong* concept of organism-environment interaction (Lerner and Spanier 1978, 1980; Overton 1973), or a concept of dynamic interaction (Lerner 1978, 1979), is associated with a developmental contextual perspective. As noted in our previous discussion of probabilistic epigenesis, this concept stresses that organism and context are always embedded each in the other (Lerner, Hultsch, and Dixon 1983); that the context is composed of multiple levels of being, with variables associated with each level changing interdependently across time (i.e., historically); and that because organisms influence the context that influences them, they are thus efficacious in playing an active role in their own development (Lerner and Busch-Rossnagel 1981).

Moreover, because of the mutual embeddedness of organism and context, a given organismic attribute will have different implications for developmental outcomes under different contextual conditions; this is so because the organism attribute is given its functional meaning only by virtue of its relation to a specific context. If the context changes, as it may over time, then the same organism attribute will have a different import for development. In turn, the same contextual condition will lead to alternative developments in that different organisms interact with it. To state this position in other, somewhat stronger terms, a given organismic attribute only has meaning for psychological development by virtue of its timing of interaction; that is, its relation to a particular set of time-bound contextual conditions. In turn, the import of any set of contextual conditions for psychosocial behavior and development can only be understood by specifying the context's relations to the specific developmental features of the organisms within it. This central role for the timing of

organism-context interactions in the determination of the nature and outcomes of development is, of course, the probabilistic component of probabilistic epigenesis (Gottlieb 1970; Scarr 1982; Scarr and McCartney, 1983).

To illustrate the nature of organism-context relations described in this view with an example to be returned to in Chapter 10, consider the implications of a child's temperamental individuality for his or her personality development. It may be argued that the significance of this individuality lies not in any organismic association between particular features of temperament (e.g., high activity level or low regularity or rhythmicity of biological functions) and specific aspects of personality (e.g., adjustment); instead, what temperament implies for personality development has been suggested (for example, in Chapter 2) to lie in the level of congruence, match, or "goodness of fit" (Lerner and Lerner 1983) between a particular aspect of temperament and the demands or presses of the psychosocial and physical context. For instance, some parents may desire or demand highly regular eating, sleeping, and toileting behaviors from their children, while for other parents such biological rhythmicity may be irrelevant (see Super and Harkness 1981). A child who is biologically arrhythmic would not match the former type of demands, and as such the import of this feature of his or her temperament might be to promote poor parent-child relations; a consequence of a history of such relations might be poor adjustment.

Three features of this illustration are important to note here: (1) the import of the person's organismic characteristics for his or her development is explained by reference to the *relation* between the organismic characteristics and the characteristics of the context; (2) therefore the presses and demands of the organism's context must be understood to be part of the explanation of individual development, and it should be emphasized that such demands vary across societies, cultures, and history (Lerner and Lerner 1983; Super and Harkness 1981);

thus, the multilevel influences on development—the person, the immediate context, and the broader societal, cultural, and historical settings—are apparent (cf. Bronfenbrenner 1977, 1979); (3) and finally, despite the importance of the context, it is the organism's characteristics—in providing a fit or a lack thereof—that establish the adaptive, maladaptive, or neutral link between organism and setting. Thus any contextual-*developmental* theory, in attempting to understand the possibilities for change provided by the context (Lerner 1984, 1985), must not ignore the structural and functional nature and characteristics of the organism. As has been noted in previous chapters and as will be stressed again below, this point has been emphasized by theorists forwarding "probabilistic epigenetic organismic" ideas of development (e.g., Gottlieb 1970, 1976a, 1976b; Lerner 1976, 1978, 1979, 1980, 1982, 1984; Schneirla 1957).

In short, several developmental psychologists have maintained that, as a consequence of person-context interdependency, a potential for plasticity exists across the life-span: That is, if intraindividual development is a synthesis of intraorganism and contextual variables, and if the context does and/or can be made to change, then the person's developmental trajectory can, at least in part, be altered. It follows that constraints on development—for example those imposed by genes or early experience—are not so great as advocates of noncontextual orientations have previously argued (Brim and Kagan 1980; Lerner 1984).

In contemporary developmental psychology there are several perspectives that are consistent with the probabilistic-epigenetic conceptions associated with a developmental-contextual model. For instance, in Chapter 1 we described Bronfenbrenner's ecological-developmental perspective and introduced the life-span developmental perspective (Baltes and Reese 1984; Baltes, Reese, and Lipsitt 1980). In their consistency with the ideas found in probabilistic epigenesis, these positions are compatible with the view that nature and nurture, organism and

context, heredity and environment, relate to each other in dynamically interactive manners; that is, the variables involved in development interact in a manner depicted in a developmental contextual model.

In the remainder of this chapter we shall explore in some detail the character, bases, and implications of three interrelated perspectives about development that are consistent with the dynamic interactionism found in the developmental contextual, or probabilistic-epigenetic, model. First, we will elaborate on our brief introduction of the life-span developmental perspective. The propositions and implications of this perspective will lead to a discussion of the theory and research of T. C. Schneirla and his students and associates. Schneirla's ideas were seminal in providing a basis for probabilistic-epigenetic thinking (Gottlieb 1970), and his work provides one systematic body of knowledge lending substantive illustration to many of the key features of the life-span perspective. Schneirla's ideas also provide a useful framework for deriving a model of human development consistent with a life-span perspective. The details and implications of such a dynamically interactive model—one reciprocally linking individual development and the social context of development—will be presented as a last major section of this chapter.

THE LIFE-SPAN DEVELOPMENTAL PERSPECTIVE

The point of view labeled life-span developmental psychology or the life-span view of human development (Baltes 1979a; Baltes and Reese, 1984; Baltes, Reese, and Lipsitt 1980) has become crystallized as a set of interrelated ideas about the nature of human development and change. In their combination, these ideas present a set of implications for theory building, for methodology, and for scientific collaboration across disciplinary boundaries. This life-span perspective has perhaps two key propositions or assumptions, which have been labeled *embeddedness* (Lerner, Skinner, and Sorell 1980) and *dynamic interaction* (Lerner 1978, 1979, 1984). From these propositions an interrelated set of implications derive, and these propositions and implications constitute the key concepts in current life-span thinking.

Embeddedness and Dynamic Interactionism

The idea of embeddedness is that the key phenomena of human life exist at multiple levels of analysis (e.g., the inner-biological, individual-psychological, dyadic, social-network, community, societal, cultural, outer-physical-ecological, and historical). At any one point in time variables and processes from any and all of these multiple levels may contribute to human functioning. However, the reason it is important to have a perspective about human development that is sensitive to the influences of these multiple levels is that the levels do not function in parallel—as independent domains. Rather, the variables and processes at one level influence and are influenced by the variables and processes at the other levels. That is, there is a dynamic interaction among levels of analysis: Each level may be a product and a producer of the functioning and changes at all other levels. It may be seen that this idea is a key component of the probabilistic-epigenetic, or developmental contextual, view of development we have discussed (Gottlieb 1970, 1976a, 1976b; Lerner 1978, 1980, 1984; Scarr 1982).

How can the dynamic interaction between person and environment emphasized in the life-span perspective be explained? Baltes, Reese, and Lipsitt (1980) specify three major influence patterns that affect this relationship: (1) normative, age-graded influences; (2) normative, history-graded influences, and (3) nonnormative, life-event influences. *Normative, age-graded influences* consist of biological and environmental determinants that are correlated with chronological age. They are normative to the extent that their timing, duration, and clustering are similar for many individuals. Examples include

maturational events (changes in height, endocrine system function, and central nervous system function) and socialization events (marriage, childbirth, and retirement). *Normative, history-graded influences* consist of biological and environmental determinants that are correlated with historical time. They are normative to the extent that they are experienced by most members of a cohort. In this sense they tend to define the developmental context of a given cohort. Examples include historic events (wars, epidemics, and periods of economic depression or prosperity) and sociocultural evolution (changes in sex-role expectations, the educational system, and child-rearing practices). Both age-graded and history-graded influences *covary* (change together) with time. *Nonnormative, life-event influences*—the third system—are not directly indexed by time since they do not occur for all people, or even for most people. In addition, when nonnormative influences do occur, they are likely to differ significantly in terms of their clustering, timing, and duration. Examples of nonnormative events include such items as illness, divorce, promotion, death of a spouse, and so on.

Thus variables from several sources, or dimensions, influence development. As such, life-span developmentalists stress that human development is *multidimensional* in character. In other words, variables from many dimensions are involved in developmental change. As I have emphasized, in the life-span perspective the relationships among these influence sources—normative, age-graded; normative, history-graded; and nonnormative, life-event—are seen as *dynamic,* that is, *reciprocal.* They may continually change, and each influence has an effect on the other and, in turn, is affected by it.

Baltes, Reese, and Lipsitt (1980) have speculated that these three sources of influence exhibit different profiles over the life cycle. Normative, age-graded influences are postulated to be particularly significant in childhood and again in old age, while normative, history-graded influences are thought to be more important in adolescence and the years immediately following it; this is thought to reflect the importance of the sociocultural context as the individual begins adult life. Finally, nonnormative, life-event influences are postulated to be particularly significant during middle adulthood and old age, promoting increasing divergence as individuals experience unique life events. Such a perspective is consonant with a concept of multidirectional development across the life span.

In sum, because of a superordinate consistency with a developmental contextual model, the ideas associated with the life-span perspective suggest that dynamic interactions among multiple, embedded levels of analysis provide bases for human development. However, the key propositions associated with a life-span perspective may be discussed not only insofar as they are associated with a developmental contextual model; they may also be discussed in regard to a set of interrelated implications derived from them.

Implications of the Propositions of a Life-Span Perspective

The import of the two key assumptions of the life-span perspective are, first, that individual developmental phenomena occur in the context of the developmental and non-developmental change phenomena of other levels of analysis; and, second, that developments and/or changes on one level influence and are influenced by developments and/or changes at these other levels. There are at least three major implications of the ideas of embeddedness and dynamic interactionism.

The Potential for Plasticity
The first implication is the one perhaps most clearly involved in our preceding discussion. The idea that changes at one level are reciprocally related to changes at other levels suggests that there is always some possibility for altering the status of a variable or process at any given level of analysis. Simply put, the character of the interaction

among levels of analysis means that there is a potential to change the functioning of any target level (or target variable) and indeed of the system of interlevel relations itself. In short, there is a potential for plasticity within any level of analysis and across the system as a whole.

However, we must emphasize that this potential for plasticity is not construed by life-span developmentalists to mean that there are no limits or constraints on change. For instance, by virtue of its structural organization a system delimits the range of changes it may undergo (Brent 1984), and such a structural constraint holds for any level of analysis. The prior developmental organization of a system constrains the potential of a later influence to lead as easily to a change in the system as would have been the case if that same influence had acted earlier in development (Lerner 1978, 1979; Schneirla 1957).

In fact, the possibility that developmental and nondevelopmental phenomena at one point in life may influence functioning at later points is explicitly recognized by life-span developmentalists in the concept of *developmental embeddedness* (Park, personal communication, December 1982). This concept indicates that there may be links among periods of life; that for any target period, prior developmental events may provide causal antecedents; and that functioning in the target period in turn may have consequences for later developmental periods. Thus, as a consequence of the potential for developmental embeddedness, life-span developmentalists emphasize that one must consider not only the changes across life but the constancies as well. Indeed, a key issue within the life-span perspective is to understand the relation between processes that serve to promote constancy and those that serve to promote change (e.g., see Lerner 1976, 1984). That is—consistent with what Werner (1957) termed the orthogenetic principle—life-span development is concerned with understanding the developmental syntheses between continuous and discontinuous processes (Lerner 1978, 1979).

Nevertheless, despite the recognition of

the limits and constraints on change, and the emphasis on the concept of developmental embeddedness, to life-span developmentalists the notion that there is a potential for plasticity means that the system is never necessarily completely limited or constrained (Brim and Kagan 1980), and that as a consequence of the dynamic interaction among multiple levels of analysis means may be found to reorganize or restructure a system—even in advanced periods of that system's development (Baltes and Baltes 1980; Baltes, Reese, and Lipsitt 1980; Greenough and Green 1981). Thus, in sum, many life-span developmentalists might agree with the geneticist R. C. Lewontin's (1981) views about the issue of constraints:

It is trivially true that material conditions of one level constrain organization at higher levels *in principle*. But that is not the same as saying that such constraints are quantitatively nontrivial. Although every object in the universe has a gravitational interaction with every other object, no matter how distant, I do not, in fact, need to adjust my body's motion to the movement of individuals in the next room. The question is not whether the nature of the human genotype is relevant to social organization, but whether the former constrains the latter in a nontrivial way, or whether the two levels are *effectively* decoupled. It is the claim of vulgar sociobiology that some kinds of human social organization are either impossible, or that they can be maintained only at the expense of constant psychic and political stress, which will inevitably lead to undesirable side effects because the nature of the human genome dictates a "natural" social organization. Appeals to abstract dependencies (in principle) of one level or another do not speak to the concrete issue of whether society is genetically constrained in an important way. ... in fact, constraints at one level may be destroyed by higher level activity. No humans can fly by flapping their arms because of anatomical and physiological constraints that reflect the human genome. But humans do fly, by using machines that are the product of social organization and that could not exist without very complex social interaction and evolution. As another example, the memory capacity of a single individual is limited, but social organization, through written records and the complex institutions associated with them, makes all knowledge recoverable for each individual. Far from being constrained by lower-level limitations, culture transcends them and feeds back to lower levels to relieve the constraints. Social organization, and human culture in particular, are best understood as negating constraints rather than being limited by them. (Lewontin 1981, 244)

The Potential for Intervention

Given the plasticity of developmental processes, a second implication of the assumptions of a life-span perspective that we may note here is that there is a potential for intervention. Given the potential for plasticity, it follows that means may be designed to *intervene*, that is, to prevent, ameliorate, or enhance undesired or nonvalued developments or behavior (cf. Baltes and Danish 1980). Moreover, the multilevel embeddedness of any target of intervention, and the dynamically interactive character of change, means that one may approach the same intervention target from any one of several levels of analysis; this possibility underscores the use of a multidisciplinary approach to intervention and, of course, to the knowledge base from which interventions should derive.

In addition, the idea of developmental embeddedness suggests that one may take a historical approach to intervention and, for instance, devise long-term preventive strategies (Lerner and Ryff 1978). However, individual ontogeny is not the only aspect of history that may be considered here. Life-span developmentalists' awareness of the features of intergenerational transmission (e.g., see Bengtson and Troll 1978) leads them to be sensitive to the possibility that one may intervene with future parents to prevent undesired outcomes in yet-to-be-conceived offspring. An example here is the possibility of changing the type of birth-control precautions of sexually active young adolescents in order to prevent the conception and birth of a child who will be at risk for several health problems as a consequence of being born to a young adolescent mother.

Finally, in regard to the implications of

the life-span perspective for intervention, let me stress that the potential for plasticity across life does *not* mean one should ignore (or not invest in treating) problems in early life. In fact, just the opposite view is promoted. The life-span perspective indicates that while plasticity may exist across life, there are always constraints on change, and plasticity is not equipotential across life; that is, the notion of plasticity for which there is most evidence is one of a ubiquitous but decreasingly narrower range of structures and functions within which the potential for plasticity may be actualized (cf. Baltes and Baltes 1980; Clarke and Clarke 1976; Greenough and Green 1981; Lerner 1984). Thus, it may be easier, more efficient, and less costly to intervene earlier in life; that is, when the system is being organized and therefore when there may be fewer constraints on the possible effects of a given intervention than if the system had progressed to a more advanced point. However, if such early intervention is not possible the implication of the life-span perspective is that all is not lost. There may still be means, albeit more difficult and/or more costly ones, to effect a desired change.

The Person as a Producer
of His or Her Own Development

I have noted that the idea of dynamic interaction suggests that any level of analysis is an influence on the other levels of analysis that influence it, and that at the level of individual psychological development this means that a person may affect the context that affects him or her. By influencing the context that influences him or her, the person provides feedback to himself or herself; in other words, the individual is a producer of his or her own development (Lerner 1982; Lerner and Busch-Rossnagel 1981).

The individual may act as a producer of his or her own development as a consequence of constituting a distinct stimulus to others (e.g., through characteristics of physical and/or behavioral individuality); the person may produce his or her own develop-

ment as a consequence of his or her capabilities as a processor of the world (e.g., in regard to cognitive structure and mode of emotional reactivity); and last, the person may also produce his or her own development as a consequence of his or her active behavioral agency (Bakan 1966; Block 1973). Indeed, the individual's developing competency to behaviorally shape and/or select his or her contexts is the instance of ultimately the most flexible means by which the person may act as a producer of his or her own development (Kendall, Lerner, and Craighead 1984; Mischel 1977; Snyder 1981). Thus the life-span emphasis on the individual as a producer of his or her own development leads to a focus on processes of self-regulation, control, and self-efficacy.

Conclusions

It will be useful to return to a discussion of these three ways in which people may act as producers of their own development when we turn to a presentation of ontogenetic bases of individual–social context relations. Here, however, it is important to note that my central point is that the dynamic interactions stressed in the life-span view of human development emphasize the inevitable, reciprocally acting embeddedness of the development of one person in the development of others. For example, from this view children raise parents as much as parents raise children. Several lines of evidence from evolutionary biology and anthropology converge to suggest that the reciprocal link between person and social context has been a key feature of human evolution.

Because this evidence not only provides support for the probabilistic-epigenetic model of human development but also because its presentation underscores the utility of many of the ideas found in the life-span perspective, I will consider these sources of information in some detail. This presentation will draw heavily on the contributions of Stephen Jay Gould, most particularly those in his book *Ontogeny and Phylogeny* (1977), and will allow me to indicate how the processes that provided the evolutionary bases of human plasticity also involved the creation of humans as social organisms, and linked the developing person reciprocally to his or her caregivers.

EVOLUTIONARY BASES OF RECIPROCAL PERSON–SOCIAL CONTEXT RELATIONS

As evident from the title of his book, Gould's (1977) interest is in detailing the relation between ontogeny and phylogeny. He contends "[t]hat some relationship exists cannot be denied. Evolutionary changes must be expressed in ontogeny, and phyletic information must therefore reside in the development of individuals" (p. 2). However, this point in itself is obvious and unenlightening for Gould. What makes the study of the relation between ontogeny and phylogeny interesting and important is that there are "*changes* in *developmental timing* that produce *parallels* between the stages of ontogeny and phylogeny" (p. 2).

However, to discuss the relation between ontogeny and phylogeny may raise the hackles (read: "Haeckels") of many scientists. This may be especially true for those trained in developmental psychology, where—as discussed in Chapter 1—the recapitulationist ideas of Haeckel (e.g., 1868), especially as they were adopted by G. S. Hall (1904), have long been in disfavor. To recall our earlier discussion, we may note that in simplified form Haeckel's theory was one of *recapitulation,* by which he meant that the mechanism of evolution was *a change in the timing of developmental events such that there occurred a universal acceleration of development that pushed ancestral forms into the juvenile stages of descendants.* For example, Haeckel (1868) interpreted the gill slits of human embryos as characteristics of ancestral adult fishes that had been compressed into the early stages of human ontogeny through a universal mechanism of accelera-

tion of developmental rates in evolving lines.

It is unfortunate for the scientific study of links between ontogeny and phylogeny that people have come to equate Haeckel's recapitulation idea with all potential types and directions of evolutionary change in the timing of developmental events. This is because there is an alternative to the changes in timing specified by recapitulation, and it provides an evolutionary basis for viewing person–social context relations in a reciprocal manner. To Gould, this alternative is the key to human evolution and to human plasticity. To understand this alternative we need to introduce three interrelated terms: heterochrony, neoteny, and paedomorphosis.

According to Gould, evolution occurs when ontogeny is altered in one of two ways. First, evolution occurs when new characteristics are introduced, at any stage of development, which then have varying influences on later developmental stages. The second way in which evolution occurs is when characteristics that are already present undergo changes in developmental timing. This second means by which phyletic change occurs is termed *heterochrony*. Specifically, heterochrony is changes in the relative time of appearance and rate of development of characters already present in ancestors.

In human evolution, a specific type of heterochrony has been predominant; as a consequence, the changes that were associated with human plasticity occurred. The type of heterochrony that has characterized human evolution is *neoteny,* which is a slowing down, a retardation, of development of selected somatic organs and parts. Heterochronic changes are regulatory effects; that is, they constitute "a change in rate for features already present" (p. 8). Gould maintains that neoteny has been a—and probably *the*—major determinant of human evolution.

For example, as explained in greater detail below, delayed growth has been found to be important in the evolution of complex and flexible social behavior and, interrelatedly, it has led to an increase in cerebralization by prolonging into later human life the rapid brain-growth characteristics of higher verte-brate fetuses. As such, this general evolu-tionary retardation of human development has resulted in adaptive features of ancestral juveniles being retained. That is, a key char-acteristic of human evolution is *paedomor-phosis,* or phylogenetic change involving retention of ancestral juvenile characters by the adult. In other words:

> Our paedomorphic features are a set of adap-tations coordinated by their common efficient cause of retarded development. We are not neotenous only because we possess an im-pressive set of paedomorphic characters; we are neotenous because these characters de-velop within a matrix of retarded development that coordinates their common appearance in human adults. . . . [and these] temporal delays themselves are the most significant feature of human heterochrony. (Gould 1977, 397, 399)

But what are some of the paedomorphic-neotenous characteristics? How do they pro-vide an evolutionary basis of human plastic-ity and of reciprocal person–social context relations? Gould himself answers these questions, and in so doing indicates that humans' evolving plasticity both enabled and resulted from their embeddedness in a social and cultural context. He notes:

> In asserting the importance of delayed devel-opment . . . I assume that major human adap-tations acted synergistically throughout their gradual development. . . . *The interacting sys-tem of delayed development–upright pos-ture–large brain is such a complex:* delayed development has produced a large brain by prolonging fetal growth rates and has supplied a set of cranial proportions adapted to upright posture. Upright posture freed the hand for tool use and set selection pressures for an ex-panded brain. A large brain may, itself, entail a longer life span. (Gould 1977, 399, italics added)
>
> Human evolution has *emphasized* one fea-ture of . . . common primate heritage—delayed development, particularly as expressed in late instruction and extended childhood. This re-tardation has reacted synergistically with other hallmarks of hominization—with intelli-gence (by enlarging the brain through prolon-

gation of fetal growth tendencies and by pro-viding a longer period of childhood learning) and with socialization (by cementing family units through increased parental care of slowly developing offspring). It is hard to imagine how the distinctive suite of human characters could have emerged outside the context of de-layed development. (Gould 1977, 400)

Thus, in linking neotony with reciprocal relations between brain development and sociocultural functioning, Gould makes an argument of extreme importance for com-parative-developmental and sociocultural-intergenerational analyses of human devel-opment. The role of the former type of analysis is raised in regard to species differ-ences (heterochrony) in the ontogeny of brain organization and their import for levels of plasticity finally attained across life; the role of the latter type of analysis is raised in regard to the role of parent-child relations in promoting the child's development to-ward a final level of functioning character-ized by plasticity. In other portions of the evolutionary biology literature and in the anthropology literature there is support for the link suggested by Gould between plastic brain development and human sociocultural functioning.

Bidirectional Organism-Context Relations in Evolution: Paleoanthropological Perspectives

Several current ideas in anthropology sug-gest that humans have been selected for so-cial dependency. The course and context of evolution was such that it was more adaptive to act in concert with the group than in iso-lation. For example, Masters (1978) notes that early hominids were hunters. These an-cestors evolved from herbivorous primates under the pressure of climatic changes that caused the African forest to be replaced with savanna. Our large brains, he speculates (Masters 1978, 98), may be the (naturally se-lected) *result* of cooperation among early hominids and hence, in an evolutionary sense, a social organ. Indeed, he believes that with such evolution the "central problem" in anthropological analysis—that of the origin of society—may be solved. Washburn (1961) appears to agree. He notes that the relative defenselessness of early man (lack of fighting teeth, nails, or horns), coupled with the dangers of living on the open African savanna, made group living and cooperation *essential for survival* (Hogan, Johnson, and Emler 1978; Washburn 1961).

There is some dispute in anthropological theory as to whether material culture or specific features of social relations—such as intensified parenting, monogamous pair bonding, nuclear family formation, and thus specialized sexual-reproductive behavior—were superordinate in these brain-behavior evolutionary relations. For example, some paleoanthropologists currently believe that there are five characteristics that separate human beings from other hominids—a large neocortex, bipedality, reduced anterior dentation with molar dominance, material culture, and unique sexual and reproductive behavior (e.g., of all primates only the human female's sexual behavior is not confined to the middle of her monthly menstrual cycle; Fisher 1982a). Some paleoanthropologists believe that early human evolution was a direct consequence of brain expansion and material culture. However, Lovejoy (1981), among others (e.g., Johanson and Edey 1981), believes that

> both advanced material culture and the Pleistocene acceleration in brain development are sequelae to an already established hominid character system, which included intensified parenting and social relationships, monogamous pair bonding, specialized sexual-reproductive behavior, and bipedality. (Lovejoy 1981, 348)

Other debates also exist. For instance, the roles that continual sexual receptivity and loss of estrus played in the evolution of human pair bonding are controversial and complex (e.g., Fisher 1982b; Harley 1982; Isaac 1982; Swartz 1982; Washburn 1982).

Such debate, however, exists in the midst of the general consensus indicated above: that the social functioning of hominids (be it interpreted as dyadic, familial, or cultural) was reciprocally related to the evolution of the human brain. Many evolutionary biologists appear to reach a similar conclusion.

For example, summarizing a review of literature pertaining to the character of the environment to which organisms adapt, Lewontin and Levins (1978) stress that reciprocal processes between organism and environment are involved in human evolution; as such this leads to a view that human functioning is one source of its own evolutionary development. Lewontin and Levins (1978, 78) state that

> the activity of the organism sets the stage for its own evolution ... the labor process by which the human ancestors modified natural objects to make them suitable for human use was itself the unique feature of the way of life that directed selection on the hand, larynx, and brain in a positive feedback that transformed the species, its environment, and its mode of interaction with nature.

Moreover, not only does Lovejoy (1981), as well as Fisher (1982a), give a graphic account of the history of the role of hominid social behavior in human evolution, but—in specific support of Gould's (1977) views—they show how the complex social and physical facets of this evolution led to human neoteny. Interestingly, while Fisher and (especially) Lovejoy tend to view the ecological presses that led to the evolution of social behaviors as eventuating in bipedalism and then rapid brain development, they nevertheless both see these links in more of a circular than a linear framework.

For instance, Lovejoy (1981) believes that it is not just that ecological changes led to social relationships, which in turn led to bipedalism and in turn to brain evolution. Instead, social relationships that led to brain evolution were then themselves altered when larger-brained—and more plastic—organisms were involved in them; in turn, new social patterns may have extended humans' adaptational presses and opportunities into other arenas, ones fostering further changes in brain, in social embeddedness, and so forth. Indeed, as Johanson and Edey (1981) describe Lovejoy's position, it is one that requires the examination of

> the mechanism of a complex feedback loop—in which several elements interact for mutual reinforcement. . . . If parental care is a good thing, it will be selected for by the likelihood that the better mothers will be more apt to bring up children, and thus intensify any genetic tendency that exists in the population toward being better mothers. But increased parental care requires other things along with it. It requires a greater IQ on the part of the mother; she cannot increase parental care if she is not intellectually up to it. That means brain development—not only for the mother, but for the infant daughter too, for someday she will become a mother.

> In the case of primate evolution, the feedback is not just a simple A-B stimulus forward and backward between two poles. It is multipoled and circular, with many features to it instead of only two—all of them mutually reinforcing. For example, if an infant is to have a large brain, it must be given time to learn to use that brain before it has to face the world on its own. That means a long childhood. The best way to learn during childhood is to play. That means playmates, which, in turn, means a group social system that provides them. But if one is to function in such a group, one must learn acceptable social behavior. One can learn that properly only if one is intelligent. Therefore social behavior ends up being linked with IQ (a loop back), with extended childhood (another loop), and finally with the energy investment and the parental care system which provide a brain capable of that IQ, and the entire feedback loop is complete.

> All parts of the feedback system are cross-connected. For example: if one is living in a group, the time spent finding food, being aware of predators and finding a mate can all be reduced by the very fact that one is in a group. As a consequence, more time can be spent on parental care (one loop), on play (another) and on social activity (another), all of which enhance intelligence (another) and result ultimately in fewer offspring (still another). The complete loop shows all poles

connected to all others. (Johanson and Edey, 1981, 325–26)

An illustration of this "complete loop," or system of reciprocal influence, is presented in Figure 5.1. This figure illustrates that the foundations of humans' plasticity evolved in a complex system of bidirectional relationships among social, ontogenetic, and neuronal variables.

Conclusions

Our analysis of the links between Gould's ideas pertinent to the role of neotenous heterochrony in the evolution of human plasticity has drawn us into a discussion of the role of reciprocal relations between organisms and their contexts in human evolution. In other words, neoteny provides adaptive advantages for members of both older and younger generations. Considering children first, the neoteny of the human results in the newborn child being perhaps the most dependent organism found among placental mammalian infants (Gould 1977). Moreover, their neoteny means that this dependency is extraordinarily prolonged, and this requires intense parental care for the child for several years. The plasticity of childhood processes, which persists among humans for more than a decade, thus entails a history of necessarily close contact with adults and places an "adaptive premium . . . on learning (as opposed to innate response) . . . unmatched among organisms" (Gould 1977, 401). Gould agrees with de Beer (1959, 930) that for the human:

> Delay in development enabled him to develop a larger and more complex brain, and the prolongation of childhood under conditions of parental care and instruction consequent upon memory-stored and speech-communicated experience, allowed him to benefit from *a more efficient apprenticeship for his conditions of life* [italics added].

In other words, the neoteny of humans, their prolonged childhood dependency on others, and their embeddedness in a social context composed of members of the older genera-

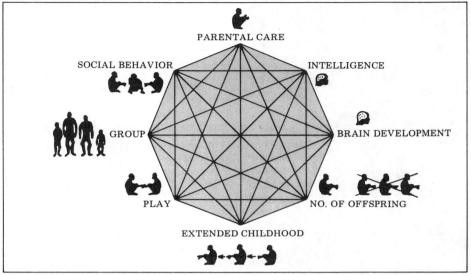

FIGURE 5.1
Components of the system of reciprocal influences that Lovejoy (1981; Johanson & Edey, 1981) believes was involved in the evolution of human neoteny and social embeddedness.
Source: Adapted from Johanson and Edey, 1981, 327.

tion who both protect them and afford them the opportunity to actualize their potential plasticity allows members of a new birth cohort to adapt to the conditions and presses particular to their historical epoch.

Of course, such development in a new cohort has evolutionary significance for members of the older cohort as well. Gould points out that neoteny and the protracted period of dependent childhood may have led to the evolution of features of adult human behavior (e.g., parental behavior). The presence of young and dependent children requires adults to be organized in their adult-adult and adult-child interactions in order to support and guide the children effectively. Furthermore, since the period of childhood dependency is so long, it is likely that human history tended to involve the appearance of later-born children before earlier-born ones achieved full independence (Gould 1977). Gould (1977, 403) sees such an occurrence as facilitating the emergence of pair bonding,

and further sees "in delayed development a primary impetus for the origin of the human family."

In sum, several lines of evidence—from developmental psychology, from evolutionary biology, from sociology, and from anthropology—converge to suggest that children and their parents interact dynamically and, in so doing, promote their own and each other's mutual development. While our discussion in this section has highlighted evolutionary bases of such person-social context reciprocity there are obviously also ontogenetic and contemporary contextual features to this relationship. My views about these features have been influenced by the theory and research of one of the most important comparative psychologists in the history of the discipline, T. C. Schneirla. As such, it is important to present his ideas, and other concepts related to them, in order to understand the basis of the dynamic interactional model of development derived from it.

T. C. Schneirla

THE CONTRIBUTIONS OF T. C. SCHNEIRLA

The work of T. C. Schneirla and his colleagues (e.g., Ethel Tobach, Daniel Lehrman, Herbert G. Birch, and Howard Moltz) represents an attempt to deal systematically with the problems of behavioral development without resorting to facile solutions; that is, Schneirla rejected as naïve and overly simplistic theoretical conceptions that stressed the exclusive role of either nature (hereditarily preformed or predetermined mechanisms) or nurture (shaping of behavior solely by environmental stimulation). Thus, consistent with the arguments presented in Chapter 3, Schneirla focused on an interaction between nature and nurture factors in attempting to find the sources of behavioral development. Because he rejected the notion that development is a simple process, he also rejected the idea that methods used to study this process can be simple. Hence, in commenting on the relation between a nature-based variable, maturation, and a nurture-based variable, experience, he said:

It would seem to be the prevalence of an intimate, dynamic relationship between the factors of maturation and experience that renders analytical study of behavioral ontogeny so difficult. Methods must be devised appropriate to the complexity and subtlety of these processes. . . . In such work, little may be expected from attempts to estimate the specific or the proportionate contributions of the innate vs. the acquired in ontogeny. (Schneirla 1956, 407)

Thus Schneirla presented a theoretical position consistent with what we have said about probabilistic-epigenetic conceptions of development. Let us turn, then, to a more detailed analysis of the ideas of Schneirla and his associates so that we may evaluate the extent to which such conceptions provide a fruitful, integrative framework with which to consider concepts of development.

Structure-Function Relations

One of Schneirla's major concerns as a comparative psychologist was with the relation between an organism's functioning (its behavior, for instance) and the structure underlying the function (e.g., the neural and hormonal processes involved in behavior). This concern arises because in comparative psychology one is interested in learning if the relation between structure and function is similar or different in different species—that is, across phylogenetic levels.

Schneirla (1957) argues that the relationship between structure and function is not always the same for organisms of different phylogenetic levels. The same functions (e.g., learning) may be present in both a rat and a human or in an infant human and an adult human, and this function may play an analogous role for each of these organisms—it may allow the organism to adapt to its environment, to survive. However, the presence of this analogous function in and of itself in no way indicates that the underlying structure of learning is the same for an infant or an adult, for a rat or a person.

Schneirla suggests, on the contrary, that the relation between structure and function is exceedingly complex and—more important here—that it will occur with varying degrees of directness at different phylogenetic and ontogenetic levels. Thus the degree of directness of relation between the two would be different for the rat, ape, horse, and human being.

Schneirla noted (1956) that behavioral patterns often reach similar developments in different phylogenetic levels as a result of parallel adaptive (evolutionary) process. To some, such a similarity indicates equivalent underlying organization, or structure. But this is neither empirically universal nor logically necessary, since the attainment of equivalently adaptive developments says nothing whatsoever about the antecedent developmental processes that brought about these adaptive functions. All mammals learn; but it is not necessarily correct to assert that because both a rat and a human being develop this adaptive function, the laws, or structures, underlying their learning are the same. The developmental processes by which learning comes about may be totally different for these two organisms. That is, antecedent developmental processes may be completely disparate for two different types of organisms, despite the fact that both demonstrate a similarly adaptive function. Thus, as Schneirla points out, these processes "may involve complex anticipations, as in a socialized human being, or may be reflex-like and automatic, as in a lower invertebrate" (1956, 392).

In essence Schneirla is suggesting that the underlying structure even of evolutionarily similar behavioral developments is different for different phylogenetic levels. Although certainly not denying that structure underlies function, he emphasizes rather that one must expect the relationship between structure and function to be differentially direct at different phyletic levels. Each level must be understood in and of itself, because the structure-function relationships of other phylogenetic levels will not hold for another level in question. In other words, the laws of one phyletic level will not apply to another, since the same structure-function relationships do not hold; and therefore one cannot

completely understand one phyletic level by merely reducing it to another. Similarly, as we will see, Schneirla views ontogenetic development in a manner analogous to phylogenetic development. That is, ontogenetic processes proceed through levels just as phylogenetic processes do. Accordingly, structure-function relations between different ontogenetic levels also can be expected to be different.

It should be clear to the reader that Schneirla is taking a now-familiar viewpoint. He is advancing the organismic notion of qualitative discontinuity between levels: Each different phylogenetic level has its own structure-function relationship or, in other words, its own law (Novikoff, 1945a, 1945b). It should be clear that, in this perspective, levels are conceived of as integrative organizations. That is:

> the concept of integrative levels recognizes as equally essential for the purpose of scientific analysis both the isolation of parts of a whole and their integration into the structure of the whole. It neither reduces phenomena of a higher level to those of a lower one, as in mechanism, nor describes the higher level in vague non-material terms which are but substitutes for understanding, as in vitalism. Unlike other "holistic" theories, it never leaves the firm ground of material reality. . . . The concept points the need to study the organizational interrelationships of parts and whole (Novikoff, 1945, p. 209).

Moreover, Tobach and Greenberg (1984, 2) stress that:

> The interdependence among levels is of great significance. The dialectic nature of the relationship among levels is one in which lower levels are subsumed in higher levels so that any particular level is an integration of preceding levels. . . . In the process of integration, or fusion, *new* levels with their own characteristics result.

Thus, because of its own laws, each different level is qualitatively different from the next. This is true, Schneirla asserts, if one is talking of different phylogenetic levels— what he calls *psychological levels*—and if one is talking of different ontogenetic levels—what he calls *functional orders*—because "on each further psychological level, the contribution of individual ontogeny is a characteristically different total behavior pattern arising in a different total context" (Schneirla 1957, 82).

In addition to adopting the organismic viewpoint, Schneirla also adopts the levels-of-organization compromise discussed in Chapter 2. Schneirla is asserting that knowledge of the structural basis of function is not sufficient for understanding behavioral developments at any given psychological level or functional order. Structure does not simply give you function because "something else" is needed, and as such, each different level must be studied in its own terms. That "something else" is, of course, the environmental, or experiential, context within which the organism develops. Structure-function relationships can be understood only in interrelation with their environmental context. Thus Schneirla asserts that a nature-nurture interactionist concept is necessary for understanding development.

Hence we may restate Chapter 2's levels-of-organization compromise in terms of Schneirla's position by indicating that for any given psychological level or functional order, the laws (variables) of the structural (lower) level are involved with (implied in) the laws of the functional, behavioral (higher) level, but function cannot be understood merely through an understanding of structure. Knowledge of structure alone is insufficient for understanding function. This is the case because function develops out of a complex interaction between structure and environmental factors, an interaction that produces a qualitatively different developmental context at each different level.

In sum, Schneirla sees phyletic and ontogenetic development as involving, at least in part, qualitative discontinuity. He sees different structure-function relationships at different levels. He maintains that the same psychological function may therefore be underlain by different processes at different points in development. Thus Schneirla takes a position that is central in developmental

theory and is shared by many other developmental theorists (e.g., Piaget, Werner, Kohlberg): The same behavior is often determined by different variables at different points in ontogeny (or phylogeny).

Behavioral Stereotypy versus Behavioral Plasticity

Schneirla has suggested that psychological levels differ qualitatively from one another because different organisms have qualitatively different structure-function relationships, which are based on different organismic structure-experience interactions. But what is the nature of these different interrelationships? What is the basis of the differences between different psychological levels? This has been a key question in comparative psychology and evolutionary biology, and it pertains to the nature of species' evolutionary changes, to the character of interspecies differences in species' evolutionary changes, and to the task of providing criteria for discriminating among species levels. In addressing these issues many evolutionary biologists and comparative psychologists have made use of the concept of *anagenesis* (Yarczower and Hazlett 1977). Although it is not an uncontroversial idea (Capitanio and Leger 1979; Yarczower and Yarczower, 1979), most scientists agree that "anagenesis refers to the evolution of increased complexity in some trait" (Capitanio and Leger 1979, 876). For example, Dobzhansky et al. (1977) note that "Anagenetic episodes commonly create organisms with novel characters and abilities beyond those of their ancestors" (p. 236), or simply that anagenesis is an "evolutionary advance or change." Similarly, Jerison (1978) notes that an evolutionary analysis of progress from earlier to later species "is called 'anagenetic' and is about progressive evolution," and indicates that in such an analysis "the objective is to identify grades in evolution" (pp. 1–2).

Thus an anagenetic (evolutionary) advance would place a species at a different evolutionary grade (Gould 1976), and location of a species at a different grade would mark interspecies differences in evolutionary changes (i.e., anagenesis; Dobzhansky et al. 1977; Jerison 1978).

However, it is clear that an advance in complexity is often difficult to identify, for example, what specific structural and behavioral criteria need to be met (cf. Capitanio and Leger 1979)? This is especially true when human social behavior is involved (Yarczower and Hazlett 1977; Yarczower and Yarczower 1979; see also Sampson 1977). However, Schneirla (1957, 1959; Tobach and Schneirla 1968), among others (e.g., Birch and Lefford 1963; Sherrington 1951; Tobach 1978, 1981), has provided a useful framework.

Schneirla (1957) proposes the use of a behavioral *stereotypy-plasticity continuum* to differentiate the levels of complexity representative of different species. If an organism's behavioral development is stereotyped, there is a relatively fixed relation between the stimulation the organism receives and the concomitant responses it emits; that is, an almost unchanging relation exists between what goes in (stimulation) and what goes out (response). What we see is little if any variability in response to stimulation. Thus if we deprive a normal frog of food for some time and then present a fly to the frog in its immediate field of vision, we will inevitably see the frog flick out its tongue to catch the fly. Assuming that we take no steps to intervene in this interaction and that the frog continues to exist in its natural habitat, we will see little variation in the response to this stimulation.

Plasticity, on the other hand, refers to the ability to show varying responses to the same stimulus input; that is, a more variable relation exists between what goes in and what will come out.

Now, some of us may be in the habit of "flicking out" our tongues whenever our favorite food goes by—for example, dessert. However, at times a reprimand from our spouse (e.g., "If you get any fatter, you won't fit through the door") will result in our varying our response to the dessert stimulus; we may take a smaller helping than usual, or

perhaps none at all. Similarly, although it would be relatively easy to train a rat to find its way in a maze, it would be extremely difficult to train it to develop a large repertoire of alternate routes that it could efficiently introduce when more habitual routes were blocked. Humans, however, develop this alternate-route repertoire quite readily. Hence, as illustrated in Figure 5.2, if our most direct—and thus habitual—route for driving from home to the market is suddenly blocked one day, we can quite efficiently adopt an alternate route.

An organism that shows stereotypy in its ontogeny develops little behavioral variability in response to stimulation. Alternatively, an organism that shows plasticity develops a relatively considerable degree of variability in response to stimulation. Moreover, as we might expect, organisms with differing degrees of plasticity or stereotypy are on different psychological levels; the more plasticity shown in an organism's development, the higher the organism's psychological level. Thus, as Schneirla has stated: "The appearance of behavioral stereotypy through ontogeny, if found characteristic of a species, indicates a lower psychological level, whereas the systematic plasticity through experiences indicates a high level" (1956, 83).

Of course, neither plasticity nor stereotypy is an all-or-none thing. One cannot say that the behavior of a particular species is either all stereotyped or all plastic. Rather, we may think of stereotypy and plasticity as forming a continuum, with stereotyped and plastic behavior at either end. Different psychological levels will fall at different points along this continuum, and the closer any species is to the plasticity end, the higher its psychological level. A hypothetical example of the ordering of species of different psychological levels along this continuum is presented in Figure 5.3. Ants are at the lower end because their behavior is less plastic than that of any other represented species. Human beings are closest to the plasticity end because human behavior is more plastic than that of the other represented species, and accordingly the human psychological

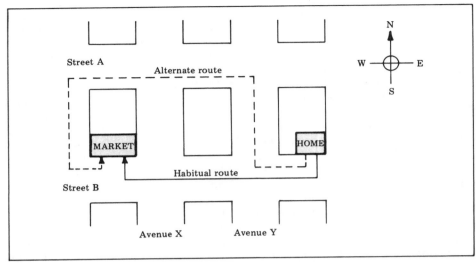

FIGURE 5.2
An illustration of human plasticity.

level is higher than that of any of the other species.

Hebb's A/S Ratio

What is the structural contribution to these contrasting functional capabilities? For example, what nervous-system structures may contribute to the plasticity or stereotypy of different psychological levels? One answer to this question might lie in a concept found in Donald O. Hebb's (1949) writings.

The cerebral cortex of the brain of mammals (e.g., rats, monkeys, dogs, or human beings) has various sections. One section is comprised of nerve cells (neurons) that constitute the cerebral centers for sensory information—information that comes from the outside world through our receptors (e.g., the rods and cones of the retina of the eye) and into our bodies. Another area of the cerebrum is comprised of neurons that constitute our motor cortex—that part of our cerebral cortex that sends messages to our muscles and thus allows us to behave. Still another section of our cortex is comprised of association neurons, cells that integrate and associate information from various parts of the brain. For example, one role of the association cortex is to integrate information

from the sensory cortex, pertaining to what is stimulating us, with information to the motor cortex, relating to our (motor, or muscular) actions or our behavior.

Now, it seems clear that the more association cortex we have, the more associations we can have between a given stimulus input and a behavioral output. That is, the more association fibers that exist, the more variable should associations be to any stimulus, and, accordingly, behavior should be more variable in relation to stimulus input. In 1949 Hebb proposed to express the relation between the amount of sensory cortex and the amount of association cortex in a species in terms of a ratio. This ratio was termed the *association cortex/sensory cortex ratio,* or simply the A/S ratio.

Some organisms have a low A/S ratio, expressed as A/S ratio = < 1.0; simply, they have more sensory cortex than association cortex. For such organisms, sensory input will be more directly related to response than it will for organisms with higher A/S ratios. With organisms that have relatively little association cortex in comparison with their sensory cortex, sensory input (stimulation) will more directly determine behavior. Such organisms can be called *sense-dom-*

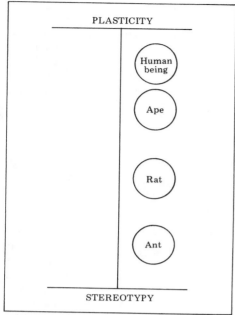

PLASTICITY

Human being

Ape

Rat

Ant

STEREOTYPY

FIGURE 5.3
An illustration of a hypothetical stereo-typy-plasticity continuum.

inated. Because such organisms have few association fibers with which to integrate their sensory input, their behavior in response to sensory input will be less variable. It will be relatively directly controlled by environmental stimulation. It will be stereotyped.

Animals with higher A/S ratios will, however, show relatively less sense domination. Animals with more association fibers relative to sensory fibers (animals whose A/S ratio = > 1.0) will integrate their sensory input with the information provided by their association fibers and thus demonstrate more variable behavior in response to stimulation. The behavior of such organisms will be more a product of an interrelation between their association cortex and their sensory cortex than would be the case with organisms having a low A/S ratio. Accordingly, their behavior will be more variable in response to stimulus (sensory) input. It will be more plastic.

Thus differences in A/S ratios may account for different degrees of plasticity and

stereotypy among different psychological levels. Consistent with Schneirla, Hebb (1949, 125) suggested that for widely differing phylogenetic levels a hierarchy of psychological complexity can be assumed that corresponds to gross differences in the proportion of sensory to association neurons. Similarly, Schneirla (1956, 411) pointed out that a deficiency in the brain's association capacity seems to be a prime condition for certain fixed responses to specific stimuli, since stereotyped response tendencies are strongest in animals with the lowest supply of association neurons.

In sum, we see that Hebb's notions allow us to speculate about a structural basis for the functional differences in stereotypy-plasticity seen on different psychological levels. Animals with more sensory cortex than association cortex are more stereotyped in their behavioral development than are animals with more association cortex relative to their sensory cortex. These latter animals are more plastic in their behavioral development than are the former. Thus the higher an animal's A/S ratio, the more functionally plastic its behavioral development. Conversely, the lower an animal's A/S ratio, the more functionally stereotyped its behavior development. To make an analogy, then, low A/S ratios are to stereotypy (and low psychological levels) as high A/S ratios are to plasticity (and high psychological levels).

Ontogenetic Implications of Stereotypy-Plasticity and of the A/S Ratio

As might be surmised, Hebb (as well as Schneirla) maintains an active interest in the developmental implications of his ideas. Accordingly, Hebb qualified his notions about the A/S ratio by pointing out differences in the ontogeny of animals with different A/S ratios. We will see that Schneirla, in talking of stereotype-plasticity, reaches conclusions similar to those of Hebb.

Animals with low A/S ratios are more stereotyped in their eventual behavioral development and, accordingly, are on low psychological levels. Yet such animals reach their final level of functional organization—

behavioral functioning—much sooner in their development than do animals with high A/S ratios. Animals with few association fibers compared to sensory fibers progress through their ontogeny relatively rapidly; they reach their final—albeit stereotyped—level in a relatively short time in their development.

One way of understanding this is to realize that such animals have comparatively few association-area cortex fibers that have to be organized through their development; they have relatively few associations that can be developed. Thus they organize their association cortex comparatively rapidly. But at the same time, because of their comparatively limited association capacity, their behavior can never develop much variability, and hence it will be relatively stereotyped.

On the other hand, animals with high A/S ratios are comparatively more plastic in their eventual behavioral development and are therefore on higher psychological levels. However, such animals develop toward their final level of development relatively slowly. These high A/S ratio animals reach their final level of functional capacity—of behavioral organization—much later in their development than do low A/S ratio animals. High A/S ratio animals have more association cortex compared to their sensory cortex, and they progress through their ontogeny relatively slowly. These animals reach a higher, more plastic psychological level, but it takes them a longer time to do so.

In sum, lower A/S ratio animals develop more rapidly, but their behavior remains relatively stereotyped; it is sense-dominated and shows little variability. On the other hand, higher A/S ratio animals develop more slowly, but their eventual behavioral development will be relatively plastic; it shows considerable variability. For example, a rat is on a lower psychological level than is a human being. Similarly, the rat has a lower A/S ratio than does a human being. But in the time span of just a few weeks a rat may be considered to be fully developed, while a human infant after only a few weeks of life is not at all, of course, like an adult human in terms of behavioral functioning. The human infant will take years to reach a level analogous to the one that the rat reaches in just a few short weeks. Yet the human, when an adult, will be capable of considerably more complex, plastic behavior than any adult rat will ever be able to produce. In fact, this will be true of the not yet fully developed human; the human will surpass the adult rat when still a child.

An empirical instance of the point can be found in the results of a classic study by Kellogg and Kellogg (1933). The Kelloggs reared a newborn ape in their home and attempted to treat it like their own newborn child, who, by the way, also happened to be living there at the time. They diapered both infants and prompted their behavioral development, including language, in the ways that parents typically do. At first the ape was ahead of their child in terms of behavioral development. Soon, however, the child overtook the ape and was never bested again.

Other lines of research support Schneirla's ideas about ontogenetic changes in stereotypy and plasticity. In order to illustrate this support, let us consider some issues in the development of perception.

Intersensory Integration: An Illustration

All species of animals have available processes that are adaptive; that is, every living species, by virtue of its existence, has processes that allow it to adapt to its environment. All species have ways of taking in food and of eliminating waste products. But I have noted that this similarity does not mean that all species have available to them the same processes. Although all species take in food and eliminate wastes, they may do these things in different ways. Thus organisms at different psychological levels may use different processes to serve the same function. Both the one-celled amoeba and human beings take in food and eliminate wastes, but they certainly perform these adaptive functions in different ways. This is because there are new processes available at different psychological levels; there is qualitative discontinuity among psychological levels.

Accordingly, although all psychological levels have the capacity to react to stimulation, it is not appropriate to attribute the capacity of perception to all psychological levels. All psychological levels must have the ability to react to stimulation in order to survive, what Schneirla (1957) terms the capacity for *sensation*. Even one-celled protozoa have this capacity. Yet it is not until we look at a much higher psychological level that we see the capacity for *perception*—that is, the ability to sense with meaning. Thus at higher psychological levels a qualitatively discontinuous capacity emerges—perception—which allows the organisms of that level to adapt to their environment. These organisms have the ability, for example, to make associations with their sensations, to integrate their purely sensory information with other information available to them. Such organisms can show different responses to the same stimulus; they can associate a different output with the same input. Thus, through their association capacity (e.g., underlain by their A/S ratio), they sense with meaning.

If the capacity of higher psychological levels is qualitatively different from that of lower psychological levels, it follows that these differences should be reflected not in the degree to which different psychological levels can organize sensory information but in the kind of organization they achieve (Schneirla 1957, 96). That is, these differences should be represented not only in how much sensory information can be handled but also in what is done with that information. Higher psychological levels should show greater associative variability—greater plasticity—than should lower levels.

Accordingly, Schneirla suggests that as one moves to higher psychological levels, one will see that sensory experiences result not merely in the *fixation* of the effects of experience—that is, in the organism being able to develop a "trace effect" of a particular sensory input-reaction experience—but also in the *correlation* of these trace effects. In other words, organisms at higher psychological levels have the capacity for a kind of organization of sensory information that is different from the capacity of phylogenetically lower organisms. They have the ability to relate information coming from one sense modality (e.g., vision) with information coming from another sense modality (e.g., touch).

Thus at higher psychological levels organisms have the capacity of *intersensory integration,* the ability to transduce (i.e., transfer, or transform) information from one sense modality to another. With this capacity, sensory input from vision, for example, may be "equated" with sensory input from touch; thus, the sensory input from the two different modalities (modes of sensing) can come to mean the same thing to the organism. For example, we can recognize a quarter by feeling or seeing the coin. We can recognize an ice cube by touching it or by seeing it. The sensations from either of these objects can mean the same thing to us even though delivered through different modalities.

Hence, as we move up the phylogenetic scale from lower psychological levels to higher psychological levels, we see perceptual ability emerging not because of new senses being present—not because higher psychological levels have more senses with which to fixate the trace effects of sensory experience than do lower levels—but because as we move to higher psychological levels better liaison emerges among existing senses. We see advances in the capacity to correlate information among the senses. We see increased intersensory integrative ability. Thus, as Birch and Lefford have pointed out: "In the emergence of the mammalian nervous system from lower forms, the essential evolutionary strategy has been the development of mechanisms for improved interaction among the separate sensory modalities" (1963, 3). Similarly, Sherrington stated: "Not new senses, but better liaison between old senses is what the developing nervous system has in this respect stood for" (1951, 289).

From the above we can see that an organism of a high psychological level—for instance, a human—has the capacity to develop considerable intersensory integrative ability, to make considerable gains through sensory experiences. However, we have also seen that humans, with their high psychological level, correspondingly have a high A/S ratio. This means that although human beings are capable of high levels of behavioral development, it takes them a relatively long period of time, as opposed to animals, to reach this developmental level—the highest point of their functional order. In essence, we can expect human beings, although capable of considerable intersensory integrative ability, to develop this ability over several years in the course of their ontogeny. Simply, we may hypothesize that human intersensory integrative ability is a developmental phenomenon.

This hypothesis was tested in an important study by Birch and Lefford (1963) of the ability of children of different ages (ranging from five to eleven years) to integrate information from three different sense modalities—vision, active touch (or the haptic sense), and passive touch (or the kinesthetic sense). The authors used geometric forms—such as blocks in the shape of a circle, square, triangle, star, and cross—as stimuli for the children. Two blocks were presented at a time. Sometimes the same object was presented for the child to see and touch; and at other times different objects were presented. In either case the child was asked to judge whether the two blocks were the same or different.

In support of the hypothesis that intersensory integrative ability increases with age (that it is a developmental phenomenon), Birch and Lefford found that "the ability to make the various intersensory judgments clearly improved with age" (p. 45). Figure 5.4 depicts some of the results of this study. The authors conclude that "the findings strongly indicate that information received by young children through one avenue of sense is not directly transduced to another sensory modality. . . . In fact, it may perhaps be argued that the emergence of such equivalence is developmental."

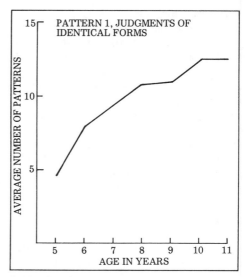

FIGURE 5.4
Some of the results of the Birch and Lefford study: Correct judgments for all intersensory pairings made when judging identical forms at different ages.

Source: Birch, H. G., and Lefford, A. *Intersensory Development in Children, Monographs of the Society for Research in Child Development 28,* p. 35. Copyright 1963 by The Society for Research in Child Development. Reprinted by permission.

In essence, Birch and Lefford (1963) provided strong evidence in support of the notion that the intersensory integrative ability of human beings reaches its eventually high level only after years of development. However, they also found that even their youngest subjects—the five-year-olds—had relatively well-developed intersensory integrative ability. They suggested, however, that at younger ages (at about three years of age) this ability would be markedly inefficient but would rapidly improve.

Accordingly, in a similar experiment, Abravanel (1968) studied intersensory integrative development in children ranging in age from 3.3 to 14.2 years. He found that the base level (the lowest level) for performing the various intersensory equivalences occurred at about three years of age. After this time, however, integrative ability improved greatly up through seven years of age, when it reached a high level of efficiency. Thus, consistent with the notions we have derived from Schneirla's ideas (1957) about perceptual development, we see that both the Birch and Lefford (1963) and the Abravanel (1968) studies provide findings that support the hypothesis that humans' ability to transduce information from one modality to another increases with age—that it is a developmental phenomenon.

Abravanel (1968) provides us with other findings that (we shall see below) support some of Schneirla's concepts other about development, those pertaining to the role of the organism's own activity as a source of its own development. Abravanel found that increases in intersensory integrative ability are associated with changes in the type of exploration activity the children showed when actively touching the stimulus. Specifically, younger, less accurate children explored the stimuli by either gross or passive movements. Alternatively, older, more accurate children used finer and more articulated movements, exploring with the fingertips, for instance, rather than with the palms.

The role of the organism's activity in the development of its own plasticity has been identified in other human data sets reported by Piaget (1961; Piaget and Inhelder 1956) and by Birch and Lefford (1967). In addition, experimental research with animals (Held and Hein 1963) confirms this role of the organism's activity. Litter-mate kittens were or were not allowed to make motor adjustments as they traversed a circular route. Those animals making the active motor adjustments later performed better on a test of depth perception—that is, a visual cliff apparatus—than did the restricted animals.

Thus the idea that human plasticity is a developmental phenomenon, advanced by Schneirla (1957) as well as by Hebb (1949), Piaget (1961; Piaget and Inhelder 1956), Bühler (1928), and Baldwin (1897), finds empirical support. In addition, support for the notion that the organism itself actively provides a basis of this progression is evident.

Conclusions

Animals of low psychological levels will develop much more rapidly than will animals of high psychological levels. However, the gains that these two levels of animals will make through their ontogeny will be quite different. Animals on a low psychological level will be able to gain little behavioral variability through their ontogeny because the nature of their development is restricted by their structural limitations, by their low A/S ratio. However, animals on a high psychological level will be able to gain considerable behavioral variability through their ontogeny because their development occurs within the context of broader structural capabilities, their high A/S ratio.

Finally, we may note that Schneirla's (1957) ideas have relevance for both the phylogenetic and the ontogenetic changes of humans. Human evolution should be characterizable by progressively greater potentials for plasticity. In turn, however, although evolution has led to the presence of this potential, its basis in structure requires organization over the course of ontogeny. As such, normative patterns of human ontogeny should be characterizable by the progressively greater presence of plasticity. There are data supporting these ideas.

In evolutionary biology Lewontin and Levins (1978) provide evidence for the link between anagenesis, complexity, plasticity, and what they term coupling-uncoupling phenomena. Lewontin and Levins (1978) cite Hegel's warning "that the organism is made up of arms, legs, head, and trunk only as it passes under the knife of the anatomist," and note that "the intricate interdependence of the parts of the body . . . permit[s] survival when they function well, but in pathological conditions produce[s] pervasive disaster" (p. 79). However, such interdependence of parts is neither phylogenetically nor ontogenetically static. Relations among parts change over the course of evolution;

often this involves the rapid evolution of some characteristics, or traits, and the relative constancy of others. In other words, whereas various aspects of an organism may be bound together as traits if they are either units of development or selection, they may lose their cohesion and evolve independently if the direction of selection is altered (Lewontin and Levins 1978).

Indeed, there are several aspects of adaptation that suggest that tight integration of traits—or in Lewontin and Levins's terms, coupling—is disadvantageous. First, a given characteristic may be subject to alternative selection pressures. If the optimal states of the characteristic under the separate pressures are not vastly different, than adaptation would be best served by a "compromise in which the part in question is determined by" all the presses. Second, the uncoupling of traits is advantageous "as the number of interacting variables and the intensity of their interaction increases" (pp. 83–84); this is so because, in the face of these increases, it becomes increasingly difficult for selective pressures to increase fitness. Thus species with very tight coupling will be unable to adapt as readily as those in which the different components that increase fitness are more autonomous. Third, the more strongly coupled and interdependent the traits of an organism, the more pervasive the damage done to an organism when some stressor overwhelms a particular trait.

Accordingly, what has occurred over the course of evolution is that the advantages of coordinated functioning and mutual regulation have come to oppose the disadvantages of excessive constraint and hence vulnerability; and that, at least at the human level, organisms may have the capacity to couple and uncouple traits successively. Ontogenetically, then, it may be that the most adaptive organisms are those that have the potential to develop the capacity to couple and uncouple traits as the context demands. We may suggest, therefore, that the direction of evolution at the human level has been to move toward providing the substrate for the coupling-uncoupling of traits. This is what

may be involved in anagenesis. That is, if higher evolutionary grades are defined as being more complex, and if greater complexity means greater plasticity, a key instance of plasticity would be the capability to couple, uncouple, and couple anew—either through recoupling or with ontogenetically unique couplings. This facility should become progressively established across ontogeny, as the physiological substrate of the psychological level of analysis becomes organized. Thus we again reach the view that evolutionary and ontogenetic progression involves progressive change toward greater plasticity of functioning.

Concepts Representing Development

From the above consideration of stereotypy-plasticity, it is clear that Schneirla was just as concerned with the problems of ontogeny as he was with those of phylogeny. He viewed both as progressing through a series of qualitatively different levels; he drew a distinction between the progression from one phylogenetic level to another, and the progression from one ontogenetic level to another, by his concepts of *psychological levels* and *functional orders,* respectively. For example, the first two years of life may correspond to the first part of the functional order of a human; the next five years to another, separate portion of the functional order; and the following five years to still another part of this functional order.

We have seen how the concepts of stereotypy and plasticity serve to differentiate between different psychological levels, and how the relative degree of stereotypy-plasticity may serve to characterize the psychological level of a particular animal species. Let us now turn to a consideration of Schneirla's concepts characterizing the functional order of a species.

A Definition of Development

To Schneirla (1957), *development* refers to successive changes in the organization of an organism, an organism that is viewed as a functional and adaptive system throughout its life. Thus development connotes successive change within a living, functioning, adaptive, individual system. By continually functioning in an adaptive manner, this system—this individual organism—develops through successive changes throughout its life.

But what are the characteristics of this system? What are the processes that comprise the determinants of the organism's development? Schneirla (1957, 86) suggests two broad concepts representing the complex factors that make up the successive changes of development.

Maturation

The first of these two concepts is maturation. To Schneirla, *maturation* means growth and differentiation of the physical and physiological systems of an organism. *Growth* refers to changes in these systems by way of tissue accretion, that is, tissue enlargement. *Differentiation* refers to changes in the structural aspects of tissues with age, that is, alterations in the interrelationship among tissues, organs, or parts of either of these. For example, at certain states in the development of the embryo a certain layer of cells exists. These cells mature not only via accretion (growth) but also through differentiation. Thus when the embryo is in its blastula stage of development, it is divided into three layers of cells. One of these layers is termed the *mesoderm*. Eventually, as the embryo goes through changes and the cells of the mesoderm grow larger and differentiate, these cells will come to form the muscles and bones of the body. Hence maturation refers to changes in the organism that results from the growth and differentiation of its tissues and organs.

Schneirla cautions, however, against thinking that maturation can occur in any way independent of environmental contribution. Consistent with what we discussed in Chapter 3 about the probabilistic-epigenetic position on the nature-nurture issue (Gollin 1981; Gottlieb 1970, 1983; Scarr and McCart-

ney 1983; Tobach 1981), Schneirla emphasizes that maturational processes must *always* occur within the context of a supportive, facilitative environment; because of this interdependence, the exact path that maturation will take will be affected by what is happening in the environmental context of the organisms. Just as maturation is not independent of environment, structure is not independent of function. Hence, as Schneirla stated:

> Maturation is neither the direct, specific representative of genetic determination in development, nor is it synonymous with structural growth. Much as an environmental context is now recognized as indispensable to any development. . . . , students of behavioral development . . . emphasize the roles of structure and function as inseparable in development. (1957, 86)

Experience

The second concept needed to represent the complexity of the factors comprising developmental changes is *experience*. To Schneirla, experience refers to all stimulus influences that act on the organism throughout the course of its life. Experience is a very broad, all-encompassing concept. Any stimulative influence, any stimulus that acts on the organism in any way, is part of experience; and this stimulative influence can occur at any time in the organism's journey from womb to tomb. Experience may affect the organism at any time in its ontogeny.

It is clear, then, that experience can affect the organism before it is born. For example, stimulative influences may act on the fetus in the form of chemicals, drugs, or disease entities. Thus a baby whose mother contracts German measles (rubella) during the early part of her pregnancy can be acted on in an adverse way. The effects of such an experience may be a deformed heart or blindness. Similarly, experience will obviously affect the organism after it is born. This may also take the form of diseases or accidents, but it can include experiences such as the type of care the infant receives.

In sum, experience is a term representing any and all stimulative influences acting on the organism as it develops. These influences may result from events taking place within the organism's body (endogenous stimulative influences) or outside the organism's body (exogenous stimulative influences). In either case, experience acting on the organism provides one of the two interacting factors determining development. Let us look, then, at how experience interacts with maturation to affect development.

The Role of Maturation-Experience Interaction in Developmental Progress

Experience is necessary for any and all developments throughout ontogeny. Experience always has an effect on the organism, and in a specific way. Experience results in *trace effects*. To Schneirla (1957), trace effects are organismic changes that result from experience and that in turn influence future experience. Experience effects changes in the organism, and these changes—these trace effects—influence how future experience will act on the organism. In other words, when experience acts on the organism it will leave a trace of its action, and this trace effect becomes part of the organism and thus changes the organism's nature. Hence any later experience that acts on the organism will act on a *different* organism— an organism that now has a residual effect, a trace effect, of its previous experience. The second experience will result in an effect different from what would have happened had the previous experience not acted.

For example, a young child may have an experience that results in a physical disability. Because of this handicap, which changes the nature of the organism, future experiences—for instance, exposure to a physical education program—will influence the child differently than if the child had not had that previous experience.

However, the possible effects of experience are limited by the maturational status of the organism. The effect of the same expe-

rience will be different at different points in the organism's development because the organism will be at different levels of growth and differentiation at those times. Thus, because the organism's sensory, association, and motor portions of the nervous system mature with time, the effects of experience are limited. For example, an infant is capable of perception and can form trace effects resulting from some types of perceptual experience (Bower 1966). At later developmental stages the same child will be capable of developing trace effects as a result of the perceptual experiences involved in reading. However, these later experiences would not have resulted in the same trace effects had they been presented to the relatively physiologically immature infant. Alternatively, the trace effects that obtain as a result of the perceptual experiences involved in reading could never have occurred when they did had the child not had a particular series of perceptual experiences, resulting in trace effects, since infancy. In sum, the nature of the behavioral gains that can result from experience are limited by the relative physiological maturation of the organism (Schneirla 1957, 90).

By this time, however, the reader should recognize that maturation in turn also has limits. These limits are imposed by experience. Consistent with the probabilistic-epigenetic interactionist position he espouses, Schneirla (1957, 90) points out that the limitation of experience imposed by maturation is in turn limited by the developmental stage of the organism—by the attained functional order the organism has reached in its ontogeny. The growth and differentiation of maturation do not occur without the supportive, facilitative effects of experience. This experience, leaving its trace effects on the organism, provides the milieu within which maturation occurs. Inappropriate experiences—such as loss of oxygen supply—will not allow maturation to proceed as it would have had the inappropriate experience not occurred. Thus maturation must interact with experience in order for development to proceed, and in turn the effects of experience are channeled by their interaction within the limits imposed by the organism's maturational status.

Hence a complex interaction between experience and maturation provides the basis of behavioral development. This complex interaction is represented schematically in Figure 5.5. Experience results in trace effects, but the nature of the trace effects is limited by the maturational status of the organism. In addition, this interaction determines what behavior the organism can develop at any particular time in its ontogeny. The experience-maturation interaction provides the basis for the developmental stage reached at a particular time in an organism's ontogeny. In turn, this developmental stage, comprising the result of the interaction between experience and maturation, provides (1) the milieu within which further maturation proceeds, does not proceed, or proceeds at a different rate; and (2) the milieu that determines what trace effects will result from further experiences. In sum, Schneirla said: "The nature of the gains made through experience is both canalized and limited by the relative maturity of species-typical afferent, neural, and efferent mechanisms, in dependence upon the developmental stage attained" (1957, 90).

What we have seen to this point, then, is that behavior emerges through the course of development as a function of an interaction between experience and maturation. If appropriate experiences do not occur or, conversely, if inappropriate experiences occur, maturation will not proceed as it otherwise would have; accordingly, the behavior that would have developed will not therefore develop at that time. In other words, if inappropriate experiences occur (such as disease, loss of oxygen supply, loss of a mother's nurturance), or if appropriate experiences occur but do so at a time too late for typical development to proceed, then maturation will not develop typically, and it follows that the behavior that would usually have developed will be altered.

Conversely, if maturation does not proceed as it typically does (because of a lack of supportive, facilitative experiences), then the effects of experience—the trace effects—will be altered; in turn, the behavior that emerges at a particular point in time will be different. What we see, then, is that the ordered emergence of behavior in development depends centrally on the nature and time of experience-maturation interactions. The attainment of developmental stages is dependent on the quality and timing of the variables involved in this interaction.

Conclusions

Thus the consistency of Schneirla's viewpoint with the probabilistic-epigenetic position discussed in Chapter 2 should be evident. Schneirla emphasizes that the nature and timing of interactions between maturation and experience are central in de-

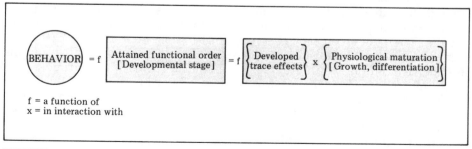

FIGURE 5.5

A complex interaction between experience and maturation provides the basis of behavioral development.

termining behavioral development. More-over, the nature and timing of this inter-action cannot necessarily be predicted in advance for every organism within a species. At best, we can say only that if the nature and timing of the maturation-experience interaction occur in certain ways, then behavior will probably develop along certain lines.

Accordingly, norms for development, which are statements about when in people's lives a particular behavior is typically seen, can be used only as general guidelines for considering development. Statements such as "babies should sit up at six months," "babies should say their first word at eleven months," or "babies should walk at fourteen months" can be considered only as state-ments that apply in general. They may apply to a given group as a whole, but they may not necesarily apply to any individual in that group. That is, such norms do not mean that babies must do these things at these times in order to be considered normal. Rather, they mean only that for a given large group of babies, an average time exists for the emer-gence of a particular behavior. At the same time that this norm exists, however, differ-ences among individuals (i.e., interindividual differences) also *necessarily* exist. Different people show a behavior either before or after the norm for their group. In fact, we would expect all people *not* to reach the same level of development at the same time.

In sum, Schneirla's ideas are an exemplar of the probabilistic-epigenetic position: Any behavioral development that occurs is ob-tained through a bidirectional (reciprocal) interaction between maturational and expe-riential factors. Thus the emergence of any behavior at any time in an organism's devel-opment is dependent on the nature and tim-ing of this interaction. In other words, behavioral development is not dependent on maturation or experience alone. This is be-cause "factors of maturation may differ sig-nificantly in their influence upon ontogeny, both in the nature and in the timing of their effects, according to what relations to the ef-fects of experience are possible under exist-

ing conditions" (Schneirla and Rosenblatt 1963, 288). Hence, from Schneirla's theoreti-cal point of view, any notion of behavioral development that stresses the exclusive con-tribution of either maturational or experien-tial factors is incorrect.

Despite the persuasiveness of Schneirla's argument, not all theorists agree with him. We will now consider two concepts that pro-vide exclusively nature explanations of be-havioral development—the *critical-periods hypothesis* and the notion of *instinct* (or in-nate behavior)—in order to illustrate how Schneirla's views allow one effectively to counter views that suggest that nature vari-ables alone can account for behavioral development. Let us first turn to the critical-periods hypothesis.

THE CRITICAL-PERIODS HYPOTHESIS

The notion of critical periods in develop-ment was formulated in embryology. Within that science the idea was advanced that the various parts of the whole organism (e.g., various organs or organ sytems) emerge in a fixed sequence; more importantly, it was held that the parts that develop in a fixed sequence do so with just a certain amount of time allowed for each; there is an overall timetable of development, and each part of the whole organism has its own fixed time of emergence, set by maturation. Each part has a critical period in which to develop.

This perspective holds that a part of the organism that is in its critical period can eas-ily be stimulated. Such a part is highly re-sponsive to both facilitating and disruptive influences. Thus, if the part does not develop normally or appropriately during its critical period, it will never have a second chance. Because the time limits of development are invariably fixed by maturation, even if the part does not develop, the focus of develop-ment will switch. It will shift to another organ system, in accordance with the prede-termined timetable of development, and that different organ system will be in *its* critical period of development. Hence any part that does not develop during its own critical period will not have another chance.

Similarly, in psychology such a critical period refers to a time in the ontogeny of a species during which it is crucial for a particular psychological development to take place; the period is crucial because certain maturational processes then occurring would allegedly place time limits on the development (Schneirla and Rosenblatt 1961). For example, as we shall see in Chapter 9, Erik Erikson divides the human life span into eight critical periods. Each emerges in accordance with a maturational "ground plan" for development, which is built into the person (Erikson 1959). Thus Erikson maintains that in the first year of life the infant must develop a certain degree of a "sense of trust." If the infant does not develop this feeling at the time when it is supposed to develop, not only will there never be another chance but the rest of that person's development will be unfavorably altered.

Clearly, the critical-periods hypothesis places complete dependence on an intrinsic, maturationally determined timetable. What this formulation clearly indicates, then, is that maturation in and of itself sets critical time limits for development; there are maturationally circumscribed periods in an organism's development and the time limits of these periods are somehow not related to experiential factors. However, from Schneirla's and others' (Gottlieb 1970, 1983; Tobach 1981; Tobach and Greenberg, 1984) probabilistic-epigenetic position we can see that such a conception of critical periods is untenable. Rather than emphasizing the independent contribution of maturation, Schneirla would opt to investigate the process by which maturation and experience interact to enable a specific development to take place at a given time in ontogeny.

Schneirla is not saying that certain developments are not critical for some later developments. He would agree to some extent with other researchers concerned with the critical-periods notion—for example, Scott (1962)—that there are critical stages, for instance for the development of learning. He would agree that what is learned at a certain time in an organism's ontogeny may be critical for whatever follows (Schneirla and Rosenblatt 1963; Scott 1962). But all this really says is that what happens at "time 1" in a person's life may be very important—in fact critical—for what can or will happen at "time 2." Such an assertion merely *describes* a relation between events that occur at two different times in ontogeny; it makes no statement about whether the first event was determined by maturation alone or by an interaction between maturation and experience (Bateson 1983).

It is the source of the "criticalness" in development about which Schneirla argues. Simply, maturationally fixed time limits for development, arising without the contribution of experience, are inconsistent with his probabilistic-epigenetic position. Rather, Schneirla proposes a theory that places "emphasis upon the fusion of maturation (growth-contributed) and experience (stimulation-contributed) processes at different stages in behavior ontogeny, together with the . . . contributions both of maturation and experience. . . , as well as the interrelations of these contributions. . . ." (Schneirla and Rosenblatt, 1963, 288). Indeed, Howard Moltz, a leading student of Schneirla's, found experimentally that the time limits of certain critical periods *could* be altered through specific manipulations (e.g., Moltz and Stettner 1961).

Weak and Strong Versions of the Hypothesis

Of course, Schneirla's view is not the only one that exists in regard to the meaning and bases of the concept of critical periods in development. Indeed, over the course of numerous reviews of the concept (e.g., Bateson 1979, 1983; Colombo 1982; Connolly 1972; Hess 1973; Hinde 1962; Nash, 1978; Scott 1962; Thorpe 1961), several definitions of critical period have been forwarded. These definitions may be divided in several ways.

For instance, Krashen (1975) distinguished between strong and weak versions of the critical-periods hypothesis. In its weak form, the hypothesis states:

> A critical period is a time during the life span of an organism in which the organism may be affected by some exogenous influence to an extent beyond that observed at other times. Simply, the organization is more sensitive to environmental stimulation during a critical period than at other times in its life. (Colombo, 1982, 261)

Similarly, in Krashen's (1975) view, the weak version of the hypothesis states that there are periods in life when the development of a system can best be furthered by particular stimulation but that the system's development can nevertheless still occur after such a period.

In essence, then, in the weak form of the hypothesis, the critical period is really only a *sensitive period,* one wherein particular experiences may most readily or efficiently promote development of a system (e.g., cognition, vision, language); nevertheless, similar or perhaps distinct experiences can foster the system's development after such a period, albeit with the requirement that the experience (the stimulus) be more intense in order to result in comparable development (MacDonald, in press). Thus this form of the hypothesis indicates that critical periods are not so critical after all, and that they are little more than labels applied to the well-known and hardly controversial observations that: (1) when a system is developing it needs stimulation to allow it adequately to do so (e.g., if we were totally deprived of light stimulation our visual system would not develop; Hebb 1949), or simply that, as Schneirla (1957) explains, our systems need to be active to function adequately; and (2) it is easier to influence a system—for better or worse—when it is in a state of development than after it has been fully organized (MacDonald, in press).

In sum, in the weak form of the critical-periods hypothesis, particular experiences play a "noncontingent" (Moltz 1973) role in development; that is, although they are not absolutely necessary for adequate development to occur, particular experiences can enhance development due to the greater efficiency of their influence at a particular time. Thus, with such not-quite-critical critical periods, developmental deficits produced by the lack of a particular experience (e.g., language deficits due to the absence of an adequate language model) may be overcome by experiences in later life. This means that while a given period may be *optimal* (Moltz 1973) for the development of a particular function, it is not a critical time for this development if recovery of function can occur. As Bateson (1983, 8) puts it: "Once the mechanisms protecting behaviour from change are stripped away by suitable treatment, change resulting from renewed plasticity is once again possible."

But we have noted that there is also a strong form of the critical periods hypothesis. In this version of the hypothesis particular stimulation is needed at a particular time in order for normal development to proceed; in other words, if the appropriate stimulation does not occur when it is supposed to in life, then what will occur is "an irrevocable result not modifiable in subsequent development" (Scott 1962). Thus in such a formulation the organism *needs* certain stimulation for its continued normal development, and given inappropriate experience, it is *vulnerable to,* or *at risk for,* abnormal development during such a period (Colombo 1982). Simply, for such a period no recovery of function by later experience is possible (Krashen 1975) and, as such, experience during this period has a "contingent" role (Moltz 1973); that is, it is absolutely necessary for normal development.

The original instance of the strong version of the critical-periods hypothesis derives from the work of Konrad Lorenz (1937). Lorenz introduced the concept of "imprinting" to describe what he believed to be an irrevocable social bond, or attachment, formed by newly hatched precocial birds (e.g., ducks, geese) to the first moving object they saw (usually their mothers) during the first hours after birth. These first few hours were claimed by Lorenz (1937, 1965) to be the critical period for imprinting to occur.

What is the evidence about the reality of such strong critical periods? Colombo (1982) has summarized data pertinent to the existence of strongly defined critical periods in regard to four areas of research: imprinting in birds, social development in rhesus monkeys, language acquisition in humans and binocular vision development in mammals. He notes:

> Nearly every demonstration of a critical period in behavioral development during the past 50 years has been followed by a demonstration of some behavioral recovery from the effects of critical period exposure or deprivation. The first example was with avian imprinting, in which Lorenz's (1937) claims of a tightly bounded period during which a permanent parent-offspring relationship was formed were rigorously tested. Subsequent evidence suggested that the critical period was not as temporally distinct (Brown 1974) nor were the effects of stimulation within it as irreversible (e.g., Ratner and Hoffman 1974; Salzen and Meyer 1968) as Lorenz had originally thought (Bateson 1966).
>
> After observing the results of social isolation during the first year of life, Harlow (1959, 1965) suggested the existence of a critical period for the development of social behavior in the rhesus monkey lasting (in one version) from birth to 250 days. The critical stimulus was apparently what he called "contact comfort," the absence of which during this early period resulted in permanent social/psychological maladjustment. Later, however, a series of experiments (Mason and Kenney 1974; Novak and Harlow 1975; Suomi and Harlow 1972) demonstrated that with special interventions and patience, the adverse effects of deprivation during this period could be overcome.
>
> Language acquisition was another major developmental process to which critical period theory was applied, only to have that application subsequently questioned. Elaborating on a suggestion by Penfield and Roberts (1959) and through the use of data on early and late unilateral brain damage (e.g., Basser 1962; Landsell 1969) and the development of language in retardates (Lenneberg, Nichols, and Rosenberger 1964), Lenneberg (1967, 1969) hypothesized a period of receptiveness to language lasting from ages two to 12. Language could be most easily acquired during this period; after this period, acquisition of a first language would be extremely difficult, if not impossible. The absolute irreversibility of the period's effects has been somewhat disconfirmed by subsequent investigation of acquisition after linguistic deprivation (Curtiss 1977; Curtiss et al. 1975; Fromkin et al. 1974) and of second language learning (McLaughlin 1977).
>
> In initial studies of the critical period for the development of binocular vision, during which monocular deprivation resulted in anatomical degeneration of the deprived eye's pathways, complete domination of cortical physiology by the deprived eye, and apparent blindness of the deprived eye (e.g., Hubel and Wiesel 1970) no recovery of function was reported (Blakemore and Van Sluyters 1974; Hubel and Wiesel 1970; Wiesel and Hubel 1965b). Subsequent studies, however, demonstrated that recovery in at least the behavioral aspects of visual function could be obtained after the end of the period (e.g., Baxter 1966; Chow and Stewart 1972; Cynader, Berman, and Hein 1976; Mitchell, Cynader, and Movshon 1977; Timmey, Mitchell, and Griffin 1978; Mitchell, 1978). It is worth noting, however, that this recovery has yet to be demonstrated in primates (Crawford et al. 1975; von Noorden, Dowling, and Ferguson, 1970). (Colombo 1982, 268–269)

Moreover, Colombo (1962) reviews additional evidence that both the presumed onsets and terminations of critical periods—that is, the times in life when these periods are believed to begin and end—are influenced by variables both endogenous and exogenous to the organism. Thus the time limits of these periods are neither as fixed and sudden as Lorenz (1937, 1965), for instance, maintains nor as impervious to contextual influences as Lorenz also believes. Colombo (1982) indicates that rather than a sudden and dramatic onset of sensitivity to a specific stimulus, sensitivity rises gradually to a peak and then gradually declines. These changes can be manipulated, for example, in regard to binocular visual development, by altering the amount of light in the rearing environment. Similar perceptual stimulation manipulations can alter the imprinting period in birds (e.g., Moltz and Stettner 1961). In addition, pharmacological manipulations can extend the imprinting period of birds or even prevent it from occurring at all (Colombo 1982).

Conclusions

There is no good evidence to support the strong version of the critical-periods hypothesis, as for instance advanced by Lorenz (1937, 1965). Nature variables *do not* prescribe fixed time limits within the life span wherein certain stimulation must occur for normal development to proceed. Rather, as a given system develops it is responsive to influences by variables outside the system but endogenous to the organism, and by variables exogenous to the organism. Indeed, Colombo's (1982) conclusions regarding the character of critical periods in development are comparable to those we would expect from the basis of Schneirla's (1956, 1957) perspective. Colombo notes that "the emergence of a critical period . . . is based on, and may be predicted by. . . , the interaction of dynamic, developing systems, and as much effort should be directed toward identifying those systems and their interactions as toward identifying the period itself" (Colombo 1982, 270).

Let us now turn to a second concept that, when also presented in its strong form, indicates that nature is the sole determinant of features of development. This is the concept of instinct, or innate behavior. This concept is quite related to Lorenz's notions regarding the critical period for imprinting, and in fact it is Lorenz whose contribution to the concept of instinct is most central.

INSTINCT: INNATE BEHAVIOR

The notion of instinct, or instinctive behavior, is today perhaps most often associated with the work of Konrad Lorenz. Beginning in the 1930s, Lorenz—an Austrian-born zoologist and physician—studied certain types of behavior he termed *instinctive behavior*. By

Konrad Lorenz

this term Lorenz appears to mean behavior that is preformed in the genotype. He contends that we inherit a genotype, and built into this genotype is a "limited range of possible forms in which an identical genetic blueprint can find its expression in phenogeny" (Lorenz 1965, 1). In essence, then, Lorenz contends that there is an isomorphism between certain genetic inheritances and certain behaviors, and this is what he means by instinctive behavior. Certain behaviors are preformed, or at least predetermined, and thus they are innate; they are built into the organism through genetic inheritance and are thus simply unavailable to any environmental influence.

More specifically, Lorenz sees as innate certain inherited properties of nervous-system structures. Certain groups of neurons, he claims, have built into them specific, distinctive properties (Lehrman 1970). They obtain these properties directly from the genotype, with experience having no influence. For example, as Lehrman (1970, 24) has pointed out, one such innate property of a given neural structure is "its ability to select, from the range of available possible stimuli, the one which specifically elicits its activity, and thus the response seen by the observer." That is, in the view of Lorenz, certain nervous-system structures come with the innate ability to select out certain stimuli from the environment; these are the stimuli that elicit (bring forth) the built-in (predetermined) functional component of the structure—that is, the response (Lorenz 1965).

Since, Lorenz (1965) contends, experience plays no role in the presence of this instinctive behavior, one does not have to bother with the issue of how the relation between the stimuli and the responses comes to be established. All one has to say is that the behavior is there because it is innate, and innate behavior comes this way. Thus to Lorenz no further analysis is needed. In advancing this argument, Lorenz "solves" the problems of behavioral development by simply avoiding them by defining them away. In essence, then, Lorenz (1940, 1965) argues that genetic inheritance represents a "blueprint" for the development and final level and form of behavior; that is, it represents a set of directives that are unalterable by environment, experience, learning, socialization, and so on (cf. Lehrman 1953, 1970). This genetic inheritance is believed able to circumscribe behavior so severely because it leads directly to the formation of an "instinct"—a predetermined, innate, and unmodifiable pattern of behavior specific to the species within which it exists. The behaviors associated with this instinct are then not capable of environmental, experiential modification.

Thus behavior is constrained by instincts; variation in behavior beyond the limits imposed by the genetically fixed instinct is not possible. Such a conception of genetic influence precludes, then, a process analysis of the ways in which genetic and environmental variables contribute to behavioral development. In other words, Lorenz's (1940, 1965) conception of instinct precludes a

consideration of how organismic and/or contextual processes may contribute to the development and organization of behavior; his conception eliminates any use for studying how behavior may be altered or enhanced.

An Example of Lorenz's Use of the Concept of Instinct

To illustrate Lorenz's use of this conception in regard to human behavior, I will cite Lorenz (translated by Eisenberg 1972). Writing in Nazi Germany in 1940, Lorenz asserted:

> The only resistance which mankind of healthy stock can offer . . . against being penetrated by symptoms of degeneracy is based on the existence of certain innate schemata . . . Our species-specific sensitivity to the beauty and ugliness of members of our species is intimately connected with the symptoms of degeneration, caused by domestication, which threaten our race. . . . Usually, a man of high value is disgusted with special intensity by slight symptoms of degeneracy in men of the other race. . . . In certain instances, however, we find not only a lack of this selectivity . . . but even a reversal to being attracted by symptoms of degeneracy. . . . Decadent art provides many examples of such a change of signs. . . . The immensely high reproduction rate in the moral imbecile has long been established. . . . This phenomenon leads everywhere . . . to the fact that socially inferior human material is enabled . . . to penetrate and finally to annihilate the healthy nation. The selection for toughness, heroism, social utility . . . must be accomplished by some human institution if mankind, in default of selective factors, is not to be ruined by domestication-induced degeneracy. *The racial idea as the basis of our state has already accomplished much in this respect.* The most effective race-preserving measure is . . . the greatest support of the natural defenses. . . . We must—and should—rely on the healthy feelings of our Best and charge them with the selection which will determine the prosperity or the decay of our people. (italics added)

Although switching his scientific focus from Jews to precocial birds after the Nazis lost the Second World War, Lorenz maintained an interest in human instincts and continued to view them in a manner consistent with a presupposition that they could not be moderated by experience. In his book *On Aggression,* Lorenz (1966) argued that aggression was instinctual in humans, that social conflict was an innate component of the human behavioral repertoire, and that there was an instinctual "militant enthusiasm" among youth. While in this book Lorenz suggests that civilization must find methods for ritualizing and containing aggressive instincts, he is basically arguing that humans must make the best of an inevitably negative situation (Schneirla 1966); that is, he sees humans as universally and unalterably destructively aggressive. The social-policy implication of this instance of Lorenz's views about "instinct" was perhaps best presented in a review of *On Aggression* written by Schneirla (1966, 16):

> It is as heavy a responsibility to inform man about aggressive tendencies assumed to be present on an inborn basis as it is to inform him about "original sin," which Lorenz admits in effect. A corollary risk is advising societies to base their programs of social training on attempts to inhibit hypothetical innate aggressions, instead of continuing positive measures for constructive behavior.

By this point the reader should be well aware of the problems inherent in Lorenz's assertions. By making a distinction between what is innate and what comes about through the environment, and by implying that there exists a genetic blueprint that imposes fixed constraints on development, Lorenz is opting for the "which one?" (nature or nurture) question, which we rejected as inadequate in Chapter 3. Thus, from our knowledge of Schneirla's probabilistic-epigenetic interactionist position and from our discussion of the norm-of-reaction concept, we know that the notion of innate, or instinctive, behavior as formulated by Lorenz (1965) is not tenable for the following reasons:

1.   Nature and nurture are inextricably bound; it is inappropriate to assert that genes can directly give you behavior. Nature variables need the supportive, facilitative influence of experiential factors in order to contribute to behavior. In turn, of course, experience needs nature variables with which to interact.

2.   Because of this interdependency, it is inappropriate to speak of "innate" as meaning developmentally fixed—that is, to speak of certain behavior as being unavailable to environmental influence or to say that an organism *must* develop certain behaviors because it inherited a certain genotype (Lehrman 1970, 23). The interdependence of the nature-nurture interaction is more complex. Because genes exert their influence through experiential interactions, and because the outcome of their influence will be different under different environmental (experiential) conditions (remember the norm of reaction), it is therefore incorrect to speak of a genetic blueprint. Simply, there is no isomorphism between genotype and eventual behavior.

Conclusions

Lorenz uses the terms *innate* or *instinctive* to refer to behavior that is genetically fixed and therefore unavailable to environmental influence. However, from our knowledge of the probabilistic-epigenetic position we can reject such notions as being overly simplistic, as being based on faulty logic, and most important, as ignoring the problems and issues of behavioral development. To study the problems of behavioral development we must avoid terms such as *innate* (at least as employed by Lorenz 1940, 1965, 1966). Such terms end scientific investigation by simply saying that a behavior develops in a certain way because the organism is built that way. Thus use of the terms *innate* or *instinctive* avoids assessing the processes by which behavior develops and hence is of little, if any, scientific use.

Perhaps the most succinct summary of the criticisms that can be leveled against Lorenz's use of these terms was made by an adherent of Schneirla's probabilistic-epigenetic position, Daniel Lehrman, in a classic paper published in 1953:

The "instinct" is obviously not present in the zygote. Just as obviously it is present in the behavior of the animal after the appropriate age. The problem for the investigator who wishes to make a closer analysis of behavior is: how did the behavior come about? The use of "explanatory" categories such as "innate" and "genetically fixed" obscures the necessity of investigating developmental *processes* in order to gain insight into the actual mechanisms of behavior and their interrelations. The problem of development is the problem of the development of new *structures* and activity *patterns* from the resolution of the interaction of existing ones, within the organism and its internal environment, and between the organism and its outer environment. At any stage of development, the new features emerge from the interactions within the *current* stage and between the *current* stage and the environment. The interaction out of which the organism develops is *not* one, as is often said, between heredity and environment. It is between *organism* and *environment!* And the organism is different at each stage of its development. (Lehrman 1953)

CIRCULAR FUNCTIONS AND SELF-STIMULATION IN DEVELOPMENT

From our above discussion we have seen how Schneirla's theoretical position provides a way to conceptualize the interactive influences of nature and nurture in behavioral development. However, Schneirla suggests that there is a "third source" of development. In addition to the interaction of nature and nurture, Schneirla says, there is another source of an organism's development: the organism itself.

A "Third Source" of Development

As the organism develops, it attains certain behavioral characteristics through the effects of the maturation-experience interaction. These individual behavioral characteristics of the organism stimulate aspects of its environment—for example, the organism's parents. This stimulated aspect then responds to the organism and this in turn again stimulates the organism. This is a *circular function:* The organism acts on its environment, and because of this action the environment acts on the organism.

In other words, the organism develops certain individual behavioral characteristics as a result of the specific maturational-experiential interaction influencing it, and as a function of these behavioral capabilities the organism behaves in its environment. This action *on* the organism's environment provides a stimulus for reactions *from* the environment. The organism's behavior may stimulate other similarly aged organisms, or the organism's parents, or even itself. The stimulation will evoke responses, which in turn will serve to stimulate the organism and will become part of the experience that shapes its further development. The circular stimulative process, initiated by the organism's own actions, creates a source of the organism's own development.

Hence, as emphasized too in the life-span view of human development discussed earlier, the organism provides an important, ever-present source of its own development. This source must be considered as important as the other sources of the organism's behavior—those that influenced the behavior that originally initiated these circular functions. In commenting on the importance of this third source of development, Schneirla said:

> An indispensable feature of development is that of circular relationships of self-stimulation in the organism. The individual seems to be interactive with itself throughout development, as the processes of each stage open the way for further stimulus-reaction relationships depending on the scope of the intrinsic and extrinsic conditions then prevalent. (1957, 86)

An illustration of the important role of circular functions and self-stimulation in the development of the organism may be offered. Because of the specifics of his maturation-experience interaction, one child develops a certain style of behavior as an infant, consisting of the following:

1. His behavior lacks regularity. For example, the child might sleep for two

hours, wake for five, sleep for three hours, and then wake for seven. Sometimes he might eliminate almost immediately after feeding, while at others there might be a considerable length of time between feeding and elimination.

2. The child, when awake, might show a considerably high activity level.

3. This might be combined with a relatively negative mood; when awake, the child cries or screams quite often.

4. And when he does cry and scream, he does so with a high intensity.

5. Finally, all of this high activity and loud crying and screaming seems to be set off by very minimal stimulation. That is, the child has a low threshold for responding.

Now, a second child may develop quite a different style of behavior as a result of the specifics of his maturation-experience interaction:

1. For example, this second child, in contrast with the first, might be regular; he wakes, sleeps, and eliminates in predictable cycles.

2. When he is awake, his activity level is of moderate magnitude.

3. He has a positive mood; he smiles and laughs a lot.

4. In addition, such behavior is of a moderate intensity.

5. And finally, he maintains a moderate threshold for responding.

What we have, then, are two markedly different sets of individual behavioral characteristics. Both sets resulted from the specifics of each child's maturation-experience interaction, yet the implications of each set of characteristics for the development of the respective children are quite disparate. One might easily agree that the former child would present obvious difficulties for his parents. He would stimulate reac-

tions that would be quite different from those stimulated in the parents of the latter child. Compared with the former child, the latter would be easy to interact with and would not create any serious problems for his parents.

If parents could choose, before the fact, either of the above sets of characteristics for an expected child, I believe they would almost without exception choose the second set. They would rather have a predictable, smiling, moderately active baby than an unpredictable, loudly crying, highly active one. But parents cannot choose their baby's behavioral characteristics. The first baby's behavioral characteristics would create reactions in his parents, and these reactions would in turn stimulate the baby and become part of his experience. For instance, the parents of such a child might find it difficult to handle the baby for long lengths of time, and so they might make their interactions with him relatively short and abrupt. Alternatively, however, if the baby's behavioral characteristics had been like those of the second child, he would have evoked different reactions in his parents, and in turn would have had different stimulation become part of his experience. Thus, if he had been easier to handle, his parents might have sought to extend their interactions with him. Moreover, the interactions might have been of a different quality (e.g., they might have been warmer).

From this example we can see that an organism's own behavioral characteristics do provide an important source of its own development, through the processes of circular functions and self-stimulation in development. In fact, the above illustration of this circular process is not quite imaginary. It is based on the research findings of Thomas and Chess (1977) and their colleagues (e.g., Thomas et al. 1963), who—basing their work on Schneirla's conceptions about circular functions in development—studied the implications of behavioral individuality for the development of more than one hundred children over the course of their infant-through-adolescent years. Their work will be a focus of our discussion in Chapter 10.

Conclusions

Schneirla highlights the necessity of focusing on the organism and its own actions in trying to understand the sources of behavioral development. His notions of circular functions and self-stimulation illustrate and emphasize a central idea in the probabilistic-epigenetic conception of development: The organism is central in its own development (e.g., Gottlieb 1983; Lerner 1982, 1984; Scarr and McCartney 1983). An organism does not just sit passively; it does not just wait for maturation and experience to interact in order for its behavior to develop; and it certainly does not just passively wait for the environment to stimulate it to respond. Rather, the organism is always active, and its own activity provides an important source of its own development. Thus development is in part a self-generated phenomenon.

This concept plays a central role in Schneirla's own ideas about the processes involved in specific psychological development, and we have seen it supported by the results of the research of Abravanel (1968) and Held and Hein (1963) on perceptual development. We have seen, too, that the idea that individuals may act to produce their own development is a key concept in the life-span view of human development. As may be expected, therefore, the dynamic-interactional model of development that I shall now present has as one of its main features an emphasis on individuals as producers of their own development. Let us turn to a consideration of this model and of its implications.

A DYNAMIC-INTERACTIONAL MODEL OF INDIVIDUAL-CONTEXT RELATIONS

To begin the presentation of this model it is useful to consider the diagram presented in Figure 5.6. Employing Schneirla's (1957) terms, this figure illustrates what I have described as a probabilistic-epigenetic conception of development; in the figure I use the term *maturation* to represent endogenous organism changes, and the term *experience* to denote all stimulative influences acting on the organism over the course of its life span. A conception of interaction levels is used in the figure. The organism's individual developmental history of maturation-experience interactions (what I term level 1 development—a term analogous to Riegel's 1975 inner-biological development level) provides a basis of differential organism-environment interactions; in turn, differential experiences accruing from the individual developmental history of organism-environment interactions, or level 2 development (a term analogous to Riegel's, 1975, individual-psychological developmental level), provide a further basis of level 1 developmental individuality.

As illustrated in the figure, endogenous maturation-experience interactions are not discontinuous with exogenous organism-environment interactions. As a consequence of the timing of the interactions among the specific variables involved in an organism's maturation-experience interactions, a basis of an organism's individual distinctiveness is provided. This organism interacts differently with its environment as a consequence of this individuality. In turn, these new interactions are a component of the organism's further experience and thus serve to further promote its individuality. Endogenous maturation-experience relations provide a basis of organism individuality, and as a consequence differential organism-environment (exogenous) relations develop.

In sum then, the target organism in the figure is unique because of the quality and timing of endogenous level 1 maturation-experience interactions; but the experiences that provide a basis of level 1 development are not discontinuous with other, extraorganism experiences influencing the target individual. The target interacts with environmental influences composed of other organisms (themselves having intraindivid-

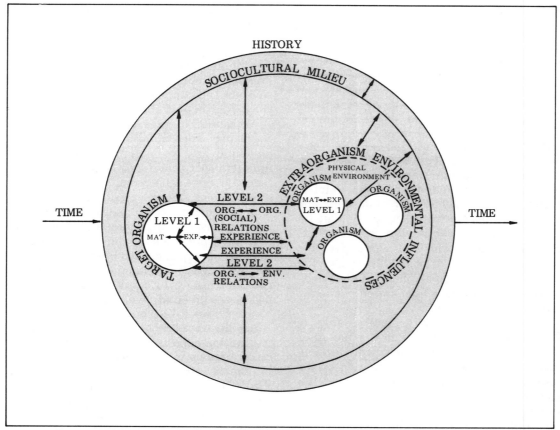

FIGURE 5.6
A dynamic interactional model of development.
Source: Lerner 1979, 277.

ual level 1 developmental distinctiveness) and of physical variables, which also show individual change over time. Indeed, all tiers of level 2—the extraorganism (social), the physical-environmental, the sociocultural, and the historical—all change over time. The timing of interactions among variables within and across all tiers not only provides a distinct experiential context impacting on the developing organism, but this distinctiveness is itself shaped by the individually different organism. In short, in the model shown in Figure 5.6 I attempt to illustrate the character of probabilistic-epigenetic development.

A "translation" of this model into one focusing specifically on child and parent development is presented in Figure 5.7. Here I have tried to illustrate the complex nature of intraindividual, interindividual, and contextual relations. As discussed earlier, children and adults—as parents—have evolved to exist in a reciprocal relationship (e.g., see Gould 1977). At the same time, both members of the dyad are not only interacting; they are also both developing. And the development of each is, at least in part, both a product and a producer of the development of the other. Moreover, however, both parents and child are embedded in a broader

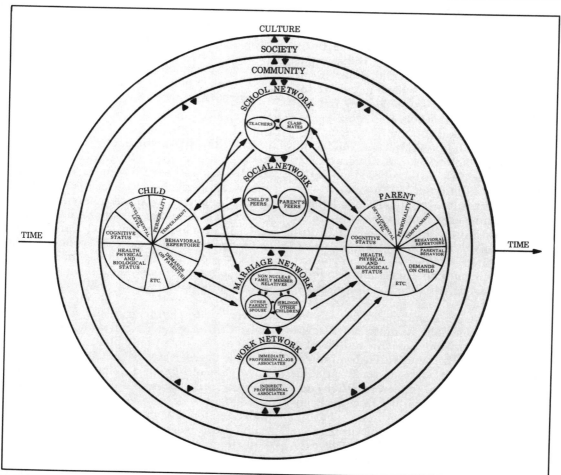

FIGURE 5.7
A dynamic interactional model of child and parent development.
Source: Lerner 1984, 144.

social network, and each has reciprocal reactions with this network, too. Furthermore, both child and parent are much more than just unirole or undifferentiated organisms. The child may also be a sibling, a peer, and a student; the parent may also be a spouse, a worker, a peer, and an adult child. Both parent and child have temperaments, cognitions, emotions, interests, attitudes, values, demands, and physical and health characteristics. And each of these attributes may be influenced by the intraindividual develop-

mental status of the remaining attributes, as well as by the developmental status of one or all of the other dyad member's attributes.

The bidirectional relations depicted in Figures 5.6 and 5.7 may be seen to be akin to those presented earlier in Figure 5.1. Indeed, in my view Figures 5.6 and 5.7 are just "translations" of the earlier figure into ones stressing ontogenetic, as opposed to evolutionary, relations.

Let me emphasize several things about Figure 5.7, however. First, the figure is only *descriptive* of the relations that theorists (e.g., Belsky 1984; Bronfenbrenner 1979; Schneirla 1957; Tobach and Schneirla 1968) and researchers (e.g., Baltes, Baltes, and Reinert 1970; Nesselroade and Baltes 1974; Thomas and Chess 1977) have noted are involved in person-context relations. Indeed, the bidirectional arrows in the figure correspond to relations identified in various portions of the child, adolescent, or adult development empirical literatures (e.g., Belsky 1980, 1984; Bronfenbrenner 1977, 1979; Lerner and Lerner 1983).

Let me stress, too, that I do not believe that it would be useful or even possible to do research testing the figure as a whole. Instead, the use of this or similar representations (e.g., Belsky 1984) of person-context relations is to guide the selection of individual and ecological variables in one's research and to provide parameters about the generalizability of one's findings. That is, this representation should remind us that we need to consider whether the results of a given study may be generalized beyond the particular individual and ecological variables we have studied, and applied to other community, societal, cultural, and historical contexts.

But let me emphasize in addition that the representation is a useful guide to theory development. What I take from this and other such figures (e.g., Belsky 1984) is that there need to be three components of theory-guided research studying person-context relations. First, one needs to have some conceptualization of the nature of the attributes of the person one is interested in studying. Second, one must have some conceptualizations of the feature of the person's context one wishes to explore *and* a rationale for why this portion of the context is pertinent to the individual attribute one is assessing. Third, and most important, one needs some conceptualization of the *relation* between the individual attribute and the contextual feature. This third point allows me to introduce some implications of the dynamic-interaction model I have described.

Some Implications of the Model

As a consequence of the reciprocity between changes at levels 1 and 2, depicted in Figure 5.6, two sets of implications arise. The first set of implications emphasizes individual development.

Individuals as Producers of Their Own Development

Level 2 interchanges will show inter-individual differences because of level 1, intraindividual distinctiveness; the feedback received as a consequence of these differential interactions will be different among individuals, and will promote further level 1 and level 2 individuality. This process provides the basis of a circular function (Schneirla 1957) between an individual and its environment, a function that allows the organism to be an active agent in its own development and allows one to characterize the processes involved in the individual's developmental trajectory as potentially plastic in character. As noted earlier, in our discussion of the life-span view of human development, one may discuss such processes around three distinct though interrelated means by which individuals function not only to shape the stimulation they receive but, in so doing, to contribute to their own development.

THE PERSON AS STIMULUS. For at least two decades some developmentalists have stressed that children influence those who influence them (Bell 1968; Thomas et al. 1963); that is, as I have stressed, development involves reciprocal relations rather than only unidirectional (e.g., from parent to child) ones (Bandura 1977; Hartup 1978; Lerner and Spanier 1978). Moreover, I have emphasized that not only do people influence those who influence them but they get feedback as a consequence of these influences.

Such circular functions arise in relation to characteristics of physical and behavioral individuality. Children who differ on physical variables relating to body build or physical attractiveness (Langlois and Stephan 1981; Sorell and Nowak 1981) or to prematurity (Goldberg 1979) stimulate differing reactions as part of their socialization. For example, physically attractive and/or mesomorphic (muscular) children are stereotyped more positively than are unattractive and/or endomorphic (chubby or obese) children (Langlois and Stephan 1981; Sorell and Nowak 1981). Environmental feedback is consistent with such reactions. For instance, peers use less personal space (they approach closer) in relation to mesomorphic children than in relation to endomorphic children (Lerner, Iwawaki, and Chihara 1976); and premature infants elicit less parental involvement during the newborn period than their full-term counterparts (probably because of their fragility) but more interaction across their first eight to nine months (because of their own inability to initiate or maintain behavioral exchanges) (Goldberg 1979). Furthermore, there is evidence that subsequent intraindividual developments are consistent with such feedback. For example, physically unattractive children have more behavioral and adjustment problems than do physically attractive children (e.g., Langlois and Downs 1979; Lerner and Lerner 1977); and premature infants, because of the extra stress they may generate for already highly stressed parents, appear to run an increased risk of being maltreated (Friedrich and Boriskin 1976).

Evidence exists for similar circular functions in regard to characteristics of behavioral individuality. Children who differ in their behavioral style, or temperament, place differing caregiving demands on their parents. For instance, to return to an earlier illustration, children who are biologically arrhythmic, intense, negative, withdrawing in their reactions, and slow to adapt to new situations are more difficult to deal with than children who are rhythmic, tend to approach and adapt early to new situations, and react with moderate intensity and positive moods (Thomas and Chess 1977). Children with such temperamental differences also interact differently with their parents and other adults (Garcia Coll, Kagan, and Reznick 1984), are differentially perceived by their caregivers (Bates 1980; Thomas, Chess, and Korn 1982), and have a differential probability of developing a problem requiring clinical intervention (Chess and Thomas 1984).

THE PERSON AS PROCESSOR. One assumption on which developmental psychology is based is that people do not remain the same over the course of their infancy, childhood, adolescence, and so on. Rather, in the normative case, physical, cognitive, social, and emotional processes undergo systematic, qualitative, and/or quantitative change. The history of the field encompasses the accumulation of a vast array of data sets supportive of this assumption, and the fact that the processes comprised by the individual undergo developmental change means that a person is, in effect, a somewhat different organism at various points in the life span. More interesting, such development means that the same experience—for instance the same parental child-rearing strategies, occurring or implemented at different points in the life course—will be processed differently and may as a consequence have different effects. Children in a period of rapid growth may process a physical-education intervention differently than will children in a period of slow or little growth; cognitively preoperational children (Piaget 1950, 1970) will be less able to use abstract rules for self-control than will cognitively formal-operational children; children who are in the process of establishing secure attachments with caregivers are likely to have different social repertoires than children who have already established such attachments.

THE PERSON AS AGENT, SHAPER, AND SELECTOR. A competent person is one who is capable of showing appropriate behavioral and cognitive flexibility (Block 1982; Block and Block 1980). And flexibility—underlain by the plasticity of the developing processes that enable the organism to change (Lerner

1984)—allows the child to change the self to meet new contextual presses *or* to change the context to better fit personal objectives. To indicate how such competency—such self-regulatory efficacy—is an instance of the child acting as a producer of his/her own development, it is useful to return to the "goodness of fit" model developed by Thomas and Chess (1977) and Lerner and Lerner (1983) and discussed in Chapter 10 in greater detail.

To reiterate the basic features of this model, just as a person brings his or her characteristics of individuality to a particular social setting, demands are placed on the person by virtue of the social and physical components of the setting. These demands may take the form of (1) attitudes, values, or stereotypes held by others in the context regarding the person's attributes (his or her physical or behavioral characteristics); (2) the attributes (usually behavioral) of others in the context with whom the person must coordinate, or fit, his or her attributes (also usually behavioral) for adaptive interactions to exist; or (3) the physical characteristics of a setting (e.g., the presence or absence of access ramps for the handicapped) that require the person to possess certain attributes (again, usually behavioral) for the most efficient interaction within the setting to occur.

The person's individuality in differentially meeting these demands provides a basis for the feedback he or she gets from the socializing environment. Thomas and Chess (1977, 1980, 1981) and Lerner and Lerner (1983) indicate that adaptive psychological and social functioning occurs when a person's characteristics of individuality match (or "fit") the demands of a particular setting.

But what are the precise competencies required to attain a good fit within and across time? To competently attain an adaptive fit a child must be able to evaluate appropriately: (1) the demands of a particular context; (2) his or her psychological and behavioral characteristics; and (3) the degree of match that exists between the two. In addition, other cognitive and behavioral skills are necessary. The child has to have

the ability to select and gain access to those contexts with which there is a high probability of match and to avoid those contexts where poor fit is likely. In addition, in contexts that cannot usually be selected—for example, family of origin or assigned elementary school class—the child has to have the knowledge and skills necessary either to change him-or herself to fit the demands of the setting or, in turn, to alter the context to better fit his or her attributes (Mischel 1977; Snyder 1981). Moreover, in most contexts multiple types of demands will impinge on the person, and not all of them will provide identical presses. As such, the child needs to be able to detect and evaluate such complexity, and to judge which demand it will be best to adapt to when all cannot be met.

In sum, as the child develops competency in self-regulation he or she will be able to become an active selector and shaper of the contexts within which he or she develops. Thus, as the child's agency (Bakan 1966) develops, it will become increasingly true that he or she "rears" his or her parents as much as they do him or her.

The Individual as a Component of Social Change

A second set of implications derives from the model presented in Figures 5.6 and 5.7. This set emphasizes social change. From the model in Figures 5.6 and 5.7 it may be seen that there is a systematic connection between individual development and social changes; this connection—implied in the immediately preceding discussion—becomes evident if one recognizes that the set of individually different and differentially developing organisms living at any one point in time constitute, in effect, a major component of the social context and, in part, social change, respectively. In other words: (1) if each person may be characterized at any one point in time as possessing both level 1 and level 2 individuality; (2) if these characteristics of individuality change systematically as a consequence of each person being reciprocally embedded in a context with other individually different people; and (3) if the set of all people surrounding a given target person represents elements of that person's social world; then (4) this set defines a key feature of the social context and the changes in this set constitute a major parameter of social change.

This analysis gives both the social context and social change two important features. First, it gives them an inherent developmental quality; this arises as a consequence of the social context being composed of developing organisms. Second, this analysis again underscores the contributions of the individual person. First, the individual affects other people (i.e., elements of the social context) and hence elicits feedback to him- or herself; second, the individual is—in respect to any other target organism—a key element of the social context.

Finally, this analysis provides a rationale for integrating the study of contextual variables marked by concepts such as "cohort effects," "normative, history-graded influences," and "non-normative events" (see Baltes, Reese, and Lipsitt 1980) into a comprehensive view of developmental processes. Such concepts are similar in that they are concerned with effects on development other than those prototypic of contributions made by individual organisms; they are part of the extraorganism environmental influences (including the physical environment) depicted in Figure 5.6. They attempt to mark contextual events that provide commonality across people—that shape the experiences of groups of individuals living at particular historical moments. In terms of the present conceptualization, the contextual experiences marked by these terms make up an important component of level 2 stimulative influences. They are components of level 2 interaction that serve to make organisms living in a context at a given time systematically alike. As such, these level 2 components are part of the systematic influences on individual development and on shaping the social context with which organisms transact.

Conclusions

From the perspective of the above model, development and its potential plasticity both contribute to and result from embeddedness in the context. Reciprocal interactions between individual and context involve functions of the active individual—for example, of his or her cognitions (sense of self or perceived self-efficacy, for instance) and repertoire of specific behaviors and skills—influencing the very context that influences him or her. With such a linkage between the active individual and his or her context, numerous avenues of research and intervention may be opened, including those attempting to enhance or alter the impact of individuals themselves, of their inner-biological functioning, of their context, or of the linkages among these levels.

In addition, if we focus on the group as our unit of analysis, we may consider ways in which the plasticity that characterizes individual developmental processes is also present in regard to these more molar units. The links between individual and context that I have outlined above suggest that levels of analysis other than the individual-psychological (e.g., the social context) may undergo developmental change. This suggestion is bolstered by the generic usefulness of a key developmental concept. This concept is the orthogenetic principle.

Werner (1957; see also Kaplan 1983) emphasized that orthogenesis is a general postulative principle of development; it prescribes that development exists when changes proceed from a state of globality, or lack of differentiation, to a state of differentiation, integration, and hierarchic organization. In other words, according to Werner (1948, 1957), Werner and Kaplan (1956), and Kaplan (1983), only changes that follow the pattern described by the orthogenetic principle are to be considered developmental changes. Thus it is not the level of analysis that is crucial for determining if development has occurred. Rather, it is the feature of the changes that take place that determine this. As such, any unit or level of analysis may undergo changes that follow an orthogenetic sequence.

In sum, I believe that the model I have presented does more than serve as a summary of the evolutionary and ontogenetic person–social context relations that I discussed in this chapter. In addition, my view is that the model constitutes a specification of the domain within which future probabilistic-epigenetic or dynamically interactive-based theory and research about individual–social context relations should be generated. No one grand theory may be able to encompass the set of reciprocal developmental relations depicted in the model; moreover, it is certainly the case that no one study can appraise all facets of the model. Nevertheless, the model is prescriptive for both theory and research.

The challenge for researchers is to dis-cover how the links between the individual and the multiple levels of his or her context may impede or facilitate the development of particular adaptive and/or valued characteristics. The challenge for future theory development is to devise other probabilistic-epigenetic models—of which the one I presented is only an instance (cf. Bronfenbrenner 1977, 1979; Riegel 1975)—that encompass the multilevel, multivariate links between individuals and their context. Research should be guided by such models. Indeed, only when we consistently design our research to be sensitive to the ubiquitous reciprocities among developing people and their changing contexts will we begin to make progress toward understanding the flexible and dynamically interactive nature of human development.

6 | The Continuity-Discontinuity Issue

A second major issue in developmental psychology can be derived from the nature-nurture issue. Granted that there are laws governing behavioral development and that these laws lie within the province of nature and nurture, how do they function across the life span of a species? Do the variables involved in determining behavioral development remain the same or do they change ontogenetically in their functioning? If the same laws, or variables, account for behavioral development at different times in the ontogeny of a species, this is *continuity*. Alternatively, if different laws account for behavioral development at different times in the ontogeny of a species, this is *discontinuity*. This, then, is the second central conceptual issue that pervades developmental psychology—that is, the continuity-discontinuity issue.

DEFINING THE ISSUE

In a general way one may say that if things stay the same, *continuity* exists, and if things change, *discontinuity* exists. However, greater precision and clarification of the continuity-discontinuity issue are necessary. The continuity-discontinuity issue pertains to issues of the description and explanation of within-person change.

Description of Intraindividual Change

In seeking to systematically represent the changes a person goes through across time—that is, in trying to describe intraindividual change—one may ask if the behavior being described takes the same form across time. Simply, does the behavior look the same? When engaging in peer-group relations, when playing, do a child, an adolescent, and an adult do the same things? If behavior seen at one point in the life span can be described in the same way as behavior at another point, then *descriptive continuity* exists. If behavior seen at one point in the life span cannot be described in the same way as behavior at another point, then *descriptive discontinuity* exists.

The former situation would exist if what a person did with his or her peers in order to "have fun" were the same in adolescence and adulthood, while the latter situation would exist if the person engaged in different activities at these two times. Further illustration of descriptive continuity and discontinuity is seen in Figure 6.1. Part *a* of the figure illustrates no change in intraindividual status (continuity), while Part *b* shows change in intraindividual status (discontinuity).

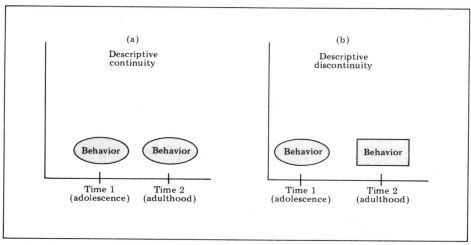

FIGURE 6.1
(a) If behavior can be represented in the same way at two times in the individual's life span, then descriptive continuity exists between these two points. (b) If behavior cannot be represented in the same way at two times in the individual's life span, then descriptive discontinuity exists between these two points.

Explanation of Intraindividual Change

Changes in the description of behavior across a person's life can occur for many reasons. In fact, even the *same* change—whether it is continuous *or* discontinuous—can be explained by many reasons. If the same explanations are used to account for behavior across a person's life, then this means that behavior is interpreted as involving unchanging laws or rules. In this case there is *explanatory continuity*. If, however, different explanations are used to account for behavior across a person's life, then there is *explanatory discontinuity*. In other words, if the variables used to account for developmental processes do not vary from time 1 to time 2 in a person's life, explanatory continuity exists; if the variables used to account for developmental processes do vary from time 1 to time 2 in a person's life, explanatory discontinuity exists.

Of course, the explanatory continuity-discontinuity issue may be considered from either a phylogenetic or an ontogenetic perspective. Thus, if the same laws account for the behavior of animals of different phylogenetic levels, this would be termed phylogenetic continuity; if different laws account for the behavior of animals of different phylogenetic levels, this would be termed phylogenetic discontinuity. On the other hand, from an ontogenetic perspective, if the same laws account for the behavior of a person at time 1 and time 2 in life, this would be termed ontogenetic continuity; if different laws account for the behavior of a person at time 1 and time 2, this would be termed ontogenetic discontinuity. Simply, then, if the laws governing behavior remain the same with time, continuity exists; if the laws governing behavior change with time, discontinuity exists. These relations are illustrated in Figure 6.2.

Descriptive and Explanatory Combinations

It is possible to have any combination of descriptive continuity-discontinuity and explanatory continuity-discontinuity. For instance, suppose one were interested in ac-

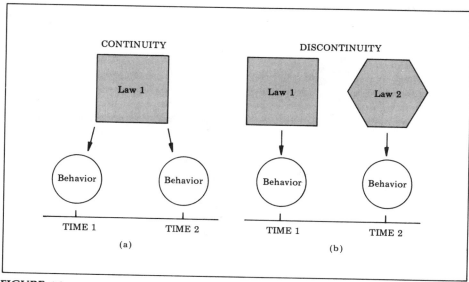

FIGURE 6.2
An illustration of (a) continuity and (b) discontinuity in development.

counting for a person's recreational behavior at different times in his or her life and tried to explain this behavior through the use of motivational ideas. There might or might not be changes in the main recreational behaviors (for example, bicycle riding) from childhood to adolescence. There might be descriptive continuity or discontinuity. In either case, however, one might suggest a continuous or a discontinuous explanation. For instance, it might be argued that recreational behavior is motivated by curiosity. Bike riding in childhood and adolescence, or bike riding in the former period and dancing in the latter, may just be determined by the person's curiosity about seeing where the bike ride can take him or her (in the former case) or about seeing what the new dance steps are (in the latter case). Thus, one would be accounting for behavior based on an explanatory continuous interpretation.

Alternatively, it might be argued that recreational behavior in adolescence is determined not by curiosity motivation but rather by sexual motivation. That is, although curiosity led to bike riding or disco dancing in

childhood, the adolescent rides bikes or goes dancing to meet members of the other sex. Here, then, one would be accounting for behavior based on an explanatory discontinuous interpretation.

Further illustration of explanatory continuity and explanatory discontinuity is presented in Figure 6.3. Part *a* is an illustration of no intraindividual change in the explanations for behavior over time (continuity). Part *b* shows intraindividual change in the explanations for behavior over time (discontinuity). In both portions of the figure the behavior being described is continuous; as indicated above, however, descriptive continuity or discontinuity and explanatory continuity or discontinuity can occur. Intraindividual change may take a form fitting into any of the quadrants shown in Figure 6.4.

With change form 1, descriptions of behavior would remain the same (for example, the person plays in the same way); similarly, the reasons used to explain why the behavior did not change would also remain the same (for example, the same motive is present). Change form 2 would involve the same de-

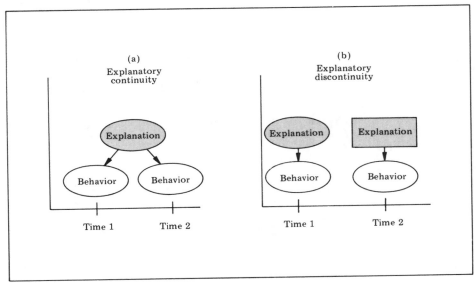

FIGURE 6.3
(a) If behavior can be accounted for in the same way at two times in the person's life span, then explanatory continuity exists between these two points. (b) If behavior cannot be accounted for in the same way at two times in the individual's life span, then explanatory discontinuity exists between these two points.

scriptions of behavior (for example, bike riding as the major form of recreation) across time, but the explanation for the identical behavior would change from time 1 (for example, the person rides to master a motor skill) to time 2 (for example, the person rides to meet members of the opposite sex). Change form 3 would involve the behavior changing from time 1 (for example, bike riding) to time 2 (for example, dancing), but the explanation for behavior would remain the same (for example, motivation to master motor skills). Finally, change form 4 involves the behavior being understood on the basis of different reasons (for example, time 1 behavior involves a motor-skill motive and time 2 involves a heterosexual-interest motive).

Quantitative versus Qualitative Changes

Explanatory discontinuity can be put forward for either of two reasons. One can assert that it is necessary to interpret develop-

ment as involving discontinuity because a *quantitative* change has occurred. Quantitative changes involve differences in how much (or how many) of something exists. For example, in adolescence quantitative changes occur in such areas as height and weight—since there is an adolescent growth spurt—and these changes are often interpreted as resulting from quantitative increases in the production of particular hormones.

In turn, one can assert that it is necessary to interpret development as involving discontinuity because *qualitative* change has occurred. Qualitative changes involve differences in what exists, in what sort of phenomenon is present. The emergence in adolescence of a drive-state never before present in life—that is, a reproductively mature sexual drive (Freud 1969)—and the emergence in adolescence of new and abstract thought capabilities not present in younger people (Piaget 1950, 1970) are instances of changes interpreted as arising from qualitative alterations in the person. It is believed that the person is not just "more

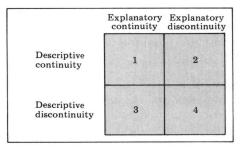

	Explanatory continuity	Explanatory discontinuity
Descriptive continuity	1	2
Descriptive discontinuity	3	4

FIGURE 6.4
Intraindividual change may take a form reflecting any combination of descriptive and explanatory continuity or discontinuity.

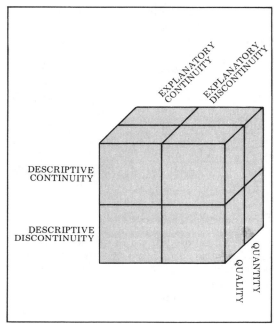

FIGURE 6.5
The intraindividual change box. Intraindividual development involves change along three dimensions—descriptive continuity-discontinuity; explanatory continuity-discontinuity; and a quantitative-qualitative dimension.

of the same"; rather, the person is seen as having a *new* quality or characteristic.

It is possible to offer an explanatory discontinuous interpretation of development involving *either* quantitative or qualitative change. For instance, when particular types of explanatory discontinuous qualitative changes are said to be involved in development, the critical-periods hypothesis discussed in Chapter 5 is often raised (e.g., Erikson 1959, 1964; and see Chapter 9 of this book). The point is that on the basis of adherence to a particular theory of development, qualitative changes are believed to characterize ontogeny, and because of this, discontinuous explanations of change are needed.

We may see, then, that virtually any statement about the character of intraindividual development involves, explicitly or implicitly, taking a position in regard to three dimensions of change: (1) descriptive continuity-discontinuity; (2) explanatory continuity-discontinuity; and (3) the quantitative versus the qualitative character of one's descriptions and explanations—that is, the quantitative-qualitative dimension pertains to both description and explanation. This situation is illustrated in Figure 6.5. As suggested by this figure, one may have descriptive quantitative discontinuity coupled with explanatory qualitative continuity, or descriptive qualitative continuity coupled with explanatory quantitative discontinuity, and so forth. The particular couplings that

one portrays will depend on the substantive domain of development one is studying (e.g., intelligence, motivation, personality, or peer group relations) and, as we shall see, primarily on one's theory of development. That is, any particular description or explanation of intraindividual change is the result of a particular theoretical view of development. This implies that commitment to a theory that focuses only on certain variables or processes will restrict one's view of the variety of changes that may characterize development.

CONTINUITY-DISCONTINUITY AS A THEORETICAL ISSUE

For a long time many psychologists held continuity-discontinuity to be an empirical issue. They contended that the existence of continuity or discontinuity for the development of a given psychological process could be determined only from the results of research. Of course, this position has a degree of validity. Whether one sees continuity or discontinuity in behavioral development *is* partially dependent on research data. The point is, however, that the results of research are not the only determining factor for the existence of continuity or discontinuity. There are other, more important factors, and these are primarily theoretical.

The Role of Theory

It may be seen that a change can take any one of several forms, and that even the same descriptive change can be interpreted (explained) in different ways. The primary reason that people interpret a given change in contrasting ways is that theoretical differences exist among them. If one adopts a theoretical position stressing the progressive, hierarchical integration of the organism (e.g., Gagné 1968), one will necessarily view development as essentially continuous. On the other hand, if one stresses the progressive differentiation of the organism, one will view development as essentially discontinuous.

For example, a given theoretical position might lead one to interpret a given piece of empirical evidence in one way (e.g., as consistent with a continuity position), while someone with a different theoretical position might interpret that same empirical fact in another way (e.g., as consistent with a discontinuity position). To illustrate, whether or not one views babbling as continuous or discontinuous with speech depends on one's particular theoretical perspective. Similarly, the events of adolescence may be interpreted as continuations of processes present in earlier ontogenetic periods or as results of processes present especially in adolescence. Thus Davis (1944) explained storm-and-stress behavior in adolescence (behavior that, by the way, was regarded as descriptively discontinuous) by proposing social-

learning principles applicable to earlier ontogenetic periods. That is, he used explanatory continuity. As will be recalled from Chapter 1, Hall (1904), however, coupled descriptive discontinuity with explanatory discontinuity, arguing that the adolescent period recapitulated a special portion of phylogeny.

The point of recasting the ideas of Davis and Hall in continuity-discontinuity terms is to indicate that whether a given behavior is seen as continuous or discontinuous is not primarily an empirical issue. It is a theoretical issue (Langer 1970; Werner 1957). Furthermore, since theoretical differences affect the ways in which one collects and analyzes data, even descriptions of behavior as continuous or discontinuous are primarily matters of theoretical interpretations and not of empirical "reality."

For example, suppose that a researcher wants to study the level of aggression in the play situations of girls from the ages of six through eleven. The researcher develops a measure of aggression that is applicable to girls throughout this age range, studies a number of girls at each age level, and obtains scores for each girl. Now let us imagine that the researcher has a theory about the development of aggression that predicts that aggression in girls of this age range should be discontinuous. Thus the researcher might specifically expect to see abrupt changes in the levels of aggression, and he or she accordingly graphs the results of the study so that any year-by-year fluctuations in aggression levels would be evident; such a graph is seen in Figure 6.6a. The graphed results would reveal abrupt fluctuations in measured aggression levels in play situations within the age range studied, and the researcher could use these results to support the notion that aggression in play situations is a discontinuous phenomenon in girls.

On the other hand, the researcher's theory might hold that aggression is a continuous phenomenon in girls of this age range. Accordingly, the researcher might not expect any abrupt changes in levels of aggression with age, but he or she might expect such de-

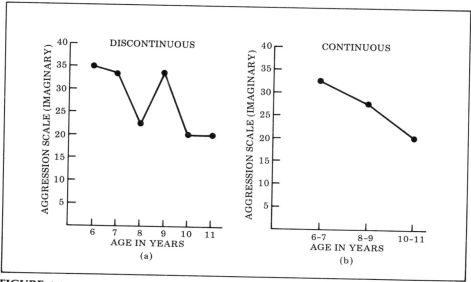

FIGURE 6.6
How one handles data may contribute to whether one views development as being discontinuous (a) or continuous (b).

velopment to be a gradual process. Thus, for ease and clarity in the analysis and presentation of the results of the study (and/or because he or she might believe it to be a more reliable procedure), the researcher might use the average scores for a combination of the six- and seven-year-olds as one data point on the graph, from the eight- and nine-year-olds as another data point, and so on; such a graph is seen in Figure 6.6b. The researcher could now use these results to support the contention that aggression in play situations decreases rather gradually over time with girls and that such aggression is therefore a continuous phenomenon.

As another example, suppose one researcher believed in a theory that learning in childhood involved general laws leading to smooth, continuous, incremental learning steps; and suppose another followed a theory that suggested childhood learning was discontinuous—that it involved jumps or spurts in knowledge and that different children spurted ahead at different times. Both researchers might do the same experiment to test their respective views, but the way they

handled their data—and what their data proved—would reflect their theoretical biases and not empirical "reality."

Suppose that, to study learning in children, ten elementary school students were selected on the basis of those factors that might influence their ability to learn (for example, their IQs, ages, educational levels, etc.). Each student would be given a list of ten nonsense syllables—two consonants and a vowel—for which no previous knowledge existed. Syllables like "guz," "wog," or "zek" might be used. After seeing the list, the students would be asked to recall the items, and the number of words correctly recalled on each of the trials would be the score the researcher would record for each student.

A researcher who believed in general laws and continuity might decide to pool the responses across students because of the belief that learning was generally the same for all children. Thus, in graphing the results, the researcher might use the group average for number of items correct on trial 1 (see Figure 6.7a). Suppose that on trial 1, subject 1 recalled all items correctly but all other sub-

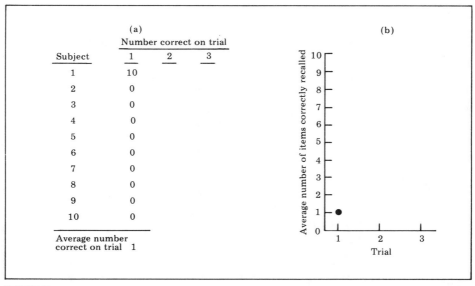

FIGURE 6.7
Results of a study of learning in childhood—the data collected and graphed for the group for trial 1.

jects recalled no items. The total number of items recalled for this trial would be 10, and the average number for the ten subjects would be 1. Thus the point on the graph of Figure 6.7b would be entered. If we further suppose that on trial 2, subject 1 continued to recall all ten items correctly, and that now subject 2 did the same—while all others continued to score zero—then the situation in Figure 6.8 would occur. The total number of correct items would be 20, the average would be 2, and the second point on the graph (see 6.8b) would be entered. Similarly, if on the third trial subject 3 got all correct—as subjects 1 and 2 continued to do—but all others still scored zero, one would have a situation like that in Figure 6.9.

If such patterns continued and the researcher connected the points in the figure, he or she would see evidence that learning was smooth and continuous. Because of the belief in general laws of learning (that all people learn in the same manner), the researcher might not look at the individual differences in the subjects' learning, and the

data graphed would be group scores. Thus, in this example (which is intentionally extreme to make a point about the theoretical basis of continuity-discontinuity decisions), the group data would support a continuity view of learning. Yet, if analyzed differently, the very same data could support a discontinuity interpretation.

If a researcher who believed in discontinuity graphed the data shown in Figures 6.7, 6.8, and 6.9, he or she would emphasize the individuality of learning processes—that children show discontinuous spurts in learning after varying lengths of time in which no learning is evidenced. Thus, from the same data, a graph like that of Figure 6.10 could be drawn, and as such, the individual data would now support the discontinuity view of learning.

It has already been stated that this example is extreme. Experienced, competent researchers would invariably be sensitive to such major trends in their data. However, this is precisely the point. Most often, trends in data are *considerably* more subtle than

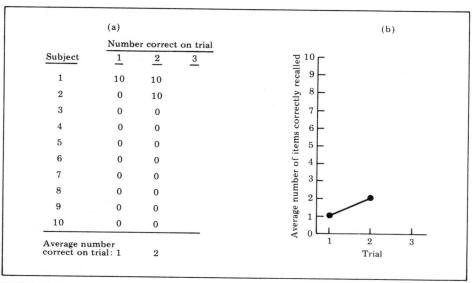

FIGURE 6.8
Results of a study of learning in childhood—the data collected and graphed for the group for trial 2.

(a)

Number correct on trial

Subject	1	2	3
1	10	10	
2	0	10	
3	0	0	
4	0	0	
5	0	0	
6	0	0	
7	0	0	
8	0	0	
9	0	0	
10	0	0	
Average number correct on trial:	1	2	

(a)

Number correct on trial

Subject	1	2	3
1	10	10	10
2	0	10	10
3	0	0	10
4	0	0	0
5	0	0	0
6	0	0	0
7	0	0	0
8	0	0	0
9	0	0	0
10	0	0	0
Average number correct on trial:	1	2	3

FIGURE 6.9
Results of a study of learning in childhood—the data collected and graphed for the group for trial 3.

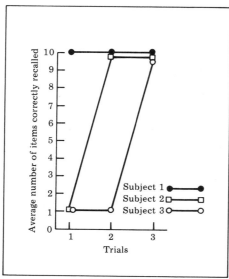

FIGURE 6.10
Results of a study of learning in child-hood—the data collected are the same as those of Figures 6.7, 6.8, and 6.9, but here they are graphed to show individual (as opposed to group) performances across trials.

those in Figures 6.7 through 6.10. As such, the impact of a theoretical orientation on the collection and handling of data is not so readily obvious. This situation not only requires vigilance about how researchers—because of their biases—may affect the nature of the "realities" they "discover"; it also highlights the need to be aware of how depictions of data relate *primarily* to theoretical issues and not to empirical ones.

In summary, both in explaining and describing intraindividual change as continuous or discontinuous, theoretical perspective is a major determinant of what particular change format (see Figure 6.5) is advanced as representative of development. Furthermore, it is important to note that even among those who agree that development must be explained by discontinuous terms, there are important differences in the discontinuities they specify as being involved in change. But here, too, the basis of

these differences involves theoretical contrasts. With theoretical issues so central, then, in the continuity-discontinuity issue, it may be of considerable use to have a means to organize these issues systematically. To do so we shall consider the work of Heinz Werner.

THE CONTRIBUTIONS OF HEINZ WERNER

The conceptual factors that influence the continuity-discontinuity issue have been specified primarily by the major contributions of Heinz Werner to the literature of developmental psychology. Like Schneirla (and like other major contributors to developmental psychology, such as Piaget) Werner conceptualized development from an organismic point of view. Werner's writings, and those of his colleagues (for example, Seymour Wapner, Bernard Kaplan, and Jonas Langer), have contributed immeasurably to the advancement of organismic theory as well as to the appropriate conceptualization of the continuity-discontinuity issue.

Werner (1957) saw that considerable confusion existed among psychologists over the continuity-discontinuity issue and that at the crux of this confusion was a lack of understanding about two different aspects of change. He saw that psychological processes could change quantitatively or qualitatively. I have already indicated (see Figure 6.5) that this dimension of change must always be considered in discussions of descriptive and explanatory continuity-discontinuity. However, it is to Werner (1948, 1957) that we owe a debt for explaining the superordinate conceptual importance of the qualitative-quantitative dimension of change.

Quantitative Change

First, there is the quantitative aspect of change. Here things change in terms of how much of something exists; quantitative

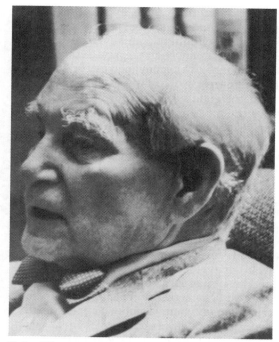

Heinz Werner

and later levels of a variable (Werner 1957, 133). The occurrence of an abrupt change is *quantitative discontinuity.*

Alternatively, the child's change in weight could have been gradual, as illustrated in Figure 6.12. By gaining 5 pounds per year, the child gradually goes from 125 to 150 pounds between his eighth and thirteenth years. With gradual quantitative changes the rate of change stays the same—is continuous—from one measurement time to the next. This is *quantitative continuity.*

Qualitative Change

The second aspect of change that Werner specifies is the qualitative one. Here we are primarily concerned not with *how much* of something exists but with *what* exists—what kind or type of thing exists. Thus we are concerned with whether or not a new quality has come to characterize an organism, whether something new has emerged in development. When we are considering qualitative change we are dealing with *epigenesis,* or emergence.

change is in amount, frequency, magnitude, or amplitude of a psychological variable or process. For example, imagine that a person's weight has been measured at the same time during each of his eighth through thirteenth years. He weighed 125 pounds when he was measured at eight, nine, ten, eleven, and twelve; but he weighed 150 pounds when he was measured at thirteen. Thus a quantitative change occurred in how much weight existed between the times of measurement occurring at twelve and thirteen. This is illustrated in Figure 6.11. This quantitative change was abrupt; there were no intermediate steps by which the person's weight gradually moved from one level (amount) to the next. In measuring this change there is a gap between one point in the measurement curve and another; that is, the curve representing the different measurements is not smooth (as in Figure 6.12) but has an abrupt change in its direction (as in Figure 6.11). There is a "gappiness" in the curve—a lack of an intermediate stage between the earlier

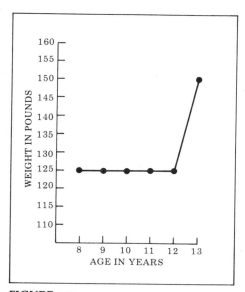

FIGURE 6.11
An example of an abrupt change (quantitative discontinuity).

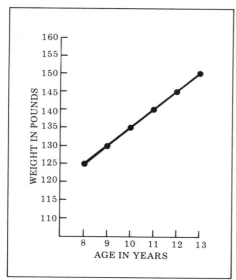

FIGURE 6.12
An example of a gradual quantitative change.

In Chapter 2 we considered the central role of epigenesis in organismic conception of development. In distinguishing between quantitative and qualitative aspects of change, Werner highlights a core conception of the organismic position. Some of the types of changes that comprise development are emergent changes. These are changes in what exists rather than in how much of something exists. Something new comes about in development, and because it is new—because it is qualitatively different from what went before—it cannot be reduced to what went before. Hence, consistent with the analogy we presented in Chapter 2, if at time 1 we can be represented by ten oranges and at time 2 we can be represented by a motorcycle, we cannot reduce our time 2 motorcycle status to our time 1 orange status.

To take another example, before puberty a person may be characterized as being (in part) comprised of several drives—for example, a hunger drive, a thirst drive, a drive to avoid pain, and perhaps a curiosity drive. With puberty, however, a new drive

emerges—the sex drive. With this emergence the adolescent begins to have new feelings, new thoughts, and even new behaviors, which may be interpreted as being a consequence of this new drive (Freud 1969). The emergence of this new drive is an instance of qualitative discontinuity. The sex drive cannot be reduced to hunger and thirst drives, for instance.

Hence qualitative changes are by their very nature discontinuous. A qualitative, emergent, epigenetic change is always an instance of discontinuity. Moreover, not only is an emergent change an irreducible change, but it is a change characterized by gappiness. As indicated above, developmental gappiness occurs when there is a lack of an intermediate level between earlier and later levels of development. It should be clear that gappiness must also be a part of an emergent change. The presence of an intermediate step between what exists at time 1 and the new quality that emerges at time 2 would suggest that the new quality at time 2 could be reduced through reference to the intermediate step. Since we have just seen that an emergent change is defined in terms of its developmental irreducibility to what went before, we should see as well that gappiness must also be a characteristic of any emergence. In sum, then, the characteristics of emergence and gappiness are needed to describe qualitatively discontinuous changes in development; on the other hand, the characteristic of gappiness (abruptness) alone seems to suffice for characterizing quantitatively discontinuous changes. Thus, as Werner stated:

> It seems that discontinuity in terms of qualitative changes can be best defined by two characteristics: "emergence," i.e., the irreducibility of a later stage to an earlier; and "gappiness," i.e., the lack of intermediate stages between earlier and later forms. Quantitative discontinuity on the other hand, appears to be sufficiently defined by the second characteristic. . . . To facilitate distinction and alleviate confusion, I would suggest substituting "abruptness" for quantitative discontinuity, reserving the term "discontinuity" only for the

qualitative aspect of change. (Werner 1957, 133)

What Werner has provided us with, then, is a clarification of the concepts involved in considering the continuity-discontinuity issue appropriately. He has given us the conceptual means with which to discriminate between quantitative continuity-discontinuity and qualitative continuity-discontinuity. But which of these two concepts (continuity or discontinuity) best characterizes the changes comprised by development? In a sense Werner's answer to this question is that *both* concepts characterize developmental changes. That is, Werner provides us with a concept that allows us to see the interrelation of continuity *and* discontinuity in development and to see, again, that the continuity-discontinuity issue is primarily theoretical. It is Werner who best allows us to see that whether one posits continuity or discontinuity as characterizing development rests primarily on the theoretical assumptions and positions one maintains. The concept that allows us to see this state of affairs quite clearly is one we have discussed in preceding chapters—the orthogenetic principle. Here we shall consider its use in organizing the key conceptual concerns involved in the continuity-discontinuity issue.

THE ORTHOGENETIC PRINCIPLE

Werner postulates that developmental psychology has one general regulative principle of development. This principle, which he terms the *orthogenetic principle,* states that "whenever development occurs it proceeds from a state of relative globality and lack of differentiation to a state of increasing differentiation, articulation, and hierarchic integration" (Werner 1957, 126).

Thus, whenever development occurs, the changes that characterize it follow a specified sequence. At time 1 in development a particular psychological process, or variable, would be relatively global—that is, general, or undifferentiated. At time 2 in development, however, this same psychological process would have become relatively differentiated—that is, more specific. In addition, the differentiated status of the process would exist in the form of a hierarchy.

An illustration of the orthogenetic principle will help us to understand its meaning. Consider a relatively young child, for example a child of about sixteen months of age. We spend a day with the child and decide to take a short walk. While doing so we see a dog. The child points and says "Doggie." We smile, perhaps, and say, "Yes, that's a doggie." But soon we see a cat and the child also points and says "Doggie." Similarly, when the child sees a picture of a raccoon in a magazine, he or she also says "Doggie."

We might conclude, then, that this child has a relatively global (undifferentiated) concept of animals. The child calls any furry creature with four legs and a tail a doggie. In other words, this child's conceptual development, at least insofar as animals are concerned, is in a state of globality, or lack of differentiation. Now suppose that we visited this same child about a year or so later. On the basis of Werner's orthogenetic principle we would expect that if the child's animal concepts had developed, they would be relatively less global—they would be more differentiated. Thus the child might now say "dog" only when a dog was in fact in view, and "cat," "raccoon," "horse," and so on when appropriate.

On another, still later visit we might notice some other things. The child might now show evidence of knowing that all dogs, cats, horses, and so on are animals and, in turn, that animals are different from trees. Thus we would see that the child's animal concepts had not only become more differentiated but had also formed into a hierarchy—that is, cats, dogs, and horses had all become instances of the class "animals." Still later, perhaps, we would see that increasing differentiation and hierarchical organization had occurred. The child would have developed a concept not only of dog but also of different breeds of dogs and, in addition, might be able to show evidence of knowing that within each breed there are puppies and adults and/or males and females of that breed. Moreover, the child might be able to differentiate among types of plants (e.g., trees from flowers from vegetables) and might know that both plants and animals are in a similar, higher-order class (living things) and are different from nonliving things.

Thus what we would see with the development of the child's animal concepts is a change from having relatively global, undifferentiated concepts to having concepts organized into a hierarchical structure. This development is illustrated in Figure 6.13, which shows that the orthogenetic principle can be used to describe the nature of developmental change. This principle holds that all developmental changes should proceed from globality to differentiation and hierarchical organization. Thus Werner asserts that the orthogenetic principle is a general, regulative law of all development. The principle describes the nature of developmental change and in so doing gives one a framework within which to consider the continuities and discontinuities that may compose a particular psychological development. Let us see how.

The Orthogenetic Principle and the Continuity-Discontinuity Issue

Jonas Langer (1970), an eminent former student of Werner's, has contributed to clarifying how the orthogenetic principle helps us to understand the continuity-discontinuity issue. He points out that *both* continuity and discontinuity may be considered to characterize development. Discontinuity occurs as the relatively global organization of earlier times in development becomes differentiated. On the other hand, continuity occurs as the differentiated organism is hierarchically integrated. One stresses developmental continuity by pointing out that earlier developments will become subsumed under later

ones—that what went before will be subordinate to later superordinate developments.

Hence development is characterized by a *synthesis,* an interweaving of two opposing tendencies. First, there is the tendency to become more differentiated. This involves the tendency for new characteristics to emerge from previous global characteristics, the tendency for global characteristics to become different, specific characteristics. This differentiation is thus discontinuity. Second, there is the tendency to become hierarchically organized, the tendency for earlier developments to be continuously subsumed under later ones. This hierarchical organization is thus continuity.

In short, what Langer (1969, 1970) and Werner (1957) are suggesting is that there are *both* continuous and discontinuous aspects of development. To maintain an appropriate perspective about development, therefore, one must recognize that the organism develops in accord with both of these perhaps seemingly opposed processes. If one focuses exclusively, however, on one or the other of these two different processes, one will miss the nature of the synthesis that characterizes psychological development, and accordingly one will have an incomplete view. Thus, if one focuses exclusively on discontinuity, one might incorrectly view development as quite a disorderly process. Alternatively, if one focuses exclusively on continuity, one will not understand the qualitative changes of the interacting, developing organism (Langer 1970, 733). What Langer and Werner are opting for, then, is a view of development that recognizes the existence of both general (continuous) and specific (discontinuous) laws of development. This general-and-specific-laws position has been outlined in Chapter 2; we shall see in Chapter 8 that Piaget, too, opts for this position and thus takes a theoretical stance quite similar to Werner's organismic position.

In sum, the orthogenetic principle highlights the fact that one must consider both the continuous and the discontinuous aspects of development, because both can be seen to characterize developmental changes.

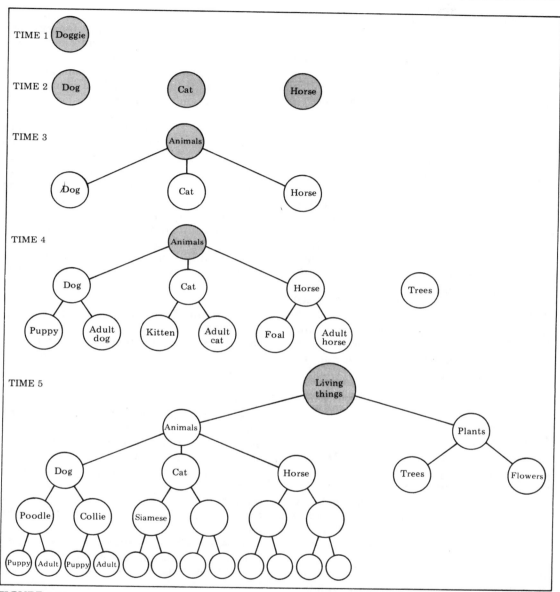

FIGURE 6.13

An illustration of the orthogenetic principle. The child's concepts of animals develop from a state of globality and lack of differentiation (time 1) to a state of differentiation and hierarchical organization (time 5).

Development proceeds from a state of globality and lack of differentiation to a state of differentiation (hence discontinuity) and integrated, hierarchical organization (hence continuity). In other words, development is actually a *dialectical* process, a synthesis between thesis and antithesis. Throughout the life span there is a dialectical integration—a synthesis—between discontinuous differentiation (thesis) and continuous hierarchicalization (antithesis).

However, despite the apparent tenability of the above assertions, arguments about whether continuity or discontinuity characterizes phylogenetic and/or ontogenetic development still occur. One such debate has centered around whether the laws governing the phylogenetic development of learning are continuous or discontinuous. It will be useful now to consider this controversy because, first, the specifics of this debate will serve to illustrate a particular and important instance of the continuity-discontinuity issue, and second, the information will be essential for our consideration of the continuity-discontinuity issue as it is applied to ontogenetic development.

THE PHYLOGENY OF LEARNING: CONTINUITY OR DISCONTINUITY?

Learning is a complex phenomenon. Although psychologists have spent a considerable amount of time and energy studying the learning process (e.g., see Kimble 1961), there is no consensus about the nature of learning. Different theorists define learning in different ways and advance different notions about what processes make up learning. For the purposes of our present discussion, though, we may consider learning as the acquisition of environmental-stimulation–behavioral-response relations, or simply, the acquisition of certain types of stimulus-response relations. If an animal acquires a bar-pressing response in the presence of a red light or a response of turning to

the right at various points in a maze in order to obtain food, we may say that learning has occurred. Although this definition certainly does not allow us to point to all the complexities involved in a consideration of learning, it is not our goal to deal with all these issues; rather, we will focus on a particular aspect of the controversies involved in the study of learning, the issue of whether learning is a continuous or a discontinuous phenomenon. Are the laws governing learning the same for all species? Or must we posit new laws to account for the learning of animals of different phylogenetic levels?

In the history of this controversy, M. E. Bitterman has come to play a central, clarifying role. In three important papers (1960, 1965, 1975), Bitterman presented arguments and empirical evidence that served to clarify the continuity-discontinuity issue in learning.

Bitterman (1960) noted that many psychologists interested in studying learning in different animals adopted as a working assumption the notion that learning processes are essentially the same in all animals. This assumption, he pointed out, had its basis in the ideas of no less eminent a figure than Charles Darwin. Darwin believed that differences among species in capacities such as learning are differences in amount (degree) and not in type (kind). Thus, relying perhaps on Darwin, many psychologists just assumed that the laws governing the learning of one phyletic level were qualitatively identical to those governing the learning of other phylogenetic levels.

This working hypothesis was extremely useful. Its adoption facilitated the experimental analysis of the learning process, because once continuity was assumed, psychologists could study one species and then apply the resulting data to other species. Hence, because it was easier to manipulate the stimulus-response relationships of laboratory rats (as compared with children, for example), rats soon become almost the exclusive organism studied. Any laws found with rats could be *assumed* to apply to humans, because the only difference between these species was in quantity, not quality, of learning. The laws of rat learning could be used to understand how humans learned. In other words, by focusing on how the rat learned one could readily discover the universal laws of learning, the laws that applied to all organisms.

As Bitterman (1960, 485) points out, however, many "learning psychologists" (those psychologists interested in the study of learning) soon lost sight of the fact that their working assumption was only just that—an assumption—and that it needed to be put to empirical tests. One needed to see if the laws of learning for one species were in fact applicable to all species. This, of course, could not be done if learning psychologists continued to focus research interest almost exclusively on the laboratory rat.

Unfortunately, many learning psychologists never did put this assumption to the test, and soon many transformed this working assumption into an article of faith, an untested belief (Bitterman 1960). Accordingly, we find such an early, famous learning psychologist as J. B. Watson saying that "in passing from the unicellular organisms to man no new principle is needed" (1914, 318). Similarly, the more modern learning psychologists Dollard and Miller maintained that "any general phenomena of learning found in rats will also be found in people" (1950, 63). Indeed, one of the most prominent psychologists today identified with the psychology of learning, B. F. Skinner, espouses an identical position. He, too, has turned the working assumption that began with Darwin into an article of faith.

For example, in 1956 Skinner published an article that contained the graph seen in Figure 6.14, which shows what we may term *learning curves* obtained by Skinner from the responses of a rat, a pigeon, and a monkey. But which curve belongs to which one of these three quite different animals? Skinner's answer to this question was, "It doesn't matter" (1956, 230). As Bitterman (1960) points out, Skinner did not present these curves to show that the learning processes of these animals are identical; rather, he as-

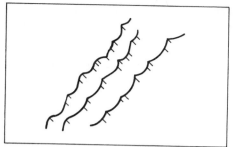

FIGURE 6.14
Learning curves for a pigeon, a rat, and a monkey.
Source: B. F. Skinner, A case history in scientific method, *American Psychologist* 11 (1956).

sumed this. Although we can see that the behavioral products of these animals—their learning curves—are markedly similar, this does not necessarily mean that it does not matter which curve belongs to which animal. By asserting this position on the basis of functional (response) similarity, one is therefore assuming that the processes, or structures, underlying these functions are identical.

Skinner is asserting, then, that it does not really matter what processes underlie an animal's behavioral capability so long as one can demonstrate that one can shape the animal's behaviors in certain ways in specific situations. If one can make an animal emit a certain response, and make another species of animal emit an identical response, then it is irrelevant if the processes by which these animals came to develop their response capabilities are different. As long as one can control the stimulus-response relations of animals and thereby demonstrate that different organisms can be made to respond in identical ways in these situations, then other differences among the animals are irrelevant. They are irrelevant because in demonstrating that one can make different animals do the same things (e.g., learn to press a bar in a given pattern), one has demonstrated that these animals are essentially the same.

In Chapter 5 we saw that such an argument is inconsistent with Schneirla's (1957) views of behavioral development and of the changing character of the relations between structure and function, which he posited existed across both psychological levels and functional orders. In that discussion we encountered some of the pitfalls of the position we now see Skinner espousing. Simply, just because we have techniques with which to manipulate the behavior of two different animals so as to make them emit markedly similar responses in similar situations does not necessarily mean that the developmental laws governing the acquisition of their response capabilities are therefore the same, or that the different animals will typically show identical responses in all other situations. To show that we can make an animal do something through use of a particular experimental manipulation does not mean that this is the way the animal comes to behave in its natural environment (cf. McCall 1981). Thus, to summarize the essential difference between Skinner's continuity position and Schneirla's probabilistic-epigenetic position, we may offer an anecdote told about a student of Schneirla's. Once, it is said, this student was called on to summarize the essential differences between the positions of Skinner and Schneirla. He did so in one sentence: "Professor Skinner is interested in finding out how animals come to do what *he* wants them to do, while Professor Schneirla is interested in finding out how animals come to do what *they* want to do!"

To Bitterman (1960) also, Skinner's reasoning is unwarranted. First, demonstrating that different animals can be made to do the same things does not necessarily prove that they learn in the same way. Again, we have seen that the assumption that even identical behaviors are underlain by identical laws is not warranted. Second, as implied above, demonstrating that animals can be made to acquire *certain* stimulus-response relations in specific situations does not prove that they acquire *all* their stimulus-response relations in all of their life situations in that same way. Third, demonstrating that *some*

animals can be made to perform the same way in a certain situation does not prove that *all* animals can be made to perform identically. For example, we know that rats, pigeons, and some apes can be made to perform identically in some situations, but what about fish, elephants, pigs, three-year-old humans, and seventy-year-old humans? In fact, when some researchers *have* compared such other animals (e.g., pigs, raccoons, and chickens) on similar learning tasks, they have found that similar behaviors cannot necessarily be made to take place (Breland and Breland 1961). In sum, a simple demonstration of similar learning curves among different species does not demonstrate any universal laws of learning. The applicability of any law of learning to all species needs empirical verification, and Bitterman (1960) emphasized that such testing had by no means been provided by Skinner or any other learning psychologist. Thus the assumption of phylogenetic continuity remains just an assumption.

Bitterman did not just point to the need for testing this assumption, however, He began a series of important experiments designed to determine if the laws of learning are continuous across the phylogenetic scale. Accordingly, he chose for subjects species of animals other than laboratory rats. In a paper published in 1965 Bitterman reported on some of the results of his studies, as well as studies by other researchers.

In some of the studies the learning capabilities of a particular species of fish were compared with rat learning. When he compared the learning of these two types of animals in four different learning situations, Bitterman found that the laws governing the learning of this type of fish appear to be different from the laws governing rat learning. For example, Figure 6.15 (adapted from Bitterman 1965), shows that the performance of rats on one of these four learning tasks clearly improved with time. As the rats were trained, they made fewer and fewer errors. On the other hand, the performance of the fish clearly did not improve. In fact, from the curve we can see that their perfor-

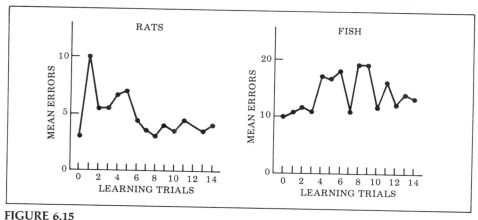

FIGURE 6.15

Performance of (a) rats and (b) fish on a specific type of learning task.
Source: Adapted from M. E. Bitterman, Phyletic differences in learning, *American Psychologist* 20 (1965). Copyright © 1965 by the American Psychological Association. Reprinted by permission.

mance seemed to get worse. The more practice they had on the task, the more errors they seemed to make. Thus, for a given type of learning task, one species improved with practice and the other species seemed to get worse. Clearly the laws governing this learning for these two species are not the same.

In addition, Bitterman compared the performance of the rats and the fish on the four types of learning tasks with the performances of other species on these four types of tasks. Not only did he again find evidence for discontinuity in the laws of learning, but he also found that on some tasks some species learned like rats, and on other tasks these same species learned in a manner similar to fish. Thus, while some species (e.g., monkeys) always learned in the way the rat learned and others seemed to learn in the way fish learned, some animals learned some problems the way rats did and other problems the way fish did. These findings by Bitterman are summarized in Table 6.1, adapted from his 1965 article.

In summary, Bitterman has argued against the seemingly well-ingrained assumption that there are universal laws of learning and only these universal laws, and

thus that the laws of learning are necessarily continuous along the phylogenetic scale. He believes that the laws of learning of one species cannot necessarily be assumed to apply to all species. We have seen that his assessments of different species of animals on different types of learning tasks allow us to conclude that, simply, the same laws of learning do not seem to apply to all species. Thus the import of Bitterman's work is to demonstrate the necessity of testing crucial developmental issues and not simply assuming that one's position on the issue is correct. Moreover, Bitterman has also provided developmental psychology with evidence against the notion that all psychological levels are the same. He has indicated that one common set of laws may not suffice to account for all the behavior of all species, and that instead there are qualitative differences among species. That is, there are differences in kind as well as in degree. One implication of Bitterman's work is that discontinuity as well as continuity may characterize the phylogeny of learning. Another is that if there are differences among animals in the laws governing learning, it is also possible that there are differences *within* a given species. That is, ontogenetic develop-

TABLE 6.1
Behavior of a Variety of Animals in Four Types of Learning Problems Expressed in Terms of Whether Their Learning Was Similar to That of the Rat or of the Fish

Animal	Learning Problem			
	1	2	3	4
Monkey	Rat	Rat	Rat	Rat
RAT	Rat	Rat	Rat	Rat
Pigeon	Rat	Rat	Rat	Rat
Turtle	Rat	Rat	Fish	Fish
FISH	Fish	Fish	Fish	Fish
Cockroach	Fish	Fish	——	——
Earthworm	Fish	——	——	——

Source: *Adapted from Bitterman (1965).*

ment may also be characterized by discontinuity in the laws governing learning.

ONTOGENETIC IMPLICATIONS OF THE CONTINUITY-DISCONTINUITY ISSUE

In 1980 Orville G. Brim, Jr., and Jerome Kagan edited a book (*Constancy and Change in Human Development*) that reviewed evidence from several disciplines about whether early experience provides a virtually immutable shaper of the entire life course—in other words, about whether events in early life necessarily constrain developments later on. With the publication of this volume, the issue of continuity-discontinuity across life came to the fore of developmental psychological concern.

In this volume studies were reviewed that indicated that features of the person's historical setting often shape personality, social, and intellectual functioning to a much greater extent than maturational- or age-associated changes (Elder 1974; Nesselroade and Baltes 1974; Schaie 1979). General historical events such as wars, economic privations, or political upheavals, as well as personal events such as marriage, divorce, illness, death, or career change, are often

seen to provide potent shapers of the quantity of life changes and of the quality of the life course (e.g., Elder 1974, 1979, 1980). These studies also indicate that there are multiple paths through life. As people age they become increasingly different from each other, and these different life paths are again linked to general historical or personal events (Brim and Ryff 1980; Baltes, Reese, and Lipsitt 1980).

On the basis of such findings, Brim and

Orville G. Brim, Jr.

Jerome Kagan

Kagan (1980) concluded that the potential for change exists across life; that as a consequence of active people reciprocally interacting in a changing world the life course is always characterized by the potential for *plasticity*—that is, systematic changes within the person in his or her structure and/or function. While not denying that constancies and continuities can and do characterize much of many people's life courses, and that plasticity is therefore not limitless, they suggested that many such features of life are not necessary ones; they contended that change and the potential for change characterize life because of the plasticity of the processes involved in people's lives.

These conclusions were controversial. One key reason for the controversy was a consequence of the fact that many of the scientific disciplines devoted to the study of human behavior, its evolution, and its development across the life span have historically been influenced by a "presupposition of limits" (Gould 1981).

The Presupposition of Limits and the Presupposition of Plasticity

A presupposition is a culturally deep-rooted, preempirical idea about the nature of reality. The term *presupposition of limits* is meant to summarize a general position or class of arguments in philosophy, one that has many instances (see Toulmin 1981). This presupposition involves the view that human functioning is unalterably constrained by one factor or by a circumscribed set of factors (e.g., genes, early experience); that is, the view is that there is a necessary "connection" (Kagan 1980, 1983) between what is given by these causal variables and a consequent form or function, and that this connection is unavailable for manipulation or alteration (Lehrman 1970). In other words, this view implies that there is one (or a limited few) developmental pathway(s), and that an individual's trajectory along a path is determined by causal factors that permit no deviation.

Although most current conceptions of development do not manifest this presupposition in terms as strong as those I have outlined, there are nevertheless relatively recent theoretical statements consistent with the presupposition of limits (e.g., Lorenz, 1965; Eysenck and Kamin 1981a, 1981b). For instance, Klaus and Kennell (1976) have introduced a notion of maternal-infant bonding that stresses that the quality of the bond established between the mother and the infant in the first few minutes or hours after the infant's birth imposes a potent constraint on the rest of the newborn's social and affective development. Klaus and Kennell (1976, 65–66) indicate:

> we strongly believe that an essential principle of attachment is that there is a *sensitive period* in the first minutes and hours after an infant's birth which is optimal for the parent-infant attachment.

They explain that one of their principles of attachment is that

> early events have long-lasting effects. Anxieties a mother has about her baby in the first

few days after birth, even about a problem that is easily resolved, may affect her relationship with the child long afterward. (Klaus and Kennell 1976, 52)

They conclude:

> This original mother-infant bond is the wellspring for all the infant's subsequent attachments and is the formative relationship in the course of which the child develops a sense of himself. Throughout his lifetime the strength and character of this attachment will influence the quality of all future bonds to other individuals. (Klaus and Kennell 1976, 1–2)

As another example of a recent position consistent with the presupposition of limits, consider the position of Fraiberg (1977); with a conceptual position not at all dissimilar to Klaus and Kennell's (1976), Fraiberg (1977) contends that throughout the life span, every instance of and/or type of expression of the emotion of love is necessarily connected to a bond that originated in the first year of life. She contends:

> Love of a partner and sensual pleasure experienced with that partner begin in infancy, and progress to a culminating experience, "falling in love," the finding of a permanent partner, the achievement of sexual fulfillment. In every act of love in mature life, there is a prologue which originated in the first year of life. (Fraiberg 1977, 31–32)

In addition to these more recent formulations, historically there have been formulations that were fairly explicitly associated with the presupposition of limits. The nineteenth century craniology of Broca involved the assumption that the size of the human skull was the factor limiting an individual's or a social group's intellectual capacity (Gould 1981). Similarly, genetic deterministic theories of both the last and the present century assume that one's biology—received at conception and represented by the genotype—constrains one's moral (Lorenz 1940), cognitive (Goddard 1912, 1914), or vocational (Terman 1916) developments (cf. Gould 1981). In short, the presupposition of limits is a preempirical—and in my view unduly pessimistic—belief in the irremediable

character of human nature. It holds that for better or for worse, we are a direct, unalterable product of our evolution, our biology, our genes; there can be no intervention to prevent, ameliorate, or enhance this "natural order."

However, a presupposition of limits may be contrasted with one of plasticity. Such a presupposition involves the belief that there may be change within a person over time, change in his or her physical, psychological, and social structures and functions. This potential for change is thought to exist because of the constant irrevocable relation that exists between a person and his/her world. In other words, the presupposition of plasticity rests on the idea that the person always exists in a world that he or she both influences and is influenced by; changes in people effect changes in their physical and social worlds—worlds that, as they are thus altered, promote further changes in people. Because of the reciprocal relations between people and their worlds, one may be optimistic that there now are (or may eventually be) ways to better the human condition. One may therefore countenance the hope that experiences at one time in life need not constrain possibilities later on—that at least some early problems, deficits, or insults to the integrity of the organism may be ameliorated (Scarr 1982; Sigman 1982).

To contrast the implications of the presupposition of limits versus the presupposition of plasticity for optimism versus pessimism about changing human functioning, we may note that beliefs in (or the presence of) fixity in human functioning and development suggest that humans are resistant to change, that they are static, immutable organisms. Beliefs in (or evidence for) plasticity suggest by definition that there is some potential for within-person (intraindividual) change, and these beliefs promote a scientific stress on studying processes fostering or constraining change. In addition, the existence of plasticity in the functioning and development of humans permits an optimistic orientation to intervention. In addition to preventative strategies, techniques aimed at ameliorating or even enhancing the human condition may appropriately be instituted (Clarke and Clarke 1976). Without plasticity, humans who possess undesired or undesirable characteristics would be, simply, without remediation (Hunt 1961).

What could be done with such people? If there is a belief that personal and social behaviors and health are fixed by genes or, in turn, by experiences in very early life—experiences that are presumed to have unmodifiable connections to functioning in later life (Kagan 1980, 1983)—then rather severe treatment policies can be instituted. Brim and Kagan (1980, 21) have depicted such perspectives by noting:

> The belief that early experiences create lasting characteristics, like the belief in biological and genetic determinism, makes it possible to assume that attempts to improve the course of human development after early childhood are wasted and without consequence. If society believes that it is all over by the third year of life, it can deal harshly with many people in later life because nothing more can be done, and social programs designed to educate, redirect, reverse, or eliminate unwanted human characteristics cannot be justified. Policies of racial, ethnic, and sex discrimination, incarceration rather than rehabilitation of criminals, ignoring urban and rural poverty, and isolation of the elderly have found shelter in the belief in the determinism of the early years of life.

Simply, the presence of plasticity holds the promise of potentially enhancing human life and the presence of fixity or immutability does not, and the empirical existence of plasticity is therefore not a point of minor practical significance. Simply, if all levels of life are available to be changed, then there is great reason to be optimistic about the ability of intervention programs to enhance human development. However, as I have noted that Brim and Kagan (1980) indicate, we, too, should emphasize that optimism about plasticity must be tempered in light of the need to understand the presence of both continuity and discontinuity—of both constancy and change—in ontogeny. As we shall

see, Werner's (1957) ideas again help us to understand this point.

Plasticity and Probabilistic Epigenesis

If discontinuity in development exists along with continuity, then any plasticity that arises as a consequence of discontinuity must be understood as a *relativistic* phenomenon. It may be recalled that I made this point about the relative character of plasticity in the discussion in Chapter 5 of Schneirla's (1957) ideas about the phylogenetic and ontogenetic implications of the stereotypy-plasticity continuum.

As a consequence of the relativity of plasticity, the issue for the study of behavioral development is to learn the organismic and contextual conditions that promote and/or constrain systematic change in structure and/or function. A similar call for the need to understand how the processes that promote plasticity also promote constraints on change has been made by Gollin (1981), who also adopts a relativistic view of the bases of an organism's plasticity across life. Moreover, similar to the theoretical stance of Schneirla (1957), we have noted in Chapter 2 that Gollin (1981) sees the variables from these bases providing plasticity because of the probabilistic character of their confluence (see also Gottlieb 1970; Lerner 1978).

In short, an emphasis on probabilistic-epigenetic development indicates that the processes that give humans their individuality and their plasticity are the same ones that provide for human commonality and constancies (cf. McClearn 1981). Indeed, Jack Block (personal communication 1982) makes this point eloquently, cautioning that when using the term plasticity one must not also imply that within the malleable system there is not a structure or structures. He notes that "if individuals are self-initiating, self-organizing systems, responsive in dynamic ways to changing contexts, this is because they have within them various ego structures, cognitive structures, perceptual structures, [and] action or knowledge structures through which experience is appre-hended, processed and behavior is forged."

In essence, then, processes of development are plastic in that they continually involve probabilistic-epigenetic transactions be-tween organism and context. The outcomes (ontogenetic products) of these develop-mental progressions are internal and behav-ioral structures affording a human the ability to change self and/or context to meet the demands of life, the ability to attain a "good fit" with the context (see Chapter 5 for a dis-cussion of the "goodness of fit" model of per-son-context relations, one derived from the more general probabilistic-epigenetic per-son–social context model also presented in that chapter).

But, as I have indicated, plasticity is not limitless. Human behavior is always in-fluenced by past events, by current condi-tions, and by the specific features of our organismic constitution. Indeed, a notion of complete or limitless plasticity is antitheti-cal to any useful concept of development (Baltes, Dittmann-Kohli, and Dixon 1984; Kaplan 1983; Lerner and Busch-Rossnagel 1981; Sroufe 1979; Sroufe and Waters 1977) and is therefore unwarranted on philosophi-cal, theoretical, and methodological—as well as on empirical (e.g., see Block 1982)—grounds.

But, on the other hand, any view that stresses complete constraints, necessary connectivity across life periods, or irremedial limits placed on later behavioral organiza-tion by antecedent experiences is similarly unwarranted. Such a view would ignore the demonstrations that at least some behav-ioral flexibility can be shown across all of life (Baltes and Baltes 1980; Baltes and Willis 1982; Brim and Kagan 1980; Greenough and Green 1981; Willis 1982; Willis and Baltes 1982) and that there is evidence for the plas-ticity of the processes producing such capa-bility.

The point I want to emphasize here, how-ever, is that the intellectual agenda pro-moted by an analysis of the plasticity concept—at least insofar as one follows the probabilistic-epigenetic route we have de-

rived from Schneirla (1957)—is *not* one of determining whether constancy or change, or whether stereotypy or plasticity, charac-terize development. *Both do.*

Indeed, let me reiterate that a key feature of Werner's (1948, 1957) orthogenetic princi-ple is that a developmental change is *defined* as one wherein processes promoting discon-tinuity (i.e., those promoting differentiation) are synthesized with those promoting conti-nuity (i.e., those promoting hierarchic inte-gration). From this orthogenetic perspective, developmental change is not only lawful and a synthesis of constancy and change, but de-velopmental change is also thereby consis-tent with the features of ontogeny that we have seen are highlighted by a probabilistic-epigenetic conception of development. Thus the task for developmental analysis is one of determining the personological and contex-tual conditions under which one will see con-stancy or change (cf. Block 1982; Lerner 1979). For instance, what developmental processes lead to a child developing a given level of "ego resiliency" (Block and Block 1980), and what conditions constrain the de-velopment of such a level of flexibility? In order to address such a question we must be concerned with the life-span character of the relation between constancy and change, of plasticity and constraints on plasticity. Some features of this character are discussed in the next section.

Plasticity as a Ubiquitous but Declining Phenomenon

An organism's plasticity does not remain at a constant level across its life span. We may introduce here several lines of work perti-nent to this point.

First, Mac Donald (1985), in an essay inte-grating the concept of sensitive period (dis-cussed in Chapter 5) with the literature pertinent to early experience effects, makes several points leading to the conclusion that plasticity is a ubiquitous but declining phe-nomenon across the life span. Mac Donald (1985) points out that the idea of sensitive period is best understood as a notion pertaining to the efficiency of environmental influences. He indicates that the two key parameters of a sensitive-period concept are the age of the organism *and*, although usually ignored, the intensity of the environmental stimulus needed to modify the age effect. He explains that the sensitive-period concept therefore means that deprivation or stimulation will be most efficient at producing effects at particular ages and that attempts to override these effects outside the sensitive period will require relatively large investments of time or energy (Mac Donald 1985).

For example, injection of testosterone propionate into newborn female mice results in greater masculinization than does injection at day 12 of life (Bronson and Desjardins 1970); and if injection is delayed until day 30 a longer injection period is needed in order to obtain the same level of masculinization (Edwards 1970). Similar findings were reported by Barraclough (1966). A progressively larger dose of testosterone propionate was needed to induce acyclicality in female rats at later ages. For instance, at five days of age, only 5 mg were needed to lower the proportion of cycling females to 56%. However, at 10 days of age, 1250 mg were needed to achieve a similar percentage. Thus Mac Donald (1985) indicates that a larger dose or more intensive treatment is needed at later ages; that is, the organism is increasingly refractory to modification by environmental stimulation.

Mac Donald (1985) reviews other nonhuman (e.g., Bateson 1964; Hoffman and Rattner 1973; Immelmann and Suomi 1981) and human (e.g., Flint 1978; McKay et al. 1978) data that support the above-described roles of the age and environmental-stimulus-intensity parameters of the sensitive-period notion. Together these data suggest that while the organism can be changed across its life, it becomes increasingly more difficult to effect change; change requires a more intensive environmental stimulus. In other words Mac Donald argues that plasticity is present across life, albeit to an increasingly narrower or more circumscribed extent

(cf. Baltes and Baltes 1980; Greenough and Green 1981).

Thus Mac Donald (1985, 116) concludes that:

> we have come a long way from supposing that behavior is absolutely fixed at an early age by genetic factors or that after a sensitive period it is impossible to change behavior. Nevertheless, there are too many data showing otherwise to reject the idea that there are important constraints on plasticity for human or animal behavior. This fact does not, of course, prevent us from finding ways to intervene with individuals who have suffered early environmental insults. Indeed, the theory of sensitive periods suggests that the intensity of an ecologically appropriate stimulus can, at least up to a point, overcome the organism's declining plasticity. . . . The fact of declining plasticity merely indicates what we already know, that successful interventions are not at present easily come by.

Plasticity and Constancy in Development

Of course, the fact that one does not see a change in behavior over time cannot be taken as proof of the absence of plasticity (Mac Donald 1985). Constancy in the individual can result from consistency in the demands and/or constraints of the environment within which the individual is functioning and to which the individual must adapt (cf. Wohlwill 1980). In addition, as a consequence of data she reviewed, Clarke (1982, 73) indicates that

> there is substantial reason to postulate a biological trajectory from which individuals may deviate when environmental deprivation is severe, but to which they will return when these stresses are removed or significantly diminished.

and that

> there is also a social trajectory determined within broad limits by accident of birth and alterable by chance or design. Normally the two trajectors are interlocking, but in studies of deviant development they may not be so. The two trajectories are helpful conceptually in explaining apparently spontaneous recovery from deprivation. The idea is derived from the

work of the British geneticist, Waddington (1957, 1966), who has drawn attention to a "self-righting tendency" which pushes deprived children towards normality whenever circumstances allow.

In addition, and especially among humans, the developing individual's progressive ability to be competent in self-regulation means that the individual becomes better able to self-select and shape the context within which he or she interacts and thereby to produce and/or maintain his or her constancy (Lerner 1982; Lerner and Busch-Rossnagel 1981; Mischel 1977; Snyder 1981). Given that the contextual pressures could be changing while such individual production processes are occurring, the maintenance of individual constancy in such a case would be evidence of considerable flexibility on the part of the individual.

Unfortunately, however, neither the environmental nor the individual sources of constancy have been well studied (Mac Donald 1985; Wohlwill 1980). Cairns and Hood (1983) have presented, however, a discussion of five factors that give rise to individual continuity in development. They note that, first, individual-specific biological variables may contribute to continuity in an individual's behavior. Such variables include genetic processes that might endure over several developmental periods, hormonal processes, and morphology (Cairns and Hood 1983). However, they caution that

> *biological factors are rarely translated directly into differences in social interaction patterns.* The *linkages* between psychobiological processes and social behavior patterns *need to be examined at each of the several points in ontogeny.* It cannot be safely assumed that biological or genetic-based differences will persist, unmodified by social encounters or interchanges in which the individual engages. (Cairns and Hood 1983, 309, italics added)

The second factor that Cairns and Hood (1983) identify as potentially contributing to the continuity of behavior includes the social network in which development occurs. They believe that, if all other factors are equal,

similarities in behavior from one time to the next will be greatest when the social network in which development occurs remains constant. This may be especially true of insulated people (Wahler 1980). The third factor Cairns and Hood (1983) identify is behavioral consolidation, based on social learning, of interactional learning experiences.

The fourth and fifth factors noted by Cairns and Hood (1983) are ones we have seen suggested before. "Social evocation and mutual control" allow individuals to contribute to the continuity of their own behavior by virtue of their being involved in a "circular function" (Schneirla 1957). That is, by virtue of their individual physical and behavioral characteristics, people evoke differential reactions in others, reactions that involve (1) classification of the person-stimulus into categories (e.g., attractive, overweight, male, black); and (2) category-specific feedback to the person (Lerner 1976; see also Kendall, Lerner, and Craighead 1984). Cairns and Hood (1983) note:

> To the extent that some stimulus properties of the individual remain relatively constant over time, the social actions contingent upon the actions of others may themselves remain relatively similar. (p. 310)

Finally, Cairns and Hood (1983) note that individuals may actively promote their own continuity. Especially as self-regulatory competency increases, individuals show choices and preferences and take actions that preserve their social network and their social relations, and maintain their environmental setting (cf. Kendall, Lerner, and Craighead, 1984; Mischel 1977; Snyder 1981).

In sum, the point involved in the Cairns and Hood (1983) presentation is that there are several processes that may maintain constancy in an organism's behavior, and that none of these processes pertains to the lasting or constraining effects of early experience or speaks directly to the level of plasticity prototypic of organisms across their development. In other words, the presence of constancy across development is not in and of itself evidence against (or for) the view that organisms remain plastic across life (Cairns and Hood 1983; Mac Donald 1985; Wohlwill 1980).

Conclusions

Plasticity not only represents a ubiquitous but declining phenomenon across life but, because an instance of plasticity may involve the organism's actively and creatively maintaining a context within which it can remain constant, the presence of plasticity may also be difficult to verify. Indeed, in this view, the presence of constancy may be an index of plasticity. Thus, the outcomes of effects of plasticity may be difficult to disentangle from other phenomena leading to constancy (or change).

To aid in this separation a clear specification of the parameters of plasticity would be useful. But attempts to make such specifications are limited by the second set of issues—that is, those dealing with theoretical, substantive, and technological problems involved in our knowledge about plasticity. Let us now consider these issues.

PARAMETERS OF PLASTICITY

First, substantively, we must recognize that despite the amount of evidence that exists for human plasticity (e.g., Gollin 1981, in press; Lerner 1984), we still cannot answer several fundamental questions about the parameters of plasticity. Are processes at different levels of analysis differentially plastic and/or are different targets within levels differentially flexible? We simply do not know.

In addition to not fully knowing the limits of plasticity that may currently characterize levels of analysis, we do not know what further substantive and technological advances may imply for the future character of these limits. For example, the geneticist D. D. Brown (1981) notes that just a few years ago we could not *imagine* how we could ever isolate a gene. Yet, Nobel laureate Paul Berg (1981) notes that today not only is such

identification quite routine, but the growth in the application of recombinant DNA methods has been truly explosive. For instance, he indicates that

> molecular cloning provides the means to solve the organization and detailed molecular structure of extended regions of chromosomes and eventually the entire genome, including man. Already, investigators have isolated a number of mammalian and human genes, and in some instances determined their chromosomal arrangement and even their detailed nucleotide sequence. (Berg 1981, 302)

Thus, if we take the idea of probabilistic epigenesis seriously, and if we recognize that science and technology represent natural parts of the human ecology, we cannot anticipate where future scientific advances may lead. As a consequence, the current limits of plasticity are not necessarily future ones. These limits are themselves plastic and will probably change in a broader and broader direction in ways that, for some of us, are beyond our imagination.

That is, as Toulmin (1981, 261) has put the issue:

> And as for the possibilities open to future, more complex cultures, there too we must be prepared to speculate open-mindedly. There, perhaps, people generally will take pride in having overcome the "illusions" of material conservation and Euclidean space alike, and may come to talk about everyday material objects with the same conceptual sophistication we ourselves display toward such un-everyday things as electrons.

But recognition that the limits of plasticity can change over time raises a developmental issue. The actualization of plasticity of course involves change, and change can only be identified over time. Numerous questions exist about the rates of change of plastic processes at the several levels of analysis that transact to provide the bases of behavior. For instance, as we discussed in Chapter 5, it is clear that there is a "nonequivalent temporal metric" (Lerner, Skinner, and Sorell 1980) across the various levels of analysis involved in person-context transactions. That is, as was illustrated in Figure 5.7 (Chapter 5), all levels of the context change over time; but time may not have an identical meaning at all the levels.

Conclusions

When the continuity-discontinuity issue is raised in regard to development across the human life span, it draws us into discussions not only of descriptions, of explanations, and of quantitative versus qualitative constancy or change. In addition, we are led into a consideration of issues of plasticity, and of constraints on development. In short, the continuity-discontinuity issue, like the nature-nurture issue, is one that pertains to more than abstract philosophical concerns. The implications of this issue pertain to several key developmental issues.

Just as the continuity-discontinuity issue is related to the nature-nurture one, another key issue of development is closely linked to that of continuity-discontinuity. We shall end this chapter by discussing the relation between the issues of continuity-discontinuity and stability-instability.

THE STABILITY-INSTABILITY ISSUE

In this chapter we have been considering the types of changes that may be undergone by the descriptions and explanations involved in development. Thus the assertion of continuity or discontinuity in an organism's development is really an assertion about how the descriptions and explanations involved in an organism's behavior may apply across its ontogeny.

Such assertions, however, necessarily specify what happens to a person as a function of the variables affecting his or her development. What happens to the person relative to other people as the relations among the variables that affect development change or remain the same? People may obviously be placed in groups—reference groups such as sex, age, race, ethnicity, or religion. What happens to the person's position in a reference group as the variables affecting the person function?

For example, let us consider the most common reference group in developmental psychology, an age group. Suppose that we have measured the IQ of every member of a five-year-old age group. We would expect that different people would get different IQ scores. In fact, we could rank every member of the age group from high to low, and any given person would therefore have a position in the age group. What happens to this person when the variables that affect behavior function? The person's position could change, or it could remain the same, relative to the other people in the age group.

Thus, whenever we consider the continuity-discontinuity issue, a second, subsidiary issue is also raised—that of *stability-instability*. The stability-instability issue describes differences that arise between people within groups as a consequence of within-person change. Thus two types of alterations involving people are occurring simultaneously. People may be changing over time, and because not all people change in the same way or at the same rate, people's locations relative to others may alter too. Accordingly, to understand all dimensions of a person's alteration over time, both aspects of change should be considered simultaneously. Only through such a joint, simultaneous focus can development across the life span best be portrayed. If a person's position relative to his or her reference group changes with development, this is *instability*. Alternatively, if a person's position relative to his or her reference group remains the same with development, this is *stability*. Thus these terms describe a person's ranking relative to some reference group. These relations are illustrated in Figure 6.16.

Notice, however, in this figure that in both the examples the IQ of the person in question (the target person) *increased* from time 1 to time 2 in development. This is an important point. Whether stability or instability occurs says nothing whatsoever about

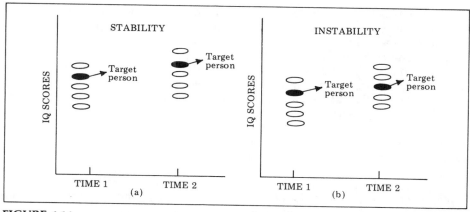

FIGURE 6.16
Examples of (a) stability and (b) instability in development.

whether or not any *absolute* change took place. A person can change, and this change may still be labeled stability. This could occur if others in the reference group also changed and if the target person remained in the same relative position. On the other hand, a person could remain the same from time 1 to time 2 and yet his or her position relative to the reference group could be termed instable. This could occur if others in the group changed while the target person did not. Hence, we should see that the terms *stability* and *instability* describe *relative,* not absolute, changes.

Let us illustrate this point. The concept of IQ, or intelligence quotient, is relative; it expresses a measure of a person's intelligence relative to his or her age group. For example, one way of expressing IQ is through use of the intelligence-quotient formula of IQ = MA/CA × 100, where MA = mental age, CA = chronological age, and 100 is used to avoid fractions. Thus, if you are as bright as a five-year-old (MA = 5 years) and you are five years of age (CA = 5 years), your IQ will equal 100. Similarly, if you are eight years old and you are as bright as an eight-year-old, your IQ will also equal 100. In this way,

then, we see that IQ is a relative concept. It expresses one's intelligence relative to one's age (reference) group.

If a five-year-old has an IQ of 120 and an eight-year-old has an IQ of 100, it would be clear that the five-year-old is brighter than the eight-year-old, because the five-year-old knows more relative to his or her age group than the eight-year-old knows relative to his or her age group. Certainly, if one could construct some imaginary scale of absolute knowledge, the eight-year-old would probably have more absolute knowledge than the five-year-old. Yet we say that the five-year-old is brighter because IQ is a relative concept, and the younger child has a higher ranking in the five-year-old reference group than does the older child in his or her reference group.

Accordingly, a person's absolute knowledge may change, but if the person's age group keeps pace, then his or her IQ would be stable. Conversely, even if a person's absolute knowledge remains the same from time 1 to time 2, his or her IQ could (1) remain the same if the age group did not change; (2) be instable and even decrease if the age group increased in its level of absolute knowledge; or (3) be instable and even increase if the age group decreased in its level of absolute knowledge.

As another example, consider the distribution of scores that would be obtained if people were measured on the characteristic of "height at puberty." Not all people would be the same height at puberty. Some would be shorter, some taller, and some of average height. People with different scores (in this case, heights) would have different positions (or locations) in the group.

When the group is tested a second time (for example, height measured at the end of the final growth spurt in adolescence), heights may have changed for most, if not all, people. However, each person's relative position in the group could have stayed the same. If persons A, B, and C each grew four inches, and all the other people in their group did as well, then despite the *absolute* increase in height, their relative positions in the group would have stayed the same. Despite intraindividual change, there were no interindividual differences in such change. This illustration is an example of stability. However, if a person's rate of change relative to the others in the group changes over time, if person C grew eight inches in height while everyone else grew only four, then person C would have changed more than those in his or her group, and instability (for this person) would have occurred. As with the IQ illustrations, notice again that in the present illustrations of both stability and instability for height the score of the person in question *increased* between time 1 and time 2.

Hence, as I have stressed, the terms *stability* and *instability* describe *relative,* not absolute, changes. Again, the terms relate to whether or not differences present among people in a group at time 1 persisted at time 2 (and hence stability occurred) or were altered, with the group distributed differently the second time (and hence instability occurred).

In sum, we can see that developmental stability and/or instability can be obtained in several ways. Stability between two times in a person's development can occur when

(1) the person remains the same and so does the reference group; or (2) the person changes and so does the reference group to corresponding extents. On the other hand, instability between two times in a person's development can occur when (1) the person remains the same but the reference group changes; or (2) the person changes but so do members of the reference group to extents not corresponding with the person's degree of change. These instances of stability and instability are illustrated in Figure 6.17, where we see the relative changes that comprise stability and instability in reference to a given target person in each instance.

Relation of Continuity and Discontinuity to Stability and Instability

What we have seen is that the concepts of stability and instability describe the relative position of a developing person, while continuity and discontinuity pertain to the functioning of the laws affecting development. In order to understand and describe the types of change that characterize development, one can and must deal simultaneously with the two concepts (e.g., see Emmerich 1968; Baltes and Nesselroade 1973). That is, the processes that determine a person's development may be either continuous or discontinuous (and in regard to both description and explanation), and the functioning of these processes may result in a person's stability or instability relative to his or her reference group.

To illustrate in respect to explanation, a developmental change may be of one of four types: (1) continuity and stability; (2) continuity and instability; (3) discontinuity and stability; or (4) discontinuity and instability. These four types of changes are indicated in Figure 6.18. In box 1 we see continuity and stability. A change that is both continuous and stable is a change in which the laws governing behavior remain the same between two points in development and the rank-ordering of people in a reference group affected by the continuous functioning of these

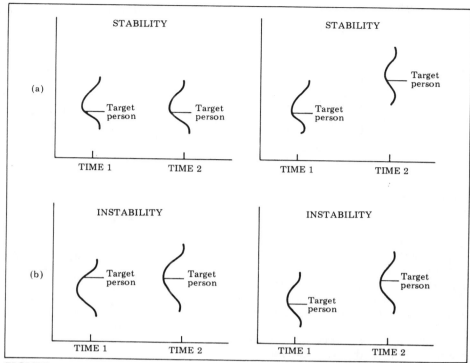

FIGURE 6.17
Two instances of the relative changes comprising (a) stability and (b) instability.

laws remains the same. Thus the variables involved in the determination of these people's behavior do not change, and the people's relative positions in the group also remain the same.

In box 2 we see a second type of developmental change, continuity-instability. In this case, although the laws affecting development remain the same over time (continuity), people's relative positions in their reference group change with development. Changes of this sort would comprise no alterations in the variables affecting development but only changes in the ranking of people in a reference group.

In box 3 we see discontinuity and stability. Here the laws affecting development are altered with time, but people's relative positions in their reference group remain the same. Such changes are constituted by the nature of the variables involved in develop-

ment changing over time (discontinuity) but people's rank-ordering in their reference group remaining the same (stability).

Finally, in box 4 we see a fourth type of developmental change, discontinuity-instability. In this instance the laws governing behavioral development change, and so do the relative positions of people in a reference group affected by these changed laws. In this kind of change the variables involved in development are altered, and the rankings of people in a reference group affected by the discontinuous functioning of these variables are also changed.

In sum, an important conclusion to draw from Figure 6.18 is that phenomena of continuity-discontinuity are distinct from those of stability-instability. Simply, continuity does not imply stability and discontinuity does not imply instability; continuity may just as readily be coupled with instability as with

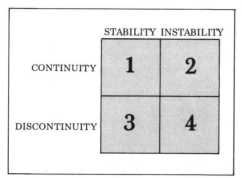

FIGURE 6.18
The interrelation of continuity-discontinu-ity and stability-instability.

stability, and discontinuity may just as readily be coupled with stability. All these relations are possible because the concepts of continuity and discontinuity pertain to the description and explanation of intraindividual change, while the concepts of stability and instability refer to interindividual differences; these latter concepts pertain to whether interindividual differences—for example, the rank-order of people along some dimension—remain the same (stability) or change (instability) across time.

It is crucial that these distinctions be kept in mind in order to avoid making mistaken inferences about the absence or presence of intraindividual change on the basis of information about stability (Baltes and Nesselroade 1973; Baltes, Cornelius, and Nesselroade 1977). The scores of a group of individuals may show complete stability. For example, the correlation between scores on two occasions of measurement may be perfect; the rank-order of a group in regard to their scores on a dimension may not change from time 1 to time 2; or the average (mean) score for the group may remain the same from time 1 to time 2. Nevertheless, considerable intraindividual change may exist in regard to most if not all of the people in the group. This possibility is illustrated in Figure 6.19, where, for a group of three people, there is complete stability in regard to rank-order and mean level and yet considerable intraindividual change in regard to two of the three people in the group. Indeed, direc-

tions of development (the trajectories of intraindividual change) are different for each of the people in this group. Another illustration of the distinction between stability and intraindividual change is presented in Figure 6.20, but here for a group larger than that depicted in Figure 6.19; again, despite complete stability in regard to their rank-order placement at two times of measurement, each member of this group shows evidence of intraindividual change, and in addition, several different change trajectories are present.

Changes Characteristic of Development

A person may show stability of location when in one group (for example, distributions formed by measuring height at age seventeen and at age twenty-one), but may show instability when considered in the context of another (for example, distributions

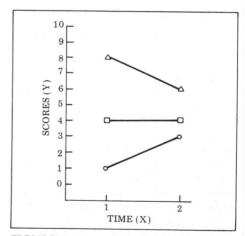

FIGURE 6.19
An illustration of why stability does not mean the absence of intraindividual change. The rank-order position along the Y axis of all people studied at times 1 and 2 remains stable, as does the group mean; however, this stability says nothing about whether intraindividual change has occurred or about the directions (the trajectories) of intraindividual change, which in this illustration are all different.

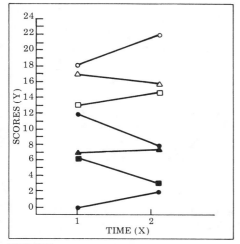

FIGURE 6.20

Another illustration of the distinction between stability and intraindividual change. The rank-order location of the group along the Y axis remains unchanged across time, indicative of complete stability, and yet all members of the group undergo intraindividual change across time.

formed by measuring knowledge of calculus at age seventeen and at age twenty-one). Not only does this underscore the point that stability-instability is a group consideration and not the property of a person, but also it suggests that when different measures of characteristics are taken, different statements about stability-instability may appropriately be made.

Within the same portion of the life span, people may show stability in regard to measures of some processes and instability in others. Any of these differences may, of course, involve either continuity or discontinuity. Thus one cannot speak of a given period of life as including just one particular type of change.

Any statements about the nature of change depend on the particular change process being focused on. More importantly, however, since the same change phenomenon (for example, storm and stress in adolescence) may be understood and measured in different ways, depending on the theoretical orientation of the researcher, statements about the nature of change relate primarily to theoretical issues.

Accordingly, to describe fully the types of changes that may characterize any portion of the life span, one should pay attention to all the levels at which change can exist and to the way in which concepts drawn from theories pertaining to processes at all these levels together may provide a more complete picture of development across life.

Conclusions

We see that any developmental change may be characterized as being either continuous or discontinuous *and* either stable or instable. As we consider the theories and research in developmental psychology in succeeding chapters, we may find this cross-characterization of developmental changes useful in that it gives us common and consistent labels to characterize any and all predicted or obtained developmental changes.

With this specification of the possible interrelations of continuity and discontinuity and stability and instability, we have concluded our presentation (begun in Chapter 2) of the core conceptual issues in developmental psychology. We shall turn now to a consideration of the various theoretical perspectives in developmental psychology. In making this transition we will find it useful to have an overview of three major types of developmental theories; they will be the topic of Chapter 7. As we consider each theoretical perspective, we will see the close and necessary interrelation of the concepts and the theories of psychological development.

7 | Theories of Development: An Overview

In the previous chapters we saw the interrelation between philosophical issues and the core conceptual issues of developmental psychology. We saw also the interrelations among various conceptual issues. In turn, as we now go on to a consideration of the various general theoretical orientations in the discipline, we shall see how these core conceptual issues are necessarily interrelated with theories of development. Just as certain philosophies of science provide an underpinning for the core conceptual issues of development, the core conceptual issues of development provide an underpinning for theories of development.

In developmental psychology several different types of theories (or approaches) have been advanced about the conceptualization of psychological development. As we will see, three of these are *stage theory,* the *differential* approach, and the *ipsative* approach. A fourth major theoretical approach to development, one involving theoretical and empirical behaviorism, will be dealt with separately in Chapter 11. Here we shall consider the similarities and differences among the stage, differential, and ipsative points of view. In developmental psychology, considerably more conceptual analysis and discussion has been associated with the developmental stage-theory approach than with either the differential or the ipsative approaches. Thus we shall need to spend more time in this chapter introducing the former approach than the latter two. In addition, we shall begin by focusing on the former approach; that is, we shall discuss first the developmental stage approach.

THE DEVELOPMENTAL STAGE-THEORY APPROACH TO DEVELOPMENT

The *stage* approach to developmental theory may also be termed simply the *developmental* approach or the *classical* approach, perhaps because it was systematized first historically. Accordingly, we will use the terms *stage theory, classical theory,* and *classical developmental theory* interchangeably.

Although, as we shall see in Chapter 8, various theorists who have used this approach have considered different aspects of development (e.g., the development of cognition, morality, and personality), all classical developmental theories have specific, common characteristics. All of these theories hold that all people pass through a series of qualitatively different levels (stages) of organization and that the ordering of these stages is invariant.

To a developmental stage theorist there are *universal* stages of development. If people develop, they will pass through all these stages, and they will do so in a fixed order. Moreover, the ordering of the stages is held to be *invariant;* this means that people cannot skip stages or reorder them. Let us use the stages in Freud's (1949) theory as an example. Freud postulates that there are five stages in development, the oral, anal, phallic, latency, and genital stages. Freud holds that if a person develops, he or she will pass through all these stages—that all of the stages apply to a given person's development and, in fact, to all people's development; moreover, Freud contends that the order of these stages is the same for all people. Thus it would be theoretically impossible for someone to skip a stage; one could not go right from the oral stage to the phallic stage; instead one would have to develop through the intermediary stage, the anal stage. Similarly, one cannot reorder the sequence; thus one could not go from the oral to the phallic and then to the anal stage. In essence, all people who develop must pass through each stage in the specified, invariant sequence.

The Definition of a Developmental Stage

But what are these entities that develop in an invariant sequence? Answering this question—and arriving, therefore, at a definition of a developmental stage—is a far from uncomplicated and uncontroversial issue. Indeed, several distinct and quite diverse theoretical stage or stage-related formulations have been forwarded in attempts to characterize human development across the life span. Runyan (1980) has commented on the breadth of the formulations that have been forwarded. He notes:

> The search for useful ways of conceptualizing the course of human lives has been a long and difficult one, approached from many different theoretical perspectives, each with distinct assets and limitations. To provide a partial list, the life course has been conceptualized as a sequence of episodes and proceedings (Murray 1938, 1959); a sequence of tasks or issues (Erikson 1963); a sequence of stages (Levinson et al. 1978; Loevinger 1976); a sequence of transitions (Lowenthal, Thurnher, and Chiriboga 1975); a sequence of personality organizations (Block 1971); a sequence of changing environments and organismic responses (Skinner 1953); a sequence of dialectical operations (Riegel 1975); a sequence of person-situation interactions (Baltes and Schaie 1973); and a sequence of behavior-determining, person-determining, and situation-determining processes (Runyan 1978). The life course has also been conceptualized from sociological and social structural perspectives that focus more on roles, life-long socialization, age norms, and the flow of populations through socially and historically structured pathways (e.g., Clausen 1972; Elder 1975, 1977; Neugarten and Datan 1973; Riley, Johnson, and Foner 1972). (Runyan 1980, 951)

Still other dimensions of diversity exist in the stage-related formulations that have been applied to understanding human development across life. For instance, as we shall illustrate by our discussions in Chapter 8, major developmental stage theorists describe changes across much, if not all, of the life span, and they focus on broad-based changes—for example, on the nature of individuals' psychosexual conflicts (e.g., Erikson 1950; Freud 1949) or on individuals' cognitive structuring of the world (e.g., Bruner 1964; Piaget 1954). More recently, however, theorists have been offering stagelike descriptions of more circumscribed domains of development (e.g., Davison et al. 1980; Fischer 1980; Kohlberg 1968; Selman 1976; Siegler 1978, 1981; von den Daele 1975). For instance, some theorists have opted to investigate relatively specific areas of ability, such as problem-solving skills (e.g., Siegler 1981) and social-cognitive development (e.g., Selman 1976; Turiel 1978). In addition, these theorists have tried to define patterns of change more precisely by limiting their focus of study, by delineating smaller and more circumscribed increments of developmental change, and by identifying procedures for measuring developmental change. Some of these theorists, for instance, have described specific sequences of development and argued against the existence of pervasive underlying structures and homogeneities in functioning across different domains of behavior. Fischer (1980), for example, portrays development as the acquisition of sequences of skills in different domains of functioning.

A final complication we may note here is that there exist several terms in the developmental literature that may relate to the stage concept, but that may vary in how they are seen to do so by different theorists. As Glasersfeld and Kelley (1982, 152) observe:

> In the field of developmental psychology we find ambiguity and occasional confusion with regard to the use of the terms *stage* and *level*. The confusion is compounded by the terms *period* and *phase* which some authors freely interchange.

Similar problems have been identified by Campbell and Richie (1983) and by Wohlwill (1973), who note the confusion that exists between the concepts of stage and sequence. One key point to be derived from these discussions is that while all developmental stages involve a sequence (of invariantly ordered qualitative changes in an organism's structures), not all sequences involve developmental stages. For example, the sequence of changes in motor behaviors that has been described by Shirley (1933) describes "steps" along a path of physical maturation; such "steps" do not involve the theoretical specification of qualitative structural changes (Wohlwill 1973). A second key point to abstract from these discussions, then, is that whatever is meant by stage is not merely an increase in the quantity of behaviors or skills; rather, a conception encompassing other, more abstract, changes is involved in the use of this term. It is the nature of such a conception that we seek here to understand.

In sum, we are faced, then, with the breadth and depth of a diverse theoretical literature that attempts to use the idea of stage and/or some stagelike notions—that is, "period," "phase," or "level" (Campbell and Richie 1983; Glasersfeld and Kelley 1982; Wohlwill 1973)—in formulations designed to characterize human development. Our task is to extract from this literature the key features of, and/or issues involved in formulating, a definition of a developmental stage. Fortunately, being able to draw on the scholarship of other developmentalists who have taken on this task (e.g., Flavell 1971, 1972; Flavell and Wohlwill 1969; Kessen 1962; Wohlwill 1963, 1973) somewhat simplifies our work. As a consequence of the analyses in this literature, I believe it is useful to start our discussion of this definitional issue by noting that, in their most general sense, developmental stages are seen as portions of the life span that are qualitatively different from each other. That is, each stage in a given theoretically specified sequence represents a qualitatively different organization—or, more precisely, a qualitatively different *structure*—from every other stage. In fact, the existence of qualitative, structural differences among portions of life is the basis of the stage formulation. That is, the reason why one portion of time in development is labeled as one stage while another portion of time is labeled as another stage, is that it is believed that within each of the two periods something qualitatively different exists. If different portions of development were not qualitatively different, there would seem to be no reason to maintain that they were in actuality different portions of development. Thus it is necessary for the classical theorist to posit the existence of qualitatively distinct stages.

Joachim Wohlwill (1973) underscores this view by noting that the concept of stage "is most profitably reserved for modal interrelationships among two or more *qualitatively* defined variables, variables developing apace" (p. 192, italics added). He adds that "conceptual links among these behavioral dimensions allow each stage to be defined in terms of a set of behaviors sharing some feature in common. In other words, 'stage' is taken as a construct within *a structurally defined system,* having the property of unifying a set of behaviors" (Wohlwill 1973, 192, italics added). Thus, in Wohlwill's view, the presence of qualitatively distinct and integrative structures differentiates one period of life from another.

In discussing the stage-related properties of cognitive development, John Flavell (1971) offers a compatible conception of stage; but he also adds more elements to the definition. Flavell asks what would be revealed if one could take a psychological x-ray in order to evaluate all the cognitive "items" present in a child who is said to be at a given stage of development ("item" is used here to refer to such things as concepts, rules, or, in fact, any cognitive "element"). Flavell's (1971) conception of stage leads him to say four things about these items. First, he believes that the items do *not* exist in an unrelated manner, as elements isolated one from the other. Rather, they interact with each other and can accordingly be said to be organized into cognitive structures. Second, Flavell (1971) contends that "the items and their structural organizations are qualitatively rather than just quantitatively different from those defining previous stages of the child's cognitive evolution; they are genuine developmental novelties, not merely more efficient or otherwise improved versions of what had already been achieved" (pp. 422–23).

Thus, in stressing that qualitative structural distinctiveness is a key defining attribute of stages, Flavell (1971) is taking a position consonant with that of Wohlwill (1973). As noted, Flavell adds two other statements to these first two in order to present what he sees as the key attributes of stages. However, even in regard to his first two statements, he introduces some qualifications that complicate the conception of stage he puts forward.

First, as seen in his above-quoted second statement, Flavell raises the issue of the role of quantitative changes in development and their relation to the qualitative structural changes that define a stage as an ontogenetically novel period in life. The presence of qualitative change does not deny the presence of quantitative change, and vice versa. Both exist in development; and, in fact, it may be that—if one focused on *how* people develop from one stage to the next, that is, if one focused on *stage transitions*—one would see "that processes which either remain the same or only change quantitatively could directly or indirectly facilitate the qualitative changes we observe" (Flavell

1971, 425; see also Flavell and Wohlwill 1969). Indeed, we shall see in Chapter 8 that within the stage theories we discuss—that is, the theories of Piaget, Kohlberg, and Freud, which are all major developmental stage theories—a role for invariancy is specified. All theorists posit that the functioning of a constant qualitatively unchanging process is the basis of a person's movement from one stage to the next; that is, from the continual application of a qualitatively constant *functional invariant* (i.e., a process that always functions in the same way) qualitative changes occur, stage transitions take place. In Piaget's (1970) and Kohlberg's (1978) theory the "equilibration process" (discussed in Chapter 8) is the functional invariant accounting for stage transition. In Freud's (1949) theory, the libido model (also see Chapter 8) plays this role. In addition, in the stage theory of Erikson (discussed in Chapter 9), his idea of the "maturational time table" has this function.

Thus it seems that to specify what is changing in development and, more basically, how this change comes about, one must posit the existence of a constant. Indeed, in a more general sense, how could change be detected unless there were some constancy against which to appraise it (Lerner 1984)?

A second complication Flavell (1971) introduces into his first two definitional statements concerns the idea that a stage involves the organization and interrelation of specific (i.e., qualitatively distinct) items into a structure. Flavell notes that to use the term *structure* correctly there must be at least two items or elements linked by at least one relationship. But Flavell contends that there exist two other properties of a structure. He believes that a structure provides a "common, underlying basis of a variety of superficially distinct, possibly even unrelated-looking behavioral acts" (Flavell 1971, 443). We have seen this view taken also by Wohlwill (1973), who adds that stages are "systematic forms of *interpatterning* among sets of developmental responses" (p. 191). However, Flavell (1971) contends also that structures involve organizations of items that are "relatively stable, enduring affairs, rather than merely temporary arrangements" (p. 443). This property of a structure is likely to generate more controversy than the others that Flavell suggests. There are at least two reasons for this.

One is that "relatively stable," "enduring," and "temporary" are not fixed or standardly agreed-on time spans. Different theorists are free to attach time spans to these terms in almost any manner they wish or, at the very least, with enough of a range that what is seen as nonenduring by one theorist may be viewed as quite stable by another. For example, a structure prototypic of an infant's early cognitive functioning for three to six months may be seen by a scholar theorizing about the early years of life as a relatively stable organization (and given this theorist's frame of reference, it is). However, a theorist who is concerned with the scope of the entire life span (e.g., Erikson 1959, 1963) might contend that such a structure was short-lived and, at best, only transitory. Moreover, even short-lived structures, such as those that are studied by comparative psychologists concerned with "transitory ontogenetic adaptations" (Gottlieb 1983), may be of great importance for the development and indeed the survival of an organism.

A second reason why controversy may exist in regard to using the length of time a given organization exists as a criterion of a structure is that stage theorists do not see "time spent" within a given stage as a key property of a stage or of development in general. As we shall note again below, although developmental stage theorists typically do not pay a great deal of attention to the topic of individual differences in development, one way (of the two) in which people *are* held to differ is in their rate of development through stages. This implies, then, that the relative duration of the existence of a stage-specific structure is of largely irrelevant concern in defining a stage as such.

Further controversy about how to define a stage is seen when we turn to the last two statements Flavell (1971) offers in regard to his view of the properties of a stage of devel-

John H. Flavell

opment. The third feature of a stage Flavell notes is that as soon as a stage is said to exist, this means that any given item involved in that stage functions at its "peak level" of efficiency—that is, it shows an adult-level state of proficiency. Flavell notes that this means, for example, that as soon as a child could perform the mathematical operation of multiplication in respect to a given set of objects, then the child "was capable of performing this particular concrete operation on all sets of classes and in all the task settings that he would ever be capable of" (Flavell 1971, 423). Moreover, as the fourth statement he makes in regard to his conception of stages, Flavell notes that all the items involved in a given stage make this abrupt transition—from not being present or functional to being present and immediately functional at an adult level—simultaneously; that is, he says that a fourth feature of stages is that all items involved in a stage become linked to it as soon as a person enters that stage.

Obviously Flavell's last two statements (1971) about what he believes is a prototypical conception of stage are statements that bring the issue of stage transition into the definition of stage per se. That is, Flavell (1971) notes that his last two statements assert that a person cannot be in a stage in a partial, ambiguous, or qualified way, "either in the sense of having only a rudimentary command of some given operation (third assertion) or in the sense of possessing only some of those operations at a given time (fourth assertion)" (p. 423). Although Flavell is clear that he proposes his statements in an admittedly overdrawn fashion (particularly in respect to the third and fourth statements), it is nevertheless the case that many developmentalists do subscribe to such a rather strict view of stage (e.g., Gibson 1969; Pinard and Laurendeau 1969). As such, issues of transitions, or developments, between and within stages are issues that must be dealt with in attempting to define a stage.

The third statement that Flavell (1971) forwards may be understood as a concern with the issue of *"abruptness";* that is, in this context this term means that "the development of individual stage-specific items is characteristically abrupt rather than gradual; that is, there is a zero-order transition period between the initial appearance of each item and its state of functional maturity" (Flavell 1971, 425). In turn, the fourth statement that Flavell (1971) forwards may be understood as a concern with *"concurrence";* that is, "The various items which define a given stage develop concurrently, i.e., in synchrony with one another" (Flavell 1971, 435). Let us consider these two issues separately.

The Issue of "Abruptness": What Is the Nature of Stage Transition?

What happens to people as they progress through the various stages within a particular sequence? Specifically, what happens to the qualitatively distinct characteristics of a first stage when the person passes into a qualitatively different second stage?

Flavell (1971) notes that there are several ways of answering such a question. One may envision, or formulate models of, types of transitions from one stage to the next. These models may vary along a dimension anchored at one extreme by complete abruptness of change and at the other by complete gradualness of change (an extreme wherein, if it existed for a given theory, the idea of stage—as a novel period of life, one having structures special only to it—would probably lose all meaning). However, while a model of stage transition located at the extreme-gradualism end of the abruptness-gradualism dimension would, in effect, be a nonstage model of development, a model of stage transition located at the extreme-abruptness end of this dimension would be a nondevelopmental model of stages.

Such an extreme-abruptness model of development is depicted in Figure 7.1a, an il-

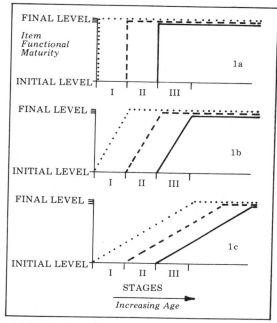

FIGURE 7.1
Three models of stage transitions. The developmental course of individual stage-specific items varies in relation to the model's location along a dimension of "abruptness-gradualism" of transition.

Source: Adapted from Flavell (1971, 426).

lustration adapted from Flavell (1971). Flavell explains why the extreme-abruptness model illustrated in Figure 7.1a is, in actuality, an adevelopmental and indeed quite static model of stage. He notes that in this model one is characterized as being "in" a particular stage of development

> because and just so long as, one *continues* to behave in some particular fashion; developmental *changes* in behavior are largely relegated to the "period of transition" from one stage to the next. If these "periods of transition" are taken to be of essentially null duration . . . , the view that stages emerge abruptly rather than gradually, leads logically to the rather paradoxical conclusion that the individual spends virtually all of his childhood years "being" rather than "becoming." . . . the termination of any stage is defined not by the cessation of developmental change in the stage-specific item (this change having both commenced and ceased at the *beginning* of the stage), but simply by the abrupt emergence of the succeeding stage. (Flavell 1971, 426–27)

Flavell goes on to note that this model

> has much to commend it on formal grounds. It lends a meaning to "stage" that is conceptually clear, theoretically strong, operationally useful, and quite congruent with the ordinary-language meaning of that term. Unfortunately, that developing system we call the child just does not seem to conform to it [therefore] Model 1a can immediately be ruled out of contention. (Flavell 1971, 428)

And indeed it is out of contention. No major developmental stage theorist takes such an abrupt view of stage transition—although such abruptness is, as noted, part of the "stereotyped" view of stages (Flavell 1971) and although some critics of stage theory (e.g., Bandura 1977; Mischel and Mischel 1976) have attributed such a conception to stage theories in the criticisms they have made. For example, Davison et al. (1980), in discussing the stage concept in theories of cognitive development, have noted:

> Such critics have assumed that stage theories imply that there will be a patterning to a subject's stage scores—All of them will be zero except one, the stage at which the subject reasons.
>
> Actually the stage theorists . . . do not say that people reason at only one stage. Their theories are more complicated than is assumed by the critics. These more complicated stage theories, however, can imply that there will be a patterning to subjects' stage scores, but not the simple patterning that would occur if subjects reason at only one stage. (pp. 121–22)

The patterning to which Davison et al. (1980) refer is explicitly recognized by stage theorists, for example in their use of concepts such as "stage mixture"—a notion indicating that people exist simultaneously at several different stages. We shall return below to this notion. Here, however, we should stress that in the extant major developmental stage theories, a model of abrupt stage progression such as that in the first model of Figure 7.1 is *not* used; stage progression is never held to be an all-or-none event. That is, people do not progress from one stage to another overnight. It is not the case that one day a person goes to sleep in stage 1 and the next day awakens in qualitatively different stage 2. Development is *not* held to be a series of qualitative leaps, of saltatory, steplike functions. Rather, transitions from one stage to the next are gradual; they take place slowly over time.

For example, one way of determining if a person is at a particular stage in development is to see if the person shows behaviors consistent with what we would expect from knowledge of that particular stage. If the person does not show such behaviors, we could say that the person has not developed into that stage. On the other hand, however, just because a person does show responses representative of a particular stage of development does not mean that the person has fully developed into that stage. Because people progress from one stage to another gradually, they will therefore show behaviors that are representative of more than one stage at the same time. In other words, because stage progression is not an all-or-none process but rather takes place gradually over time, we would expect a person to show behavior representative of more than one stage of development at the same time.

How, then, may we determine what stage a person is in? Clearly, one behavior or even a few would not be a sufficient sample to allow us to determine unequivocally a person's representative stage of development. Rather, it is necessary to get a large sample of the person's behaviors. Once we know which behaviors are representative of which stages of development, we have to observe many instances of the person's behavior. Only then can we make a stage determination. Then we may know within which stage the majority of the person's behaviors fall. Thus we are determining to which stage most of the person's behaviors relate. By determining the most frequently occurring (i.e., the modal) behavior, we are finding out what stage best represents the person's level of development.

Hence, whenever we say that a person is at a particular stage of development, we are saying this on the basis of the person's most frequently occurring (modal) behaviors. We are not saying that a person at a particular stage of development is functioning only at that one stage; in fact, as we have seen, we would expect quite the opposite to be the case. Yet, if we are judicious enough to obtain a large sample of a person's behaviors, we will also be able to ascertain which stage is most representative of his or her behaviors.

In sum, whenever we speak of a person as being at a particular stage of development, we are making a relative, not an absolute, statement—a statement that should ideally be based on that person's modal response pattern. We are saying that relative to other stages of development, the person's modal behavior is representative of a particular stage. In other words, people may function at more than one developmental level at a time, and attributing the status of a particular stage to a person should be based on a large sampling and determination of the person's modal behaviors. However, if people also simultaneously possess attributes of

more than one stage as a consequence of less than completely abrupt transitions between stages, then we need to inquire into the form that may be taken by these more gradual stage changes. Thus it is useful to refer to the other models illustrated in Figure 7.1.

Figure 7.1b represents a model of stage transition wherein the functional maturity of a stage-specific item increases gradually throughout the stage. Development of this item continues until the very end of the stage, when full maturity is reached. However, at the end point of the stage the items specific to the next stage are beginning their development. Therefore Flavell (1971) notes that in this model the end point of a stage is defined by the completion of development of its own items *and* by the initiation of development of the items of the next stage. Thus in this model a stage is not a static state of being. Rather it is a state of constant "becoming." The stage's own items are becoming more developed (i.e., functionally mature) throughout the stage and, while this achievement is being attained the stage is also a period of preparation for the development of the items of the next stage.

This view of stage transition is found in Piaget's (1955) own writings. As translated by Flavell (1971), Piaget has indicated that "a stage thus comprises both a level of *preparation,* on the one hand, and of *achievement,* on the other" (Piaget 1955, 35). Flavell (1971, 427) himself notes that "a stage here is not a state but a process—it is *itself* the 'period of transition.'"

However, models can be formulated that are even more extreme in their emphasis on the gradualness of development. One such model, formulated by Flavell (1971), is represented in Figure 7.1c. In this model a stage's items do not reach complete functional maturity within the stage with which they are modally associated or, in other words, with the stage within which the major proportion of their development occurs. In this third model, an item's development can continue into subsequent stages. Thus a feature of development present in this model, but not in the other two suggested by Flavell (1971), is that items from two different stages can be developing at the same time. An item from a former stage can be completing its development in a subsequent stage while, at the same time, items from that subsequent stage can also be developing.

Flavell (1971) observes that since the three models illustrated in Figure 7.1 lie on a continuum of abruptness-gradualness, it is possible to formulate models representative of other points along this continuum. A general implication of this observation is that there may be several different ways to conceptualize the characteristics of stage transition. Indeed, scholars other than Flavell (1971) have formulated different sets of models, or schemes, of stage transition (e.g., Emmerich 1968; van den Daele 1969, 1974; Wohlwill 1973). Despite starting from perhaps different conceptual bases, because these scholars deal with the same issues addressed by Flavell (1971), their schemes of transition are often substantially compatible. To illustrate another approach to the topic of the ways in which stage transitions may occur, and to indicate this compatibility among scholars, let us consider the views of Walter Emmerich (1968), a scholar whose work has served to clarify issues pertinent not only to the stage approach but also to the other approaches we shall consider in this chapter (i.e., the differential and the ipsative approaches). As such, we shall have reason to return again in this chapter to Emmerich's views. Here, however, let us note only Emmerich's ideas regarding stage transition.

Emmerich believes that one of three things may happen to the characteristics (or "items," in Flavell's 1971 terms) of a previous stage when a person develops into the next stage. He points out that the first thing that could happen when a person completes a transition from one stage of development into the next is that the characteristics of the first stage become completely displaced. This is the most extreme view of what may happen when transition from one stage to the next is complete. This component of

Emmerich's first alternative is compatible with the outcome of abrupt change depicted in Flavell's (1971) first model. That is, both views hold that when transition is complete, the person will be completely newly organized and the characteristics of the previous stage will be lost. However, there is no requirement in Emmerich's first alternative that the change from stage 1 to stage 2 be totally abrupt. That is, even this radical transition may take place gradually over time; and accordingly, even in this case the person will show evidence of behavioral characteristics of both developmental stages while the transition is still occurring.

In the second type of transition, the later stage becomes the dominant level of functioning, but the behavioral characteristics of the previous stage are still seen. This possibility is similar to the general notions of gradual stage transition already discussed, and it is a view consonant with features of the second and third models illustrated by Flavell (1971). However, this second alternative suggested by Emmerich (1968) places greater emphasis on stage development as a modal phenomenon. This alternative, then, stresses the notion that current stages are dominant in that behaviors representative of that stage are most frequent. However, although they do occur at a lower frequency than the modal behaviors, the behavioral characteristics of earlier stages are not lost. In fact, it is sometimes held that under some circumstances the lower-frequency behaviors can for a time become dominant in frequency (Emmerich 1968, 674).

The third possibility is similar to the second. Here, however, when the new stage has fully emerged, the behavioral characteristics of the earlier stage do not typically occur. That is, the characteristics of the new stage will be the only characteristics that are typically seen. The characteristics of the earlier stage lie dormant, or are latent, and are not typically seen. In certain special circumstances, however, the earlier characteristics may emerge (Emmerich 1968, 674).

In sum, scholars such as Flavell (1971) and Emmerich (1968), among others (e.g., van den Daele 1969, 1974; Wohlwill 1973), have suggested several types of transitions that may occur between the stages proposed within developmental stage theories. Different stage theories may opt for any one of these alternatives. Of course, the difficulty for the researcher who wants to test these different alternatives lies in measuring the differences that each alternative predicts. It would be difficult to discriminate among these three types of transitions because, in any event, all the transitions take place gradually. Hence, by the time a given stage has almost completely displaced a previous stage as a person's dominant level of functioning, another stage may be beginning to displace this now-dominant stage. Hence, because of this stage *mixture* (Turiel 1969), stage development is very complex, and it is most difficult to ascertain which model or scheme of stage transition best fits the data—that is, best characterizes development. However, this very complexity is the major point of our present discussion. Because of the gradual nature of stage transition, a person functions at more than one qualitatively different stage at the same time. Thus stage mixture is an essential component of any adequate stage theory of development and is a key feature of an appropriate conceptualization of a developmental stage.

We have noted, however, that at least one other concept—that of concurrence—needs to be evaluated in respect to its role as a feature of the definition of stage. We have seen that the concept of abruptness with which we have just dealt pertains to the issue of the development—the transitions—between stages. We noted in turn that the concept of concurrence pertains to the issue of development within a stage. Let us turn, then, to a consideration of this last concept.

The Issue of "Concurrence": Is There Synchrony in the Development of the Items within a Stage?

Is the time course of the development of the stage-specific items that define a stage com-

mon across all these items? "Being in" a stage means possessing certain stage-specific attributes. But does this mean, too, that all items begin and end their development at the same time? These questions are involved in considering the concept of concurrence.

The best answer to the above questions seems to be no. Time differences are typically, indeed almost invariably, found in the attainment of the different attributes (or items) that are specific to a stage (Flavell 1971). In fact, we shall see in Chapter 8 that such lacks of concurrence are quite specifically included in the ideas of some stage theorists. For instance, in the Chapter 8 presentation of Piaget's theory, we shall see that his notion of *décalage* (Piaget 1950, 1970) is used to refer to systematic time differences in the cognitive attainment of particular stage-specific concepts. Accordingly, and although the point is not held without some exceptions (e.g., Pinard and Laurendeau 1969), we may agree with Flavell (1971) that *complete* concurrence is not a requirement of a developmental stage theory, be it Piaget's (1950, 1970) or any other.

Wohlwill (1973) appears to agree with this point but adds some important qualifications, noting

> that despite *the undeniable fact of asynchrony,* a considerable degree of order and regularity—or, to put it another way, of constraints on the forms which the interrelationships of developing elements of a structure may take—still obtains. (Wohlwill 1973, 239, italics added)

In other words, despite a lack of complete concurrence, the elements or items of a stage do not develop in a completely haphazard fashion. And, just as one may model the nature of developments, or transitions, between stages—as varying along an abruptness-gradualness continuum (Flavell 1971), for instance—one may model the nature of developments, or concurrences, within a stage—as involving differing degrees of concurrence (or synchrony). Wohlwill (1973) has formulated some models representing different degrees of concurrence, and they are summarized in Table 7.1.

TABLE 7.1
Degrees of Within-Stage Concurrence or Synchrony: Wohlwill's Models of Developmental Stages, Arranged in Order of Complexity of Interrelationship Among Component Sequences

Model	Major Hypothesis	Implications for Concepts of Stages
IA: Synchronous progression	Changes in level for all sequences occur in synchrony	Structural network tying together ordered sequences of responses at equivalent levels, with developmental progression occurring in unison in all sequences, linked in one rigid system
IIA: Horizontal décalage, convergent	Changes in level occur in synchrony, with exceptions for certain sequences, taking the form of staggered progression	Structural network integrating ordered sequences of responses at equivalent levels, with sequence-specific or extraneous factors resulting in temporary lags between systems at intermediary levels
IIB: Horizontal décalage, divergent	As in IIA above	As in IIA above, except that sequence-specific or extraneous factors have cumulative effect, with progressively widening gaps between sequences
III: Reciprocal interaction	Changes in level occur in synchrony, with exceptions for certain sequences, taking the form of intersecting developmental functions	Structural network integrating ordered sequences of responses at equivalent levels, with interdependence among particular sequences resulting in temporary perturbations in developmental timetable
IV: Disequilibration-stabilization	Attainment of levels of stage consolidation occurs synchronously for all sequences, separated by intermediary levels marked by behavior oscillation; irregular relationships among sequences	Structural network representing nodes at which ordered sequences of response become functionally integrated, with developmental progression occurring in fluid fashion between these nodes

Source: *Wohlwill 1973, 206.*

Thus Wohlwill's (1973) position is akin to Flavell's (1971): A concept of stage necessarily involves relative concurrence. Absolute concurrence is neither a theoretical requirement of developmental stage theories nor is it empirically ubiquitous. Wohlwill (1973, 192) summarizes his position by noting that his:

> underlying assumption is that in certain areas of development, particularly in the cognitive realm, but not necessarily confined to it, there exist regulating mechanisms that modulate the course of the individual's development so as to ensure a degree of harmony and integration in his functioning over a variety of related behavioral dimensions. The mechanism might be thought of in part as a mediational generalization process, permitting acquisitions in one area, for example number conservation, to spread both to equivalent aspects of different concepts (e.g., conservation of length) and to different aspects of the same concept (e.g., cardinal-ordinal correspondence). The result is the formation of a broad structural network of interrelated concepts appearing, not all at once to be sure, but within a fairly narrowly delimited period, with further progress along any component concept or dimension being assumed to be deferred till the consolidation of this network—that is, the attainment of the "stage." Stage development thus provides for relative consistency of behavior, economy in the acquisition of new responses, and harmony and interrelatedness in the development of diverse concepts or skills across successive levels.

Conclusions

We may abstract from the controversy surrounding the conception of developmental stages a definition of a developmental stage as a component of a sequence of qualitative structural reorganizations. Between-stage developments are never completely abrupt, and there is no complete concurrence or synchrony in the within-stage development of the elements or items comprising a specific stage.

Finally, we may note that in positing the universal applicability of the stages they describe—that is, the invariant applicability of

Joachim F. Wohlwill

the stages to all people—stage theorists are proposing features of development that are common to all people. Thus such theories describe the development of the *generic* human being, the general case of humanity, and thus the laws of development proposed by stage theorists are laws that apply to all individuals. Such laws are termed *nomothetic* laws. That is, the stage-theory approach is concerned with the postulation of general (group, nomothetic) laws of development— laws that apply to the generic human being.

Individual Differences within Stage Theories

Despite their overriding attention to laws that characterize all people, stage theorists do recognize that people differ, but they hold these individual differences to be relatively minimal. That is, stage theorists maintain that there are only two ways in which people may differ (Emmerich 1968). First, as we noted earlier, people may differ in their *rate of progression* through the stages, in how fast they develop. It may take one individual one year and another individual two years to pass through the same stage, but all people pass through the same stages in the same order.

The second way that people may differ within developmental stage theories is in the *final level of development* they reach. Not all people go through all the stages—for example, because of illness or death, the development of such people stops. The point is, though, that as far as the development of such people does go, it will necessarily be in accord with the specified stage progression; and if these people had developed, they would have progressed through the stages in accordance with the specified sequence. In sum, according to stage theory, people may differ in how *fast* they develop (rate of stage progression) and in how *far* they develop (final level of development reached).

Relation of Concepts of Development to Stage Theories

We have seen that the stage concept is used to denote an ordered, qualitative structural change in development. It should be clear that such an approach to development contrasts fundamentally with perspectives that describe developmental change as quantitative or incremental—that is, as occurring only continually and gradually, and involving only the addition of "molecular" (e.g., stimulus-response) units to the behavioral repertoire (e.g., Bijou 1976; Bijou and Baer 1961). As we shall see in Chapter 11, such mechanistic approaches typically take an empirical-behaviorist or a theoretical-behaviorist approach to conceptualizing developmental changes. In the empirical-behaviorist approach, for instance, the processes through which behaviors are shaped, and through which an increasing number of skills are acquired, are seen to involve an individual's response to contingencies in the external environment (e.g., Bijou and Baer 1961).

A key basis of this difference between de-

velopmental stage theorists and mechanistic theorists is, as noted in Chapter 2, that stage theories of development are predicated on a commitment to an organismic philosophy of science (see Reese and Overton 1970). Within this tradition, the characterization of the nature of development is an idealized one, and it provides a formal conceptual metric against which observed behavioral change is compared in order to ascertain whether a given change constitutes development (e.g., see Kaplan 1966, 1983).

From this perspective there are two key components of a developmental analysis. First, a stage theory must provide descriptions of the stages themselves—that is, descriptions of the structural properties of each stage in the sequence. Second, a stage theory must posit mechanisms by which the individual progresses through these stages. However, the difference with mechanistic positions arises because these stages—and the progression through them—are explained by concepts different than those associated with the systems of explanation employed in mechanistic views of development (e.g., Bijou 1976; Brainerd 1978, 1979). Specifically, these stage components of development are explained from the perspective of formal causality (e.g., see Berndt 1978; Buss 1979; Neimark 1978; Olson 1978; Sigel 1979). The role of formal causality in developmental stages has, however, not often been understood or appreciated by mechanistically oriented developmentalists—who either prefer to focus solely on notions of efficient causality (Bijou 1976; Bijou and Baer 1961) or who cannot appreciate the idea that there may be a useful notion of causality other than efficient cause (Brainerd 1978, 1979). In short, the concern with formal cause within stage theory stands in contrast to the focus on efficient cause in mechanistic approaches to development, and this difference stands as a key contrast between the two types of approaches.

Stage theorists take stands on developmental issues other than those pertinent to causality, however, and it should be clear where stage theorists stand in terms of at least some of the concepts we have considered in earlier chapters—for example, the continuity-discontinuity issue. By definition, stage theorists consider development to include qualitatively discontinuous phenomena. In specifying that the sequential emergence of qualitatively different levels of functioning characterizes development, stage theorists are defining development as being qualitatively discontinuous.

On the other hand we have noted that stage theorists also recognize that there are certain laws that function invariantly across a person's life span. Hence the postulation of such functional invariants indicates that most stage theorists recognize that development is characterized by continuity as well as discontinuity. In short, even though stage theorists define development as being qualitatively discontinuous, continuous laws that exist throughout development are recognized as well. Consistent with the ideas of Werner (1957), development involves, then, a *synthesis* of processes making a person the same across life with processes making a person different across life.

Second, stage theorists—committed to an organismic philosophy of science—to differing extents take an interactionist viewpoint in respect to the nature-nurture controversy. Thus, to some extent, all stage theorists look at an interaction between intrinsic (nature) and extrinsic (nurture) variables in accounting for behavioral development. However, different theorists put differing degrees of emphasis on nature and nurture factors. Thus Piaget (1950, 1970) puts greater emphasis on an interaction between nature and nurture factors than do Freud (1949) and Erikson (1963, 1964), who place greater emphasis on nature variables and view the nurture variables as either facilitators or inhibitors of primarily intrinsic emergences (Emmerich 1968; Kohlberg 1963a). For example, we will see in Chapter 9 that Erikson (1959, 1963) places a good deal of emphasis on the "maturational ground plan" that he believes exists in all people. Thus, to Erikson, although a child must interact within society in order to develop

normally, the stage emergences that characterize a child's development are primarily maturational in origin; they will emerge and exert a particular influence on development independent of the character of the child's interactions in society.

Moreover, just as stage theorists differ to some extent on the specifics of the nature-nurture interaction, they also differ about the critical-periods issue. It may be said that in one sense all stage theorists support a critical-periods notion, in that in each qualitatively different stage something unique is developing. This unique development, which gives the stage its qualitative distinctiveness, is by definition supposed to be developing at this particular point. Because stage theorists define development as comprising qualitatively distinct phenomena that arise in a universal, invariant sequence, they therefore maintain that not all periods in development have equal potentiality for any particular development. Thus each specific stage has its own specific emergence, which by its very existence serves to define that period in ontogeny as a stage. In this sense, each stage has its own critical development.

Yet different stage theorists have different ideas about "how critical is critical." Given the different views about stage transition that we have discussed, and therefore the different models of transition to which stage theorists may adhere, it is understandable that they disagree about the implications for later development of inappropriate development within a given stage. For some stage theorists, if one does not develop what one should develop in a given stage, one will never have another chance for such development. Thus each given stage of development is truly critical, in that if one does not develop appropriately within a given period, irreversible unfavorable implications will be inevitable. Such extreme views, which we have discussed in Chapter 5, will be illustrated in Chapter 8 by the theory of Freud and in Chapter 9 by the theory of Erikson.

In addition, as might be surmised from the above differences of opinion, stage theorists also differ about the source of critical periods. Just as different stage theorists place contrasting emphases on nature and nurture factors in explaining the interactive basis of development, they correspondingly place different emphases on these factors in accounting for the critical nature of different stages. Those theorists who lay greater emphasis on nature (maturational) factors in accounting for stage development similarly place greater stress on maturation as the source of the criticalness of critical periods.

In sum, we see that all stage theorists present theories that speak to the various core conceptual issues of development. In the next two chapters we shall see how different stage theorists deal with these issues within the contexts of their specific theories. At present, however, let us turn to a second type of approach one may use to conceptualize development.

THE DIFFERENTIAL APPROACH TO DEVELOPMENT

Those concerned with a differential approach to development begin their inquiry by posing what is basically an empirical question: "How in the course of development do groups of people become assorted into subgroups, subgroups which are differentiated on the basis of status and behavior attributes?" (Emmerich 1968, 671).

In its most basic form the differential approach to development is primarily empirical rather than theoretical; it uses particular research methods to study differences among groups of people and individuals within these groups. Thus, as we shall see, the differential approach does not necessarily connote any given theoretical point of view, but it can be used by people with various theoretical perspectives.

The main focus of the differential approach is to discover how people become sorted into subgroups over the course of their development. Subgroups are formed, or differentiated, on the basis of one of two types of attributes. The first type is *status*

attributes. Status attributes are characteristics that place people in particular demographic categories or groups, such as those based on age, sex, race, religion, and socioeconomic status (SES). A differentiation of people into subgroups on the basis of age, sex, and race is illustrated in Figure 7.2.

Obviously, however, there is nothing really psychological about differentiating a group of people on the basis of their status attributes. The psychological component of the differential approach arises when people are further differentiated on the basis of the second type of attribute, *behavioral attributes.*

Behavioral attributes may be considered as bipolar behavioral, or psychological, dimensions. For example, a behavioral attribute would be any dimension such as:

extraversion————introversion
dominance————submission
aggression————passivity
high activity level————low activity level
independence————dependence
trust————mistrust

A behavioral attribute is really a continuum that has opposite traits, or characteristics, at either end. A differential psychologist using the term *behavioral attribute,* then, is referring to psychological attributes conceptualized along a bipolar continuum. For instance, behavioral attributes such as independence-dependence or high activity level–low activity level are seen as bipolar traits running along a continuum, and people grouped toward one end of each of the continua might be termed independent or high-active, while people grouped toward the other end of the continua might be termed dependent or low-active, respectively.

The goal of a scientist using the differential approach for the study of psychological development would be, then, to discover the subgroups into which people become assorted on the basis of both their behavioral and status attributes. The differential psychologist would choose some behavioral attributes (e.g., aggression-passivity and independence-dependence) as well as some

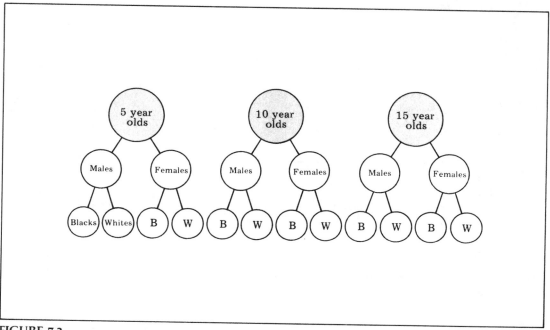

FIGURE 7.2

A group of people differentiated into subgroups on the basis of the status attributes of age, sex, and race.

selected status attributes (e.g., age—for instance, five-year-olds and ten-year-olds—and sex) for study and then try to discover how people in these groups become differentiated in the course of development.

For example, the psychologist would ask questions to see if the five-year-old boys as a subgroup are located at different points along the aggression-passivity and the independence-dependence continua than are the five-year-old girls. The psychologist would also ask these same questions of the ten-year-old male and female subgroups. Thus, in relation to the status attributes of age and sex, the psychologist would be able to discover if these people form subgroups located at different points along the behavioral dimensions. The psychologist would be able to see if five-year-old girls as a subgroup are more or less aggressive than five-year-old boys, for example; for that matter, the psychologist would be able to see how each subgroup compares with every other subgroup

in terms of relative location along each of the bipolar dimensions studied.

The design of such an inquiry is illustrated in Figure 7.3a, and in Figure 7.3b some imaginary results are depicted in order to illustrate the above points. In this figure we see that the four subgroups differentiated on the basis of status attributes are also differentiated on the basis of their location along the bipolar behavioral dimensions. That is, the subgroups occupy different spaces on these dimensions.

Individual Differences within the Differential Approach

The differential approach is primarily concerned with groups—or better with subgroups—of people. Accordingly, in attempting to ascertain how such subgroups become differentiated with development, the differential approach is concerned with discovering nomothetic laws. Those taking the

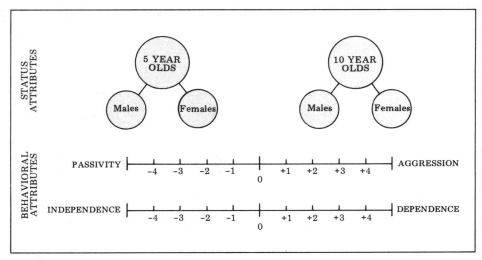

FIGURE 7.3a
Design of a differential study of the relation of two status attributes to two behavioral attributes.

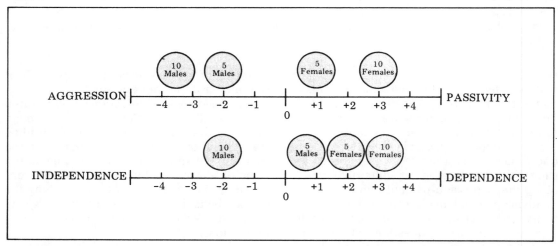

FIGURE 7.3b
Some imaginary findings of the study illustrated in Figure 7.3a.

differential approach do not necessarily posit universal group laws of development, and they are thus different from the nomothetically oriented stage theorists. Yet differential psychologists *are* concerned with nomothetic laws, insofar as they are concerned with ascertaining the variables that predict how groups are differentiated into subgroups over the course of development.

However, differential psychologists are more interested than are stage theorists in ascertaining the dimensions of individual differences in development. Consistent with how they conceptualize subgroup differ-

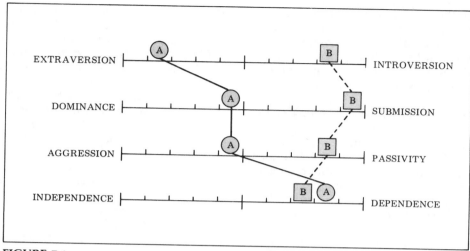

FIGURE 7.4

Individuality within the differential approach. Individual A and individual B have different locations on each of the four dimensions.

ences, they define individual differences in terms of people's different locations along various bipolar dimensions. Just as subgroups have different locations along each of these dimensions, so do individuals. In turn, then, each individual may also have his or her own location in multidimensional space. This is illustrated in Figure 7.4 for two individuals, each of whom takes up a different space along each of the four dimensions shown. In sum, then, within the differential approach individuality is defined as one's location in multidimensional space (Emmerich 1968, 678).

The Study of Development within the Differential Approach

Although the differential approach can be used simply as an empirical approach within which to consider development, we shall see that it can also be combined with specific theoretical formulations. For example, we will see in Chapter 9 that Erik Erikson, primarily a stage theorist, employs a differential formulation within each of his "eight stages of man" (Erikson 1959, 1963). Similarly, just as stage theorists may use the dif-

ferential approach within their qualitatively discontinuous theoretical point of view, other theorists may use differential ideas within theoretical approaches that stress continuity throughout development (e.g., Cattell 1957). The point here is that the differential approach does not constitute a perspective mutually exclusive from other approaches.

We have said, however, that the differential approach may be used in an essentially empirical way. A researcher may have no previously formulated ideas about whether development is characterized by, for instance, developmental stages and/or by continuity or discontinuity; the researcher may thus adopt the differential approach in order to see which of these concepts best describes the development of certain subgroups of people.

Particular types of research methodology and statistical analyses of results—for example, statistics that can readily show how many dimensions are needed to characterize subgroups of people—are typically employed by differential psychologists. Thus such statistical procedures as correlational analysis, factor analysis, or cluster analysis are used. These procedures have common bases and, when used within the context of the differential approach, a common goal. Their intent is to see how variables—composed of status and behavioral attributes—group together over the course of development.

For example, do the same groups of behavioral attributes characterize females when they are five, ten, fifteen, and twenty years of age? Or do the dimensions that must be used to group females of different ages differ over the course of development? Questions such as these are addressed by statistical procedures such as the above. For instance, factor analysis, one of the more sophisticated of these procedures, would be used to discern whether the number of dimensions that differentiated the groups stayed the same or changed over time, and whether the group of behavioral attributes that related to each other at time 1 in development remained in the same relation at time 2 (Baltes and Nesselroade 1973).

To specify the exact details of these statistical procedures is beyond the purposes of the present discussion. Still, a simplified illustration of the use of these procedures within the differential approach will clarify and convey their utility. Suppose a researcher is studying boys and girls aged five, ten, and fifteen years. In relation to these status attributes (age), the researcher wishes to learn how these people form into subgroups on the basis of fifty behavioral attributes, fifty bipolar dimensions. The researcher labels the fifty variables by their number and measures each of the subjects on each of the variables. He or she next performs a factor analysis on each of the age-sex subgroups; that is, the researcher statistically analyzes the scores on the variables (the behavioral attributes) to determine if some of them seem to have a high degree of relationship (thus forming a *factor*) while not similarly relating to the other variables. The researcher finds that for both the five-year-old males and the five-year-old females the same variables seem to group together— that is, the scores on each of the first twenty variables are consistent (correlated) with each other but are not so related to any of the remaining thirty variables.

Thus the first twenty variables form a factor. Similarly, the next fifteen variables form a second factor, and the last fifteen variables form a third factor. Thus the five-year-old males and females are found to be similarly differentiated on the basis of three similar groupings of variables. The structure of the relationship among the variables—*the factor structure*—is the same. With both subgroups of subjects the same variables cluster together.

This finding may not mean, however, that the males and females have identical sets of scores on each of the variables within a factor. Suppose that factor 1 is aggression-passivity and that some of the behavioral bipolar dimensions comprised by this factor are:

looks for fights——stays away from fights
teases others——gets teased
yells when bothered——quiet when bothered

Other variables within the factor are similar to these, and thus the researcher might reasonably opt to give this factor a name such as "aggression-passivity." In order for each of the variables in this factor to relate to each other and thus form a factor, we would expect the scores on the variables within the factor to be consistent. For instance, we would expect a person scoring high (or low) on one variable in the factor to score similarly high (or low) on each of the other variables. Thus, despite whether a subgroup scores high and/or low on all of the variables, the variables would form a factor as long as all the people in the subgroup scored similarly on each of the variables. The same factor could be obtained for both the five-year-old boys and girls even if each group's scores were not identical. For instance, the boys could have higher aggression scores than the girls on all the variables comprising the factor. Of course, this would not mean that boys and girls do not vary among themselves. The point here is that the boys may vary along the aggression-passivity continuum at points closer to the aggression end of the continuum than do girls.

With the above findings about the factor structure of the five-year-old males and females, the differential psychologist may proceed to assess developmental changes or consistencies in the ten- and fifteen-year-old subgroups. In doing so, the psychologist will necessarily be addressing some of the core conceptual issues of psychological development—the continuity-discontinuity and the stability-instability issues.

Continuity-Discontinuity

When looking at results across age levels, the differential psychologist will be primarily concerned with whether the subgroup differentiations found at earlier age levels (e.g., with the five-year-olds) remain the same or change at older age levels. If the same variables seem to relate to each other in the same way at all age levels, this is continuity. If, however, differences from earlier patterns are found, this is discontinuity. Specifically,

the differential psychologist may find continuity if, for example, the same number of factors, comprised by the same variables, exist in the older subgroups (Baltes and Nesselroade 1973). Alternatively, discontinuity may be discovered if, for example, a different number of factors exists within the older subgroups. Also, discontinuity may be found even if the same factors exist but if different behavioral attributes make up the factors. That is, bipolar dimensions not included in earlier age-level factors may be related to older age-level factors or vice versa.

In Figure 7.5 we see an imaginary example of such differential research, illustrating the discovery of both continuity and discontinuity using this approach. Continuity exists between both the five-year-old male and female subgroups and both the ten-year-old male and female subgroups. The same number of factors exists in each subgroup and, in addition, the variables comprised by each factor remain the same. However, discontinuity exists between the ten-year-old and fifteen-year-old subgroups. With the males,

	5 YEAR OLDS		10 YEAR OLDS		15 YEAR OLDS	
	Males	Females	Males	Females	Males	Females
	Variables		Variables		Variables	
FACTOR A	1–20	1–20	1–20	1–20	1–15	1–20
FACTOR B	21–35	21–35	21–35	21–35	16–30	16–25
FACTOR C	36–50	36–50	36–50	36–50	31–50	26–40
FACTOR D						41–50

FIGURE 7.5

An example of hypothetical findings of differential research, illustrating both continuity (between five and ten years of age) and discontinuity (between ten and fifteen years of age).

the same number of factors still exist at both age levels, but the meaning of the factors is different because different variables make up the factors of the fifteen-year-old males as compared with the ten-year-old males. With the females, discontinuity also exists. Here, however, the reason is primarily the emergence of a new factor among the fifteen-year-old females.

Stability-Instability

In addition to being able to analyze whether or not the same variables account for differentiation throughout development (continuity-discontinuity), the differential psychologist is able to determine whether a person's rank on a variable, and on a factor within his or her subgroup, remains the same or changes with time. Each subgroup is, of course, composed of individuals who have scores on each of the measured variables. Although these scores may be similar, it will still be possible to rank-order all of the individuals in a subgroup, from high to low. Thus a person's rank for a variable may change with development; as we have seen in Chapter 6, when such a change relative to one's reference group occurs, we term this instability. If a person's rank on a variable remains the same across time, we term this stability.

Consistent with what we have said in Chapter 6, Emmerich (1968, 676–77) points out that any thorough analysis of development from the differential point of view must consider the continuity-discontinuity and stability-instability issues at the same time. As illustrated in Chapter 6, any combination of continuity-discontinuity and stability-instability may occur. In reference specifically to the differential approach, Emmerich (1968, 677) points out the following:

1. *Continuity and stability* may occur when the factors (and the variables within them) remain the same for subgroups from time 1 to time 2 and, accordingly, individuals' rankings within their respective subgroups remain unaltered.

2. *Continuity and instability* may occur when the factors (and the variables within them) remain the same for subgroups from time 1 to time 2 but, despite this consistency, individuals' rankings within their respective subgroups change.

3. *Discontinuity and stability* may occur when factors (and/or the variables within them) are altered for subgroups from time 1 to time 2 but, despite these changes, individuals are ranked in similar ways within these new subgroupings.

4. *Discontinuity and instability* may occur when the factors (and/or the variables within them) change for subgroups from time 1 to time 2 and individuals' rankings are accordingly altered.

We shall have reason to return to some of these possible interrelations in Chapter 9, in order to understand the results of a specific instance of research done with a differential approach—the longitudinal study of Kagan and Moss (1962). At present, however, let us conclude our discussion of the differential approach by reviewing the relation of this approach to the conceptual issues of development we dealt with in earlier chapters.

Relation of Concepts of Development to the Differential Approach

We have seen that those employing a differential approach deal primarily with the continuity-discontinuity and stability-instability issues and that the differential approach may be interrelated with other approaches to the understanding of development. When this approach is interrelated with stage theories of development, as in the case of Erikson's (1959, 1963) theory of psychosocial development, the stage formulations, in a sense, take theoretical precedence. That is, when Erikson uses differential formulations within the context of his stage theory, the continuity-discontinuity of behavioral development does not remain an empirical question; rather, development is held to proceed through eight qualitatively different stages.

The above interrelation by Erikson really does not alter the substance of the differential approach. As more of an approach to the study of development, rather than a theoretical view of development, the differential approach does not a priori maintain a position relative to the continuity-discontinuity issue. Moreover, it in no way speaks to the nature-nurture or related issues. That is, the differential approach in no way offers formulations that specify the sources of differential developmental subgroupings; rather, in its use within the context of contrasting theoretical perspectives, it can be integrated with virtually any position on a nature-oriented to a nurture-oriented conceptual continuum.

In sum, while we have seen that developmental stage theories take a priori theoretical stands relative to the continuity-discontinuity and nature-nurture issues, this is not necessarily the case with the differential approach. It is more the case, however, with the ipsative approach, the last conceptual approach to the study of development that we shall consider in this chapter. Let us turn, then, to the ipsative approach to development.

THE IPSATIVE APPROACH TO DEVELOPMENT

In an *ipsative* analysis an individual is compared to himself or herself, as opposed to being compared to other people. As compared with the stage and the differential approaches to developmental psychology, the ipsative approach is much more *idiographic* in orientation. Idiographic laws are regularities associated with an individual instead of a group, and the goal of the ipsative approach is to discover individual (rather than group) laws or regularities of behavioral development. Those opting for an ipsative approach might argue that the nomothetic laws of behavioral development, which

apply only to groups and not to the individuals within them, are meaningless; they would thus try to ascertain the variables involved in an individual's development. If these findings could then be applied to larger groups of people (e.g., to better understand any qualifications in the application of group laws to individuals), so much the better for the science of psychological development. However, if the findings of ipsative research indicated that group laws were too general to be useful for understanding the character of an individual's life course, then again so much the better for science. Here the contribution would be, however, that scientists would not be misled by relatively vacuous general principles of human functioning.

In sum, the rationale for an ipsative analysis of development is that the variables providing the bases of human functioning may coalesce in each person in a unique way. As such, laws of behavioral and psychological functioning that apply only to groups may have no direct meaning for a given individual's functioning, although they may constrain that individual's social interpersonal behaviors.

Accordingly, development at the individual level must be understood, and the ipsative approach to development considers intraindividual consistencies and changes in the development of the person (Emmerich 1968). The approach asks whether or not the variables that comprise the individual remain the same or change throughout the individual's ontogeny.

It should be noted that psychologists from diverse theoretical perspectives have argued for the need for ipsative analyses of human behavior. For example, the need for such analyses may derive from an individual's unique genotype and genotype-environment interaction (Hirsch 1970), from the person's individual reinforcement history (Bijou 1976; Bijou and Baer 1961), or from the person's unique interrelation of his or her temperament attributes (Thomas and Chess 1977) or his or her personality organization (Allport 1937; Block 1971). It should be noted, however, that while all such theorists would agree that ipsative analyses are necessary to describe an individual's functioning, not all would agree that idiographic laws need to be used to account for intraindividual uniqueness. For example, Bijou and Baer (1961) might argue that while each person would have a unique reinforcement history and would therefore have a unique response repertoire, the laws governing the acquisition of any of the responses (e.g., laws of associative learning or conditioning) are applicable to all organisms.

When ipsative analyses are used in developmental research, however, the scientist seeks to understand the makeup of the individual in two ways. First, an attempt is made to ascertain the specific *attributes,* or psychological variables, that make up the person (Emmerich 1968) over the course of development. These attributes may be characteristics such as personality traits (e.g., dependency, aggression), temperamental styles (e.g., high activity level, low threshold of responsivity), or, in fact, any set of psychological/behavioral variables. Moreover, these attributes may be unique to the person or common among many people (like the personality traits illustrated above). In any event, the first task of the ipsative approach is to find out what attributes comprise the individual, to discover the individual's *attribute repertoire* across development. For example, a psychologist may be interested in discovering a person's values. Accordingly, the psychologist might discover that at age fifteen a given person was comprised of four values (e.g., values about one's body, about sex, about education, and about religion), while at age twenty-five an additional two values had become part of this person's value attribute repertoire (e.g., values about a career and about raising a family).

Second, attributes certainly have an organization. Some attributes may be central in that they serve to organize other attributes, while others may be subordinate. Alternatively, we may think of the organization of attributes in terms of attribute clusters. For instance, some attributes may be grouped together while others may not. By analogy, one might view this attribute organization in

terms of intraindividual attribute factors. In fact, one form of factor analysis—P-technique factor analysis—is aimed at identifying intraindividual factors (Nesselroade 1983); in other words, P-technique factor analysis provides an ipsative analysis of the structure of attributes that exists within a single person over the course of his or her development. In Chapter 10 we shall discuss still another method used to study the development of intraindividual structures—that is, the Q-sort methodology used in Block's longitudinal study (1971).

However, no matter which particular data analysis technique is used, a person may be found to have several personality attributes clustered together, and these attributes may be independent of, for example, the person's cluster of value attributes and of temperamental attributes. Moreover, within a particular cluster, a specific attribute may be superordinate. Thus the sexual value may be superordinate to a person at a particular time in life, with all other values subordinate, at least if they are viewed in terms of the overriding importance of the sexual value. In any event, the second task of the ipsative approach is to attempt to understand a person's *attribute interrelation* across development, how the attributes comprised by the person are related to each other over the course of the person's life.

To illustrate, suppose an individual has three types of value attributes—religious, sexual, and economic. Although it is possible that these same three values may make up the person's attribute repertoire at different times in life, the values may be interrelated differently over time. For instance, at age seventeen, the person's sexual value may be most important (superordinate), with the others subordinate. This attribute interrelation may stay the same over time, but it might also change. For instance, at age thirty-eight, the economic value may be superordinate and the sexual value not as important—it has now fallen to second-order importance, perhaps; however, the religious value may maintain its previous intraindividual position. Still later, however, perhaps at age sixty-seven, these same three values may still make up the person's repertoire, but once again they are interrelated differently. Thus at this age the person's religious value may be most important, while the economic value has fallen to second and the sexual value to third place.

In sum, those taking an ipsative approach to the study of development seek to discover the regularities involved in an individual's development by attempting to find the person's attribute repertoire—those characteristics comprising the person—and attribute interrelation—the intraindividual organization of these attributes. Thus the ipsative problem in development is to discern intraindividual consistencies and changes in attributes and their organization over the course of an individual's development.

To illustrate how, in an ipsative analysis, one may identify how a person may change over the course of development as a function of new attributes existing in his or her repertoire, consider the attribute repertoire depicted in Figure 7.6. Here we see that at time 1 the person was comprised of seven attributes (a–g), while at time 2, three new variables (h–j) are in the repertoire.

But even if the attributes in a person's

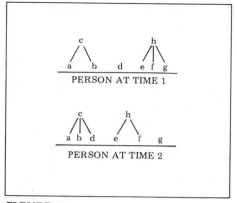

FIGURE 7.7
An example of ipsative change. The attributes in a person's repertoire are interrelated differently at time 1 and time 2.

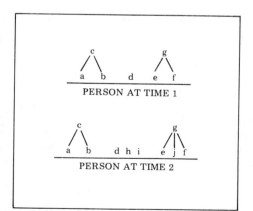

FIGURE 7.6
An example of ipsative change. The person's attribute repertoire changes from time 1 to time 2.

repertoire remain the same in development, the person may change if the attributes are interrelated differently over time. This second type of change that can be identified by the ipsative intraindividual approach to development is depicted in Figure 7.7. Here we see that although the same number of attributes exists in the person's repertoire at times 1 and 2 in development, the interrelation of the attributes is different at these two times. At time 1, attributes a, b (subordinate), and c (superordinate) cluster together, as do attributes e, f, g, and h. Attribute d does not cluster with either of these two groups. At time 2, however, the organization of the attributes is different. Here we see that attribute d now clusters along with attributes a, b, and c, while attribute g has now become independent of the attribute cluster composed of e, f, and h.

Of course, *both* the number of attributes in the person's repertoire and the attribute interrelation may change over the course of development. If the attribute repertoire changes, then of course the person will have changed; but even if the attribute repertoire remains the same, the person can still change through a change in the attribute interrelation. Either or both of these changes may constitute an individual's development.

Individual Differences within the Ipsative Approach

It should be clear that individual differences are the essence of the ipsative approach. The goal of this approach is to ascertain laws or regularities lying closer to the idiographic than to the nomothetic end of an idiographic-nomothetic continuum (Block 1971). Thus the concern in this approach is to identify laws applying to an individual's development. Accordingly, a result of an ipsative analysis may be the formulation of highly specific generalizations about the course of an individual's development. Analysis begins at the level of the individual because, it is held, general laws of development may not apply equally to all individuals. Hence within this perspective one should first understand how the individual develops before one tries to understand how large groups of individuals develop.

In stressing this view, however, those taking an ipsative approach are not denying either the validity or the necessity for study of general laws of development. Rather, they are stressing a different aspect of the problem of developmental analysis. They are trying first to understand the role of the individual in his or her own development. Accordingly, they would suggest that particular attributes of a person may be unique, but they would not disregard the possibility that other attributes of the individual may be similar to those of other individuals. Thus the stress of the ipsative approach is not that all people are *completely* different, but rather that in order to understand all of the phenomena of development, one must deal with the particular intraindividual features of development.

There are other issues that may be raised in respect to the focus of the ipsative approach on the individual and on intraindividual differences over time—instead of on interindividual differences within time, as is more often the focus with nomothetically oriented approaches. First, theorists differ as to the ability of idiographic laws to account for substantial proportions of the variance in behavioral development, both absolutely and especially in comparison to nomothetic laws. A second scientific issue is that the interpretation of the individual differences described in ipsative analyses is open to debate. Do such individual differences reflect qualitatively unique, individual laws or only quantitative (and perhaps "error") variance around some more general (group or universal) law? If the former is the case, then both basic research and more applied endeavors of assessment and intervention need to focus primarily on the individual, deferring for secondary analysis any focus on the group or on general laws. If the latter is the case, then given the practical problems (of cost and time) of designing and implementing plans for separate assessment of every individual, it may be that the appropriate role of basic research is to remain focused on designing research to assess general laws. Similarly, if the latter is the case, the same practical problems of cost and time would suggest that those interested in applied issues should be primarily concerned with assessments and interventions aimed at the more general components of human functioning.

Developmental Changes within the Ipsative Approach

We have seen that within the ipsative approach people may change through development on the basis of changes in their attribute repertoire and/or their attribute interrelation. But are such intraindividual changes systematic? Do they follow a predictable pattern or are they unique to each and every individual? In other words, are there any principles that may be used to understand the nature of the intraindividual changes constituting development?

Thanks to the clarifications provided by Emmerich (1968, 679–81), the answer to all these questions may be considered to be yes. Although Emmerich points out that traditionally there was little evidence of systematic ipsative developmental theorizing, he suggests that a principle exists allowing such conceptualization to proceed. This is a general, regulative principle of development, describing the course of developmental changes *whenever* development occurs. This principle is one we are familiar with—Werner's *orthogenetic principle.*

As discussed in Chapter 6, the orthogenetic principle holds that whenever development occurs, it proceeds from a state of globality and lack of differentiation to a state of differentiation, integration, and hierarchical organization. Individuals, of course, develop. Therefore we would expect the orthogenetic principle to hold for the intraindividual development of a person. It would imply that no matter what the specific attribute repertoire of a person may be, the developmental changes in this attribute repertoire follow a specific, systematic course. All changes in a person's intraindividual attributes would proceed in accordance with the orthogenetic principle.

Hence, even if all individuals were completely unique in the repertoires of attributes they possessed, the development of the interrelations of their attributes would still be in accord with the descriptions provided by the orthogenetic principle. Therefore, we would expect that as an individual develops from time 1 to time 2, his or her attribute repertoire and attribute interrelation should develop along specific, systematic lines. Specifically, we would expect that:

1.   An individual's attribute repertoire should be relatively global and undifferentiated at time 1 in development but more differentiated at time 2. In other words, as an individual develops, new and more differentiated attributes should emerge in his attribute repertoire. Thus, in terms of the ipsative attribute repertoire, the orthogenetic principle suggests that *discontinuity* should characterize development. Differentiated attributes should emerge from global attributes.

2.   An individual's attribute interrelation should change, increasing in hierarchical integration with development. At time 1 a person's attribute interrelation would be less

integrated, less hierarchically organized than at time 2. Thus, in terms of the ipsative attribute interrelation, the orthogenetic principle suggests that *continuity* should characterize development. The attribute interrelation should become increasingly more hierarchically organized over the course of an individual's development.

In sum, then, we see that when the orthogenetic principle is applied to intraindividual development, ipsative development may be held to follow certain systematic changes. There will be discontinuous changes when the person develops from time 1 to time 2 in his or her ontogeny, because the attribute repertoire will go from a state of globality to a state of differentiation. In addition, there will be continuous changes when the person develops from time 1 to time 2, because the attribute interrelation will become increasingly more hierarchically organized.

Relation of Concepts of Development to the Ipsative Approach

We have seen that when the ipsative approach is interrelated with the orthogenetic principle, the ipsative approach takes a clear position on the continuity-discontinuity issue. As discussed in Chapter 6, the orthogenetic principle implies the existence of both continuity and discontinuity in development, and accordingly, when this principle is applied to the ipsative approach, this approach also characterizes development as having both continuous and discontinuous components. Thus, when this interrelation is achieved, the continuity-discontinuity issue does not remain an empirical issue for those taking the ipsative approach but becomes instead a theoretical issue; those taking this approach would now maintain that development is both continuous and discontinuous in character.

The ipsative approach also has specific applicability to the nature-nurture issue. We have seen that an essential consideration of the ipsative approach is the role of the laws governing the individual. This focus leads, in my view, to a concern with the contribution the individual makes to his or her own development. This point may be explained by reference to our discussion of the ideas of Schneirla (1957), presented in Chapter 5. As Schneirla (1957) suggested, the experience-maturation interaction that provides the source of all individuals' development functions to give each person a lawfully singular set of behavioral characteristics; this behavioral individuality provides, then, a third source of the individual's development through the establishment of circular functions and self-stimulation in ontogeny.

Thus, ipsatively oriented psychologists, in focusing on a person's behavioral individuality, can ascertain how the individual—in interaction with his or her environment—provides a source of his or her own development. Thus such psychologists would necessarily be taking an interactionist stance in respect to the nature-nurture controversy; and they would, by attempting to discover the contributions of the individual to his or her own development, be ascertaining important evidence bearing on this aspect of the nature-nurture interaction. In Chapter 10 we shall review two ipsatively oriented studies—that of Thomas et al. (1963) and that of Block (1971)—which bear on this argument.

Here, however, we should note that another notion involved in the ipsative approach is in accord with a stress on person-environment interactions. We have noted that the ipsative approach recognizes that while it is possible for people to have completely unique attribute repertoires, it is also possible for people to have attribute repertoires that are very similar, if not identical. Accordingly, from an ipsative point of view we may identify people who have similar attribute repertoires at time 1 in their development and study them longitudinally—that is, across time. Some of these people will remain similar at time 2, while some will be different. Thus, by focusing on the different types of person-environment interactions these people experienced, we

may discover how specific interactions provide a source of an individual's development. By discovering the laws that function to change people who were similar at time 1 into people who either remained similar or were different at time 2, we may learn about the specific characteristics of organism-environment interactions that enable the person to provide a third source of his or her behavioral development.

Alternatively, of course, we could also focus on people who had different attribute repertoires and/or interrelations at time 1 and study those people who remained different and who became similar at time 2. By assessing the organism-environment interactions of these groups we might further discover how the characteristics of the individual in interaction with his or her environment provide a source of the individual's own development. In sum, we may see that the ipsative approach can be considered to take a stand on the continuity-discontinuity issue and to be potentially extremely useful in providing information about nature-nurture interactions as a source of development.

Conclusions

The ipsative, the differential, and the stage approaches represent contrasting orientations to the study of development. Yet all of them put forward concepts that bear on the core conceptual issues of development. These approaches—along with the fourth major theoretical view of psychological development, the approach emphasizing empirical-behavioristic and theoretical-behavioristic (Reese 1976; White 1976) formulations (which shall be discussed in Chapter 11)—provide different theoretical ideas about development; and accordingly, the empirical questions and concomitant research studies done by those concerned with each respective approach are quite different. Still, all of the approaches to the conceptualization of development do provide us with ideas, and eventually with facts, which are essential in attempting to understand the complexities of psychological development.

Accordingly, in the following chapters we shall deal with specific examples of the three approaches discussed in this chapter. Thus in Chapter 8 we shall discuss some major stage theories (those of Piaget, Kohlberg, and Freud); in Chapter 9 we shall consider two examples of differential approaches (the theory of Erikson—who combines differential ideas within a stage-theory framework—and the research of Kagan and Moss); and in Chapter 10 we shall discuss two examples of the ipsative approach (the longitudinal studies of Thomas and Chess, 1977, and of Block, 1971). Finally, in Chapter 11 we shall consider a last major orientation that may be used to conceptualize development, the empirical- and theoretical-behaviorism approaches (and the ideas of such scientists as Skinner, Bijou and Baer, Gewirtz, White, Reese, and Bandura).

8 | *Stage Theories of Development*

In this chapter we shall consider three of the most prominent stage theories of psychological development: those of Piaget, Kohlberg, and Freud. In addition, Anna Freud's (1969) extension of her father's theory (Freud 1949) will also be considered. Although these theories deal with different aspects of the developing person, they have certain similarities. Whether talking about the development of cognition (Piaget), of moral reasoning (Kohlberg), or about psychosexual development (Freud), these theorists all hold that all people who develop pass through the stages specified in the theory in an invariant sequence. These stages represent universal sequences of development—that is, qualitatively different developmental levels through which all people must pass in the same order if they develop. As we pointed out in Chapter 7, the essential ways in which people are thought to differ, from a classical stage point of view, are in the final level of development they reach (how far they eventually develop) and in the amount of time it takes them to move from one stage to the next (how fast they develop).

The stage theories we shall consider in this chapter are also similar in that they take definite stands on the major conceptual issues we have considered in earlier chapters. Thus these stage theories take a more or less interactionist viewpoint on the nature-nurture controversy. Similarly, they make specific statements about the continuity and the discontinuity of behavioral development. Because of their essential commitment to an organismic point of view in regard to the nature-nurture controversy, stage theorists specify that development is in part characterized by qualitatively different phenomena across ontogeny. One portion of development is distinct from another because of the emergence of qualitatively different attributes arising out of the interaction between the organism's characteristics and the features of its experience. Hence the term *stage* is used to denote this ontogenetic qualitative distinctiveness.

However, we shall see that stage theorists also maintain that there are continuous elements in development. Thus, consistent with the organismic notions advanced by Heinz Werner (1957), the stage theorists considered in this chapter more or less explicitly view development as a dialectical process, an organismic synthesis of the discontinuous *and* continuous variables affecting development. In sum, then, while we shall see that Piaget, Kohlberg, and Freud are often talking about different aspects of the developing person, they are also doing so within the context of some markedly similar views about the nature of psychological development.

I should reemphasize here a point made earlier in regard to my purposes in reviewing the theories of development discussed in this chapter, as well as in other chapters of this book. My goal is not to present an in-depth description of each theory. This could not readily be accomplished within the confines of one chapter, since there are literally dozens of books devoted to each theory alone; moreover, to learn what a particular theorist says it is best to read his or her own words (i.e., to read primary sources) rather than a brief review in a secondary source. Thus my goals are to indicate the relationships between key conceptual issues in development and exemplars of each of the major types of theories of development, and to show how these issues pertain both to the features of one theory *and* to the sorts of research derived from or related to it. For instance, these goals have led me to focus more on the research associated with Kohlberg's theory than with Piaget's. While Kohlberg's theory may be viewed as an instance of the application of Piaget's more general cognitive-structural-developmental approach to a particular domain of cognition (moral reasoning), the conceptual issues with which we are concerned (e.g., continuity-discontinuity, plasticity, the role of interactions with the social context, and multidirectionality) are more readily focused on by a review of Kohlberg's (1963, 1973) theory and the research associated with it. Let us turn, then, to a consideration of each of the above theorists' ideas; we will begin with the developmental theory of cognition of Jean Piaget.

Jean Piaget

PIAGET'S ORGANISMIC DEVELOPMENTAL THEORY OF COGNITION

Jean Piaget was born in Switzerland in 1896. He died there in 1980. The young Piaget was quite intellectually precocious; for example, he published his first scientific paper at the age of ten, and while still a teenager he published so many high-quality research papers on mollusks (sea creatures such as oysters and clams) that he was offered the position of curator of the mollusk collection in a Geneva museum (Flavell 1963). As a culmination of these early research interests, Piaget received his doctorate in the natural sciences at the advanced age of twenty-two!

Although his doctorate was in the natural sciences, Piaget maintained broad intellectual interests. Thus, soon after receiving his

degree in 1918, he found himself involved with work in psychology. In addition, he maintained an active interest in epistemology, an area of inquiry concerned with the philosophy of knowledge. Perhaps it seemed to Piaget that the best way to understand knowledge was to study how it develops. In any event, he began to study the development of cognition in his own children. Piaget's first books resulted from these initial studies. What he began to devise, then, in his first endeavors, was a developmental theory of cognition rather than a cognitive theory of development. He viewed cognition as a developmental phenomenon rather than viewing all development as a cognitive phenomenon.

In terms of Piaget's theory, the study of cognitive development can be defined as the study of knowledge and of the mental processes involved in its acquisition and utilization (Elkind 1967). Moreover, as we have said, Piaget came to his interest in cognitive development from his training in natural science and his interest in epistemology. Thus not only is his theory colored by these intellectual roots, but as he himself pointed out (see Flavell 1963), he never took a course in psychology or even passed a test in the subject! Most of us forgive Piaget this limitation. He is one of the two (the other is Freud) unquestioned geniuses who have ever contributed to the field. However, like Freud, and due most probably to his doctoral training, Piaget's theory has a strong biological basis. To begin our assessment of Piaget's theory, then, let us consider first his views concerning the biological basis of intelligence.

STAGE-INDEPENDENT CONCEPTIONS

Although Piaget's theory is a stage theory, he advances several important conceptions relevant to all stages of cognitive development. That is, Piaget proposes certain stage-independent conceptions, principles of cognitive development that apply to all stages of development. These are general laws of development that continually function to provide a source of cognitive development throughout ontogeny. To understand them we must first focus on the biological basis of Piaget's theory.

To Piaget, *cognition* and *intelligence*—terms we treat as synonymous for our purposes here—are just instances of a biological system. Digestion, respiration, and circulation are also examples of biological systems. Intelligence, to Piaget, is a biological system just like any of the above, governed by the laws that govern any other biological system; the functions and characteristics of the biological system "cognition" are identical to those involved in the organism's digestive, respiratory, and circulatory systems.

Like all biological systems, then, cognition has two basic aspects that are always, invariantly, present and functioning: *organi-*

zation and *adaptation*. Cognition always functions within an organization, and it is always an adaptive system—that is, its functioning allows the organism to adapt to its environment; it has survival value.

The functional invariants of organization and adaptation are present throughout the organism's development; they are general characteristics of cognitive functioning applicable to any and all points in the organism's ontogeny. Although he recognizes the fundamental importance of both of these general laws of cognitive functioning, Piaget chooses to devote the major portion of his theorizing to the second functional invariant, adaptation. By focusing on how cognitive development allows the organism to adapt to its environment—to survive—we can understand the dynamic interrelation between the organism and its environment; this interrelation provides a source of intellectual development.

To Piaget, the process of adaptation is divided into two complementary component processes: *assimilation* and *accommodation*. Both of them are always involved in the functioning of cognition to allow the organism to adapt to its environment.

Assimilation

Let us first consider assimilation. This concept is used in a manner identical to that used in any biological discussion; that is, when a cell assimilates food, what does it do? It takes the food in through its membrane and breaks it down to fit its needs. In other words, when food is taken into a cell, it does not retain its original form or structure but is altered; it is converted into energy and water, for example, in order to fit the already existing cellular structure. Thus when a cell assimilates food, it alters it in order to integrate it into its already existing characteristics. Hence, Piaget indicates, "From a biological point of view, assimilation is the integration of external elements into evolving or completed structures of an organism" (1970, 706–7).

Cognitive assimilation functions in a similar manner. Let us imagine that a child has knowledge of a particular stimulus object, say an isosceles triangle like the one presented here:

Now the child is presented with another triangle, a right triangle like this one:

How may the child know what this second stimulus object is? If the child assimilates, the external object (the right triangle) will be integrated into the child's already existing cognitive structure; knowledge of that object will be distorted, or altered, so that the object will take the form of an isosceles triangle. When assimilation occurs the person distorts reality by changing the object—external to the subject—to fit the already existing internal structure of the subject.

Thus an infant may have knowledge of its mother's breast. It has gained this knowledge through its *actions* on this external stimulus object. The infant has sucked on its mother's nipple and has developed an internal cognitive structure pertaining to this action-based knowledge. The infant "knows" the mother's breast through the actions it performs in relation to it. Hence the subject has an internal structure, derived from its actions on an external stimulus, which allows it to know that stimulus. Thus objects are known through the actions performed on them. In other words, to Piaget the basis of knowledge lies in action.

When, however, the infant discovers its thumb and begins to suck on it, knowledge of this other external stimulus may be gained by assimilating it into the already existing action-based cognitive structure. That is, instead of changing its cognitive structure in order to know this new object, the infant may act on the thumb as it did the nipple, thus integrating the thumb into the already existing cognitive structure pertaining to the mother's breast. We may say that the infant alters its actions on the thumb—or rather fits its actions on the thumb—so as to incorporate these actions into an already existing

cognitive structure. Thus the infant would be changing the object to fit, or match, the structure of the subject; the infant would be assimilating.

Accommodation

As we have already noted, however, there is a process that is the complement of assimilation. This process is termed accommodation. Instead of the subject's altering the external object to match his or her internal cognitive structure (assimilation), accommodation involves the altering of the subject to fit the object. For example, think of two people seated very comfortably on a rather small sofa. A third person comes along and asks to sit down. Either or both of the already seated people will have to alter their positions on the sofa to accommodate this third person. The people seated on the sofa will have to change their already existing structure to incorporate this intrusion by an external stimulus. They will have to accommodate, to change themselves, to fit with the external object.

Thus cognitive accommodation involves the altering of already existing cognitive structures in the subject to match new, external stimulus objects. Rather than changing the object to fit the subject, accommodation involves changing the subject to fit the object. In the triangle example we offered above, accommodation would involve an alteration of the child's cognitive structure pertaining to triangles. Instead of altering the right triangle to fit in with the existing isosceles-triangle cognitive structure, the child would change the existing structure; he or she would accommodate by now changing the structure to include knowledge of both isosceles and right triangles.

Similarly, the infant could accommodate to its thumb rather than assimilate it. Instead of acting on the thumb as it did on its mother's nipple, hence assimilating the thumb through integrating it into an already existing cognitive structure, the infant could incorporate different actions through an alteration of its own already existing cognitive structure. The infant could alter this structure to include its differential actions on this new object, thus gaining a new knowledge. By the subject's altered actions on the different object, a corresponding alteration in the subject's cognitive structure would occur. Rather than matching the object to the subject, in this case the subject—through differential actions—would match the object. Hence accommodation would have occurred.

Equilibration

Why are assimilation and accommodation complementary processes? Piaget answers this question by postulating what he believes to be a fundamental factor in development. This factor he terms *equilibration.* Piaget proposes that an organism's adaptation to its environment involves a balance, an equilibrium, between the activity of the organism on its environment and the activity of the environment on the organism.

When an organism acts on its environment it incorporates the external stimulus world into its already existing structure (assimilation); alternatively, when the environment acts on the organism, the organism is altered in order to adjust to the external stimulus world (accommodation).

Hence, Piaget proposes, a balance must be struck between these two tendencies. In essence he hypothesizes that there is an intrinsic orientation in the organism to balance its actions on the environment with the environment's actions on it. In order for the organism to be adaptive, it must be able to incorporate the environment into its already existing structure and to adjust itself to fit the exigencies imposed on it by the environment. Piaget proposes that, if the organism is to be adaptive, neither of these two tendencies must always override the other. An equilibration between these two tendencies is needed in order for the organism to be adaptive.

Hence for every assimilation there must be a corresponding accommodation. One process must balance the other. Just as the subject changes the object to fit its internal structure, the internal structure of the subject must be changed to fit the object. Thus, to Piaget, equilibration is the balance of interaction between subject and object (Piaget 1952). There is an inherent tendency in the organism to equilibrate, to balance between assimilation and accommodation. This tendency exists because of its fundamental biological significance; that is, it is the basis of an organism's adaptation to its environment. Thus, as Piaget has stated:

> cognitive adaptation, like its biological counterpart, consists of an equilibrium between assimilation and accommodation. As has been shown, there is no assimilation without accommodation. But we must strongly emphasize the fact that accommodation does not exist without simultaneous assimilation either. (1970, 708)

In essence Piaget proposes that there is a general, biologically based adaptive tendency that applies to the organism throughout its development. This factor—equilibration—is the moving force behind all cognitive development. There must be a balance between subject and object, between assimilation and accommodation. Whenever the organism alters the environment to incorporate it into its already existing internal structure, there must also be a compensatory alteration of the organism's structure to match the objects in its external environment. There must be a balance in action—the basis of all knowledge—between the organism and its environment.

Functional (Reproductive) Assimilation

If, as we have seen, cognitive development tends to move toward a balance—an equilibration—between assimilation and accommodation, then why does cognitive development not just stop when such a balance is reached? Why, after the infant assimilates its mother's nipple and then accommodates to its thumb, does cognitive development not simply stop there? If equilibration is the end point, or goal, of cognitive development, why does such development continue after a given equilibration is reached?

It is not enough to argue that there are many things that impinge on the infant's world that necessitate further assimilations (and ensuing accommodations). If the infant is in equilibrium, there would seem to be no reason to bother with other impinging stimuli. Let me make an analogy. Most of us have a favorite food. For example, let us suppose that we cannot resist cheeseburgers. Whenever we have the opportunity to eat a cheeseburger we do so. (We "assimilate" as many cheeseburgers as we can.) However, let us imagine that we have just finished Thanksgiving dinner at Grandma's house. If we were offered a cheeseburger now, we certainly would not assimilate it; we would be more likely to turn away, protesting the inappropriateness of more food at that time. We would be in gastronomical equilibrium and would not bother with any food stimuli that we would otherwise assimilate.

Of course, we do not remain in gastronomical equilibrium forever. Rather, our digestive system continues to function, and as a result food is assimilated and we are no longer in equilibrium. Similarly, we do not appear to remain in cognitive equilibrium. Thus the problem for Piaget is to account for continuing cognitive development while maintaining that equilibrium is the point toward which all cognitive development tends.

To address this problem, Piaget specifies that there exist several other aspects of assimilation. Discussion of one of these—*functional* (or *reproductive*) *assimilation*—will illustrate how cognitive development continues to progress. In essence, the concept of reproductive assimilation refers to the fact that any cognitive structure brought about through assimilation will continue to assimilate. That is, it is the nature of assimilatory functioning to continue to assimilate. This is the case for any biological system; although a biological system may be in equilibrium, this balance is necessarily temporary because the system must continue to function

if its adaptive role is to be maintained. (Although ingested food may place the digestive system in equilibrium, such balance is transitory since the food must necessarily be assimilated if digestion is to continue to subserve its adaptive function.) The cognitive system works like any other biological system. When a simple cognitive structure is developed on the basis of assimilation—such as that involved in our example of the infant's sucking on its mother's nipple—it continues to assimilate; it functions to reproduce itself. That is, such structures "apply themselves again and again to assimilate aspects of the environment" (Flavell 1963, 55). Thus, the concept of functional (or reproductive) assimilation indicates that it is a basic property of assimilatory functioning to continue to assimilate. (In the same way, it is a basic property of the digestive system to continue to digest.)

Hence any equilibrium that the infant establishes will be only transitory. The child assimilates and then accommodates and reaches an equilibrium. But cognitive development goes on to higher and higher developmental levels. This happens because reproductive assimilation occurs even though an equilibrium is reached. Thus the child assimilates other components of the environment, which in turn require compensatory accommodation. Hence an equilibrium is again reached, but this, too, is short-lived because a disequilibrium will inevitably result when the child continues to assimilate. Once again, this assimilation will be balanced by a corresponding accommodation, again establishing a transitory equilibrium. Thus, because of the disequilibrium resulting from the child's continued functional assimilation, higher and higher levels of cognitive development are reached.

Schematically, the steps in this continuous process of cognitive development may be seen as (1) *assimilation;* (2) *accommodation,* which results in (3) *equilibration;* (4) *reproductive assimilation;* resulting in (5) *disequilibrium,* which necessitates a return to accommodation and a repetition of the sequence.

Hence the occurrence of disequilibrium (through the process of reproductive assimilation) provides the source of cognitive development throughout all stages of life. In other words, with the postulation of this model Piaget has offered a set of stage-independent concepts about cognitive development; that is, these concepts apply at all stages of cognitive development. They represent general laws of development applicable to the development of cognition throughout all stages. In fact, these stage-independent concepts account for the person's continual cognitive development. With this understanding, then, let us now turn to a consideration of Piaget's stage-dependent concepts.

STAGE-DEPENDENT CONCEPTS: THE STAGES OF COGNITIVE DEVELOPMENT

There are four stages in Piaget's theory. They span the age range from birth through adolescence (with no fixed point associated with the end of the last stage, since it is presumed to continue throughout adulthood).

The Sensorimotor Stage

The first stage of cognitive development in Piaget's theory is the sensorimotor stage. Although the age limits of any stage may vary from individual to individual, we may suggest rough boundaries for each stage. Thus the sensorimotor stage may be held to last from birth through two years of age.

When the child is born and thus begins its sensorimotor stage, it enters the world with what Piaget terms *innate schemes*. We need not argue here about whether or not his use of the term *innate* means that Piaget believes these "schemes" are unavailable to experiential influences. In fact, we might even assume that he does *not* mean this; as we have already noted in our discussion, Piaget is quite aware of the necessity of conceptualizing development within an interactionist model. Hence let us just assume that by "in-

nate schemes" Piaget means "congenital schemes"—schemes that are present at birth.

But what is a scheme? A scheme to Piaget is the essential component, the main building block, of cognitive development. Precisely defined, a *scheme* is an organized sensorimotor action sequence. By this term, then, Piaget refers to a structure

1. that has an organization;

2. that has a sensory, or input, component—that is, a component comprising stimulation derived from the external environment;

3. that has a motor component—that is, a component comprising in part some output component like a muscular movement; meaning

4. that some action on the environment follows the sensory portion of this structure; and finally

5. that the components of this structure function in a sequential order; that is, there is a sequence to the organized sensory and motor actions that occur.

It may seem to you that a scheme resembles what we typically term a reflex. In fact, the schemes that the child is born with—as well as the schemes existing throughout this first stage—may conveniently be thought of as reflexive in nature. Like a reflex, a scheme is a rigid cognitive structure. That is, although the development of schemes throughout the sensorimotor stage represents considerable development in the child's cognitive functioning, at the same time, the existence of schemes during this period tends to place limitations on the child's cognition. As we shall soon see, schemes tend to be unidirectional; that is, the direction of the sequence involved in the scheme is always the same. Thus a scheme is in many ways analogous to a reflex. For example, in an eye-blink reflex a puff of air would always precede and lead to an eye blink. Schemes are also unidirectional in that the motor component of their sequences cannot be reversed.

In essence, when we say that the newborn enters the world with a complement of innate schemes, we may think of this as the beginning of the sensorimotor stage, characterized by the presence at birth of an assortment of reflexes, or sensorimotor structures. Such innate schemes may be illustrated by the grasping reflex; the infant will grasp tightly an object placed in its palm. Another example would be the Babinski reflex, a backward curling and fanning of the toes in response to tactile stimulation of the sole of the foot. (This reflex, by the way, disappears early in ontogeny due to the development of portions of the brain; in fact, the presence of this reflex in an older child is an indication of brain damage.) Yet another example of an innate reflex, or scheme, would be the rooting reflex. Here, if the infant's cheek is stimulated—say by lightly running a finger from the bottom of the ear to the corner of the mouth—the infant will turn its head in the direction of the stimulation and promptly begin to suck. This is obviously an adaptive reflex. It is typically the mother's nipple that so stimulates the infant, and head-turning and sucking actions will increase the infant's proximity to the mother's nipple and hence food. In sum, then, the infant enters the world with a complement of innate schemes.

However, these schemes do not remain innate for long. That is, they do not retain their original structures. In functioning for the very first time, they change. They begin to assimilate from the environment and hence become *acquired schemes*. In other words, once the scheme functions it does so by assimilating. This, of course, changes its structure and requires a complementary accommodation. Then, because of functional or reproductive assimilation, the structure of the scheme continues to change.

To understand how schemes develop throughout the sensorimotor stage and the concomitant cognitive developments are attained through these alterations in schematic structure, we must point out some other facets of the sensorimotor stage. First, Piaget divides this stage into six sequential

periods. Within each period the concept of circular reaction is involved.

Circular reaction refers to one repetition or to a series of repetitions of a sensorimotor response. The first response in any of these series is always new to the infant. When a scheme first functions, the infant cannot anticipate its specific results; the results were not intended before the response was made. The important aspect of a circular reaction comes about, however, after this first, new response is made. Because of reproductive assimilation the infant will tend to repeat this new, chance adaptation over and over (Flavell 1963, 93). What we see, then, is that a circular reaction involves the repetition of a given scheme's functioning.

Thus the first period of the sensorimotor stage involves the alteration of the infant's innate schemes to acquired schemes. Again, this alteration—this bringing into existence of initial acquired schemes—comes about through the functioning of reproductive assimilation. In period two of this stage, circular reactions are involved with and affect the infant's body itself; these circular reactions are termed *primary*. In period three, the infant's circular reactions come to involve objects in the outside world, such as toys or mobiles hanging over the crib; these circular reactions are termed *secondary*.

To this point in the sensorimotor stage, one could use the phrase "out of sight, out of mind" to describe the infant's cognitive development. The infant interacts with objects in the external world as if their existence depended on their being sensed (Piaget 1950). When objects are not in the infant's immediate sensory world, the infant acts as if they do not exist. In other words, infants are *egocentric;* there is no differentiation between the existence of an object and the sensory stimulation provided by that object (Elkind 1967).

Although all stages of cognitive development contain functioning that may be described as egocentric, overcoming this sensorimotor egocentrism will involve the child's most important cognitive attainment during this stage. We may think of all of the remaining periods within the sensorimotor stage as involving the elaboration of schematic structures that subserve the crucial function of allowing the infant to know that there is object permanency in the world—that is, that objects continue to exist even when he or she is not observing them.

We may think of numerous instances of the infant's apparent lack of a scheme of object permanency. Before a certain point in cognitive development, games, such as peekaboo, hold the child's attention. The child acts as if the person playing peekaboo with him or her appears and disappears throughout the game by going into and passing out of existence. Thus the person jumps in and out of the child's immediate sensory purview, and when the person is in the reappearing phase, the child responds with "surprise" (a smile or a laugh). Similarly, if an attention-getting toy or object is brought in and out of the child's sensory purview, at these initial points in cognitive development the child will not follow the object (for example, visually) when it leaves his or her immediate sensory world. It is only after a series of circular reactions, involving many different objects, that the child is finally able to represent an object that is not in its immediate sensory world. Only after repeatedly acting on objects does the child become able to represent these objects internally. Thus, as a consequence of these repeated sensorimotor actions, resulting in an internalized representation of an object, the child comes to know that an object exists even though he or she is not perceiving it. Thus the child has *conquered the object* (Elkind 1967). The child's egocentrism has diminished enough—the child has decentered enough—now to know the difference between an object and the sensory impression it makes. This *representational ability,* this ability to represent an absent object internally and thus to act as if one knows it continues to exist, constitutes the major cognitive achievement of the sensorimotor stage. It is an achievement enabling the infant to progress to the ensuing stage of cognitive development.

The Preoperational Stage

The age range associated with this second stage is usually from two through six years of age. The major cognitive achievements in this stage involve the elaboration of the representational ability that enabled the child to move from the sensorimotor stage to the present one. In the preoperational stage, true systems of representation, or symbolic functioning, emerge. In fact, Elkind (1967) has termed this stage the period of *the conquest of the symbol.*

The most obvious example of the development of representational systems in this stage is language. Here the child's use of language develops extensively, as words are used to symbolize objects, events, and feelings. There are other indications of this representational ability as well. During this stage of life we see the emergence of symbolic play; for example, the child uses two crossed sticks to make an airplane or uses his or her finger to make a gun. In addition we see the emergence of delayed imitation; for example, the child sees someone perform an act—for example, Daddy smoking a pipe and pacing across the room—and then imitates the act hours later.

Although cognitive development in the preoperational stage does have positive characteristics—by virtue of the fact that such elaborate systems of representational ability do develop—it has limitations too. The child in this stage is also egocentric, but here the egocentrism takes a form different from that seen in the previous stage. The child now has the ability to symbolize objects with words, to use words to refer to objects. But at the same time, the child fails to differentiate between the words and the things the words refer to. For example, the child believes that the word representing an object is inherent in it, that an object cannot have more than one word that symbolizes it (Elkind 1967). The child does not know that an object and the word symbolizing the object are two independent things. The child does not differentiate between symbols and what the symbols refer to (Elkind 1967).

David Elkind

This type of egocentrism has several consequences. One is that the child acts as if words carry much more meaning than they actually do (Elkind 1967). For instance, it is not uncommon to see a child in this stage of development ask someone for the "thing" and act as if enough information has been conveyed to the other person to have the request fulfilled. Since the child does not differentiate between symbols and their referents, he or she thinks the word belongs to (inheres in) the object.

A broader consequence of this egocentrism is the child's inability to hold two aspects of a situation separately in mind at the same time. That is, the child does not differentiate between objects and the words that refer to them and thus joins, or merges, these two dimensions of a stimulus—the object and the symbol. This failure suggests a more general lack of ability to take into account two different aspects of a stimulus array at the same time. One indication of this general inability may be found in the preoperational child's failure to show conservation ability.

Conservation refers to the ability to know that one aspect of a stimulus array has remained unchanged although others have changed. To understand this concept, let us imagine that we present a five-year-old with two dolls, a mommy doll and a daddy doll. We then take four marbles and place them in a row beside the mommy doll, and we place four more marbles beside the daddy doll in positions directly corresponding to the mommy doll's marbles. Our materials would look like those in Figure 8.1a. Now, if we show the five-year-old these materials arranged in this way and ask, "Which doll has more marbles to play with—the mommy doll or the daddy doll?" the child will most probably say that both dolls have the same amount of marbles to play with. However, if we spread out the mommy doll's marbles in the full view of the child (but leave the daddy doll's marbles in their original position), so that we have an arrangement that looks like Figure 8.1b, and then ask which doll has more, the preoperational five-year-old will answer that the mommy doll has more!

What we see from this example, then, is the inability to conserve number. The child does not know that one aspect of the stimulus array—the number of marbles—has remained unchanged, although another aspect of the array—the positioning of the marbles—has changed. It would seem that the child cannot appreciate these two dimensions of the stimulus array at the same time. A cognitive error is made because, in not being able to put these two dimensions in their proper interrelation, the child fails to know that the movements of the mommy doll's marbles can be reversed and be put back into the original stimulus-array arrangement. As we will learn when we discuss the next stage of cognitive development—the concrete operational stage—the child cannot yet understand this *reversibility*. The child's thought is still dominated by schemes, and as we have seen, such structures are rigidly unidirectional. Thus, even though we spread out the marbles right in front of the child, the child will still maintain that the altered array has more marbles. We

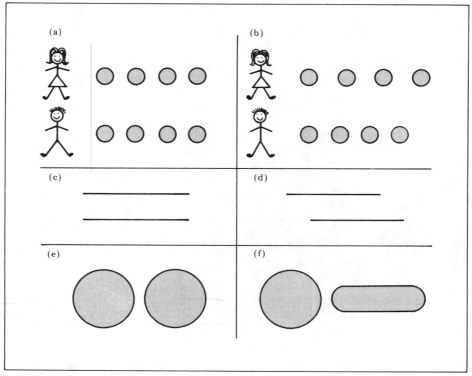

FIGURE 8.1
Examples of tests of number conservation (a and b), length conservation (c and d), and mass conservation (e and f).

might even return the array to its original form and again ask which doll has more. The child will now probably say once again that they both have the same amount, and even if we repeat these steps several times the child's answers might correspondingly alternate between "same" and "more."

The lack of conservation ability seen with the quantitative dimension of number applies, too, to other quantitative aspects of stimuli. Thus, if we present two equal lengths of rope—as in Figure 8.1c—and ask which rope is longer, the child will probably answer that the ropes are equal in length. If, however, we move the location of one of these pieces of rope—as in Figure 8.1d—and repeat the question, the child will now claim that one piece of rope is longer than the other. Similarly, if we take two equal-sized pieces of clay and roll them up into balls of

equal size and shape and present them to the child—as in Figure 8.1e—the child will say that each ball contains the same amount of clay. If, however, we reshape one of these clay balls into a sausage—as in Figure 8.1f—again doing this right in full view of the child, and then ask which ball contains more clay, the child's answer will be different; the child will now say that the sausage-shaped piece contains more clay. In this example we see an instance of the inability to show conservation of mass. The child does not know that one aspect of the stimulus array—its mass—remains the same although another aspect of the array—its shape—is altered.

In sum, then, the preoperational child does not generally show conservation ability; this manifests itself not only in respect to quantitative aspects of stimuli such as mass, length, and number, but to other quantitative aspects of stimuli such as area and volume as well. Thus, although the pre-operational child's thought has progressed well beyond that of the sensorimotor child—due mostly to extensive representational abilities—the preoperational child's cognition still has the above limitations. However, as the cognitive conflicts produced by being unable to differentiate between symbols and the objects they refer to increase, and as instances of the inability to simultaneously appreciate two different aspects of a stimulus array similarly increase and cause conflict, the child must accommodate more and more. As the equilibrations and the disequilibrations involved in this process occur, the child's cognitive structure will be altered. When enough alteration has taken place, the child will enter into the next stage of cognitive development.

The Concrete Operational Stage

Up to the point when a child enters the concrete operational stage (which spans a period from about six years through eleven or twelve years of age), the child's cognitive structure is composed predominantly of schemes. However, because a scheme is a unidirectional structure, the child is generally unable to simultaneously appreciate contrasting aspects of a stimulus array. This limitation, as we have seen, is illustrated by the lack of conservation ability. Preoperational thought thus limits a child in not providing the ability to reverse various physical events. That is, if we as adults see two balls of clay and decide that each contains an equal amount of clay, we would continue to maintain this even if one of the balls were reshaped to look like a sausage. If this were done we would know—without having to see the action performed—that by reversing the action of reshaping the clay we would be back to the original two clay balls. Because nothing was added to or subtracted from either ball—because reshaping does not alter the mass—we would assert that both pieces of clay are the same.

The emergence of *operational structures* gives the child this ability. An operation is an internalized action that is reversible. As opposed to schemes, operations allow the person to know that actions can be counteracted by reversing them. Moreover, operations *are* internalized actions. That is, we do not have to see the action of rolling the sausage back into a ball to know that we can return the clay to its original shape. We can just think of this action. Our thought about concrete, physical actions does not depend on our actually seeing these actions. We can reverse the actions in our heads and come to the same conclusion about them as if we actually, concretely viewed them.

Thus the emergence of operational cognitive ability extends the child's capacity to deal with the world. Because thought is now reversible—because the child can now appreciate the reciprocity in concrete actions on and with physical stimuli—the concrete operational stage is the period in which the child begins to show the conservation abilities lacking in the preoperational stage. Moreover, because operations are internalized actions, the child's cognitive abilities are also extended in that now he or she need not actually see actions performed in order to know about them. Thus the child now has cognitive structures that enable him or her to think about the actions of the world without actually having to experience these actions. Simply, operations extend the scope of action by internalizing it.

But despite the great cognitive accomplishments inherent in the concrete operational stage, thought in this stage also has its limitations. Notice that the label for this stage is concrete operational. What this denotes is that although thought is operational, it is bound by concrete, physical reality. Although the child can deal with objects internally—that is, without having to actually experience them—these actions and objects must have a concrete, real existence. Things or events that are counterfactual—that are not actually represented in the real world—cannot be understood by the concrete operational child. An illustration of this point, which is offered by Elkind (1967), is helpful. Suppose someone asks you to imagine that coal is white, and then further asks you to indicate what color coal would be when burning at its hottest. Most probably you would have an answer to this counterfactual question. You might think that since coal is actually black and when burning at its hottest is white, then if it were white, it would be black when burning at its hottest. The point here is not the particular solution, but the fact that you can deal with the counterfactual question. The concrete operational child, on the other hand, cannot do this. For example, the response of the concrete operational child might typically be, "But coal is black!" (Elkind 1967). In essence, then, a major limitation of concrete operational thought is that it is limited to thinking about concrete, real things.

There are other limitations of concrete thought, too, however. As Elkind (1967) has pointed out, the concrete operational child is also egocentric. Here, however, the egocentrism takes the form of an inability to differentiate between actions and objects experienced directly and actions and objects the child thinks about. We have seen that the child's thought is now independent of experience, so that he or she can now deal with an action whether it is experienced or just thought about. However, the child fails to distinguish between knowledge gained through experience and knowledge gained from thought alone. If given some information about a physical situation (say a scientific problem) and asked to give a solution to the problem, the child will not have to see the actual physical objects in order to reach a solution; instead, he or she will think about it and form an answer, a hypothesis. But the child will not recognize that the answer is just a hypothesis, just one possible solution to the problem. Rather, the child will think that the answer is one and the same with the physical situation. The child will not see any difference between what he or she thinks and what is! Even if the child's ideas about experience are challenged and/or evidence is presented contradicting those ideas, the child will not alter the answer, but will just reinterpret the opposing evidence to fit into his or her ideas (Elkind 1967).

Unable to think counterfactually, and equating perceived and actual reality, the child cannot recognize that his or her thoughts about reality represent only hypotheses; that they are arbitrary; that they are not necessarily imposed by or part of reality but are just one of many possible interpretations of reality. Thus a child is egocentric in failing to view thoughts and experience as two independent phenomena. With further cognitive development, however, the child attains the ability to think counterfactually, to see that thoughts about reality and reality are different. Hence, the child's final stage of cognitive development begins.

The Formal Operational Stage

The last stage of cognitive development in Piaget's theory is termed the *formal operational stage*. It begins at about eleven or twelve years of age and continues for the rest of life, according to Piaget (1972). It is because of the lower age limit typically associated with this stage in both theory and research (see Neimark 1975) that the study of formal operations is linked with the period of adolescent development.

In the formal operational stage, thought becomes hypothetical in emphasis. Now discriminating between thoughts about reality and actual reality, the child comes to recognize that his or her thoughts about reality have an element of arbitrariness about them, that they may not actually be real representations of the true nature of experience. Thus the child's thoughts about reality take on a hypothetical "if . . . then" characteristic: "*If* something were the case, *then* something else would follow." In forming such hypotheses about the world, the child's thought can be seen to correspond to formal, scientific, logical thinking. This emergence accounts for the label applied to this stage—the formal operational stage.

Another perspective on the quality of this stage is provided by Neimark (1975). She explains the distinctive quality of adolescent thought by noting:

Although the properties and relations at issue during the concrete operational stage are abstract in the sense of being derived from objects and events, they are still dependent upon specifics of the objects and events from which they derive; that is, they are empirically based abstractions rather than pure abstractions. In this sense the elements of concrete operational thought are "concrete" rather than "abstract" or "formal." On the other hand, propositions, the elements of formal operational thought, are abstract in the sense that the truth value of a statement can be freed from a dependence upon the evidence of experience and, instead, determined logically from the truth values of other propositions to which it bears a formal, logical relationship. This type of reasoning, deriving from the form of propositions rather than their content, is new in the development of the child: deductive rather than inductive thought. (Neimark 1975, 547–48).

In other words, because the concrete operational child can only form abstractions relevant to phenomena or problems that exist, thoughts about a given topic cannot be integrated with *potentially* relevant but nonempirical (that is, hypothetical) aspects of the problem. In this sense, mental operations are not coordinated, and the child cannot reach solutions by means of general theories or by the postulation of all possible solutions to a problem (Wadsworth 1971). In turn, the formal operational person does show these qualities of thought.

Thus, to be able to deal with all potentially relevant aspects of a problem, a person has to be able to *transform* (that is, alter, or rearrange) the problem so as to contend with all its possible forms. The cognitive structure that characterizes formal operations allows such complete transformations. Piaget terms this structure the INRC group (Inhelder and Piaget 1958; Piaget, 1950, 1952, 1970). That is, all transformations of a problem may be obtained though the application of the components of this group: identity, negation, and reciprocal and correlative transformations. Simply, one can think of all the aspects of a problem by, for instance, recognizing the problem in terms of its singular attributes (an identity transforma-

tion), canceling the existence of the problem (a negation operation), taking its opposite (a reciprocal transformation), or relating it to other problems (a correlative transformation).

Since only the coordinated use of all these transformations allows all potentially applicable aspects of a problem to be dealt with, it is not until the INRC group is established that the person possesses a cognitive structure appropriate for dealing with pure abstractions—with a set of all the propositions pertinent to a problem that is the "object" of thought in the formal operational stage. To indicate the attributes of thought characteristic of people in the formal operational stage, it is useful to discuss some examples of tasks typically used to measure such cognitive functioning.

The Measurement of Formal Operational Thought

In discussing preoperational thinking, some of the various conservation tasks used to index the child's level of functioning were noted. Different types of problems are presented to children and adolescents in order to assess whether they show the types of mental functions that represent formal operational thought. Inhelder and Piaget (1958; Piaget and Inhelder 1969) describe several such formal operational tasks.

One of these tasks tests *combinatorial* thought. To explain the meaning of this term, Piaget and Inhelder (1969) describe a task wherein a subject is presented with five jars, each containing a colorless liquid. Combining the liquids from three particular jars will produce a color, while any use of the liquids from either of the other jars will not produce a color. The subject is shown that a color can be produced but is not shown which combination will do this.

Concrete operational children typically try to solve this problem by combining the liquids two at a time, but after combining all pairs or possibly trying to mix all five liquids together, their search for the workable combination usually stops. However, the formal

operational child will explore all possible solutions, typically testing all possible combinations of two and three liquids until a color
is produced.

Tasks involving certain types of *verbal
problems* cannot usually be solved without
formal operational ability (Piaget and Inhelder 1969; Wadsworth 1971). One such
verbal problem is represented by the question, "If Jane is taller than Doris, and is
shorter than Francine, who is the shortest of
the three?" (Wadsworth 1971). Although
concrete operational children may be able to
solve an analogous problem—for example,
one dealing with sticks of various lengths—
when the elements of the problem (the
sticks) are physically present, abstract
verbal problems are usually not solved until
formal operations have emerged.

Although formal operational thought can
be illustrated by particular solutions to
problems presented by many other tasks
(Inhelder and Piaget 1958), I may mention
one other task, the *pendulum problem,* to illustrate the quality of thought at this period
of functioning. A pendulum can be made to
swing faster by shortening the string holding
it. Conversely, it can be made to swing
slower by lengthening the string. Concrete
operational children typically adjust the
weight of a pendulum when asked to alter its
speed (Wadsworth 1971). Alternatively, they
may adjust string length and weight simultaneously and attribute any change in speed to
the weight alteration (Wadsworth 1971).
However, in the formal operational period,
subjects separate weight and string length,
deal with them separately, and show knowledge that it is string length that is the variable relevant to the speed of swinging
(Inhelder and Piaget 1958).

In summary, with formal operations the
child's thought is completely free from any
dependence on concrete reality. Now the
child can and does think not only in the "if
. . . then" or "as if" manner, but the child
thinks counterfactually and completely abstractly as well. In reviews of research on adolescent intellectual development, Neimark
(1975, 1979) notes that there exists strong

research evidence for the validity of formal
operational thought as an empirical phenomenon distinct from concrete operational
thought. There have been repeated demonstrations of age-related improvements in
formal thought during adolescence (for example, Martorano 1977). Indeed, presentations by Moshman (1977) and Flavell and
Wohlwill (1969) support Piaget's ideas about
the structure of adolescent thought, as well
as about how this stage is formed. Similarly,
Roberge (1976) found that the formal operational structures necessary to solve complex
problems and to deal with conditional reasoning emerge in early adolescence, and a
report by Strauss, Danziger, and Ramati
(1977) shows that formal thoughts, which
dominated college students' thinking, cannot
easily be changed back to concrete operational ones. Thus, formal operations emerge
as a distinct stage in adolescence and continue to characterize thought thereafter.
However, several qualifications of these conclusions are necessary.

Issues in the Assessment of
Formal Operations

As will be noted below, the emergence of
formal operations in adolescence does not
say anything about whether another stage of
cognition follows. Moreover, there is evidence that the emergence of a formal operational thought structure is not a
characteristic of all people. As reviewed by
Neimark (1975), studies done with older adolescents and adults in Western cultures show
that not all individuals attain the level of
formal operations. Neimark (1979) notes:

> while there is increasing acceptance of the ex-
> istence of a level of adult thought qualitatively
> different in structure and properties from the
> stage of concrete operations, there is also a
> great deal of healthy skepticism as to its gen-
> erality, the methodology of its assessment, and
> theoretical characterization of its essential in-
> gredients. (p. 61)

For instance, Jackson (1965) found that
only seven of sixteen persons thirteen to fifteen years old reached a conventional stage

of formal thought, and less than 75 percent of the fifteen-year-olds that Dale (1970) studied reached such a stage. In fact, on the basis of results from two studies (Elkind 1962; Towler and Wheatley 1971), Neimark (1975) notes there is evidence that only about 60 percent of college students sampled show appropriate performance on tasks requiring the conservation of volume. Similarly, Martorano (1977) found that in a sample of sixth-to-twelfth-grade females, there was a grade-associated improvement on average scores for ten different tests of formal operations. However, not even the oldest group of subjects showed formal operations across all ten tasks.

Moreover, although not all people may attain the formal operations level, once attained in adolescence it may not be continuous throughout the rest of life. Papalia (1972) found that less than 60 percent of her sixty-five- to eighty-two-year-old sample conserved volume, and Tomlinson-Keasey (1972) found evidence of formal operations in just about 50 percent of her middle-aged female sample. These latter two studies could be interpreted as showing that formal operations are not present in the post-adolescent life periods of people of some (older) cohorts. This may be due either to their never having reached this stage or to their losing their ability after having attained it. However, without longitudinal data on subjects' life-span performance, this issue presently cannot be decided.

Generalizations about the course of formal operations across the life span within a culture are tentative, but so, too, are such statements when made from a cross-cultural perspective. As summarized by Neimark (1975), people in many cultural settings do not attain formal operational abilities at the average, early-adolescent time that is typical within Western cultural settings. For example, Douglas and Wong (1977) reported that American adolescents (thirteen- and fifteen-year-olds) were more advanced in formal operations than Hong Kong Chinese of corresponding ages. In fact, in some non-Western groups there is a failure ever to attain such

thinking ability. Piaget (1969, 1972) himself noted such failures. Reasons for these differences have been suggested to lie in the contrasts in experience found between rural and urban settings (Peluffo 1962; Youniss and Dean 1974), and in the kind of schooling experiences encountered (Goodnow 1962; Goodnow and Bethon 1966; Peluffo 1962, 1967).

Although these explanations might lead one to expect socioeconomic or educational differences to be associated with formal operational attainment, the data do not support such a view. Neimark (1975) finds that socioeconomic status has no known effect on the development of formal thought, and in addition she notes that only very profound differences in education seem to be associated with the development of formal thought. Moreover, variables such as sex and psychometric intelligence, which might be thought to mark differences in experience associated with formal thought development, do not seem useful. Some studies find sex difference (for example, Dale 1970; Elkind 1962), and some do not (for example, Jackson 1965; Lovell 1961). Moreover, IQ score differences do not relate to differences in formal operational development (Kuhn 1976). Indeed, it seems that after some minimal level of psychometric intelligence is reached, variables other than those associated with IQ scores contribute to formal operational development (Neimark 1975).

I have just suggested that the variables readily thought of as possible facilitators of such progression do not seem consistently functional. Thus it might be appropriate to try directly to train formal operational thought. But few studies have attempted this. Although Tomlinson-Keasey (1972) facilitated formal thought through training on one task, subjects did not generalize formal thinking ability to other tasks. Schwebel's (1972) attempt at training also met with limited success, and Lathey (1970) had no success at all in attempting to produce volume conservation in eleven-year-olds. Kuhn and Angelev (1976) did succeed in their intervention attempt, however. Fourth and fifth graders were given a fifteen-week program in which they confronted problems requiring formal operational thought. The frequency of exposure to the problems (once every two weeks, once a week, or twice a week) was related directly to amount of advancement on three formal operational problems.

In sum, the formal operational stage does not represent a level of thought reached universally by all people in all cultures. Even though uncertainty remains about the variables that provide a transition to this level of thinking, there is strong evidence that formal operations does represent a distinct level of thought beyond concrete operations. Moreover, for most adolescents living in contemporary Western culture—and for all those people now reading these words—formal operations represents an attained stage of thought. Although we have seen the assets of this type of thought, it must be noted that—as with preceding levels of thought—formal operational thinking also has limitations. These are now considered.

Adolescent Egocentrism

Because anything and everything can become the object of the adolescent's newly developed abstract and hypothetical cognitive ability, the person may not only recognize his or her own thoughts as only one possible interpretation of reality, but may also come to view reality as only one possible instance of a potentially unlimited number of possible realities. The concrete predomination of what is real is replaced by the abstract and hypothetical predomination of what can be real. All things in experience are thought about hypothetically, and even the adolescent's own thoughts can become objects of his or her hypothesizing.

In other words, one can now think about one's own thinking. Since the young person spends a good deal of time using these new thought capabilities, the person's own thought processes thereby become a major object of cognitive concern. This preoccupation, or *centration* on one's own perspective, leads, however, to a limitation of the newly

developed formal operational thought. It leads to egocentrism within the formal operational stage. Elkind (1967) has labeled the egocentrism of this stage *adolescent egocentrism,* and sees it as having two parts.

First, we have seen how the adolescent's own thoughts come to dominate his or her thinking. Because of this preoccupation, the adolescent fails to distinguish, or discriminate, between his or her own thinking and what others are thinking about. Being preoccupied with self and not making the above discrimination, the adolescent comes to believe that others are as preoccupied with his or her appearance and behavior as he or she is (Elkind 1967). Thus the adolescent constructs an *imaginary audience.*

As an illustration of the functioning of the imaginary audience and of some emotional consequences of this cognitive development, think back to your early-adolescent days. Assuredly, some new fad—perhaps in regard to a particular style of clothing—sprang up among your peers. Some adolescents perhaps were stuck with wearing the old, outdated style and were literally afraid to be seen in public. They were sure that as soon as they appeared without the appropriate clothes, everyone would notice the absence.

There is a second component of adolescent egocentrism. The adolescent's thoughts and feelings are experienced as new and unique by him or her. Although to the adolescent they *are* in fact new and unique, the young person comes to believe that they are *historically* new and unique. That is, the adolescent constructs a *personal fable,* the belief that he or she is a one-of-a-kind individual—a person having singular feelings and thoughts.

Here, too, it is easy to think of an illustration of the personal fable. Think back to your early-adolescent years and your first "love affair." No one had ever loved as deeply, as totally—no one had ever felt the intense compassion, the devotion, the longing, the overwhelming fulfillment that you felt for your one true love! Then remember a few days or weeks later, when it was over. The pain, the depression, the agony—no one had ever suffered as deeply, no one had ever been so wrongfully abused, so thoroughly tortured, so spitefully crushed by unrequited love! You sat in your room, unmoving. Your mother would say, "What's wrong with you? Come and eat." The inevitable answer: "You don't understand. What do you know about love?"

Although the formal operational stage is the last stage of cognitive development in Piaget's theory, the egocentrism of this stage diminishes over the course of the person's subsequent cognitive functioning. According to Piaget (Inhelder and Piaget 1958; Piaget, 1969, 1972), the adolescent decenters through interaction with peers and elders and—most importantly—with the assumption of adult roles and responsibilities: "The focal point of the decentering process is the entrance into the occupational world or the beginning of serious professional training. The adolescent becomes an adult when he undertakes a real job" (Inhelder and Piaget 1958, 346).

In sum, Piaget (1950, 1970, 1972) claims that with the attainment of formal operations, the person has reached the last stage of cognitive development. To him and his followers, no new cognitive structures emerge over the course of life (Flavell 1970; Piaget 1972); however, the person may change through a differentiation or specialization of abilities within the common formal structure (Neimark 1975; Piaget 1972). By way of summary, Table 8.1 presents the four stages in Piaget's theory and shows the cognitive achievements and limitations involved in each stage.

Some Concluding Comments

What we have seen is that Piaget offers a theory of cognitive development that includes both continuous, stage-independent

TABLE 8.1
Piaget's Stages of Cognitive Development

Stage	Approximate age range	Major cognitive achievements	Major cognitive limitations
Sensorimotor	Birth to 2	Scheme of object permanency	Egocentrism: lack of ability to differentiate between self and external stimulus world
Preoperational	2 to 6 or 7	Systems of representation: symbolic functioning for example, language, symbolic play, delayed limitation	Lack of conservation ability. Egocentrism: lack of ability to differentiate between symbol and object
Concrete operational	6 or 7 to 12	Ability to show experience-independent thought (reversible, internalized actions) Conservation ability	Egocentrism: lack of ability to differentiate between thoughts about reality and actual experience of reality
Formal operational	12 on	Ability to think hypothetically, counterfactually, and propositionally	Egocentrism: imaginary audience, personal fable

phenomena and discontinuous, stage-dependent phenomena. Piaget's is an organismic account of development; he views development as the outcome of organism-environment interactions and hence as an active, self-generated process. Action—the action of the organism on the environment and the action of the environment on the organism—is the basis of cognitive development. The disequilibriums continually caused by these actions provide the moving force of cognitive development, and the changes brought about by this process are characterized by developmental stages.

Although he is a stage theorist, Piaget does not view the person as making abrupt modal transitions from one stage of development to the next. Rather, as is true of other stage theorists, he recognizes in several ways that people function at more than one stage of development at the same time. For instance, children do not gain the ability to make conservations in all quantitative dimensions at one time. Rather, number and length conservations appear first, area conservation appears later, and volume conservation typically develops last. Thus, in some areas of cognitive functioning a child may show behaviors indicative of the preoperational stage, while in other areas the child may show evidence of concrete operational functioning. Thus, stage transition becomes a matter of shifts in modal type of functioning.

Moreover, through his concept of *décalage,* Piaget also recognizes the fact that people frequently show similar cognitive phenomena at different points in their ontogeny. Piaget terms a repetition of a cognitive phenomenon that takes place within the same, single stage of development and involves a single, general level of functioning a *horizontal décalage.* The circular reactions that occur throughout the sensorimotor stage are illustrations of horizontal décalage. In addition, repetitions of the same phenomena at different stages of development are termed by Piaget *vertical décalage* (Flavell 1963, 21–22). Showing conservation ability at two different stages of development is an

instance of vertical décalage, as is the continuous functioning of reproductive assimilation across ontogeny.

Thus, although different stages of development have different stage-specific laws governing their functioning, vertical décalage suggests that there are laws general to all levels of functioning. This, then, is the second "compromise" between the organismic and the mechanistic philosophies of science discussed in Chapter 2. This is the general-and-specific-laws compromise. That is, there are phenomena at all ontogenetic levels that can be understood by one or a common set of laws or principles; however, this does not alter the fact that each level may also be governed by specific laws— whose specificity in fact serves as the criterion for calling a stage a stage. Thus Piaget, in agreement with Werner, sees both continuity and discontinuity as characteristic of developmental processes. Piaget's recognition of stage mixture as characterizing cognitive development and functioning is an indication of his understanding of the modal nature of stage transition and his belief in the orthogenetic nature of cognitive development; these points will also be salient in our discussion of Kohlberg's related stage theory, which we consider next.

KOHLBERG'S STAGE THEORY OF THE DEVELOPMENT OF MORAL REASONING

Before detailing the features of Lawrence Kohlberg's stage theory, it will be useful to note the many reasons why morality is of major scientific concern. Most developmental theorists see morality as a basic dimension of a person's adaptation to his or her world. Although different theorists define moral behavior and development in markedly distinct ways, all ideas about moral functioning suggest an adjustment by the person to the social world, an adjustment that serves the dual purpose of fitting the person to his or her society, and at the same time, contributing to the maintenance and perpetuation of that society.

Thus moral development appears to be a basic component of human adaptation and societal survival. This view is reflected in the position taken by Hogan and Emler:

> The capacity of human groups to survive and to extend their domination over the environment is a direct reflection of their ability to solve the problems of social organization and cultural transmission.
>
> Most scholars who have thought seriously about these problems have concluded that they are rooted largely, if not mainly, in the moral socialization of the group. The great social philosophers of recent times—Emile Durkheim, Karl Marx, Max Weber, L. T. Hobhouse, and Sigmund Freud—have all taken the view that human societies are at the core embodiments of moral orders. If we wish to understand that uniquely human invention, culture, we must analyze the relation of the individual to this moral issue. (1978, 200)

However, despite this general agreement, there are substantial theoretical differences involved in the specification of this bidirectional relation. Thus one should understand the different meanings attached to the term *moral development* in order to place Kohlberg's theory of the development of moral reasoning in its proper theoretical perspective.

DEFINITIONS OF MORAL DEVELOPMENT

Despite the practical and scientific importance given to moral functioning, there is no consensus about what constitutes such functioning. What is morality? How does one know if a person is or is not moral? When and how does morality develop, and what are the changes that people go through as they show this development? Theories derived from the nature, nurture, and interactionist conceptions discussed in previous chapters provide different answers to these questions. Indeed, three major types of

theories of moral development are present in the current study of human development: theories that stress the role of *nature,* of *nurture,* or of *interaction.*

Freud's Nature-Oriented Theory

Sigmund Freud's (1949) psychoanalytic theory of psychosexual stage development will be discussed next in this chapter. Both to presage this discussion and to reflect our present concern with alternative theoretical views of moral development, suffice it to say that Freud (1949) takes a weak interactionist stance regarding nature and nurture, and as such he sees each stage emerging in an intrinsically determined, universalistic manner. Accordingly, all people experience an oedipal conflict in their third psychosexual stage (the phallic stage). The successful resolution of this conflict will result in the formation of the structure of the personality Freud labeled the superego. This structure has two components, the ego ideal and the conscience. The latter represents the internalization into one's mental life of society's rules, laws, codes, ethics, and mores. In short, by about five years of age (with the end of the phallic stage) superego development will typically be complete. When this occurs, the person's conscience will be formed as much as it ever can be, and this in turn means that by about five years of age the person will have completed his or her moral development.

Of course, there are reasons for incomplete moral development. Freud (1949) specified that females did not experience the same type of conflict in the phallic stage as did males. Males were thought to develop based on an emotional reaction termed castration anxiety; females, not having an identical genital structure, developed based on an emotional reaction termed penis envy. Freud held that only castration anxiety could eventually lead to full superego development (and hence conscience formation). Because of their biologically fixed anatomical difference, females could never have complete conscience formation. Females would never be as morally developed as males (Bronfenbrenner 1960). In addition, moral development could be hampered by particular experiences occurring within the third psychosexual stage (for example, absence of an appropriate same-sex model might lead to an inability to resolve the oedipal conflict). However, because such experiences are moderated in their possible influence on the basis of whether or not they occur within the third stage, even such experiences are shaped by the nature of the person. Hence Freud's view of moral development is a nature-based one, and one that emphasizes the completion of moral development in early childhood.

One may recognize two attributes of Freud's psychoanalytic view of moral development. First, Freud would identify a person as morally developed or not on the basis of whether that person showed *behavior* consistent with society's rules. Because of the internalization involved with conscience formation, Freud would only be able to know when a person had completed this formation on the basis of behavioral consistency with these external social rules. Accordingly, to Freud (1949), moral development involves increasing behavioral consistency with society's rules, and as soon as a person shows such behavioral congruence (at about five years of age), he or she is completely morally developed. This conception indicates then that as long as two people—say a five-year-old and a twenty-year-old—show an identical response in a moral situation, they are identically morally developed.

This observation raises the second point about Freud's views on morality. Freud does not deal with the content of behavior. He does not concern himself with whether a particular response in a situation should be judged as moral in some universalistic sense. Rather, as long as the response conforms to the particular rules of the society, then that response shows internalization, conscience formation, and thus moral development. Hence, because different societies can and do prescribe different sorts of rules for behavior, Freud says there is no universal

moral behavior. Rather, what is seen as moral behavior is defined *relative* to a particular society.

In summary, Freud's nature-based view focuses on response consistency with society's rules as an index of moral development and takes a *moral relativism* stance about the ethical appropriateness of any given behavior. Interestingly, a theoretical position often diametrically opposed to Freud's takes an identical stance regarding moral responses and moral relativism. That is, some nurture-based social-learning theories converge with psychoanalytic conceptions of moral development.

Nurture-Oriented Social-Learning Theories

Some social-learning theorists see behavior as a response to stimulation (Davis 1944; McCandless 1970). Such responses may arise either from external environmental sources, such as lights, sounds, or other people, or from internal bodily sources, such as drives (McCandless 1970). Nevertheless, in either case responses become linked to stimulation on the basis of whether reward or punishment is associated with a particular stimulus-response connection (Bijou and Baer 1961). Those responses leading to reward stay in the person's behavioral repertoire, while those associated with punishment do not. The social environment determines which responses will or will not be rewarded, and as such, behavior development involves learning to emit those responses leading to reward and not to emit those responses leading to punishment.

Although social-learning theorists differ in regard to the details of how such learning takes place (Bandura and Walters 1963; Davis 1944; McCandless 1970; Sears 1957), there is general consensus that development involves behavior that increasingly conforms to social rules. Thus the comparability of this position with Freud's is evident. Moreover, it is clear that behavioral development and moral development are virtually indistinct. There is no qualitative difference between behavior labeled as moral and behavior labeled as social, personal, or anything else for that matter. All behavior follows the principles of social learning, and as such, all behavior involves the conformity of the person's responses to the rules of society.

Thus, like all classes of behavior, moral development involves increasing response consistency to the rules of society; and since there is an *arbitrary* relation between a response and a reward—that is, any particular society may reward any given behavior—there are no responses that necessarily (universally) *have* to be rewarded. Hence, any response may be defined as moral in a given society, and this means that a morally relativistic stance is taken by social-learning theorists. By focusing on how nurture processes come to control a person's behavior, social-learning theorists derive a conception of moral development that, like the nature-based psychoanalytic one, stresses increasing response consistency with society's rules as the index of moral change. This view also takes a morally relativistic stance regarding the content of moral behavior.

Although basing their views on quite distinct ideas about the *basis* of response conformity to societal rules, both psychoanalytic and social-learning theorists would judge that if a young child and an adult emitted the same response in a moral situation, they would therefore be equally morally developed. Moreover, theorists from both persuasions might say that if killing of certain other people were condoned in a particular society and, in fact, rewarded (for example, the murder of Jews by Nazi Germany or the institutionalized killing of some female infants in some primitive societies), this would be morally acceptable behavior insofar as that society was concerned. That is, because of moral relativism, any society may establish any behavior as moral.

Structural Cognitive Developmental Theories

Another view of moral development has become increasingly prominent in American social science since the late 1950s. This conception not only rejects the focus on responses as an index of moral development but also stresses that a *universalistic* view of moral development must be taken.

Rejecting moral relativism, this view might lead to the claim that those societies that condone killing of other humans are in fact immoral societies. This third type of theory is based on the work of Jean Piaget. It has, however, been more prominently advanced by theorists who, working from a cognitive developmental position like Piaget's, have expanded his initial conceptions.

Piaget (1965) became a major contributor to the topic of moral development by offering a theory that, consistent with his general theory of cognitive development, saw a child's morality as progressing through phases. That is, he saw the child as having "two moralities"—as progressing through a two-phase sequence. However, the target of concern in this sequence is not behavior that might require moral action but rather it is *reasoning* about moral responses in such situations. Thus, in his major statement of his views regarding moral development, Piaget (1965, 7) cautions readers that they will find "no direct analysis of child morality as it is practiced in home and school life or in children's societies. It is the moral judgment that we propose to investigate, not moral behavior. . . ."

Kohlberg (1958, 1963a, 1963b), Turiel (1969), and other followers of the cognitive developmental view (e.g., Colby 1978) believe that there must be a focus on reasoning and not on responses, since the same moral response may be associated with two quite distinct reasons for behavior. Unless one understands the reasons why people believe an act is moral or not, one will be unable to see the complexity of moral development that actually exists (Turiel 1969).

On the basis of his research, Piaget (1965) formulated two phases of moral reasoning development in children. In the first phase, labeled *heteronomous morality,* the child is objective in his or her moral judgments. An act is judged right or wrong solely in terms of its consequences. If one breaks a vase, a child in this phase would judge one as morally culpable, whether or not the breaking was accidental. This type of judgment is based, Piaget believes, on the child's moral realism. Rules are seen as unchangeable externally (that is, societally) imposed requirements for behavior; these rules are imposed by adults on the child and require unyielding acceptance. Such a "relationship of constraint" is seen as necessary because punishment for disobedience to rules is seen as an automatic consequence of the behavior. In short, acts are objectively judged as good or bad, and if a bad act is committed, there will be *imminent justice*—that is, automatic, immediate punishment.

However, in the second phase, labeled *autonomous morality,* children become subjective in their moral judgments. This means that, when judging the moral rightness or wrongness of an act, children take intentions into account. If one breaks a vase out of spite or anger, one would be judged morally wrong. But if one breaks the vase because of clumsiness, no moral culpability would be seen. This second type of judgment Piaget believes is based on the child's *moral rationality*. Rules are seen as outcomes of agreements between people in a relation not of social constraint but rather of cooperation and autonomy. That is, each person is an equal in such a relation, and as such, rules are made in relation to the mutual interest of those involved. Thus acts are judged good or bad in terms of the principles of this "contract." Whatever punishment is associated with violation of contract rules is determined by humans and is not a consequence of some reflexive, automatic punisher.

Accordingly, although a seven-year-old and an eighteen-year-old might behave in similar ways in a moral situation—for example, neither might cheat on a test or steal from a friend—the similar responses would not mean that the reasons underlying the responses were similar. The younger child might not cheat or steal simply because of a belief that he or she would be physically punished for it. However, the eighteen-year-

old might see such reasoning as "immature." Here the reason for not stealing might involve an *implicit* agreement among friends to respect each other's rights and property. The fact that there may be physical punishment associated with stealing would be irrelevant to a reason based on such a conception of mutual trust. Thus, to Piaget, because of the presence of such different types of moral reasoning, the seven-year-old and the eighteen-year-old would not have similar levels of moral development, despite their similar responses.

In summary, Piaget (1965) believes that all people pass through these two phases of moral reasoning. In other words, he suggests a sequence that first involves an objective and concrete morality based on constraints imposed by the powerful (for example, adults) on the nonpowerful (for example, children). Second, a subjective morality follows, based on an abstract understanding of the implicit contracts involved in cooperation and autonomy relationships.

Piaget's denial of the importance of focusing *just* on the moral response and his stress on orderings to morality represented an approach to the study of moral development that was quite distinct from the morally relativistic, response-centered approaches of psychoanalysis and social-learning theory. As such, it stimulated considerable interest among developmental researchers, especially because it offered a provocative framework for assessing changes in morality beyond the level of early childhood. However, the interest it stimulated soon led to Piaget's theory being replaced as the focus of developmental research inquiry. Following Piaget's general cognitive developmental theoretical approach, Lawrence Kohlberg (1958, 1963a, 1963b) obtained evidence that Piaget's two-phase model was not sufficient to account for all the types of changes in moral reasoning through which people progressed. Kohlberg devised a theory involving several stages of moral-reasoning development in order to encompass all the qualitative changes he discerned. Interest in moral development in the 1960s and 1970s was centered on assessing the usefulness of Kohlberg's universalistic theory. Accordingly, to determine what is currently known about moral development, one must deal with the research and theory generated in relation to Kohlberg's stage theory.

FEATURES OF KOHLBERG'S THEORY OF MORAL-REASONING DEVELOPMENT

Kohlberg's theory of moral development, like Piaget's, is based on the idea that by focusing only on the response in a moral situation, one may ignore important distinctions in people's moral reasoning at different points in their life span, reasoning differences that in fact may give different meaning to the exact same response at various developmental levels. Because the response alone does not necessarily give a clue about underlying reasoning, "an individual's response must be examined in light of how he perceives the moral situation, what the meaning of the situation is to the person responding, and the relation of his choice to that meaning: the cognitive and emotional processes in making moral judgments" (Turiel 1969, 95).

Because of these issues, Kohlberg rejected response-oriented approaches to understanding moral development and chose to investigate the reasons underlying moral responses (Kohlberg 1958, 1963a). He devised a way to find the underlying reasons through his construction of a moral-development interview. Information from this interview provided the data for the theory he formulated. As such, to understand the empirical origin of Kohlberg's ideas, one must consider his method of studying moral reasoning.

Kohlberg's Method of Assessing Moral Reasoning

To study moral reasoning, Kohlberg devised a series of stories, each presenting imaginary moral dilemmas. We will present one such story and then evaluate the features it offers in providing a technique for assessing moral reasoning.

> One day air raid sirens began to sound. Everyone realized that a hydrogen bomb was going to be dropped on the city by the enemy, and that the only way to survive was to be in a bomb shelter. Not everyone had bomb shelters, but those who did ran quickly to them. Since Mr. and Mrs. Jones had built a shelter, they immediately went to it where they had enough air space inside to last them for exactly five days. They knew that after five days the fallout would have diminished to the point where they could safely leave the shelter. If they left before that, they would die. There was enough air for the Joneses only. Their next door neighbors had not built a shelter and were trying to get in. The Joneses knew that they would not have enough air if they let the neighbors in, and that they would all die if they came inside. So they refused to let them in.
>
> So now the neighbors were trying to break the door down in order to get in. Mr. Jones took his rifle and told them to go away or else he would shoot. They would not go away. So he either had to shoot them or let them come into the shelter.

What features of this story make it a moral dilemma? First, like all of Kohlberg's moral dilemma stories (Turiel 1969), the story presents the listener with a conflict. In this particular story the conflict involves the need to choose between two culturally unacceptable alternatives: killing others so that you may survive or allowing others and yourself and your family to die. The story presents a dilemma because it puts the listener in a conflict situation in which no response is clearly the only conceivably acceptable one. As such, the particular response is irrelevant. What is of concern is the reasoning used to resolve the conflict. Thus Kohlberg asks the listener not just to tell him *what* Mr. Jones should do, but *why* Mr. Jones should do it.

Thus Kohlberg would first ask, "What should Mr. Jones do?" Next he would ask, "Does he have the right to shoot his neigh-

Lawrence Kohlberg

bors if he feels that they would all die if he let them in since there would not be enough air to last them very long? Why?" Then, "Does he have the right to keep his neighbors out of his shelter even though he knows they will die if he keeps them out? Why?" And finally Kohlberg would ask, "Does he have the right to let them in if he knows they will all die? Why?"

On the basis of an elaborate and complicated system for scoring the answers people give to questions about this and other dilemmas in his interview (Kohlberg 1958, 1963a; Kurtines and Greif 1974), a system which has undergone considerable revision (Colby et al. 1983), Kohlberg classified people into different reasoning categories. This classification led him to formulate the idea that there existed a sequence in the types of reasons people offered for their responses to moral dilemmas. The types of moral reasoning people used passed through a series of

qualitatively different stages. However, contrary to the two cognitive developmental phases Piaget (1965) proposed, Kohlberg first (1958, 1963a) argued that there are six stages in the development of moral reasoning and asserted that these stages were divided into three levels, with each level being associated with two stages. Currently, however, Kohlberg (1976, 1978) and his collaborators (Colby 1978, 1979) have revised and refined the theory somewhat. It appears that evidence for only five stages exists (Colby et al. 1983; Kohlberg 1978); that is, the last level has only one stage. In addition, with the stages redefined, new systems of scoring moral development have been developed. Nevertheless, in both the present and the former version of the theory, both the levels and the stages within and across them are seen to form a universal and invariant sequence of progression.

STAGES OF MORAL REASONING IN KOHLBERG'S THEORY: FORMER AND CURRENT LEVEL AND STAGE DESCRIPTIONS

In this section I present a description of the stages and levels in both the former and the current formulation of Kohlberg's theory. I present both versions for several *quite* important reasons. First, human development is an active scientific discipline. It is important for students of the science to realize that scientific theories are not "carved in stone" but are themselves developing sets of ideas; Kohlberg's theory is a case in point. Second, Kohlberg and his associates revised the theory because of research evidence and conceptual criticism that the theory as it stood could not adequately treat. Because this revision is a relatively recent one, and because much of the existing data pertinent to moral development were collected in regard to the former version, we need to see what the former characteristics of the theory were in order to (1) understand a lot of the already collected data about moral development and (2) judge if appropriate revisions now exist in the theory. We will see that the theory may be able to handle more, but certainly not all, of the criticism advanced against it.

No age limits are typically associated with Kohlberg's stages or levels. However, since in both versions of the theory the very first stage does seem to rest on some minimal representational ability, we may presume it does not emerge prior to the preoperational period of Piaget's theory—that is, somewhere between two to six or seven years of age. Moreover, many of the subsequent stages of moral reasoning seem to be dependent on formal operational thinking (Kohlberg 1973). As such, they may be expected to be involved more typically with adolescence and adulthood, at least insofar as Western culture is concerned (Simpson 1974).

Levels and Stages in the Former Version of Kohlberg's Theory of Moral-Reasoning Development

Kohlberg's (1958, 1963) earlier formulation of his theory included three levels of moral-reasoning development; there were two stages within each level. Let us now consider the levels and stages of the former version of Kohlberg's theory.

Level 1: Preconventional Moral Reasoning

The first two stages of moral reasoning emerge within the first level. Although these two stages involve qualitatively different thought processes about moral conflicts, they do have a general similarity. For both stages a person's moral reasoning involves reference to external, physical events and objects—as opposed to such things as societal standards—as the source for decisions about moral rightness or wrongness.

STAGE 1: OBEDIENCE AND PUNISHMENT ORIENTATION. The reference to external, physical things is well illustrated in this first stage of moral development. Kohlberg sees this stage as being dominated by moral reasoning involving reference merely to obedience or punishment by powerful figures. Thus an act is judged wrong or right if it is or is not associated with punishment. Reasoning here is similar to what we have seen involved in Piaget's first stage of moral reasoning. In stage 1, a person reasons that one must be obedient to powerful authority because that authority is powerful—it can punish you. Acts, then, are judged as not moral only because they are associated with these external, physical sanctions.

STAGE 2: NAIVELY EGOTISTIC ORIENTATION. Reference to external physical events is also made in this stage. However, an act is judged right if it is involved with an external event that satisfies the needs of the person or, sometimes, the needs of someone very close to the person (e.g., a father, mother, husband, or wife). Thus even though stealing is wrong—because it is associated with punishment—reasoning at this level might lead to the assertion that stealing is right if the act of stealing is instrumental in satisfying a need of the person. For example, if the person was very hungry, then in that instance stealing food would be seen as a moral act.

Although this second stage also involves major reference to external, physical events as the source of rightness or wrongness, the perspective of self-needs (or, sometimes, the needs of significant others) is also brought into consideration (albeit egocentrically). Thus the development in this second stage gradually brings about a transition of perspective, a perspective involving people. This transition then leads to the next level of moral reasoning.

Level 2: Conventional Moral Reasoning

In this second level of moral reasoning, the person's thinking involves reference to acting as others expect. Acts are judged right if they conform to roles that others (i.e., society) think a person should play. An act is seen as moral if it accords with the established order of society.

STAGE 3: GOOD-PERSON ORIENTATION. Here the person is oriented toward being seen as a good boy or a good girl by others. The person sees society as providing certain general, or stereotyped, roles for people. If you act in accord with these role prescriptions, you will win the approval of other people, and hence you will be labeled a good person. Thus acts that help others, that lead to the approval of others, or that simply should—given certain role expectations by society—lead to the approval of others will be judged as moral.

STAGE 4: AUTHORITY AND SOCIAL-ORDER MAINTENANCE ORIENTATION. A more formal view of society's rules and institutions emerges in this stage. Rather than just acting in accord with the rules and institutions of society to earn approval, the person comes to see these rules and institutions as ends in themselves. That is, acts that are in accord with the maintenance of the rules of society and that allow the institutions of social order (e.g., the government) to continue functioning are seen as moral. The social order and institutions of society must be maintained for their own sake; they are ends in themselves. A moral person is one who "does his or her duty" and maintains the established authority, social order, and institutions of society. A person is simply not moral if his or her acts are counter to these goals.

Reasoning at this level involves a consideration of a person's role in reference to society. In addition, at stage 4, in contrast with stage 3, moral thinking involves viewing the social rule to do one's duty as the basis of being moral; however, this thinking may lead the person to consider the alternative, or the reverse side of the issue. The person may begin to think about what society must do in order for it to be judged as moral. If and when such considerations begin to emerge, the person will gradually make a transition into the next level of moral reasoning.

Level 3: Postconventional Moral Reasoning
This is the last level in the development of moral reasoning. Moral judgments are made

in reference to the view that there are arbitrary, subjective elements in social rules. The rules and institutions of society are not absolute, but relative. Other rules, equally as reasonable, may have been established. Thus the rules and institutions of society are no longer viewed as ends in themselves, but as subjective. Such postconventional reasoning, which is related to formal operational thinking—and thus to adolescence as well—also develops through two stages.

STAGE 5: CONTRACTUAL LEGALISTIC ORIENTATION. In this stage, similar to Piaget's (1965) second phase, the person recognizes that a reciprocity, an implicit contract, exists between self and society. One must conform to society's rules and institutions (do one's duty) because society in turn will do its duty and provide one with certain protections. Thus the institutions of society are not seen as ends in themselves but as part of a contract. From this view a person would not steal because this would violate the implicit social contract, which includes mutual respect for the rights of other members of the society.

Thus the person sees any specific set of rules in society as somewhat arbitrary. But one's duty is to fulfill one's part of the contract (e.g., not to steal from others), just as it is necessary for society to fulfill its part of the contract (e.g., it will provide institutions and laws protecting one's property from being stolen). The person sees an element of subjectivism in the rules of society, and this recognition may lead into the last stage of moral-reasoning development.

STAGE 6: CONSCIENCE, OR PRINCIPLE, ORIENTATION. Here there is more formal recognition that societal rules are arbitrary. One sees not only that a given implicit contract between a person and society is a somewhat arbitrary, subjective phenomenon, but also that one's interpretation of the meaning and boundaries of such a contract is necessarily subjective. One person may give one interpretation to these rules, while another person may give a different interpretation. From this perspective, the ultimate appeal in making moral judgments must be to one's own conscience.

The person comes to believe that there may be rules that transcend those of specific given social contracts. Since a person's own subjective view of this contract must be seen as legitimate, a person's own views must be the ultimate source of moral judgments. One's conscience, one's set of personal principles, must be appealed to as the ultimate source of moral decisions. To summarize, Stage 6 reasoning involves an appeal to transcendent universal principles of morality, rules that find their source in the person's own conscience.

Levels and Stages in the Revised Version of Kohlberg's Theory of Moral-Reasoning Development

In the present version of the theory (Colby 1978; Colby et al. 1983; Kohlberg 1976, 1978), there are again three levels of moral-reasoning development, generally labeled as in the former version. The last level, however, includes only one stage. The first two levels each have two stages. The major change in the theory is in the definition of these five stages. They focus on the person's social perspective *moving toward increasingly greater scope* (i.e., including more people and their institutions) *and greater abstraction* (i.e., moving from physicalistic reasoning to reasoning about values, rights, and implicit contracts). The levels are seen in essentially the same way as in the former version; however, the characteristics of each stage within each level have been changed in the ways I have described.

Level 1: Preconventional

STAGE 1: HETERONOMOUS MORALITY. Here the person has an egocentric point of view. The person does not consider the interests of others or recognize that they differ from his or hers; the person does not relate two points of view. Actions are considered physically rather than in terms of the psychological interests of others. There is a confusion of authority's perspective with one's own.

STAGE 2: INDIVIDUALISM, INSTRUMENTAL PURPOSE, AND EXCHANGE. Here the person has a concrete individualistic perspective. The person is aware that everybody has interests to pursue and that these can conflict. From this perspective, right is relative.

Level 2: Conventional

STAGE 3: MUTUAL INTERPERSONAL EXPECTATIONS, RELATIONSHIPS, AND INTERPERSONAL CONFORMITY. Here the perspective of the individual exists in relationships with other individuals. The person is aware of shared feelings, agreements, and expectations—which take primacy over individual interests—and he or she relates points of view through the concrete "golden rule" of putting oneself "in the other guy's shoes." The person does not yet consider a generalized system perspective.

STAGE 4: SOCIAL SYSTEM AND CONSCIENCE. Here the person differentiates the societal point of view from interpersonal agreements or motives. At this stage, the person takes a point of view of the system that defines roles and rules and considers individual relations in terms of the roles they play in the system.

Level 3: Postconventional, or Principled

STAGE 5: SOCIAL CONTRACT OR UTILITY AND INDIVIDUAL RIGHTS. This stage may also be termed the "prior-to-society perspective." The rational individual is aware of values and rights prior to social attachments and contracts. Such a person integrates perspectives by formal mechanisms of agreement, contract, objective impartiality, and due process; he or she considers moral and legal points of view. The person recognizes that these sometimes conflict, and may find it difficult to integrate them.

Characteristics of Moral-Reasoning Stage Development

Kohlberg and his associates (e.g., Colby 1978, 1979; Colby et al. 1983; Turiel 1969) have done more than just describe the ordering and nature of the above stages. They have also attempted to describe the nature of intraindividual *change* from one stage to another. Turiel (1969), for example, notes that development through the stages of moral reasoning is a gradual process. Transition from one stage to another is not abrupt; rather, movement is characterized by gradual shifts in the most frequent type of reasoning given by a person over the course of development. Thus at any given point in life a person will be functioning at more than one stage at the same time. Stage movement is characterized, then, by gradual shifts in the modal type of reasoning given by a person over the course of development. Thus, as explained in Chapter 7 and illustrated again in the present chapter in our discussion of Piaget's concept of décalage, such stage mixture means that at any given time a person will be functioning at more than one stage.

Accordingly, one must have a large sample of instances of a person's moral reasonings in order to accurately determine that person's stage of moral reasoning. Only such a large sample will allow one to discover the modal (i.e., the most frequently occurring) type of reasoning the person uses to make moral decisions. Although research and writing by some psychologists interested in moral development (e.g., Bandura and McDonald 1963) has not attended to the existence and implications of stage mixture, Turiel (1969) believes that stage mixture is an ever-present facet of the developmental processes involved in moral reasoning.

In addition Turiel (1969) has indicated that stage mixture is a necessary component of the development of moral reasoning. From a cognitive developmental perspective, changes in moral reasoning level should come about as a result of disequilibrium, which of course would necessitate the reestablishment of equilibrium. Turiel (1969) has demonstrated that when children are exposed to reasoning at a level one stage higher than their own, disequilibrium is

caused. That is, the child perceives a contradiction between his or her own level of moral reasoning and the next higher one, and the conflict produced by this recognition is the product of disequilibrium. In order to achieve equilibration the child must accommodate to this higher stage, and this results in the child's movement toward a higher stage of moral reasoning.

But how is the child able to perceive a discrepancy between his or her own reasoning and reasoning that is from one stage higher and thus not modally the child's? Turiel suggests that the answer lies in stage mixture. Since the person is functioning at more than one stage at the same time, reasoning structures available from the higher stage enable the person to perceive the discrepancy. Stage mixture, then, is not only a ubiquitous but a necessary component of moral-reasoning development. As Turiel has said, "Stage mixture serves to facilitate the perception of contradictions, making the individual more susceptible to disequilibrium and consequently more likely to progress developmentally" (1969, 130).

Data reported by Colby et al. (1983) provide support for the presence of stage mixture. Kohlberg (1958) studied a group of males who have been followed longitudinally since original testing. When first tested, the people ranged from late childhood to middle adolescence. Today they are all in their adult years. Figure 8.2. shows the percentage of reasoning at each of five stages of development for the various age levels through which the people progressed over the course of this continuing study. For example, at the ten-year-old level, most moral reasoning was at stage 2, but there were several instances of reasoning at other stages. In turn, at the thirty-six-year-old level, most reasoning is at stage 4, but reasoning at several other stages is also evident.

Of course, people may experience differing degrees of cognitive conflict—and therefore disequilibrium—in their lives. Accordingly, they may pass through the stages of moral reasoning at different rates—if in fact they pass through them at all. Thus different

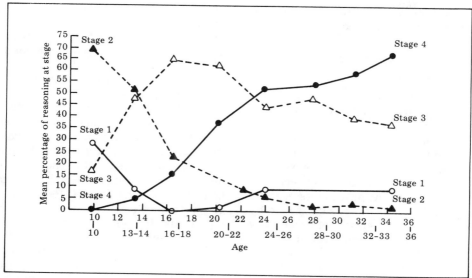

FIGURE 8.2
Mean percentage of reasoning at each stage for each age group.
Source: Colby et al. 1983.

people are likely to reach different levels of moral thinking at any one time in life. In fact, Turiel (1969) has said that his research indicates that most Americans are modally at stage 4 in their moral-reasoning development. That is, for the majority of today's Americans, moral correctness, or right, is evaluated in reference to the maintenance of established social order and the institutions of that order.

This last observation leads beyond just description of the attributes of Kohlberg's theory. We are led to consider whether his formulations are useful for indicating what processes lead or do not lead to advances in moral reasoning. Why do some people advance beyond stage 4, while other people do not typically show such thinking?

To deal with these issues it is necessary to review the formulations and data generated in relation to Kohlberg's work. This review will address the methodological and empirical issues involved in this approach and, in so doing, will lead us to a formulation of moral development somewhat different from

that of Kohlberg's moral-universalism theory.

A CRITIQUE OF KOHLBERG'S THEORY

Evaluations of Kohlberg's work can be classified into two areas. First, there are those who have considered Kohlberg's method of evaluating moral-reasoning development. Second, there are those who have tried to determine if moral reasoning follows the stagelike sequence Kohlberg formulated. Consideration of the first area of evaluation will make us cautious about generalizing information about moral reasoning derived from the use of Kohlberg's interview. Consideration of the second area will support the idea that there are indeed qualitative changes across life in moral reasoning (although not necessarily completely consistent with the order Kohlberg suggests), and that these changes are related to behavior change processes ranging from the psychological to the sociocultural and historical.

Methodological Appraisals of Kohlberg's Theory

A major methodological critique of Kohlberg's approach to the study of moral development was presented by Kurtines and Greif (1974). Writing essentially in respect to methods used to collect data pertinent to the former version of Kohlberg's theory, and about techniques that are not now necessarily prototypic of current procedures used by Kohlberg and his associates (e.g., see Colby et al. 1983), it is nevertheless useful to review the critique of Kurtines and Greif if only to see problems associated with Kohlberg's initial period of research devoted to testing his theory. Kurtines and Greif identified several major problems with how scores were derived from Kohlberg's interview. The scores represent the basic data for evaluating a person's level of moral reasoning. Kurtines and Greif contended that because there were many areas of methodological concern associated with his interview, it was most difficult to evaluate unequivocally the usefulness of Kohlberg's theory. Because several of the major objections Kurtines and Greif raised about Kohlberg's method are unanswered (see Kuhn 1976 and Colby 1978 for some exceptions), it is still important to remain appropriately cautious.

First, Kurtines and Greif (1974) noted problems with the administration and scoring of Kohlberg's interview. Together these problems related to the interview's reliability. A measure is reliable when consistent scores are repeatedly obtained from its administration. Because of issues relating to lack of standardization, subjectivity, and ambiguity, there may have been problems with getting consistent appraisals of moral reasoning from Kohlberg's interview.

In regard to administration of the interview, Kurtines and Greif noted that the questioning process was quite time-consuming and unstandardized, and that precise instructions for administration were not easy to obtain. The instructions were presented in an unwieldy manual, which it was often necessary to learn to use from Kohlberg or one of his associates. This made independent use of the interview quite difficult. Moreover, the questions used to evaluate people's reasoning were different for different people, and this made comparing data across subjects problematic, since different subjects were being measured in different ways. Furthermore, since the content (and number) of the dilemmas presented in the interview was different in different studies, it was again difficult to generalize the results of one investigation to another, because in effect different measuring devices of unknown comparability were used (Kurtines and Greif 1974).

Complicating the administration problems were scoring problems. The classification of answers to interview questions was based on subjective evaluation by the researcher (Kurtines and Greif 1974). Thus the potential for introduction of scorer-bias into the results was great. Furthermore, the subjectivity in scoring gave rise to considerable variability in scoring. Moreover, the fact that the rules for scoring were often ambiguous (Kurtines and Greif 1974), was another reason for independent researchers not to use the interview.

A study by Rubin and Trotter (1977) illustrates some of the problems with the reliability of measuring moral reasoning through Kohlberg's approach. Three of the interview dilemmas were administered to elementary-school children in grades three and five. Two weeks later the children were retested. This time half the children were again given the interview stories, while the other half received a multiple-choice test based on the interview (that is, rather than being asked open-ended questions, the children were asked to choose a solution to a dilemma from among some alternatives). Across the two-week period there was low-to-moderate consistency in reasoning scores for the children, but those in the second group had significantly higher scores. Moreover, since several answers were given to each dilemma, Rubin and Trotter (1977) wanted to see if a person showed consistency in moral reasoning within a given dilemma. Looking at all the answers within each dilemma for the first time of testing, the researchers found no consistency in the moral-reasoning scores obtained by a subject answering different questions about the same dilemma.

In addition to administration and scoring problems, Kurtines and Greif identified problems with the content of the dilemmas. These problems related to the validity of the interview measure. A measure is valid if it assesses what it is supposed to assess. Does the interview provide, as Kohlberg (1958, 1963a, 1971) claimed, a measure of *universal sequences* of moral reasoning (sequences that apply equally to all people of all cultures at all times of measurement)? Kurtines and Greif (1974) noted that the main characters in the dilemmas are male. If a person recognizes the different role expectations for males and females in traditional Western culture, then the gender of the main character in the dilemma may influence that person's moral reasonings. In light of this, it is not surprising that some research using Kohlberg's scale shows females to be less morally mature than males (Kohlberg and Kramer 1969), although it must be noted that most studies using Kohlberg's measures show males and females to be quite similar in their reasonings (Maccoby and Jacklin 1974, 114–117). Yet Kurtines and Greif's criticism of sex bias in the content of the dilemmas is consistent with other objections to the content of the interview.

Eisenberg-Berg (1976) notes that all dilemmas pertain only to constraint situations—that is, to a person's being pressured by two moral values affecting himself or herself. However, prosocial issues, such as risking one's own life to save someone else's, are never evaluated. Thus there is a value bias in Kohlberg's interview.

A broader and more profound bias is noted by Simpson (1974). She sees Kohlberg's dilemmas and his past scoring system as culturally biased. Simpson (1974) notes that while dilemmas were revised in content for cross-cultural research, this procedure

was not sufficient because the scoring system was kept the same. This was done because of the belief in the universality of principles and issues in moral reasoning. However, she argues that Kohlberg sees morality from an American viewpoint, and as such, only those answers that are consistent with American moral values can be scored as moral. Thus, if the content of a dilemma raises an issue not relevant to a given culture or if the culture has different moral values, lower moral reasoning would be scored.

To illustrate this cultural bias in the content and scoring of the interview, Simpson (1974) notes that one typical dilemma contrasts *property rights* with the *value of human life*. A man's wife is dying of a disease for which a pharmacist has developed a cure. However, the drug is quite expensive, and because the man cannot afford it, he breaks into the pharmacy to steal the pharmacist's property (the drug) so that his wife may be saved.

Simpson sees cultural bias in the content and scoring of this dilemma. First, not all cultures have notions of property rights that would make the above situation a dilemma. She notes: "The Americans who believe that one has a right to anything one can pay for and that taxes on income and private property and restrictive use laws are wrong or bad have very little content in common with members of a culture where little or no property is seen as private and rights over it are group rights and held in common" (Simpson 1974, 96). Simpson notes, too, that the scoring attached to this interview story is also biased in that Kolberg (1971, 174) believes that "anyone who understands the values of life and property will recognize that life is morally more valuable than property." Simpson contends that this view not only falsely reflects actual moral practice even in the United States but also reflects a lack of appreciation of the nature of other cultures.

First, she notes that in America it is human life, and not all life, that is seen as sacred. However, even the value of human life may be secondary to other values. Those who kill or rape others are often put to death, and insofar as property is concerned, those "who steal secrets from the government to give to other governments" (Simpson 1974, 97) are liable in times of war to receive the death penalty. In turn, in cultures such as that of the Eskimo, it was appropriate to kill the aged or newborns because they might consume resources needed for the survival of the major part of the group.

In sum, because of the potential biases in the content and past scoring of his dilemmas, there is reason to be wary about whether Kohlberg's past and present techniques can accurately assess universal sequences in moral-reasoning development. In addition, the past lack of standardization in administration and scoring procedures involved with the interview, and the subjective component involved in scoring, led to questions about the reliability of the interview. Despite these limitations, Kohlberg's approach continues to be an important one in studying moral development, especially since he and his co-workers continue to address many of the above criticisms of his work. They have revised the system of interview scoring and even the number and definitions of the stages themselves (Colby 1978; Colby et al. 1983; Kohlberg 1978). Furthermore, there is some empirical support for the specifics of Kohlberg's theory and for the more general idea that there are indeed qualitative changes in moral reasoning across life. Keeping the methodological limitations of this work in mind, we now turn to research relevant to Kohlberg's theory.

Empirical Appraisals of Kohlberg's Theory

Two major interrelated issues have been involved in the empirical assessment of Kohlberg's theory (1958, 1963a, 1963b, 1971, 1976). First, it has been investigated whether moral reasoning progresses through a sequence akin to that suggested by Kohlberg. Second, if such a sequence does exist, is it universal and irreversible, as is a requirement of all stage theories of development

like Kohlberg's? Finally, a third issue has arisen as a consequence of interest in the first two. People have concerned themselves with the variables that may moderate the stage sequences of moral-reasoning.

Sequences in Moral Judgments

Most research relevant to Kohlberg's ideas has dealt with whether reasoning proceeds in a sequence consistent with this theory. Although many studies have not used his exact measures, there is strong evidence for the existence of an age-associated development toward principled reasoning. However, although older people are more likely than younger ones to offer principle-based moral judgments that take into account the intentions—rather than merely the actions—of a person, the sequence does not appear as inevitable, as unfluctuating, or as smooth as Kohlberg might predict.

Data collected in the longitudinal study being conducted by Kohlberg and his colleagues (Colby et al. 1983) provide the strongest support of the view that people from late childhood to the early part of the middle-adult years go through the stages of moral reasoning in the manner Kohlberg specifies. Figure 8.3 shows a smooth, continuous increase from age ten to thirty-six in the average moral maturity score derived from responses to the dilemmas of the interview. In turn, the data in Table 8.2 show that there is an age-associated increase in the percentage of people reasoning at each of the succeeding stages.

Data other than those provided by Kohlberg and his colleagues also suggest an age-associated progression toward principle- or intention-based, as opposed to consequence-based, moral reasoning. Eisenberg-Berg and Neal (1979) studied a small group of forty-eight- to sixty-three-month-old preschoolers. The children were observed and questioned by a familiar researcher about their spontaneous prosocial behaviors (helping, sharing, or comforting) over a twelve-week period. The children justified their behaviors primarily by references to others' needs and pragmatic considerations. They used little

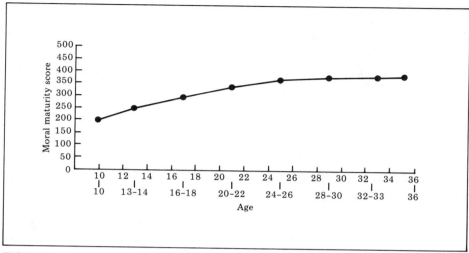

FIGURE 8.3
Mean moral maturity score for each group.
Source: Colby et al. 1983.

punishment-and-authority-oriented, stereo-typed, approval-oriented, or hedonistic rea-soning. There were no age or sex differences in this sample. Thus these very young chil-dren showed moral reasoning that appears associated with the first level of reasoning in Kohlberg's theory.

In turn, Eisenberg-Berg (1979) examined the development of older children's reason-ing about prosocial moral dilemmas. She studied 125 elementary- and high-school students. Elementary-school children's rea-soning tended to be hedonistic, stereotyped, and approval-oriented, and interpersonally oriented and/or tended to involve labeling of others' needs. Stereotyped images of persons and interpersonally oriented or approval-oriented reasoning decreased with age, and alternatively the use of empathic considera-tions and judgments reflecting internalized values increased with age. Again consistent with a general progression toward more principled reasoning, associated with the highest level in Kohlberg's theory, the moral reasonings of people at older ages had more abstract bases. Similar progressions are found in other studies.

Weiner and Peter (1973) studied 300 peo-ple, aged four to eighteen years. In making moral judgments, subjects were asked to take the intentions and abilities of the actor and the outcome of the act into account. At higher age levels the main determinant of moral evaluation was the subjective inten-tions of the actor rather than the objective outcome of his or her act. Similarly, Hewitt (1975) read Dutch male children and early adolescents (age eight to twelve years) stories about a harm-doer. The harm-doer's intentions were either good or bad, and the results of the harm were either minor or seri-ous. The older males differentiated the harm-doer's behavior as being naughty or not on the basis of intentions and provoca-tions for the harmful acts. The younger males did not make these distinctions. This developmental trend toward a predomina-tion of abstract reasons for judging moral acts is supported by data reported by Kea-sey (1974). Child and adult (i.e., college) females rated responses to Kohlberg's di-lemmas. Their ratings were given in the con-text of being presented with (1) an *opinion* as to how the dilemma should be resolved; and (2) a moral *reason,* at various stages, that supported the opinion. Opinion agree-

TABLE 8.2
Percentage of Subjects at Each Stage within Each Age Group

Stage	Age, in Years							
	10	13–14	16–18	20–22	24–26	28–30	32–33	36
1/2	71	21	7	0	0	0	0	0
2	39	33	28	0	0	0	0	0
2/3	8	57	22	8	5	0	0	0
3	2	12	42	21	6	13	4	0
3/4	0	1	16	18	17	27	15	6
4	0	0	0	21	14	25	25	14
4/5	0	0	0	0	31	39	23	8

Source: *Colby et al. 1983.*

ment had a greater relative influence than stage of moral reasoning in shaping the ratings of the children as opposed to the college students.

Similarly, evidence for development toward a more abstract conceptualization of morality is provided in a report by Edwards (1974). Seven hundred seven- through fifteen-year-olds were asked to define terms like "right" and "wrong." Older groups had higher moral-development scores, and although there were no socioeconomic status differences, females did better on these evaluations than did males. This finding is consistent with the higher verbal ability noted for females of the age range studied (Maccoby and Jacklin 1974) and suggests that depending on how moral thinking is measured, there may be either no sex differences or differences favoring females (which is counter to Freud's [1949] views, of course).

Further evidence exists for a sequential movement to stages involving more abstract, principle-based, and intentionality-oriented forms of judgment. Davison, Robbins, and Swanson (1978) studied 160 people ranging in school level from junior high school through graduate school. To measure moral reasoning, they used a scale developed by Rest et al. (1974). Using this device, Davison, Robbins, and Swanson found that a subject's pattern of stage scores was generally consistent with the ordering of stages in Kohlberg's theory and that as one instance in support of this, reasoning at adjacent stages

(e.g., stages 3 and 4) was more similar than reasoning at nonadjacent stages (e.g., stages 3 and 5).

Recall Turiel's (1969, 1974) claim that movement from one stage to another is dependent on information that causes conflict and hence a disequilibration. This, he contends, requires a reevaluation of the existing way of thinking and the construction, therefore, of a new, higher stage of thought in order to reestablish balance (Turiel 1974). If this idea is correct, we should see people at a given stage of reasoning respond differently to reasoning below or above their own. The former should be seen as inferior (or "immature"), while the latter, causing conflict, should influence the subjects intellectually or be seen as better. Turiel and Rothman (1972) reported stage 4 subjects to be influenced in their responses by reasoning above but not below their own level. Although this finding supports Turiel's (1969, 1974) ideas about cognitive conflict, the fact that the Turiel and Rothman (1972) subjects who reasoned predominantly at stages 2 and 3 were unaffected by moral justifications does not lend such support.

However, some additional support for the idea of the role of cognitive conflict in moral reasoning development is provided by the data reported by Lazorowitz, Stephen, and Friedman (1976). The subjects were a large group of college students. These subjects tended to be positively influenced (to show altruism to a partner in a laboratory experiment) by reasoning above their own. Moreover, those subjects at the highest levels of moral reasoning did react negatively to reasoning below their own. However, inconsistent with the idea of the role of cognitive conflict was the finding that those subjects at the lowest levels of moral reasoning (stages 1 and 2) were not differently affected by reasoning similar to their own (that is, a stage 2 reason given to a stage 1 person) and, in fact, reacted somewhat *negatively* to reasons above their own (that is, stage 3).

Thus there is some evidence to indicate that although people generally seem to progress toward intentional, principled reasonings, they do not *necessarily* conform to a stagelike progression. Data reported by Surber (1977) support this view. Surber studied kindergarten-through-adult subjects. At all these age levels—that is, *not* just at the older ones—the intentions of the actor and the consequences of the act influenced judgments. As Kohlberg might predict, the major age trend was a decrease in the importance of consequences in making moral judgment. Yet the fact that intentions were used continuously from early childhood through adulthood suggests that moral reasoning is less stagelike than outlined in Kohlberg's universalistic theory.

Moreover, there are other reasons why Kohlberg's universalistic stage divisions—of consequence-based moral reasoning being associated with early stages and intention-based reasoning being associated with only the latter or last stages—are not compelling ones. Hill and Enzle (1977) found that first-, third-, and fifth-grade children could be trained to consider intentions rather than consequences when making moral judgments. Moreover, even without any explicit training, kindergarteners, second-, and fourth-graders have been found to take the intentions of an actor in a story into account when making moral judgments about that actor (Elkind and Dabek 1977). Furthermore, in a study (Darley, Klosson, and Zanna 1978) that involved the measurement of people ranging in age from five to forty-four, it was found that mitigating circum-

stances involved in a harmful act in a story were taken into account by subjects at *all* age levels. That is, mitigating circumstances led to less recommended punishment for the harm-doer across the entire age range sampled.

In turn, how one measures moral reasoning seems to affect whether people make consequence- or intention-based judgments. Chandler, Greenspan, and Barenboim (1973) found that when seven-year-olds were asked to make moral judgments in response to a verbally presented dilemma, their judgments were largely based on consequences. However, when responding to videotaped dilemmas, their judgments were largely based on intentions. Similarly, Feldman et al. (1976) report that whether four- to five-year-olds and eight- to nine-year-olds make intention- or consequence-based judgments depends on the order in which questions about such reasonings are presented to them. Moreover, in a review of the literature, Karniol (1978) concludes that children do use intentions and ignore consequences when the acts they are asked to judge are explicitly specified. Finally, Kohlberg might suggest that the absence or presence of reciprocity between actors in a moral situation should be taken into account only at the highest stages of moral reasoning (e.g., stage 4 or 5). However, there are several studies that show that children in kindergarten and elementary school make judgments—moral and otherwise—based on the reciprocity between actors and thus reason like those adults assessed in the same studies (Berndt 1977; Brickman and Bryan 1976; Peterson, Hartmann, and Gelfand 1977).

In sum, many data suggest that reciprocity and intention information can be and is used from early childhood through the adult years in making moral judgments. As noted above, this indicates that moral reasoning does not have the universalistic stage features Kohlberg suggests. Further evidence of the lack of universalism of Kohlberg's ideas is derived from cross-cultural studies. We now turn to them.

The Universality of Kohlberg's Stages

Most cross-cultural studies of moral development have been cross-sectional in design. Although they provide data somewhat consistent with the notions of stage progression outlined by Kohlberg for the first four stages, they do not tend to show invariant progression into the highest level of moral reasoning—that is, the principled one. This in itself is not necessarily contrary to a stage theory. Such a theory does not say that people will necessarily reach the highest levels but only that if they do they will go through the specified sequence. Yet since cross-sectional studies assess only age-group differences and not age changes, they cannot be regarded as providing unequivocal support for Kohlberg's theory. Indeed, in one cross-cultural study that used a longitudinal design (White, Bushnell, and Regnemer 1978), effects related to variables other than age (i.e., in this case time of testing) were seen to contribute most to moral-reasoning scores.

To be specific, all cross-cultural research before 1978 had been cross-sectional in design. For instance, studies done in British Honduras (Gorsuch and Barnes 1973), Canada (Kohlberg and Kramer 1969), Kenya (Edwards 1974), Great Britain (Kohlberg and Kramer 1969), the Bahamas (White 1975), and Taiwan (Kohlberg and Kramer 1969) had consistently indicated age differences in moral reasoning through Kohlberg's stages 1 through 4. However, reasoning beyond these first four stages appeared so infrequently in these studies that their age-related development in populations other than those derived from the United States remained uncertain.

This cultural difference may be due to the absence of particular, but largely unknown, variables that may moderate reasoning development in cultures other than the United States. Some support for this idea is found in the data of Edwards (1975), who reported that people in highly industrialized settings move through lower stages more rapidly, and achieve higher stages more often, than people in less industrialized and less urban settings (Salili, Maehr, and Gillmore 1976). In turn, the cultural difference may be due to the cultural bias in Kohlberg's theory and scoring system identified by Simpson (1974). Other cultures may not include as morally relevant the types of situations or values used by Kohlberg to score the higher stages of moral reasoning.

Although current data cannot decide between these two alternatives, the study by White, Bushnell, and Regnemer (1978) suggests that any changes in moral-reasoning scores are more attributable to events occurring within the cultural milieu when people are tested than to age- or stage-related phenomena. White, Bushnell, and Regnemer studied 426 Bahamian males and females aged eight through seventeen. All subjects were interviewed repeatedly over a three-year period using Kohlberg's interview; that is, the design involved repeated testing of the initial cross-sectional sample over the course of the three-year period. There was an upward stage movement within and between age groups. In other words, the cross-sectional data at each year showed age-group differences; older age groups showed higher scores. Morever, *within* each age group there was an upward movement in reasoning scores from initial to final testing.

However, not only did none of the subjects in the sample show reasoning above stage 3, but the age differences in reasoning scores were associated much more with time of testing than age or age group (i.e., birth cohort). The time-of-testing effect was 3.5 times greater than the age effect. This was the major effect found in the study; for example no sex differences were found. Thus the results of the within-cohort longitudinal comparison suggest that variables in the milieu of the subjects at the times they were tested, rather than those variables that may covary with age, account for the age differences found in the study.

It is clear that with such time-related effects playing the major role in contributing to changes in moral development, the universality of Kohlberg's stages is in doubt. Similar doubt about the adequacy of his stage theory is derived from the few studies directly assessing the irreversibility of the stages he posits.

The Irreversibility of Kohlberg's Stages

Kuhn (1976) used a short-term longitudinal design to assess the continuity in moral reasoning of five- to eight-year-olds as measured by Kohlberg's interview. Across each of two six-month intervals, subjects were as likely to show progressive change (an increase in scores) as regressive change (a decrease in scores). However, over the longer period (one year) encompassed by the study, subjects tended to show progressive change, most of which involved *slight* advancement toward the next stage in Kohlberg's sequence. Although these data bear only on the sequence-irreversibility of the first three stages of Kohlberg's theory—since these were the stages at which subjects reasoned—they do provide partial support for his theory.

The considerable short-term (i.e., six months) fluctuation could have been due to several sources. Other studies (Bandura and McDonald 1963) have shown that children can be *induced* to move forward or backward in their moral reasoning. Since subjects have the reasoning structures of several stages available to them, such inducement would be expected to be obtained on the basis of stage mixture (Turiel 1969). However, the subjects in Kuhn's (1976) study were not prompted to show either continuity or discontinuity in their reasoning. Thus the observed fluctuation could be due either to measurement unreliability associated with Kohlberg's interview or to genuine fluctuation in judgment (Kuhn 1976)—fluctuation perhaps naturally moderated by variables that happened to be acting at the particular times at which Kuhn's subjects were longitudinally tested. Indeed, such a time-of-testing effect in a longitudinal study is possible, given the data of White, Bushnell, and Regnemer (1978).

However, despite the variables that may be operating to produce fluctuation or continuity in reasoning, there are data suggesting that when the irreversible sequencing of Kohlberg's stages is evaluated at age levels beyond childhood, their universal ordering does not hold. Holstein (1976) studied the individual developmental sequences of fifty-two middle-class adolescents, forty-eight of their fathers, and forty-nine of their mothers. These family groups were followed longitudinally for a three-year period. Over this sequence there was a stepwise progression in moral-reasoning development *but not from stage to stage*. Rather, people progressed from level to level. However, even this held only for levels 1 and 2 of Kohlberg's theory; that is, people only progressed sequentially from preconventional to conventional morality. Moreover, insofar as irreversibility is concerned, regression in reasoning was found in the higher (postconventional) stages. Futhermore, since the subjects in Holstein's study were of different ages and from different cohorts, and since all these groups nevertheless showed the progression limitations and reversibility characteristics, we may infer that time-of-testing effects again are most associated with whatever age differences were obtained.

In conclusion, characteristics of universality and irreversibility do not seem to be associated with Kohlberg's stages. Rather, variables acting in the particular historical contexts of people at particular times seem to be most related to whether one sees qualitative changes in moral reasoning and to what directions those changes take. In other words, although evidence exists for a general progression from objective morality to subjective, intentional, and principled reasoning, it appears that the nature and direction of this sequence is a changeable phenomenon; it is dependent on other than stage-related variables. In the next section, we consider evidence pertaining to those non-stage-related variables that may moderate the shift in moral thinking from objective to principled reasoning.

VARIABLES RELATING TO MORAL DEVELOPMENT

Moral development involves an orientation of the person toward others in his or her world. This relation suggests the social relational character of morality. There are data suggesting that children who do have different levels of moral reasoning also have different types of social-interactional experiences. Most of these data relate to interactions with other psychological and/or behavioral variables and/or with a model, with family members, or with peers.

Interactions with Psychological and/or Behavioral Variables

As noted earlier, Rest et al. (1974) attempted to construct a scale that could be scored objectively to measure "Kohlbergian" moral development. To do this, statements were written to exemplify each of Kohlberg's stages, and subjects were asked to pick the statement defining the most important issue in a moral dilemma. The importance attributed to principled (stages 5 or 6) moral statements (a measure termed the P score) showed age-related differences. In a group of junior-high-school through graduate-school students, the P score correlated about +.6 with age, with comprehension of social and moral concepts, and with the scores from Kohlberg's interview. While the first correlation is consistent with an age-progression or stage-progression theory and the last correlation shows some validity for Kohlberg's interview measure, the correlation between P score and moral and social comprehension suggests that perhaps intelligence plays a major moderating role in moral reasoning.

However, although the P score did correlate with IQ, it was a much lower correlation. Alternatively, there was an indication that subjects chose important moral issues on the basis of attitudes and values rather than just intelligence. The P score correlated about +.6 with various political attitude measures.

Similarly, an independent study by Eisenberg-Berg (1976) considered the relation of moral reasoning to prosocial moral reasoning, and to various political and humanitarian attitudes. Subjects were seventy-six white adolescents ranging in grade level from seven to twelve. Not only did Eisenberg-Berg find a significant relation between constraint reasoning and prosocial moral reasoning, and a grade-associated increase toward more principled judgments, but she also found that attitudes may moderate these moral-reasoning differences. Political liberalism significantly related to both constraint and prosocial moral reasoning, while humanitarian political attitudes related to prosocial, but not to constraint, reasoning.

Rest (1975) reports longitudinal data bearing on the relation of attitudes to moral reasoning and on the role of other moderating influences. After two years, eighty-eight adolescents (aged from sixteen to twenty) were retested with the scale Rest et al. (1974) had devised. In addition, they were retested with the measure of their comprehension of social and moral concepts and with a measure of their "law and order" political attitudes. Both younger and older adolescents showed increases in their P scores, and the younger group showed shifts from preconventional to conventional thinking. Moreover, there were also increases in the measures of comprehension and attitudes that coincided with the reasoning differences.

While again suggesting the possible role of attitudes, other features of Rest's (1975) data also indicated that variables other than psychological (here, attitudinal) ones may exist to foster the development of moral reasoning. Among those adolescents in his sample who were high-school graduates, those who went away to college changed twice as much in principled reasoning as did the noncollege subjects. Rest (1975) found that at the time of their first testing in 1972:

> The college-bound subjects were not significantly different from the noncollege-bound subjects on any of the three measures. By 1974, however, the college group was different from the noncollege group on the P score, and on the Law and Order test score. (The college group also showed greater average gains on the comprehension test, but was not significantly different from the noncollege group in 1974.) In fact, on the P score each group gained significantly over two years, but the college group gained over twice as much as the noncollege group (p. 745).

Thus—although both college and noncollege adolescents did not differ at the first testing, and even though they maintained nonsignificantly different levels of comprehension regarding social and moral concepts, and despite the fact that they both advanced toward more principled reasoning levels—there was something in the college environment that facilitated the development of adolescents.

Although other studies have also shown that the moral reasoning of adolescents varies in relation to their situational context (McGeorge 1974), there have been no direct tests of just what variables might lead an adolescent in one setting to advance and an adolescent in another setting not to. There are some indirect clues, however.

Perspective Taking, Formal Operations, and Principled Reasoning

Yussen (1976) studied thirty subjects at each of grades nine, ten, twelve, and in college. He asked the subjects to answer a moral-reasoning questionnaire for the social roles of "self," "average policeman," and "average philosopher." As expected by Kohlberg's theory, there was an age-associated increase in principled responses, and this held for answers in regard to all three roles. In addition, however, there was also an age-associated increase in differentiation among the contrasting social roles. Older subjects were more able than younger ones to take the moral perspective of people playing different social roles. Similarly, Costanzo et al. (1973) found that an age-associated increase from five to eleven years in use of information about intentions in making moral judgments coincided with an increase in social perspective-taking ability in this age range. Moreover, Eisenberg-Berg and Mussen (1978) found that a measure of *empathy* (the ability to take the perspective of another and feel what that person feels) was related to measures of both constraint and prosocial moral reasoning among seventy-two adolescents in grades nine to twelve.

Together these studies suggest that the ability to take the perspective of someone in another social role or social situation may be related importantly to the presence of principled moral reasoning. Such a relation is consistent with the quality of postconventional morality, in that a mutual pact, a reciprocal relation, among equal partners in a social relation is involved as a basis of such an orientation. It might seem that if one could not take another's perspective, and see the world from the role orientation of the other, the reciprocal social relation that provides the basis of principled moral thinking could not emerge.

Three ideas are therefore suggested. First, inability to take another's perspective should be associated with a failure to show advanced moral reasoning, while in turn, perspective-taking ability should be related to principled reasoning. The above-noted studies by Yussen (1976), Costanzo et al. (1973), and Eisenberg-Berg and Mussen (1978) support this idea. Also supporting this idea are data reported by Moir (1974), who found that scores of eleven-year-old females on Kohlberg's interview were correlated with scores on non-moral-role-taking tasks.

Similarly, data by Arbuthnot (1975) bear on this first idea. College students showed both immediate and delayed increases in moral judgment scores when required to role-play a moral dilemma against an opponent who used reasoning above the subject's reasoning stage. These data suggest that role playing at a higher moral level than one's own may encourage reasoning change. It is possible that such role playing produces cognitive conflict and induces disequilibrium. But disequilibrium from what level?

Here the second idea is raised. Moir (1974), in the above-noted study, suggested that role playing coincides with principled judgment, because being able to take another's perspective requires being able to overcome a form of egocentrism involving seeing oneself as central (imaginary audience) and quite special (personal fable). In other words, principled morality rests on overcoming the egocentrism of the formal operational stage of cognitive development because such egocentrism involves an inability to take others' perspectives and hence to show the cognitive ability apparently necessary for more advanced moral thinking.

Thus, Arbuthnot's (1975) data may be interpreted as showing that required role playing led to moral reasoning increases because it stimulated a typical, naturally occurring process wherein conflict produced by having to take others' roles makes the person decenter from his or her adolescent egocentrism. In support of this idea, it may be noted that Arbuthnot found that those college students who were reasoning at levels below the highest ones were the ones who showed the most change toward principled reasoning through role playing.

Together the above data and reasoning suggest that processes of cognitive change typically associated with adolescence in Western culture may be those most involved with advances to higher levels of moral reasoning. In other words, principled morality rests on the attainment of cognitive processes typically associated with adolescence—that is, formal operations. Indeed, not only did Kohlberg (1973) himself advance such a hypothesis, but data reported by Tomlinson-Keasey and Keasey (1974) support it. Among subjects who had just begun to acquire formal operations (thirty sixth-grade females) and subjects who were assumed to be well practiced in formal thought (twenty-four college females), there were high positive relations between being at advanced levels in both areas of functioning. Similarly, Langford and George (1975) found that among sixty-five females aged twelve to fifteen years, there were positive relationships between scores at Kohlberg's higher stages and scores on a task of formal operational ability. Comparable relationships have been reported among male and female college students (Faust and Arbuthnot 1978).

If principled morality seems to be so related to that form of cognition most associated with adolescence, then it may be that those sociocultural and historical influences that promote one type of functioning also promote the other. This observation leads us to the third idea involved in interrelating perspective taking and principled morality. This idea suggests a reason why the college students in Rest's (1975) study showed more advancement in principled morality than their noncollege peers. Earlier, we noted Turiel's (1969) report that certain groups of people living in today's world were more likely than other groups to show advanced moral thinking. These groups are late adolescents and young adults who are involved in a college environment. It may be that the demands of college involve more intense perspective-taking requirements for adaptation than is the case in other settings. Being exposed to people from varied backgrounds and having at least in part to interact with these others (for example, in dormitories or in class projects), as well as being exposed to and tested about thoughts (for example, of philosophers, about other cultures) typically quite different from one's own, require personal adaptation. The functional assimilation of this information would require accommodation and thus a movement away from knowledge of the world through one's own, possibly egocentric point of view.

Although people outside the college setting can certainly obtain the information necessary for decentering, and hence perspective taking and principled morality (and Rest's noncollege subjects did show an increase in P scores), it appears that the college setting facilitates this process.

Of course, given the fact that there is a relation between IQ, formal operations, and principled morality (Rest et al. 1974), and that there are marked individual differences in the attainment of formal operations, not all adolescents who go to college will show similar changes in moral reasoning. Thus, in order to understand the course of moral development, one must take into account characteristics of the person as well as characteristics of the situation. This conclusion is complicated by the fact that it is not just the cognitive egocentrism processes of the person that interact with the situation to foster moral development. Other psychological variables—even beyond those of attitudes, which we have already noted—interact with sociocultural variables to facilitate moral functioning.

Personality–Moral Reasoning Relations

An interaction among individual-psychological processes relating to identity, formal operations, and morality has been found. It will be recalled that earlier in this chapter I noted that Piaget believes that the transition from earlier to later formal operational thought involves attainment of a role (Inhelder and Piaget 1958). Piaget believes that an adolescent becomes an adult cognitively when he or she has attained a firm role to play in society. In Erikson's (1959, 1963) terms, the adolescent has found an identity; Erikson (1959) believes that successful transition to a stage beyond adolescence also involves such identity achievement. Kohlberg (1973), too, has said that identity achievement is a prerequisite for principled morality.

Stage theories of personality and social development other than Erikson's (1959, 1963) illuminate the relation between moral and other psychological developments (for example, emotional and ego developments). Indeed, Loevinger's (1966; Loevinger and Wessler 1970) stage theory of ego development includes milestones of development that appear to correspond to the stages Kohlberg sees as involved in moral reasoning. Following the psychoanalytic conception of seeing the ego as a personality structure involved in controlling impulses from the id, Loevinger (1966; Loevinger and Wessler 1970) describes seven stages of ego development and the type of control the ego, at each of these stages, can exert on impulses. As seen in Table 8.3, the stages of ego development appear to involve many of the functions Kohlberg relates to moral stages. This seems to be especially true in the last five stages. The last column of Table 8.3 represents the possible relation between the ego stages in Loevinger's (1966; Loevinger and Wessler 1970) theory and the moral-reasoning stages in Kohlberg's theory. In sum, the

TABLE 8.3
Some Possible Relations Between Loevinger's Stages of Ego Development and Kohlberg's Stages of Moral-Reasoning Development

Loevinger's Stages	Impulse Control Involved in the Stage	Possible Relation to the Stages in Kohlberg's Theory
Presocial Impulse-ridden	—— Impulse-ridden fear of retaliation	Level 1 Preconventional reasoning Stage 1 Obedience and punishment Stage 2 Naïve-egoistic orientation
Self-protective Conformity	Expedient, fear of being caught Conformity to external rule	Level 2 Conventional reasoning Stage 3 Good-person orientation
Conscientious	Internalized rules, guilt	Stage 4 Authority and social-maintenance orientation
Autonomous	Coping with conflict, toleration of differences	Level 3 Postconventional reasoning Stage 5 Contractual legalistic orientation
Integrated	Reconciling inner conflicts, renunciation of the unattainable	Stage 6 Conscience or principle orientation

ideas of Loevinger, as well as those of Piaget and Erikson, suggest interrelation among ego, cognitive, and moral processes.

There is some empirical support for these hypothesized interrelations among individual-psychological processes. As noted, Tomlinson-Keasey and Keasey (1974) found that older adolescents (female college students) who should be more practiced in formal operational thought showed more advanced moral judgments than younger adolescents (sixth-grade females) who had just begun to acquire formal operations. The findings were interpreted as suggesting that although formal thought may be a prerequisite of higher levels of moral reasoning, there may be a time-lag between the acquisition of formal thought and its use in moral reasoning.

Evidence also exists about relations between ego functioning and moral-reasoning level. Podd (1972) studied a group of about 100 white middle-class male college students. Subjects who had achieved an ego identity were generally characterized by the higher levels of moral judgment, while those with a relative lack of ego identity were generally characterized by either the least advanced level of moral reasoning or a transitionary level between intermediate and high levels of reasoning. Moreover, those who were in a crisis over their identity were inconsistent in their reasoning levels.

While Podd's data are consistent with the ideas of Piaget, Kohlberg, and Erikson, there are some studies in the literature that provide either no support (Cauble 1976) or only indirect support for the interrelation between identity and morality (Bachrach, Huesmann, and Peterson 1977). In the latter study, for instance, if it can be assumed that feeling that one controls one's own destiny is an emotion consistent with feeling a sense of self-knowledge (identity), then the relation between data about this feeling (labeled "internality" by the authors) and intentionality-based moral reasoning is consistent with an identity-morality relation. Among 130 seven- to eleven-year-olds, Bachrach, Huesmann, and Peterson (1977) found that intentionality of judgments and internality

of control develop in a related manner, and that heightened internality significantly enhances the ability to attain intentionality in moral reasonings.

Behavior–Moral Reasoning Interrelations

Harris, Mussen, and Rutherford (1976) administered both Kohlberg's interview and an intelligence test to thirty-three fifth-grade boys. In addition, the boys' peers rated their moral conduct, and the boys' honesty was evaluated in a structured test. Higher levels of moral reasoning were associated with better cognitive ability. Moreover, on a behavioral level, higher reasoners showed greater resistance to temptation and were rated by their peers as behaving in a prosocial manner (for example, as being concerned with the welfare of others).

Not only are moral-reasoning differences thus associated with behavioral differences in late childhood, but such associations exist among late adolescents and young adults as well. Norma Haan, M. Brewster Smith, and Jeanne Block (1968) studied about 500 University of California and San Francisco State College students and Peace Corps volunteers-in-training, about equally divided into male and female groups. Because of the study's major empirical and theoretical implications, we shall consider its details quite carefully.

All subjects in the study had responded to Kohlberg's interview. The students participated in various campus activities and groups. They showed a wide range of behavioral and social involvement. Some students had been arrested as a consequence of their participation in a protest advocating free speech. Others were members of such groups as the Young Democrats, Young Republicans, California Conservatives for Political Action, a student-body-sponsored community involvement program, or a tutorial group. On the basis of answers to Kohlberg's interview the subjects were divided into one of five "pure" moral-type groups, basically one for each of the stages from 2 to 6.

Haan, Smith, and Block (1968) obtained

several biographical, behavioral, and cognitive-personality test measures on the subjects. Together, the data provide a profile of the behavioral as well as the personality characteristics of members of each moral-reasoning group. In addition, the data provide clues about the bases of differences among these groups.

CHARACTERISTICS OF PRINCIPLED REASONERS. The members of the principled-reasoning groups were more likely to have interrupted their college careers, to live in apartments or houses on their own, to be politically more radical, and to have been in strong support of the protest movement. Indeed, the political-social activity of these people was the highest of all groups studied. They affiliated with more organizations—and thus played more roles as members of different groups—and were more involved with them. They were active participants in a lot of groups; they were not just passive joiners.

In addition to these behavioral characteristics, male members of this principled group described their own personalities as "idealistic," and conceived of the ideal good man in society as being perceptive, empathic, and altruistic. These ideas emphasize their commitment to taking the roles of others (Haan, Smith, and Block 1968). The principled women saw themselves as guilty, doubting, restless, impulsive, and altruistic. Their idea of the ideal woman was one who is rebellious and free.

CHARACTERISTICS OF CONVENTIONAL REASONERS. The members of the conventionally reasoning moral groups were the least likely to interrupt their college careers, lived mainly in institutional, adult-approved arrangements, were politically more conservative, and were the groups least in support of (although still approving) the protest movement. Members of these groups affiliated with few political-social organizations and were relatively inactive.

The self-descriptions that coincided with these behaviors for the males in these groups reflect traditional social values: conventional, ambitious, sociable, practical, orderly, and not curious, individualistic, or rebellious. The women saw themselves as ambitious and foresighted, and not as guilty, restless, or rebellious. Both sexes shared an idea of the good person in society as one who had efficient control of the self and was socially skillful.

CHARACTERISTICS OF PRECONVENTIONAL REASONERS. Finally, with those people who reasoned predominantly at a *preconventional, naive egotistic* moral level, Haan, Smith, and Block found a high likelihood of college-career interruption. The men in this group were more likely than the women to live on their own; both men and women strongly supported the protest movement. The men in this group belonged to only a moderate number of organizations, but they participated intensely. On the other hand, the women in this group had joined the most organizations but had been the most inactive.

The personal descriptions of these behavioral orientations show that both men and women see themselves as rebellious. The men's self-descriptions reflect a lack of involvement with others, and their ideal person is someone who is aloof, stubborn, uncompromising, playful, and free. Similarly, women also reject interpersonal obligations, see themselves as stubborn and aloof, and idealize such characteristics as practicality and stubbornness.

In summary of the Haan, Smith, and Block (1968) findings, it seems that differences in moral-reasoning level indeed relate to contrasts in attitudes, personality, and behavior. Principled thinkers are actively involved in the role orientations of others and see themselves as altruistic and idealistic. Their principled view of a person's relation to his or her social world permeates their own self-conceptions and provides a basis for their active involvement in their world. Alternatively, preconventional thinkers, although showing some behavioral similarities to principled thinkers (for example, living

TABLE 8.4

Percentage of Subjects from Each of Five of Kohlberg's Moral-Reasoning Stages Who Were Arrested in a Free-Speech-Movement Protest

| | Stage* | | | | |
	2 Naïvely egotistic	3 Good-person	4 Authority and social-order maintenance	5 Contractual legalistic	6 Conscience or principle
Men	60	18	6	41	75
Women	33	9	12	57	86

* There were no stage 1 thinkers reported in the sample.

Source: *Adapted from Haan et al. (1968). Copyright © 1968 by the American Psychological Association. Reprinted by permission.*

alone, engaging in protests), do so for entirely different reasons (ones consistent with their naïvely egotistic orientation). They are unconcerned with the welfare of others, show little concern for interpersonal obligation, and engage in protest behaviors to abet their individual rights or goals. In contrast, the conventional thinkers are not actively involved in many organizations, tend to live in situations and behave in accordance with traditional and adult-approved values, and show additional ideas and values that are also consistent with their conventional reasoning and behavior.

As a final instance of the moral-reasoning and behavior differences among these groups, we may consider the data in Table 8.4. This table presents the percentage of men and women in the Haan, Smith, and Block sample from each moral-reasoning group who were arrested in a protest demonstration regarding the free-speech movement. As expected, the conventional thinkers (stages 3 and 4) as a group had by far the lowest proportion of arrests. Similarly, the postconventional group (stages 5 and 6) had the highest percentage. However, while the preconventional thinkers (stage 2) also had a high proportion of arrests, their involvement was for reasons qualitatively different than those used by the principled groups. Consistent with their egotistic, nonsocially concerned orientation, the stage 2 thinkers were mostly concerned with their individual rights in a power conflict. The

principled thinkers apparently used their perspective-taking abilities behaviorally; they based their involvement on concerns with basic issues of civil liberties and rights, and on the relation of students as citizens within a university community. Thus these data show that there are behavioral consequences of moral thought. But as stressed by Piaget (1965), Kohlberg (1958, 1963a), and Turiel (1969), it is necessary to focus on the thought, because the same behavior (for example, protest) can be based on qualitatively and developmentally different individual-psychological levels of functioning.

These conclusions indicate that adolescents and young people who may be described as differing in their levels of moral reasoning may also be described as differing in their personal characteristics (for example, in regard to identity, attitudes, values) and behavioral attributes. However, these descriptions do not suggest an explanation for these differences. Some of the elements for a potential explanation lie in some of our previous discussions as well as in other data from the Haan, Smith, and Block (1968) study, presented below.

SOCIAL INTERACTIVE BASES OF MORAL DEVELOPMENT

In reviewing the Rest (1975) data about college students' greater increase in principled reasoning than their noncollege peers, it was suggested that if one brings certain characteristics to a social situation having facilitative characteristics, then moral development will be fostered. Interacting in an environment that fosters social perspective taking may foster moral development among those adolescents who have certain levels of formal operational egocentrism, IQ, and identity. The time-of-testing effects found (White, Bushnell, and Regnemer 1978) or implicated (Holstein 1976; Kuhn 1976) in moral-development research may in fact represent the outcome of a time-specific interaction between individuals having such predispositions and the forces in a setting that promote such change.

However, a question remains as to what brings a person into a facilitative setting, such as college, with a predisposition amenable to influence. Why do some adolescents show principled morality as a consequence of their college experience, while others remain at levels not as high? Indeed, why do people enter *into* their college years with different levels of morality? One suggestion we may make is that adolescents show such differences because of differences in their history of social interactions. It may be that if adolescents experience different interactional histories, they will develop at different rates after entering potentially facilitative settings.

Although the longitudinal research needed to test this idea has not been done, there are data that suggest that, at the very least, young people who do have different levels of moral reasoning also have different types of social interactional experiences. Most of these data relate to adolescent-parent interactions.

Adolescent-Parent Interactions

Haan, Smith, and Block (1968) found that the preconventional, conventional, and postconventional subjects they studied all reported different types of family interaction patterns. Subjects were evaluated on how different their own political views were from those of each of their parents (for example, in regard to commitment to various issues), how different their views were from those of their parents on various social issues pertinent to the two generational groups, and how much conflict they had with their parents. These measures were combined to form one index of conflict and disagreement.

As seen in Figure 8.4, there is a curvilinear relation between conflict and moral reasoning for the men. Intense family conflict, especially with the father, is associated with preconventional thinking. Alternatively, and as expected on the basis of their moral orientation, there is least conflict found with the conventional thinkers. A moderate level of conflict exists for those with principled reasoning. For the women, there is a trend toward increased conflict with mother being associated with higher moral reasoning. Although this trend is not as evident with the father, it seems that for both males and females, conflict with the parent of the same sex is most related to moral reasoning.

Thus, among students measured at a given time, there is a relation between differing reports of conflict in family interactions and contrasts in moral reasoning. From such data we do not know if differing levels of conflict produced moral development, or the reverse. Hoffman (1975), however, in a study of fifth- and seventh-grade white middle-class children and their parents, concluded that differences in the moral orientation of children (for example, in their consideration for others or feelings of fear or guilt upon transgression) are at least in part due to different discipline and affection patterns of parents.

Data reported by Santrock (1975) provide direct support for this idea. Subjects were 120 six- to ten-year-old predominantly lower-class boys from either an intact home environment or a family where the father was absent (due to separation, divorce, or death). Based on reports by the subjects, the sons of divorced women experienced more power-assertiveness discipline (as opposed, for instance, to love-withdrawal discipline) than did the sons of widows. Such inter-

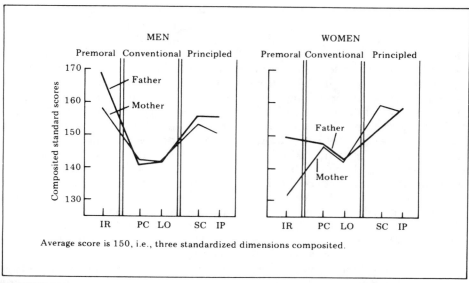

FIGURE 8.4

Degree of conflict and disagreement with parents for males and females from preconventional, conventional, and postconventional groups.

Source: Haan, Smith, and Block, 1968.

action differences influence moral behavior. According to teachers' ratings, the sons of divorced women have more social deviation, but more advanced moral judgment, than do the sons of widows. Moreover, in relation to interaction differences associated with being in a father-absent or a father-present home, there were also differences in moral functioning. Teachers rated the former group of boys as less advanced in moral development than the latter group.

Thus social interactions involving parents and children do seem to provide a basis for differences in moral development. Yet such family social interactions are not the only ones that an adolescent experiences. Not only do adolescents show development toward more social interactions with peers, but even insofar as their interactions with parents are influential, they do not seem to imitate the moral reasoning orientations of their parents. Haan, Langer, and Kohlberg (1976) found that in a large sample of people (ranging in age from ten to thirty) and their parents, there was little relation between

moral stages among family members. Although husbands' and wives' moral stages were correlated at a low level, there was no relation among siblings' moral levels. Parents' and daughters' stages were also unrelated, and parents' and sons' stages were related only among younger sons. Mussen et al. (1970) studied honesty and altruism among early adolescents, ranging in age from 11.6 to 12.6 years. Girls who showed high levels of honesty and altruism were found to have warm, intimate interactions with their mothers and high self-esteem. However, for boys honesty was negatively related to gratifying relationships with parents and peers and with self-esteem, but altruism was associated with good personal ego strength. Thus, although family interactions do contribute to moral functioning, they do not seem to shape it totally.

Parents are not the only people who shape the developing person's moral functioning through interaction with him or her. Peers as well as other sorts of "models" of moral functioning can influence the person.

Peer Interactions

Social interactions outside the family may be more likely to advance moral development because, by avoiding the inevitable power differences between parents and children, they may promote more readily the reciprocal and mutual interactions involved in decentered, morally principled thinking. It may be that children's greater interaction with their peers, who by definition are equal to them, provides them with the precise context necessary to facilitate moral development.

Findings reported by Gerson and Damon (1978) and by Haan (1978) support this position. Gerson and Damon studied children aged four to ten. The longer the children took part with their peers in a group discussion of how to distribute candy, the more likely they were to agree to an equal distribution of candy. This was true at all ages but most markedly among the older children. That is, 77 percent of all children in the study made an equal distribution their final choice, but 100 percent of the eight- to ten-year-olds did so.

In turn, in the study reported by Haan (1978) six adolescent friendship groups (sexually mixed but either all black or all white) participated in a series of moral "games" to see whether behavior was accounted for better by Kohlberg's formal, abstract reasoning ideas or by an interpersonal formulation stressing that "moral solutions are achieved through dialogues that strive for balanced agreements among participants" (Haan 1978, 286). The games presented to subjects, aged thirteen to seventeen, included having to role-play life in two cultures, competing or cooperating as teams in a game having only one winner, constructing a society, and role playing being the last survivors on earth and deciding what to do.

Haan scored the subjects on the Kohlberg and "interpersonal" measures of morality across games. Although these scores fluctuated between games, the interpersonal scores were more stable than the Kohlberg scores, particularly in games involving stress (e.g., the competition one). Moreover, in all situations requiring action, all subjects used interpersonal morality—which required a balance of positions among all those who were interacting—more than the type of moral reasoning associated with Kohlberg's theory. Thus, insofar as moral behavior was concerned, moral reasoning involved establishment of social-interaction agreements among the adolescents and was not primarily based on principled thoughts independent of the group consensus.

Yet the use of such interaction-based, social-reciprocity morality facilitated development of both the interpersonal and Kohlberg-related measures of morality. After the games, the levels of scores of both these types of morality increased for all six adolescent groups, as compared to a control group that did not play any moral games. This suggests that any explanation of moral development is enhanced by considering the interaction between abstract reasoning and the demands of the particular social situation.

Effects of Models

Several studies show that exposure to a person modeling behaviors in a moral situation can lead to people, across a wide age range, showing comparable behaviors. Walker and Richards (1976) exposed first- and second-grade children to a model who made moral judgments on the basis of the motives underlying an act (intentions), to a model who made moral judgments on the basis of the consequences of an act, or to no model at all. While children in the last group showed no changes in the type of moral judgments they offered, children in the other two groups showed change in their moral reasoning in the direction of the particular model they were exposed to. In turn, Eisenberg-Berg and Geisheker (1979) exposed third- and fourth-graders to empathic, normative, or neutral speeches, or "preachings," in their terms, delivered by a principal or a teacher. Empathic preachings significantly enhanced children's generosity behavior (donating a portion of their earnings anonymously). Similarly, Brody and Henderson (1977) report that children exposed to adult and peer models who consistently displayed advanced moral judgments themselves produced advanced moral judgments.

Conclusions

We have seen that Kohlberg, like Piaget, offers a stage theory that deals essentially with the development of aspects of cognition. However, Kohlberg's theory has been subjected to theoretical criticism (e.g., Simpson 1974), and research based on the theory has some important methodological problems (e.g., Kurtines and Greif 1974). Such criticism has resulted both in reactions by Kohlberg (1978) and in some revisions of his ideas (Colby 1978; Colby et al. 1983); yet such activity indicates that Kohlberg's theory represents an example of a current, provocative stage theory of an aspect of moral development, a theory perhaps not in its own final stage of development.

Processes other than cognitive ones also develop, of course. Let us turn, then, to the last stage theory we will present in this chapter. Our analysis of Sigmund Freud's theory of psychosexual development will provide us with an instance of how other facets of the development of people—in this instance, their affective, or emotional, development—may be also conceptualized within the framework of a stage theory.

FREUD'S STAGE THEORY OF PSYCHOSEXUAL DEVELOPMENT

Sigmund Freud was born in Freiberg, Moravia (now Czechoslovakia), in 1856 and died in London in 1939. He lived most of his life, however, in Vienna, where in 1881 he obtained his medical degree. Although thus able to practice medicine, Freud became a research physician after graduation and undertook a series of studies of the nervous system. However, Freud was forced to leave the university setting and his neurological research; although he had shown himself to be an excellent scientific researcher, he was unable to support his family on the basis of the limited income given to low-status faculty members, and he was unable to receive faculty advancement because of anti-Semitism that was prevalent in Austrian universities at that time. Freud thus left university life and entered medical practice.

Freud began this private practice as an associate of another physician, Joseph Breuer. Breuer had been working to a great extent in the treatment of hysteria, a disease believed to afflict only women because it was held that the source of the disease was damage to the uterus. Breuer had successfully treated this disorder through the application of what he termed the "talking cure" (Boring 1950). Breuer hypnotized his patients and allowed them to talk about the emotional events associated with their difficulty. Thus, through use of this *catharsis,* or emotional release, Breuer was able to cure his hysterical patients. Freud readily adopted this method but soon modified its use. He found it equally, if not more, effective to allow his patients to talk completely freely about whatever was on their minds. Thus, by supporting such *free association* in his patients, Freud found that the same emotional releases could be produced without the use of hypnosis. Freud soon found that once such emotions were released, his patients would talk about things that they themselves thought they had forgotten.

With this use of the free association method, Freud was able to get his patients to reveal to him, and to themselves, what he termed *repressed* memories. These were memories of unpleasant feelings (affects, or emotions) or events that patients had experienced and—because of their negative emotional valence—had actively kept out of their awareness. Because of the negative affective connotation of these experiences, they had repressed the memory of them; they had actively kept these unpleasant memories in an area of their mind, the un-

Sigmund Freud

conscious, that contained only material normally not present in awareness. Thus, through the use of such methods as free association, as well as a subsequent method he developed—dream interpretation—Freud was able to discover the repressed, emotion-laden memories stored in the unconscious of his patients. He was also giving himself the major tools for the method of therapy he was developing and discovering information for his theory of development and personality. Thus Freud's practice resulted in two things: a method of treatment of emotional, or neurotic, disorders, termed *psychoanalysis*, and a psychoanalytic theory of development.

Freud's methods allowed him to ascertain his patients' repressed memories. He saw that most of these memories were of events that had occurred very early in the lives of his now-adult patients—in fact, in the first five years. On the basis of these retrospective accounts by adult patients of their early years of life, Freud was able to formulate a theory of affective, or emotional, develop-

ment. Let us see the characteristics of this theory. To do this we must first deal with a core concept in this theory necessary for the understanding of all the developments that concerned Freud. This is the concept of libido.

The Concept of Libido

Freud was trained as a scientist and understandably was influenced by work in many areas of scientific inquiry, including the field of physics. In that field, notions relating to the concept of physical energy were being investigated, and one such idea—the law of the conservation of energy—appears to have had a profound influence on Freud's thinking. This principle states that physical energy can neither be created nor destroyed, but only transformed. For example, in the human visual system, energy in the form of light rays is transformed into chemical energy (when light hits the retina of the eye), which in turn becomes electrical energy (when the chemicals decompose and cause a nerve-cell firing to occur). When this electrical energy reaches the appropriate area of the brain, we experience vision.

Freud saw a parallel between the transformation of energy in the physical world and events that occur in people's mental life. That is, Freud hypothesized that humans are really just complicated energy systems (Hall 1954). By this he meant that human mental life is energized just as other physical systems are energized. Human mental life, he hypothesized, is governed by its own energy, and this human mental, or psychic, energy he termed *libido*. Thus, libido could not be created or destroyed. Humans are born with a finite amount of libido. Instead of this psychic energy being transformed into another type of energy, an alternative type of transformation was seen to take place: Libido changes its area of localization within the body over the course of development. Thus people are born with psychic energy—libido—which energizes their psychological functioning, enabling them to perform such functions as thinking, perceiving, and remembering. But although a person is born with a finite amount of libido, this libido is transformed throughout the course of a person's development in that it changes its area of localization within the body. As we shall soon see, this alteration in bodily location is the essential determinant of a person's developmental stages. The law governing the movement of the libido is the factor accounting for developmental stage progression. Analogous to Piaget's equilibration model, libido movement is the continual process underlying stage development. But before we turn to a consideration of how libidinal movement accounts for stage progression, let us first consider some implications of the fact that libido is centered in different bodily areas, or zones, at different times in development.

As we have seen, libido is energy. This energy is not held to be distributed evenly across all parts of the body, but rather, at different points in time, it is thought to be localized in specific bodily zones. When energy is present in a zone, all the person's libido is concentrated in that one bodily area. Such an accumulation of energy would lead to an excessive amount of tension if there were not some way for this energy-produced tension to be released. Freud specified, however, that such excessive tension could be avoided, that it could be released, if stimulation were applied to the appropriate bodily area. For example, if one's libido were centered in the area of the mouth, then stimulation of this zone would release tension. An unpleasant feeling-state (tension) would be gotten rid of, and in turn a pleasurable feeling (tension reduction) would occur. We may term this tension reduction resulting from appropriate stimulation *gratification*. Stimulation of the appropriate bodily zone would provide libidinal gratification.

The area of the body wherein the libido is centered is termed an *erogenous zone*. This term implies sexual arousal, but we will see that Freud had a broad view of what "sexual" meant. Sexual gratification was seen as involving not only the genital areas (although, as we will see, at specific stages it did mean this); rather, any bodily area wherein

the libido was centered was an erogenous zone of the body and therefore capable of providing as much sexual gratification as that provided by any other such zone. Accordingly, such sexual gratification could be obtained through appropriate manipulation and stimulation of that area (Hall 1954).

In sum, Freud said that a person's libido "travels" to different zones of the body over the course of development, and depending on where the libido is centered, the person may receive sexual gratification from stimulation to that area. That is, such stimulation would give pleasure to the person in that it would diminish the tensions that tend to accumulate in such an erogenous zone due to the focusing of libido there. Hence we see that Freud conceptualized the way in which people's emotions were gratified. By implication, we also see how a person's emotions cannot be gratified. If the appropriate stimulation to a bodily area does not occur, then an unpleasant feeling-state will remain. Freud believed that such an event would have a profoundly negative effect on the person's emotional-sexual, or psychosexual, development. To learn of these effects, let us now turn to our consideration of the sequences that Freud postulated as characterizing the changes in bodily localization of the libido.

THE PSYCHOSEXUAL STAGES

Freud saw the libido as changing its site of bodily localization several times in the course of development. Hence, several psychosexual stages resulted from this libidinal movement.

The Oral Stage

Freud believed that the location of the libido at a particular point in a person's development follows the sequence of what he saw to be invariant universal stages. To Freud, the emergence of these stages is primarily maturationally determined, but as we shall see, the effects of these emerging stages on a person's psychosexual functioning are dependent on the specifics of that person's experience.

Accordingly, Freud postulated that the first erogenous zone in development is the oral zone. Here the libido is centered in the mouth region, where it remains for approximately the first year of the child's life. The infant of this stage obtains gratification through stimulation of this oral area, which can occur in two ways. The infant can bring things into its mouth and suck on them, or later, when teeth develop, it can bite on things. Accordingly, the first portion of the oral stage can be thought of as the oral incorporative (or oral sucking) period. Again, stimulation appropriate for the obtaining of gratification would involve sucking on things such as the mother's nipple or the thumb.

We have indicated, however, that it is possible for such sexual gratification not to occur. For example, an infant might be deprived of some needed oral stimulation because of frequent or prolonged mother absence. When the infant's attempts to obtain appropriate stimulation are blocked, or frustrated, serious problems in the infant's psychosexual development may ensue. If such frustration is extensive enough, *fixation* may occur. That is, there may be an arrest of libidinal development. Some of the infant's libido will remain fixed at the oral zone; when the infant develops to the next stage—in accordance with its maturational timetable—all the libido that could have moved on to the next erogenous zone will not now do so. Thus some libido will always be tied into the person's oral zone, fixated there for the rest of life. Such an oral fixation during the oral stage will mean that for the rest of his or her life the person will attempt to obtain the gratification missed earlier. To put it another way, the emotional and/or psychosexual problems the person has as an adult will be based on these early, stage-specific fixations.

Accordingly, a fixation in the incorporative portion of the oral stage might result in an adult who is always attempting to take things in, to acquire things (Hall 1954). This might manifest itself through attempts to acquire wealth or power or, more obviously, through the taking in of excessive amounts of food. Other examples might be an older child who relentlessly sucks on his or her thumb or an adult who chain smokes.

Alternatively, a fixation in the oral biting period of the oral stage might result in an adult who continually uses orality to be aggressive. Thus, someone who constantly makes "biting remarks" about others—for example, an extremely sarcastic or cynical person—might be seen to be fixated in the oral biting portion of the oral stage.

The Anal Stage

From about the end of the first year of life through the third year, the libido is centered in the anal region of the body. Here the child obtains gratification through exercise of the anal musculature, the muscles opening and closing the anal sphincters allowing the fecal waste products to be let out or kept in. In this stage we may also speak of two subperiods: an anal explusive period, wherein the child obtains gratification from loosening his or her anal musculature and allowing the feces to leave; and an anal retentive period, wherein gratification is obtained through keeping the feces in.

Fixations may result from frustrating experiences in this stage also. For example, since this stage usually corresponds in our culture to the time in which people are toilet trained, anal expulsive fixations may result from too-severe toilet training. This may result in an adult who "lets everything hang out"—a messy, disorderly, wasteful, or excessively demonstrative person (Hall 1954). Alternatively, an anal retentive fixation might result in an adult who is excessively neat and orderly. Such an adult might also be seen to be "up tight," keeping everything in, including his or her emotions.

The Phallic Stage

Here, for the first time in our discussion of psychosexual development, we must distinguish between the development of boys and of girls. Although for both sexes the phallic stage, which spans from about the third through the fifth years, involves the moving of the libido to the genital area, it is necessary to discuss the sexes separately because of the structural differences in their genitalia.

The Male Phallic Stage

The libido has moved to the boy's genital area. Here sexual gratification is obtained through manipulation and stimulation of the genitals. Although masturbation would certainly provide a source of such gratification, Freud believed that the boy's mother is the person most likely to provide this stimulation. Because mother is providing this stimulation, the boy comes to desire his mother sexually. That is, the boy experiences incestuous love for his mother. However, at the same time, he recognizes that his father stands in the way of the fulfillment of his incestuous desires. This recognition arouses considerable negative feeling toward the father in the boy.

This complex of emotional reactions Freud labels the *Oedipus complex*. Oedipus was a character in Greek mythology who (unknowingly) killed his father and then married his mother. Freud saw a parallel between this myth and events in the lives of all humans. Freud believed that the stages of his theory are universally applicable to all humans and, further, that phenomena occurring within each stage—such as the Oedipus complex—are biologically imperative. They are biologically based developments and hence cannot be avoided, although their effects on the person's psychosexuality are dependent on experience. Thus, all males experience an Oedipus complex; all experience incestuous love for their mother and feelings of antagonism toward their father.

However, when the boy realizes that the father is his rival for the mother's love, a new problem is presented. The boy comes to fear that the father will punish him for his incestuous desires and that this punishment will take the form of castration. Thus, as a result of his Oedipus complex, the boy experiences

castration anxiety. Because of the power of this castration anxiety, the boy gives up his incestuous desires for his mother and, in turn, identifies with his father.

This identification with the father is a most important development for the young boy. As a result of this identification, the boy comes to model himself after the father. That is, the boy forms a structure of his personality that Freud terms the *superego*. As noted earlier, the superego has two components. The first, the *ego-ideal,* is the representation of the perfect, or ideal, man (the "father figure"), and the second is the *conscience,* the internalization of society's standards, ethics, and morals. Thus as a result of castration anxiety, the boy models himself after his father and in so doing becomes a "man" in his society. That is, the modeling, or identification, process results in the formation of the superego, whose ego-ideal component represents the internalization of the attributes that are required to become an ideal man in society. Moreover, as a result of this process, the boy develops a conscience, the second superego component, and as discussed earlier in this chapter, this internalization brings about moral development in the boy (Bronfenbrenner 1960).

At many points in this complex series of events, experiences can unfavorably alter the outcome of this stage. For example, if for some reason the boy does not successfully resolve his Oedipus complex, he may not give up his love for his mother. Thus as an adult he may be inordinately tied to her, or he may in fact identify with her instead of with his father. If this event occurs, the male might incorporate the mother's superego; this might express itself in the choice of a sexual partner when the boy reaches adulthood. Part of the mother's ego-ideal involves the type of person she wants or has as a mate. Whatever her preference, however, the point is that she chooses a male as a mate and as a sexual partner. The young boy who adopts his mother's ego-ideal might also choose a male sexual partner when an adult. Thus one possible outcome of an unresolved

Oedipus complex would be male homosexuality.

The Female Phallic Stage

Freud himself was never fully satisfied with his own formulation of the female phallic stage (see Bronfenbrenner 1960). Here, too, the libido moves to the genital area, and gratification is obtained through manipulation and stimulation of the genitals. Although presumably it is the mother who provides the major source of this stimulation for the girl, the girl (for reasons not perfectly clear even to Freud himself) falls in love with her father. Then, analogous to what occurs with boys, she desires to possess her father incestuously but realizes that her mother stands in her way. At this point, however, the similarity with male development is markedly altered.

The female is afraid that the mother will punish her for the incestuous desires she maintains toward the father. Although it is possible that the girl first fears that this punishment will take the form of castration, her awareness of her own genital structure causes her to realize that in a sense she has already been punished. That is, the girl perceives that she does not have a penis but only an inferior organ (to Freud, at least), a clitoris.

Hence, the girl is unable to resolve her oedipal conflict in the same way as the male does. The male experiences castration anxiety and this impels him to resolve his Oedipus complex. However, since the girl does not have a penis, she cannot very well fear castration. Thus the girl experiences only a roughly similar emotion; she experiences *penis envy*. The girl envies the male his possession of a genital structure of which she has been deprived.

The effect of penis envy is, however, to impel the girl to resolve her oedipal conflict. She relinquishes her incestuous love for her father and identifies with her mother. She then forms the superego component of her personality, which again is composed of the ego-ideal (here the ideal female, or "mother figure") and the conscience. However, to reiterate a point made earlier in this chapter, Freud believed that only castration anxiety could lead to complete superego development, and thus, because females experience penis envy and not castration anxiety, they do not attain full superego development. This lack, Freud believed, takes the form of incomplete conscience development. In short, to Freud (1949), females are never as morally developed as males.

Finally, as with males, difficulties in the female's phallic stage could have profound effects on adult psychosexual functioning. Thus, in a manner analogous to that discussed for males, female homosexuality could result from extreme difficulties occurring in the female's phallic stage.

The Latency Stage

After the end of the phallic stage—at about five years of age—the libido submerges, in a manner analogous to that of an iceberg. The libido is not localized in any body zone from the end of the phallic stage until puberty occurs—typically at about twelve years of age. Freud said that the libido is latent. Because it does not localize itself in any bodily zone until puberty, no erogenous zones emerge or exist.

The Genital Stage

At puberty the libido again emerges. Once more it emerges in the genital area, but now it takes a mature, or adult, form. If the person has not been too severely restricted in his or her psychosexual development in the first five years of life, adult sexuality may now occur. Sexuality can now be directed to heterosexual union and reproduction. Although remnants—or traces—of the effects of the earlier stages may significantly affect the person at this time in life, it is only when the genital stage emerges that the person's libido can be gratified through directing it into reproductive functions.

A CRITIQUE OF FREUD'S IDEAS

We have seen that Freud described five stages involved in the development of one's psychic energy. This libido, he believed, changes its bodily localization over the course of development, and this change determines where in the body tensions are built up (through the presence of the libido in one concentrated area) and how these tensions may be diminished. That is, where the libido is centered determines how the person may be gratified. Thus psychosexual development and modes of psychosexual gratification involve the stage-dependent alteration of libido localization. Moreover, since anything that can adversely affect adult psychosexual functioning seems to have to occur in the first three stages, one major implication of Freud's theory is that the first five years of life are most crucial for adult psychosexual functioning.

Thus, for Freud, the form of development after childhood—that is, the form of adolescent and adult life—was determined in early life. To him, the first five years of life, involving the first three psychosexual stages, were critical stages for functioning in later life. As such, Freud's concerns with adolescence and adulthood were only secondary. The behaviors in these periods were shaped in earlier life, and if one wanted to understand an adolescent or an adult, one had to deal with the fixations, conflicts, and frustrations that had occurred in the first five years.

Several objections can be raised to these conclusions from Freud's ideas. Freud was a critical-periods theorist. As such, he saw nature as having a primary role in development independent of the contribution of nurture. Such a conception is inadequate on both logical and empirical grounds, as was discussed in Chapter 5. Moreover, one may object to Freud's ideas because of the sources of information he used to form his idas.

That is, although Freud believed his stages to be biologically based and universal, Freud had a very biased source of "data." He worked in Victorian Europe, a historical pe-

riod noted for its repressive views about sexuality. As a practicing psychiatrist, his main source of data was the memories of *adult* neurotic patients, people who came for treatment of emotional and behavioral problems interfering with their everyday functioning. Freud used his psychoanalytic therapy methods to discover the source of his patients' emotional problems. Through work with such patients he attempted to construct a theory of *early* development. But these patients were adults from one particular historical period—*not* children. Thus Freud constructed a theory about early development in children without actually observing children.

Freud's adult patients reconstructed their early, long-gone pasts through *retrospection*. With Freud's help they tried to remember what had happened to them when they were one, two, or three years of age. This is how Freud obtained the information to build his theory. But it is quite possible that adults may forget, distort, or misremember long-ago events. Therefore, because his data were unchecked for failures of early memories, the possibility that he obtained biased information cannot be discounted. Furthermore, Freud's patients cannot necessarily be viewed as representative of other nonneurotic Victorian adults or, for that matter, of all other humans living during other times in history.

Thus one may question whether Freud, if he were working today, would devise the same theory of psychosexual development. For example, would Freud today find females viewing their genital structure as inferior and thus experiencing penis envy? Would he still maintain that females are not as morally developed as males, and would he find no evidence of pychosexual functioning during the years of latency?

Finally, even if one were to ignore all the above criticisms, one might question whether Freud's ideas represented all the possible developmental phenomena that could occur in each stage of life. Is latency necessarily a period of relative quiet, a time when few significant events occur for the child? Is adolescence just a time when events in preceding life make themselves evident? Or are there characteristics of adolescence that are special to that period? Interestingly, although accepting most of Freud's ideas as correct, it was other psychoanalytically oriented thinkers who led the way in showing that Freud's depiction of developmental phenomena within and across stages was incomplete. Erikson (1959, 1963), for instance, showed that by attending to the demands placed on the individual by society as the person developed, important phenomena could be identified in latency, in adolescence, and across the rest of the life span as well. Similarly, Anna Freud (1969) said that if one focused on events that occurred only at puberty, one would see special characteristics of the adolescent period.

Erikson and Anna Freud did not so much contradict Freud as they transcended him. Both reached this point not by adding anything new to Freud's basic ideas but rather by focusing on the implications of one aspect of Freud's theory to which he himself did not greatly attend. We now consider Freud's ideas about the structure of personality; the different focus taken by Anna Freud is discussed in order to illustrate the implications of this alteration in focus. In addition, this presentation will presage the ideas of Erikson, discussed in Chapter 9.

Structures of the Personality

Freud believed that the human personality is made up of several different mental structures. We have noted that one of these structures, the superego, arises out of the resolution of the oedipal conflict. Another of these, termed the *id,* was defined by Freud as an innate structure of the personality. The id "contains" all the person's libido. The id is thus involved in all of the person's attempts to obtain pleasure, or gratification, through appropriate stimulation. In fact, because the id is the center for the libido, and since the libido creates tensions that require appropriate stimulation, resulting in pleasure, Freud said that the id functions in accordance with the *pleasure principle.* Thus, in emphasizing the implications of the gratification of libidinal energy, Freud emphasized the implications of the biologically based id on human functioning.

However, in addition to the superego and the id, Freud specified a third structure of the personality, the *ego.* The function of the id is solely to obtain pleasure. Thus the id compels a person in the oral stage to seek appropriate stimulation—for example, the mother's nipple. When the stimulation is not available, the id functions in a particular way that Freud termed the *primary process.* Simply, the primary process is a fantasy, or imagining, process. When the mother's nipple is not present, the child imagines that it is there. But such fantasies are not sufficient to allow the child to obtain appropriate stimulation. One cannot just fantasize. One must interact with reality. Accordingly, another structure of the personality—the ego—is formed, and the sole function of the ego is to adapt to reality, to allow the person actually to obtain needed stimulation and hence to survive.

Because the ego develops only to deal with reality, to allow the person to adjust to the demands of the real world and hence to survive, Freud said the ego functions in accordance with the *reality principle.* The ego has processes that enable it to adjust to and deal with reality. This *secondary process* involves such factors as cognition and perception. Through the functioning of these processes, the ego is capable of perceiving and knowing the real world, and thus of adapting to it.

Although Freud spoke about the implications of all three of the structures of the mind—the id, the ego, and the superego, the sum of which constitute a person's personality structures—he emphasized the implications of the id on human functioning. Thus, in describing human psychosexual development, Freud was viewing human beings as essentially governed by inner biological and psychological variables. On the other hand, Freud did not spend a good deal of time discussing the implications of the ego. This focus is what was provided by Anna Freud (and by others, e.g., Erikson 1959, 1963, whom we shall discuss in Chapter 9).

ANNA FREUD: ADOLESCENCE AS A DEVELOPMENTAL DISTURBANCE

In agreement with her father, Anna Freud (1969) notes that all structures of the personality are present when the ego and the superego form to join with the innately present id. Moreover, like her father, she believes that all three of these structures are present by the end of the third psychosexual stage, the phallic stage, or in other words, by about the end of the fifth year of life.

Both Freuds contend that when all structures are present, they present different directives to the person. The id only "wants" pleasure (gratification). It is not concerned with either survival or morality. The superego, at the other extreme, contains the conscience and cares nothing for pleasure. Only morality (and a stern Victorian view of it at that!) is important. Thus, while the id might pressure the person for sexual gratification, the superego would condemn the person for such a desire. The ego, however, has to balance these two counterdirected types of pressures.

The ego's only function is survival. It must defend itself from dangers to that survival, whether those dangers are from within or without. The conflict between the id and the superego represents a danger to survival. If the person spent all his or her time in conflict about action, there would be no energy left to deal with the demands placed on the person from outside the self (for example, from society). Accordingly, the ego develops defense mechanisms, that is, ways to avoid dealing with at least one set of the conflicting demands imposed from within. Such avoidance would rid the person of the internal conflict, and "free up" energy for external adaptive demands.

The defense mechanisms developed by the ego (mechanisms like *repression, rationalization, substitution, projection*) involve taking the pressures imposed by the id and placing them in a particular area of the mind—the *unconscious*. This area contains material most difficult to bring into awareness (into the conscious). The reason that the id pressures are defended against, and not those of the superego, is that the latter's pressures represent the demands and rules of society. If one got rid of these demands—internalized as one's conscience—this would mean getting rid of one's morality. We term people who apparently have no internalized morality, who do not obey rules of society, *sociopaths*. Typically, society has severe sanctions against sociopaths, often defining their behavior as illegal and sometimes imprisoning them. Accordingly, it would not be adaptive for the ego to put the superego in the unconscious, and so it is the id material that is placed in this area of the mind.

To both Freuds, the typical person establishes a balance among the id, ego, and superego by five years of age. By the time

Anna Freud

latency has been reached, ego defenses appropriate for dealing with all pressures, or drives, from the id have been established. The person is thus in equilibrium. However, although people may differ in regard to the character of this balance, depending on events in the first three stages of life, Anna Freud (1969) claims that all people will have their balance *destroyed* in adolescence.

Unlike her father, Anna Freud sees adolescence as a period in life presenting demands for the person that are not *just* those relating to earlier life. These demands involve new pressures being put on the ego, and they require new adaptational solutions for the person. The new demands on the ego are universal, she contends, because the pressures that create them are universal, too. To understand this, let us consider the special alterations that Anna Freud (1969) associates with adolescence.

Alterations in Drives

With puberty comes an adult genital drive. Thus the balance among the id, ego, and superego is upset as this new feeling-state comes to dominate the person's being. Because this alteration is an inevitable, universal one, Anna Freud argues that an inescapable imbalance in development occurs. As such, adolescence is necessarily a period of *developmental disturbance*. Although for theoretical reasons that differ from theorists such as Hall (1904), Anna Freud also says that adolescence is a period of storm and stress.

In sum, because of the universal emergence of the genital drive at puberty, the adolescent is necessarily involved "in dangers which did not exist before and with which he is not accustomed to deal. Since, at this stage, he lives and functions still as a member of his family unit, he runs the risk of allowing the new genital urges to connect with his old love objects, that is, with his parents, brothers, or sisters" (Freud 1969, 7). Since such incestuous relations are not condoned in any known culture (Winch 1971), some

defense against them must be established. The genital alteration thus requires a personality alteration.

Alterations in Ego Organization

Anna Freud claims that the new drive throws the person into upheaval. It causes unpredictable behavior, as the person tries out all the formerly useful defenses to deal with the new drive. This, she contends, puts strain on the person since what is involved is using a set of mechanisms balanced for one state on another, quantitatively greater and qualitatively different state. As such, not only does the adolescent try more of the same defenses, but also he or she eventually forms new types of mechanisms. For example, in relation to the new cognitive abilities that emerge in adolescence, the adolescent comes for the first time to use highly abstract, intellectual reasons to justify his or her behavior. This new ego-defense mechanism is thus termed *intellectualization*. However, such alterations are still not sufficient to resolve the adolescent disturbance.

Alterations in Object Relations

Despite the new ego defenses, the danger of inappropriately acting out the genital drive is so great that "nothing helps here except a complete discarding of the people who were the important love objects of the child, that is, the parents" (Freud 1969, 8). Indeed, the new defenses are useful in helping the adolescent to alter the relations he or she has had with these "love objects." Defenses like intellectualization often involve quite involved rationales for why the parents are "stupid," are "ineffective," or possess "useless . . . beliefs and conventions" (Freud 1969, 8). Of course, in moving away from parents as the major object of social relations, the adolescent does not necessarily become nonsocial. To the contrary, in fact, there is a last alteration that follows from the break in ties with parents.

Alterations in Ideals and Social Relations

When the adolescent has broken the ties with the parents, he or she has also rejected the attitudes, values, and beliefs formerly shared with them. Anna Freud argues that the adolescent is thus left without social ties or ideals. Substitutes are found for both of these in the peer group, she suggests. Moreover, these new social relations are "justified" not only on the basis of shared ideology (for example, in accordance with the intellectualization defense, adolescents might say that the peers understand them while parents do not). More importantly, attachment to the peer group provides a mechanism wherein the new genital drive—which started all alterations initially—may be dealt with in a setting less dangerous to the adolescent's adaptation than the family setting.

A Critique of Anna Freud's Ideas

Anna Freud, her father, and others who use nature bases for their ideas share the limitations of such an orientation. Because she sees the alterations of adolescence as biologically imperative and hence universal, she clearly describes adolescence in terms that acknowledge little plasticity within people and few differences between people. She is led to a depiction of adolescence as necessarily stormy and stressful.

However, such statements simply are not consistent with a vast amount of existing data. Contrary to what she indicates, the data of Bandura (1964), Douvan and Adelson (1966), and Offer (1969), which we reviewed in Chapter 1, clearly indicate that most young people (1) do not have stormy, stressful adolescent periods; (2) do not break ties with parents; (3) continue to share the ideals of their parents; and (4) choose friends who, like themselves, have ideals consistent with those of their parents. By taking a weak interactionist stance in regard to the nature-nurture issue, both Sigmund and Anna Freud are led to describe human development in a manner inconsistent with the known character of the transition that occurs from childhood to adolescence.

Conclusions

Although problems exist in his formulations pertaining to the universal nature of the psychosexual stages, the cultural bias of his theory, and the nature of the methods he used to obtain information relevant to his formulations, Sigmund Freud did posit an extremely influential view of emotional development. Moreover, his views have had considerable heuristic significance, influencing other psychoanalytically oriented scholars—for example, Anna Freud and Erik Erikson—as well as scientists working from a more mechanistic perspective—for example, Miller and Dollard (1941).

Thus, despite the problems and limitations of Freud's theory, we do see that he provided developmental psychology with a provocative and influential—if not readily empirically testable—stage theory of aspects of emotional development.

With our analysis of Freud's theory we have seen three instances of stage theories of psychological development. These positions are similar in that they all view development as proceeding through a series of qualitatively different levels of organization. Moreover, while the positions thus see development in part as being qualitatively discontinuous, they also include notions of continuity. That is, they posit general as well as specific laws. Thus to Piaget and Kohlberg it is disequilibrium that continuously accounts for stage progression, while to Freud it is the continual movement of libido. Finally, to differing extents, these three positions share an organismic, interactionist view of behavioral development; in differing ways these three theorists see the outcomes of behavioral development resulting from an interaction between the organism's characteristics and the characteristics of its experience.

We have thus completed our presentation of stage theories of development. Although we have treated these theories separately from our consideration of other approaches to the conceptualization of development, stage conceptualizations are not necessarily mutually exclusive with these other approaches. Accordingly, we shall see, as we next consider the differential approach to the study of behavioral development, that it is possible to combine both stage and differential concepts into one integrated theory of development. Thus we will begin our next chapter with a consideration of the developmental theory of Erik Erikson. A follower of Freud, Erikson however went beyond both Sigmund and Anna Freud in that he contributed to the refocusing of the major directions of psychoanalytic theory.

9 | *The Differential Approach*

As discussed in Chapter 7, the differential approach to the study of behavioral development considers how people become sorted into various subgroups over the course of their development. Psychologists taking such an approach are concerned with the developmental interrelations among selected status and behavioral attributes. For instance, status attributes such as age, sex, and race are considered as they interrelate across development with behavioral attributes, which are conceptualized as bipolar dimensions, such as dominance-submission, extraversion-introversion, or aggression-passivity. The specification of the developmental location of various subgroups of people—defined in terms of their status attributes—along these dimensions is, then, a major goal of the differential developmental psychologist. Also, given individuals can be denoted in terms of their own locations in multidimensional space.

The concern with the developmental interrelation of status and behavioral attributes may be expressed either in primarily theoretical terms or as a primarily empirical interest. Psychologists employing differential concepts as components of their theoretical writings may specify how specific status attributes will be interrelated with specific behavioral attributes. Such theoretical attempts may first posit particular status attributes and then specify, along with each status attribute, characteristics that are thought of in behavioral-attribute terms— for example, characteristics thought of as bipolar trait dimensions (e.g., activity-passivity).

On the other hand, differential psychologists whose orientation is primarily empirical do not a priori specify the exact interrelation of these attributes. They certainly may have theoretical orientations that affect their choices of particular status and behavioral attributes for study, and they certainly may make predictions about how status and behavioral attributes will interrelate, but they are primarily concerned with empirically discovering or verifying these interrelations. Thus this approach attempts to ascertain empirically how people become differentiated into subgroups over the course of their development.

In the present chapter we shall consider examples of both the theoretical and the empirical uses of the differential approach to psychological development. First, as an instance of the use to which differential concepts may be put within a given theoretical context, we shall consider the theory of Erik Erikson. Next we shall consider an instance of the empirical use of the differential approach through our review of the classic work of Jerome Kagan and Howard Moss (1962). Let us now consider the developmental theory of Erik Erikson.

ERIK H. ERIKSON'S STAGE AND DIFFERENTIAL THEORY OF PSYCHOSOCIAL DEVELOPMENT

Erik Erikson is a psychoanalytically oriented stage theorist who, following Freud, proposes a stage theory of human emotional development. But, in addition, within each of the eight stages of development that Erikson specifies, we shall see the inclusion of an emotional crisis in development which is conceptualized in differential terms. We shall see, then, that Erikson combines both stage and differential concepts of development and provides a theoretical account of the development of human beings across their entire life span. In other words, Erikson sees development *within* each of the eight stages of his theory as involving a person's location along a stage-specific differential dimension; in addition, the location one attains on a dimension within any later stage of development is influenced by one's location(s) in previous stages.

Of course, Erikson's primary use of differential notions as theoretical constructs does not obviate the fact that research may be derived from his theory. Moreover, this research is also of a differential character; that is, the research derived from Erikson's stage-differential theory leads empirically to the differential categorization of people into subgroups on the basis of status attributes such as "stage" and/or sex. Thus, after we review the features of Erikson's stage-differential theory, we shall consider several lines of differential research derived from it. It is useful to begin our discussion by reference to some of the events in Erikson's life.

A Brief Biographical Sketch

Erik H. Erikson was born in Frankfurt, Germany, in 1902 and moved to the United States in the early 1930s. While still a young man, Erikson served as tutor to the children of some of Sigmund Freud's associates. While working in this capacity, Erikson came under the influence of both Sigmund Freud and his daughter Anna. Accordingly, Erikson received training in psychoanalysis, and after moving to the United States and settling in the Boston area he soon established his expertise in the area of childhood psychoanalytic practice.

Through his practice, as well as through the results of some empirical investigations

Erik H. Erikson

(see Erikson 1963), Erikson began to evolve a theory of affective—or emotional—development that complemented the theory of Sigmund Freud. Erikson's theory altered the essential focus of psychoanalytic theorizing from a focus on the id to one on the ego. To understand this alteration, let us consider first some of Sigmund Freud's views about the mental structures that comprise the human personality.

THE ID AND THE EGO

As indicated in Chapter 8, Freud's theory emphasized the biologically based components of a person's psychosexual development. That is, he emphasized an interrelation between inner, biologically imperative presses and psychological functioning. Simply, Freud emphasized the effects of the human inner biological level on human psychology. In the terminology of psychoanalysis, the above relation might be cast in terms of Freud's emphasis on the id in psychological functioning.

In Chapter 8 we saw that Freud specified several different mental structures comprising the human personality. To review this discussion briefly, we noted that one of these structures, the *superego,* arises out of the resolution of the oedipal conflict. Other personality structures were held to exist, however, and as we discussed, Freud termed these the *id* and the *ego.* To Freud, the id is an innate structure, a part of the personality present at birth "containing" all the person's psychic energy, the libido. As we have seen, the libido functions in accordance with biological imperatives. For all people it changes its site of bodily localization in accordance with an intrinsic timetable of development. Thus the id, originally possessing all of a person's libido, is intrinsically involved in all the person's attempts to obtain pleasure, or gratification, through appropriate stimulation. In fact, because the id is the center for all of the biologically based libido, and since the focusing of the libido creates tensions necessitating appropriate stimulation for their release, and since the release of such tensions results in pleasure, Freud said that the id functions in accordance with the pleasure principle. Thus, in emphasizing the implications of the gratification or frustration of libidinal tensions, Freud was emphasizing the implications of the biologically based id for psychological functioning.

Thus the function of the id is solely the obtaining of pleasure, the gratification of libidinal tensions. For example, the id impels a person in the oral stage to seek appropriate stimulation—for instance, the mother's nipple. Sometimes, however, the nipple is not present. At such times the id has available a particular type of functioning, or process, which Freud termed the primary process. Thus, when the mother's nipple is not present the child can imagine that it is there. Simply, the primary process was held to be a fantasy process. Clearly, however, such fantasies are not sufficient to allow the child to obtain the appropriate stimulation. To do this, one cannot just fantasize, one has to interact with reality. Because of this situation, Freud hypothesized that another structure of the personality—the ego—is formed, a structure whose sole function is to adapt to reality, to allow the person actually to obtain needed stimulation and hence to adapt and survive.

Thus we see that the ego develops in order to deal with reality; it comes about to allow the person to adjust to the demands of the real world and hence to survive. Accordingly, Freud said that the ego functions in accordance with the reality principle. Moreover, the ego must have processes available that enable it to adjust to and deal with reality. Thus, the secondary process available to the ego involves such things as cognition and perception. Through the functioning of the secondary process the ego is capable of perceiving and knowing the real world, and hence of adapting to it.

Although Freud spoke about the implications of all three of the structures of the mind—the id, the ego, and the superego, the sum of which comprise a person's personality structure—we have seen that he emphasized the implications of the id for human psychological functioning. Hence, in describing human psychosexual development, Freud was viewing human beings as essentially biological and psychological in nature. On the other hand, Freud did not spend a good deal of time discussing the implications of the ego. This focus is what Erikson provides.

Implications of the Ego

When one turns one's focus from the id to the ego, one immediately recognizes the necessity of dealing with the society in which the person is developing. The function of the ego is survival, or adjustment to the demands of reality. That reality is shaped, formed, and provided by the society in which the person is developing. An appropriate adjustment to reality in one society, allowing the person to survive, might be inefficient or even totally inappropriate in another society. Hence when we say that the child is adapting to reality we are saying, in effect, that the child is adapting to the demands of his or her particular society. How the ego fulfills its function of reality adaptation will necessarily be different in different societies.

For instance, although it is held that all infants pass through the same oral stage and need to deal with reality in order to obtain the appropriate oral stimulation, the way they obtain it may be different in different societies. In one society, for example, there may be prolonged breast-feeding by the mother. Here the infant need only seek the mother's breast, which may never be very far away, in order to obtain the needed oral stimulation (Super and Harkness 1981). In another society, however, infants may be weaned relatively early. A few days after birth the mother might return to work and leave the infant in the care of a grandparent or older sibling (see DuBois 1944). Although the latter infant also still needs oral stimulation, adjustments to reality different from those involved with the former infant will have to be made. We see, then, that the specifics of a child's society must be understood when we consider the implications of the ego's functioning. In some societies learning to hunt, to fish, and to make arrowheads are necessary for survival. In other contexts such skills are not so useful as learning to read, to write, to do arithmetic, and to program a computer.

Thus society, the roles it evolves, and the process of socialization within society are all components of adaptive individual and social functioning. To Erikson, the aspect of the person that attains the competency to perform these individual-social linkages is the ego, that element of the personality believed in psychoanalytic theory to be governed by the reality principle. Whether or not one chooses to talk of an ego as being in-

volved in these linkages, the person must attain the skills requisite for survival in his or her society.

Yet it is clear that the demands placed on the person (or the ego) are not constant across life. Although society may expect certain behaviors from its adult members—behaviors that both maintain and perpetuate society—similar behaviors are not expected from infants, children, and (in some societies) adolescents. In other words, the adaptive demands on an infant are not the same as those on a child or an adolescent or an adult, and one must understand the person's social context to understand the specific adaptational demands placed on him or her.

Such a conclusion was reached by Erikson. Along with other psychoanalysts practicing after Sigmund Freud (e.g., Anna Freud), Erikson believed that Freud had not given sufficient attention to the implications of the ego for human psychological functioning. When such attention was given, however, it seemed clear that humans are not only biological and psychological creatures; they are *social* creatures as well. To Erikson, a child's psychological development can be fully understood only within the context of the society in which the child is growing up. Perhaps we can see why Erikson's most famous book is entitled *Childhood and Society* (1963).

In sum, Erikson changed the focus of Freud's psychoanalytic theory by giving primary consideration to the implications of the ego rather than the id. Although Erikson, too, deals with the development of affect—or feelings—his alteration in theoretical focus broadens the scope of Freud's theory beyond just concern with the psychosexual stages of development. Erikson's theory stresses the interrelation of the ego and the societal forces affecting it; thus, rather than being concerned with biologically based psychosexual development, Erikson is concerned with a person's *psychosocial* development throughout life. He sees that human emotional development involves far more than only psychosexual development.

As psychosocial development proceeds,

the ego has to alter continuously to meet the changing demands of society. At each stage of psychosocial development, new adjustment demands are placed on the ego and, accordingly, new emotional crises emerge. Hence, Erikson's consideration of the ego and society led him to the formulation of stages of development different from those of Freud, and to the formulation of psychosocial emotional crises specific to each stage of development. It is these emotional crises that are conceptualized in differential terms and that, accordingly, allow us to use Erikson's theory as an instance of the interrelation of stage and differential theories of development. In order to understand both Erikson's use of these concepts as well as the details of his theory of psychosocial development, let us consider the eight stages of ego development he specifies. As a necessary introduction to these stages, however, we must focus on Erikson's epigenetic principle and his concomitant concept of critical periods. The former notion provides us with Erikson's model for stage transition, while the latter indicates the central importance of each stage for effective, integrated psychosocial functioning.

ERIKSON'S EPIGENETIC PRINCIPLE

As the ego develops, new adjustment demands are continually placed on it by society. The ego must adapt to these new demands if healthy or optimal development is to proceed. Yet when new adjustment demands are placed on the developing ego, new ego capabilities must be gained in order for these demands to be met; each new societal demand requires a different adaptation by the ego—a different capability to be developed—if the ego is to continue to develop optimally. Simply, healthy ego development involves appropriate adjustments to the demands of society.

Society alters its specifications for adaptive behavior at different times in a person's life. In infancy, society (specifically the fam-

ily) expects "incorporation" from an infant. All that an infant must do in order to be deemed *socially* adaptive is to be stimulated by and to consume food from caregivers. We would not expect a person of this age to do much more than this. Certainly we would not expect the infant to get a summer job or to follow career goals. Yet we might expect such behavior from an eighteen-year-old. Indeed, if all one did during one's summer vacation from college were to take in stimulation (from the sun) and incorporate food (from the kitchen), this probably would not be considered very appropriate behavior by one's parents.

Thus a behavior deemed adaptive at one time in life is not going to be seen as similarly functional over the rest of life. Rather, new behaviors must emerge. Although we still have to be incorporative at eighteen, we have to do more. Identity-related behaviors (i.e., behaviors related to finding an adult role to play in society) may come to predominate at this time of life. Unless one shows these behaviors, and shows them to sufficient degrees, one may be judged as unadaptive. One may not meet the demands of his or her society. In summary, a person must always meet the societally shaped demands of his or her world, but these demands are altered continually across the person's life span.

A similar conception has been advanced by Robert Havighurst (1951, 1953, 1956), who believes that as people progress across their life spans, they must master certain tasks at different portions of life. He terms such change-related requirements *developmental tasks* and notes that the specific tasks that occur at each particular portion of life arise out of particular combinations of pressures from inner-biological (e.g., physical maturation), psychological (e.g., aspirations in life), and sociocultural (e.g., cultural expectations) influences (Havighurst 1956). These pressures require an adjustment on the part of the person. Since at different times in the life span the combination of pressures from each of the levels is different, then at each successive portion of life a distinct set of adjustment demands is placed on the developing person. Consequently a developmental task "arises at or about a certain period in the life of an individual, successful achievement of which leads to his happiness and to success with later tasks, while failure leads to unhappiness in the individual, disapproval by society, and difficulty with later tasks" (Havighurst 1953).

In other words, as each new demand is placed on the ego, a new crisis must be faced. Can the ego meet the demands of the society by developing this new capability? Can it thus continue to function adaptively? In essence, psychosocial development involves the development of the ego's emerging capabilities to meet society's demands; it involves the person's attempts to resolve the emotional crises provoked by these changing demands. Hence each new demand placed on the ego causes an emotional crisis, a new adjustment challenge. If the ego develops the appropriate capabilities, the crisis will be successfully resolved and healthy development will proceed. In turn, if the appropriate ego attributes are not developed, negative emotional consequences will ensue. Of course, for this view to be of use, infants must be capable of manifesting a range of emotional reactions, and current research indicates that they are (Hiatt, Campos, and Emde 1979; Izard et al. 1980; MacDonald and Silverman 1978). For example, Izard et al. (1980) report that one- to nine-month-old infants can reliably be shown to express at least eight different emotions (interest, joy, surprise, sadness, anger, disgust, contempt, and fear).

But how does the ego develop the appropriate capabilities to deal with the changing demands of reality and hence to effectively resolve the concomitantly changing emotional crises? To use Erikson's (1959, 52) terms, "How does a healthy personality ... accrue ... increasing capacity to master life's outer and inner dangers ... ?" To address this question Erikson offers an *epigenetic principle*. As defined by Erikson, "This principle states that anything that grows has a ground plan, and that out of this ground plan the *parts* arise, each having its *time* of special ascendancy, until all parts have arisen to form a *functioning whole*" (1959, 52).

Thus, to account for healthy ego development, Erikson offers a principle that is basically maturational in its emphasis. This predetermined epigenetic principle asserts the existence of a maturational ground plan, a timetable, for ego development. Various capabilities make up a fully developed ego. These capabilities are not, however, present or fully developed at birth. Rather, each part of the ego has a particular period of time, or stage, in the life span when it must develop if it is ever to do so. When one capability is developing, the focus of development is centered around this function. However, when the next stage of development comes about, again in accordance with a maturationally fixed timetable of development, the focus of development has switched to it. This predetermined epigenetic, maturationally fixed alteration in developmental focus is represented schematically in Figure 9.1.

Clearly, we see that Erikson proposes a stage theory of psychosocial development. The emergence of each stage of development—of each ego part—is fixed in accordance with a maturational timetable. Since

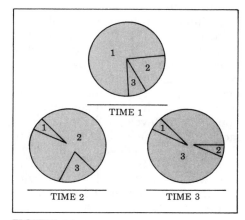

FIGURE 9.1
Schematic representation of maturationally fixed alterations in developmental focus. Here we see a developmental pattern involving three parts of a whole; each part has its own time period of ascendancy.

each stage involves the development of a specific ego capability, a person has only a limited time to develop each stage-specific capability. Time is limited because the time-table of development will move on to the next stage, whether or not the necessary capability is developed. Thus to Erikson each stage of psychosocial development is a *critical period*.

Critical Periods of Psychosocial Development

Because stage development is governed by a predetermined epigenetic maturational time-table, a person *must* develop what is supposed to be developed in each stage of development or else there will *never* be another chance. The timetable of development will move on, and another part of the whole— another capability—will be in *its* time of ascendancy. Thus each stage of psychosocial development is critical in that if the appropriate capability does not develop when it is supposed to, two things will happen. First, that capability is doomed as a completely adequate entity. The potential for its optimal development will be lost. Second, if what was necessary in order for healthy ego development to proceed did not develop, the rest of development will be unfavorably altered. When all parts of the whole should have formed a synthesized, functioning whole, the person will be lacking the complete, or adequate, development of one ego part, one ego capability. Because to Erikson there are no second chances in development, once appropriate development of part of one's ego is missing, one will never be able to regain it, and the rest of development will be unfavorably altered. Hence, to that extent, the person will be ineffective in dealing with reality. In this sense the second outcome of inappropriate development within each critical period of development is neurotic, as opposed to healthy, personality development.

In sum, Erikson proposes that ego development proceeds through eight stages of psychosocial development. In each stage a different ego capability must be developed in order for healthy ego development to proceed. Simply stated, developments within each psychosocial stage are critical for the final development of a fully integrated, whole ego. Such an ego will have all the capabilities necessary to meet all the societal demands imposed on it. Thus, within each stage of development, the component emotional crisis—which Erikson conceptualizes in differential terms—must be successfully resolved in order for healthy ego development to proceed.

STAGES OF PSYCHOSOCIAL DEVELOPMENT

As a follower of Freudian psychoanalysis, Erikson saw the stages of psychosocial development as complementary to Freud's psychosexual stages. Accordingly, the id-based psychosexual stages exist, but along with the ego-based psychosocial stages. Hence, while these psychosocial stages have some similarity to the psychosexual stages, they go beyond them in that they constitute stages in the ego's continual functioning.

Stage 1: The Oral-Sensory Stage

Freud's first stage of psychosexual development is termed the oral stage. In that stage the infant is concerned with obtaining appropriate stimulation in the oral zone. Erikson believes, however, that when one's focus shifts to the ego, one sees that the newborn infant is concerned not merely with oral stimulation. Rather, the infant has newly entered the world, and therefore all its senses are being bombarded with stimulation—its eyes, ears, nose, and all other sense-receptor sites. Thus, in order to begin to deal effectively with the social world, the infant must be able to incorporate all this sensory information effectively. Hence Erikson terms this psychosocial stage the oral-sensory stage, and in so doing he indicates that the ego must develop the capability of dealing with the wealth of sensory stimulation constantly impinging on it.

However, the need to deal with all this stimulation evokes a stage-specific emotional crisis for the infant. If the infant experiences the sensory world as relatively pleasant or benign, one sort of emotion will result. Alternatively, if the child's sensory-stimulation experiences are negative or harsh, another type of feeling will result. If the infant has relatively pleasant sensory experiences, he or she will come to *feel* that the world is a relatively benign, supportive place—that it will not hurt or shock him or her. According to Erikson, then, the infant will develop a sense of basic trust. If, however, the infant experiences pain and discomfort, he or she will feel that the world is not supportive—that there is pain and danger in the world. Here the infant will develop a sense of mistrust.

The infant thus faces an emotional crisis, precipitated by the nature and quality of the sensory world he or she attempts to incorporate. The infant will develop a sense of trust or a sense of mistrust. It is this emotional crisis that Erikson conceptualizes in differential terms. The emotional crisis, then, is between *trust* versus *mistrust*. (We may delete the words "a sense of" for the sake of brevity of presentation, with the understanding that they are always to be applied to all of the alternative stage-specific sets of feelings.) Erikson thinks of these two alternative feelings as forming a behavioral attribute. That is, they represent bipolar, alternative end points along a single dimension. Erikson would represent the emotional crisis of trust versus mistrust as:

trust————mistrust

The ends of this bipolar continuum represent the alternative emotional outcomes of this stage of psychosocial development. In other words, Erikson stresses the point that people do not, and should not, develop *either* complete trust *or* complete mistrust. Rather, a given person will develop a feeling that falls somewhere *along* this dimension.

If a person develops complete trust, Erikson points out, it will be as unadaptive as developing complete mistrust—the person will not recognize the real dangers that exist in the world (e.g., the person will never look when crossing the street because of a belief that no driver would ever hurt him or her, or the infant might never strive to provide for him- or herself because he or she feels that the world will surely do that). On the other hand, however, a person on the far end of the mistrust side of the continuum will never venture interactions with the world, feeling that the world will assuredly hurt him or her. In a sense we might say that such a person would have absolutely no hope; he or she feels that there is no chance of anything but pain resulting from his or her interactions, his or her incorporations of the world.

Thus we see that it is necessary to develop a feeling that lies somewhere between the two end points of the bipolar continuum. If one develops more trust than mistrust, Erikson believes that healthy ego development will proceed. If, however, one develops greater mistrust than trust, then unhealthy, unoptimal ego development will proceed. Having a feeling located closer to the trust end of the continuum means that the ego has developed the appropriate incorporative capabilities allowing it to deal effectively with the world's sensory input. Having a feeling located closer to the other side of the continuum means that the appropriate ego capabilities have not developed. (Of course, one can develop a location at any point along this continuum.)

In other words, for this first status attribute—the oral-sensory psychosocial stage of development—a ratio of trust-mistrust greater than 1.0 will result in healthy ego development. For any status attribute (stage of development), a behavioral attribute location that results in a ratio (from positive end to negative end) greater than 1.0 means that the appropriate ego capabilities have developed, while a corresponding ratio less than 1.0 means that the appropriate ego capabilities have not developed.

We see that each stage of psychosocial development may be construed as a status attribute, and that within each status attribute there exists an emotional crisis that is conceptualized as a bipolar dimension, as a behavioral attribute. One's location along this dimension defines the extent to which one has successfully resolved the emotional crisis precipitated by the reality demands put on the ego at this stage of development; thus the location reflects the extent to which the appropriate ego capability has been developed. Further, this location will affect the ego's functioning as the child enters the next stage of psychosocial development.

Stage 2: The Anal-Musculature Stage

Freud's second stage of psychosexual development is termed the anal stage. Here we may remember from Chapter 8 that the infant obtains gratification through the exercise of his or her anal musculature. To Erikson, however, psychosocial development involves the other muscles of the body as well. Here, then, psychosocial development involves developing control over all of one's muscles, not just those involved in psychosexual development. Analogous to use of his anal muscles, the infant must learn when to hold on to and when to let go of all his or her bodily muscles (Erikson 1963). He or she must develop the capability of being able to control his or her overall bodily movements.

Accordingly, if the child feels that he or she is in control of his or her own body—that he *himself* or she *herself* can exert this control over himself or herself—the child will develop a sense of autonomy. To the extent that the child can control his or her own movements, he or she will feel autonomous. On the other hand, if the child finds him- or herself unable to exert this independent control over his or her own bodily musculature, if he or she finds that others have to do what he or she feels expected to do him- or herself, then the child will develop a sense of shame and doubt. He or she will feel shame because he or she is not showing the ability to control his or her own movements (e.g., bowel movements, movements involved in feeding himself or herself), and this may evoke dis-

approval from significant other persons (e.g., parents). Moreover, because the child experiences this inability to control him- or herself, he or she will feel doubt about his or her capabilities to do so. He or she feels shame because he or she experiences others doing things for him or her that both the child and these others feel the child should be doing for himself or herself; thus feeling shame for this lack of effectiveness, he or she further feels doubt about whether or not he or she has the capability to perform these expected functions. In sum, the second bipolar psychosocial crisis is one between *autonomy* versus *shame and doubt*.

Stage 3: The Genital-Locomotor Stage

Here, if the child has appropriately developed within the anal-musculature stage and gained the ability to control his or her own movements, he or she will have a chance to use these abilities. This third psychosocial stage corresponds to Freud's psychosexual phallic stage. Although Erikson does not dismiss the psychosexual implications of the oedipal conflict, he specifies that such a development also has important psychosocial implications. That is, if the child is successfully to resolve the oedipal conflict, he or she must begin to move away from the parental figures. He or she must begin to employ the previously developed self-control over his or her muscles, take his or her own steps into the world, and thereby break his or her oedipal ties. What Erikson says is that society expects the child not to remain "tied to the mother's apron strings," but rather to locomote (walk off) independently and thereby eliminate such attachments. The child him- or herself must be able to move freely in interaction with the environment.

Accordingly, if the child can move in the world without a parent's guiding or prodding, he or she will develop a sense of initiative. He or she will feel able to decide when to use his or her locomotor abilities to interact with the world. On the other hand, if the child does not do this, if he or she remains tied to the parent for directives about the exercise of his or her locomotor functioning, he or she will not feel a sense of initiative. Rather, the child will feel a sense of guilt. That is, the child's oedipal attachments will remain relatively intact, and to the extent that they continue to exist while at the same time the society expects him or her to show evidence of their elimination, he or she will feel guilt. Thus in this stage a child will develop either toward *initiative* or *guilt,* and again, of course, this emotional crisis is conceptualized as a bipolar dimension. People should develop toward the initiative side of this emotional attribute continuum so that the ratio of initiative to guilt is greater than one.

Stage 4: Latency

Freud did not pay much attention to the psychosexual latency stage because of his belief that the libido is submerged; consequently, the stage had little if any psychosexual importance for him. However, Erikson attaches a great deal of psychosocial importance to the latency years. Erikson believes that in all societies children begin at this stage to learn the tasks requisite for being adult members of society. In our society this psychosocial directive takes the form of the child's being sent to school. In other societies this same psychosocial orientation may take the form of teaching the child to farm, cook, hunt, or fish.

Accordingly, if the child learns these skills well, if he or she learns what to do and how to do it, he or she will develop a sense of industry. The child will feel that he or she knows what to do to be a capably functioning adult member of society. He or she will feel able to be industrious, that he or she has the capability to *do.* On the other side of the continuum lies the feeling associated with failures in these psychosocial developments. If the child feels that he or she has not learned to perform capably the requisite tasks of his or her society (while feeling that others around him or her *have* acquired this), he or she will feel a sense of inferiority.

Thus, to the extent that children feel that they have or have not developed the requisite skills of their society, they will develop feelings toward either *industry* or *inferiority.*

Stage 5: Puberty and Adolescence

This stage of development corresponds to the genital stage of psychosexual development in Freud's theory. Erikson, too, is concerned with the implications of the emergence of a genital sex drive occurring at puberty. But, as with the previous stages of psychosocial development, Erikson here looks at the broader, psychosocial implications of all the physical, physiological, and psychological changes that emerge at puberty.

Numerous changes occur when a person enters puberty. In fact, one may even suggest that every dimension of the person undergoes a quantitative and/or qualitative change. With puberty comes the emergence of the secondary sexual characteristics (e.g., pigmented pubic hair, changes in the voice, changes in bodily muscle and fat distributions, menarche and breast development for females, the first ejaculation and pigmented facial hair for males). There are even changes in the primary sexual characteristics, the genitalia; for instance, in males there is a thickening and an elongation of the penis. Moreover, the person now has a sexual drive—a genital capacity—and this evokes new bodily sensations that have to be dealt with and understood. Furthermore, the person's mental structures also undergo a qualitative change at about this time. As we have seen in our discussion of Piaget's theory in Chapter 8, the person at this time begins to think differently; formal operations emerge, and this means that the person will become predominantly centered on him- or herself (we have seen this centration termed adolescent egocentrism). In addition, the person will think about him- or herself abstractly and hypothetically.

Erikson sees all these changes occurring with puberty as presenting the adolescent—

for this is the label that society now attaches to the person—with serious psychosocial problems. The child has lived for about twelve years and has developed a sense of who he or she is and of what he or she is and is not capable. If he or she has developed successfully, he or she will have developed more trust than mistrust, more autonomy than shame and doubt, more initiative than guilt, and more industry than inferiority. In any event, all the feelings the child has developed have gone into giving him or her a feeling about who he or she is and what he or she can do. Now, however, this knowledge is challenged. The adolescent now finds him- or herself in a body that looks and feels different, and further finds that he or she is thinking about these things in a new way. Thus all the associations the adolescent has had about him- or herself in earlier stages may not be relevant to the new person he or she now has become.

Accordingly, the adolescent asks him- or herself a crucial psychosocial question: Who am I? Moreover, at precisely the time when the adolescent feels unsure about this, society begins to ask him or her related questions. For instance, in our society the adolescent must now begin to take the first definite steps toward career objectives (e.g., deciding whether or not to enter college preparatory courses). Society asks adolescents what role they will play in society and wants to know when these soon-to-be-adult persons will contribute to its maintenance. Society wants to know what *socially prescribed set of behaviors*—behaviors functioning for the adaptive maintenance of society—will be adopted. Such a set of behaviors is a *role,* and thus the key aspect of the adolescent dilemma is that of finding a role. Yet how can one know what one can do and wants to do to contribute to society (and to meet its demands) if one does not know who one is?

In summary, this question—Who am I?—is basically a question of self-definition, necessitated by the emergence of all the new feelings and capabilities arriving during adolescence (e.g., the sex drive and formal thought) as well as by the demands placed on the adolescent by society. The adaptive challenge of finding a role one can be committed to, and thus achieving an identity, is the most important psychosocial task of adolescence. Erikson terms the emotional upheaval provoked by this challenge the *identity crisis.* To resolve this, and to achieve a sense of identity, Erikson (1959) sees it necessary to attain a complex synthesis between psychological processes and societal goals and directives:

> At one time, it will appear to refer to a conscious sense of individual identity; at another to an unconscious striving for a continuity of personal character; at a third, as a criterion for the silent doings of ego synthesis; and finally, as a maintenance of an inner solidarity with a group's ideals and identity. (Erikson 1959, 57)

To achieve identity, then, the adolescent must find an orientation to life that fulfills the attributes of the self while being consistent with society's expectations. As such, this orientation must be both individually and socially adaptive. That is, such a role cannot be something that is self-destructive (e.g., sustained fasting) or socially disapproved (e.g., criminal behavior). Indeed, Erikson terms the adoption of a role such as the latter *negative identity formation* and notes that although such roles exist in most societies, they have—by definition—severe sanctions associated with them. In trying to find an orientation to life that meets both individual and societal demands, the adolescent is searching for a set of behavioral prescriptions—a role—that fulfills the biological, psychological, and social demands of life. To put it another way, a role represents a synthesis of biological, psychological, and social adaptive demands. This is why Erikson (1959, 1963) sees ego identity as having these three components.

To find such an identity, the adolescent must discover what he or she believes in, what his or her attitudes and ideals are. These factors, which can be said to define one's *ideology,* provide an important component of one's role. When we know who we are, we know what we do, and when we know what we do, we know our role in society.

Along with any role (e.g., wife, father, student, teacher) goes a set of orientations toward the world that serve to define that role. These attitudes, beliefs, and values give us some idea of what a person engaged in a particular role in society thinks of and does. Thus there is an ideology that serves to define a societal role. We know fairly well what the ideology of a Catholic priest is and how it is similar to and different from the ideology associated with a professional soldier or a professional artist or a professional politician. The point is that along with any role goes a role-defining ideology. To solve one's identity crisis, one must be committed to a role, which in turn means showing commitment toward an ideology. Erikson (1963) terms such an emotional orientation *fidelity*.

If the adolescent finds his or her role in society, if he or she can show commitment to an ideology, he or she will have achieved a sense of identity. Alternatively, if the adolescent does not find a role to play in society, he or she will remain in the identity crisis. He or she might typically complain of not knowing "where I'm at" or of being unable to "get my head together." In an attempt to resolve this crisis, the adolescent may try one role one day and another the next, perhaps successfully—but only temporarily—investing the self in many different things. Accordingly, Erikson maintains that if the adolescent does not resolve the identity crisis, he or she will feel a sense of *role confusion* or *identity diffusion*. These two terms denote the adolescent's feelings associated with being unable to show commitment to a role and hence to achieve a crisis-resolving identity.

Several possibilities exist for an adolescent who is in his or her identity crisis. One is to simply adopt a readily available role supplied by society. For instance, the adolescent could go into his or her father's or mother's business, enter military service, or get married and define him- or herself as a husband or wife. Another possible route would be to adopt an identity also readily available but deemed socially unacceptable by society; for example, one could become a delinquent. We have seen that Erikson terms such an occurrence negative identity formation.

Finally, instead of finding a role first, one could adopt an ideology. That is, one could show intense commitment to some set of beliefs (e.g., those associated with some current social cause) and thus achieve a feeling of having a role. Since ideology and role go hand in hand, if one adopts an ideology, one must therefore have a role. One would be someone who stands for that cause, and this would give a feeling of having found one's role. Thus one would feel "older now"; one would feel that one had moved past one's identity crisis. Perhaps, however, because such a solution does not represent a true internalization of a role, this intense commitment to an ideology and the concomitant sense of being "older now" are not enduring. One might become disillusioned with the ideology; then, if one develops further and finally achieves an actual identity, one might look back at these previous commitments and feelings as immature.

In summary, it may be seen that the identity crisis of adolescence is provoked by individual changes in the person and societal changes toward the person; the identity crisis can only be resolved through commitment to a role balancing the individual and social demands raised by these changes. The terms *crisis* and *commitment* become hallmarks of the fifth stage of psychosocial development. Yet not only is the adaptive struggle in this stage preceded by events in earlier ones but its outcome is also influenced by them. As Constantinople (1969, 358) points out:

> In order to achieve a positive resolution of the identity crisis, the adolescent must sift through all of the attitudes toward himself and the world which have occurred over the years with the resolution of earlier crises, and he must fashion for himself a sense of who he is that will remain constant across situations and that can be shared by others when they interact with him.

Furthermore, the identity the adolescent attains as a consequence of the psychosocial crises preceding and during adolescence will influence the rest of the life span. To Erikson, self-esteem is a feeling about the self that tends to remain constant across life and thus gives the person a coherent psychological basis for dealing with the demands of social reality. In one essay (1959) in which he casts the notion of identity in terms of self-esteem, Erikson says:

> Self-esteem, confirmed at the end of a major crisis, grows to be a conviction that one is learning effective steps toward a tangible future, that one is developing a defined personality within a social reality which one understands. (Erikson 1959, 89)

Constantinople (1969, 358) elaborates that in adolescence,

> this self-esteem is the end product of successful resolutions of each crisis; the fewer or the less satisfactory the successful resolutions, the less self-esteem on which to build at this stage of development, and the greater the likelihood of a prolonged sense of identity diffusion, of not being sure of who one is and where one is going.

Where one is going is on to the early portion of one's adulthood. There yet another psychosocial crisis will be faced. As implied, its successful resolution, as well as of the remaining crises of the adult years, will rest on the attainment of an adequate identity.

Stage 6: *Young Adulthood*

In this and the last two psychosocial stages, Erikson departs from the psychosexual model and provides a description of the psychosocial stage changes involved with the rest of the human life span. Thus after the adolescent years the person enters into young adulthood and accordingly is faced with a new set of psychosocial requirements.

In young adulthood the person is oriented toward entering into a marital union. The person should by now have achieved an identity and should know who he or she is. The society now requires the person to enter into an institution that will allow the society to continue to exist. Accordingly, the formation of a new family unit must be established—for example, through marriage. The young adult must form a relationship with another person that will allow such an institution to prosper. This psychosocial directive, however, leads the person into another emotional crisis.

Erikson argues that to enter into and successfully maintain such a relationship, a person must be able to give of him- or herself totally. Such openness and complete give-and-take is not limited, according to Erikson, only to sexual relations. Rather, Erikson means that by giving of oneself totally, all the facets of one person (e.g., feelings, ideas, goals, attitudes, and values) must be unconditionally available to the other; moreover, the person must be unconditionally receptive to these same things from the partner. Accordingly, to the extent that one can attain such interchange, one will feel a *sense of intimacy*. Again, this is not limited just to sexual intimacy but includes the mutual interchange of both partners' most intimate feelings, ideas, and goals. If, however, one has not achieved an identity in Stage 5 and thus does not have a total sense of self (to give of completely), then of course one will not be able to achieve this sense of intimacy. One cannot give of one's self if one does not have a self to give. Thus, rather than being able to have a complete mutual interchange, one will be restricted in what one is capable of giving. Accordingly, there are limits to intimacy with another; if one cannot (for whatever reason) share and be shared, then one will feel a *sense of isolation*.

Erikson's theorizing provides a suggestion about why divorce is becoming so prevalent in today's society. Perhaps people enter into marriage unions with the expectation of finding their identities. They expect to define themselves through marriage and thus discover who they are. However, because, according to Erikson, less than two identities can never be made to equal two identities, such people will be disillusioned by marriage. Instead of finding out who they are, they experience feelings of isolation. Although they are now joined with another person, this union, this other person, is a disappointment. This other person has not provided them with what they expected—an identity—and this union has instead brought on feelings of being alone.

Stage 7: Adulthood

If a successful, intimate union has been formed, however, the person can now attempt to meet the next set of psychosocial requirements, the ones presented by adulthood. In this stage society requires the person to play the role of a productive, contributing member of society. Farmers must grow produce, artists must paint pictures, and professors must generate ideas (and publications).

Accordingly, if the person is successfully playing the role society expects, if he or she is contributing and producing what is expected, then the person will have a *sense of generativity,* a feeling that he or she is performing his or her role appropriately. The person will feel he or she is being generative. On the other hand, if the person finds that he or she is not fulfilling the requirements of his or her role, if the person is not producing as he or she should, the person will feel a *sense of stagnation.* The person will find that his or her output is below expectations.

Traditionally, American society has drawn important distinctions between men and women in what behaviors they may appropriately engage in. Thus how men and women achieve feelings of generativity has been different. While men's generative feelings could be achieved through engaging in professional or business activities, women's generational feelings traditionally could be attained only through the generation (or production) of children. Women who chose not to have children or opted for entering the "men's world" (of business or professionalism) were negatively evaluated by society and were viewed as inappropriately fulfilling women's roles. Such pejorative orientations toward women obviated the possibility of women making their maximal contribution to our society. This situation is, of course, changing, and Erikson points out that well it should. If women are limited to the production of children as their only way of attaining

this needed feeling of generativity, then, Erikson feels, eventually our society and the world will be faced with a severe problem: overpopulation.

Thus, in addition to the moral and human-rights reasons for widening women's roles in society, Erikson provides us with a psychological and an ecological reason for this alteration. Women must, he argues, be allowed to channel their generational behavior in other directions—to fulfill their generational feelings in all possible ways—if society is to survive, and society must come to view this as appropriate. The choice for women should not remain one of children versus stagnation. If this choice is not altered, then we will enter into a most dangerous spiral. More and more people will be produced, and they in turn will produce more and more people. However, while Erikson believes that women should engage in roles other than wife and mother he does *not* believe women and men should engage in the same exact set of roles, and/or play roles in the exact same ways. Erikson's reasons for this view will be discussed later in this chapter. Here, however, let us discuss the last stage he proposes.

Stage 8: Maturity

In this stage of psychosocial development the person recognizes that he or she is reaching the end of his or her life span. If the person has successfully progressed through his or her previous stages of development—if he or she has experienced more trust than mistrust, more autonomy than shame and doubt, if he or she has had an identity, had an intimate relationship, and been a productive, generative person—then the person will face the final years of life with enthusiasm and eagerness. The person will be childlike, says Erikson, in his or her enthusiasm for life. Thus, Erikson argues that he or she will feel a *sense of ego integrity.* The person will feel that he or she has led a full and complete life.

Alternatively, if the person has not experienced these events—if, for example, he or she has felt mistrustful, guilty, has had a sense of identity diffusion, isolation, and stagnation—then he or she will not be enthusiastic about these last years of his or her life. Rather, the person will perhaps feel cheated or bitter. The person might be "childish" in his or her behavior, as if trying to go back to earlier years and attain the feelings that he or she never experienced. In this case, Erikson says, the person would feel a *sense of despair*. The person would feel that time was running out and that he or she had not gained everything from life that he or she needed.

Conclusions

Erikson's theory of ego development involves changes encompassing the human life span. His theory represents a synthesis between psychoanalytically based, classical stage notions and an explicit differential orientation to development. Erikson's (1959, 1963) theory has, at least in the last two decades, led to more research in developmental psychology than has any other psychoanalytically oriented theory (Conger and Petersen 1984; Lerner and Spanier 1980; Muuss 1975a). This research considers both the stagelike and the differential features of Erikson's ideas. We shall review two general lines of research derived from—or, perhaps better, associated with—Erikson's ideas in order to illustrate how theories such as his may be "translated" into research and to evaluate several key conceptual issues of development associated with his ideas (e.g., the universal sequentiality versus the plasticity of development, the criticality of one developmental stage for later functioning, and the degree to which intrinsic, nature variables predetermine epigenetic change).

The general areas of research we shall review are, first, studies devoted to investigating the ego-developmental sequence posited by Erikson and, second, studies devoted to verifying Erikson's views about sex differences in ego (and specifically, identity) development. As we shall see, several subareas of research are associated with these two

general ones. Nevertheless, to anticipate the conclusion that I believe we shall be able to draw from the review of all areas, we shall see that, while ego development does differentiate on the basis of the status variable of "age" and in some cases on the basis of the status variable of "sex" as well, there is not strong evidence for the nature-based and universal stagelike sequence posited by Erikson (1959, 1963, 1964, 1968). I believe the review will indicate, too, that there exists considerable plasticity in ego development and that this plasticity derives from the sort of dynamic interactions discussed in earlier chapters—that is, interactions between organism and context. To defend these previews of my conclusions, let us turn to a first area of research associated with Erikson's ideas.

EGO DEVELOPMENT: RESEARCH DIRECTIONS

Research about ego-development processes has fallen into three interrelated categories. First, there has been research assessing whether ego identity occurs in a stagelike progression such as Erikson specifies. Do issues of industry versus inferiority invariably precede those of identity versus role confusion, and do these issues in turn always become of concern before problems of intimacy versus isolation? If such universality of sequencing were found, then it would support Erikson's (1959) ideas about the critical importance of successful development in a prior stage for subsequent stage functioning. If such universality were not found, then it would be appropriate to search for those variables that provide a basis for the various sequences of ego development that could occur.

A second focus of research has been on the adolescent identity crisis—as an exemplar or representative one in the life span—and a concern with what changes, if any, occur in a person's identity status over time. Erikson describes the identity crisis (as he does the basic crisis of each stage) as a bipolar continuum ranging from identity to role confusion. Thus a person may occupy any position along this continuum or, in other words, a person may have any one of a number of statuses along this dimension. A person may have a location along this continuum close to the identity end, have a status close to the confusion or diffusion end, or be located at any one of several points in between. Researchers (e.g., Marcia 1964, 1966) have tried to describe the array of different statuses a person may have along this dimension and how these statuses may change across life.

Because Erikson's sequences have not been found to be universal, and because one's identity status within the adolescent stage of life has also been found to change, a third area of research pertinent to ego identity has arisen. People have been concerned with what variables are related to ego development and identity status changes. Although such work has been largely descriptive, we shall see that it provides ideas about the explanation of these changes that differ from the relatively predetermined epigenetic ones of Erikson (1959, 1963).

Sequences in Ego Development

Does the emergence of, for instance, an identity crisis in adolescence occur in a stagelike manner? Is the adolescent crisis, as Erikson described it, inevitably preceded by the specified childhood crises and followed by the hypothesized adult ones? Although much research supports the idea of adolescence as a time of change in self-definition, the universal stagelike characteristics of this change are in doubt.

Several studies, independent of Erikson's framework, do show adolescence to be a period of change in self-definition. Montemayor and Eisen (1977) found that self-concept development from childhood to adolescence followed a sequence from concrete to abstract. This change was assessed by analyzing responses to the question Who am I?—a question we have seen to be of central import in the identity crisis. Significant increases from grades 4 through 12 were seen in self-definitions relating to occupational role, individuality of one's existence, and ideology. All these are concerns of the adolescent role-search as Erikson (1959, 1963) describes it. Decreases in self-definitions pertaining to territoriality, citizenship, possessions, resources, and physical self were also seen across this grade range.

Additional support for the view that adolescence is a time of personal reorganization, and one involving ego development, is found in studies by Haan (1974) and by Martin and Redmore (1978). In the former study, involving a longitudinal assessment of ninety-nine adolescents, it was found that being able to cope with adaptive demands in adulthood was apparently preceded by progressive reorganization of personality characteristics during adolescence. In the latter study, of thirty-two black children studied longitudinally from the sixth to the twelfth grade, thirty children showed an increase in level of ego development, and these increases showed intraindividual stability (the correlation in ego scores between the two grades was +0.5).

Thus people's egos do develop, their personalities reorganize, and their self-definitions come to include occupational and ideological concerns, but such alterations do not necessarily correspond to a stagelike progression. Research aimed directly at assessing such a conception has not provided complete support for Erikson's ideas. In the largest study involving an assessment of the presence of stagelike qualities in adolescent development, Constantinople (1969) tested more than 900 male and female college students from the University of Rochester. Her study was complex, involving both cross-sectional and longitudinal comparisons. In 1965 she tested members of the first-year through senior classes, and then in 1966 and again in 1967 she retested portions of these original groups.

To study Erikson's stages of ego development, she devised a test containing sixty items. She wrote five items for each of the first six stages in Erikson's theory to reflect the successful, or positive, end of the bipolar continuum and five items to reflect the negative end. Although there was some evidence that people's answers were somewhat influenced by how socially desirable a particular response to an item seemed, Constantinople (1969) nevertheless concluded that high scores on positive continuum ends (e.g., industry, identity) *and* low scores on negative ends (e.g., inferiority, diffusion) indicated successful resolution of a stage crisis. Let us consider Constantinople's (1969) findings regarding the crises of industry versus inferiority, identity versus identity diffusion, and intimacy versus isolation.

Insofar as the scores for these crises are concerned, it appeared that, in general, scores on the positive continuum ends increased, while those for the negative ends decreased across groups. There was increasingly more successful stage resolution among males and females having higher college standing. Moreover, since between-cohort differences (people studied at different times but in the same college class) did not appear great, it seems that the age-group differences may reflect age changes. Another characteristic of the cross-sectional data was a trend involving stage resolution being less evident for the intimacy-versus-isolation crisis, a finding consistent with Erikson's idea that identity issues must be resolved first before intimacy ones can be dealt with. These college students may just have resolved their identities and made career plans by the senior years, and they may just have begun to focus on intimacy. But although seniors scored higher than first-year students on the positive industry and identity ends, and lower on the negative inferiority end, there were *no* college-class differences for diffusion or isolation—negative crisis ends that should have been lower had successful development occurred in accordance with Erikson's stage theory. This failure to show the expected developmental trend was particularly evident for females (Constantinople 1969).

Constantinople (1969) undertook longitudinal follow-ups of the subjects in order to provide further information about the differences in successful resolution of stages in the cross-sectional data. These three-year repeated measurement studies gave unqualified support to the suggestion of developmental changes in the cross-sectional data insofar as alterations in identity and identity diffusion were concerned. There were consistent increases in the successful resolution of identity from the first year to the senior year across subjects *and* from one year to the next within subject groups. Even here, however, there are problems for Erikson's theory. Only males showed consistent decreases in the scores for identity diffusion. Changes in scores for the other crises did not always decrease or increase in accordance with Erikson's theory, and furthermore, the changes that did occur were often more associated with time of testing and group (cohort) membership than age. Figure 9.2 shows the increase in identity scores for males and females from their first year through their senior year, as well as the degrees of decrease in the diffusion scores for these subjects during this period.

Constantinople's (1969) data provide, at best, only partial support for the stagelike character of ego development. Similarly, Ciaccio (1971), studying ego development in male five-, eight-, and eleven-year-olds through use of a projective test, found only partial support for Erikson's theory. In support of Erikson, the youngest group showed the most interest with stage 2 crisis issues (autonomy versus shame and doubt), while the older two groups showed the most interest for the crises of stages 3 and 4. But support for Erikson's idea that the ego develops as it meets the different crises of succeeding stages was not found, since despite their varying interests, all groups showed most conflict for the stage 2 crisis.

Similarly, LaVoie (1976) studied sophomore, junior, and senior male and female high-school students with Constantinople's (1969) measure of stage-crisis resolution. LaVoie classified these adolescents on the basis of their degree of successful stage 5 crisis resolution (identity achievement) and found

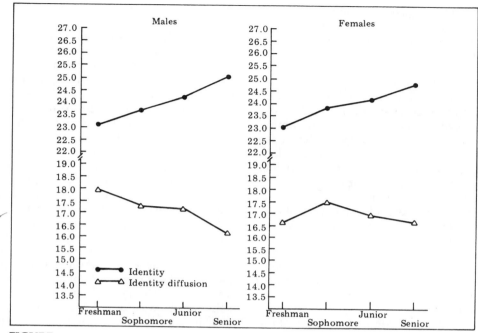

FIGURE 9.2

Changes in identity and identity diffusion scores for male (*left graph*) and female (*right graph*) college subjects.

Source: Adapted from Constantinople (1969, 364–366).

that although those who were high on identity scored higher on the positive crisis ends for stages 1 and 4, there were no differences between high- and low-identity achievers for the positive scores for stages 2, 3, and 6.

In summary, it appears that ego development does not proceed in the stagelike manner that Erikson suggests. Thus the ego-identity crisis does not necessarily arise after the crises typically associated with earlier portions of life or precede those typically associated with later portions. Instead, a more plastic ordering of crises seems to exist among individuals (Douvan and Adelson 1966; Gallatin 1975). However, there does seem to be a progressive increment in resolution of issues dealing with identity. For instance, the major consistency between cross-sectional and longitudinal data that Constantinople (1969) reported was the general movement across life toward a change in location along the identity–identity diffusion

continuum. Most students changed in the direction of increased identity and decreased diffusion scores.

Hence there do seem to be developmental progressions involved in the resolution of the identity crisis of adolescence. Adolescents' changing status along this crisis continuum has thus become the second major focus of research on identity development.

The Differentiation of Identity Status

What are the major types of ego changes adolescents go through in meeting the challenge of the identity crisis? Are there adolescents who occupy locations along the identity–identity diffusion continuum other than at or near its two extremes? If so, what is their location or status? These were the major issues that James Marcia (1964, 1966) confronted as he began a series of provocative studies of identity development in adolescence. Rather than viewing identity as a global phenomenon, Marcia hypothesized that more differentiation existed. Erikson (1959) suggested this possibility, and in this idea Marcia found the basis of his own notions about identity status.

Erikson noted that the adolescent period involves a crisis in self-definition and that in order to resolve this crisis one must commit oneself to a role. As discussed earlier, such commitment means adoption of an ideology (attitudes, values, beliefs) that coincides with the behavioral prescriptions for one's adopted role or occupation. Accordingly, to ascertain the adolescent's identity status, one should appraise his or her degrees of crisis and commitment. Using a semistructured open-ended interview, Marcia (1966) evaluated adolescents' levels of crisis and commitment insofar as issues of occupational choice, religion, and political ideology were concerned.

Using eighty-six male college students as subjects, Marcia (1966) found evidence for four identity statuses. As Erikson (1959, 1963, 1968) said, one of these statuses was held by adolescents who had achieved identity and another involved those who were in a state of identity diffusion. The former group had had a crisis period but had now showed commitment to an occupation and to an ideology. The latter group may or may not have had a crisis; however, their defining characteristic was their lack of commitment. Moreover, they were not concerned about this lack of commitment.

The first of the two other statuses Marcia identified he labeled as *Moratorium*. Students here were in a crisis and had, at best, only vague commitments to an occupation *or* to an ideology. However, young people in the Moratorium status were actively trying to make commitments. They were in a state of search.

The last identity status Marcia identified was termed *Foreclosure*. Those in this status had never experienced a crisis, yet they were highly committed. Their interviews showed they had adopted the identities their parents had wanted them to take and that they had

done so with little or no question and with no crisis.

Marcia (1966) found some evidence that there were differences among these four groups that were consistent with Erikson's theory. As such, his research provided some support for the validity of each status. *Identity Achievers* were found to have the highest scores on an independent test of ego identity and did not follow authoritarian values (e.g., the belief that one should conform, a stress on obedience to authority) as much as members of some other statuses (e.g., Foreclosure adolescents). In addition, the Achievers maintained their feelings of self-esteem (i.e., positive self-regard) more than did members of other groups in the face of experimental manipulations involving negative information about them. Foreclosure adolescents endorsed authoritarian values more than did other groups, and their self-esteem was more vulnerable to negative information than that of the Identity Achievers.

Evidence regarding the validity of the other two statuses was not as compelling. In a concept-attainment task involving experimentally induced stress, the Moratorium subjects showed more variability than others but were otherwise not distinguishable from the Identity Achievers. Furthermore, the *Identity Diffusion* subjects performed lower than did the Identity Achievement subjects on the stress task, but in no other way did their behavior conform to theoretical expectations (Marcia 1966).

However, the results of other studies have been offered as evidence that these four identity statuses exist. Schacter (1968) found that even among emotionally disturbed adolescent males, resolution of the identity crisis was positively related to attainment of occupational commitment. Marcia (1967) found that Identity Achievement and Moratorium adolescent males were less vulnerable to attempts to manipulate their self-esteem than were Foreclosure or Diffusion males, and Marcia and Friedman (1970) found that Identity Achievement adolescent females chose more difficult college majors than did Identity Diffusion females. In addition, Foreclosure females, although like Identity Achievers in many respects, were higher in authoritarianism. However, they also had higher self-esteem and lower anxiety than did the Achievers, a finding seemingly inconsistent with those of other studies.

Similarly, partial support for the fourfold differentiation of identity status comes from a study by Toder and Marcia (1973). Attempts were made to induce conformity to group demands experimentally among sixty-four college females. Identity Achievers conformed less than those having unstable statuses (the Moratorium and Diffusion subjects). However, the Foreclosure subjects also conformed less than those in the other two groups. Although this lack of conformity to group pressure would be expected on the basis of the Foreclosure subjects' stable identity status, it would not be expected by virtue of their authoritarian and hence conforming and obedient values.

Thus these data are far from unequivocal in showing distinctions among the four different statuses. Other data, however, provide some additional support. Several studies have shown that when adolescents are studied longitudinally, they progress through the four identity statuses in ways consistent with theoretical expectations (Waterman 1982). For instance, Waterman and Waterman (1971) longitudinally studied ninety-two male adolescents through the course of their first college year. Using Marcia's (1966) interview, changes in occupational and ideological status were assessed. In regard to occupational commitment, there was a significant increase in the number of Moratorium subjects—that is, those people actively searching—and a significant decrease in the number of Identity Diffusion subjects—that is, those people not searching for a commitment. Thus there was a group movement toward trying to make commitments and hence to play an adaptive, functional role in society.

Insofar as ideology was concerned, there was a significant increase in the number of Identity Diffusion subjects. Indeed, about 44 percent of the subjects changed identity status for occupation over the course of their first year, and about 51 percent did so in regard to ideology; *but* people who had an Identity Achievement status at the beginning of the first-year period were just as likely to change as those who initially had other statuses.

These one-year longitudinal data do not provide compelling support for general progression toward more adaptive identity statuses in adolescence. However, the first year of college may involve demands on the person that produce discontinuity in identity. Progressively more continuity in identity achievement might be found if adolescents were followed beyond the first year. Longer-term longitudinal assessments support this expectation.

Waterman, Geary, and Waterman (1974) studied fifty-three male college seniors, all of whom had been subjects in the Waterman and Waterman (1971) study of identity development in the first year of college. Over this longer time period there were significant increases in the frequency of subjects falling in the Achievement status, for *both* occupation and ideology ratings. Moreover, although about fifty percent of these subjects stayed in the same status from the first to the senior year, the Achiever status had the most continuity across this period. In turn, the Moratorium status had the least continuity. Similarly, Marcia (1976), in a reinterview of thirty males who were given identity-status interviews six to seven years earlier, found the Moratorium status to show a 100 percent rate of change. Moreover, Waterman and Goldman (1976), reinterviewing eighteen seniors studied as first-year students in 1970 and forty-one seniors studied as first-year students in 1971, found with both cohorts that there were significant increases in the frequency of Identity Achievement and decreases in Moratorium and Diffusion statuses. In summary, there was a very high probability for resolution of the identity crisis. About 75 percent of those subjects studied over the entire period of their college experience reached a status of Identity Achievement.

We may conclude, therefore, that there is some evidence for differentiation among ego-identity statuses within adolescence. Most people move adaptively from other statuses toward Identity Achievement, and hence crisis resolution, by virtue of occupational and ideological role commitment. However, it is clear that there is variability in this pattern. Not all people go through this sequence. For instance, some begin and end adolescence in the Foreclosure status. People differ in their rates of development, and some never seem to attain an identity of either Achievement or Foreclosure. For example, Waterman, Geary, and Waterman (1974) found that a substantial proportion of subjects completed their college years in the Identity Diffusion status. In their study, 13 percent of seniors were Diffuse on both occupational and ideology ratings, and an additional 33 percent were Diffuse in one or the other of these areas.

In summary, not only is there considerable plasticity of when in the sequence of other psychosocial crises the identity crisis occurs, but there is also plasticity in developments within this adolescent crisis. Because of this variability, the third area of research pertaining to adolescent identity has arisen. Researchers have become concerned with what variables may interrelate with those pertaining to identity processes. Through describing how identity may be moderated by those other variables to which it is related, this research provides an explanation of the basis of ego identity and, as such, its changing character.

Identity: Psychological Dimensions

Processes of cognitive and moral development are intertwined with those of identity. Podd (1972) found that principled moral reasoning, formal-operational thought, and identity achievement were positively related. Those adolescents whose identity status was diffuse tended to show preconventional moral thought (Podd 1972).

Furthermore, independent data show the interrelation between advances in identity development and other theoretically relevant psychological functions. Advances in formal operations involve progressions in dealing with abstract thought. If such development is indeed related to identity formation, then one should expect to see those who engage in abstraction processes tending to have the Identity Achievement status. If one construes the writing of poetry as an activity at least in part based on abstract thought, then support for this relation is found in a report by Waterman, Kohutis, and Pulone (1977). In two studies of college students, these investigators found that those people who wrote poetry were more likely to be in the Achievement status than those who did not write poetry. Moreover, poetry writers were less frequently found in the Foreclosure and Diffusion statuses than people who did not write poetry. Yet writing per se was not related to identity status, since there were no identity differences among students who did or did not keep a personal journal or diary.

Similarly, Waterman and Goldman (1976) found that among the two cohorts they studied longitudinally from the first year of college to the senior year, an interest in literary and other art forms was predictive of becoming Identity Achievers by the end of college for those who were not in this status as first-year students. Moreover, that identity status is related to school attainments is a finding reported by Jones and Strowig (1968). A group of 150 female and 167 male rural Wisconsin high-school seniors were asked the Who am I? question, and answers were scored for identity development. Higher scores were positively related to achievement.

Thus advanced cognitive performance is associated with an advanced identity status. This relation suggests that a generally greater level of adaptive functioning is associated with identity attainment. Data reported by LaVoie (1976) support this idea. Male and female high-school students who were measured as having high identity had lower scores on measures of defensiveness, general adjustment, and neurosis than did students measured as low in identity. Moreover, the self-concepts of the high-identity scorers were more positive than those of the low-identity scorers. Similarly, Matteson (1977) found that among ninety-nine Danish young people aged seventeen to eighteen, more advanced identity status was related to the ability to control the expression of impulses among males, and to the rejection of compliance with authority among both males and females. It may be that in rejecting authority, high-identity subjects see themselves as more capable of controlling their own lives.

Two studies support these interpretations. Waterman, Beubel, and Waterman (1970) found that Identity Achievers (and also Moratorium subjects) saw their own behavior as more controlled by phenomena internal to and thus dependent on them than by events external to and thus independent of their control (e.g., luck or "fate"). In turn, the reverse ideas about the locus of control for one's behavior were held by subjects in the Foreclosure and Diffusion statuses. Similarly, Schenkel (1975) found that Identity Achievers were least dependent on extraneous cues from the environment in performing a perceptual task, while the reverse was the case with Identity Diffusion adolescents.

Thus the development of identity is associated with cognitive, adjustment, perceptual, and other psychological processes. However, the character of these psychological interactions may be moderated by their reciprocal relations with interindividual social processes.

Identity: Social Dimensions

Since achieving an identity denotes finding a role meeting society's demands, identity processes are basically interpersonal ones. They link the person to society in a way that facilitates both individual and social maintenance and survival. One might expect, then, that people who have achieved identity should engage in interpersonal relationships useful in advancing this individual and social functioning—that is, intimate relations. Orlofsky, Marcia, and Lesser (1973) found evidence of just such a relation. In a study of fifty-three college males, it was found that those subjects who were in the Identity Achievement status were among those who had the greatest capacity for intimate interpersonal relationships. The interpersonal relationships of Foreclosure and Diffusion students were stereotyped, superficial, and hence not very intimate. The searching Moratorium students showed the most variability between these two extremes. Similarly, Kacerguis and Adams (1980) studied forty-four male and forty-four female college students and found that those people of either sex who were in the Identity Achievement category were more likely to be engaged in intimate relationships than were males or females in the Foreclosure, Moratorium, and Diffusion categories. People in these latter three groups were much more variable in their level of intimacy.

Because identity links the adolescent to his or her social world, a basis of the different interpersonal styles of adolescents differing in identity status may lie in their social interaction history; perhaps this involves the family, since it is the major social institution delivering those societal demands to which the person must adapt. Recalling Erikson's (1959) conception of identity as being in part composed of, or indexed by, self-esteem, O'Donnell's (1976) finding that in eighth- and eleventh-grade adolescents the degree of positive feelings toward parents was generally more closely related to self-esteem than was degree of positive feelings toward friends may be taken as support for the saliency of family relationships in identity development. Other studies show that different family structures, for example, the presence of a working or a nonworking mother (Nelson 1971) or father absence (Santrock 1970), are associated with contrasts in levels of adjustment in adolescence or in ego development prior to adolescence, respectively. However, neither these reports nor O'Donnell's suggests what sort of parental or familial functions may facilitate ego-identity development.

Several studies suggest that, in the context of the family milieu the parents help to create, parental personal and interpersonal characteristics may be transmitted to their offspring and this may act to foster identity development. LaVoie (1976) reports that male high-school students high in identity reported less regulation and control by their mothers and fathers and more frequent praise by their fathers than did males low in identity. Similarly, LaVoie found that high-identity high-school females reported less maternal restrictiveness and greater freedom to discuss problems with their mothers and fathers than did low-identity females. Thus high-identity adolescents appear to be characterized by a family milieu involving less parental restrictiveness and better parent-child communication than do low-identity adolescents. Waterman and Waterman (1971) and Matteson (1974) provide further data to support this conclusion.

In their longitudinal study of first-year college students Waterman and Waterman (1971) found that those students who showed stable Identity Achievement status for the entire year—and it will be recalled that many did not—scored significantly higher on a measure of family independence than did those who changed out of the Achievement status. In addition, these students who were initially in the Foreclosure status and then left it by the end of the first year were also significantly higher scorers on a measure of family independence than those students who did not change out of this status.

In the study by Matteson (1974), involving ninth-grade students, a measure of adolescent self-esteem and of communication with parents was taken. In addition, the adolescents' parents completed questionnaires about parent-adolescent communication and their own marital communication. Matteson reported that adolescents with low self-esteem viewed communication with their parents as less facilitative than did adolescents with high self-esteem. Moreover, parents of adolescents with low self-esteem perceived their communication with their spouses as less facilitative and rated their marriages as less satisfying than did parents of adolescents with high self-esteem.

Thus family milieu variables relating to communication quality among *all* family members and to patterns of parental control appear to relate to identity development. A family milieu with open communication and low restrictions on the individual seems to be most facilitative in providing a context for successful resolution of role search. Of course, the milieus having such characteristics need not be just conventional American or Western European familial ones. Although there have been few studies, other types of family structures, on the one hand, or other types of social milieus, on the other, can promote such development.

Long, Henderson, and Platt (1973) studied fifty-one Israeli male and female adolescents aged eleven to thirteen, reared in a kibbutz, comparing them to two groups of same-age early adolescents reared in more traditional family settings. In the kibbutz system, children are reared collectively by adults who are not necessarily their parents. In fact, in this system children may often spend at most a few hours a day with either biological parent. Yet, in the kibbutz system, the individual's contribution to the group is emphasized, as is equality of all group members despite their age or role. The adolescents reared in this setting showed more social interest and higher self-esteem than those adolescents reared in other settings.

Moreover, the college environment may be seen as a nonfamilial social milieu involving open communication of ideas and minimal restrictiveness of search for roles. Sanford (1962) has speculated that because of these properties the college experience promotes movement toward Identity Achievement status. The longitudinal data of Waterman and Waterman (1971), Waterman, Geary, and Waterman (1974), and Waterman and Goldman (1976) support this view. Most college students experience an identity crisis during their college years, and of these, 75 percent reach the Achievement status.

Although future research is needed to evaluate the appropriateness of these interpretations, it does appear that if an adolescent is placed in a social setting involving openness of social communication and minimal restrictions on role-search, an adaptive coordination between self and society will be attained. An identity will be achieved.

In sum, ego development appears to be a more plastic process than that specified in Erikson's (1959, 1963) theory. This plasticity appears to derive from the interaction between organism and contextual variables. In other words, the maturational ground plan posited by Erikson (1959) does not appear to function in the predetermined epigenetic manner he suggests. Simply, one's nature acts neither directly nor independently of contextual influences to determine one's ego development. A similar set of conclusions can, I believe, be drawn from a review of a second area of research associated with Erikson's (1959, 1964, 1968) theory.

SEX DIFFERENCES IN EGO DEVELOPMENT

There are obvious differences between the sexes. Structural differences in primary and secondary sexual characteristics and functional differences in reproduction are universal contrasts between males and females. Only women can *menstruate, gestate* (carry children), and *lactate* (breast-feed). Only men can *impregnate* (Money and Ehrhardt 1972). However, Erikson (1964, 1968), as well as Freud (1923), has suggested that personality and social functioning are innately tied to the physical and physiological characteristics of males and females. Such a *nature* view says that there are inevitable differences between the sexes, since there are universal biological contrasts between them. Just as it is biologically adaptive (for species survival) to engage in male or female reproductive functions, it is also "biologically imperative" (Freud 1923, 1949) to engage in those personal behaviors that are innately linked to one's biological status as a male or

female. It is in this sense that sex differences in personality and social relations are seen as universal. To proponents of this position such as Erikson (1964, 1968), *autonomy is destiny!*

Three sets of predictions regarding sex differences in ego development, or more generally personality, may be derived from Erikson's (1959, 1964, 1968) nature-based theory. As we shall see, these predicted sex differences pertain to (1) body concept, (2) self-concept and self-esteem, and (3) vocational role orientation.

ERIKSON'S THEORY OF INNER AND OUTER SPACE

As I have indicated, Erikson (1959, 1963) believes that healthy or adaptive ego development requires a synthesis of the biological, psychological, and societal demands placed on the person. At each stage of ego development, the person is placed in a psychosocial crisis that can best be dealt with through such a synthesis, or integration.

In adolescence the identity crisis can only be resolved adequately through the attainment of a role. Such a role must involve the adoption of a set of behaviors and an ideology that allow the individual to contribute to society in a biologically appropriate way. Erikson (1964, 1968) believes that since males and females differ in terms of their physiological functions and reproductive organs, there will be different implications for role adoption. In other words, because of the basic biological differences between men and women, they will necessarily have to adopt different role-related behaviors and ideologies in order to be psychosocially "healthy." Thus, for Erikson (1964, 1968), the anatomical and physiological differences between the sexes relate directly to differences in ego development:

> Many of the testable items on the long list of "inborn" differences between human males and females can be shown to have a meaningful function within an ecology which is built, as any mammalian ecology must be, around the

fact that the human fetus must be carried inside the womb for a given number of months, and that the infant must be suckled or, at any rate, raised within a maternal world best staffed at first by the mother (and this for the sake of her own awakened motherliness, as well) with a gradual addition of other women. (Erikson 1968, 281)

The Inner-Space Orientation of Females

Thus Erikson sees women's reproductive role as the dominant force in shaping their ego identities. However, his idea is more pervasive than this. He argues that because of their anatomical structure and the biological demand for carrying and nurturing the child of a man, women's whole sense of self is necessarily involved with motherhood and mothering. He says:

> The stage of life crucial for the emergence of an integrated female identity is the step from youth to maturity, the state when the young woman, whatever her work career, relinquishes the care received from the parental family in order to commit herself to the love of a stranger and to the care to be given to his and her offspring. (Erikson 1968, 265)

To Erikson identity development in females moves in the direction of being a wife and a mother. Accordingly, Erikson believes that to fulfill her biologically based role appropriately an adolescent female must be oriented to her *inner space*. To bear children in fulfillment of her biological directive, a female must be oriented toward *incorporation*—toward bringing a man's penis into her inner space, into her body. Only through such incorporation can the woman create a situation allowing adaptation. Only through incorporation can she create *within* herself the child that will fulfill her biological destiny. Because of this biologically based orientation to inner space, the female will undergo identity-formation processes different from the male's. The behaviors females will be committed to, or show fidelity toward, will be markedly different than those of males. Indeed, by asking some rhetorical

questions, Erikson (1968) argues that whether or not a woman chooses a career outside marriage (as we have seen he, in fact, espouses in order to avoid overpopulation), at her core the woman is always disposed to, and indeed dominated by, her orientation toward being a mother and mothering:

> But how does the identity formation of women differ by dint of the fact that their somatic design harbors an "inner space" destined to bear the offspring of chosen men and, with it, a biological, psychological, and ethical commitment to take care of human infancy? Is not the disposition for this commitment (whether it be combined with a career, and even whether or not it be realized in actual motherhood) the core problem of female fidelity? (p. 266)

To become a mother and to engage in mothering, a female obviously needs a male. Thus, her inner-space-incorporative orientation leads to an interpersonal orientation. She needs to admit a male to her inner space so that her biologically imperative psychosocial role can be achieved. In short, because of her inner-space demands, a female becomes interpersonally oriented to search for a man to incorporate.

Although a female can prepare for this before she meets a particular male, she must keep her identity somewhat open in order to adjust herself to the specific characteristics of the particular male she attracts. Indeed, Erikson (1968) notes:

> Young women often ask whether they can "have an identity" before they know whom they will marry and for whom they will make a home. Granted that something in the young woman's identity must keep itself open for the peculiarities of the man to be joined and of the children to be brought up, I think that much of a young woman's identity is already defined in her kind of attractivenes and in the selective nature of her search for the man (or men) by whom she wishes to be sought. (p. 283)

Hence a female needs to attract a male in order that a biologically adaptive incorporation into her inner space may occur. Thus a female is dependent on a male for the attainment of her identity, since without a literal or at least symbolic incorporation of the penis, she cannot attain her requisite role. Indeed, all her psychosocial activities are directed toward this fulfillment of inner-space pressures. In fact, Erikson (1968) says: "But since a woman is never not-a-woman, she can see her long-range goals only in those modes of activity which include and integrate her natural dispositions" (p. 290). Moreover, he notes that identity can only be achieved, that "womanhood arrives [only] when attractiveness and experience have succeeded in selecting what is to be admitted to the welcome of the inner space for keeps" (1968, 283).

In sum, Erikson sees a female's inner-space, incorporative *mode of functioning* as making her committed to a role involving interpersonal orientations and dependency on others. Because of the invariant biological basis of these relations, Erikson appears to be taking a weak interactional, and hence nature-based, view of the basis of females' ego development. Indeed, he is quite explicit about this stance:

> Am I saying, then, that "anatomy is destiny"? Yes, it is destiny, insofar as it determines not only the range and configuration of physiological functioning and its limitation but also, to an extent, personality configurations. The basic modalities of woman's commitment and involvement naturally also reflect the ground plan of her body. (Erikson 1968, 285)

If "anatomy is destiny" for females, it must also be so for males. Yet the different structure of male reproductive organs leads to quite different implications for them.

The Outer-Space Orientation of Males

According to Erikson (1968), males must also use their reproductive organs in ways consistent with their biological roles. If they are to use their bodies appropriately, then they cannot be incorporative. Rather, they must seek to *intrude upon,* or enter into, objects external to their own bodies. They must be oriented to *outer space* and develop an *intrusive mode* of dealing with the environment outside themselves in order to use

their bodies for reproduction. Although Erikson believes that a female needs a male, either literally or symbolically, in order to attain an appropriate identity, the reverse is not the case for males: A man does not need a woman in order to be a man. Instead, the outer-space orientation of men requires only that they develop ego capabilities allowing for intrusion on target objects outside the body. Although such objects may be females, they need not be. As long as any object in the environment is being successfully intruded on—or in other words, *dominated, manipulated,* or *controlled*—then (at least symbolically) the male is conforming adaptively to his outer-space, intrusive mode of functioning.

Thus as long as males are oriented toward, and effective in, gaining dominance over objects in their outer space, they are behaving in a biologically appropriate manner. Indeed, while the inner-space orientation of females leads to an inevitable *press* toward being a mother and mothering, males' outer-space orientation leads to quite distinct behaviors. Since appropriate use of the body involves intrusion upon any objects external to the self, the male does not need another person to show this orientation. Thus the adaptive male should develop an independent, *individual* orientation. In fact, if the male depended on others in any way for his psychosocial functioning, this would mean he was not dominating his outer space but instead that he was dependent on objects external to himself.

In contrast with a female, whose basic "unit" of reproduction—the ovum—must passively wait for the male's sperm for impregnation and thus fulfillment of the inner space, the male must play an active role in life to meet the demands of the outer space (Erikson 1968). That is, if sperm are not active and mobile, then reproduction will not occur. Analogously, if males do not show behaviors that are effective, independent, and active manipulations of their environment, they cannot fulfill the demands of their outer space. Thus roles allowing for these behaviors are appropriate for males.

In summary, the linkage between differences in reproductive anatomy and physiology and differences in the personality and social behavior of males and females is a nature-based and hence invariant one in Erikson's (1964, 1968) view. The biological basis of these differences is construed to mean that females' identities must, at their core, be oriented to being a mother or to mothering, while males' identities must, at their core, involve mastery of the external world. These sex differences not only reflect the different ways the genitals of the two sexes are structured, but they also mirror the function of the reproductive cells of each sex. Additionally, they pervade each sex group's entire orientation to the world.

Furthermore, Erikson believes that childhood play behaviors reflect the psychosocial preparation of the person for a role consistent with his or her anatomical and physiological characteristics. As evidence, Erikson (1968) reports that when he asked a group of ten- to twelve-year-old males and females from the Berkeley Guidance Study (discussed in Chapter 10) to construct scenes with materials such as dolls and blocks, they portrayed scenes consistent with their respective genital structures. Although not instructed in any way about what sort of scene to construct, males built scenes figuratively related to an intrusive penis, or an organ attaining or losing its erect state. Females' scenes were symbolically related to their vaginal opening or to their internal genitalia. Erikson's report and interpretation of these data are instructive:

> Girls' enclosures consist of low walls, i.e., only one block high, except for an occasional elaborate doorway. These interiors of houses with or without walls were, for the most part, expressly peaceful. Often, a little girl was playing the piano. In a number of cases, however, the interior was intruded by animals or dangerous men. Yet the idea of an intruding creature did not necessarily lead to the defensive erection of walls or closing of doors. Rather the majority of these intrusions have an element of humor and pleasurable excitement.
> Boys' scenes are either houses with elaborate walls or facades with protrusions such as cones or cylinders representing ornaments or cannons. There are high towers, and there are entirely exterior scenes. . . .
> The male and female spaces, then, were dominated, respectively, by height and downfall and by strong motion and its channeling or arrest; and by static interiors which were open or simply enclosed, and peaceful or intruded upon. It may come as a surprise to some and seem a matter of course to others that here sexual differences in the organization of a play space seem to parallel the morphology of genital differentiation itself; in the male, an external organ, erectable and intrusive in character, serving the channelization of mobile sperm cells; in the female, internal organs, with vestibular access, leading to statically expectant ova. (Erikson 1968, 270-71)

DIMENSIONS OF SEX DIFFERENCES PREDICTED BY ERIKSON'S THEORY

In their play, in their social behaviors, and in their ideologies, males and females show differences related, Erikson (1964, 1968) believes, to their respective biological status. The basis and nature of these differences converge to suggest three major domains, or indicants, of ego-identity, or personality, difference between males and females.

Body Concept

If females use their bodies appropriately, they will incorporate a male into their inner space and fulfill their role regarding being a mother and mothering. Thus they are oriented to use their bodies interpersonally, to attract a man and thus to fulfill the inner-space demands. In other words, the more a female uses her body as a vehicle for interpersonal attraction of males, the more likely she is to be in a position to play her incorporative role and thus form a healthy, adaptive identity. The more a female views her body as physically attractive to others, the better sense of self—the better self-concept—she should have. The self-concept would be enhanced because of the greater likelihood of inner-space fulfillment.

An alternative set of relations should exist for males. If males use their bodies appropriately, they will use them individually, to intrude upon, show mastery over, or manipulate objects external to their bodies. To fulfill outer-space demands, the male must be effective in this intrusion. If he is not, he will be dependent on others for functioning in the environment, since he himself could not master it. And this reliance on others for survival is incompatible with male biological demands. Thus the more a male uses his body as an instrument for individual physical effectiveness, the more likely he is to be playing an intrusive role and thus forming a healthy, adaptive identity. The more a male views his body as physically effective, the better self-concept he should have.

In sum, different body concepts should develop in males and females, and these different body concepts should be related to self-concept and inner-versus-outer-space orientation. Females should conceive of their bodies more in terms of physical attractiveness than physical effectiveness, while the reverse should be the case for males. This means that conceptions about body attractiveness should be more highly related to the self-concept of females than of males and that conceptions about body effectiveness should be more highly related to the self-concepts of males than of females. In addition, it may be predicted from Erikson's (1964, 1968) conceptions that females' body concepts and self-concepts should be more highly related to inner-space than to outer-space orientation, while males' body concepts and self-concepts should be more highly related to outer-space than to inner-space orientations. These predicted relations lead directly to the second domain of differences that can be predicted from Erikson's ideas.

Self-Concept and Self-Esteem

Self-concept may be defined as the set of knowledge one maintains about oneself.

Self-esteem is the level of positive or negative evaluation one associates with the self-concept. One person might know himself or herself to be aggressive, intelligent, and calculating—and evaluate all the "traits" in this concept as positive. Thus this person would have a high (positive) self-esteem. On the other hand, another person having an identical self-concept might have negative feelings about the first and the third traits; if this were the case, the person would be said to have lower (negative in this case) self-esteem.

Erikson's ideas have implications for the self-concepts and self-esteems of males and females. First, it is clear that the items or traits that make up the self-concept will show sex differences. Erikson depicts the female as dependent because of her incorporative, interpersonal orientation and as passive because of the nature of her reproductive functioning. Males, in turn, are independent because of their individual orientation and are active because of the nature of their reproductive functioning.

Thus, if she is playing her role appropriately, a female's self-concept should include the traits of dependency and passivity. Moreover, since she is dependent on and passive to a male, she should be characterized as dominated and as conforming to the suggestions of others. Furthermore, because she is oriented to using her body—and thus herself—in ways promoting interpersonal physical attractiveness, she should not focus on effectiveness or mastery endeavors. Thus she should not be task-oriented but rather person-oriented.

A male's self-concept, however, should include the traits of independence, activity, and instrumental effectiveness, if he is playing his intrusive role appropriately. This would mean that he would not be conforming to the suggestions of others, but rather would attempt to assert himself in order to dominate the objects in his world, be they physical objects or people. This effectiveness, dominance, and activity style should lead to aggressive interaction with his physical and social world, and promote a task-mastery orientation rather than a person orientation.

Erikson (1964, 1968) thus predicts that males and females should define themselves differently. However, because the predicted attributes characterizing the male self-concept (e.g., independence, individuality, dominance, assertiveness, aggressiveness, activity, instrumental effectiveness, nonconformity, task orientation) tend to be ones generally judged positively (Block 1973; Broverman et al. 1972), males should have a positive self-esteem. In turn, because the predicted attributes characterizing the female self-concept (e.g., dependence, submission, passivity, instrumental ineffectiveness, conformity) tend to be ones generally judged negatively (Block 1973; Broverman et al. 1972), females should have a negative self-esteem, or certainly one less positive than that of males.

Accordingly, because they think about and regard themselves differently, males and females should not *do* the same things in their societal setting. They should play different roles. The understanding of such role differences is, of course, the central concern of Erikson's ideas about identity. The nature and direction of such role differences make up the third domain of differences that can be predicted on the basis of Erikson's ideas.

Vocational Role Orientation

It is obvious that in the modern world men and women do not always perform the same tasks. They tend to engage in different vocations and thus are oriented to playing different roles in their lives. It is clear what Erikson's views are about the bases of these differences. Since "anatomy is destiny," there are biological reasons seen as *necessarily* fostering role adoption along particular paths. Thus, to Erikson, not only do men and women adopt different vocations but it is biologically adaptive that they show an orientation toward maintaining these vocational role distinctions. If women denied the demands of their inner space, there would be no one to perpetuate and nurture society.

Accordingly, women should be oriented to adopt vocational roles consistent with their inner space. Obviously, the traditionally feminine roles—most notably of wife and mother—are those toward which they should be oriented. Indeed, these roles are traditional because of their survival value for the species (Erikson 1968). However, there are other traditionally feminine roles—endeavors that also have a component of nurturance associated with them—for example, nurse and elementary-school teacher, and Erikson sees women's adoption of these other roles as having societal usefulness.

Moreover, because the commitment to interpersonal attractiveness exists to enhance the woman's chance to fulfill her inner space and thus her reproductive function, no vocational orientations requiring a commitment of effort and time inconsistent with a mothering or a nurturant role would be appropriate. This orientation—coupled with the fact that the body concept of females promotes a self-concept involving passivity and instrumental ineffectiveness, and a negative self-esteem as well—suggests that only lower-status roles would be seen as appropriate for females. Such roles are those typically seen as feminine. Stated differently, roles that are traditionally feminine are also traditionally of lower status in society (O'Leary 1974, 1977).

An alternative vocational role orientation would be expected for males. Because of their orientation toward individual intrusion and effectiveness, males should seek vocations allowing mastery, independence, dominance, and competent control over their world. This vocational role orientation is fostered by their body concepts, their self-concepts, and their self-esteem. These attributes promote an orientation toward competence-effectiveness and/or high-status roles (e.g., those involving power, leadership, prestige), which are of course conventionally those defined as traditional masculine endeavors. Thus, because of their outer-space body orientations, their self-concepts, and their self-esteem, males should be oriented toward adopting vocational roles that are traditionally masculine ones (e.g., those requiring mastery or strength, such as engineer, truck driver, or farmer) and/or those having high status in society (for example, doctor, lawyer, or banker).

In summary, Erickson's theory of sex differences in ego identity and role behaviors leads to distinct predictions about the nature and direction of development in several domains of psychosocial functioning. The rather negative picture he draws of the types of behaviors developed by the female is all the more disconcerting because Erikson sees these sex differences as biologically based. Moreover, because he believes that a biological contribution is innate and hence stereotyped, fixed, and not amenable to basic alteration either by proximal environmental or by more distal historical or societal processes, there is very little one can do to alter the basic character of these sex differences. For example, although the particularities of a culture determine how, for instance, mothering may be expressed and how it may relate to other components of a woman's role, the weak interactional, predetermined epigenetic view that Erikson takes does not allow for a shaping of that biological basis that he presumes innately disposes one to a mothering orientation.

We may turn now to an evaluation of Erikson's ideas, and to a discussion of how well they integrate existing data pertinent to his views. To begin our evaluation, it is useful to discuss first the concept of sex-role stereotypes.

SEX-ROLE STEREOTYPES

Erikson (1964, 1968) describes males' and females' development in stereotypic and traditional ways. In Chapter 3 I defined a social stereotype as an overgeneralized belief— that is, some combination of cognition and feeling, some *attitude*—that invariantly characterizes a stimulus object (for example, a person). A stereotype allows for little exception (Allport 1954). Because of this rigid-

ity, a social stereotype is relatively resistant to change and, as such, may become accepted as always true in a given society. The sex differences that Erikson describes are consistent with traditional social stereotypes regarding males and females in American society. Such stereotypes are widely held in America today.

A *sex role* may be defined as a socially defined set of prescriptions for behavior for people of a particular sex group; *sex-role behavior* may be defined as behavioral functioning in accordance with the prescriptions; and *sex-role stereotypes* are the generalized beliefs that particular behaviors are characteristic of one sex group as opposed to the other (Worell 1978). Broverman et al. (1972) report a series of studies they conducted using a questionnaire that assessed perceptions of "typical masculine and feminine behavior." In order to study sex-role stereotypes, Broverman et al. gave a group of college males and females a long (122-item) list of traits, with each trait presented in a bipolar manner (for example, "not at all aggressive" to "very aggressive"). They conceptualized sex roles as "the degree to which men and women are perceived to possess any particular trait" (Broverman et al. 1972). They found forty-one items for which at least 75 percent agreement existed among males and females as to which end of the bipolar dimension was more descriptive of the average man or the average woman. These were the items they concluded formed the sex-role stereotypes for these students. These items are presented in Table 9.1.

From this table, it can be noted that those item ends associated with males, as judged by *both* males and females, are markedly consistent with the expectations derived from Erikson. For instance, we find males described as very aggressive, very independent, very dominant, very active, very skilled in business, and not at all dependent. These items form what Broverman et al. (1972) term a *competency cluster;* and this is indeed identical to the competency-effectiveness set of behaviors that Erikson predicts to be associated with males.

TABLE 9.1
Stereotypic Sex-Role Items

Competency cluster (masculine pole is more desirable)

Feminine	Masculine
Not at all aggressive	Very aggressive
Not at all independent	Very independent
Very emotional	Not at all emotional
Does not hide emotions at all	Almost always hides emotions
Very subjective	Very objective
Very easily influenced	Not at all easily influenced
Very submissive	Very dominant
Dislikes math and science very much	Likes math and science very much
Very excitable in a minor crisis	Not at all excitable in a minor crisis
Very passive	Very active
Not at all competitive	Very competitive
Very illogical	Very logical
Very home-oriented	Very worldly
Not at all skilled in business	Very skilled in business
Very sneaky	Very direct
Does not know the way of the world	Knows the way of the world
Feelings easily hurt	Feelings not easily hurt
Not at all adventurous	Very adventurous
Has difficulty making decisions	Can make decisions easily
Cries very easily	Never cries
Almost never acts as a leader	Almost always acts as a leader
Not at all self-confident	Very self-confident
Very uncomfortable about being aggressive	Not at all uncomfortable about being aggressive
Not at all ambitious	Very ambitious
Unable to separate feelings from ideas	Easily able to separate feelings from ideas
Very dependent	Not at all dependent
Very conceited about appearance	Never conceited about appearance
Thinks women are always superior to men	Thinks men are always superior to women
Does not talk freely about sex with men	Talks freely about sex with men

Warmth-expressiveness cluster (feminine pole is more desirable)

Feminine	Masculine
Doesn't use harsh language at all	Uses very harsh language
Very talkative	Not at all talkative
Very tactful	Very blunt
Very gentle	Very rough
Very aware of feelings of others	Not at all aware of feelings of others
Very religious	Not at all religious
Very interested in own appearance	Not at all interested in own appearance
Very neat in habits	Very sloppy in habits
Very quiet	Very loud
Very strong need for security	Very little need for security
Enjoys art and literature	Does not enjoy art and literature at all
Easily expresses tender feelings	Does not express tender feelings at all easily

Note: These results are based on the responses of seventy-four college men and eighty college women.
Source: *Adapted from Broverman et al. (1972, 63).*

Moreover, not only are females judged by both males and females to be at the opposite (low) ends of these competency-effectiveness dimensions, but they are also judged to be high on the warmth-expressiveness items. For example, they are seen to be very gentle, to be very aware of the feelings of others, to be very interested in appearance, and to have a very strong need for security.

Moreover, although Table 9.1 shows that for competency items the masculine end of the trait dimension is more desirable, while for the warmth-expressiveness cluster the feminine end is more desirable, we see also that there are more competency items than warmth-expressiveness items. Thus, there are more positively evaluated traits stereotypically associated with males than with females. Broverman et al. (1972) found evidence that these attitudes are quite pervasive in society. They report that their questionnaire has been given to 599 men and 383 women, who varied in age (from seventeen to sixty), education level (from having completed elementary school to an advanced graduate degree), religious orientation, and marital status. Among all the respondents there was considerable consensus about the different characteristics of males and females; the degree of consensus was not dependent on age, sex, religion, educational level, or marital status (Broverman et al. 1972).

In fact, one of the most striking instances of the high consensus regarding sex-role stereotypes was derived from a special sample that the researchers studied. They administered the questionnaire to seventy-nine practicing mental health workers (clinical psychologists, psychiatrists, and psychiatric social workers). Of the forty-six men in this sample, thirty-one had a Ph.D or M.D., while of the thirty-three women studied, eighteen had one of these degrees. The clinical experience in this group ranged from internship to extensive professional practice. These professionals were asked to respond to the questionnaire three times—to describe "a mature, healthy, socially competent adult male"; to give a corresponding

description for an adult woman; and to provide a description for an adult (with no sex specified).

First, it was found that these male and female clinicians did not differ significantly from each other in their descriptions of men, women, and adults, respectively. Second, for each of these three categories there was high agreement about which end of the trait dimension reflected more healthy behavior. Thus these clinicians had a generalized belief about what constituted good mental health. Third, it was found that these clinical judgments regarding mental health were highly consistent with college students' corresponding depictions.

Finally, and most importantly in terms of sex-role stereotypes, these professionals' judgments regarding what constituted the healthy male and the healthy female were consistent with sex-role stereotypes. The desirable "masculine" end of the competency cluster was attributed to the "healthy man" rather than to the "healthy woman" more than 90 percent of the time, while the desirable "feminine" end of the warmth-expressiveness cluster was attributed to the "healthy woman" rather than to the "healthy man" more than 60 percent of the time (Broverman et al. 1972, 70). Thus, if one considers the content of the items attributed by these mental health workers to males and females, respectively:

> Clinicians are suggesting that healthy women differ from healthy men by being more submissive, less independent, less adventurous, less objective, more easily influenced, less aggressive, less competitive, more excitable in minor crises, more emotional, more conceited about their appearance, and having their feelings more easily hurt. (Broverman et al. 1972, 70)

Moreover, the mental health workers' judgments about what constitutes a "healthy adult" and what constitutes a "healthy man" did not differ. However, there was a difference when their view of the healthy adult was compared to their view of the "healthy woman." That is, among both the male and female professionals, the general idea of mental health for a sex-unspecified adult is

> actually applied to men only, while healthy women are perceived as significantly less healthy by adult standards. (Broverman et al. 1972, 71)

Not only is there evidence that sex-role stereotypes are fairly consistent across sex, age, and educational levels within society, but there is also evidence for considerable cross-cultural consistency in sex-role stereotypes. In fact, Block (1973), in a study of six countries (Norway, Sweden, Denmark, Finland, England, and the United States), found not only marked cross-cultural consistency but also empirical verification of the differential emphases on competence-effectiveness and warmth-expressiveness for the two sexes that Erikson predicted to exist and

that Broverman et al. (1972) found people *believed* to exist.

Jeanne H. Block's (1973) term for the type of behaviors we have labeled competence-effectiveness is *agency*. As seen in Tables 9.2 and 9.3, the items she sees as characteristic of agency (for example, assertive, dominating, competitive, and independent) correspond to those in the Broverman et al. (1972) competency cluster. Block's (1973) term for the type of behaviors we label warmth-expressiveness is *communion*. The items she sees as constituting communion (for example, loving, affectionate, sympathetic, and considerate) correspond to those in the Broverman et al. warmth-expressiveness cluster.

Block (1973) had four psychologists classify all these items into either the agency or the communion category. Those items that showed high agreement among the judges

TABLE 9.2

Adjective Attributions Among Students in Six Countries: Items on Which Males Are Stereo-typically Associated

Agency-communion classification	Adjective	Country					
		United States	England	Sweden	Denmark	Finland	Norway
Agency	Practical, shrewd	X	X	X	X	X	X
Agency	Assertive	X	X		X	X	X
Agency	Dominating	X	X			X	X
Agency	Competitive	X	X				
Agency	Critical	X					X
	Self-controlled	X				X	
Agency	Rational, reasonable	X				X	
Agency	Ambitious						
	Feels guilty						X
	Moody		X				
Agency	Self-centered						
	Sense of humor				X		
	Responsible					X	
	Fair, just					X	
Agency	Independent						X
Agency	Adventurous						X

Note: X = significant differences found in number of attributions to males and females.
Source: *Adapted from Block (1973, 518).*

TABLE 9.3
Adjective Attributions Among Students in Six Countries: Items on Which Females Are Stereotypically Associated

Agency-communion classification	Adjective	Country					
		United States	England	Sweden	Denmark	Finland	Norway
Communion	Loving						
	Affectionate	X	X		X	X	X
	Impulsive	X	X	X		X	X
Communion	Sympathetic		X			X	
Communion	Generous			X			X
Agency	Vital, active	X		X			X
	Perceptive, aware						X
Communion	Sensitive	X	X				
	Reserved, shy	X	X				
Communion	Artistic					X	
	Curious						X
	Uncertain, indecisive					X	
	Talkative					X	
Communion	Helpful		X				
	Sense of humor		X				
	Idealistic				X		
	Cheerful						X
Communion	Considerate						X

Note: X = significant difference found in number of attributions to males and females.
Source: *Adapted from Block, (1973, 519).*

are shown by classification in the first column of Tables 9.2 and 9.3. Table 9.2 shows that among the university students in the samples there were sixteen items on which males were more stereotypically associated than were females. In this group, *all* items receiving a classification were agency (competence) ones. Moreover, although there are cross-cultural differences, the implications of which will be discussed below, we see that in at least four of the six cultural groups, both males and females within *and* across cultures agreed that males are higher than females in regard to being practical, shrewd, assertive, dominating, competitive, critical, and self-controlled.

Table 9.3 shows that there were seventeen items on which females were more stereotypically associated than males. Of those eight items receiving a classification by the judges, seven were communion (warmth-expressiveness) ones. Moreover, in at least four of the six cultural groups, males and females within and across cultures agreed that females are higher than males in regard to being loving, affectionate, impulsive, sympathetic, and generous.

In summary, across groups in American society and in comparisons among samples from other societies, there is clear evidence that stereotypes exist that specify that different sets of behaviors are expected from males and females. This evidence shows that the male role is associated with individual effectiveness, independent competence, or agency. On the other hand, the evidence shows that the female role is associated with interpersonal warmth and expressiveness, or communion. Although the existence of these stereotypes means that people believe males and females differ in these ways, the existence of the stereotypes does not necessarily mean that males and females *actually* behave differently along these dimensions. Thus, although people's stereotypic beliefs do correspond to Erikson's theoretical expectations, this correspondence does not necessarily confirm his views, because as noted, stereotypic differences need not correspond to behavioral differences. Moreover, even if a correspondence between the stereotypes and behaviors does exist, this relation would not provide unequivocal support for Erikson's theory. Other processes, unspecified by him, could be involved. Thus, before we evaluate data pertinent to the relations between sex-role stereotypes and sex differences in ego development and role behavior, it will be useful to consider some implications of the character of existing sex-role stereotypes.

Implications of Sex-Role Stereotypes for Socialization

Chapter 3 presented some ideas about the potential role that stereotypes could play in behavioral and social development. On the basis of initial stereotypic appraisals of people categorized in a particular group (for example, adolescents, endomorphs, blacks, women), behavior is channeled in directions consistent with the stereotype. As a consequence, stereotype-consistent behavior often develops. Once this self-fulfilling prophecy is created, behavior maintains the stereotype and a circular function is thus perpetuated. There is evidence that a self-fulfilling-prophecy process is involved in the creation of sex differences in ego development and role behavior.

The socialization experiences of males and females differ in ways consistent with traditional sex-role stereotypes, and hence with the existence of a self-fulfilling-prophecy process. Miller and Swanson (1958) found that a majority of urban Midwestern mothers who were studied channeled the behaviors of their children in accordance with traditional ideas about divisions of labor (e.g., about "women's work" such as dishwashing). In Norway, Brun-Gulbrandsen (1958) found results similar to those of Miller and Swanson (1958) and, in addition, found that mothers put more pressure on girls than on boys to conform to societal norms.

In a series of investigations involving the mothers and fathers of boys and girls ranging in age from early childhood through late adolescence, Block (1973) found further evidence pertaining to stereotype-related differences in the ways males and females are socialized. The parents were asked to describe their child-rearing attitudes and behaviors regarding one of their own children. Block assumed that parents of boys are not (at least beforehand) intrinsically different from parents of girls. Therefore, differences in the way parents socialize males or females should reflect sex-role stereotyping imposed by parents on the children.

In comparing the parents of boys with the parents of girls, Block (1973) reports that the socialization practices for boys across the age range studied reflected an emphasis on achievement, competition, an insistence on control of feelings, and a concern for rule conformity (for example, to parental authority). However, for girls of the age range studied, the socialization emphasis was placed—particularly by their fathers—on developing and maintaining close interpersonal relationships; the girls were encouraged to talk about their problems and were given comfort, reassurance, protection, and support (Block 1973, 517).

Thus there appears to be evidence that parents strive to socialize their children in accordance with sex-role stereotypes. At least the *attempt* by parents to channel behavior, in a manner consistent with a self-fulfilling-prophecy process, is apparent. But before data are reviewed pertaining to whether developing children and adolescents conform to these attempts, one must address the more basic issue of what is the source of behaviors that compose the definition of the role for each sex.

THE ADAPTIVE BASIS OF SEX DIFFERENCES IN ROLES

Why are there traditional, stereotypic sex-role prescriptions, and why does their content exist as it does? To answer these questions it is useful to discuss the adaptive significance of roles. The function of roles is to allow society to maintain and perpetuate itself. Indeed, it may be that the anatomical and physiological constitution of the sexes resulted in the first social roles being differentiated on the basis of sex. Although there is no way to test this idea directly, sex roles—like all other social roles—should have some basis in the functions of people and their society. Accordingly, from this reasoning it follows that sex differences in role behavior arose, at least initially, from the different tasks males and females performed for survival, including reproduction (cf. Fisher 1982a, 1982b; Lovejoy 1981).

Maintaining these sex differences—that is to say, making them traditional—could continue to serve this survival function if the survival demands on people remained the same. However, it is also possible that sex roles could become traditionalized despite a change in the adaptive demands facing society. Indeed, not only is there cross-cultural empirical evidence consistent with these speculations about the basis of sex-role differences, but there is also at least some indirect support for the possibility that sex roles may not be evolving apace with social changes promoting new adaptive demands.

Barry, Bacon, and Child (1957) reviewed anthropological (ethnographic) material that described patterns of socialization in mostly nonliterate cultures. They reported a general trend of greater socialization pressures toward nurturance, responsibility, and obedience for females, and greater socialization pressures toward self-reliance and achievement behaviors for males. In these relatively primitive societies, these different socialization pressures were seen to be associated with the contrasting biological and socioeconomic functions each sex had to assume when adult. Accordingly, as argued by Block (1973), such findings suggest that:

> When hunting or conquest is required for societal survival, the task naturally and physically falls upon the male because of his intrinsically superior physical strength. So, boys more than girls receive training in self-reliance, achievement, and the agentic corollaries. Child-bearing is biologically assigned to women, and because, in marginally surviving societies, men must be out foraging for food, child rearing, with its requirement of continuous responsibility, is assigned to women. Thus, girls more than boys are socialized toward nurturance responsibility, and other qualities of communion. (p. 518)

Cultural-Historical Change and Sex-Role Evolution

In modern countries, the demands of day-to-day life are considerably different than those of primitive, marginally surviving societies. Accordingly, the meaning and function of the traditional sex roles may be different. As Block (1973) states the issue:

> The heritage and functional requiredness of sex typing in early or marginal cultures seem clear. The question for our times, however, is to what extent past socialization requirements must or should control current socialization emphases in our complex, technological, affluent society where, for example, physical strength is no longer especially important and where procreation is under some control. Under present conditions, and for the future, we might ask: What is necessary? What is "natural" in regard to sex typing? (p. 519)

One way of addressing this issue is to reconsider the data on cross-cultural analyses of sex-role stereotypes presented in Tables 9.2 and 9.3. If sex roles do reflect to some extent the requirements placed on men and women in their particular societal settings, then differences in these settings should—to some extent—relate to differences in sex-role prescriptions in the different cultures. Thus, despite the fact that all countries studied by Block (1973) are Western societies, and despite the fact that we have seen general trends in *all* cultures toward agency stereotypes for males and communion stereotypes for females, there are nevertheless differences in the socioeconomic, political, and physical environmental pressures on people in the respective societal settings.

Bakan (1966) found a relationship between socialization pressures for agency (competency-effectiveness) and the presence of a capitalistic social and economic system, which he believed required an intensification of the agency orientation. Consistent with this view, Block (1973) reported that in the two countries in her research that had long and widespread commitments to social welfare—Sweden and Denmark—there were fewer sex differences and less emphasis on agency than in the United States. In fact, Block (1973) found that American males were significantly different from the males of the other countries studied; they placed greater emphasis in their ratings on depictions of the male role as being adventurous, self-confident, assertive, restless, ambitious, self-centered, shrewd, and competitive. Their emphasis on these characteristics reflects their greater orientation to agency.

Moreover, also consistent with Bakan's (1966) idea of a relation between capitalism and agency—and with our more general idea that behaviors associated with the roles of each sex necessarily reflect the sociocultural (for example, economic, political, and environmental) demands placed on people at a particular time in their society's history—are Block's findings regarding the females. Despite being more oriented to communion than to agency, American women nevertheless placed greater emphasis in their ratings on agency terms than did women in the other countries studied (Block 1973). To a significantly greater extent than did the women from the other cultural settings, the American women gave higher ratings to traits such as practical, adventurous, assertive, ambitious, self-centered, shrewd, and self-confident in their responses about a woman's role (Block 1973). These characteristics are also all agency ones.

The United States is the most capitalistic of the countries studied by Block (1973); and if we can assume that this characteristic is an important one differentiating the countries, then the differences between the sex-role stereotypes of males and females in the United States and those of the other countries may be better understood. Thus differences in the behavior expected from males and females in a particular society are understandable on the basis of the sociocultural forces acting on the people over time. Moreover, not only should these different sociocultural-historical pressures influence behavioral expectations but they should also influence child-rearing (socialization) practices. If the adaptive demands placed on people in a society are different, then the socialization of people to meet these demands should be different too.

In support of this idea, Block (1973) reported that students' ratings of parental child-rearing practices differed between the United States sample and those of the five other countries. In the United States, it was found that significantly greater emphasis was placed on early and clear sex typing and on competitive achievement, and less importance was placed on the control of aggression in males (Block 1973).

Thus these differences between American and European child-rearing orientations and sex-role stereotypes show not only that there can be (and are) contrasts among societies (Block 1973)—although they are highly similar, Western ones—but also that these contrasts are related to familial, sociocultural, and historical differences. Moreover, the character of the sex differences in some cultural settings shows that because of its long-term nature, a presumably adaptive narrowing of some of the agency-communion differences found traditionally in other cultural settings (for example, American ones) can occur. This suggests that, insofar as sex-role stereotypes and socialization practices are concerned, humans can overcome the divisions between the sexes that remain as perhaps less than optimal remnants from earlier times (Block 1973).

Conclusions

The above evidence and arguments suggest that a biological theory that stresses that anatomy is destiny is a limited view. Biology certainly does exert pressures on psychosocial development. However, this influence does not occur independently of the demands of the cultural and historical setting. The biological basis of one's psychosocial functioning relates to the adaptive orientation for survival. Hence, although it may be adaptive at some time in a given society to perform roles highly associated with anatomical and physiological differences, these same roles may not be adaptive in other societies or at other times in history. The agency-communion differences that were functional in primitive times may no longer be so in a modern society having greater leisure time, nearly equal opportunity for employment, and almost universal formal education. A similar argument has been advanced by Self (1975).

In fact, Block (1973) shows that at least one measure of more developed psychosocial functioning—the presence of a principled level of moral reasoning—is associated with American college-age males and females who have less traditional sex-role definitions of themselves. In a series of studies by Bem (1974, 1975, 1977), it has been found that among men and women who have an orientation to *both* traditional male and traditional female behaviors, there is evidence for adaptive psychosocial functioning. Bem (1974, 1975) argued that internalization of the culturally stereotypic sex role inhibits the development of a fully adaptive and satisfying behavioral repertoire. Instead, a male or female who identifies with both desirable masculine and desirable feminine characteristics—an *androgynous* person—is not only free from the limitations of stereotypic sex roles but should be able to engage more ef-

Jeanne H. Block

fectively in both traditional male *and* traditional female behaviors across a variety of social situations—presumably because of his or her flexibility—than should a nonandrogynous person (Jones, Chernovetz, and Hansson 1978). Several studies (Bem 1974, 1975, 1977; Spence and Helmreich 1978; Worrel 1978) have provided data validating this general idea.

If one views individual development as reciprocally related to sociocultural change, then one may be led to predict that the current historical context presses males and females to forego the traditional vocational roles, perhaps adaptive in earlier times; instead, today's cohorts of males and females may be encouraged to adopt sex-role orientations showing flexibility and independence from traditional sex-role prescriptions in order to be adaptive in the current social context. Thus anatomy is *not* destiny.

Rather, it is just one component of biology that may be of relevance for the adaptive roles in a particular sociocultural-historical setting (Self 1975).

As such, at any point in history, a person's behavior in his or her cultural setting appears to involve a coordination of the cultural, political, and economic values of one's society—as that society exists in a physical environmental setting that places changing survival demands on the people embedded within it, and in the context of family rearing pressures and psychological (for example, moral) developments.

In sum, this analysis leads to conclusions about the nature and bases of ego development and role behaviors that differ substantially from Erikson's (1964, 1968). We now consider the three major domains of functioning predicted by Erikson to show sex differences, in order to determine whether data directly relevant to these predictions support his views or the alternative ones I have just presented.

BODY ATTITUDES: ATTRACTIVENESS VERSUS EFFECTIVENESS

Predictions derived from Erikson's theory suggest that because females are incorporatively and interpersonally oriented they should be oriented to their inner body space and to seeing their bodies in terms of physical attractiveness rather than physical effectiveness. For instance, there should be a higher relation between inner-space orientation (and/or attractiveness attitudes) and self-concept than between outer-space orientation (and/or effectiveness attitudes) and self-concept. For males the opposite situation should exist. Because of their presumed proneness toward an intrusive and individual orientation, males should stress their outer body space and see their bodies in terms of physical effectiveness rather than physical attractiveness. For instance, there should be a higher relation between outer-

space orientation (and/or effectiveness attitudes) and self-concept than between inner-space orientation (and/or attractiveness attitudes) and self-concept.

Some studies provide data relevant to these predictions. In a group of 118 male and 190 female late-adolescent college students Lerner, Karabenick, and Stuart (1973) found a significant correlation between a measure of body satisfaction and self-esteem for males ($r = +.3$) and for females ($r = +.4$). The two groups did not differ significantly, and thus, for both, the more satisfied an individual was with his or her body, the higher was the self-esteem. However, people can differ about *why* they are satisfied with their bodies. One can be satisfied because one's body is physically attractive and/or because it is physically effective. The study did not question subjects about the bases of their body satisfaction, and it was not directly relevant to a test of the male-female effectiveness-attractiveness predictions.

However, in a study of 70 male and 119 female late-adolescent college students, correlations between a measure of self-esteem and one of how physically attractive one assumed one's body to be showed sex differences consistent with what Erikson would predict (Lerner and Karabenick 1974). The relation between the two scores for females was $r = +.4$, while for males it was $r = +.2$. Thus—more so for females than for males—the more attractive they thought their bodies, the higher their self-esteem.

Data speaking to the converse of this relation—that is, pertaining to the relation between effectiveness and self-esteem for the two sexes—have also been reported (Lerner, Orlos, and Knapp 1976). In addition to self-esteem and attractiveness measures, a measure of how physically effective one assumed one's body to be was included in this study. Using 124 male and 218 female college students as subjects, this study found sex differences that, at least in part, were consistent with the ideas derived from Erikson. The combined (multiple) correlation for *females* between all items involved in the attractiveness ratings and self-esteem was higher (R =

+.52) than was the combined correlation between the effectiveness ratings and self-esteem (R = +.37); with males the combined correlation between the effectiveness ratings and self-esteem was slightly higher (R = +.58) than was the combined correlation between the attractiveness ratings and self-esteem (R = +.50). These data suggest that females' self-esteem is more strongly related to their attitudes about their body's physical attractiveness than its physical effectiveness. However, males' self-esteem appears to be only somewhat more related to their attitudes about body effectiveness than body attractiveness; indeed, these two types of body attitudes may be highly related in males.

Although these findings are consistent with Erikson's ideas, they do not speak to all aspects of his views. All the measures of body attractiveness and effectiveness dealt only with ratings of *external* body parts. That is, in all the above studies subjects were asked to rate such items as face, eyes, or general appearance in terms of each one's attractiveness or effectiveness. As such, the findings may pertain more directly to the outer "world" of the body than to its inner domains; in any event, the findings do not directly show females to be more oriented to their inner space than are males, or that such contrasting orientations relate differentially to the self-esteems of the two sexes.

A test for the presence of this differential relation was involved in a study by Lerner and Brackney (1978). Using 107 female and 72 male college students as subjects, these investigators measured self-esteem and, in addition, assessed the degree of emotion (affect) attached to inner and outer (external) body parts. They asked subjects to rate a list of body parts in terms of how important each was in making them attractive and effective. For Erikson's ideas to find support, females should place more importance on their inner parts than their outer ones, while males should show the reverse.

In addition, if females show greater inner-space orientation, they should also have more knowledge about their inner space than should males. To test this, subjects were also presented with an asexual frontal outline of a human figure and asked to draw and label their internal organs inside the figure. It was found that females rated their outer (external) body parts as more important than did males, and that the sexes did not differ in regard to the importance placed on their internal common parts. However, females did place more importance on sex-specific internal parts than did males on theirs. Furthermore, females showed more knowledge of the parts inside their bodies than did males (e.g., they drew more internal parts than did males).

These data provide only partial support for the idea that females are more inner-space oriented than are males. Although females had more knowledge about their inner bodies than did males about theirs—and although this knowledge was combined with more affect for sex-internal parts—the females did not show more affect than did males for most internal parts. Moreover, they showed more affect than did males for their external body parts, and this finding is counter to males' presumably greater outer-space orientation. Thus it appears that females are just generally more attuned to their bodies—both internal and external—than are males.

However, despite the appropriateness of these interpretations, it may be argued that the crucial issue for testing Erikson's inner-space–outer-space ideas pertains to the level of relation between inner-outer orientation and self-esteem. The relation between self-esteem scores and the affect and knowledge scores did differ for the sexes. But the correlation between a measure of inner body importance on the one hand and self-esteem on the other was *zero for females*. However, *for males* the correlation between the level of importance placed on internal body parts and self-esteem (r = +.3) was significant. Contrary to what would be expected if females had a greater inner-space orientation than males (and if males had a greater outer-space orientation than females), males and *not females* maintained affects about inner space that were positively related to self-esteem.

Together the above studies suggest that the differing orientations to attractiveness and effectiveness shown by adolescents do not exist in relation to a greater inner-space orientation for females and a greater outer-space one for males. Indeed, if any conclusion can be drawn, it is that inner space is more important in the self-esteem of males than of females. Even the greater emphasis on attractiveness for females is uncertain since in two of the above three studies that measured attractiveness (Lerner and Brackney 1978; Lerner, Ortos, and Knapp 1976), the correlation between self-rated physical attractiveness and self-esteem was as high for males as for females.

In essence, then, Erikson's views do not find great support in the above data, and as such, the first prediction drawn from his ideas is not a powerful one. Data relevant to the second prediction are reviewed in the next section.

ROLE BEHAVIOR, SELF-CONCEPT, AND SELF-ESTEEM

Considerable data exist on the quality of the self-esteem of adolescents and on sex differences in self-esteem (Block 1973, 1976; Maccoby and Jacklin 1974; O'Leary 1977). However, important problems in integrating this literature are that researchers often do not distinguish between self-concept and self-esteem; they often define either of these terms in quite different ways, and they use different instruments to measure these constructs (Wylie 1974). Because there is no extensive information about how these different measures of self-esteem and/or self-concept relate to each other, important issues of interpretation are raised. For instance, one often does not know—when a study using a particular measure shows that groups of people (e.g., adolescent males and females) differ in their self-concepts—

whether these differences reflect true differences between the groups, differences due to the fact that a particular measure was used, or some combination of the two. These methodological problems make it difficult to assess unequivocally whether males and females differ in their self-concepts and self-esteem in ways that Erikson predicts.

Moreover, this problem is complicated by a related one. Some data can be found to support the view that (*a*) males' self-concepts are characterized by individual competency, independent effectiveness (that is, agency), and high, positive self-esteem; and (*b*) females' self-concepts are characterized by warmth-expressiveness and dependency-passivity (that is, communion) and a lower, more negative self-esteem than that found in males. However, data can also be found to contradict these views.

For example, the longitudinal study reported by Kagan and Moss (1962), which we shall discuss in greater detail later in this chapter, showed that males' scores relating to aggression and dominance (both agency characteristics) tended to be stable and continuous from the early years of life through young adulthood, but males' scores relating to dependency and passivity (communion characteristics) tended to be unstable and discontinuous. In turn, communion-type characteristics were found to be stable and continuous for females during the age span, whereas agency-related characteristics tended to be unstable and discontinuous (Kagan and Moss 1962). Similarly, in a study of the self-images of over 2,000 children and adolescents in the late 1960s, Rosenberg and Simmons (1975) report that adolescent females have images of themselves that are more people-oriented, while the view adolescent males have of themselves stresses achievement and competence. Indeed, more females than males view their own sex with displeasure, and this is related to females having a more negative self-image than do males (Simmons and Rosenberg 1975). Moreover, cross-sectional data derived from 139 male and 142 female high-school students, reported by Hakstian and Cattell (1975), are consistent with the above data, in that males were shown to be more tough-minded and realistic, while females were seen to be more tender-minded, dependent, and sensitive.

Yet other data are not consistent with these findings. For instance, although as a consequence of their presumably greater dependency and domination by others, females should be more prone than males to conform to group pressures, studies of male and female five- to nineteen-year-olds (Collins and Thomas 1972) and of male and female thirteen- to fourteen-year-olds and eighteen- to twenty-one-year-olds (Landsbaum and Willis 1971) found no difference between the sexes in their incidence of conformity.

Thus the issue is not whether there are absolute, nonoverlapping differences between males and females in regard to the agency and communion behaviors thought to differentiate them. Rather, the issue is the extent of overlap found between the sexes. Further, one must not only determine whether there are *behavioral* differences between the sexes relating to the incidence of agency-related and communion-related behaviors, but one must also see the correspondence between any such differences and self-concept and self-esteem.

Although the methodological problems identified above becloud the certainty of any interpretation, the range of findings existing in the literature shows that Erikson's predictions find some support, but not without exceptions. As such, we shall see that the most important issue for science will become one of trying to learn what particular types of biological, psychological, sociocultural, and historical processes promote what seem to be relatively changeable behaviors in members of each sex.

Differences in Agency-Related and Communion-Related Behaviors

The first issue to address is whether the existing literature indicates that males and females differ in agency-related and communion-related behaviors. If so, to what extent are these differences consistent with

Erikson's views? Literally hundreds of studies may be considered in order to address this issue, and fortunately there have been several attempts to integrate these studies (e.g., Block 1976; Maccoby and Jacklin 1974; O'Leary 1977). One of these (Maccoby and Jacklin 1974) was sufficiently encompassing to serve as a basis for our presentation.

Maccoby and Jacklin (1974) evaluated the results of about 1,600 research reports, published for the most part between 1966 and 1973. They derived these studies from those professional research journals that frequently include information about psychological sex differences, as well as from other sources (such as review chapters and theoretical papers). The studies they reviewed were classified into eight major topical areas (e.g., perceptual abilities, intellectual abilities, and achievement motivation). Moreover, within each of these areas, studies were sorted on the basis of their relevance to particular behaviors or constructs—for example, aggression, dependency, helping, or anxiety. The number of studies dealing with the more than eighty behaviors or constructs evaluated by Maccoby and Jacklin differed from topic to topic, and tables were formed for each of these behaviors or constructs. These tables included information about the authors of the study, the ages and numbers of the people studied, and whether or not statistically significant differences between males and females had been found. Depending on the proportion of studies done on a topic for which significant sex differences occurred, Maccoby and Jacklin drew conclusions about whether sex differences were or were not well established.

However, there are some problems with the conclusions they drew. First, the proportion of findings used to decide whether a sex difference was well established varied for different domains of behavior. In addition, not all studies pertinent to a particular behavior were of the same quality. For example, some studies assessed very small samples. In such cases it is difficult for statistics confidently to confirm a difference between the sexes. At these times it is said that the statistics lack power, and in deciding whether a sex difference was well established, Maccoby and Jacklin (1974) did not consider "how the poor statistical power of certain studies may have influenced adversely the trend of the findings they are attempting to integrate" (Block 1976, 287).

Another problem with Maccoby and Jacklin's conclusions (1974) was an unevenness in the representation of various age groups in the research they reviewed. Seventy-five percent of the studies on which Maccoby and Jacklin based their conclusions involved people twelve years of age or younger, and about 40 percent studied preschool children (Block 1976). Age is important because there is some evidence (Terman and Tyler 1954) that sex differences increase in frequency during adolescence. Thus, Maccoby and Jacklin (1974) may have underestimated the proportion of sex differences that actually exist for a particular behavior by their review of studies of preadolescent samples.

Because of such problems with the conclusions that Maccoby and Jacklin reached, Block (1976) attempted to draw her own conclusions by tallying the number of studies reviewed by Maccoby and Jacklin that pertained to various domains of behavior. In other words, for each of several behaviors, Block took the studies reviewed by Maccoby and Jacklin and calculated the ratio of significant differences favoring one or the other sex in each set of studies. We may here adapt Block's (1976) tallying method and, for each of several behaviors, discuss the percentage of studies in which females were significantly higher, the percentage in which males were significantly higher, and the percentage not showing a significant difference.

In addition, I have classified each of the behaviors I will discuss into either an agency or a communion category, based on the criteria for such behavior presented by Block (1973), Bakan (1966), and Broverman et al. (1972). The behaviors I have classified as communion ones include the following behaviors surveyed by Maccoby and Jacklin (1974): sensitivity to social reinforcement; touch and proximity to parent and resis-

tance to separation from parent; touching and proximity to nonfamily adult; proximity and orientation to friends; positive social behavior toward nonfamily adult; positive social interactions with peers; self-report of liking for others; trust in others; sensitivity to social cues ("empathy"); helping; sharing; cooperation; compliance with adult requests and demands; conformity; compliance with fears; susceptibility to influence; and spontaneous imitation.

The behaviors I have classified as agency ones include the following behaviors surveyed by Maccoby and Jacklin (1974): achievement striving; task persistence and involvement; curiosity and exploration; confidence in task performance; internal locus of control; activity level; aggression; competition; and dominance.

The study of most communion behaviors is not generally associated with sex differences. Indeed, for the 419 comparisons of male and female communion behaviors surveyed by Maccoby and Jacklin (1974), females scored higher than males in 19.8 percent of the cases, males scored higher than females in 13.4 percent of the cases, and the sexes did not differ significantly in more than two-thirds of the cases: 66.8 percent. Indeed, if one considers such communion behavior in relation to studies done at successive age levels, then—for the combinations of behavior by age grouping associated with thirteen of the fifteen communion behaviors—the sum total of the studies showing sex differences was *50 percent or less.* Thus more often than there were sex differences in a communion behavior, there were no such differences when the same behavior was assessed in males and females of the same age levels.

Similarly, most agency behaviors are not generally associated with sex differences. Of the 289 comparisons of male and female agency behaviors surveyed by Maccoby and Jacklin (1974), females scored higher than males in 10.4 percent of the cases, males scored higher than females in 40.1 percent of the cases, and the sexes did not differ significantly 49.5 percent of the time. Moreover, if one considered each agency behavior separately, then with seven of the nine agency behaviors assessed the sum total of studies showing sex differences was 50 percent or less. Specifically, except for fifteen studies of confidence in task performance and ninety-four studies of aggression, a general trend in the 180 (62.3 percent) additional comparisons of agency behaviors surveyed by Maccoby and Jacklin (1974) is that sex differences are much more likely to be absent than they are to be present. That is, of the fifteen comparisons made by Maccoby and Jacklin (1974) regarding confidence in task performance, sex differences favoring males were found in twelve and no comparison found a sex difference favoring females; similarly, of the ninety-four comparisons regarding aggression, fifty-two comparisons showed males scoring higher than females, five comparisons showed females scoring higher than males, and the remaining comparisons showed no sex differences. However, if one considers the remaining agency behaviors, then of the 180 comparisons across these latter behaviors, females scored higher than males in 13.9 percent of the cases, males scored higher in 24.2 percent of the cases, and the two sexes did not differ significantly in the majority of comparisons: 61.7 percent.

Although the data regarding communion and agency behaviors suggest that *when* sex differences are found in communion behaviors, the differences most often "favor" females and, in turn, *when* sex differences are found in agency behaviors, the differences most often favor males, the point is that these differences are *not* seen in most of the studies.

It can be concluded, then, that most studies of either agency or communion behaviors *do not* show that the sexes differ. However, when they do differ, females tend to score higher on communion behaviors—such as dependency, social desirability, compliance, general anxiety, and staying in the proximity of friends (Block 1976)—and males tend to score higher on agency behaviors—such as aggression, confidence in task performance,

dominance, and activity level (Block 1976). Thus only a minority of the studies are consistent with the agency and communion differences in males and females posited by Erikson. As such, researchers must search for those biological-through-historical processes that produce such wide variations (such plasticity) in the presence and quality of communion and agency behaviors in *both* males and females.

In order to best discuss information pertinent to such interactive processes, I now consider data relevant to the question of whether the self-concepts and self-esteem of males and females differ in the ways predicted by Erikson.

Agency and Communion in Self-Concept and Self-Esteem

As with Erikson's predetermined-epigenetic, nature predictions about role differences between males and females, self-concepts should reflect an orientation toward agency for males and toward communion for females. Moreover, because agency is composed of more positively evaluated traits than is communion (Broverman et al. 1972), the self-esteem of males would, from Erikson's perspective, be predicted to be higher (more positive) than those of females. Of course, the interactionist view I favor leads one to expect more plasticity.

Data relevant to self-concept and self-esteem differences are numerous and have also been integrated by Maccoby and Jacklin (1974) and evaluated by Block (1976). However, as noted earlier, major methodological problems are involved with these data (Block 1976; Maccoby and Jacklin 1974; Wylie 1974). In addition to these problems of definition and instrumentation, which we have already discussed, other problems exist that limit the usefulness of the data. Most studies assessing self-concept and/or self-esteem have used the person's own ratings of these constructs as the basis for measurement. Not only are such judgments obviously subjective (and probably considerably biased), but if only self-ratings are used, it is difficult to check the validity of the appraisals. In addition, Broverman et al. (1972) have shown that both males and females share the same sex-role stereotypes and tend to apply these stereotypes to themselves when characterizing their own behaviors. This stereotype-consistent appraisal may bias the self-concept and self-esteem scores in the direction of the predicted agency-communion differences. These methodological problems make it difficult to assess unequivocally whether males and females differ in their self-concepts and self-esteem in the ways that Erikson predicts. Nevertheless, there is *at best* only partial support for self-concept and self-esteem sex differences.

Seven of the eight studies that Maccoby and Jacklin (1974) summarize for levels of strength and potency of the self-concept (i.e., agentic self-concept) showed males scoring higher than females. In the one remaining study, there was no sex difference. Five of these eight studies involved five- to seventeen-year-olds and three involved eighteen-year-olds. Of nine studies of social self-concept (i.e., communion self-concept) done among eight- to seventeen-year-olds and of an additional three studies of social self-concept done with eighteen- to forty-five-year-olds, females scored higher than males on four of the nineteen and on two of the three studies within the two age groupings, respectively. In turn, males scored higher on one of the nine and on one of the three studies within the two age groupings, respectively. However, the more agency-oriented self-concepts of males and the more communion-oriented self-concepts of females do not appear to translate into self-esteem differences between the sexes.

Among those studies reviewed by Maccoby and Jacklin (1974) that looked at self-esteem sex differences, in the majority (61 percent) of the thirty-nine studies the sexes did not differ. Age level did not seem to moderate these results. There were two studies done among three- to four-year-olds, eighteen studies done among six- to twelve-year-olds, one study done among eleven- to seventeen-year-olds, and eighteen studies done among eighteen- to eighty-eight-year-olds.

There were no sex differences reported in the studies done at the first and the third age-level groupings. Females scored higher than males on five and on four of the studies within the second and fourth age-level groupings, respectively; males scored higher than females on two and on four of the studies within these two age-level groupings, respectively. Thus, on the majority of studies within each of these last two groupings, the sexes did not differ.

Although the sexes may differ in regard to the items that they use to define themselves (Maccoby and Jacklin 1974; O'Leary 1977), they do not evaluate the items differentially when applying them to themselves. This means that males and females are likely to have comparable levels of self-esteem. In fact, in a series of studies pertinent to sex differences in self-esteem (Lerner, Karabenick, and Stuart, 1973; Lerner, Orlos, and Knapp 1976; Lerner and Karabenick 1974; Lerner and Brackney 1978), virtually identical levels of self-esteem were found in four independent cohorts of male and female late adolescents.

In summary, it is clear that agency and communion sex differences are not characteristic of most males and females who have been studied and are not necessarily translated into the self-esteems of the sexes in any event. Accordingly, the question we are faced with is: What are the conditions under which such sex differences do occur? Aid in answering this question is derived from a consideration of data relevant to sex differences in vocational role development (and to an evaluation of Erikson's nature predictions).

SEX DIFFERENCES IN VOCATIONAL ROLE DEVELOPMENT

Erikson predicts that males and females should expect and aspire to play roles in society that are traditionally sex-oriented. Such role orientations, it is held, are adaptive (for biological reasons). The data to be reviewed provide both some support for and some refutation of these ideas.

Differences in Vocational Role Behavior

Independent of the expectations and aspirations of males and females or of their implications for adaptive functioning, it is clear that the vocational roles of men and women in today's society are different. For instance, in the data reported in the 1980 U.S. Census, it was found that over 80 percent of the people engaged in the vocations of doctor, lawyer, dentist, truck driver, and farmer were males. Over 80 percent of the people engaged in the vocations of nurse, secretary, librarian, telephone operator, and elementary-school teacher were females.

Moreover, in society the primary role assigned to women is that of wife (O'Leary 1977). In this country, only 5 percent of women never marry, and the average age of becoming a wife is twenty-one years (Spanier and Glick 1979). In addition, the role of wife is associated with that of mother; indeed, most people entering marriage expect to have children. Another reason is that wives who are voluntarily childless are viewed negatively (Veevers 1973) and are often characterized as neurotic or selfish (Bardwick 1971). In fact, Russo (1976) notes that the number of children a woman has is sometimes used as a measure of her success in the mothering role. Although men are expected to marry and be fathers, there are role expectations for them outside of the marital union, and their success in these outside roles is of more import than their success as husbands and fathers (Block 1973; O'Leary 1977).

As suggested by Block (1973), it is not certain that the role-behavior divisions are adaptive, despite their traditionality. There is a higher incidence of mental illness among married women than among single women (O'Leary 1977), and Gove and Tudor (1973) suggest that this difference may reflect the difficulties involved in engaging in traditional female roles which are not highly valued.

Findings by Block (1973) support these ideas. Block notes that the traditional socialization process widens the sex-role definitions and behavior options of men; we have just noted that in addition to being husbands and fathers, men are expected to (successfully) play roles outside marriage. However, the traditional socialization process narrows the sex-role definitions and behavior options of women—wifing and mothering are the major roles some women play. About half the married American women are not employed outside the home (Hoffman, 1985). Thus, in her research about sex differences in ego development, Block (1973) concluded that it is more difficult for women to achieve higher levels of ego functioning because it involves conflict with prevailing cultural norms. As a consequence, few women of the cohort she studied had sex-role definitions that combined agency and communion orientations. Block (1973, 526) concludes that "it was simply too difficult and too lonely to oppose the cultural tide." Yet she notes that some balance of agency and communion was apparently necessary for advanced ego functioning. Highly socialized men had this adaptive status, but because of restricted socialization, highly socialized women did not (Block 1973).

There is some evidence that adaptive behavior is associated with women who do engage in somewhat nontraditional role behavior. Although there are differences found in relation to socioeconomic status (Nye 1974; Shappell, Hall, and Tarrier 1971), employed women have been found to be more satisfied with their lives than are homemakers (Hoffman and Nye 1974). Similarly, Birnbaum (1975) reports that middle-aged career women, whether single or married, had higher self-esteems than homemakers and even felt that they were better mothers. Moreover, Traeldal (1973) found that Norwegian women who were homemakers had stable feelings of life satisfaction across age but that the life satisfaction of women who were employed increased with age.

Contrary to expectations derived from Erikson's notions, then, traditional role behavior does not appear maximally adaptive for either males or females. Rather, the available evidence suggests that combinations of agency and communion behaviors can facilitate psychological and social processes related to ego development and life satisfaction (Block 1973; O'Leary 1974, 1977). However, Block (1973) suggests that most women do not achieve this; instead, they remain oriented toward traditional female vocational patterns.

Sex Differences in Vocational Role Orientation

Most data indicate that men and women remain oriented to traditional sex differences in vocational roles, despite the fact that the complexion of the American work force continues to change (Block 1976). From 1900 to 1978 the percentage of all adult women (aged twenty to sixty-four) who were in the labor force rose from 20 to 58 percent. The percentage of married women who were employed rose from 5.5 percent in 1900 to 48 percent in 1978 (Bureau of Labor Statistics 1978). The percentage of mothers with children under 18 years who were employed rose from 8.6 percent in 1940 to 60.5 percent in 1984 (Hoffman 1985).

The female work force shows uneven representation in relation to educational level and race. In 1977, 62.3 percent of women with college degrees and 71.5 percent of those with at least some graduate work were employed, while only 23 percent of women with eight or less years of education were employed. Black women were more likely than white women to work outside the home, and this difference is maintained across various educational levels (Bureau of Labor Statistics 1978).

Furthermore, since the number of women receiving college degrees and the proportion of women in professional graduate schools are increasing rapidly, the future complexion of the American work force will certainly be altered. In fact, Kreps (1976) estimates that the average woman's work life will be only about ten years shorter than that of the average man.

Despite the continuing changes in the proportion of women in the work force, the vocational role orientations of females—and of males—remain quite traditional. In fact, stereotypes of females as vocationally incompetent, emotional, and unable to handle high-level jobs persist (Huston-Stein and Higgins-Trenk 1978). Indeed, in a review of the literature by Huston-Stein and Higgins-Trenk, it was concluded that most studies show that females accept this stereotyped view of themselves, particularly in vocations that are traditionally "male."

Given the apparent acceptance of these stereotypes by males and females, it *might* be expected that vocational aspirations and expectations will be traditional. Data support this inference.

Looft (1971) asked first- and second-grade males and females to indicate their *personal* vocational role orientations—that is, the vocations that they themselves expected to engage in as adults. The aspirations of both sexes were traditional. Boys commonly named football player and police officer as personal role orientations, while girls often named nurse or teacher. No girl mentioned vocations such as politician, lawyer, or scientist, although these were frequently noted by the boys.

In a comparable study, Bacon and Lerner (1975) interviewed second-, fourth-, and sixth-grade females about their personal vocational role orientation and in addition assessed the females' *societal* vocational role orientation—that is, their conception of the roles in which the sexes could engage in society. At the higher two grade levels, females were more egalitarian (i.e., nontraditional) in their societal responses than were females in the second grade; however, at all grade levels, most females had personal vocational orientations that were traditional. Thus, for most females, there was a self-other discrepancy between the nature of the vocational orientations associated with others (males *and* females) and the nature of the vocational orientation they associated with themselves. Others could have egalitarian vocations, but *they* aspired and expected to be traditional.

Lerner, Vincent, and Benson (1976) retested most of the second- and fourth-graders when they were in the third and fifth grades, respectively, and found this self-other discrepancy still evident. Furthermore, in an independent sample of fourth-, fifth-, and sixth-grade females and males, the self-other discrepancy was confirmed (Lerner, Benson, and Vincent 1976). Both males and females at all grade levels showed similar and high levels of societal egalitarianism, but insofar as personal vocational orientations were concerned, both groups were traditional. Thus males associated themselves with the highly evaluated traditional male roles while associating others with egalitarian possibilities; females had personal associations with the less favorable traditional female roles and associated others (i.e., females) with more favorable egalitarian opportunities.

In my view, however, the fact that the vocational role orientations of both sexes are, at least in part, egalitarian and nontraditional in character is both encouraging—if one favors social equality for the sexes—and, at the same time, a basis for suggesting that the third prediction derived from Erikson's writings is not supported.

Erikson would hold that there should be comparability between personal and societal orientations, since for Erikson this relation would be necessary for biological adaptation. Moreover, there would be difficulty for Erikson's views when attempting to integrate the data about the dually directed personal-societal vocational orientations of both males and females. Also, it would be problematic that there is increasing evidence that some females, especially college-educated ones, are expecting to combine agency-type careers with marriage and family goals (and hence communion) or, in turn, are placing emphasis on the former and not on the latter.

The percentage of college women who obtain graduate degrees, pursue careers, and yet get married has increased in recent years. Furthermore, fewer young women expect to be solely homemakers and mothers. There has been a decrease in recent years in women's involvement in marriage and childbearing. Birthrates reached an all-time low

in the 1970s, while female employment rates reached an all-time high. Only about one in four married women in the eighteen- to twenty-four-year-old age range expects to have three or more children, although the proportion of young married women who desire to remain childless (one in twenty) has not changed much in recent years (U.S. Bureau of the Census 1978c). In addition, it appears that there are the beginnings of some acceptance among males of this revised vocational role orientation among women. Although there are some data to indicate that middle-class males, especially those with high IQs, are the most traditional regarding vocational roles for males and females (Entwisle and Greenberger 1972), other studies show that from 40 to 60 percent of college males would favor an interrupted career pattern for their wives; however, most define this pattern as meaning that wives should not work until children have completed school (Huston-Stein and Higgins-Trenk 1978).

In conclusion, the vocational role predictions of Erikson do not appear very consistent with existing data. Nontraditional vocational role behavior appears to be adaptive for both sexes and seems to involve a combination of agency and communion orientations. Moreover, the vocational role ideologies of males and females involve the perception—at least societally—of equal opportunity for males and females in endeavors traditionally defined as agency or communion. Not only may the self-other discrepancy in the personal vocational orientations of females facilitate social change, but there is also some tentative evidence that at least among people in a college setting, some increasing orientation toward combining agency and communion behaviors is occurring.

Thus, in again rejecting the utility of the Erikson position, we find evidence that complex alterations in the ego development and role behaviors of males and females are occurring and these developments involve changes associated with particular cohorts who are embedded in particular social settings (e.g., college).

INTERACTIVE BASES OF THE DEVELOPMENT OF INDIVIDUALITY

Because of the particular combination of forces acting on a person, the individual character of development stands out. Block (1973, 513) notes that one's characterization of the attributes of the sexes "represents a synthesis of biological and cultural forces." I have noted that variables associated with many processes play a role in the ego development and role behaviors of males and females, and one may conclude that few sex differences must necessarily apply across time, context, and age. Indeed, the major implication of the analysis of this chapter is that such individual differences are dependent on the person's developmental context. One component of this context is composed of phenomena associated with time of testing. In support of this view, Nesselroade and Baltes (1974) report that the main basis of personality changes in the adolescents they studied longitudinally from 1970 to 1972 was the type of social change patterns that made up the adolescents' environmental milieu during their period of assessment.

Perhaps the best example of how the changing social context provides a basis of individual development is derived from a study by Elder (1974), who presented longitudinal data about the development of people who were children and adolescents during the Great Depression in the United States. Elder reports that among a group of eighty-four males and eighty-three females born in 1920 to 1921, characteristics of the historical era produced alterations in the influence of education on achievement, affected later adult health for youths from working-class families suffering deprivation during this era, and enhanced the importance of children in later adult marriages for youths who suffered hardships during the depression.

Other components of a person's context can be the physical and social characteristics of his or her school environment. Simmons,

Rosenberg, and Rosenberg (1973) found that changes in the school context may influence personality. In a study of about 2,000 children and adolescents, they found that in comparison to eight- to eleven-year-old children, early adolescents—and particularly those twelve and thirteen years of age—showed more self-consciousness, greater instability of self-image, and slightly lower self-esteem. However, they discovered that contextual rather than age-associated effects seemed to account for these findings. Upon completion of the sixth grade, one portion of the early-adolescent group had moved to a *new* school—that is, a local junior high school—while the remaining portion of the early adolescents stayed in the same school (which offered seventh- and eighth-grade classes). The group of early adolescents who changed their school setting showed a much greater incidence of the personality changes than did the group that remained in the same school. Thus variables related to the school context seem to influence the personality of young people.

Still another component of a person's context is provided by his or her family setting. Family interaction differences seem to provide a basis of different personality developments. For instance, I noted earlier that Matteson (1974) found that adolescents with low self-esteem viewed communication with their parents as less facilitative than did adolescents with high self-esteem. Moreover, parents of low-self-esteem adolescents perceived their communication with spouses as less facilitative and rated their marriages as less satisfactory than did parents of high-self-esteem youths. Similarly, Scheck, Emerick, and El-Assal (1974) found that feelings of internal (personal) control over one's life, as opposed to believing that fate or luck was in control, were associated with adolescent males who perceived parental support for their actions. Furthermore, interactive differences associated with different types of families promote individual differences in personality development. Similarly, we have noted that Long, Henderson, and Platt (1973) found that among eleven- to thirteen-year-old Israeli children of both sexes, rearing in a kibbutz, as compared to more traditional familial rearing situations, was associated with higher self-esteem and social interaction among both sexes.

The cultural context can also be influential. Evidence suggests that development in different cultures is differentially related to the presence of sex differences. For instance, Offer and his colleagues (Offer and Howard 1972; Offer, Ostrov, and Howard 1977) report variation in sex differences from culture to culture. For example, the differences between the sexes in the United States are not as great as they are in Israeli and Irish cultural settings. However, there seem to be no differences between the types of sex differences found in American and Australian adolescent samples (Offer and Howard 1972).

In sum, it is my view that the nature of individual differences between the sexes is dependent on interactions among biological, psychological, sociocultural, and historical influences. In other words, I stress the implications of all aspects of the person's context in attempts to understand his or her individual development.

Some Concluding Comments

We have seen that Erikson describes eight stages in the psychosocial development of human beings, and within each of these eight stages, Erikson conceives of an emotional crisis, conceptualized in differential [text cut off]. That is, while each of the stages may [be] thought of as a separate status attribute, each concomitant emotional crisis is conceptualized as a bipolar trait dimension. A person develops a feeling within each stage that lies somewhere between the end points of each feeling dimension. Thus each of these bipolar dimensions may be thought of as representing a behavioral attribute. In turn, since a person may develop a feeling at any particular location along each of these continua, a person's individual psychosocial developmental pattern may be represented as his or her location in this multidimensional feeling-space. Table 9.4 presents the eight psychosocial stages in Erikson's theory, along with the bipolar emotional crisis associated with each stage.

In sum, then, Erikson uses differential concepts to theoretically conceptualize people's psychosocial development. He uses his stages as analogous to status attributes, and in addition he specifies theoretically the existence of differentially conceptualized emotional crises within these stages. Thus, through our presentation of Erikson's theory, we have seen how a differential approach to the understanding of psychosocial development may be employed within what is primarily a theoretical framework. Erikson uses differential concepts to best depict what he considers to be the theoretically important components of psychosocial devel-

TABLE 9.4
Erikson's Theory of Psychosocial Development

Psychosocial stage	Bipolar emotional crisis		
	A sense of	versus	A sense of
1. Oral-sensory	basic trust		mistrust
2. Anal-musculature	autonomy		shame, doubt
3. Genital-locomotor	initiative		guilt
4. Latency	industry		inferiority
5. Puberty and adolescence	identity		role confusion
6. Young adulthood	intimacy		isolation
7. Adulthood	generativity		stagnation
8. Maturity	ego integrity		despair

/ould take issue with ,pecific formulations— ,scussions in Chapters 2 ,babilistic-epigenetic po- .re-nurture controversy— preceding research reviews ,c to support the ideas de- riveu , ,son's (1959) essentially pre- determineu igenetic theory (and instead seem consistent with ideas associated with the probabilistic-epigenetic view)—Erikson's theory is still important. It represents a unique integration of stage and differential conceptualizations of human development within a theory that attempts to describe aspects of development across the entire life span.

I have said, however, that the differential approach may also be utilized as a primarily empirical mode of investigating the phenomena of psychological development. Thus one may employ research methods that allow people who possess different status attributes to be differentiated into subgroups on the basis of studied behavior attributes. Hence the use of such methods will allow one to make an empirical determination of the developmental interrelation of status and behavioral attributes. Although numerous examples exist of such an empirical use of the differential approach, we will now consider one of the major examples of such work, the longitudinal study by Kagan and Moss (1962).

THE KAGAN AND MOSS STUDY OF BIRTH TO MATURITY

In their 1962 book, *Birth to Maturity*, Jerome Kagan and Howard Moss report the results of a longitudinal study of psychological development. As noted already at several points in our discussion, a *longitudinal study* involves the study of the same group of people over the course of their development. Through such repeated measurement the researcher obtains data allowing an assessment of the continuity-discontinuity

and/or the stability-instability of the developing behaviors being studied. Accordingly, studies that have a long duration (like those of Kagan and Moss) are suited for studying these issues.

However, longitudinal studies are difficult to do, and they usually have important limitations. As I shall discuss in greater detail in Chapter 12, it is difficult to obtain a large group of people who are willing to submit to repeated, and often intensive, psychological investigation. Accordingly, longitudinal samples are usually comprised of a small number of people, and these people can be presumed to be different from other people in important ways. After all, these people are willing to take part in a long-term psychological investigation of their own lives. Thus longitudinal samples may not be representative of any larger population. This makes results from such a study difficult to generalize to other groups of people. In addition, longitudinal studies are expensive, both in terms of money needed to pay for ongoing research costs and because of the great deal of time it obviously takes to do such studies. As the years go by, some subjects may drop out (possibly making the sample even more unrepresentative), or in one way or another the researchers themselves may drop out of the study. In addition, repeated measurements with the same subjects may allow practice to affect responses. Yet, despite these limitations, longitudinal studies seem suited for assessing the continuity-discontinuity and/or the stability-instability of selected behaviors. Indeed, longitudinal assessment is the *only* means by which we can study intraindividual change.

The expense, difficulty, and requisite commitment involved in longitudinal research allows one to recognize why major longitudinal studies of psychological development are few and far between. Our consideration of the Kagan and Moss study allows us to focus on one of the most important major longitudinal studies of psychological development. Let us now turn to a consideration of the methods that Kagan and Moss used to assess the development of various psychological phenomena from birth to maturity.

The Methods of the Kagan and Moss Study

Kagan and Moss present a summary of the results of a longitudinal study of personality development that began in 1929 and continued through the late 1950s. Because Kagan and Moss believed that "only systematic longitudinal observations can discover those behaviors that are marked for future use and those that will be lost along the way" (1962, 1), they employed longitudinal observations to assess personality development. Thus children enrolled in the Fels Research Institute's longitudinal population during the years between 1929 and 1939 were selected for such repeated observations. In this way eighty-nine children (forty-four boys and forty-five girls) were selected for study. Subjects were mainly from the Midwest, Protestant, white, of middle-class backgrounds, and the children of relatively well-educated parents. In other words, among the differential status variables that Kagan and Moss considered were, of course, age and sex; in addition, religion, socioeconomic status, and parents' educational backgrounds were also considered.

Obviously, not everyone who develops has the above status characteristics. Thus we see that one limitation of the Kagan and Moss longitudinal study is that the sample is not representative of broader populations. Accordingly, while we may be unsure about the extent to which we may generalize the specific results of the Kagan and Moss study, we may at least expect the findings to provide us with some interesting (if tentative) suggestions about the general course of personality/behavioral development. For instance, the biased samples inevitably involved in longitudinal studies may limit generalizations about mean levels of behavior, but they may not be similarly restrictive in regard to learning about basic processes and/or the structure of developmental changes.

Sources of data

The major purpose of the Kagan and Moss study was to discover the interrelation of selected status variables (primarily age and sex) and various behavioral dimensions. Through such an interrelation an indication of the relation between psychological development in childhood and adult psychological functioning might be discovered. Accordingly, information about the subjects was gathered in a manner allowing the information to be divided into two broad age periods.

The initial information about the children pertained to their development from birth through early adolescence. The children were administered various intelligence and personality tests, and these assessments were combined with observations of them in their homes, their nurseries, and later, their schools and day camps. In addition, assessments of the children's mothers were made and teacher interviews were conducted. Through these procedures, data allowing for the measurement of many different variables across the first fourteen years of life were obtained. Each variable was conceptualized as representing a differential (behavioral) dimension, with end points lying at 1 and 7. For example, for the variable "dependency," a score of 7 might indicate high dependency and a score of 1 might indicate low dependency, and a person's score could fall anywhere along this dimension.

Before interrelation between these attributes began, the status variable of age was further reconceptualized. Instead of differentiating their subjects continuously—that is, into fourteen consecutive age groups, one year to the next—Kagan and Moss reduced the first fourteen years of data into four consecutive and overlapping age periods: birth to three years (infancy and early childhood); three to six years (preschool); six to ten years (early school years); and ten to fourteen years (preadolescent and early adolescent years). In sum, for the first fourteen years of their subjects' lives, status variables such as age period and sex were interrelated with several psychological variables, each conceptualized as seven-point behavioral attribute dimensions.

Of the eighty-nine subjects studied in their first fourteen years of life, seventy-one participated in the second phase of data gathering. When they returned, from about mid-1957 through late 1959, they were between nineteen and twenty-nine years of age. Thus, a final age period—adulthood—was now introduced into the study. Again, these subjects had to be tested and measured to ascertain their locations along the various psychological dimensions under study.

Kagan and Moss now had a considerable amount of data bearing on the psychological development and later adult functioning of a group of people, a group whose development from birth to maturity had been longitudinally studied. They now began the arduous process of interrelating these measurements in their attempt to discover how these people were differentiated into various subgroups over the course of their development. They began to analyze their information in order to discover how development in the first fourteen years of life (the first four age periods) related to the psychological functioning of the adult.

Did behaviors seen early in life remain present throughout the remaining childhood years, and further, did early behavior relate in any way to the psychology of the developed adult? How did one's multidimensional location throughout childhood relate to one's multidimensional location as an adult? Let us now turn to the results of the Kagan and Moss study to see how the information they obtained answered such questions.

The Status Variables of Age Period and Sex

Perhaps the most consistent finding obtained by Kagan and Moss was that many of the childhood behaviors shown in the third age period (the early school years, from six to ten years of age) were fairly good predictors of similar early-adulthood behaviors (Kagan and Moss 1962, 266). Similarly, a few behaviors seen in the second age period (the preschool years, from three to six years of age) were also related to theoretically similar adult behaviors. Thus such adult behaviors as dependency (on the family) or anxiety (in social interactions) seemed to be related to analogous behavior/personality characteristics in these early or middle-childhood periods. In this way Kagan and Moss found that knowledge of a child's position on a given variable at a particular age period in the child's life allowed one to make at least some predictions about that child's related adult functioning. In other words, the person's position along some dimensions seemed to remain stable, and in turn, because these same variables seemed to characterize the person at these different age periods in his or her life, at least some continuity of personality development seemed to exist. Accordingly, Kagan and Moss conclude that such findings offer support to "the popular notion that aspects of adult personality begin to take form during early childhood" (1962, 266–67).

Despite such overall continuity in personality development, however, an important qualification must be made. Despite the fact that changes in the status variable of age period were often associated with continuity in the expression of various behavior/personality attributes, another status variable—sex—affected this relation. Kagan and Moss found that age-period continuity in various behavioral characteristics was essentially dependent upon whether or not that behavior was consistent with traditional sex-role standards. For example, degrees of childhood passivity and childhood dependency remained continuous for adult women but were not similarly continuous for adult men. Kagan and Moss argue that traditional sex-role standards in our culture place negative sanctions on passive and dependent behaviors among males. As we have seen earlier in this chapter, studies of stereotypes about the ideal masculine figure in our society find that the most positively evaluated male figure is one who is viewed as dominant, aggressive, and instrumentally effective (e.g., Broverman et al. 1972). Men who do not display such characteristics are negatively evaluated (Lerner and Korn 1972). Kagan and Moss believe, however, that no corresponding negative sanctions about such behaviors exist for women in our society. Thus the authors found continuity between childhood passivity and dependency and adult passivity and dependency for females. A similar relation for males was not found.

On the other hand, through an analogous argument we might expect aggressive, angry, and sexual behaviors to be continuous for males but not continuous for females. In fact, such a finding was obtained. For example, "Childhood rage reactions and frequent dating during preadolescence predicted adult aggressiveness and sexual predispositions, respectively, for men but not for women" (Kagan and Moss 1962, 268).

Of course, certain behaviors could be expected to remain similarly continuous for both sexes. Intellectually oriented behaviors (e.g., attempting to master schoolwork) and sex-appropriate interest behaviors (e.g., fishing for males, knitting for females) are consistent with traditional sex-role standards for either sex. Society approves such behaviors among members of both sexes. Accordingly, Kagan and Moss found that such behaviors showed a marked degree of continuity for both sexes from their early school years through their early adulthood.

In sum, Kagan and Moss found overall age continuity for at least some personality/behavior characteristics. For many of these characteristics one could predict the adult's type of functioning through knowledge of his or her functioning in respect to conceptually consistent childhood variables. Yet whether or not such overall continuity was found depended on whether a particular behavior was consistent with traditional societal sex-role standards. Those behaviors that were consistent with sex-role standards remained continuous; for those that were not, discontinuity was seen. Kagan and Moss summarize this portion of their results by stating:

> It appears that when a childhood behavior is congruent with traditional sex-role characteristics, it is likely to be predictive of phenotypically similar behaviors in adulthood. When it conflicts with sex-role standards, the relevant motive is more likely to find expression in theoretically consistent substitute behaviors that are socially more acceptable than the original response. In sum, the individual's desire to mold his overt behavior in concordance with the culture's definition of sex-appropriate responses is a major determinant of the patterns of continuity and discontinuity in his development. (1962, 269)

The Sleeper Effect

The above results present an important illustration of the potential empirical outcomes derived from longitudinal application of the differential approach. However, this technique provides the opportunity for finding other types of results. For instance, it may be the case that an important event occurs early in a person's life. The event will provide a cause for some of the person's behaviors but this effect may not be seen right away. Simply, "there may be a lag between a cause and open manifestation of the effect" (Kagan and Moss 1962, 277). In other words, one may see a *sleeper effect* in development.

The Kagan and Moss method was well suited for the discovery of such sleeper effects. Through their repeated measurements of the same people over the course of their development, Kagan and Moss could ascertain if a behavior or event measured early in a person's life, while not showing effects at middle periods, was highly related to similar behavior found in later adult life.

Three instances of a sleeper effect in development occurred in the Kagan and Moss study. First, among males, passivity and fear of bodily harm measured in the first age period (zero to three years) were found to be better predictors of a conceptually similar adult behavior (e.g., love-object dependency) than were other measurements of the childhood behaviors. Thus, males who were passive and feared bodily harm in their first three years of life (and thus may be surmised to have been dependent on their mothers for support and protection) were found to be similarly dependent on their love objects (e.g., their wives) when they reached adulthood. Yet measurements of passivity and fear of bodily harm in the other three childhood/adolescent age periods did not predict adult male dependency.

Although one may attempt to account for this finding through reference to possible problems in the measurement of dependency (perhaps the measures used during the intervening periods were not sensitive enough to measure dependency adequately), one may also speculate that this sleeper effect is an instance of qualitative continuity and quantitative discontinuity. For some males there was an abrupt change in their measured dependency-related behaviors between the first age period and the next three, and in turn between these three periods and the adult period. These two abrupt changes represent quantitative discontinuity. Yet—because the first-period behavior measurements *were* predictive of adult behavior measurements, and because these two sets of measurements seem to be reflective of analogous behavioral tendencies—one may say that the same underlying personality characteristic was expressed in these two measurements. Thus one may interpret the relation between the two widely separated age periods as being reflective of qualitative continuity and speculate that perhaps factors related to differential social situations can account for this complex finding.

Perhaps quantitative discontinuity was seen because the dependency-related behaviors measured in the first period and in adulthood were measures of the male in relation to a female (mother and wife, respectively), while the measures of dependency-related behaviors in the intervening three age periods were measures of the male in relation to his peers (presumably mostly other males). Since we know that such dependency-related behaviors are negatively sanctioned for males, it may be the case that although the personality characteristic remained present, it was not manifested in the later-childhood/adolescent age periods because these periods presumably involved major interaction with males and not females. Admittedly, this is speculation, but the point is that the discovery of sleeper effects in development, through the application of longitudinal differential methodology, provides rich bases for future research.

A similarly interesting sleeper effect was also found with females, when certain measures of the mother's behavior toward the child during the first three years of the child's life were related to various aspects of the child's own adolescent and adult functioning. If mothers had critical attitudes toward their daughters during the first age period (zero to three years), this was highly predictive of adult achievement behavior on the part of the daughter. However, a similar attitude in the middle three age periods was not related to such adult female behavior. Similarly, maternal protection of the female child during the child's first three years of life was related to a conceptually consistent adult female behavior on the part of the daughter (e.g., withdrawal from stress), while similar maternal behaviors during the child's later age periods were not related to these adult female behaviors. Thus through these findings we see that Kagan and Moss were able to discover events and/or behaviors that occurred early in a child's life that—while not relating to similar behaviors in immediately succeeding age periods—did relate highly to later, adult functioning.

Some Concluding Comments

We see, then, that the application of a longitudinal differential approach allowed Kagan and Moss to discern some important ways in which people may become differentiated into subgroups over the course of their development. Although their specific results are certainly provocative, as noted above, they are difficult to generalize to broader populations of people. Yet their method and findings do suggest the importance of employing a longitudinal strategy if one wants to discover the continuities and the discontinuities in a child's development. A cross-sectional approach might not have been able to uncover the fact that sex-appropriate behaviors in a child seem to be destined for continuity, while sex-inappropriate behaviors seem to be discontinuous. Moreover, a cross-sectional approach certainly would not have been able to discover the sleeper effects involved in particular children's development. Since a cross-sectional study assesses different children at different ages, it would not have been possible, for example, to discover that if a female had a protective mother in her first three years of life, she would show withdrawal from stress as an adult. Still, despite the wealth of empirical findings that are possible from longitudinal differential studies, such studies do have their limitations. We have seen some of these in earlier discussions in this chapter, and we will have reason to refer to these points again in Chapter 12.

10 | *The Ipsative Approach*

In this chapter we turn to a consideration of the last of the three approaches to the study of human development described in Chapter 7. We learned there that the ipsative approach to developmental psychology assesses intraindividual consistencies and changes in the attribute repertoire and the attribute interrelation of a person over the course of development. As opposed to the relatively more nomothetically oriented stage and differential approaches, the ipsative approach is relatively more idiographic in orientation. That is, it seeks to understand the laws that govern an individual's behavior; it attempts to formulate highly specific generalizations, those potentially applicable to the development of a single individual.

However, in seeking to understand the variables involved in an individual's development, those taking an ipsative point of view are not necessarily formulating specific laws of development applicable only to that given person (Block 1971). Rather, they stress that an understanding of the individual is a necessary basis for any more general understanding. Although developmental psychology must be concerned with ascertaining nomothetic, or group, laws as well as idiographic laws, those taking this point of view suggest that the science would suffer if the former were emphasized to the exclusion of the latter. As pointed out in Chapter 7, general laws of development may not apply equally (or at all) to all the individuals in a group. Hence one must also understand intraindividual laws if one wants to get a full account of development. In other words, one must understand the contributions that an organism's own individuality makes toward its own development in order to comprehend development more fully.

We see, then, that a basic, necessary orientation of the ipsative approach is an assessment of the role of the organism's own characteristics in its own development. An organism's lawful, systematic characteristics of individuality provide an important source of that organism's own development. This is a key reason why those taking an ipsative point of view seek to assess an individual's attribute repertoire and the concomitant interrelation of this repertoire over the course of the individual's development. From this perspective, ipsatively oriented developmentalists follow an organismic developmental point of view in focusing on how the organism itself contributes to its own development. While not necessarily denying the validity of other approaches to the study of psychological development (e.g., the stage approach), the ipsative approach suggests that these other orientations are incomplete because they do not pay sufficient attention to the organism's lawful (and potentially unique) characteristics of individuality and the contributions of this individuality to the organism's own development.

It may be concluded then, that the ipsative approach shares with other organismically oriented positions, such as those of Schneirla (1957), the idea that the organism's own characteristics play an active role in its own development. Yet, despite the similarities between the ipsative approach and other organismically oriented positions, little systematic developmental research has been conducted from an essentially ipsative point of view. (Some of the reasons for this have been suggested in Chapter 7.) However, we may discuss two major, longitudinal studies of development that involve research from the ipsative point of view. One study, the New York Longitudinal Study, has been conducted by Alexander Thomas and Stella Chess, and their collaborators Herbert Birch, Margaret Hertzig, and Sam Korn. A second study, conducted by Jack Block, involves reanalyses of two longitudinal data sets derived from research conducted at the Institute of Human Development at the University of California, Berkeley. These two studies represent the best examples of ipsative research about psychological development in the literature, and they have especially important theoretical and practical implications. As such, the rest of this chapter will review their features and implications.

This review will serve several purposes. First, it will give us some knowledge and appreciation of how major studies of psychological development are initially conceptualized. Second, it will illustrate how developmental psychologists move from conceiving of a study to implementing it. Third, it will illustrate the problems very often encountered in developmental research and some ways in which developmental psychologists seek to address these problems. Fourth, our analysis will allow us not only to appreciate two major ipsative studies of development but, further, to make some more general statements about conceptions of the role of organismic individuality in development. Let us begin our discussion with a review of the research and theory associated with the New York Longitudinal Study.

THE THOMAS AND CHESS NEW YORK LONGITUDINAL STUDY

The New York Longitudinal Study (NYLS) began in 1956 in New York City and continues through this writing. The major sample in the study involves a longitudinal assessment of a relatively large (i.e., for a longitudinal study) group of children (i.e., 133 males and females) from their first days of life onward. Although, of course, it is essential for us to understand the methods, findings, and implications of this study, we must first focus on the theoretical issues that led to the study. Only by beginning here can we understand the rationale for the entire NYLS and thus see why the study took the form that it did.

Why Are Children Different?

Any developmental psychologist would of course admit that children are different. We have seen, for example, that both stage and differential approaches to the study of child development incorporate concepts of individuality into their respective systems. Thus any debate about developmental individuality does not focus on whether or not children are different. Rather, it concerns either

Alexander Thomas

Stella Chess

vironmental influence. Those taking an environmentalist position (e.g., Bijou and Baer 1961) have stressed stimulus-response relationships, acquired through the empirical laws of conditioning. In its extreme, this position views people as malleable balls of clay. Where the genetically oriented preformationists stress that a person enters the world as an already formed ball, the environmentalists opposingly argue that the person enters the world with little but the potential to be completely shaped by stimulus-response relations. Thus the environmentalists suggest that instead of different genetic inheritances being the source of individuality, different—although lawfully identical—stimulus-response relations provide the source of individuality.

Furthermore, we have seen that such organismic individuality may have profound influences on the organism's own development. We have seen that Schneirla (1957), in describing a "third source" of development,

Herbert G. Birch

the ways in which children differ (e.g., stage theorists say children may differ in their rates and final levels of development, while differential psychologists conceptualize individuality as one's location in multidimensional space) or the sources of differences. In other words, people may recognize all children as having individualistic characteristics, yet they may debate about from where these differences derive.

If such a debate seems reminiscent of the controversy surrounding the nature-nurture issue dealt with in Chapters 3, 4, and 5, this is because nature-nurture is precisely the issue involved in such debate. Arguments about the source of behavioral individuality have traditionally involved either a *preformationist* viewpoint or an environmentalist viewpoint. Those taking a preformationist view (e.g., Sheldon 1940, 1942) have essentially stressed inborn sources of individuality, which are thought to be largely genetic in origin and apparently unavailable to en-

Margaret Hertzig

Sam J. Korn

has indicated that an organism's characteristics of individuality, arising out of its unique maturational-experiential interaction, stimulate differential reactions on the part of the other organisms in the organism's environment. These differential reactions then feed back to the organism, providing a further source of the organism's experience and thus contributing to the organism's development.

Because Thomas et al. (1963, 1968, 1970) subscribed to this organismic interactionist view, they rejected both the preformationist and the environmentalist views of behavioral individuality. Rather, they conceptualized the source of a child's characteristics of individuality as being the interaction between the organism's intrinsic and extrinsic factors; further, because of the theoretical implications of this interactionist points of view, they sought to ascertain the role that such behavioral individuality plays in contributing to a child's development. Thus, the Thomas et al. (1963, 1) study was "concerned with identifying characteristics of individuality in behavior during the first months of life and with exploring the degree to which these characteristics are persistent

and influence the development of later psychological organization."

Because of this theoretical point of view, Thomas et al. felt it necessary to focus on intraindividual consistencies and changes in the characteristics of a child over the course of development. Such an ipsative analysis would yield, they believed, information regarding the contribution that such behavioral individuality makes to the child's own development. In other words, such an assessment of the contributions and implications of a child's individually different *style of behavioral reactivity*—the child's style of responding or reacting to the world—might supply important information bearing on unanswered but crucial problems of child development.

Implications of the Thomas et al. Theoretical Position

I have developed the general theoretical stance of Thomas et al. through addressing the question, Why are children individually different? An exploration and empirical assessment of this point of view would seem to have important theoretical implications. That is, if the Thomas et al. view of the source and the implications of behavioral individuality is correct, some revisions in our thinking about both preformationist and environmentalist views would be warranted. In addition, the approach and findings of Thomas et al. (1963) might have implications for other controversies in child-development study. For instance, as Thomas and Chess (1970) have suggested, an approach such as theirs might provide answers about such important developmental questions as:

> Why do youngsters exposed to the same kind of parental influences so often show markedly different directions of personality and development? ... Why do some parents who show no evidence of any significant psychiatric disturbances and who provide a good home for their children sometimes have a child with serious psychological disturbances? Why do the rules for childcare in feeding, weaning, toilet training and so on never seem to work equally well for all children, even when applied by intelligent and conscientious mothers? (p. 531)

Clearly, we see the theoretical suggestion that some portion of the answers to these questions must lie in the fact that children have important characteristics of individuality. These individual differences serve to promote two things. First, different children will have different reactions to the same environmental stimulus situation. The probabilistic epigenetic interactionist viewpoint suggests that as a result of an organism's unique maturation-experience interaction, the organism will develop its own characteristics of individuality; this means that though an identical stimulus may impinge on two different children, the resulting reaction may not be the same. For example, one child might react intensely to a loud noise, while another may hardly react at all. Thus, because of such individual differences in a child's style of reactivity, what might be a part of the *effective stimulus environment* for one child—that is, a stimulus in the child's environment that evokes a reaction—may not be part of the effective environment for another.

Second, because the same environmental event (e.g., a particular parental child-rearing practice) will have different effectiveness for different children, such differential reactivity characteristics will differently influence others in the child's environment. Because different children may be expected to interact differently, each individual child will influence even similarly acting parents in different ways. The child who reacts intensely to even the slightest noise will certainly evoke parental responses different from those that would be evoked by a child who showed hardly any response at all to noise. Thus one's characteristic style of reactivity to the world will differentially influence and stimulate other people in one's world. The reactions from these other people will, in turn, provide a further component of the child's stimulus-world. Since such experiences play an integral role in affecting the child's further development, we see that here, too, the child's style of reactivity plays an active contributory role in the child's own development.

To represent a child's style of reactivity, Thomas and Chess (1977) use the term *temperament,* by which they mean only the person's style of behavior—*how* he or she does whatever is done. When studying personality one may focus on *what* people do (the content of the behavioral repertoire), or *why* they do it (the motivation underlying components of the behavioral repertoire), or on *how* they do it. As we have just noted, it is this last component of personality that Thomas and Chess (1977) study and label as temperament. To illustrate, because all people engage in eating, sleeping, and toileting behaviors, the absence or presence of such contents of the behavior repertoire would not differentiate among them. But whether these behaviors occur with regularity (i.e., rhythmically), or with much or little intensity, might serve to differentiate among people.

Although the New York Longitudinal Study was initiated just as a study of temperamental individuality, like other major longitudinal studies it has become an extremely rich and diverse data set. Thus the data on temperament are embedded in a wealth of other longitudinal data pertinent to, for example, other personality variables (e.g., anxiety, adjustment, self-image), cognitive development and academic achievement, family structure and function and parent-child relations, the development of clinical symptoms, peer relationships, the development of sexuality, drug use and abuse, vocational interests and career development, and health and physical development. Moreover, these data were obtained through the use of several different methodological strategies—for example, parental interviews, subject interviews, home observations, school observations, teacher interviews, and standardized personality and cognitive tests.

Accordingly, with a data base as rich and complex as the New York Longitudinal Study, we can do no more than provide an overview of the methodological and substantive features of the study, especially since this data set extends over a quarter-century of people's lives and is still an active investigation. That is, at this writing the subjects are still being followed. Accordingly, in order to discuss the uses of the data found in this study, we must consider how Thomas et al. (1963) translated their theoretical concerns about organism individuality and about temperament into a longitudinal research investigation.

From Theory to Research

Given the basic theoretical rationale for the Thomas et al. study, we may see that the investigation holds the promise of providing data bearing not only on the accuracy of the probabilistic epigenetic interactionist position but on important empirical and practical concerns of child development as well. Moreover, in light of the theoretical rationale of the study, the use of the focus on a child's characteristics of temperamental individuality should be evident. If the contributions of a child's temperamental individuality are to be found consistent with the study's theoretical rationale, then Thomas et al. will have to demonstrate not only

that such behavioral style may play a role in the child's behavior at a given point in life, but also that such individuality continues to contribute to the child's functioning over the course of development.

Accordingly, in order to translate their theoretical ideas into empirical facts, Thomas et al. will have to do several things.

First, of course, they must have some idea how to measure individual characteristics of temperament. They must know exactly what behaviors or aspects of behavior constitute such behavioral style and how to measure these behaviors in children as they develop.

Second, they must be able to find out the extent to which children's individual temperament styles remain individually different or are similar at various points in their development.

Third, they must continually assess the ways in which such individuality (to the extent that it is found to exist) continues to provide an important source of the child's development. Thus they must ascertain how children with different temperamental styles interact differently with the world over the course of their development, and how such differential interactions continue to provide a source of the child's development. Given these requirements, it is clear why Thomas et al. had to study their subjects longitudinally.

In sum, we see both the theoretical rationale of the Thomas et al. study and the general manner in which this theoretical viewpoint must be translated into an empirical procedure in order for the ideas to be tested. Let us turn now to a consideration of the methodology of the Thomas et al. study.

The method of the Thomas et al. NYLS
The New York Longitudinal Study (NYLS) is one of the world's longest ongoing longitudinal studies. Indeed, its founders—the psychiatrists Alexander Thomas and Stella Chess—continue at this writing to be actively involved in the project. Although there has been continuity in the major staff of the NYLS, there has been an evolution in the interests of these scientists and thus in

the features and foci of the study. These constancies and changes in the study (a prototypic phenomenon of research continuity-discontinuity, by the way, in major longitudinal studies) may be evidenced by a discussion of the samples in the NYLS and the data available about them over time.

Characteristics of the NYLS samples

The NYLS involves three samples. First, what may be termed the *core sample* of the NYLS is composed of 133 children (66 males, 67 females). Over 99 percent of the sample is white. The sample seems to be an especially committed, cooperative one. The sample members have been followed from their early infancy to, today, their adulthood. Begun in 1956, sample recruitment was completed six years later. Originally the sample consisted of 136 subjects, but in the early portion of the study three subjects were dropped. To date, the remaining 133 subjects are still being followed. Thus the data from the core NYLS sample provide a depiction of the life courses of a group of people from early infancy to young adulthood that is remarkably unbiased by selective attrition.

The families of the core sample are of middle- or upper-middle-class backgrounds. Almost all parents were born in the United States. Throughout the study, information has been obtained about the parents (e.g., regarding career, health, employment, and marital status). Forty percent of the mothers and 60 percent of the fathers had both college educations and postgraduate degrees, and less than 10 percent had no college at all. The parents of the core sample are predominantly Jewish (78 percent), while the remainder are Catholic (7 percent) and Protestant (15 percent). Eighty-four families are involved. Forty-five have one child participating in the study (although these families may have more than one child), thirty-one have two, six have three, and two families have four children participating in the study.

The NYLS has also included a population of a contrasting socioeconomic background.

This sample is involved in a second study, which was initiated in 1961; it involves ninety-eight children (fifty males, forty-eight females) of working-class Puerto Rican parents. These families were mostly intact and stable; eighty-six percent lived in low-income public housing projects in New York City. This group was longitudinally followed from 1961 to 1968, with the same general approach to data collection and analysis as in the core NYLS sample.

Another sample composed of fifty-two children (thirty-six males, sixteen females) with mildly retarded intellectual levels but without gross evidence of motor dysfunction or body stigmata are also part of the NYLS. They were followed for various lengths of time, beginning at age five and ranging up to their middle teen-age years (i.e., thirteen to seventeen).

Features of the NYLS data set

A longitudinal study that has extended over the course of a quarter-century, and that has included a core sample as well as auxiliary ones, obviously contains considerable data. As such, we may only briefly describe the data present in the NYLS.

DATA EXISTING ON THE CORE SAMPLE. Upon entry into the study, demographic information about the parents and family was obtained. This information included the educational and employment history and status of the parents, the structure of the family, and the type of residence in which the family resided. Families—recruited into the study during the end of pregnancy or shortly after the birth of the children—also made available the mothers' obstetrical histories (e.g., complications during pregnancy), birth information (e.g., use of medication), and neonatal information (e.g., weight and length).

Starting in the first few months of life, parents were interviewed periodically (e.g., every three months in the children's first year of life) about the children's behaviors in numerous content areas (e.g., sleeping, feeding, bathing, toileting, mobility, social responsivity, and sensory functioning). Along with this interview, parents were asked questions pertaining to responsibilities for daily child care and to details of daily living. For the first two years of the study these interviews represent the major source of information about the children. However, after this age the data set includes several other sources of information about them.

That is, as the children became older, data collection was expanded to include the other contexts within which they interacted. As the children entered nursery school or elementary school, detailed teacher interviews were conducted about the children's adaptation and overall functioning, and classroom observations of the child were made; both interviews and observations were done periodically throughout the school years. In addition, psychometric measures (e.g., IQ tests) of cognitive functioning, standardized achievement-test scores, and school grades were also obtained throughout the school years.

When the children were approximately three years of age, 100 of the mothers and 93 of the fathers of the core NYLS children were interviewed about their child-care practices, parental attitudes, parental and spousal roles, and the effects of the children on them and the family. Each parent was interviewed independently by two interviewers who were blind to data already gathered. All interviews were audiotaped. After the interview each parent completed a Parental Attitude Research Instrument, PARI (Schaefer and Bell 1958). This interview sought to obtain information pertinent to parental permissiveness, consistency of rules, and discipline strategies. Questions about child dominance and independence were specifically asked. The interview also sought to assess parental liking and approval of the children. In addition, questions about the marital relationship, attitudes toward the spouse, and attitudes toward the parental role were included, and there were questions about attitudes toward working mothers. Finally, to obtain additional data relevant to the children's effects on the fam-

ily context, the parents were questioned on their expectations about the children, as well as the concrete effects the children were felt to have had on the family milieu.

In addition, there is an evaluation of the home environment of the subjects and of any special environmental circumstances (e.g., separations, divorces, remarriages, deaths). Information also exists about any significant handicaps possessed by the children; and in those cases where behavioral and/or emotional disorders were identified, there are additional psychometric data and clinical psychiatric evaluations.

In adolescence and early adulthood, interviews were conducted separately with both the subjects and their parents. These interviews were structured much like the earlier ones, with additional questions about new spheres of functioning (i.e., college plans, career goals, sexual and social functioning). Additionally, during the adolescent assessment, one-third of the subjects responded to the Offer (1969) Self-Image Questionnaire.

DATA EXISTING ON THE PUERTO RICAN SAMPLE. The procedure for data collection for this sample was similar to that in the core sample; that is, birth history and family demographics were initially gathered. Subsequently, throughout the seven years (1961–68) of data collection, detailed parental interviews about the children's psychological and social functioning were conducted, and direct observations of the children's behavior were made. In addition to this information, data about the home environment and any significant events that had occurred were periodically obtained.

As in the core sample, once the children entered school, teacher interviews, classroom observations, and grades and achievement scores were collected. IQ data also exist for this sample. There is information as well on any significant handicaps possessed by the children; and in those cases where behavioral and/or emotional disorders were identified, additional psychometric data and clinical pychiatric evaluations exist. Finally, single-occasion behavioral evaluations and IQ scores were obtained on 116 of the older sibs of these subjects, who ranged from six to sixteen years of age at the time of their one assessment.

DATA EXISTING ON THE MENTALLY RETARDED SAMPLE. As in the other samples, parental home reports and observations, teacher interviews, school observations, and grades were collected from the subjects in this sample. However, because there was a clinical sample, much more detailed clinical information exists on these subjects, along with numerous psychological, intelligence, and achievement tests. For most subjects, additional data were collected three (and also six) years after initial data collection was completed. These assessments involved interviewing the children's parents and teachers in manners comparable to those with the other NYLS sample subjects.

In my presentation of the NYLS I will obviously not be able to discuss every analysis reported on each of the longitudinal samples. One reason precluding such an attempt is the great productivity of Thomas and Chess and their associates (e.g., Chess and Thomas 1984; Chess, Thomas, and Birch, 1965, 1966; Thomas and Chess 1970, 1977, 1980, 1981; Thomas, Chess, and Birch 1968, 1970; Thomas et al. 1963; Thomas, Chess, and Korn 1982). Our discussion will focus primarily, then, on the core sample and, for comparative purposes, at times on the Puerto Rican sample as well. Finally, although we shall need to draw on diverse information in the NYLS data set, given the theoretical concerns of Thomas et al. with the role of organismic individuality in development, the major data we shall draw on will be those pertinent to temperament.

However, our interest in temperament raises a question that confronted Thomas and Chess when they initiated the NYLS. Let us consider it.

What Is Temperament?

At the time of the study's inception there existed no acceptable definition of the dimensions of a child's temperament. Al-

though other psychologists (e.g., Sheldon 1940, 1942) had provided definitions of temperament (or behavioral style), these had been linked to preformationist theoretical conceptions and were thus unacceptable to the probabilistic epigenetic orientation of Thomas et al. (1963; Thomas and Chess 1970). Accordingly, although Thomas et al. wanted to study objectively the aspects of a child's behavioral style, they had no preformed ideas about what constituted such aspects. They knew that they wanted to concern themselves with the *how* rather than the *what* of behavior, but they were uncertain about how to measure it in any precise way. They had no preconceived ideas about what sort of different characteristics comprised a child's temperament.

Simply, the immediate crucial conceptual problem facing Thomas et al. as they began the NYLS was that although they knew generally what aspect of a child's development they wanted to study (characteristics of temperament), they did not know what constituted the various aspects of temperament. In terms of the ipsative approach, they did not know what attributes were comprised by the child's intraindividual attribute repertoire. The dilemma faced by Thomas et al. was, as already implied, associated with a second unanswered question.

How Does One Measure Temperament?

Even more basic than this definitional problem was the problem of temperament measurement. Assuming for the moment that Thomas et al. knew the particular attributes of temperament in which they were interested, how were they going to go about obtaining measures of these attributes? Where was the information about the development of the child's temperament going to come from?

This problem was complicated by the fact that the authors felt it crucial to obtain measures of the child's temperament in all situations in which the child engaged. There were two reasons for this. First, Thomas and

Chess (1977) believed that the significance of a child's particular characteristics of temperamental individuality lay in how it fit with what other people in the child's world wanted from the child. They believed that if a child fit well with most of the situations, or contexts, in which he or she found him- or herself, then healthy development would proceed; poorly fit children would not show healthy adjustment, however. This idea may be recognized as the "goodness of fit" model noted in earlier chapters. We shall have reason to discuss this model and the NYLS data relevant to it again later in this chapter. Here we should note that the second reason for the Thomas et al. interest in assessing the child in multiple contexts is that if the concern was with ascertaining how the child did *whatever* he or she did, and not just with how he or she went about doing *certain* things (for instance, those things that might be involved in a once-a-month experimental assessment session), Thomas et al. would have to observe the child's temperamental style continuously. They would have to observe the child each and every day of the child's life. Thus observations could not be limited to those at the Thomas et al. laboratory but would have to include observations of the child in the real, nonlaboratory world.

A possible way to obtain such observations would be to hire and train a large set of observers to live in each child's household around the clock and thus observe and rate the child in how he or she does everything. Such a procedure presents problems, however. The hiring and training of, for example, 133 observers (one for each core sample subject) would be economically prohibitive. Moreover, probably three times as many observers would have to be hired, since the observers would probably work no more than eight hours a day. Furthermore, few if any families would allow one (not to mention three) people to enter their homes permanently to observe each and every interaction made by their child. Thus how were Thomas et al. to obtain the necessary continuous, total observations of each of their subjects?

Fortunately, someone did exist who observed the child continuously, who at no cost to the researchers lived with the child daily and who always worked a twenty-four-hour day. This, of course, was the child's parent (typically the mother). Hence the Thomas group decided to use each child's parent as the observer of the child's temperament; thus, through interviews with each parent, the researchers were able to obtain the needed information about the child's style of reactivity in all daily interactions with the world. Since the parent continually observed the child, an appropriately designed interview of the parent could turn these observations into data about the child's developing temperament.

Problems of data accuracy

We have noted that after the subjects were about two years of age, data from parental interviews were regularly supplemented with data from other people (e.g., teachers were interviewed and, as the subject got older, he or she was interviewed as well). In addition, data collected with methods other than interviews (e.g., through nursery-school observations) were also included after two years of age. However, a reliance on parental interviews continued to exist throughout childhood, and such reliance presents problems. Obviously, one would not be quick to nominate a child's parent if one wanted an objective description or appraisal of the child. Such parental observations hold the danger of being subjectively biased. Yet Thomas et al. decided that there was a way to avoid the subjectivism typically involved in parental reports. The interview of each parent was structured so that *descriptions,* rather than *interpretations,* of behavior were elicited. Although the interviewer recorded both interpretations and descriptions, only descriptions were considered for use as data. At times, when parents insisted on interpreting rather than describing, the interviewer carefully reworded, rephrased, or repeated the question so as to obtain in each case a step-by-step description of the behavior in question. This insistence on description rather than interpretation was illustrated by Thomas et al. (1963, 25) in the following example of a segment of a parental interview:

INTERVIEWER: "What did the baby do the first time he was given cereal?"

PARENT: "He couldn't stand it."

INTERVIEWER: "What makes you think he disliked it? What did he do?"

PARENT: "He spit it out and when another spoonful was offered he turned his head to the side."

Thus when questions were asked about bathing or meeting new people, for example, and the parent responded with an interpretation (e.g., "He likes to be bathed," or "She is afraid of new people"), the interviewer always insisted on a description. The only answers used for data about temperament were those that responded to the question, "What did the child do?"

In this way Thomas et al. took a first step toward ensuring that the data derived from parental interviews were accurate. However, other steps were also followed. In Chapter 8 we saw that one of the major limitations of Sigmund Freud's method was that he obtained retrospective accounts of the early lives of his adult patients. He asked adults to reconstruct their long-gone past by remembering back to their early years of development. Such retrospections may be biased through such factors as selective remembering or forgetting, or distortion. Similarly, biases could enter into the parental responses. Such retrospective accounts are less accurate than *prospective* descriptions, descriptions of a child's behavioral development given at about the same time the behavior is occurring. Thus the Thomas group used prospective interviews, conducted at three-month intervals during the child's first year of life. For example, the first

interview occurred when the child was about three months old and was used to provide information about the child's temperamental development during these first three months; the second interview, conducted when the child was six months old, was used to obtain temperamental information about his or her fourth, fifth, and sixth months of life. After the first year, subsequent interviews were conducted at six-month intervals for year two of life. Generally, yearly interviews were conducted for periods beyond the first two years.

Further steps were taken to ensure data accuracy. A loss of accuracy could have resulted from the researchers' scoring of these parental interview responses. Because of the large number of response descriptions resulting from each of the several interviews of each of the many parents, different people would have to be used to score and interpret these answers. The researchers had to be sure that each different person would score the same responses in the same way and, moreover, that the same person would always score the same response in the same way; if such consistency was not achieved, considerable inaccuracy would be introduced into the information. To check for such consistencies the researchers had different people score the same set of parental responses and had the same people score the same parental responses twice (after a three-month interval had gone by). In both cases, there was over 90 percent agreement between the two sets of responses.

In sum, we see that after taking several necessary steps to ensure the accuracy of their data, Thomas et al. were able to conclude that they had consistent, accurate descriptions of the children's development. Yet they still did not have an indication of what constituted the temperamental-attribute repertoire of their subjects. Although they now considered that they had accurate, consistently scored information describing the "how" of children's behavior in the world, they did not know the particular aspects of temperament that were present. What were the variables, or attributes, comprising the child's temperamental repertoire? Although such knowledge lay in their already-obtained information, they now had to tease this knowledge out. Let us consider how they went about ascertaining this knowledge and what, in fact, they discovered.

The Attributes of Temperament

Thomas et al. did not have any predetermined theoretical notions concerning what the attributes of temperament were. Accordingly, the researchers could not decide deductively what particular temperamental attributes should be derived from their data; they could not say that since their theory about temperament said "x," there should be evidence of a particular attribute of temperament.

Moreover, Thomas et al. wanted to avoid limiting the analyses of the interviews to a scoring of just one or two possible temperamental attributes; this methodological route would clearly introduce the possibility of ignoring large or important aspects of the data. On the other hand, there was so much information contained in the interviews that some categorization of the descriptions was necessary. One had to score, or place, the various parental descriptions into categories in order to reduce the vast number of bits of data; however, at the same time, one did not want to produce as many different categories as there were bits of information. Thomas et al. wanted to move from data to more general organizational categorizations; they wanted to induce (discover) categories in the data that would organize it.

Accordingly, a sample of parental interviews was read, and by a careful review and discussion of the contents of these interviews Thomas et al. were able to identify nine categories of temperament. That is, by performing an *inductive content analysis* of their data, they were able to generate nine attributes of temperament, which could be reliably scored and into which the various behavioral descriptions in the interviews could be placed.

Although there was evidence in *some* of the parental descriptions for temperamental attributes other than the nine on which Thomas et al. focused, the group decided to concentrate on the nine attributes of temperament induced by the above method since these nine attributes were present in all of the interview data. The nine attributes were:

1.   *Activity level.* This category refers to descriptions of the child's motor behavior (muscle functioning). Such descriptions answered several questions: Was the child very highly active all the time or were very low levels of general activity seen? Did the child move around a lot or a little when eating, playing, sleeping, and so on?

2.   *Rhythmicity.* This category refers to the cyclicality or regularity of behavior. Was the child's behavior very predictable? For example, did the child sleep for four hours, wake for four hours, sleep for four hours? Did the child always eliminate one hour after eating or always get hungry at the same time? Or was the child's behavior irregular? Did the child sleep for seven hours, wake for two, then perhaps sleep for three, but then wake for five? Did he or she sometimes eliminate right after eating and sometimes hours after? Was he or she sometimes hungry a short time after eating, while at other times he or she might go for hours without getting hungry?

3.   *Approach or withdrawal.* Did the child tend to move toward—approach—new stimuli (for example, toys, people) or to move away—withdraw—from all such stimuli?

4.   *Adaptability.* Did the child tend to adjust easily to new situations (after his or her initial approach or withdrawal response was made), or did the child tend to take a good deal of time to adjust to new situations and stimuli?

5.   *Intensity of reaction.* This attribute refers to the strength of a response. Whenever the child responded to a situation or stimulus, was this response indicative of a high level of energy? Did the child respond with vigor or with little energy? For exam-

ple, did the child tend to whimper rather than scream loudly when crying?

6.   *Threshold of responsiveness.* A threshold refers to the smallest amount of energy necessary to evoke a response. If, for example, a noise has to be very loud for it to bother you, then you have a high threshold; if even a pin dropping causes you to react, you have a low noise threshold. This category, then, relates to the child's general threshold for responding.

7.   *Quality of mood.* Was the child generally pleasant and friendly? Did he or she smile and laugh a lot and thus have a positive mood? Or was the child's behavior generally unpleasant? Did he or she cry and frown a lot and thus have a negative mood?

8.   *Distractibility.* Once the child was engaged in a given behavior (e.g., watching television), was it very easy to alter this behavior (e.g., by calling him or her to dinner)? That is, was the child easily or highly distractible in that external stimulation would easily change his or her ongoing behavior? Or was the child hard to distract? Was it difficult to change his or her ongoing behavior through introduction of another stimulus to the situation? Did the child thus show low distractibility?

9.   *Attention span and persistence.* How long did the child tend to stay at a given behavior in which he or she was engaged? Did he or she tend to persist in doing a task for a long time, or did he or she stay with one task for a few minutes or so and then move to another task, and then another? If the child tended to stay with tasks for a long time, he or she would have a long (or high) attention span. He or she would be persistent. If the reverse were true, then he or she would have a short (or low) attention span. He or she would not show high persistence.

These categories comprise the nine attributes of temperament identified by Thomas et al. (1963). Note that the nine categories refer to descriptions of the "how," the style, of behavior. They refer to how a child goes about doing the behaviors in which he or she engages. Thus the nine attributes make up a

description, rather than an interpretation, of the dimensions of a child's style of behavioral reactivity to the world. Thus the parental descriptions of how the child behaved in respect to such content topics as sleep, feeding, toilet training and toilet activities, bathing, grooming, meeting other people, playing, learning rules, talking, and so on, were used by Thomas et al. to obtain a broad sample of descriptions of the child's characteristics of reactivity; these descriptions were then placed in one of the nine categories of temperament that Thomas et al. identified. Each of these nine attributes was scored on a three-point scale. For example, for threshold of responsiveness, a child could be scored as having a low threshold, a high threshold, or a moderate threshold. The nine attributes of temperament and the three levels of scoring—or rating—for each attribute are presented in Figure 10.1.

In terms of the ipsative approach, the attribute repertoire of temperament for any given child would be made up of the child's "score" on each of the nine attributes. Since a child's score on one dimension would not necessarily affect his or her score on any other attribute, the attribute interrelation of the repertoire could be different for different children. In other words, with the discovery and scoring of the nine attributes of temperament, Thomas et al. defined a temperamental-attribute repertoire that could exist differently in different children; that is, different children could have different scores on the various attributes; therefore, of course, the interrelation of the attributes would then be different for these different children. One child might combine a low threshold with high activity and a positive mood, while another child might combine a moderate threshold with low activity and a negative mood.

Was this in fact the case? Did different children show different attribute repertoires? Were different attribute interrelations seen? And did the children's repertoires remain the same as the children developed? To address these questions let us turn to some of the results of the NYLS.

ATTRIBUTE OF TEMPERAMENT	POSSIBLE "SCORES" FOR EACH ATTRIBUTE		
Adaptability	/ adaptive /	variable /	nonadaptive /
Rhythmicity	/ regular /	variable /	irregular /
Activity level	/ high /	moderate /	low /
Approach—Withdrawal	/ approach /	variable /	withdrawal /
Threshold	/ high /	moderate /	low /
Intensity	/ intense /	variable /	mild /
Mood	/ positive /	variable /	negative /
Distractibility	/ yes /	variable /	no /
Attention span; persistence	/ high /	variable /	low /

FIGURE 10.1

The nine attributes of temperament found by Thomas et al. (1963), and the possible "scores," or ratings for each attribute.

Results of the NYLS

Temperamental individuality in infancy and childhood

As I have discussed, the NYLS is an ongoing longitudinal project. The data from the study are still being analyzed, and the children of the project are still being studied, although these children are now—at this writing—in their late twenties and some have children of their own. Accordingly, we have a rich and extensive data base from which to draw in order to address the issues of whether children possess individually distinct temperament repertoires and/or interrelations of these repertoires and of what the developmental course of temperament might be. However, for clarity of presentation we shall not try to present all pertinent data in this vast data set. Instead, we shall focus on what are quite representative results—those describing intraindividual consistencies and changes in the individual's temperamental-attribute repertoire and repertoire interrelation over the course of the first ten years of development (Chess and Thomas 1984; Chess, Thomas, and Birch 1965; Thomas and Chess 1970, 1977, 1980, 1981; Thomas, Chess, and Birch 1968, 1970; Thomas et al. 1963).

The first task of data analysis for Thomas et al. (1963) was to discover if children did in fact possess individually different temperamental repertoires in early infancy. Second, the group had to determine the developmental course of such individuality. The first major finding, then, was that children do show individually different temperamental repertoires and interrelations; moreover, these individual differences in temperament do become distinct—they can be discerned—even in the first few weeks of the child's life. Although some children tend to be similar in their temperamental styles—a point whose implications we shall consider below—different arrays of scores for each of the different attributes were found. Thus, in particular for the attributes of activity level, threshold, intensity, mood, and distractibility, marked individual differences in temperamental repertoires were evident (Thomas et al. 1963, 57).

Moreover, these individually different temperamental styles were not systematically related either to the parents' method of child rearing or to the parents' own personality styles (Thomas et al. 1970). This finding indicates not only that children are individually different but also that these characteristics of individuality are not simply related to what a parent does to a child or to a parent's own personality characteristics.

The second major finding of the NYLS is that these characteristics of individuality, first identified in the child's first three months of life, tend to remain relatively continuous in the child over the course of later years. For example, one may look at a child's most frequent score for each of his various nine temperamental attributes. That is, although in various instances a child may score high, moderate, or low in threshold, most of the ratings might be one of these scores, for example, high. If one looks at these scores, one sees that the child's temperament tends to remain in the same category over his or her childhood years; for example, the preponderance of his or her threshold scores across life tends to be high (Thomas et al. 1963, 71). Moreover, the child's other scores, both within a particular attribute category and between the different attribute categories, tend to remain similar over the course of the first ten years of life as well. This finding indicates not only that the child's attribute repertoire tends to remain fairly consistent but also that the attribute interrelation tends to remain consistent. The expression of such temperamental similarity over the course of the first ten years of life is illustrated in Table 10.1. This table displays two ratings for each of the nine categories of temperament, along with behaviors indicative of the consistency in temperament at each of the age periods ranging between two months through ten years of age.

We may conclude that to a great extent a child is born with an individually different temperament and that this individuality tends to remain with the children over the course of his first ten years of life. The ipsative longitudinal study of Thomas et al. indicates that individually different attribute repertoires and attribute interrelations characterize the individual over the course of his or her childhood development. These findings, of course, have important theoretical implications for organismic, dynamic interactionist theory, as well as important practical implications. However, before

turning to a consideration of these implications it is useful to consider some other aspects of the results of the study. Although children were found to be characterized by individually different temperamental styles, we have also said that certain characteristics of temperament tended to be similar in some children. That is, for some children—although not for all, by any means—certain attribute scores on one dimension tended to occur at the same time with certain other attribute scores on other dimensions. Let us see the implications and meaning of such occurrences.

Temperamental types

Among some children, scores on some temperamental attributes tended consistently to go along with scores on some of the other attributes. That is, a cluster, or grouping, of attribute scores was found for some children. For instance, for some children low thresholds tended to go along with high adaptability and high attention spans. In fact, Thomas et al. were able to identify three such temperamental clusters. Some children had one type of temperamental-attribute grouping, while other children possessed another type. These three types were given different labels to describe the temperamental patterns of the children who possessed them.

THE EASY CHILD. Some children were characterized by a temperament comprising a positive mood, high rhythmicity, low- or moderate-intensity reactions, high adaptability, and an approach orientation to new situations and stimuli. About 40 percent of the children in the NYLS sampler possessed this temperamental type (Thomas, Chess, and Birch 1970). Such children slept and ate regularly as infants, were generally happy, and adjusted readily to new people and events. As older children, they also adjusted easily to changing school requirements and adapted and participated easily in games and other activities. Hence, the Thomas group labeled such a child as easy because such a child obviously presents few difficul-

TABLE 10.1
Illustrations for Ratings of the Nine NYLS Temperamental Attributes at Ages Two Months Through Ten Years

Temperamental quality	Rating	Two months	Six months	One year
Activity level	High	Moves often in sleep. Wriggles when diaper is changed.	Tries to stand in tub and splashes. Bounces in crib. Crawls after dog.	Walks rapidly. Eats eagerly. Climbs into everything.
	Low	Does not move when being dressed or during sleep.	Passive in bath. Plays quietly in crib and falls asleep.	Finishes bottle slowly. Goes to sleep easily. Allows nail-cutting without fussing.
Rhythmicity	Regular	Has been on four-hour feeding schedule since birth. Regular bowel movement.	Is asleep at 6:30 every night. Awakes at 7:00 A.M. Food intake is constant.	Naps after lunch each day. Always drinks bottle before bed.
	Irregular	Awakes at a different time each morning. Size of feedings varies.	Length of nap varies; so does food intake.	Will not fall asleep for an hour or more. Moves bowels at a different time each day.
Distractibility	Distractible	Will stop crying for food if rocked. Stops fussing if given pacifier when diaper is being changed.	Stops crying when mother sings. Will remain still while clothing is changed if given a toy.	Cries when face is washed unless it is made into a game.
	Not distractible	Will not stop crying when diaper is changed. Fusses after eating even if rocked.	Stops crying only after dressing is finished. Cries until given bottle.	Cries when toy is taken away and rejects substitute.
Approach/Withdrawal	Positive	Smiles and licks washcloth. Has always liked bottle.	Likes new foods. Enjoyed first bath in a large tub. Smiles and gurgles.	Approaches strangers readily. Sleeps well in new surroundings.
	Negative	Rejected cereal the first time. Cries when strangers appear.	Stays away from strangers. Plays with new toys only after some time.	Stiffened when placed on sled. Will not sleep in strange beds.

(Continued on next page)

TABLE 10.1 (continued)

Temperamental quality	Rating	Two months	Six months	One year
Adaptability	Adaptive	Was passive during first bath; now enjoys bathing. Smiles at nurse.	Used to dislike new foods; now accepts them well.	Was afraid of toy animals at first; now plays with them happily.
	Not adaptive	Still startled by sudden, sharp noise. Resists diapering.	Does not cooperate with dressing. Fusses and cries when left with sitter.	Continues to reject new foods each time they are offered.
Attention span and persistence	Long	If soiled, continues to cry until changed. Repeatedly rejects water if he wants milk.	Watches toy mobile over crib intently. "Coos" frequently.	Plays by self in playpen for more than an hour. Listens to singing for long periods.
	Short	Cries when awakened but stops almost immediately. Objects only mildly if cereal precedes bottle.	Sucks pacifier for only a few minutes and spits it out.	Loses interest in a toy after a few minutes. Gives up easily if she falls while attempting to walk.
Intensity of reaction	Intense	Cries when diapers are wet. Rejects food vigorously when satisfied.	Cries loudly at the sound of thunder. Makes sucking movements when vitamins are administered.	Laughs hard when father plays roughly. Screamed and kicked when temperature was taken.
	Mild	Does not cry when diapers are wet. Whimpers instead of crying when hungry.	Does not kick often in tub. Does not smile. Whimpers and moves when temperature is taken.	Does not fuss much when clothing is pulled on over head.
Threshold of responsiveness	Low	Stops sucking on bottle when approached.	Refuses fruit he likes when vitamins are added. Hides head from bright light.	Spits out food he does not like. Giggles when tickled.
	High	Is not startled by loud noises. Takes bottle and breast equally well.	Eats everything. Does not object to diapers being wet or soiled.	Eats food he likes even if mixed with disliked food. Can be left easily with strangers.

(Continued on next page)

Temperamental quality	Rating	Two years	Five years	Ten years
Quality of mood	Positive	Smacks lips when first tasting new foods. Smiles at parents.	Plays and splashes in bath. Smiles at everyone.	Likes bottle; reaches for it and smiles. Laughs loudly when playing peekaboo.
	Negative	Fusses after nursing. Cries when carriage is rocked.	Cries when taken from tub. Cries when given food she does not like.	Cries when given injections. Cries when left alone.
Activity level	High	Climbs furniture. Explores. Gets in and out of bed while being put to sleep.	Leaves table often during meals. Always runs.	Plays ball and engages in other sports. Cannot sit still long enough to do homework.
	Low	Enjoys quiet play with puzzles. Can listen to records for hours.	Takes a long time to dress. Sits quietly on long automobile rides.	Likes chess and reading. Eats very slowly.
Rhythmicity	Regular	Eats a big lunch each day. Always has a snack before bedtime.	Fall asleep when put to bed. Bowel movement regular.	Eats only at mealtimes. Sleeps the same amount of time each night.
	Irregular	Nap time changes from day to day. Toilet training is difficult because bowel movement is unpredictable.	Food intake varies; so does time of bowel movement.	Food intake varies. Falls asleep at a different time each night.
Distractibility	Distractible	Will stop tantrum if another activity is suggested.	Can be coaxed out of forbidden activity by being led into something else.	Needs absolute silence for homework. Has a hard time choosing a shirt in a store because they all appeal to him.
	Not distractible	Screams if refused some desired object. Ignores mother's calling.	Seems not to hear if involved in favorite activity. Cries for a long time when hurt.	Can read a book while television set is at high volume. Does chores on schedule.

(Continued on next page)

TABLE 10.1 *(continued)*

Temperamental quality	Rating	Two years	Five years	Ten years
Approach/withdrawal	Positive	Slept well the first time he stayed overnight at grandparents' house.	Entered school building unhesitatingly. Tries new foods.	Went to camp happily. Loved to ski the first time.
	Negative	Avoids strange children in the playground. Whimpers first time at beach. Will not go into water.	Hid behind mother when entering school.	Severely homesick at camp during first days. Does not like new activities.
Adaptability	Adaptive	Obeys quickly. Stayed contentedly with grandparents for a week.	Hesitated to go to nursery school at first; now goes eagerly. Slept well on camping trip.	Likes camp, although homesick during first days. Learns enthusiastically.
	Not adaptive	Cries and screams each time hair is cut. Disobeys persistently.	Has to be hand led into classroom each day. Bounces on bed in spite of spankings.	Does not adjust well to new school or new teacher; comes home late for dinner even when punished.
Attention span and persistence	Long	Works on a puzzle until it is completed. Watches when shown how to do something.	Practiced riding a two-wheeled bicycle for hours until he mastered it. Spent over an hour reading a book.	Reads for two hours before sleeping. Does homework carefully.
	Short	Gives up easily if a toy is hard to use. Asks for help immediately if undressing becomes difficult.	Still cannot tie his shoes because he gives up when he is not successful. Fidgets when parents read to him.	Gets up frequently from homework for a snack. Never finishes a book.
Intensity of reaction	Intense	Yells if he feels excitement or delight. Cries loudly if a toy is taken away.	Rushes to greet father. Gets hiccups from laughing hard.	Tears up an entire page of homework if one mistake is made. Slams door of room when teased by younger brother.

(Continued on next page)

Mild	When another child hit her, she looked surprised, did not hit back.	Drops eyes and remains silent when given a firm parental "No." Does not laugh much.	When a mistake is made on a model airplane, corrects it quietly. Does not comment when reprimanded.
Threshold of responsiveness Low	Runs to door when father comes home.	Always notices when mother puts new dress on for first time. Refuses milk if it is not ice-cold.	Rejects fatty foods. Adjusts shower until water is at exactly the right temperature.
High	Can be left with anyone. Falls to sleep easily on either back or stomach.	Does not hear loud, sudden noises when reading. Does not object to injections.	Never complains when sick. Eats all foods.
Quality of mood Positive	Plays with sister; laughs and giggles. Smiles when he succeeds in putting shoes on.	Laughs loudly while watching television cartoons. Smiles at everyone.	Enjoys new accomplishments. Laughs when reading a funny passage aloud.
Negative	Cries and squirms when given haircut. Cries when mother leaves.	Objects to putting boots on. Cries when frustrated.	Cries when he cannot solve a homework problem. Very "weepy" if he does not get enough sleep.

ties to raise. Such a child is easy to interact with.

As we shall see below, when we consider the data in the NYLS pertinent to the goodness-of-fit model, it is the implications of the child's temperamental style for social interaction with others that provide the significance of a given temperamental style for the child's healthy psychosocial functioning. Simply, the functional significance of a temperament type (i.e., the significance for healthy or unhealthy behavior and development) lies in the impact of the type on other people.

THE DIFFICULT CHILD.   In contrast to the easy (to interact with) child, there is the child who possesses a temperamental style that makes for difficult interactions. These children are characterized by low rhythmicity, high-intensity reactions, a withdrawal orientation to new situations and stimuli, slow adaptation, and a negative mood. About 10 percent of the NYLS children had this temperamental type. As infants they ate and slept irregularly, took a long time to adjust to new situations, and were characterized by a great deal of crying. To say the least, such a child would be difficult for a parent to train or a teacher to educate. Such a child would be difficult even just to interact with. Parents and teachers would have to show both tolerance and patience in order to have favorable interactions with such children.

THE SLOW-TO-WARM-UP CHILD.   Here we find a child who has a low activity level, a withdrawal orientation, slow adaptability, a somewhat negative mood, and relatively low reaction intensities. Such children comprised 15 percent of the NYLS sample (Thomas, Chess, and Birch 1970). These children would also present interaction difficulties and problems for their parents and teachers. It would take some time to get such a child involved in new activities and situations, and similarly, the child's slow adaptability and somewhat negative mood would suggest that the slow-to-warm-up

child would not interact favorably with new people. Clearly, the temperamental characteristics of this type of child would provide a basis for parental and teacher interactions different from that of easy children.

One indication of the different functional significance of these three types of temperamental styles is found in the proportion of children in each temperamental group who eventually developed behavioral problems severe enough to call for psychiatric attention. Of the total number of children in the Thomas et al. project, 42 percent were seen (i.e., screened) at one time or another for the presence of such problems. (This high percentage is due, probably in large part, to the fact that the NYLS parents had free access to the advice of Stella Chess in regard to any behavioral or emotional problems in their children; this opportunity may have elevated the proportion of parents who would seek out a psychiatrist for advice or treatment of their children.)

About 70 percent of the difficult children developed behavior difficulties, while only 18 percent of the easy children did so; the proportion of slow-to-warm-up children who developed such problems was between these two groups. Thus, although only 65 percent of the NYLS sample children had temperamental types falling into one of these three distinct clusters, each of these types was suggestive of a different functional significance.

The various temperamental-attribute scores of the easy, difficult, and slow-to-warm-up child are presented in Table 10.2. From this table and from our preceding discussion, we may infer that the distinct temperamental styles associated with these three types might have different implications for healthy psychosocial functioning because of their import for social interaction. That is, easy children are easy because they are not hard people with whom to interact; they possess the temperamental attributes that many parents and teachers might desire in children. In turn, difficult children are difficult by virtue of the fact that it is hard to interact with them; they possess tempera-

TABLE 10.2
Temperamental Attributes Of the Easy, Difficult, and Slow-To-Warm-Up Child

Type of child	Activity level	Rhythmicity	Distracti-bility	Approach/Withdrawal	Adaptability
	The proportion of active periods to inactive ones.	Regularity of hunger, excretion, sleep, and wakefulness.	The degree to which extraneous stimuli alter behavior	The response to a new object or person.	The ease with which a child adapts to changes in his environment.
"Easy"	Varies	Very regular	Varies	Positive approach	Very adaptable
"Slow to warm up"	Low to moderate	Varies	Varies	Initial withdrawal	Slowly adaptable
"Difficult"	Varies	Irregular	Varies	Withdrawal	Slowly adaptable

Type of child	Attention span and persistence	Intensity of reaction	Threshold of responsiveness	Quality of mood
	The amount of time devoted to an activity, and the effect of distraction on the activity.	The energy of response regardless of its quality of direction.	The intensity of stimulation required to evoke a discernible response.	The amount of friendly, pleasant, joyful behavior as contrasted with unpleasant, unfriendly behavior.
"Easy"	High or low	Low or mild	High or low	Positive
"Slow to warm up"	High or low	Mild	High or low	Slightly negative
"Difficult"	High or low	Intense	High or low	Negative

Source: *A. Thomas, S. Chess, and H. G. Birch, "The Origin of Personality."* Scientific American *223 (1970).*

mental attributes that many parents and teachers might not want, desire, or prefer in children.

A study by Gordon and Thomas (1967) is consistent with these ideas. Gordon and Thomas (1967) found that kindergarten teachers were able to rate their students in respect to their temperamental styles. The teachers were also asked to estimate the intelligence of these students, and Gordon and Thomas independently measured these chil-

dren's intelligence. It was found that the teachers distorted the students' intelligence; that is, the teacher ratings of intelligence were biased by the students' temperamental styles. For instance, children who had temperaments similar to that of the easy child were rated as more intelligent than children who had temperamental styles similar to the slow-to-warm-up child. Yet these estimates tended to represent an overestimation of the easy children's intelligence and an underestimation of the slow-to-warm-up children's intelligence. It is reasonable to assume that teachers will interact differently with children they believe to be brighter than with children they believe to be duller. For example, they may attempt to provide remedial work for the "duller" children and might leave the "brighter" children alone to work by themselves more often. These distortions suggest that different children, possessing different temperamental types, will experience different interactions with their teachers over the course of their educational development; these different interactions are based, in part at least, on the different meanings attached by teachers to different child-temperament styles (Pullis and Caldwell 1982).

Thus, if the functional significance of a child's easy, difficult, or slow-to-warm-up temperamental style lies in the impact the style has on the child's social context, it is important to understand the nature of the relations between the child's temperament and his or her social settings. Such understanding is the goal of those who use the goodness-of-fit model. We turn now to a discussion of this model, and the NYLS data pertinent to it.

The goodness-of-fit model

We may recall from our discussions of the nature-nurture controversy in previous chapters that both a person and his or her context will be individually distinct as a consequence of the unique combination of genotypic and phenotypic features of the person and of the specific attributes of his or her context. The presence of such individuality is central to understanding the goodness-of-fit model. We have noted that as a consequence of characteristics of physical individuality—for example, in regard to body type or facial attractiveness (Sorell and Nowak 1981)—and/or of psychological individuality—for instance, in regard to conceptual tempo or temperament (Kagan 1966; Thomas and Chess 1977)—children promote differential reactions in their socializing

others; these reactions may feed back to children, increase the individuality of their development milieu, and provide a basis for their further development. As we have seen, Schneirla (1957) termed these relations circular functions. It is through the establishment of such functions in ontogeny that people may be conceived of as producers of their own development (Lerner and Busch-Rossnagel 1981). However, this circular-functions idea needs to be extended since it is mute regarding the specific characteristics of the feedback (e.g., its positive or negative valence) a child will receive as a consequence of its individuality.

We have noted that a basis of the feedback a child receives comes from his or her fit with the demands placed on the child by virtue of the physical and/or social components (i.e., by the significant others) in the setting, or in the "context" in other terms (Lerner and Lerner 1983). If a given temperament attribute is congruent with the demands of a significant other (e.g., a parent) we expect positive adjustment (adaptation), while if that same attribute is incongruent with such demands we expect negative adjustment.

To illustrate, let us consider the case of the child in his or her family context and of the psychosocial and physical climate promoted by the parents. Parents can vary in their cognitive and behavioral attributes (e.g., in regard to their child-rearing attitudes and parenting styles; Baumrind 1971); parents can vary, too, in the physical features of the home they provide. I conceive of these parent-based psychosocial and physical characteristics as constituting presses for, or demands on, the child to adapt. Simply, parent characteristics are "translated" or "transduced" into demands on the child.

As explained earlier these demands may first take the form of attitudes, values, or expectations held by parents (or in other contexts by teachers and/or peers) regarding the child's physical or behavioral characteristics. Second, demands exist as a consequence of the behavioral attributes of parents (or, again, of teachers and/or peers); these people are significant others with whom the child must coordinate, or fit, his or her behavioral attributes for adaptive inter- actions to exist. Third, the physical charac- teristics of a setting (such as the noise level of the home) constitute contextual demands. Such physical presses require the child to possess certain behavioral attributes for the most efficient interaction within the setting to occur. The child's individuality in dif- ferentially meeting these demands provides a basis for the feedback he or she gets from the socializing environment.

Considering the demand "domain" of atti- tudes, values, or expectations, teachers and parents may have relatively individual and distinct expectations about behaviors de- sired of their students and children, respec- tively. Teachers may want students who show little distractibility, since they would not want attention diverted from the lesson by the activity of other children in the class- room. Parents, however, might desire their children to be moderately distractible—for example, when they require their children to move from television watching to dinner or to bed. Children whose behavioral individu- ality was either generally distractible or generally not distractible would thus dif- ferentially meet the demands of these two contexts. Problems of adjustment to school or to home demands might thus develop as a consequence of a child's lack of match, or "goodness of fit," in either or both settings.

In short, the key idea within the goodness- of-fit-model is that adaptive psychological and social functioning do not derive directly from either the nature of the person's char- acteristics of individuality per se or the na- ture of the demands of the contexts within which the person functions; instead if a per- son's characteristics of individuality fit or exceed the demands of a particular setting, *adaptive outcomes* (i.e., those associated with good personal adjustment and positive social interaction) in that setting will accrue, while if the characteristics are incongruent with (i.e., fall short of) the demands of a set- ting, personal maladjustment and/or nega- tive social functioning will occur.

TESTS OF THE GOODNESS-OF-FIT MODEL IN THE NYLS. Much of the research litera- ture supporting the use of the goodness-of-fit model is derived from the Thomas and Chess (1977) NYLS. Let us consider, then, the contribution of these data from the NYLS.

Within the NYLS data set, information relevant to the goodness-of-fit model exists as a consequence of the multiple samples present in the project. We have noted that the NYLS core sample is composed of 133 middle-class, mostly white children of pro- fessional parents and that, in addition, a sample of 98 New York City Puerto Rican children of working-class parents has been followed for about seven years. Each sample was studied from at least the first month of life onward. Although the distribution of temperamental attributes in the two sam- ples was not different, the import of the attributes for psychosocial adjustment was quite disparate. Two examples may suffice to illustrate this distinction.

First, let us consider the impact of low reg- ularity or rhythmicity of behavior, particu- larly in regard to sleep-wake cycles. The Puerto Rican parents studied by Thomas and Chess (1977; Thomas et al. 1974) were quite permissive. No demands in regard to rhythmicity of sleep were placed on the in- fant or child. Indeed, the parents allowed the child to go to sleep at any time the child de- sired and permitted the child to awaken at any time as well. The parents molded their schedule around the children. Because par- ents were so accommodating there were no problems of fit associated with an arrhyth- mic infant or child. Indeed, neither within the infancy period nor throughout the first five years of life did arrhythmicity predict adjustment problems. In this sample ar- rhythmicity remained continuous and inde- pendent of adaptive implications for the child (Korn 1978; Thomas et al. 1974).

In the middle-class families, however, strong demands for rhythmic sleep patterns were maintained. Thus an arrhythmic child did not fit with parental demands, and con- sistent with the goodness-of-fit model, arrhythmicity was a major predictor of problem behaviors both within the infancy years and across time through the first five years of life (Korn 1978; Thomas et al. 1974).

It should be emphasized that there are at least two ways of viewing this finding. First, consistent with the idea that children influence their parents, we may note that sleep arrhythmicity in their children resulted in problems in the parents—for example, reports of stress, anxiety, anger (Thomas et al. 1974; Chess and Thomas 1984). Such an effect of child temperament on the parent's own level of adaptation has been reported in other data sets; for instance, infants who had high thresholds for responsiveness to social stimulation, and thus were not easily soothed by their mothers, evoked intense distress reactions in their mothers and a virtual cessation of maternal caregiving behaviors (Brazelton, Koslowski, and Main 1974). Thus it is possible that the presence of such child effects in the NYLS sample could have altered previous parenting styles in a way that constituted feedback to the child that was associated with the development of problem behaviors in him or her.

In turn, a second interpretation of this finding arises from the fact that problem behaviors in the children were identified initially on the basis of parental report; thus it may be that irrespective of any problem behavior evoked in the parent by the child and/or of any altered parent-child interactions that thereby ensued, one effect of the child on the parent was to increase the probability of the parent labeling the child's temperamental style as problematic and so reporting it to the NYLS staff psychiatrist. Unfortunately, the current state of analysis of the NYLS data do not allow us to discriminate between these obviously non-mutually-exclusive possibilities.

However, what the data in the NYLS allow us to indicate now is that the parents in the middle-class sample took steps to change their arrhythmic children's sleep patterns; and as most of these arrhythmic children were also adaptable, and since temperament may be modified by person-context interactions, low rhythmicity tended to be discontinuous for most children. That the parents behaved to modify their children's arrhythmicity is also an instance of a child effect on its psychosocial context. That is, the child "produced" in his or her parents alterations in parental caregiving behaviors regarding sleep. That these child effects on the parental context fed back to the child and influenced his or her further development is consistent with the above-noted finding that sleep arrhythmicity was discontinuous among these children.

Thus in the middle-class sample early-infant arrhythmicity tended to be a problem during this time of life but proved to be neither continuous nor predictive of later adjustment problems. In turn, in the Puerto Rican sample infant arrhythmicity was not a problem during this time of life, but it was continuous and—because in the Puerto Rican context it was not involved in poor fit—it was not associated with adjustment problems in the child in the first five years of life. (Of course, this is not to say that the parents in the Puerto Rican families were not affected by their children's sleep arrhythmicity; as with the parents in the middle-class families, it may be that the Puerto Rican parents had problems of fatigue and/or suffered marital or work-related problems due to irregular sleep patterns produced in them as a consequence of their child's sleep arrhythmicity; however the current nature of data analysis in the NYLS does not allow us to investigate this possible child effect on the Puerto Rican parents.)

The data do allow us to underscore the importance of considering fit with the demands of the psychosocial context of development, in that they indicate that arrhythmicity did begin to predict adjustment problems for the Puerto Rican children when they entered the school system. Their lack of a regular sleep pattern interfered with their getting sufficient sleep to perform well in school and, in addition, often caused them to be late to school (Korn 1978; Thomas et al. 1974). Thus before the age of five only one Puerto Rican child presented a clinical problem diagnosed as a sleep disorder. However, almost 50 percent of the Puerto Rican children who developed clinically identifiable problems between ages five and nine were diagnosed as having sleep problems.

Another example may be given of how the differential demands existing between the two family contexts provide different presses for adaptation. This example pertains to differences in the demands of the families' physical contexts.

As noted by Thomas et al. (1974), as well as Korn (1978), overall there was a very low incidence of behavior problems in the Puerto Rican sample children in their first five years of life, especially when compared to the corresponding incidence among the core-sample children. However, if a problem was presented at this time among the Puerto Rican sample, it was most likely to be a problem of motor activity. In fact, across the first nine years of their lives, of those Puerto Rican children who developed clinical problems, 53 percent presented symptoms diagnosed as involving problematic motor activity. Parents complained of excessive and uncontrollable motor activity in such cases. However, in the core sample only one child (a child with brain damage) was characterized in this way. We may note here that the Puerto Rican parents' reports of "excessive and uncontrollable" activity in their children does constitute, in this group, an example of a child effect on the parents. That is, a major value of the Puerto Rican parents in the NYLS was child "obedience" to authority (Korn 1978). The type of motor activity shown by the highly active children of these Puerto Rican parents evoked considerable parental distress, given their perception that their children's behavior was inconsistent with what would be emitted by obedient children (Korn 1978).

Of course, if the middle-class parents had seen their children's behavior as excessive and uncontrollable, it may be that—irrespective of any major salience placed on the value of child obedience—problems would have been evoked in them, and feedback to the children would have ensued. Thus an issue remains as to why the same (high) activity level should evoke one set of appraisals among the Puerto Rican parents but quite another set among the middle-class parents (i.e., in the latter group no interpretation of "excessive and uncontrollable" behavior was evoked). Similarly, one may ask why high activity level is closely associated with problem behavior in the Puerto Rican children and not in the middle-class children. I believe that the key information needed to address these issues relates to the physical features of the respective groups' homes.

In the Puerto Rican sample the families usually had several children and lived in small apartments. Even average motor activity therefore tended to impinge on others in the setting. Moreover, and as an illustration of the embeddedness of the child-temperament–home-context relation in the broader community context, I may note that even in the case of the children with high activity levels, the Puerto Rican parents were reluctant to let their children out of the apartment because of the actual dangers of playing on the streets of East Harlem. In the core sample, however, the parents had the financial resources to provide large apartments or houses for their families. There were typically suitable play areas for the children both inside and outside the home. As a consequence, the presence of high activity levels in the home of the core sample did not cause the problems for interaction that they did in the Puerto Rican group. Thus, as Thomas et al. (1968, 1974) emphasize, the mismatch between temperamental attribute and physical environmental demand accounted for the group difference in the import of high activity level for the development of behavioral problems in the children.

In sum, the results of the NYLS tests of the goodness-of-fit model that I have reviewed allow the inference that at a given point in development neither children's attributes per se nor the demands of their setting per se are the key predictors of their adaptive functioning. Instead, the *re-*

lation between the child and his or her context—one described by the goodness-of-fit model—seems most important in home and school settings. This conclusion leads to some important practical implications. However, before we turn to these implications of the results of the NYLS, let us first consider the theoretical implications of this important ipsative longitudinal study of child development.

Theoretical Implications of the NYLS

The results of the Thomas et al. NYLS strongly indicate that children have present at birth characteristically individual, or unique, attributes of temperament. That is, children tend to show stylistically different reactive repertoires to the stimuli and situations with which they interact. This individual pattern of reactivity is presumed to arise out of an interaction between the intrinsic and extrinsic variables that provide a source of the child's development. In other words, on the basis of the child's individual maturational-experiential interaction, the child develops characteristics of individuality, which are furthered on the basis of interactions between this individually different child and his or her environment. In fact, we have seen that because the child does have such characteristically different attributes of reactivity, he or she will react to a given environmental situation differently than will another individually different child. Thus, because different children can be expected to react differently to the same environmental situation, these differential reactions will differentially influence significant other persons in their respective environments; and these influences on others are consistent with what would be expected on the basis of the goodness-of-fit model. Similarly, these different reactions in significant others will then feed back to the child and provide a further experiential source of his or her own development.

Thus, even if parents attempt to provide the same child-rearing environment for their different children and even if such parents possess markedly similar personalities, such parental similarities will not have the same effect on different children. Because a child's temperament is at least in part unrelated to his or her parents' personalities and child-rearing practices (Thomas, Chess, and Birch, 1970), this suggests: (1) that such parental-environmental variables cannot be viewed as the *only* source of a child's temperament; and (2) that the same environment will have a different effect on different children. One may not appropriately focus solely on either hereditary or experiential sources of influences if one wants to deal accurately with the actual source of individuality and development. Rather, one must study hereditary sources, prenatal and perinatal sources and influences, and later, life-course experiences, all of which may interact to contribute to the development of the individual (Thomas et al. 1963, 81).

In sum, the results of the Thomas group's NYLS indicate the following:

1.   Extremely early in their lives children appear to possess, and to maintain, characteristically different patterns of reactivity, or temperament; this individuality is believed to find its source in the interactions of the intrinsic and the extrinsic factors affecting the development of organisms. In any event, the functional significance of this individuality lies in the relation between the child and his or her context.

2.   Because of this interactively based individuality, different children will react differently even to the same environmental influences. Thus the same stimulus will not have the same effect on different children, and any analysis of behavioral development that attempts to account for development simply by reference to stimulus factors is inappropriate, naïve, and destined to remain incomplete (Scarr 1982; Scarr and McCartney 1983).

3.   On the basis of the child's individuality and the circular feedback functions that arise out of this individuality (Schneirla 1957)—functions that are consistent with the goodness-of-fit model—the child must be

viewed as playing an active, participatory role in his or her own development.

Thus the ipsative study of the Thomas group has found results consistent with the organismic, dynamic-interactionist developmental position we have been stressing throughout this book. Consistent with other such organismic theories (e.g., Gottlieb 1970, 1983; Schneirla 1957), the child's development is seen by Thomas et al. (1963) as finding its source in an interaction between the child's organismic characteristics and the characteristics of experience; hence the organism itself plays an active, contributory role in its own development. We will be able to draw similar conclusions from the second major ipsative study of development we shall discuss in this chapter, the study by Block (1971). However, before we turn to this study, let us first consider the important practical implications of the Thomas et al. NYLS.

Practical Implications of the NYLS

Many parents consult various how-to books about child rearing to gain information about how to raise their children. Often such books tell the parent what a child is like at a particular age period and what child-rearing practices to employ. One important practical implication of the NYLS is that such cookbook approaches to child rearing are inappropriate.

Because children are individually different, because they possess characteristically different and potentially continuous attributes of reactivity, one may not appropriately make generalized statements about what children at a particular age level are like. One may not imply that a given type of rearing procedure will work equally well with all children. Although children do share general, age-related characteristics, they also possess important characteristics of individuality. Thus, a child-rearing book must help parents understand that to an important extent their child is an individual person (see Chess, Thomas, and Birch 1965).

Moreover, the cookbook approach to child rearing is also inappropriate because, again, one cannot accurately specify how a general method of child rearing will affect all children. Since children have individually different temperamental repertoires, they will not react in the same way to the same rearing procedure. Different children will react differently to the same exact procedure. For instance, adoption by the parents of a fixed schedule of feeding may work well for an easy child but might prove unfavorable for either a difficult child or a slow-to-warm-up child.

Another practical implication of the Thomas et al. study relates to parental responses to children's development. If emotional or behaviorial problems arise in a child, the typical parental response is guilt. Perhaps because the parents believe the environmentalist doctrine—that anything a child becomes is solely an outcome of his or her environmental experiences—the parents feel that they are responsible for the child's problems. They feel guilt because they believe that they are responsible for their child not only in a moral sense—which, of course, one may maintain that they *are*—but also in a behavioral-determinancy sense. They believe that they are the major environmental determinants of their child's behavior, and in turn they believe that the environment provides a primary source of their child's behavioral development. Such parents are not aware of the fact that the child plays an active contributory role in his or her own development (Lerner 1982; Lerner and Busch-Rossnagel 1981). Thus their guilt is misdirected because they do not understand that a child's behavioral or emotional problems arise in part from an interaction between his or her temperament and conflicting environmental demands. For instance, while it is easy to imagine that almost any environmental circumstance would be adapted to by an easy child, a difficult child would probably have interactional difficulties with almost any environment.

Thus parents should not feel guilty. Rather, they should be made aware of the importance of understanding the implications of their child's individuality, and they should attempt to alter their procedures to achieve a more favorable interaction between the child's temperamental characteristics and their child-rearing practices.

In summarizing the implications of their work for both theory and practice in psychiatry, Thomas, Chess, and Birch (1970) have said:

> Theory and practice in psychiatry must take into full account the individual and his uniqueness: how children differ and how these differences act to influence their psychological growth. A given environment will not have the identical functional meaning for all children. Much will depend on the temperamental makeup of the child. As we learn more about how specific parental attitudes and practices and other specific factors in the environment of the child interact with specific temperamental, mental and physical attributes of individual children, it should become considerably easier to foster the child's healthy development. (p. 109)

Some Concluding Comments

With this specification of the practical implications of the NYLS we have concluded our assessment of how this ipsative study of development may be used to understand the complexities of psychological development. Although the ipsative approach, as represented in the work of Thomas et al., is quite different in its procedural orientation from either the stage or the differential approaches, we have seen that the Thomas et al. approach to ipsative analysis addresses similar issues of development. Thus, consistent with the general organismic, interactionist theoretical positions found in the ideas of stage theorists (e.g., Piaget, Kohlberg), the Thomas et al. ipsative approach provides evidence for the interactive basis of psychological development and supports organismic notions about the important role that the individual him- or herself plays in his or her own development. As noted above, the importance of a focus on individuality in attempting to understand development, and

the use of an ipsative approach in implementing this focus, are illustrated in the second major study that we shall consider in this chapter. We turn, then, to our discussion of the research of Block (1971).

BLOCK'S STUDY OF "LIVES THROUGH TIME"

For more than one-half century the Institute of Human Development at the University of California, Berkeley, has been the leading center for the long-term longitudinal study of human development. The multidisciplinary group of scientists who have worked at the Institute of Human Development (IHD) over this period have been prolific in regard to the important theoretical, methodological, and empirical contributions they have made to the study of human development across the life span (e.g., Bayley 1949; Block 1971; Eichorn et al. 1981; Haan 1974, 1977; H. Jones 1938, 1939a, 1939b, 1958; Jones and Bayley 1950; Livson and Peskin 1967, 1980; Macfarlane 1938a, 1938b; Mussen and Jones 1957; Tuddenham 1959).

Two major longitudinal studies conducted by the scientists at the IHD provide the data base for the second ipsatively oriented research project we shall discuss in this chapter—the research project conducted by Jack Block (with the collaboration of Norma Haan), entitled "Lives Through Time" (1971). That is, Block used the data from two IHD longitudinal studies "to trace, more closely than before, the ways of personality development and change from adolescence to adulthood" (1971, 2). Block reorganized, recoded, and reanalyzed the already-collected data from these two IHD studies in order to indicate

> the importance of studying personality development and personality change in a differentiated way, of identifying and understanding the alternative paths along which people evolve over time. (1971, 1)

By addressing this issue Block not only provided a demonstration of the usefulness of an ipsative approach to understanding personality in a more refined, singular way; in addition, he showed that when sound and creative scientific procedures are followed, substantial use can be made of existing longitudinal data—that is, of a longitudinal data archive—in the study of human development.

The first of the longitudinal studies that Block drew upon was started in 1929 by Jean Macfarlane and involved the quite intensive study of people (and their families) from their infancy through their childhood, adolescence, and into their adulthood. These people were intensively studied as a consequence of their placement in what was termed a guidance group—a group whose families had agreed to participate in an indepth long-term study of normal children. The seventy-four children who were involved in this long-term longitudinal enterprise (and who were studied in Block's 1971 research) are referred to as the Berkeley Guidance Study (BGS) subjects. The second longitudinal study that Block employed was started by Harold Jones in 1932. Here children were studied from the fifth grade onward. The sample was drawn from the Oakland, California, area, and therefore the ninety-seven children who were involved in this longitudinal study (and who were part of Block's 1971 research) are referred to as the Oakland Growth Study (OGS) subjects.

Both the BGS and the OGS subjects took part in repeated, often quite time-consuming testing sessions over much, if not most, of their lives; we have to recognize that such commitment may not be present among all people, and that—as is true of *all* samples in long-term longitudinal research—issues of representativeness, bias, and generalizability are present. However, as Block (1971) well argues, one must live with such problems because the long-term longitudinal "approach can respond to questions regarding psychological development not otherwise scientifically accessible" (p. 1). Indeed, without longitudinal research such as Block's (1971), the conditions, causes, and consequences of constancy and change—of continuity and discontinuity—could not be de-

Jack Block

scribed or understood. Let us turn, then, to a discussion of Block's study to discern how his ipsative approach allows one to understand the nature and implications of individual constancies and changes across life.

The Orientation of the Study

Block wanted to combine the BGS and the OGS samples in order to increase his sample size and thus the power of his statistical analysis and his ability to discern possible subgroups of people whose personality development was of a particular type. Because the OGS sample was not studied until late childhood/early adolescence (that is, they were recruited in the fifth grade), it was not possible to combine the samples—that is, to use information from the BGS prior to the adolescent period. Thus Block's study is, as we noted above, an assessment of personality development from adolescence to adulthood—that is, from junior high school to the time the subjects of the study were established in their families and their careers. Consistent with contemporary views of the adolescent period (e.g., Brooks-Gunn and Petersen 1983; Lerner 1981) as one in which substantial personality and social development and change may occur, Block argued that,

> contrary to the view still largely held within psychoanalysis, with its emphasis on the irreversible and determinative significance for character formation of the first few years, adolescence is a time of considerable change and considerable consequence. Contrary to the cumulative, continuous view of personality evolvement held within reinforcement theory, which heavily influences the field of developmental psychology, adolescence is a time often of dramatic personality flux, consolidation, and redirection. (1971, 2)

Thus Block asserts, as I have argued, too, in previous chapters, that the course of life is not irrevocably set in the early years; he also argues (and we shall see that his study provides evidence) that there is often individually distinct change—as well as constancy—across the years following childhood.

Accordingly, although Block does not deny the relevance of nomothetic laws or the usefulness of nomothetic analyses, he believes that

> developmental psychology has been hampered in its progress to date because, in its preferred world, it has staked much and clung too long to the assumption of uniformity of relationships ... the presumption ... that *all* people develop in the same way ... [and that] in the main, temporal correspondence or stability is to be expected if measurement has been adequate and important, central variables are considered. (Block, 1971, 10)

Thus, while "normative trends and continuities in personality development" have been emphasized in previous work,

> the emphasis in the present work, to achieve more complete understanding, is upon consideration of *different life trends* and the significance of *personality changes* for later behavior and adjustment. (Block 1971, 10)

Block contends that life paths that differ in kind and direction, as well as in rate, represent an idea antithetical to a nomothetic one, which emphasizes universal laws that apply to all people. But as we discussed in Chapter 7, in our presentation of the ipsative perspective, "universal applicability and lawfulness need not go together" (Block 1971, 11); in addition, the presence of laws of development pertinent to one or only to relatively few people does not deny that there are features of these people's development to which universal laws may apply. In fact, I noted in Chapter 7 that—despite the potentially unique intraindividual developmental courses of different people—it may be that the structural development of any individual life trajectory may be capable of description by the orthogenetic principle (Block 1982; Lerner 1978; Werner 1957). Indeed, it may be that individual ontogenesis is characterized by a synthesis of singular (idiographic) and generic (nomothetic) developments (Block 1971; Lerner 1984). Such a possibility leads Block (1971) to posit that development is best viewed as neither idiographic nor nomothetic, but rather as a phenomenon that may be identified as existing along a continuum anchored at its extremes by the concepts of nomothetic and idiographic.

Block (1971) marshals considerable evidence in support of this notion, which is reminiscent of the often-cited observation of Kluckhohn and Murray (1948, 35) that in certain respects every person is (*a*) like all other people (e.g., the orthogenetic principle may be used to describe any person's structural pattern of change); (*b*) like some other people (e.g., people's personality development may be divisible into subgroupings on the basis of their sex, race, ethnicity, child-rearing experiences, etc.); and (*c*) like no other person (e.g., the particular constellation of personality or behavior attributes possessed by a person may be singular to him or her). To understand how Block (1971) was able to provide data illustrating all three of these features of development we must discuss his research methodology.

Methods of Research

When one wants to study intraindividual change across a substantial portion of the life span, one has at least two major options. One can plan one's own study and select subjects, methods, measures, and times (ages) of observation. Then one can implement these plans and—for instance, if one is concerned with intraindividual change from early adolescence through middle adulthood—begin the twenty-year-or-so process of conducting one's study. On the other hand, one can turn to one of the relatively few longitudinal data archives that exist and try to address one's interest by capitalizing on these already-existing data. Of course, the characteristics of the subject population and of the methods and the measures, as well as the ages of observation, may not match ideally with what one desires. In fact, as Block (1971) found—and as I believe is generally the case in regard to broad-based, long-term longitudinal archives—data available for one subject may not be exactly the same as that available for any other subject in the archive; some subjects miss testing sessions, others supply additional information—such as letters, school reports, or hospital records—and still others are simply more cooperative than others.

However—if the longitudinal archive is rich in depth and breadth of coverage, if the researcher is willing to live with methodological features he or she would not have wanted, and if the unevenness of data across subjects can be surmounted through the researcher's conceptual and methodological ingenuity—the advantages in time (and cost) of using an archive to address one's concerns may be greater than those to be gained by initiating a new study. In fact, given the extreme commitment in time and money of such an enterprise, as well as the difficulty in locating and maintaining a longitudinal sample for a substantial portion of the life span, the practical reality may be that if questions of long-term constancy and change are to be addressed, a researcher has no recourse *other* than to use a longitudinal archive. If such a decision is indeed taken, then the procedures of Block—who himself was faced with the above methodological issues and chose to use the IHD archival data—serve as excellent examples to follow. Block was faced with issues involving the subjects, the measures, the methods, and the incommensurability of data across subjects.

Let us discuss these issues and see how Block dealt with them.

Subjects

We have already seen some of the characteristics of the BGS and the OGS samples. Let us note some others, which underscore the fact noted earlier—that longitudinal samples tend to have characteristics different from those that would be seen in a random sample of the population. Both IHD groups were, in general, brighter than average, although the former group scored somewhat higher. The mean IQ score of the BGS subjects was 123 (standard deviation = 15.99), and the mean IQ of the OGS subjects was 116 (standard deviation = 11.81). Moreover, within both the BGS and the OGS groups there tended to be a greater-than-typical representation of families of higher socioeconomic standing. In addition, for 81 percent of the subjects, their families were intact through their adolescence.

Finally, we should note again that the way in which Block made sure that at least the age periods were commensurate across both groups was to study only the junior-high-school-to-adulthood age range. This left him with 171 subjects, about equally divided in regard to sex (e.g., 84 males and 87 females were studied in adulthood), but this sample was much smaller than the original one of 212 for the OGS and 248 for the BGS. Accordingly, sample attrition is a problem in this study; this means that not only may results be difficult to generalize precisely to a broader population, but it also means that we do not know the extent to which the 171 subjects—who remained in the study from early adolescence through adulthood—provide data comparable to what could be derived from the 289 subjects who did not remain in the study.

The nature of the longitudinal archive

We have already noted that the IHD archives did not provide exactly the same information for each of the subjects. This lack of equivalence presented a problem that manifested itself in several ways. First,

Block (1971) notes that at least some data was missing for a great number of subjects. Second, across the years the procedures needed to test subjects changed; this made it difficult to determine if differences over time were due to developmental or methodological changes. Third, across the two IHD samples (BGS and OGS) there was some difference in conceptual frame of reference; in turn, Block approached the research with a set of concepts that differed from those of either the original BGS or the original OGS researchers. This difference in conceptual orientation means that the variables of interest to the original IHD scientists, and about which data were collected, were not those of greatest interest to Block. For example, he notes that in the 1920s and 1930s, when the BGS and the OGS were initiated, there was major interest in such relatively overt and practically applicable variables as "leadership" and "behavior problems"; at the time of Block's (1971) research, however, major interest was in more covert variables such as "identity formation" and "ego mechanisms."

Another problem Block faced pertaining to the nonequivalence of data across subjects arose from the presence of considerable naturalistic data about each subject. That is, in addition to the quantitative tests and measures for each subject, there was anecdotal information about each subject—about his or her behavior at home, in school, or in peer groups. In addition, news clippings (if any) about subjects were included, as well as records of any informal encounters they had with IHD staff members. Lastly, Block (1971) notes, "Unpredictable events happen, and people react complexly" (p. 35). That is, nonnormative events occur in the lives of some people—for example, death, divorce, sudden illnesses—and these may influence the course of development in major ways. Information about these events was also in the subjects' files, and since different people have different histories of life events, this represents a major basis of lack of equivalent information across subjects.

In sum, the IHD archives provided a rich source of quantitative and qualitative information about each subject. However, this richness—which existed in regard to both the BGS and the OGS samples at the early-adolescent (junior high school), middle-adolescent (high school), and adulthood (the fourth decade of life) age levels—was not present in exactly equivalent ways across subjects. Block wanted to discern what, if any, differentiated patterns of personality development existed across the early-adolescent-to-adulthood age range; more specifically, he wanted to identify potentially distinct patterns of constancy and change in personality development from the first measurement time (early adolescence) to the second (middle adolescence), and from the second to the third (adulthood). But how could he score, or rate, the available data to address this concern in a manner that would allow him to know whether differences in personality development were "real" or merely a reflection of the fact that the different sorts of information about each subject made likely different depictions of personality change? Block needed to find a way to rate the different sets of information so as to provide comparable data bases for each subject; only then could he begin to see if personality developed in a differentiated or in a universal way. The means Block took to address this issue resulted in the main data of the "Lives Through Time" study and, in addition, constituted his ipsative methodological approach to understanding personality development.

The Q-sort procedure

Block assembled a group of twenty-seven clinically experienced mental health professionals (eleven males and sixteen females). These clinicians served as a panel of "judges," or raters, of the subjects' personalities. That is, at least two, and typically more, of these judges read through a complete file on a given subject for one of the three age periods in question (early or middle adolescence or adulthood). Each judge then independently contributed ratings of the subject's personality via the Q-sort procedure.

As described by Block (1971):

> The Q-sort procedure is simply a set of mildly technical rules for the scaling of a group of personality-descriptive variables (Q items) vis-à-vis a particular individual, so that the ultimate ordering of the Q items expresses well the judge's formulation of the personality of the individual being evaluated. (p. 37)

The Q items Block (1971) presented to the judges to rate the subjects during their adulthood was a version of the California Q set (CQ set), which was developed by Block (1961). There are 100 items in the CQ set. Some of these are "is critical, skeptical, not easily impressed"; "basically submissive"; "has warmth; is compassionate"; "responds to humor"; "has fluctuating moods"; and "is verbally fluent; can express ideas well."

Corresponding versions of the CQ set were used to rate the subjects as adolescents. That is, a 104-item adolescent CQ set was used by the judges to assess adolescent personality structure and dynamics. Ninety items in the adolescent CQ parallel those in the CQ set used to rate the subjects as adults (Block 1971). Some representative items are "seeks reassurance from others"; "feels satisfied with self"; and "questing for meaning, self-definition or redefinition."

Finally, a sixty-three-item interpersonal Q set was used by judges to rate the subjects' behavior, during adolescence, in regard to peer-group relations, attitudes toward parents, and differential behavior with peers and with adults. Some representative items are "subject (S) respects his parents"; "is competitive with peers"; and "is dependent on peers."

But how does a judge use a given Q set to formulate his or her ratings of a subject? After reading a file and formulating an impression of the subject, the judge—in order to quantify his or her impression—is instructed to

> order the Q items into a designated number of categories and, most important, with an as-

signed number of items placed in each category. At one end of the judgmental continuum are placed those items most characteristic of the person being described or most "salient" in describing him. At the other end of the continuum are placed the items most uncharacteristic or most "salient" in a negative sense in formulating the personality description of the designated subject.

> Conventionally, the Q items are printed separately on cards, a convenience which permits easy arrangement and rearrangement until the desired ordering is obtained. After the sorting, the placement of each item is recorded. The categories into which the judge has placed the Q statements are themselves numbered, from 9 through 1, with 9 by convention referring to the most characteristic end of the continuum and the number 1 to the least characteristic end. For each item, the number of the category in which it was placed is recorded as that item's value in the personality description. With the data entered in this fashion ready for subsequent analysis, the procedure is completed. (Block 1971, 38)

Thus, despite missing data, procedural changes, new conceptual foci, or the differential presence of life-event data, judges—after reading a file—can rate each subject on a set of Q items that are consistent across subjects at a given age period. To illustrate, with the CQ set used by the judges to rate the subjects as adults, the 100 items are required to be sorted into nine categories: Five items (cards) must be placed in category 1, eight into category 2, twelve into category 3, sixteen into category 4, eighteen into category 5, sixteen into category 6, twelve into category 7, eight into category 8, and five into category 9. Scores of 1 through 9, respectively, are assigned to the cards put into each of the above categories. Similarly, the 104 items of the adolescent CQ set are required to be distributed among the nine categories according to the following distribution: 6, 9, 13, 15, 18, 15, 13, 9, and 6.

The judges were instructed by Block to formulate their ratings from an *ipsative* frame of reference. That is, for each Q item it was the judge's task to appraise "the saliency or the decisiveness of the item in shaping or characterizing" (Block 1971, 46) that particular subject's personality. Thus the placement of an item into a category (1 through 9) was *not* made on the basis of how a given subject compared to any other subject. Rather the placement of an item was made by "comparing the subject against himself or herself." That is, how important was this item, as compared to the others used to constitute the subject's personality, in *shaping* the subject's personality? Thus ratings were intraindividual. As we saw in respect to the Thomas and Chess (1977) NYLS, wherein nine categories of temperament were used to characterize all subjects, Block's (1971) use of the Q-sort procedure "imposed," or defined, the attribute repertoire for each subject (i.e., the 100- or 104-item Q set used to rate the subjects as adults and as adolescents, respectively, constituted each subject's attribute repertoire). However, it was the judges' ratings (and the ratings' statistical analyses, e.g., factor analyses) that determined the attribute interrelation of the subjects.

In sum, by using the Q-sort procedure, Block (1971) was able to move the IHD archival data set from one providing incommensurate information across subjects to one allowing for a common set of ratings at each of the three age levels studied. Thus application of Q-sort methodology allowed Block to capitalize on the richness present in the IHD archive.

However, as with virtually any methodological strategy, its uses exist along with its limitations (see Chapter 12 for a fuller discussion of this point). Thus the Q-sort procedure has liabilities as well as assets. For example, given the requirements of sorting Q items in a fixed frequency distribution, there is an imposed (and negative) expected-average correlation among the items; that is, the statistically conventional null hypothesis—which here would be that there is no correlation among the items (that there is, for instance, no personality structure discernible in the ratings of the Q items)—does not hold for Q items rated by the Q-sort procedure (Nesselroade, personal communication, September 1982). This nonzero and, in fact, neg-

ative-expected-average correlation makes difficult the interpretation of the significance levels of correlation coefficients (which are typically judged for their statistical significance on the basis of whether they differ from an expected correlation of zero, i.e., from the null hypothesis of "no correlation").

In addition to this statistical issue, a conceptual one may be raised. Mischel (1983) has noted that the Q items are not all conceptually independent. That is, putting a given item into one category—for example, category 9, which indicates high salience in depicting the person—means that other items are likely to be rated with similar salience levels; in turn, if a Q item might "carry" other Q items with it, this also suggests that there may be items that, for reasons of a "negative carrying effect," may be placed in a category far from the item in question. For instance, in the adult CQ set, placement of item 57 ("is an interesting, arresting person") in a category of a given salience may imply that item 88 ("is personally charming") be placed in the same or in a close-by category, and that item 48 ("aloof, keeps people at a distance; avoids close interpersonal relationships") be placed further away.

Block (1971) was, of course, aware of these potential problems with the Q-sort procedure, and he took steps to address them. Thus he trained his judges extensively to avoid making stereotypic ratings. In addition, he instructed them that they could rate conceptually similar items in distinct ways. Finally, his use of multiple judges for each subject meant that reliable composite ratings could be (and indeed were) formed; in addition, the presence of multiple judges meant that a subject's scores were not a product of the biases (e.g., the implicit personality theory or stereotype) of a single judge. Thus while Block acknowledges that his results are, of course, a function of his particular method of assessment, he does not believe his findings are merely an artifact of his method. He states:

> Although the results are inevitably a function of the variable set employed, this variable set

appears to have sufficient degrees of freedom so that personality diversities can be manifested. Thus, the dependency of the relationships found upon the particular Q items employed is not methodologically bothersome. The limitation, to the extent it exists, is the limit on current ways of viewing personality rather than a deficiency of a particular method. (Block 1971, 114)

But what are the results found by Block? What evidence exists for the presence of stability and for change? What evidence is there that personality develops in other than a nomothetic, universal fashion? To answer these questions we turn to a presentation of some of the key results of Block's research.

The Findings of Block's (1971) Study

Block's findings are presented in well over 200 pages of his 1971 book. As a consequence we may here consider only a summary of some of the key findings of his data analyses. It should be noted that these analyses are complicated as well as numerous. Although Block strives to analyze his data in as straightforward a manner as possible, the large number of variables he had to deal with simultaneously required that some relatively sophisticated multivariate procedures be used to reduce the complexity of the data. For example, the adolescent CQ set included 104 variables and the adult CQ set had 100 variables; thus, to reduce the complexity of dealing with interrelationships among so many variables, at times Block used factor analysis as a multivariate data-analysis technique with which to identify patterns of relationships among variables. We shall see that factor analysis was used, for instance, to identify particular types of personality development. Before considering these types, however, it is useful to discuss other bases of differential personality development that were found in the data.

Sex differences in personality attributes studied over time

Block first sought to ascertain whether the men in the sample followed courses of personality development that differed from those of the women in the sample. Simply, he was concerned with whether, *in general,* the sex of the subject was associated with differential patterns of personality constancy and change. Of course, to address this concern Block had to specify what he meant by pattern, type, or category of continuity or of change. To define such types or categories of continuity or change, Block had to deal with three features of developmental change in his data.

1.   *Correspondence.* This facet of change refers to the *correlation* between personality attributes (Q items) studied at one time (e.g., early adolescence) and those same attributes studied at a second time (e.g., middle adolescence).

2.   *Salience level.* This facet of development refers to the mean (average) level of the rating given to personality attributes. The higher the rating, the more salient that attribute in depicting the person.

3.   *Salience heterogeneity.* This facet of development refers to the dispersion (variation) among salience levels. Here the concern is with whether attributes have similar (homogeneous) or dissimilar (heterogeneous and, therefore, dispersed) salience levels.

Using these three components of development, Block generated seven categories of continuity and change. Figure 10.2 lists these categories and, in addition, diagramatically portrays their meaning. For each of the seven categories presented in the figure, the statistical criteria used by Block (1971) to define the category are shown. For each category there is a presentation of the statistical criterion for either (1) correspondence, expressed as a correlation coefficient (r) calculated between two measurement times; and/or (2) salience level, expressed as a t-ratio between means derived from two measurement occasions; and/or (3) salience heterogeneity, expressed as a t-ratio of differences between the standard deviations (as a measure of variability) associated with the means derived from two measurement occasions.

Using these categories, we may turn now

to the issue of whether males in general showed a different pattern of personality continuity or change than did females. We should note that the time interval between measurement times 1 and 2—that is, from junior high school (JHS) to senior high school (SHS)—was only three years. However, the time interval between measurement time 2 (SHS) and measurement time 3 (adulthood) was about twenty years. Thus we might expect that if change was found, it would be more evident among both sexes between time 2 and time 3 than between time 1 and time 2. This was in fact found. For both sexes, there were more Q items in the sameness and order-maintained categories across the JHS-SHS period than across the SHS-adulthood period. However,

women tended to change more than men; in the time 2–time 3 comparison forty-eight Q items showed significant changes for women, while only thirty-one Q items showed such changes for men.

But what were the specific patterns of continuity and change found for men and women? Table 10.3 shows some of the Q items for which significant personality continuities and changes were found within the IHD male and female samples studied by Block (1971). This is an admittedly complicated table. Nevertheless, it is possible to summarize some of the trends in personality-development it displays. For males, the JHS-SHS period was marked by continuity with respect to Q items related to expressiveness, personal resiliency, and a cognitive

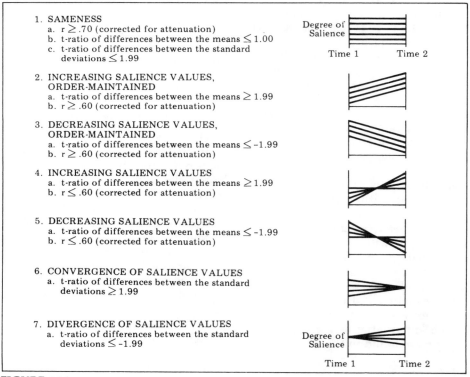

FIGURE 10.2
The criteria employed by Block (1971) to define categories of continuity and change.
Source: Block 1971, 63.

orientation; there were changes in this period as well, and these were in regard to Q items related to cognitive concerns, sexual interest, and dependence. In turn, the males' SHS-adulthood period was marked by continuity in respect to such attributes as cognitive orientation, dependability and by change in such attributes as self-assurance, aggressiveness in interactions, and preoccupation with somatic concerns.

For females, the JHS-SHS period was marked by a continuity in expressiveness, a concern for interpersonal relatedness, and a cognitive orientation, and by change in regard to an intensification of reflecting on life, an increase in heterosexual interests, and greater interpersonal deviousness. In turn, the SHS-adulthood period shows continuity for females in respect to a passive/conforming-versus-expressive/aggressive orientation and in respect to a cognitive-intuitive orientation; change, however, was seen in respect to movement toward a "psychological-mindedness" (e.g., introspectiveness) and toward a culturally stereotypical definition of femininity (see the discussion of this stereotype in Chapter 9).

In sum, by the time the IHD subjects reach adulthood they have shown, from early adolescence on, substantial sex differences in their patterns of personality continuities and change. As Block (1971) concludes, these sex differences are as much reflective of stereotypic cultural pressures regarding sex roles as they may be of biological pressures. Thus the IHD males became more goal-oriented and self-satisfied and, in addition, changed in the direction of becoming less esthetically reactive, less responsive to humor, less straightforward, and more narrow in their interests. In turn, the IHD women became more psychologically-minded and showed greater tenderness in close interpersonal relationships; in addition, they showed more esthetic orientation, more protectiveness, and more sympathy. In short, as we saw in our discussion of the Kagan and Moss (1962) study, Block's (1971) study indicates that both constancy and change characterize people's development

across life, and that sex is an important differential variable in such development; sex differences in personality development exist, and they often reflect culturally stereotypic sex-role prescriptions.

Block (1971) points out, however, that this pattern of sex differences in development reflects only a general trend in the IHD sample. Not all males show the same pattern of personality development and, similarly, not all females follow an identical course of personality development. Indeed, Block posited that there may be as much, if not more, within-sex as between-sex variation. Block was, in fact, quite correct about this point. Although we may profitably discuss numerous other facets of Block's (1971) data, let us turn to the findings that provide evidence for the presence of different kinds, or types, of personality development within both males and females.

Different courses of personality development among the IHD males and females: Block's typological approach

As we noted earlier, Block contended that personality development was a phenomenon that existed at some midway point on a continuum whose end points were idiographic and nomothetic. Block's view translates into the contention that while, on the one hand, there may be no one completely universal (nomothetic) course to personality development, on the other hand, there should not be completely singular development either. While people are not completely alike, not everyone is completely different from everyone else. Thus, while there may not be one universal pattern of personality development, there may be coherent subgroups of people—that is, people who have a particular pattern of personality development, one shared by some but not all others. Indeed, Block's (1971) identification of sex differences in the personality development of the IHD sample illustrates two general subgroupings; the male type of personality development and the female type. However, as noted, Block believed that grouping just by

TABLE 10.3

Some of the Q Items for Which Significant Personality Continuities and Changes Were Found Within the IHD Male and Female Samples Studied by Block (1971)

Category of Continuity and Change	MALES		FEMALES	
	JHS-SHS	SHS-Adulthood	JHS-SHS	SHS-Adulthood
1. Sameness	Arouses liking Turned to for advice Warm Socially perceptive Plus ten additional items	Values intellectual matters Verbally fluent	Values intellectual matters Aesthetically reactive Overcontrolled Undercontrolled Plus ten additional items	No items met the criterion for this category
2. Increasing salience, order maintained	High intellectual capacity Philosophically concerned High aspiration level Questing for meaning	Dependable Prides self on objectivity	Philosophically concerned Questing for meaning Deceitful Basic hostility	Wide interests Values intellectual matters Philosophically concerned Submissive
3. Decreasing salience, order maintained	Dependable Fantasizes Extrapunitive Thin-skinned Plus two additional items	Intellectual capacity Aesthetically reactive Undercontrolled Fantasizing	Dependable Productive Arouses liking Warm Plus four additional items	Rebellious Intellectual capacity
4. Increasing salience	Calm Interesting Affected Eroticizing Interested in opposite sex	Feels satisfied with self Philosophically concerned Fastidious Overcontrolled Plus nine additional items	Distrustful Affected Interested in opposite sex	Introspective Straightforward Cheerful Feels guilty Plus thirteen additional items

(Continued on next page)

TABLE 10.3 (*continued*)

Category of Continuity and Change	MALES		FEMALES	
	JHS-SHS	SHS-Adulthood	JHS-SHS	SHS-Adulthood
5. Decreasing salience	Self-defensive Projective Favors status quo Fearful Plus three additional items	Responds to humor Interesting Sensuous Lacks personal meaning Plus seven additional items	Expresses hostile feelings directly	Fantasizing Sensuous Undercontrolled Power-oriented Plus eighteen additional items
6. Convergence	No items converged	Productive Eroticizes Interested in opposite sex Physically attractive	No items converged	Expressive Responds to humor Intellectual capacity Dependable Plus nine additional items
7. Divergence	Affected Favors status quo Calm Philosophically concerned	Self-defensive Somatizes Brittle Expresses hostile feelings directly Plus two additional items	Prides self on objectivity Interesting Questing for meaning Deceitful Plus three additional items	Introspective Satisfied with self Evaluates situation in motivational terms Arouses nurturance Plus four additional items

Source: *Based on Block (1971, 66-68, 70, 72-73).*

sex did not provide a sufficiently fine discrimination for the course of personality development. He believed that several different *types* of personality development might exist among males and females.

Block (1971) defined a type "as a subset of individuals characterized by a reliably unique or discontinuously different pattern of covariation across time with respect to a specifiable (and non-trivial) set of variables" (pp. 109–10), and he believed that the reliable identification of types would help psychologists accept the view "that the nomothetic, monolithic view of personality functioning is gross, misguided, and outworn" (p. 110).

Block's procedure to identify reliably different personality types is perhaps the best illustration of the ipsative character of his research. The Q-sort procedure involves the intraindividual distribution of a set of Q items, such that one achieves an ordering of items—from those highly salient (or characteristic) to those of low salience—*within* a person. Block (1971, 114) believes that this "ordering of variables . . . [is the] sufficient basis for defining the personality configuration of a subject." In order to have an empirical indication of the presence of a resemblance in the order of Q items for different subjects sufficient to categorize them as having the same type of personality, Block calculated product-moment correlation coefficients among the orderings found for the IHD subjects. He then factor analyzed the resulting matrix of correlations in order to see if types emerged as the results of these analyses.

As Block notes, factor analysis is a multivariate statistical procedure for reducing the complexity of a set of relationships. The procedure allows one to estimate the number of dimensions to which some (larger) set of relationships (e.g., correlations) may be reduced; the procedure—of which there exist many variants—allows one to discern the structure that exists in a matrix of relationships. For instance, in a correlation matrix involving 100 variables (all related each to the other), there are too many interrelations

to summarize without some attempt at reduction of this complexity. Factor analysis might reveal, however that the relationships in the matrix could be described by reference to only a relatively few higher-order relationships, or "factors"; for example, it may be that one group of twenty of the items correlate highly with each other but do not relate highly to any other items; that another group of twenty items similarly interrelate highly among themselves but not highly with any other items; and so forth. Thus it may be, in this example, that the 100-item correlation matrix could be reduced to a five-factor structure. That is, there may be five groupings of items—five dimensions—each with twenty items, that constitute the factor structure for that matrix.

Thus factor analysis, when used to analyze correlations among items (or variables), can reveal how variables form together to form factor dimensions. However, one can also apply factor analysis to a matrix of correlations among people—that is, the sort of matrix that Block (1971) generated when he intercorrelated the IHD subjects' ordering of Q items. When factor analysis is used to analyze correlations among people, *factor types* are derived, and one may interpret these types as the categories into which different people may be placed. The technical term for this type of factor analysis—one that identifies clusters, or types, of people (as opposed to clusters, or "types," of variables)—is Q-factor analysis.

Block performed one Q-factor analysis for the IHD males and another for the IHD females. As he expected, evidence was found within each sex group for different personality types. In fact, although a relatively few subjects in each sex group did not have personality structures clearly classifiable into a given type, most subjects fell rather well into one of the Q-factor-analysis-derived categories. Block identified five male types and six female types. The labels associated with these types are presented in Table 10.4. Let us discuss briefly some of the key features of the course of personality development associated with each of these male and female types.

THE MALE TYPES. For each of the five male types identified by Block we shall note some of the Q items found to be most characteristic of their personalities at each of the three times of measurement.

1. The Ego Resilients

During JHS, Q items found to be highly characteristic of Ego Resilient males were "dependable, productive, ambitious, bright, values intellectual matters, likable, has a wide range of interests, verbally fluent, poised, straightforward, sympathetic, and interesting" (Block 1971, 139). Many of these items were found in SHS to remain as highly characteristic of these males. Similarly, in adulthood, these males continued to be highly characterized by such items. In short, throughout the JHS-SHS-adulthood period these males are characteristically goal-oriented and individually and interpersonally effective people. As Block (1971, 149) puts it, the Ego Resilient male "was blessed with more than his share of native intelligence, good health, and physical endowment ... [he] has been favored by circumstance from the beginning and he did not muff his opportunities."

2. The Belated Adjusters

During JHS, Q items found to be highly characteristic of Belated Adjuster males were "basically hostile, withdraws when frustrated, self-indulgent, self-defeating, bothered by demands, extrapunitive, brittle, projective, and negativistic" (Block 1971, 151). However, the presence of this relatively negative set of items began to diminish by SHS. Although these males were still characterized by items such as "gives up and withdraws when frustrated," "negativistic," and "testing of limits," Block notes that these subjects became significantly *more* warm, aware of their impression on others, valuing of intellectual matters, and internally consistent, and *less* irritable, extrapunitive, hostile, and self-indulgent. The more positive picture of these males found in SHS was evident also in their adulthood assessments. Items found to be characteristic of these males were "dependable, sympathetic, giving, protective, productive, likable, warm, calm, straightforward, cheerful, and internally consistent." Thus, the Belated Adjusters show substantial change from JHS to adulthood. They develop from being what Block (1971, 158) terms a "nasty adolescent" that is, an adolescent marked by "narcissistic, sulky, fitful and fickle" behavior—to being an adult who is cheerful, parental, relaxed, a steady worker—in short, a contributing member of society.

3. The Vulnerable Overcontrollers

During their JHS period the Vulnerable Overcontroller males were found to have several Q items that characterized their personalities. These were overcontrolled, aloof, thin-skinned, ruminative, uncomfortable with uncertainty, and distrustful. Many of these attributes continued to characterize these males in SHS; for instance, they were still overcontrolled, distrustful, aloof, and uncomfortable with uncertainty. In addition, they were seen now to be critical, emotionally bland, delaying of action, and guilty.

TABLE 10.4
Types of Personality Development Identified by Block (1971) in the IHD Male and Female Samples

Male Types	Female Types
1. Ego Resilients	1. Female Prototypes
2. Belated Adjusters	2. Cognitive Copers
3. Vulnerable Overcontrollers	3. Hyperfeminine Repressives
4. Anomic Extraverts	4. Dominating Narcissists
5. Unsettled Undercontrollers	5. Vulnerable Undercontrollers
	6. Lonely Independents

Similarly, in adulthood, these males were characterized along similar lines—for example, they were aloof, basically hostile, self-defensive, thin-skinned, ruminative, distrustful, and uncomfortable with uncertainty. They also felt cheated and victimized by life and were self-defeating, projective, and submissive. Thus, although there is continuity from JHS to adulthood in these males' overcontrolled, "uptight," anxious, and introverted characteristics, and in their uneasiness in interpersonal situations, there seems to be some change as well. Block (1971) notes that by adulthood there has been a "cost" for the lifetime of overcontrol. These males are barely tolerable to themselves. The Vulnerable Overcontroller has been now defeated by life, and he "is exposed to his despairs, confronted with his failures, and is resourceless before them" (Block 1971, 168).

4.   The Anomic Extroverts

Males who were categorized as Anomic Extroverts were characterized in JHS as gregarious, masculine, assertive, likable, cheerful, poised, and conventional. This outgoing interpersonal style shows continuity into SHS. These males continue to be gregarious, assertive, and cheerful; in addition, they become emotionally involved with members of the same sex, have a rapid personal tempo, test limits imposed on them, and are undercontrolled. By the time of their adult testing, a major change occurs with these males, however. The prototypic males they seemed as JHS adolescents (e.g., gregarious, cheerful, and vigorous), and to a great extent as SHS adolescents as well (e.g., they remained gregarious, but in addition they changed to show undercontrol), is not now apparent. As adults they are characterized by such Q items as "uncomfortable with uncertainty, basically hostile, self-defensive, repressive, brittle, irritable, conventional, and moody." Block (1971) characterizes these males, as adults, as having a repressive character structure and a sense of anomie; that is, he notes that they lack personal meaning and an inner life, and that they are suspicious, bitter, and valueless.

5.   The Unsettled Undercontrollers

During their JHS period the Unsettled Undercontroller males were rebellious and covertly hostile with adults. Indeed, these males perceived their parents as restraining their activities and viewed their family life as conflicted. In turn, with peers they were talkative, attention-getting, initiating of humor, and assertive. The relatively negative characteristics seen in JHS tended to become accentuated in SHS, when these males were characterized as being rebellious, hostile toward others, thin-skinned, self-defeating, undercontrolled, irritable, bothered by demands, and negativistic; in addition, they showed fluctuating moods and lacked a sense of meaning in life. Rebelliousness, moodiness, and undercontrol continued to characterize these males when they were assessed as adults. In addition, however, they were rated as talkative, interesting, rapid in tempo, and bright. Thus Block characterizes these males, as adults, as impulsive and unsettled. In essence, then, these males showed a continuity in their being rebellious and undercontrolled.

THE FEMALE TYPES.   As noted in Table 10.4, Block identified six female types. As with the male types, we shall note some of the Q items found to be most characteristic of the personalities of each type at each time of measurement.

1.   The Female Prototypes

In JHS the Q items rated to be characteristic of the Female Prototype females were "likable, poised, cheerful, gregarious, dependable, warm, productive, giving, sympathetic, straightforward, fastidious, physically attractive, socially perceptive, turned-to-for-advice and reassurance, protective, and aware of her social stimulus value" (Block 1971, 190). In SHS many of these same attributes continue to characterize the females; in addition, seemingly compatible items ("responsive to humor, talkative, and feminine") are also seen to characterize them. Similarly, there is continuity into adulthood for many of the JHS and SHS attributes. In addition, the attribute of "over-controlled" is seen to characterize these women. Block (1971) sees these females as having needs and capacities that are highly congruent with the prototypic societal demands and values regarding the women's roles (see also our discussion in Chapter 9 of Jeanne Block's 1973 work on this societal perspective). Thus these females show substantial continuity from JHS to adulthood and are, as adults, at ease with themselves and others and are optimistic, nurturant, and attractive people.

2.   *The Cognitive Copers*

During JHS the females categorized as Cognitive Copers were characterized as overcontrolled, thin-skinned, aloof, distrustful, and basically hostile; in addition, they felt guilty, fearful, and victimized, and they were bothered by demands, uncomfortable with uncertainty, ruminative, self-defensive, and tended to fantasize. This essentially negative depiction in early adolescence may be expected to bode ill for these females. However, in SHS these females were seen as having a high degree of intellectual capacity and as being dependable and productive; in addition, they were also seen to continue to be overcontrolled and to be hostile toward others and judgmental in regard to human conduct. Thus, and perhaps as a means of coping with their negative characteristics, we find these females in SHS combining positive cognitive attributes with those other personality characteristics seen in JHS. This cognitive emphasis is found to be more prominent in adulthood. Here these females are seen as having high intellectual capacity, as valuing intellectual matters, and as verbally fluent; in addition, these females are rated as dependable, introspective, ambitious, esthetically reactive, and as valuing their independence. Thus, as Block (1971) describes her, the Cognitive Coper "blossomed with the years, going from inadequacy in adolescence to an admirable competence as an adult" (p. 209).

3.   *The Hyperfeminine Repressives*

In JHS, females in the Hyperfeminine Repressive category were rated, as the label implies, as feminine and repressive. In addition they were seen as dependable, but as uncomfortable with uncertainty and as people who compared themselves to others. In SHS these females continued to be characterized as feminine, as calm and relaxed in manner, as sympathetic, and as accepting of their dependency. In addition these females favored the status quo and continued to show something of a repressive characteristic in that they handled anxiety and conflicts by attempting to exclude them from awareness. It is this repressive characteristic that implied potential problems for these females and, indeed, their adult personality characteristics seem essentially negative. They are seen as basically hostile, brittle, self-defensive adults who—as in JHS—are uncomfortable with uncertainty and, in addition, are distrustful, thin-skinned, aloof, irritable, self-defeating, extrapunitive, moody, and negativistic. They feel cheated and victimized by life, are bothered by demands put on them, and have concerns about their bodily integrity. Thus, although showing only a moderate and certainly not unique set of personal inadequacies in adolescence, the Hyperfeminine Repressive became in adulthood "a characterological shambles, unhappy, self-pitying [and] explosively but ineffectively reactive to frustrations" (Block 1971, 218).

4.   *The Dominating Narcissists*

In JHS the Dominating Narcissist females were characterized as both self-indulgent and self-defensive. In addition they were interested in the opposite sex, they eroticized, and they were undercontrolled. They were also rebellious, extrapunitive, assertive, and conventional. They expressed hostile feelings directly. In SHS these females continued to be self-indulgent and self-defensive as well as eroticizing and extrapunitive. However, in addition, they were seen as irritable, as bothered by demands, and as distrustful. In adulthood, the Dominating Narcissists were characterized by Q items that suggested both continuity and change between SHS and their later lives. The items associated with these females during adulthood were "assertive, power-oriented, proffers advice, condescending, and expresses hostile feelings directly." In addition, they were rated as socially poised, straightforward, and as feeling satisfied with themselves. Thus Block sees continuity in these females' aggressive, direct, interpersonal style, and a personality characterized by condescension, self-indulgence, and undercontrol. However, these women have become highly poised adults, a manner quite distinct from the pushy and "nasty" characteristics seen in adolescence.

5. *The Vulnerable Undercontrollers*

During their JHS period the Vulnerable Undercontroller females were characterized as talkative, self-dramatizing, and self-indulgent. In addition, they were seen as pushing the limits imposed on them, and as changeable and undercontrolled. In SHS these females continued to be seen as undercontrolled, and their fluctuating mood is consistent with their changeable style in early adolescence. In addition the females tended toward fantasizing and identified and romanticized individuals and causes. They enjoyed sensuous experiences, were facially and gesturally expressive, and sought reassurance from others. Finally, they were rated as brittle—that is, vulnerable to being easily hurt. As adults, these females continued to seek reassurance from others and were submissive to and aroused nurturance in others. They also continued to be emotionally changeable, that is, moody; in addition, they were concerned about their bodies, were self-defeating, and felt a lack of personal meaning in their lives. Block (1971) summarizes the changes involved in these females' personality development from early adolescence to adulthood as involving a "move toward a personal unpleasantness and undercontrol in adolescence and on to a pathetic self-unsureness in adulthood" (p. 236).

6. *The Lonely Independents*

In their JHS period the Lonely Independent females were seen as assertive, ambitious, and as valuing independence. In addition, they were seen as interesting and

expressive young adolescents. In SHS these females are still characterized as valuing their own independence and autonomy, as ambitious, and as interesting. In addition they valued intellectual matters and in fact had a high degree of intellectual capacity. However, they were now seen as rebellious, as irritable and bothered by demands imposed on them, and as critical and introspective. In their adulthood, these females continued to value their independence and to have high intellectual capacity. However, they also continued to be bothered by demands on them, and in addition they were seen now as basically hostile, skeptical, aloof, and distrustful. They felt cheated and victimized by (and felt a lack of personal meaning in) their lives. Thus over their early-adolescence-to-adulthood period these females experienced a continuity in their self-assertiveness and desire for autonomy. However, an increasingly more prominent social unconnectedness came to characterize them, and by adulthood they felt cheated by a life that held no personal meaning for them.

Conclusions

As noted earlier, there are several other quite significant features of Block's (1971) findings that we might review. However, I believe that the details we have presented are sufficient to allow us to see the merit of Block's approach to studying development *and* the substantive importance of his findings. His concern with the individual distinctiveness of people's lives led him to employ a longitudinal ipsative analysis of the changing intraindividual salience of a large set of personality attributes. His approach illustrates, then, the usefulness of merging a conceptual concern about individuality with a method of analysis designed to allow one to focus directly on what is developing within a person. Moreover, the "Lives Through Time" research stands as an excellent example of the use that can be made of a rich longitudinal archive by a capable and creative scientist.

The substantive import of Block's (1971) research is equally noteworthy. First, Block's findings amply demonstrate that both constancy *and* change characterize development. For all of the eleven (five male and six female) personality types that Block identified, we have seen instances of constancy from one time of measurement to the next; at the same time, and within the same personality type, we have seen instances of change as well. Thus, as noted in Chapter 6, both continuity and discontinuity exist simultaneously across life periods. Debate, then, should *not* be focused on which one is present. Rather, science must ask the more appropriate—but more difficult—questions, What are the bases and implications of the synthesis of continuity and discontinuity at particular times of life (and for particular types of people)? and What are the conditions under which constancy and/or change will be seen in a particular developmental process at a given point in time?

A second major substantive contribution of Block's (1971) research is the identification of the different courses of personality development present in the IHD sample. As we have seen also in respect to the Thomas and Chess (1977) NYLS, the presence of numerous distinct courses of development across life speaks to the empirical uselessness and conceptual limitations of any completely nomothetic, universalistic view of human development. People exist as distinctive and, in many ways, singular entities. Block's data, along with those of other scientists sensitive to ipsative analysis and the relative singularity of development across life (e.g., Lerner 1982; Nesselroade 1983; Nesselroade and Ford, in press; Thomas and Chess 1977; Thomas et al. 1963), serve to underscore the importance of focusing on each individual's attribute repertoire and the intraindividual changes in the content and structure of that repertoire over the course of life. Through such a focus the organizing role of the individual, as a central contributor to his or her own development, may best be understood.

11 | Theoretical- and Empirical- Behaviorism Approaches

In the preceding chapters we have focused predominantly on predetermined-epigenetic organismic or probabilistic-epigenetic organismic conceptions of development. These theoretical formulations view a person's psychological development as arising out of an interaction between the intrinsic (nature) and the extrinsic (nurture) variables involved in development. Moreover, such organismic, interactionist viewpoints imply that qualitative discontinuity in part characterizes psychological development, although—because of adherence to such ideas as the orthogenetic principle—they also see aspects of development as being continuous in nature. Thus, to differing extents, organismic developmentalists believe that development arises out of an interaction between the organism (and/or the characteristics of the organism) and its environment; furthermore, to different extents, organismic developmentalists represent such development as proceeding through qualitatively different stages.

Although such organismic conceptions have been given most attention in our presentation, we have also at points indicated that an important opposing point of view exists. This approach falls within the "family of theories" (Reese and Overton 1970) associated with a mechanistic, nurture-oriented view of development. Family members include positions labeled as empirical behav-

iorism—that is, the behavior-analysis or the operant-psychology approach (Reese 1976; White 1976)—or as theoretical behaviorism—that is, the learning-theory or the social-learning theory approaches (Reese 1976; White 1976).

In Chapter 6, in our discussion of the continuity-discontinuity controversy, we introduced some of the basic components of this general point of view and considered some of the ideas of perhaps the most famous contributor to the formulation of this mechanistic, nurture approach, B. F. Skinner. We saw that Skinner views the laws of classical and operant conditioning as being invariantly involved not only in the behavior of humans but, moreover, in the behavior of all animals. Thus Skinner maintains that the laws of classical or operant conditioning are universal; that is, they are continuously applicable to the behavior of all organisms. After one "corrects for" the (seemingly trivial) differences among animals in their anatomical or morphological makeup, one can use the same set of laws of conditioning to account for the behavior and the development of all animals. Skinner suggests that some animals behave in a certain way, for example by pressing a bar with a paw; other types of animals might have to use the beak, and still others might use a hand. Yet, after such differences are accounted for, one sees that all animals behave in accordance with the very same set of laws, those of classical and operant learning.

We may surmise, then, that as opposed to organismic theorists, developmentalists taking this approach or other variants of the mechanistic, nurture approach stress the continuities of behavioral development. They stress the view that the continuous applicability of mechanistic laws accounts for the development of behavior.

Thus mechanistic, nurture theories of development stress the influence of experiential and environmental variables on behavior change. However, it is important to understand that such a conception of nurture theories is a broad one. Not all nurture theorists whose ideas fall within this family of theories would label themselves as either learning theorists, social-learning theorists, or behavior analysts of the functional role of stimuli in the acquisition of behavior. In other words, they might differ about what is involved in the acquisition of behavior as a consequence of experience.

SOME DIMENSIONS OF DIVERSITY IN NURTURE-BEHAVIORIST THEORIES

There is great diversity among nurture theorists. Some, for instance, tie their accounts of behavior to the "laws" of classical and operant conditioning, and thus present their views of behavior change in terms of the functional relations between externally manipulable stimuli and objectively verifiable responses (Bijou 1976; Bijou and Baer 1961). Such an approach is often called a *functional analysis of behavior* (Bijou 1976, 1977) or is termed *behavior analysis* (Baer 1976, 1982; Reese 1976, 1982) because behavior (actually a response, R) is seen to be a function (f) of stimulation (S), or simply R = f(S). Reese (1976) labels this approach empirical behaviorism and notes that in this type of nurture theory the stress is on the

experimental analysis of developmental phenomena; indeed, it is this stress that leads Baer (1976, 1982) to label the approach as behavior analysis.

Because of the commitment to completely empirical stimulus-response (S-R) relations, nurture theorists who take a behavior-analysis aproach do not necessarily consider themselves "learning theorists" (Bijou 1977). Learning theorists are, instead, those who include in their systems phenomena that are not directly (extrinsically) empirically observable. This type of nurture theorist is a "theoretical behaviorist," and as Reese (1976, 70) explains, mental activities are given operational definitions, and organization of this activity is handled by assumed interdependencies among variables intervening between stimuli and responses.

For instance, theoretical behaviorists might talk about internal "mental" or "cognitive" responses and stimuli being involved in linking external S-R connections (e.g., Hull 1952; Kendler and Kendler 1962). Thus by including phenomena in their theories that, although derived from previous experience, are not present for extrinsic empirical observation, such learning theorists differ from those nurture theorists who adopt a behavior-analysis approach.

Moreover, further differentiations can be made among those committed to a nurture view. One can differentiate between those theoretical and empirical behaviorists who view behavior change as involving the necessary role of *reinforcement* (any stimulus that produces or maintains behavior or, in other words, makes a behavior more probable; Skinner 1950) and those who see nurture as capable of controlling behavior independent of the presence of any reinforcing stimulus (e.g., Bandura 1965; Bandura and Walters 1959, 1963). In other words, one can differentiate on the basis of the role given to reinforcement or to other nurture phenomena—for instance, the experience of observing others—in the control of behavior.

Bandura and Walters (1963), for example, assert that by observing others behave, a person can acquire new responses not previously in the behavior repertoire or come to show again a response that had been dropped from the response repertoire because of previous experience. By observing a model behave, they argue, a person can show such changes although there is no direct reinforcement to the person. Seeing the response consequences to the person who serves as the *model* of behavior (i.e., the person who displays the behavior a subject observes) and the social status of the model can affect the observer's behavior independently of any direct reinforcement (Bandura and Walters, 1963). Thus such nurture theorists contend that an observer—free of specific reinforcement for a particular response—may imitate a model's behavior if the status of the model is high (Bandura and Huston 1961) and if the response consequences to the model are positive. Such theorists are often termed *observational learning* ones. Alternatively, however, those who consider themselves reinforcement theorists say that an observer being influenced by a model does indeed involve reinforcement of the observer's behavior, albeit of a more general response than that involved in a specific, single act by a model (Gewirtz and Stingle 1968).

This discussion of the diversity among those who adopt nurture behaviorist positions neither raises nor resolves all the many issues dividing such scholars. Rather, it suggests that a range of views exists within the nurture theoretical camp and highlights the difficulty, if not the impossibility, of defining the precise attributes of "the" nurture view. In fact, differences between empirical behaviorism (e.g., the behavior-analysis approach) and theoretical behaviorism (i.e., the learning-theory position) on the one hand, and between reinforcement theory and observational learning theory on the other, are just two of the many dimensions of disparity that might be mentioned (cf. Baer 1982; Reese 1976, 1982; White 1976).

To facilitate our discussion, let us use the term *nurture behaviorism* to refer to a general, mechanistic, nurture view of development, one that is composed of two major

instances—empirical behaviorism and theoretical behaviorism. In addition, and because of precedents in the literature (Reese 1976; White 1976), let us use these two instances of nurture behaviorism as the major division among the numerous ones that could be forwarded. This division will allow us to discuss, where relevant, other divisions of opinion that exist among nurture-behaviorist theories (e.g., regarding the role of reinforcement in learning); it will also allow us to present as well key commonalities that exist among these theories.

However, a point we should note here—and one that it will be useful to reiterate—is that whatever theoretical statements are made about the nurture basis of human development, be they derived from either empirical-behavioristic or theoretical-behavioristic positions, they are going to be ones derived from data collected primarily from organisms other than humans. Complicating this situation is the fact that there has never been a nurture theory devised *solely* to address phenomena of either human development in general or any portion of the life span in particular (White 1970). Nevertheless, as we shall see, there are some major applications of nurture-behavioristic ideas to human development.

The Nurture-Behaviorist Position and the "Passive" Organism

The empirical behaviorists Sidney Bijou and Donald Baer have, both collaboratively (Bijou and Baer 1961, 1965) and independently (Baer 1970, 1976, 1982; Bijou 1976), sought to devise a systematic and empirical theory of child development. Their position has been prominent in developmental psychology for over a quarter of a century (Bijou and Baer 1961) and continues to attract attention and provoke controversy (e.g., Morris et al. 1982). Although, as noted, neither their position nor that of any other scholar working within the nurture-behaviorist framework can be considered a prototype of all nurture-behaviorist positions, we shall pay particular attention in this chapter to the position of Bijou and Baer (e.g., 1961, 1965) because it does constitute the most significant effort to date to evolve a nurture-behaviorist theory specifically pertinent to human developmental phenomena.

Moreover, our attention to the ideas of Bijou and Baer will allow us to raise several conceptual issues common to all extant nurture-behaviorist positions, despite whether they are examples of a theoretical-behaviorist approach or an empirical-behaviorist approach. Most centrally, these issues pertain to the concept of the "passive" organism and to the role of the environment in providing the organism with any behavioral structure it may develop. White (1976) explains that an active organism (e.g., the one posited to exist in organismic developmental conceptions) is one that gives form to its experience. However, a passive organism is one that receives form from its experience. White goes on to note:

> Theoretical behaviorism—the learning theory movement— . . . was built around a basic conception of a passive organism, one that is pushed by experience to learn, one that is reactive rather than active. (White 1976, 99)

This idea of the passive organism is found not only in theoretical behaviorism (e.g., Hull 1952), however, but in empirical behaviorism (e.g., Bijou and Baer 1961) as well. Indeed, Reese, (1976, 108) notes that in the model involved in both theoretical behaviorism and empirical behaviorism, there exists the conception of the organism as either passive, reactive, or responsive. This last term is Baer's. Reese (1976) points out why this term is a preferred one:

> "Passive" misleadingly implies a lack of behavior, and "reactive" misleadingly implies classical conditioning or respondent behaviors. The behavior of a "responsive" organism is clearly under stimulus control, but the stimulus can be US, CS, S^D, or S^R, that is, the behavior can be respondent or operant (Unconditioned Stimuli and Conditioned Stimuli control respondents; Discriminative Stimuli and Reinforcing Stimuli control operants). (Reese 1976, 108)

The terms *unconditioned, conditioned, discriminative,* and *reinforcing* stimuli, and the symbols used to represent them (US, CS, S^D, and S^R, respectively), are terms associated with the processes of classical (or respondent) conditioning and operant (or instrumental) conditioning. Often these two types of conditioning are seen to be instances of one of the major types of "learning" that exists; that is, they are seen to be instances of what is termed associative learning. However, our discussion of the diversity that exists among those taking a nurture-behaviorist position indicated that there are some scholars who would object to the use of the term *learning* as a summary of the empirical phenomena they are studying; for instance, some adopting a behavior-analysis position (e.g., Bijou 1976) would contend that in analyzing the functional relation between stimuli and responses—or in studying how behavior is brought under stimulus control—there is no need to resort to a term—such as learning—which refers to unseen, "mentalistic" phenomena intervening between the stimulus and the response. Other behavior analysts, however, use the term *learning* but take care to anchor its meaning in empirical stimuli and empirical responses that are linked through the associative mechanisms of respondent and operant conditioning (e.g., Baer 1976). Indeed, this latter definitional stance is used to underscore the view that the organism is passive—or better, perhaps, responsive—when seen from the perspective of behavior analysis.

For example, Baer (1976) explains:

> When the laws of learning are stated as the principles of respondent and operant conditioning, they are statements about the control of responses through environmental contingencies. These statements need not specify the organism, and usually do so only implicitly. (p. 88)

Learning, anchored as an empirical concept describing links between environmental stimuli and responses, excludes, then, any reference to phenomena intervening between stimulus and response, and to Baer (1976, 1982) this exclusion apparently applies to the organism too. In fact, he makes this point quite explicit. He contends that

> organisms are not reinforced, responses are . . . the procedures that accomplish learning are, *in fact,* applied not to organisms but to selected responses of organisms [p. 87] . . . it is not the organism that changes, but the responses. (p. 88)

Thus, in this view, the organism is so passive as not even to be involved in "learning," in changes in responses. Indeed, Baer (1976) contends that the organism is merely the "host" of its responses. That is, in explaining his position he notes that

> responses are the basic entities of this account. They lead lives of their own, dictated by their separate interactions with the surrounding environment, and by their interactions with one another, because, to a considerable extent, they are the surrounding environment of one another. However, they lead their own lives as guests of the organism; the organism is their host. (Baer 1976, 89)

In sum, from the perspective of the behavior-analysis position of Baer (1976, 1982), of Bijou and Baer (1961) and, as noted, from the position of theoretical behaviorism also (White 1976), the organism is passive—it receives form from its experience; its form is under environmental-stimulus control. Thus, the phenomena of learning, defined either as an empirical and/or as a theoretical construct, account for changes in responsivity. It is perhaps ironic that the position forwarded by Bijou and Baer (1961, 1965; Bijou 1976) is one that is the most systematic at attempting to use principles of operant and respondent conditioning to account for human developmental phenomena, and yet is also the most insistent on the view that it is not the human who develops. It is instead only the responses to which the human is host that change.

Nevertheless, despite this irony, it is clear that in order to adequately understand the nurture-behaviorist approach to development, we must first understand something about the nature of the laws, or variables, involved in the process linking stimuli and responses. As we have seen, however, there is diversity among scholars who study this linkage in regard to whether they summarize the focus of their study with the term *learning.* However, we shall use this term to reflect a concern with the processes by which behaviors (responses) are acquired as a function of stimulus presentation. Let us inquire further into the nature, then, of the "learning" process. Accordingly, we will now turn to a consideration of what learning is; after this discussion we will be able to interrelate our knowledge of the learning process with our previous discussions of the philosophical basis of this approach, the mechanistic philosophy of science. This presentation will allow us to present and evaluate several instances of nurture-behaviorist positions—the behavior-analysis views of Bijou and Baer (1961) as well as those of other nurture-behaviorists, that is, theoretical-behavioral ones. Our goal will be to indicate the uses of as well as the problems involved in adopting nurture-behaviorist approaches to understanding human development.

WHAT IS LEARNING?

As with any complex psychological phenomenon, there is no general theoretical agreement about what constitutes learning. Although it is fair to say that in general more attention has been paid by psychologists to learning than to any other psychological process, different workers in this area maintain markedly different conceptualizations about what variables are actually involved in learning and what, in fact, constitutes learning (see, for example, Gewirtz and Stingle 1968; Bolles 1972). Despite this controversy there is, to some extent, a general agreement about the *empirical* components of learning. Even though we must recognize that even this empirical analysis might raise some controversial points, we are making a relative choice; that is, there is relatively more agreement about the empirical components of the learning process than there is about its theoretical characteristics.

Accordingly, we may focus on a classic empirical definition of learning offered by Kimble (1961). Learning is a relatively permanent change in behavior potentiality that occurs as a result of reinforced practice, excluding changes due to maturation, fatigue, and/or injury to the nervous system. This is obviously a complex definition, including many important component concepts. In order to understand this empirical definition, let us consider the various key words in this definition.

Relatively permanent

Learning is defined as a relatively permanent change in behavior. By this we mean that the changes comprised by learning are changes that tend to remain with the person. When a person learns, he or she acquires a behavior; that is, the behavior in the person's repertoire has been changed, and this addition tends to remain. Although you might question this component of the definition, there is considerable empirical support for it. Let us take an extreme example for the purposes of illustration. Many people study a particular subject early in their educational careers (e.g., a foreign language). As adults, they may believe that they no longer remember anything they learned. Yet, if they attempt to relearn the foreign language, they might find that it takes them a shorter time to reach their previous level of competence. Such a *savings effect,* which has frequently been experimentally verified, indicates that previously acquired changes in the person tend to remain relatively permanent. Although when the person began relearning, he or she did not retain everything previously acquired, the fact that he or she relearned the material more easily than when it was originally learned suggests that some of the learning had been saved; it was relatively permanent.

Change

Learning constitutes a modification of behavior. The person has a repertoire of behavioral responses. With learning, however, this repertoire is altered. More responses are

added to the repertoire, and thus a change has occurred. This is illustrated in Figure 11.1.

Behavioral potentiality

This terms refers to a most important concept we must deal with when attempting to understand learning. One never actually sees learning; learning is not a directly observable phenomenon. This lack of direct observability is a basis for the difference between empirical behaviorists (e.g., Baer 1976, 1982)—who eschew the term *learning*—and theoretical behaviorists—who focus on the term precisely because of their interest in formulating ideas about the variables intervening between observable stimuli and responses (White 1976).

Thus, what one typically sees when studying learning is performance. One sees an animal perform a task. As such, on the basis of relatively permanent changes in such performance, one may infer that learning has taken place. In other words, the term *learning* may be used as a summary term describing a process involving changes in performance. Hence the term *behavior potentiality* refers to the *learning-performance distinction.* We do not see learning per se; rather, we see performance changes and we summarize these changes by the term *learning.*

For example, a student may be given a pretest in mathematics. After a certain score is achieved on that pretest, the student is ex-

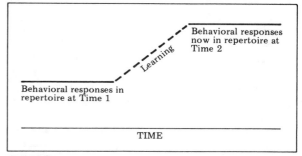

FIGURE 11.1
Learning involves a change in the behavioral-response repertoire of an organism.

posed to a given type of instruction designed to improve his or her score (performance) on a posttest. If the student's score increases, if his or her performance is enhanced through exposure to this instructional technique, we say that the student has learned. Yet we do not actually see this phenomenon called learning. We only see an alteration in performance. Still, we infer that learning has taken place on the basis of the observed change in performance. Simply, then, learning is not a variable we directly observe. It has the status of an *intervening variable in psychology;* that is, it summarizes observed changes in performance.

Reinforced practice

This term, too, is particularly important for our understanding of learning. Practice per se of a behavior might lead only to fatigue. Yet many—but not all (e.g., see Bandura 1965)—learning psychologists would contend that if practice is combined with reinforcement, learning will occur. In other words, when a behavior is reinforced, a relatively permanent change in behavior potentiality will be obtained. Reinforcement, then—to many nurture behaviorists—is an essential component of an empirical conceptualization of the learning process. The application of reinforcement will make the acquisition of a relatively permanent change in behavior potentiality more likely. The exclusion of reinforcement, on the other hand, will not lead to such incremental changes.

What, then, is reinforcement? As noted earlier, reinforcement, or a reinforcing stimulus, may be defined as any stimulus that produces or maintains behavior. For instance, salivation is a form of behavior. Given the appropriate stimulus conditions, our salivary glands will excrete a liquid substance termed saliva. One way of eliciting this salivary behavior is to show a hungry person his or her favorite food. The person will probably salivate, and the production of this salivary behavior is under the control of the food stimulus. In other words, the food is a reinforcing stimulus because it produces the salivary behavior.

Another form of behavior involves the muscular responses involved in digging a ditch. It is obvious that each time we shovel dirt up from the ground we are behaving. If someone comes up to us and simply gives us a shovel and tells us to start digging, we might readily decline this request. However, if the person says that for each shovelful of dirt we will be given one dollar, most of us will engage in shoveling behavior quite readily. What leads to the emission of shoveling behavior in this instance? Clearly, it is that the attainment of money is made contingent upon our performing the behavior. The money that follows our behavior maintains it. (If no money were to follow the behavior, we would probably not shovel.) Hence in this example money is a reinforcing stimulus; it leads us to emit an appropriate response. Our response emission is maintained because a reinforcing stimulus follows (is contingent upon) our behavior.

In sum, a reinforcing stimulus is a stimulus that will lead either to the elicitation of a response (as in the case of the food producing salivation) or to the emission of a response in order to obtain the reinforcing stimulus (as in the case of digging). In either case the relation between behavior and reinforcement is that a reinforcing stimulus makes a behavior more probable. It is more likely that behavior will occur when it is reinforced. In general, many nurture behaviorists contend that reinforcement is needed for learning because a reinforcing stimulus is a stimulus that increases the probability of a behavior.

Excluding changes due to maturation, fatigue, and/or injury to the nervous system

Not all changes in behavior involve alterations due to the learning process. Only those relatively permanent changes in behavioral potentiality that occur as a result of reinforced practice may be attributable to the learning process. Changes that may not reasonably be attributed to learning are accounted for by variables involved in such things as maturation, fatigue, or nervous-system injury. We may have learned, for example, that cookies are kept in a jar on tcp of the refrigerator. Yet because we are not tall enough (and because there are no chairs around) we will not perform the behavior of reaching into the cookie jar. However, when the appropriate maturation has occurred (e.g., we have grown ten inches), such behavior may be very typical. Fatigue may also lead to changes in behavior. Even if we are digging a ditch for one dollar per shovelful of dirt, our rate of shoveling will decrease after a time. Although our behavior might still be maintained by the monetary reward, it will change; it will slow down simply because we experience muscular fatigue. Finally, it is obvious that after some injury to our nervous system (e.g., serious brain damage following a car accident) our behavior will change, but such changes are attributable to the injury rather than to learning.

Types of Learning

We have seen some of the components many (albeit not all) nurture behaviorists would include in an empirical conceptualization of the learning process; however, we have not considered the ways in which these components may interrelate in order to produce learning. What is the way, or ways, in which learning takes place? How does learning occur? How do stimuli interrelate with responses to produce learning?

Generally, learning psychologists maintain that two types of relations between stimuli and responses account for learning. First, there is associative learning, of which there are two main instances—classical conditioning and operant conditioning. Second, there is cognitive learning. Here mental processes (e.g., schemas, memory) are involved in learning, and the role of reinforcement is not stressed for the acquisition of behavior, although it is needed for the performance of behavior (Bandura 1965). As noted earlier, processes such as the observation and/or imitation of a model are thought to be central in this cognitive type of learning. Be-

cause such models represent social stimuli, this view of learning is often termed social-learning theory (Bandura 1971), and/or cognitive social-learning theory (Bandura 1978, 1980a, 1980b).

Our purposes in this chapter do not involve an exhaustive treatment of the associative-learning and the cognitive-learning paradigms. Instead, our interest lies in a consideration of how ideas derived from these approaches are used to formulate theories of human development. Phenomena of associative learning have been used most generally in the extant attempts of empirical behaviorists—for example, behavior analysts (Bijou and Baer 1961)—to devise a systematic theory of development. Cognitive-learning phenomena play a prominent role in the ideas of those theoretical behaviorists who have attempted to devise social-learning, or cognitive social-learning, accounts of development. We shall discuss instances of both empirical-behavioristic and theoretical-behavioristic theories of development. Because, as noted, the behavior-analytic ideas of Bijou and Baer (1961) represent the most major extant attempt to formulate a nurture-behavioristic theory of development, and because their ideas constitute a position based on the application of principles of associative learning, we shall review their ideas first.

BEHAVIOR ANALYSIS AND ASSOCIATIVE LEARNING

Empirical behaviorism involves the analysis of the functional relations that exist among stimuli and responses. As we have noted, this approach is best illustrated by the behavior-analysis system of Bijou and Baer (1961; Baer 1970, 1976, 1982; Bijou 1976). Behavior analysis involves accounting for behavioral development through reference to the phenomena of associative learning.

There are two types of associative learning—classical and operant conditioning. That is, these two instances of the ways in which stimuli and responses interrelate are thought to be the means by which associative learning occurs. As we shall see, classical conditioning involves behavior that is elicited by preceding reinforcing stimuli, while operant conditioning involves behavior that is controlled by succeeding reinforcing stimuli (Bijou and Baer 1961). Accordingly, because of the centrality of classical and operant conditioning phenomena in the behavior-analytic system of Bijou and Baer, we will now consider the essential components of each of these two types of associative learning.

The Classical Paradigm

Many of us are probably familiar with what is termed the *classical learning paradigm* through knowledge of the work of Ivan P. Pavlov, the Russian physiologist who discovered this type of learning. We know that through happenstance Pavlov discovered that the dogs he was using as experimental subjects would salivate to stimuli other than food (e.g., his white lab coat, a bell). His studies of the variables involved in such associations led to an understanding of the nature of one of the two types of associative learning, classical conditioning.

To understand how classical conditioning functions we must first focus on initial associations the organism has when it enters the learning situation. Let us first posit that there exists a stimulus that reliably (i.e., regularly) elicits a response of strong magnitude. For example, let us assume that food elicits salivation. If we further assume that no prior association, or learning, is necessary to establish this relation between the stimulus and the response, between the food and the salivation, then we may assume that food is a stimulus that will reliably elicit a salivary response. Given this assumption, we may term the food stimulus an *unconditional, or unconditioned, stimulus* (*UCS*). A *UCS,* then, is a stimulus that reliably elicits a response of strong magnitude without previous learning. Hence a UCS is an unlearned stimulus. Moreover, since no previous asso-

ciation, or learning, is necessary in order for the UCS to elicit the salivation, this salivation response is an *unconditioned response* (*UCR*), an unlearned response. Thus, to begin with, the classical paradigm may be represented as

(1) UCS (food) → UCR (salivation).

Of course there exist numerous stimuli in the organism's environment that do not elicit this particular UCR. That is, they are neutral in respect to the above UCS → UCR relation; such neutral stimuli do not elicit the UCR. However, if one takes such a neutral stimulus (for example, a bell) and repeatedly pairs it with the UCS, a different state of affairs will soon exist. For instance, suppose one rings the bell (that is, presents the neutral stimulus) and then presents the UCS; after such repeated pairings the previously neutral stimulus will come to elicit a response markedly similar to the UCR. Because of the repeated pairings of the bell and the food, the bell begins to acquire some of the properties of the food: it, too, leads to salivation. We say, then, that the bell—previously a neutral stimulus—has become a conditioned stimulus (CS), a learned stimulus. Through repeated pairings of the bell and the food, the bell becomes a CS and comes to elicit a learned response, or a *conditioned response* (CR). In this case the bell comes to elicit salivation. However, this salivation is not a UCR; rather, it is a response to a stimulus that obtained its control over behavior through its associations with another stimulus. Since the organism learned this CS-UCS association, the response to the CS is a learned, or a conditioned, response. Hence, because of

(2) CS (bell) − UCS (food),

a learned response is acquired. A learned association, one that did not previously exist, between a previously neutral stimulus and a response to this stimulus, is acquired. This association may be represented as

(3) CS (bell) → CR (salivation).

This, then, is the classical conditioning, or learning, paradigm. A previously neutral stimulus precedes an unconditioned stimulus, and after repeated pairings of this CS and UCS, the CS comes to elicit a response markedly similar to the original unconditioned response. A summary of this paradigm may be represented as

(4) CS − UCS → UCR − CR
(bell) − (food) → (salivation) − (salivation).

CHARACTERISTICS OF CLASSICAL CONDITIONING. We see that in classical conditioning, the CS or the UCS is said to elicit the response. The term *elicit* is used to signify the fact that classical conditioning typically involves the autonomic nervous system and the body's involuntary musculature. Hence we do not have to learn to salivate in response to food. We do not have to learn to blink in response to a puff of air directed at our eyes. Rather, such responses are reflexive in nature. They are involuntary responses. Hence classical conditioning ordinarily involves the conditioning of our involuntary, reflexive responses. Such responses are almost literally pulled out of us by the stimulus in question (e.g., the food or the puff of air), and this is why we say that classical responses are elicited.

Moreover, since classical conditioning involves our involuntary nervous system, many of our emotional responses are acquired through classical conditioning. For example, a rat will show unconditioned emotional behavior in response to a strong electric shock delivered to the floor of its cage. The shock is a UCS and the emotional response is a UCR. If a buzzer is always sounded two seconds before the shock begins, however, then after some time the rat will show a similar emotional response to the buzzer. The buzzer will become a CS and the emotional response will be a CR, a *conditioned emotional response* (*CER*). Similarly, if a pedestrian witnesses a particularly bloody auto accident at a certain street corner, he or she might experience unpleasant emotional reactions in response (e.g., fear and disgust). The sight of the blood will be a UCS and the emotional response will be a UCR. If at some time later, however, the person is walking by that same street corner and is again overcome with fear and disgust,

this might indicate that the particular corner had been established, in just one trial, as a CS and the emotional response was a CR.

Reinforcement plays an essential role in classical conditioning. In this form of associative learning the role of the reinforcing stimulus is to *produce* behavior. That is, classical responses are elicited, they are produced, by the UCS. Thus, since the UCS (e.g., food) produces the response (e.g., salivation), it represents the reinforcing stimulus within the classical conditioning paradigm. However, after classical learning has been accomplished—that is, after the CS has become able to produce (elicit) the CR—there is obviously another stimulus that now elicits responding: The CS also produces a response. However, because the CS obtained its reinforcing power (or efficacy) through its association with the UCS, we must distinguish between these two levels of reinforcers. Accordingly, we may term the UCS a *primary* reinforcing stimulus and the CS a *secondary* reinforcing stimulus. In the case of both the UCS and the CS, though, reinforcement always produces a response within the classical conditioning paradigm. In classical conditioning the reinforcing stimulus always leads to the response.

Finally, we may note that terms other than *classical conditioning* are used to represent this type of associative learning. For example, some psychologists refer to classical conditioning as *Pavlovian conditioning*. Others refer to it as *associative shifting*—in recognition of the shift in association between the UCS and the response to the CS and the response—while still other psychologists use the term *stimulus substitution*, for similar reasons. Lastly, another major term representing this type of learning is *respondent conditioning;* this term is used by behavior analysts, for instance, and is employed to highlight the fact that this type of learning involves responses to previous stimulation (Bijou and Baer 1961; Skinner 1938). However, all these terms refer to a type of learning involving responses elicited by preceding, reinforcing stimulation. On the other hand, the other major type of associative learning that exists—operant conditioning—works in quite another way. Let us now turn our attention to a consideration of the operant conditioning paradigm.

The Operant Paradigm

Many of us have had the experience of being in a bus or subway station on a hot day. Suppose we are in such a situation and that we are hot and tired. Looking around the station, we might see two machines—a telephone on the wall and a soft drink machine. Being hot, tired, and perhaps a bit thirsty, we might put some money in the soft drink machine and get a cola. Certainly, however, we would not put the money in the phone if we wanted something to drink. Such a response would not be followed by the appropriate (needed) stimulus. In other words, only if we emit the appropriate response (putting coins in a slot) in the presence of the correct stimulus (the soft drink machine) will we get the "needed" stimulus. If in the presence of a certain stimulus we emit a certain response, this response will be followed by an appropriate stimulus. Emission of the same response, but in the presence of an inappropriate stimulus (the telephone), will not be followed by the appropriate stimulus (the cola).

The above description represents an analogy of the *operant conditioning paradigm.* Certain stimuli in the environment are *discriminated* (responded to differentially) from other stimuli in the environment on the basis of the fact that responses emitted in the presence of some stimuli are followed by a reinforcing stimulus, while responses in the presence of other stimuli are not followed by a reinforcement. We know from our above discussion of reinforcement that if a response is followed by a reinforcing stimulus, the future occurrence of that response will be more probable. That is, if the occurrence of a reinforcing stimulus is made contingent upon the emission of a response, then the probability of the emission of that response will increase. A response of putting coins into a slot will be followed by a reinforcing

stimulus (a cola) if that slot works the dispensing mechanism of a soft drink machine. Since a response to that stimulus (the machine) will be followed by a reinforcement (the drink), while responses to another stimulus (e.g., the telephone) will not be followed by the reinforcement, a discrimination between these two stimuli is established: Responses in the presence of the soda machine are quite probable and responses in the presence of the telephone are not. This is so because the former responses are reinforced while the latter are not. Thus stimuli are discriminated on the basis of the consequences of responses made in their presence.

Hence operant conditioning involves learning to emit a response (R) in the presence of an appropriate, or discriminative, stimulus (S^D); responses in the presence of such discriminative stimuli are followed by a reinforcing stimulus (S^R). Simply, in terms of the above analogy, the presence of a drink is contingent upon the emission of a correct response—a response to a soda machine and not a telephone.

A discriminative stimulus (S^D), then, is a stimulus that cues the occasion for a response. This is the case because a response (R) in the presence of an S^D will lead to the attainment of a reinforcing stimulus (S^R). Thus, since the attainment of reinforcement is contingent upon the emission of responses only in the presence of certain stimuli, operant learning involves the acquisition of responses in the presence of S^Ds and the absence of the responses in the absence of S^Ds. We may represent the operant paradigm as

(5) $S^D - R \rightarrow S^R$.

The work of Skinner (e.g., 1938, 1956) is, of course, most associated with operant conditioning. Most of his work has dealt with animals, and an example of operant conditioning with animals may be used to further illustrate this paradigm. Suppose you place a rat in a small experimental chamber (what some have termed a Skinner box). Protruding from the wall is a small lever (or bar); behind the wall is a container capable of delivering food into a cup, which also protrudes from the wall. When placed in the chamber, the animal will assuredly move around in it and eventually press the bar. If food is delivered when this happens, the rat will continue to press the bar if—and as long as—it is hungry. That is, if the rat has been deprived of food and if the bar-press leads to food, it will bar-press until satiated. However, if there is also a light in the chamber that can be turned on or off by the experimenter, this light could soon be established as an S^D. As long as the rat is not satiated, it will continue to bar-press. However, if the light is turned on and off at random intervals, and only bar-presses occurring when the light is on are followed by food, then responses when the light is off will soon diminish (or cease entirely). Only responses in the presence of the light will remain. This example of operant conditioning may be represented as

(6) S^D (light on) − R (bar press) → S^R (food).

Thus operant conditioning involves the acquisition of responses in the presence of certain (i.e., discriminative) stimuli, stimuli cuing the occasion for a response to be followed by a reinforcement. Responses emitted in the presence of such stimuli will be followed by a reinforcement; responses emitted when such stimuli are not present will not be followed by a reinforcement. The attainment of reinforcement is contingent upon the emission of a response in the presence of a discriminative stimulus.

CHARACTERISTICS OF OPERANT CONDITIONING. We see that within the operant conditioning paradigm, responses are emitted in the presence of a discriminative stimulus, and in fact a discriminative stimulus is established as such because such responses are followed by a reinforcing stimulus. An organism emits a response in the presence of an S^D because such responses are associated with succeeding reinforcement. In other words, responses are *maintained* in the presence of an S^D, and an S^D is in turn established as such because the occurrence of a reinforcement is contingent upon such responses. Thus responses are maintained because they are followed by reinforcing stimuli, or conversely, the stimulus following

B. F. Skinner

the response in the operant conditioning paradigm maintains the production of that response.

In operant conditioning, then, the response produces the reinforcement (as opposed to classical conditioning, wherein the reinforcement produces the response). The organism must respond—in the presence of the appropriate stimulus (the S^D)—in order to obtain reinforcement. In other words, the organism is instrumental in obtaining reinforcement; it must operate in its environment in order to obtain reinforcement. In the presence of the appropriate, cuing, discriminative stimulus, the organism must itself respond (through pressing a bar, pecking a key, turning a handle, putting a foot on a pedal, etc.) for a reinforcement to be obtained. The organism itself must operate on its environment, it must be instrumental itself, to obtain reinforcement. As opposed to classical learning, wherein responses are elicited by the UCS (the reinforcing stimulus), the organism must learn to emit the appropriate response—that is, the response that will lead to the production of an S^R in the presence of an S^D. The animal must behave in order to obtain a reinforcement.

Thus, since the organism itself is instrumental in obtaining an S^R, another name typically applied to operant conditioning is *instrumental learning*.

The term *emit* is used within the context of this paradigm to signify the fact that operant responses involve typically the body's voluntary musculature. Thus, operant conditioning ordinarily involves learning to use the voluntary musculature to emit a response that will be followed by a reinforcement. However, this is not to say that operant responses are not controlled. Rather, such responses are under the complete control of the stimulus environment (Reese 1976). Since operant responses are maintained by succeeding, reinforcing stimuli, their probability of occurrence is determined by the degree of absence or presence of reinforcing stimuli; since operant responses are reinforced only when emitted in the presence of the appropriate discriminative stimuli, they are also set by discriminative stimuli. We see, then, that although operant learning typically involves the voluntary musculature, such responses are in the final analysis maintained and controlled by the reinforcing stimuli following them.

However, because operant responses generally involve the voluntary muscles of the body, the major portion of motor behavior is thought to be acquired through operant conditioning (e.g., see Bijou 1976). Such broad involvement in the majority of behaviors emitted by organisms may be illustrated by various kinds of seemingly disparate motor behaviors. If, while driving a car, we see a stop sign at the end of the road, we take our foot off the accelerator pedal and place it on the brake pedal. Soon after this response the car comes to a halt. This motor-behavior series may be interpreted as an instance of an operant sequence. The stop sign represents an S^D, cuing the occasion for the motor response (R) of lifting the foot off one pedal and placing it on another. The S^R in this instance is the halting of the car. Another example may be seen in learning a foreign language. If our teacher shows us the word *garçon* and we respond "boy," some sort of approval or indication of correctness is offered by the teacher. In this case the French word *garçon* may be seen as an S^D, the emission of the word "boy" is an R, and the approval is an S^R. Operant conditioning may also be involved in the exploratory behavior of young children. A toddler may be exploring the kitchen while a roast is cooking in the oven. He or she puts his or her hand on the oven and then, of course, rapidly removes it. In further explorations he or she continues to move away from the oven. Here we may say that the oven is an S^D, which is associated with the R of moving away. The reinforcing stimulus in this instance is the heat from the oven, and as we will soon see, it is a negatively reinforcing stimulus. The point now is that the occurrence of most motor behaviors may be construed as consistent with the operant paradigm.

Yet it is obvious that most of our daily motor behavior is much more involved than the behaviors described above. People typically emit long sequences, or *chains,* of behaviors mediated by the voluntary musculature, rather than single, discrete responses. Still, in principle, such complex chains of responses can be completely accounted for within the operant conditioning paradigm. However, such an accounting again requires reference to the principle of secondary reinforcement.

SECONDARY REINFORCEMENT AND CHAINING. In our discussion of classical conditioning we saw that after repeated pairing with the UCS, the CS too obtains reinforcing power. Through its association with the primary reinforcing UCS, the CS thus becomes a secondary reinforcement—that is, a stimulus that acquires its ability to reinforce behavior through association with another reinforcer. Similarly, within the operant conditioning paradigm, the S^D, through its association with the S^R, becomes a secondary reinforcing stimulus (S^r). The S^D cues the occasion when an R will be followed by an S^R, and this covariation between the occurrence of the discriminative stimulus and that of the reinforcing stimulus establishes the S^D as a secondary reinforcement. Because of the nature of its association with the S^R, reinforcing efficacy accrues to the S^D, establishing it as an S^r—secondary reinforcement. Thus, simply,

(7) $$S^D = S^r$$

Because the S^D is also an S^r, this means that other responses may be acquired with the S^D used as the stimulus maintaining those responses. In turn, another S^D, which may be used to signal the occasion in which a certain response will now lead to the occurrence of the first S^D, will also—through its association with the latter discriminative stimulus—acquire reinforcing properties. In turn, then, this new S^D may be used to reinforce yet another response. In this way, long sequences (chains) of behaviors may be established. Let us consider an illustration.

Earlier we considered an example in which a rat learned to press a bar (R) when a light was on (S^D) to obtain food (S^R). The stimulus that maintained bar-pressing behavior was the food, and on the basis of our above analysis we know that the light represented both a discriminative stimulus and a secondary reinforcement. Accordingly, if the light is in fact a secondary reinforcing stimulus (an S^r), then it should be able to maintain another response, say a hook-pull. That is, let us create a state of affairs in which the light will only go on when the rat pulls a hook protruding from the side of the chamber. The light going on is contingent upon a hook-pull. However, let us further specify that a hook-pull will cause the light to go on only when it occurs during the sound of a buzzer. After some training with these contingencies, we would have a situation like this:

(8) S^D - R - S^D - R - S^R, or (buzzer on) - (hook-pull) - (light on) - (bar-press) - (food).

Thus the rat's hook-pulling behavior is maintained by the light going on, and when the light goes on the rat's bar-pressing behavior is in turn maintained by the consequent food.

Let us continue this chain. Let us now specify that the buzzer will go on only when the rat jumps in the air, and further that a jump will lead to the occurrence of the buzzer only when a bell rings. After some training with such contingencies, the rat will respond in accordance with the following sequence:

(9) S^D - R - S^D - R - S^D - R - S^R, or (bell-ring) - (jump) - (buzzer on) - (hook-pull) - (light on) - (bar-press) - (food).

Thus in the presence of a bell-ring the rat jumps up, which leads to a buzzer going on, which cues the occasion for a hook-pull, which is followed by a light going on, which allows a bar to be pressed and food to be obtained.

Obviously, we could continue this chain almost indefinitely, linking one response to another through the use of secondary reinforcement. Since an S^D is also an S^r, each response in a chain is maintained by the succeeding stimulus event. In this way a complex series of behaviors may be built up. Yet each unit (link) of the chain is basically composed of the same operant unit: S^D – R – S^R. In other words, even complex behavior series may be broken down (reduced) to the same constituent elements. All portions of the chain are composed of the same basic stimulus-response elements. The content of a particular segment of the chain may be different from the content of another component (for example, in one case a bar-press may be involved, while in another case a hook-pull is necessary). Nevertheless, all segments are just basically the same discriminative stimulus–response–reinforcing stimulus unit, linked together on the basis of an S^D being equivalent to an S^r.

Hence even complex adult behavior may be interpreted as consistent with this chaining model. The alarm clock going off in the morning is an S^D, which "allows us" to get out of bed to "obtain" the bathroom, which in turn allows us to wash, which in turn allows us to dress, which in turn allows us to eat breakfast, leave the house, get in the car, drive to work, earn our salary, and buy food.

One may tear this series of behaviors apart attempting to find the various discriminative stimuli that link the secondary reinforcing functions, which chain these discrete, voluntary musculature behaviors into a seemingly complex behavioral series.

In sum, with this model, then, complex human behavior is only apparently complex. In actuality, complicated series of motor behaviors really comprise the building up of a series of links on a chain. All behavior is made up of the same constituent elements, the $S^D - R - S^R$ connections.

At this point some important conceptual implications of this chaining model may be pointed out. Our presentation of this model enables us to see certain basic similarities between it and the reductionistic, mechanistic position discussed in Chapter 2. The notion of chaining implies that to understand complex (e.g., adult) behavior all one must do is *reduce* this behavior to its constituent elements, these stimulus-response-stimulus connections. Hence, the development of behavior only involves building up these chains; as the child develops, he or she continually adds more of these identically constituted links to his or her repertoire. Moreover, since these chaining units are composed of the same type of elements, all that behavioral development thus involves is the addition of more similarly composed units. Although there have been some arguments to the contrary (see Gagné 1968), this position implies that development is the continuous addition of qualitatively identical chaining units; hence the only difference between different points in development is in the *quantity* of these units; and since all levels of development are therefore composed of these similarly constituted units, any and all behavior can be reduced to these common elements.

Thus this view of the operant conditioning paradigm places it within the context of the mechanistic philosophy of science (Harris 1957; Reese and Overton, 1970) discussed in Chapter 2. Since this interrelation is a most crucial one, we will provide further clarification and expansion of it. However, we should first consider one last important component of associative learning phenomena. To this point in our discussion of the classical and the operant conditioning paradigm, the concept of reinforcement has been a central one. It is clear that this concept is the core principle in the phenomena of associative learning. Hence we should consider in greater detail some other important aspects of the phenomenon of reinforcement.

POSITIVE AND NEGATIVE REINFORCEMENT. We have defined a reinforcing stimulus as any stimulus that produces or maintains behavior. As we have seen, in classical conditioning the reinforcement precedes the response, while in operant conditioning the reinforcement follows the response. In either case, however, the reinforcing stimulus increases the probability of a response. In our previous discussion we indicated a distinction between primary and secondary reinforcers. Another clarification, that between positive and negative reinforcement, should be mentioned.

In the example of the rat pressing the bar (in the presence of a light) to obtain food, we have an instance of positive reinforcement. That is, in this example food is a positively reinforcing stimulus. We saw that the food maintained the rat's bar-pressing behavior; in other words, bar-pressing behavior was maintained because this behavior produced a stimulus. If an organism behaves (i.e., emits a response) in order to produce a stimulus, then that stimulus may be termed a *positive reinforcement*. We may define a *positive-reinforcing stimulus* as a stimulus that maintains behavior through its production. We will behave to produce such stimuli as food, water, or money. We will emit responses in order to produce a positive reinforcement, an S^{+R}. Hence, such S^{+R}s maintain behaviors (as do all S^Rs, of course) because they are produced by those behaviors. In short, one way in which behavior may be maintained is through the production of such positively reinforcing stimuli; one result of a behavior may be the production of an S^{+R}.

However, behavior may result in something else. There is another type of reinforcing stimulus that may follow (be produced by) a behavior, a *negative-reinforcing stimulus*. If we are placed in a situation in which a painful electric shock will continue to be delivered to us until we press a bar, we will soon press the bar to terminate (turn off) the electric shock. If we have a very bright light shining in our eyes, we will emit a behavior (turning off the light) that will terminate the stimulus. What maintains the bar-pressing or light-turning-off behaviors in these examples? Clearly these behaviors are maintained by the stimulus events following them—the termination of the shock and the bright light, respectively. Thus these behaviors are also maintained by consequent stimulus events, but in these instances the behaviors lead to a termination of the stimulus. Responses are emitted in order to terminate a stimulus. In such instances we may term the stimulus a negative reinforcement, an S^{-R}. If an organism behaves in order to terminate a stimulus, we say the behavior is maintained through negative reinforcement. Hence we may define an S^{-R} as a stimulus that maintains behavior through its termination.

Hence a given response may be followed by one of two types of stimuli, an S^{+R} or an S^{-R} (excluding responses that are followed by neutral stimuli, which in any event would not maintain the emitted response). In other words, responses are maintained either by a positive reinforcement (a stimulus that maintains behavior through its production) or a negative reinforcement (a stimulus that maintains behavior through its termination).

One may view behavioral functioning, then, in terms of only two categories, responses and succeeding stimuli. A given behavioral response may either produce a stimulus or terminate a stimulus, and the stimulus that is either produced or terminated may be either an S^{+R} or an S^{-R}. That is, sometimes we emit a behavior that produces an S^{+R} (for example, doing our chores and earning, or producing, our allowance), while at other times we emit a behavior that terminates an S^{+R} (for example, hitting our

brother and losing, or terminating, our allowance). On the other hand, sometimes we emit a behavior that produces an S^{-R} (for example, hitting our brother, which is followed by, or produces, a reprimand from a parent), while at other times we emit a behavior that terminates an S^{-R} (for example, saying—with sobbing sincerity—that we are sorry, which terminates, or ends, a parent's spanking). Thus any given behavior may be conceptualized simply in terms of whether or not it produces or terminates an S^{+R} or an S^{-R}.

Since any and all behavior may be conceptualized in this manner, we may attempt to represent the phenomena resulting from these combinations of responses and stimuli. When our responses either produce a positive reinforcement or terminate a negative reinforcement, our responses become strengthened. Thus our behavior results in a *reward*. In other words, it is rewarding to produce a positive reinforcement or to eliminate a negative reinforcement; responses that do these things tend to remain in our behavioral repertoire and are said to be strengthened. Moreover, responses that terminate an S^{-R}, such as a shock, may be labeled as a special type of reward. In ending the presence of such a noxious stimulus state, we may say that the response allows the organism to *escape* from it. Hence the state of reward in which an R terminates an S^{-R} is considered escape.

However, when our responses either terminate a positive reinforcement or produce a negative reinforcement, our responses become weakened. That is, behavior that terminates an S^{+R} or produces an S^{-R} constitutes *punishment,* and such behavior tends to drop out of our behavioral repertoire. Because they are punished, such responses tend to be seen with decreasing frequency and are said to be weakened.

Simply, then, the responses that exist in a person's behavioral repertoire at any time in development may be accounted for by the past history of rewards and punishments that person has experienced. Hence a person's behavioral repertoire may be under-

TABLE 11.1
The Establishment of Rewards and Punishments Resulting from the Primary Reinforcement Consequences of Responses

	S^{+R}	S^{-R}
Response produces	Reward	Punishment
Response terminates	Punishment	Reward (escape)

Source: *Adapted from Bijou and Baer (1961).*

stood simply by reference to the nature of the stimulus-response relationships the person has experienced. A person's behavioral repertoire may be conceptualized as, or reduced to, the sum total of the strengthened and weakened responses that have resulted from the stimulus consequences of those responses. Following the presentation of Bijou and Baer (1961, 37), we present in Table 11.1 these relations between responses and consequent stimulus events, which lead to the establishment of rewards and punishments.

The notion of secondary reinforcement may also be included in this discussion. Obviously not all stimuli that maintain responses are either primary positive reinforcers (S^{+R}s), such as food or water, or primary negative reinforcers (S^{-R}s), such as shock. As we have seen, stimuli can acquire either positive or negative reinforcing characteristics through their association with other stimuli. Yet responses that either produce or terminate such secondary positive reinforcing stimuli (S^{+r}s) or secondary negative reinforcing stimuli (S^{-r}s) similarly result in either reward or punishment. Thus a response that either produces an S^{-r} or terminates an S^{+r} would be a weakened, punished response, while a response that either pro-

duced an S^{+r} or terminated an S^{-r} would be a strengthened, rewarded response. Moreover, since responses that terminate the presence of S^{-r}s constitute a case in which a stimulus associated with (or leading to) an S^{-R} is terminated, such responses may be seen as eliminating the eventual presence of this primary negative reinforcement. Thus, by terminating the secondary negative reinforcement, the organism is *avoiding* the eventual presentation of the primary negative reinforcer. Hence this situation constitutes a special case of reward—avoidance. These relations between responses and secondary reinforcing stimulus events, which also lead to the establishment of rewards and punishments, are represented in Table 11.2.

Conclusions: Associative Learning and the Mechanistic Paradigm as Bases of the Behavior-Analytic Approach

We have reviewed above the two major types of associative learning; these are the instances of learning that are used most typically by those adopting an empirical-behav-

TABLE 11.2
The Establishment of Rewards and Punishments Resulting from the Secondary Reinforcement Stimulus Consequences of Responses

	S^{+r}	S^{-r}
Response produces	Reward	Punishment
Response terminates	Punishment	Reward (avoidance)

Source: *Adapted from Bijou and Baer (1961).*

ioral, or behavior-analysis, approach to child development study (e.g., Baer 1976, 1982; Bijou 1976; Bijou and Baer 1961, 1965). We have seen that classical conditioning typically involves the autonomic nervous system and the involuntary musculature, and it can be used to account for the acquisition of reflexive and emotional responses. Operant conditioning, on the other hand, ordinarily involves the central nervous system and the voluntary musculature and can be used to account for the majority of our "voluntary" motor behavior. Moreover, in our discussions of the concepts of secondary reinforcement, chaining, and positive and negative reinforcement, we saw that even seemingly complex human behavior can be understood on the basis of these basic conditioning paradigms.

The notions of secondary reinforcement and chaining allow one to reduce seemingly complex series of behaviors to identically constituted constituent elements. If the developing behavior of a person is just regarded "as a cluster of interrelated responses interacting with stimuli" (Bijou and Baer 1961, 14–15), then one may reduce these clusters to their constituent stimulus-response connections, connections that may be acquired only on the basis of either of two processes: classical or operant conditioning. These two forms of associative learning may be used continually to represent the acquisition of any and all behavior because it is assumed that all behavior is learned behavior (White 1970, 662) and that these two types of associative learning are regarded in empirical behaviorism to be sufficient to account for the occurrence of "learning." Thus the same laws of learning are continually applicable to a person's behavior, whatever that person's level of development. This is the case because any level of behavioral development can be reduced to the stimulus-response clusters, formed on the basis of the same laws of learning.

Thus all that behavioral development amounts to is the quantitative addition of similarly acquired stimulus-response associations. The behavior seen in a person's repertoire at any time in development is present as a result of the stimulus consequences of that person's responses. That is, stimulus-reponse associations are strengthened or weakened on the basis of whether or not a response produces or terminates a positive or negative reinforcement. The number of responses and the content of the responses a person has in his or her repertoire, and how many responses will be added to this repertoire, are totally dependent on the stimulation the environment provides (Bijou and Baer 1961).

In sum, we see that behavior at any level of development may be understood by reduction of the behavior into its constituent elements. These elements—lawfully identical stimulus-response associations—are continually quantitatively added to the person's developing response repertoire. Hence, if all behavior is learned behavior, and if such learning proceeds on the basis of the simple stimulus-response mechanisms involved in the laws of associative learning, all that is involved in the study of behavioral development is the analysis of two types of events in the natural environment: responses and the environmental stimuli that control them (Baer 1976, 1982).

It is clear that this position, with its concepts of reduction, mechanism, continuity, and quantitative addition, is consistent with the mechanistic philosophy of science discussed in Chapter 2. The reductionism and mechanism of this philosophical position may be seen to have been translated into the mechanistic, reductionistic theoretical orientation of those using the phenomena of associative learning to formulate an empirical-behaviorist, or behavior-analytic, approach to development. In order to better understand this interrelation we will now consider the basic assumptions and characteristics of the behavior analysis approach. Although we will draw upon the work of several learning-approach developmentalists, we will focus on the work of Bijou and Baer (1961). As we have noted, their behavior-analytic approach is the exemplar of the application of empirical behaviorism to understanding human developmental phenomena.

CHARACTERISTICS OF THE BEHAVIOR-ANALYSIS APPROACH TO DEVELOPMENT

Learning is a behavioral function that obviously has fundamental biological significance. If the organism's behaviors were unalterable in the face of environmental changes, then the chances of that organism's survival would be severely diminished. Accordingly, stimuli in the organism's environment that promote such modifications of behavior have primary adaptive significance. Such stimuli function to modify the organism's behavior in its environment and thus allow the organism to survive. If psychology is to be an objective, empirical science, it has to study the observable sources of behavior.

Such reasoning has led many psychologists to adopt an empirical-behaviorist approach as a framework with which to conduct psychological investigations, because the essence of this approach is a scrutiny of the interrelations among observable stimuli and responses. Then, to offer a rationale for this emphasis, these psychologists emphasized the biologically adaptive role that reinforcement plays in organism survival. As we have noted, such environmental stimuli serve to select naturally those behaviors that will be strengthened or weakened as the organism's responses interrelate with the stimulus world. Hence the study of such "learning" allows one to assess the processes by which organisms acquire the essential functional characteristics—behaviors—allowing them to survive. Thus early followers of this approach believed that the study of learning allows psychology to be an objective, empirical discipline within the tradition of natural science. As White put it: "There was a vision of reinforcement as a natural selection process in the environment which could select out adaptive animal behaviors—hence the justification for an intensive

Sidney W. Bijou

examination of learning as a reinforcement process" (1970, 661). Some current nurture-behavioral psychologists have retained this initial orientation and, implicitly, this underlying rationale. Hence, in describing their work, Bijou and Baer assert: "We present here an approach to the understanding of human psychological development from the natural science point of view" (1961, 1).

Accordingly, Bijou and Baer stress that this point of view focuses on observable events—responses and environmental stimuli—and the theory they advance merely represents "generalized summaries and explanations of observable interactions between behavior and environment" (1961, 5). However, their use of the term *interaction* must be contrasted with the use of this term by organismically oriented psychologists. To Bijou and Baer this term is tied solely to environmental stimulation: "An *interaction* between behavior and environment means simply that a given response may be ex-

Donald M. Baer

pected to occur or not, depending on the stimulation the environment provides" (1961, 1). Thus an interaction in this sense involves what Baer (1982) terms a "response function"—that is, "the environmental contingency that controls a response and explains why it occurs" (p. 357).

Bijou and Baer's theory looks at all behavior as ultimately controlled by environmental-stimulus events. Whether or not an organism will respond is dependent just on the stimulation in the environmental situation. Such *situational dependency* implies that the organism is a passive recipient of environmental stimulation, and it accounts for why some scholars—for example, Bowers (1973)—use the term "situationalism" to represent the empirical-behavioral approach (Reese 1976).

In this approach, behavior is equated with responses, and whether or not a response will be given is dependent on the stimuli in the organism's environment. Hence, as noted earlier, responses (or behaviors) are not dependent on the organism itself. In contrast to the organismic point of view—

which holds that the organism plays an active participatory role in its own behavior— this view asserts that the source of all behavior lies merely in the effects that environmental stimulation has on responses, to which the passive, nonparticipatory organism is merely a "host" (Baer 1976). Thus psychological development consists only of "progressive changes in the way an organism's behavior interacts with the environment" (Bijou and Baer 1961, 1). All that a child's development consists of is the ongoing accumulation of responses-in-control-by-environmental-stimulation.

As implied in our discussion of associative learning, the behavior of the developing child is thought of as "being made up of two basic kinds of responses—*respondents and operants*" (Bijou and Baer 1961, 15). Hence all one must actually know about in order to understand, predict, and control a child's development are the laws of classical and operant conditioning. These learning processes are inextricably linked to observable responses and stimuli present in the child's environmental situation, and thus a child's behavior and development may be accounted for merely through an analysis of the stimuli and responses in a particular situation (Bowers 1973).

We see, then, that this situationalist, behavior-analysis approach to development assumes the following:

1. All human behavior is learned behavior, that is, all behavior is the product of responses controlled by situation-specific environmental stimuli (White 1970, 662).
2. These stimuli exert their control over behavior in accordance with the laws of classical and operant conditioning. Human beings are passive, and they function essentially as a machine; their outputs (responses) are evoked or maintained by antecedent or consequent conditioning mechanisms. Thus, as White has pointed out (1970, 662), all human behavior is seen merely as a simple mechanical contrivance.

3. Since all human behavior is composed of mechanical stimulus-response respondents or operants, then stimuli are the cause of human behavior and responses are the effect of these causes (Bowers 1973; White 1970).

Although, as White has noted, "no learning theory has ever been constructed from studies of children or been specifically directed toward them" (1970, 667), psychologists working from the nurture-behaviorist point of view have tended to generalize the results of some studies with nonhuman animals as well as with children into a general account of the behavior of all humans at all ages, and even in some cases of all animals of all phylogenetic levels (see our discussion of this point in Chapter 6, and White, 1970, 681). This integration is done on the basis of the assumption that behavior at any level of analysis may be reduced to the objectively verifiable operants and respondents that make up any and all behavior, and only in this way may the study of behavior remain within the objective framework of natural science (White 1970, 666).

In sum, the behavior-analysis approach to developmental psychology—as represented by Bijou and Baer—views development as merely the accumulated acquisition of operant and respondent behaviors, responses acquired by situationally specific environmental stimulation. The laws of associative learning involved in classical and operant conditioning, and the phenomena involved in these processes (e.g., secondary reinforcement, positive and negative reinforcement, chaining), may be used to account for the behavioral functioning of a person at any level of psychological development. That is, behavior at any of these levels may similarly be analyzed as being made up of operants and respondents. Because of this identical composition there is continuity in the variables involved in psychological functioning and development. Behavior at any level of development is qualitatively the same as behavior at any other level, and thus the only difference between levels of development lies is in the quantity of these similarly acquired elements.

A succinct summary of the key features of the empirical-behaviorist, behavior-analytic approach to development has been provided by Sheldon White (1970). White notes five core assumptions of this approach:

1. The environment may be unambiguously characterized in terms of stimuli.

2. Behavior may be unambiguously characterized in terms of responses.

3. A class of stimuli exist which, applied contingently and immediately following a response, increase it or decrease it in some measurable fashion. These stimuli may be treated as reinforcers.

4. Learning may be completely characterized in terms of various possible couplings among stimuli, responses, and reinforcers.

5. Unless there is definite evidence to the contrary, classes of behavior may be assumed to be learned, manipulable by the environment, extinguishable, and trainable. (White 1970, 665–66).

It will be necessary, of course, to evaluate the assumptions and the features of the behavior-analytic approach to development in order to draw conclusions about the usefulness of this position—the most systematic and extensive attempt to use empirical behaviorism to formulate a theory of human development (Baer 1970, 1976, 1982; Bijou 1976; Bijou and Baer 1961, 1965). However, I noted earlier that there exist instances of theoretical-behavioristic formulations that are also pertinent to human development. Moreover, as we have indicated too, White (1976) contends that theoretical-behaviorism shares with empirical behaviorism several key assumptions—for example, the idea of the "passive organism." Accordingly, because of this commonality as well as because of their relevance to ideas about the bases and character of human development, let us review some of the key theoretical-behaviorist attempts to use learning principles

Sheldon H. White

to account for development. After this review, we shall turn to an evaluation of nurture-behavioristic theories.

THEORETICAL-BEHAVIORISM AND SOCIAL-LEARNING THEORIES OF HUMAN DEVELOPMENT

Theoretical behaviorism has a long history and a rich, active, and diverse present (Boring 1950; Hilgard and Bowers 1966; Horton and Mills 1984), one that over the years has increasingly involved reference to the role of cognitive phenomena in learning—for example, encoding processes, memory processes, and schemata (see Horton and Mills 1984). For this reason, theroretical behaviorism is today often labeled as cognitive learning,

and is seen to encompass a set of phenomena that stand in contrast to those involved in associative learning. However, as White (1970) has observed, these theoretical formulations have not been devised either because of a primary interest in development or on the basis of data derived from the study of developing organisms (i.e., infants, children, early adolescents, etc.). Thus, as with our discussion of empirical behaviorism, our interest in theoretical behaviorism is not in presenting a broad-based review of this area of scholarship per se. Rather, we are concerned with those instances of theoretical behaviorism that have been used to account for human developmental phenomena. The most prominent instances of these formulations have been ones that may be termed social-learning or cognitive social-learning theories. Our discussion will therefore stress these positions.

In the 1940s and 1950s, some theorists (e.g., Miller and Dollard 1941; Dollard and Miller 1950) used nurture-based learning principles to explain how the social environment comes to control human behavior. Although the principles eventually generated in such *social-learning* interpretations of human behavior were, in the main, derived from data collected on laboratory rats, they represented influential views of how nurture is involved in human functioning.

As with the nurture-behavioristic view in general, there is no one social-learning theory of human functioning. Numerous theories, all labeled social-learning ones by their formulators, were devised. For instance, one such position is the theory of socialized anxiety of Davis (1944). Davis (1944) argued that what people learn in their social environment is to anticipate reward for approved behavior and punishment for disapproved behavior. Anticipation of punishment represents an unpleasant feeling-state—termed *socialized* (learned) *anxiety* for the person—and people behave in ways that will diminish or avoid this anxiety. For example, Davis argues that, in adolescence, the behaviors society will reward and/or punish are less certain for the person, and thus there is no definite way to decrease socialized anxiety. Accordingly, storm and stress are involved in this period.

Other social-learning theories have different components. McCandless (1970), for example, proposed a "drive theory" of human behavior. He views a drive as an energizer of behavior and specifies that there exist several drives in the person (e.g., a hunger drive, a drive to avoid pain, and, emerging in adolescence for the first time in life, a sex drive). The nurture component of McCandless's theory involves the direction that behavior takes as a consequence of being energized by a particular drive.

One learns in society, through the principles of classical and operant conditioning, that certain behaviors will appropriately *reduce* drive-states. Certain behaviors will reduce hunger, or pain, or sexual arousal. McCandless asserts that those behaviors that reduce drives are most likely to be learned (repeated again in comparable social situations). Drive-reducing behaviors are those that are rewarded (as a consequence of having the drive diminished), while behaviors that do not diminish a drive-state are, therefore, punished behaviors. Such behaviors are less likely to be repeated.

As a consequence of repeating behavior, people form habits. Thus when a particular drive is aroused, it is probable that an individual will behave by emitting the habit. Thus, like Davis, McCandless says people learn to show certain behaviors (habits) because the habits reduce an internal state. However, unlike Davis, to McCandless these states involve more than just socialized anxiety, which is a learned association to behavior. McCandless says the states individuals act to reduce are drive-states, and these states (e.g., hunger or sex drive) need not be learned. They may be biologically based. Nevertheless, what people do in response to the arousal of *any* drive is a socially learned phenomenon.

Like Davis, McCandless sees a specific relevance of his ideas to adolescent development; again, however, this relevance differs from the one that Davis specifies. For instance, as already implied, adolescence is special for McCandless because of the emergence of a new drive: sex. New social learning, new habits, must be formed to reduce this drive in a way that will be rewarded. However, McCandless specifies that society does not reward males and females for the same drive-reducing habits; consequently, males and females are channeled into developing those habits that are socially prescribed as sex-appropriate. Thus, because of the sex drive, adolescence becomes a time of defining oneself in terms of new, sex-specific habits—habits that are socially defined as leading to reward for people of one or the other sex. Until new habits are formed, and thus new self-definitions attained, McCandless (1970) would argue that adolescence could very likely be a period of undiminished drives and hence of stress and emotional turmoil.

Still other versions of social-learning theory exist. The version formulated by Bandura (1965, 1971, 1977; Bandura and Walters 1963) has evolved over the last quarter of a century to become the most prominent instance of this class of theories. Moreover, congruent with the trend over the years for the increasing prominence of cognitive-learning phenomena in the general field of learning, is Bandura's (1974, 1977) increasingly greater stress on cognitive phenomena in social learning. Indeed, Bandura (1980a, 1980b) labels his position as a cognitive social-learning one. As we shall see, as we now focus on Bandura's ideas, the stress on cognition occurs because Bandura argues that people learn through the mere observation of others as a consequence of their possession of cognitive processes such as attention, symbol formation, and memory.

Observational Learning: Modeling and Imitation

The type of learning phenomena studied by Bandura may be termed *observational learning*. As discussed by Liebert and Wicks-Nelson (1981) this type of learning "occurs through exposure to the behavior of others, the others being presented either live or symbolically in literature, films, television, and the like" (p. 170). As evidence that observational learning has occurred, the observer produces behaviors that are an *imitation* of those that were observed. Thus this form of learning is often labeled *imitative learning,* and the actor that produced the to-be-copied or to-be-imitated learning is labeled the *model.*

Because one learns from observing others in one's social milieu, it is clear why this form of learning is treated as an instance of social learning. As I have noted, the position of Albert Bandura (1971, 1977, 1978, 1980a, 1980b) today is most often thought of when people discuss principles of either observational learning or social-learning theory.

Both classical and operant conditioning stress the role of reinforcement in the acquisition of behavior. In addition, insofar as operant learning is concerned, a response must first occur (and then be reinforced) in order for learning to occur (Shaffer 1979). However, Bandura (1971) contends that neither classical nor operant learning principles are sufficient to explain the rich, complex, and often rapid development of behaviors in the repertoire of even very young children. In his view, learning can occur *vicariously*—that is, through observation of others' behaviors and its consequences for them (Bandura 1971). That is, children need not receive reinforcement, or even respond, in order to learn from a model.

A classic experiment by Bandura (1965) illustrates this view. Bandura presented a short film to nursery-school children, studied individually. In the film an adult was shown making a series of aggressive behaviors—for example, hitting a large, inflated plastic doll with a hammer or yelling at the doll. The children watching this film were divided into one of three groups, differentiated on the basis of the ending of the film. Group one was a "model rewarded" group. Here at the end of the film a second adult gave the first some candy for his "excellent" performance. Group two was a "model pun-

Albert Bandura

ished" one; a second adult scolded and spanked the first one. Children in group three saw neither reward nor punishment given to the model; here there were "neutral" consequences shown to the model.

After the film ended, children in all groups were individually placed in a room having many of the same toys that had been available to the model. Hidden observers recorded each child's behavior. Children in both the "model rewarded" and the "neutral" groups imitated more than did children in the "model punished" group.

However, despite these performance differences there was evidence that children in all three groups equivalently learned the model's actions. Bandura (1965) offered children in all three groups rewards (e.g., a glass of fruit juice) if they would demonstrate what they had seen the model do in the film.

This inducement canceled out the above-described performance differences, and children from all groups showed comparable amounts of imitative learning.

From these data it is possible to see why Bandura (1965) makes a distinction between learning and performance. It appears that reward or punishment influences whether or not children will perform observed behavior; it does not appear to influence their learning of the behavior (Shaffer 1979). In other words, the response consequences to the model affects whether an observationally learned behavior will be imitated. However, the mere observation of the model may be sufficient for learning to occur.

OBSERVATIONAL LEARNING PROCESSES. What are the requisite processes that determine the acquisition and performance of actions observed in a model? Processes both intrinsic and extrinsic to the child seem to play a role (Shaffer 1979). As I have noted, because social-learning theorists like Bandura (1977, 1978, 1980a, 1980b) emphasize intrinsic, cognitive processes in the acquisition of behaviors observed in a model, the theoretical approach is today often termed *cognitive social-learning theory* (e.g., see Bandura 1980a, 1980b; and Mischel 1973, 1977). Shaffer (1979) has presented an excellent summary of both the cognitive and behavioral processes thought to be involved in observational learning. Among these are:

1. *Attentional processes.* The child must attend to the model in order to observe him, her, or it. What sort of variables influence the child's attention? The status of the model (e.g., his or her age) and the response consequences to the model (e.g., whether he or she is punished or rewarded) are features of the model and of his or her social interactions to which the child attends (Bandura and Walters 1963). A child's past learning history is also important for attention. For example, whether the model is a novel person or figure plays a role in evoking attention (Bandura and Walters 1963). In addition, whether the model is presented in a medium of "intrinsic" interest to the children of a particular age—for instance, a cartoon figure presented to a young child—is an important variable in evoking attention (Shaffer 1979). Finally, current situational influences, such as a teacher's instructions, can evoke attention.

2. *Memory processes.* To retain the information that has been observed, the child must use the cognitive processes involved in encoding, storage, and retrieval of the information.

3. *Motor processes.* The child must have the ability to translate the attended-to and remembered behaviors into overt actions. He or she must have the *skill* to enact the behavior.

4. *Self-monitoring processes.* People are often aware that their performance may not conform to their image (memory) of the behavior they observed in others. For example, I often observe (on television) professional basketball players making graceful drives and jump shots. When I am in the process of trying to imitate these observations on the basketball court in my driveway, I am quite aware of how my actions do not correspond—either in grace or outcome (sinking the ball in the hoop)—with those I have witnessed. Often my lack of correspondence leaves me with a feeling of great frustration—especially after repeated attempts at performance. As this example suggests, people may also have ideals of performance that they use as standards against which to compare the behaviors they observe in themselves. These standards can be acquired through observational learning and/or through direct instruction—for instance, through a verbal statement, independent of observation (Bandura 1978; Shaffer 1979). Through applying these memories and standards, children can self-regulate, and self-reward or self-punish, their performance (Bandura 1978).

5. *Motivational processes.* Here we return to reward and punishment. As noted earlier, rewards and punishments may not affect the acquisition of behaviors observed in a model (Bandura 1965); however, they

are the variables that appear to affect performance.

In sum, observational learning processes are quite distinct from those involved in classical and operant conditioning. Moreover, their distinction is today thought to lie to a great extent in the role that cognitive processes play in observational learning (Bandura 1978, 1980a, 1980b). However, cognitive processes show quite significant developmental changes throughout life. Thus it is important to ascertain whether there is evidence that observational learning and imitation develop in ways that would be expected on the basis of the often dramatic changes in cognitive functioning, especially as they occur in the early, infant years of life. Let us now turn to such an evaluation.

DEVELOPMENTAL CHANGES IN IMITATION IN INFANCY. There is some evidence that even in the first days, and certainly after the first few weeks and months, of life infants can imitate some behaviors. For example, data reported by Meltzoff and Moore (1977) indicate that twelve- to twenty-one-day-old infants can exhibit tongue protrusion in response to seeing an adult display a similar action. Meltzoff and Moore (1977) believe that such tongue protrusion represents the earliest form of selective imitation. However, this view has been criticized because their research did not consider the possibility that matching behavior can be elicited by events other than the modeled behavior. To appraise whether this criticism is applicable, Jacobson (1979) studied thirty-four infants at six, ten, and fourteen weeks of age. She found that a moving pen and ball were as effective as the tongue model in eliciting tongue protrusion at six weeks of age. In turn, a dangling ring elicited as much hand-opening and -closing behavior at fourteen weeks as did a model showing this behavior. More recently, Field et al. (1982) found that newborns could discriminate three facial expressions—happy, sad, and surprise—posed by a live model. Most interestingly, the infants' expressions corresponded

with those of the model at better than a chance level.

Most infants can imitate some adult sounds by twelve weeks of age, and many can imitate motor movements of the face, hands, and so on, by the second half of the first year of life. In turn, by the end of the period of life that most scholars identify with the end of infancy—that is, by the time the child is twenty-four months old—infants' imitative capacities have increased so dramatically that the imitation of new words is a typical occurrence.

There are numerous data sets that document the development of imitative capacity through the infancy period. A major report of this development has been provided by McCall, Parke, and Kavanaugh (1977). One portion of their work involved the study of twelve- to twenty-four-month-olds. Infants watched a live adult perform several different behaviors (e.g., vocalizing, making a wooden puzzle, playing with some toys). After each behavior was performed, McCall, Parke, and Kavanaugh noted whether the infant imitated the adult's behavior. They found that the amount of imitation increased rapidly from twelve to twenty-four months of age.

Another portion of the McCall, Parke, and Kavanaugh report involved the representation of televised as well as live models. Other investigators have addressed similar issues. Slaby and Hollenbeck (1977), for instance, found that six-month-olds looked at a TV showing children's programs 49 percent of the available time. Returning to the McCall, Parke, and Kavanaugh (1977) study, they provide evidence that such television observation is increasingly combined during infancy with imitative outcomes. Between eighteen and thirty-six months of age children attended to a live model nearly all the time but showed an increasing tendency to attend to a televised model. At eighteen, twenty-four, and thirty-six months of age the percentage of time spent watching the televised model was 68, 78, and 95 percent, respectively. Moreover, although both live and televised models were imitated at all age levels, at eighteen and twenty-four months the live model was imitated more than the televised one. However, by thirty-six months of age imitation toward both models was virtually the same.

In sum, throughout infancy there is an increasing tendency to imitate behaviors observed in both live and televised models. Moreover, as the child makes the transition from infancy to childhood, there is evidence that either type of model is equally capable of evoking imitation. Given that at this time imitative capacity begins increasingly to involve language, and that the child therefore becomes exposed to potential models through oral and written, as well as televised, media, it is clear that the potential richness of sources of observational learning experiences is quite great. Thus Bandura's (1971) point that much of the learning of the early years of life primarily involves observational learning—the imitation of models—seems an excellent one.

Conclusions: The Cognitivization and Contextualization of Theoretical-Behavioral Views of Human Development

As Bandura's formulation of social-learning theory grew to include cognitive processes, including those that monitored the person's interactions in his or her environment (e.g., recall the example given above of my basketball-playing performance), two quite significant features were included in his position. First is the one we have stressed above—that is, the role of cognitive processes in learning; this "cognitivization" of social-learning theory corresponds, as we have noted, to the cognitivization that has occurred in theoretical behaviorism over the course of the last two to three decades. However, Bandura's (1978, 1980a, 1980b) concern with self-monitoring, or self-regulatory, processes—ones involving people's relationships to their settings—reflects an interest in the context of social learning. This interest has been construed by Bandura

(1978) to involve *reciprocally deterministic relations* between the person and his or her context.

This view of the bases of human functioning has been discussed in preceding chapters as one consonant with the developmental-contextual, probabilistic-epigenetic view of development; it arises in Bandura's (1978) theorizing as a consequence of his recognition that through their cognitive processes—their activity—"people create and activate environments as well as rebut them" (Bandura 1978, 344). In other words, because organisms are active—or, in White's (1976) terms, because organisms give form to their experience—Bandura (1978) rejects a "unidirectional environmental determinism" and contends that "psychological functioning involves a continuous reciprocal interaction between behavioral, cognitive, and environmental influences" (p. 344). In other words, Bandura's (1977, 1978, 1980a, 1980b) cognitive social-learning theory—which in my view is a major, current instance of the application of theoretical-behaviorist ideas to human development—has become, to a great extent, an active-organism position: The organism is seen to influence its context as much as that context influences it.

This transition in theoretical behaviorism has been observed, at least in part, by White (1976); he noted that, at least insofar as the research program of theoretical behaviorism is concerned, "more and more evidence for active factors in the causation of behavior" (p. 100) was discovered over the years. Perhaps because Bandura's laboratory has been one of the most productive of those associated with the theoretical-behaviorist movement, his research activity led to the development of his views regarding reciprocal determinism and of the person as a producer of his or her own development.

If it is the case, then, that theoretical-behaviorist formulations relevant to human development have become developmentally contextualized, it is left to the versions of empirical behaviorism that are designed to be pertinent to human development to defend the ideas associated with the concepts of the "passive organism" and with the view that associative learning principles suffice to account for human development. As such, as we turn now to an evaluation of nurture-behavioral theories, the empirical-behaviorist position—and more specifically, the behavior-analysis view of Bijou and Baer—will be the instance of nurture behaviorism on which we shall focus most.

AN EVALUATION OF NURTURE-BEHAVIORAL APPROACHES

In turning to our evaluation of nurture-behavioral approaches, we shall continue to consider the comments provided by Reese (1976), by White (1970, 1976), as well as those found in another, particularly important critique written by Bowers (1973); this latter essay evaluated the "situationalist" (or behavioral-analysis; Reese 1976) approach to development.

The nurture-behavioral approach clearly attempts to place developmental psychology within an objective, empirical, natural-science framework. In fact, proponents of this view contend that "the preservation of objectivity in psychology depends upon the observability of truly causal variables" (Bowers 1973, 308). By focusing on stimuli and responses, it is believed that such causal observations are made. Simply, it is believed that stimuli in an organism's environment cause the organism's responses and as a consequence provide the basis of the organism's behavioral form or structure.

Using the behavior-analysis approach as the exemplary case of a systematic nurture-behavioral theory of human development, we may illustrate the above reasoning by referring to a discussion by Reese (1982). In contrasting the behavior-analysis approach with alternative, organismic approaches to developmental psychology, Reese points out that the key issue dividing behavior analysis from the other approaches

is about the process of development. A rose, for example, does not learn to be a rose, according to a nativist position; its rose-ness unfolds epigenetically. And persons do not learn to be human; their humanness—and their cognition—unfolds with maturation and experience. The nativist does not deny an effect of experience; however, experience is a *condition* or material base for development rather than a *cause* of development. The environmentalist, in contrast, presumes that the causes of development are environmental, and that heredity provides the conditions for development. The latter position is well illustrated by Baer's [1970, 244] statement, "It seems to me implicit in modern behavioral technology that there must be quite some number of environmental programs, or sequences, which will bring an organism to any specified developmental outcome." (Reese 1982, 355)

Thus adherents of the behavioral-analysis approach to developmental psychology appeal to situational stimuli as the cause of all behavior. Accordingly, it is believed that this orientation not only makes developmental psychology an objective natural science, but provides other important assets too. For instance, in discussing the advantages of their theoretical orientation, Bijou and Baer assert: "We can point out as advantages the simplicity of this approach, its frequent fruitfulness, and its freedom from logical tangles which ultimately turn out to be illusory rather than real" (1961, 4). Admittedly, the behavioral-analysis approach is a relatively simple one. Yet the belief that in the stimulus situation lies the cause of behavior raises several potentially problematic issues. Let us consider them.

The Role of Organismic Factors

In behavior analysis the excessive concern with the stimulus situation is associated with what is, in effect, an almost complete disregard of the organism, organismic factors, and the active role these variables may play in behavioral functioning and development. Clearly, however, there is an organism in any stimulus situation. It is the organism upon which the stimuli act, and it is the organism that behaves in any situation. Yet the behavior-analysis approach categorically eliminates the possibility that the organism may play an active, participatory, and potentially unique role in its own behavior and development (Baer 1976).

Thus individual behavioral differences among organisms in seemingly identical situations are held to be, in principle, merely reducible to potential empirical stimulus differences in the situation. This reliance on the stimulus situation as the cause of the behavior of any organism and as the basis for any differences among organisms in their behavior "is limited by the tendency either to ignore organismic factors, or to regard them as ... subsidiary to the primary impact of the external stimulus" (Harré and Secord 1972, 27). The categorical dismissal of active organismic factors and, in turn, the appeal to the stimulus situation as the cause of all behavior raise, however, the very sort of logical problems that Bijou and Baer (1961) claim are obviated by the behavior-analysis approach. Let us see how.

The Environment as the Cause of the Organism's Structure

The core notion in the behavior-analysis approach is that a stimulus causes a response, whatever characteristics the organism might possess. Simply, it is held that one may essentially disregard the organism and focus just on the stimulus in the situation, because the stimulus is the cause of behavior. This, then, is the idea we have discussed earlier, the notion of the "passive organism," or of the "organism as host" (Baer 1976); that is, an organism that receives its form from its environmental experience (White 1976). Given this view of the organism, it seems clear that if the passive organism has a form—a structure—it must be one derived from the environment. If the environment were a nonstructured entity it could not easily give a structure to the organism. Therefore, it seems likely that it must be the case that the structure of the organism is received from the structure of the environment it experiences. In this regard Reese (1976), commenting on Baer's (1976) formulation of behavior analysis, has noted that:

> Baer's structures are sets of behaviors that have organization imposed on them but that are potentially independently controllable by the environment. The structure is a product of common environmental action and is not intrinsic to the behaviors nor to the organism. However, it must then be intrinsic to the environment, as Kohlberg (1968) also noted. The environment must be intrinsically structured to yield an environmental account of cognitive structure. Thus, one could characterize Baer's model as attributing cognitive structure—or, better, behavioral structure—primarily to the structure of the environment. (Reese 1976, 110–11)

But while this behavior-analysis view explains the basis, or cause, of the organism's structure, it does not account for the structure of the environment. As Reese (1976, 111–12) points out:

> The structured nature of the environment is not explained in Baer's model. Why does it have the structure it has? More basically, why does it have any structure at all?

Reese notes, too, that similar questions may be raised in regard to the structure of the organism in nature-based maturationalist models, such as those of Hall (1904) and Gesell (1929, 1946, 1954), and in regard to the structure of the organism-environment interaction in the structuralist model (e.g., Overton 1976). Thus, he concludes, "Apparently, the nature of the causal structure must be accepted as given" (Reese 1976, 112).

In short, the behavior-analysis model shares with other approaches to development a problem of identifying the cause of causal structure. But the behavior-analysis position has problems specific to it as a consequence of its belief that it is the stimulus environment that provides the cause of the organism's structure. The nature of these problems has been succinctly noted by White (1970). He points out that: "The problem is that one cannot seem to find a part of the environment which in and of itself, disregarding the subject, is always a stimulus for behavior" (1970, 669). Thus the appeal of the behavior-analysis approach to the stimulus as a source of all behavior seems to be limited by the fact that a stimulus simply cannot be found in every situation to account for every behavior.

The Definition of the Environment

The presence of this lack of stimulus specification may suggest that there exists a vague, or an unclear, conception of the stimulus-environment among nurture-behaviorists, such as behavior analysts. This point has been made by Wohlwill. He notes:

> One of the criticisms that environmentalists have been prone to level against those who would attribute a functional role to hereditary variables in human behavior is that they represent little more than a cloak for our ignorance, given the virtual impossibility, in the foreseeable future, of isolating the contribution of specific genes to behavior at the human level. Whether or not one accepts this argument on its merits—and it is a debatable one—it ignores the fact that the standard equation, B = f (H, E) is in fact an equation in *two* unknowns. The fact is that environmentalists have, by and large, been woefully unspecific in their reference to the role of "environment" as a determinant of behavior; particularly in the human differential psychology literature on the heredity-environment question, little consideration has typically been given to specifying the meaning of "environmental" influences or of the variables presumed to be operating to mediate such influences. Environment has, in fact, represented a catchall for everything from mere opportunity for the exercise of a motor response to the broad complex of forces operating in the child's familial, social and cultural milieu. The term has been used interchangeably to refer to ill-defined aspects of the physical, the interpersonal and the institutional environment, encompassing such diverse aspects as child-rearing practices, schooling and the trappings of our material civilization.

This diffuseness in our use of the term "en-vironment" and our thinking about its role in behavior is reflected in the basic ambiguity surrounding the closely related term "experience," which has been at the core of the environmentalist's vocabulary. Upon even cursory examination, it appears that there is a remarkable lack of consistency in the use of this term, even with respect to as fundamental an issue as to whether it is intended to refer to a variable on the stimulus or the response side of the ledger. (Wohlwill 1973, 90–91).

Overgeneralizing the Role of the Environment

In Chapter 6, and again in this chapter, I noted that one of the problems with the nurture-behavioral approach is overgeneralization. We saw that although one might be able to manipulate some behaviors of some animals in some situations and make these animals perform with marked similarity, one is not therefore justified in assuming that one can manipulate all behaviors in all animals in all situations to produce similar performance. In the present discussion we see another instance of such overgeneralization. Although in some situations there may exist stimuli that provide a source of some behaviors, this does not mean that in all situations there exist stimuli that provide a source of all behaviors.

Despite this problem, the behavior-analysis approach, for instance, continues to appeal to a stimulus in any account of a behavioral response. If this appeal were not maintained, then according to this position an objective natural-science orientation could similarly not be maintained (Bowers 1973, 317). Yet, as Bowers (1973) has pointed out, many experiments done by those testing this approach do not show changes in behavior as a function of situational stimulus alterations. Those following a behavior-analysis approach do experiments in which differing stimulus situations are presented to subjects in an attempt to assess the effect of these altered situations on subjects' behavior. However, the researcher often finds that the differing situations used in the experiment do not result in differing subject behaviors. This is true even though the situations were not randomly selected; that is, they were in fact selected *because* they were thought to be capable of differentially affecting behavior. Most active researchers know that even the best-designed experiments often do not work out—that is, the subjects behave in the same way in different situations.

When such results occur the researcher may often consider the experiment a failure. After all, is it not the case that different situational stimulus conditions cause different responses? Since this assumption may be treated by the researcher as if it were a fact, then when different situations do not effect different responses in subjects, the researcher may view the results as negative and the study as a failure. As pointed out by Bowers (1973), many editors of scientific journals might agree with the researcher's appraisal of the study, since the results from such studies are typically not accepted for publication.

Yet it is possible to offer a different interpretation of such findings. If we assume that all of an organism's behavior is *not* determined just by the situationally specific stimuli impinging upon it, then we may view the results as supportive of another idea. If we assert that organisms possess characteristics that continue to characterize the organism and play an active, contributory role in its behavior apart from any specific situation, then when we see the failure of differing situations to differentially influence the organism's behavior, we may take this "as evidence regarding the relative stability of behavior across situations" (Bowers 1973, 317). We may view such experimental results as supportive of the assumption that in addition to situation-specific stimulus determinants of behavior, there exist organismic (situation-general) determinants of behavior.

Of course, the researcher who believes in the situational determinancy of behavior could always argue that the experiment failed to show situational differences because the study inadvertently used stimulus situations that were not *really* different. However, Bowers (1973, 317) points out that such an argument raises serious logical problems. If one hypothesizes that behavior is situation specific, then it must in some way also be possible to show that it is *not* situation specific. If one hypothesizes that "A" is the case, then in order for this assertion to be scientifically verifiable one must be able to subject it to a test, one possible result of which is the conclusion that "A" is *not* the case. If one makes hypotheses that can in no way be proved incorrect, then those hypotheses are useless for science. To fairly test one's assertions one must offer them in such a way that they can be tested for their truth or falsity.

Hence Bowers (1973) notes that if a researcher finds that situational manipulations fail to effect behavioral change and then *always* concludes that this only means that the situations were thus not *really* different—rather than taking such findings as evidence of the cross-situational generalizability of behavior—then the researcher is advancing a nonfalsifiable and scientifically useless assertion. Thus Bowers concludes that "if (truly) changed environments can only be inferred from changed behavior, then the potential circularity of the situationalist model becomes actual and vicious" (1973, 317). That is, Bowers characterizes the situationalist approach as involving a completely circular argument: "When does behavior change? When the situation does. How do you know when the eliciting and evoking conditions change? When the behavior does. Viewed in this way, behavior becomes situation specific because it is impossible for it not to be situation specific" (1973, 317).

We see, then, that in addition to the specific problems introduced into the behavior-analysis position by its disregard of organismic characteristics and its overreliance on the stimulus situation as *the* cause of behavior, some logical problems are involved in a complete adherence to this approach. Some other logical problems may still be noted, however.

The Definition of Reinforcement

We know from our earlier presentations in this chapter that if a response is reinforced it will be maintained because a reinforcing stimulus is by definition a stimulus that increases the probability of a behavior. Thus, as Bowers (1973) points out, the assertion that behavior that is reinforced is accordingly maintained is necessarily true because it follows logically from the definition of what a reinforcing stimulus is. However, Bowers argues that those following a behavior-analysis approach often "glide noiselessly from this initial assertion to a more problematic one that is *not* true by definition, nor does it follow logically from the definition of reinforcement, namely, behavior which is acquired and maintained is reinforced" (1973, 311).

We may see that this second assertion involves the notion that any behavior that occurs must occur on the basis of reinforcement. Here, then, is the assumption that all behavior is learned behavior and the idea that reinforcement (in accordance with classical or operant conditioning) is the mechanism by which behavior is learned. In other words, while it is true by definition that one may shape an animal's behavior by reinforcement, it does not follow that therefore whenever an animal shows behavior it does so because it was reinforced.

Here we see another instance of overgeneralization as well as of circular reasoning. To rephrase some of Bowers's (1973) earlier arguments: What does reinforcement do? It increases the probability of behavior occurrence. When a behavior increases in probability of occurrence, what causes this? Reinforcement!

Let us illustrate the problems, then, with the logic of this use of the concept of reinforcement. From knowing that one can increase the probability of a rat's bar-pressing response by making food reinforcement contingent on that response, behavior analysts have moved toward arguing that when one sees any behavior whatsoever one may account for its presence simply by asserting that its basis lies in reinforcement. Why does one paint a picture, sew a dress, write a book, vote for a particular political candidate, or love a certain person and not another? One does any and all of these things because one is reinforced. People show love behavior, political behavior, artistic behavior, or moral behavior because stimuli in their environment reinforce (shape) these behaviors. Thus, because all such human behaviors are merely caused, and therefore controlled, by the external stimulus situations people find themselves in, and because these situations exist apart from people—in the sense that people themselves do not have controlling influence on situational characteristics—people themselves have no "freedom or dignity." Such concepts as freedom and dignity are fictitious and fallacious, put forth by those who do not "know" that every aspect of human behavior is controlled by situation-specific reinforcing stimuli.

This view suggests that the human organism (or any organism, for that matter) has no integrity, in the sense that it plays no active, contributory role in its own development. Humans are merely passive machines, malleable balls of clay, waiting to be shaped and controlled by the stimulus-environment, which provides the cause of all behavior.

But where are the stimuli that reinforce these behaviors? As we have seen White (1970) and Bowers (1973) point out, such controlling stimuli cannot readily be found for these situations. Thus, the appeal to situation-specific controlling stimuli as the cause for all behavior becomes an overgeneralized, logically circular, and objectively and empirically unverifiable assertion. On the basis of circular reasoning and thus the seemingly unfounded belief that all behavior is reinforced behavior, those taking a behavior-analytic approach to development attempt to fit all behavior into a "situationalist paradigm." Yet, since in many cases the presence of reinforcement is not seen but only inferred on the basis of the fact that behavior has occurred, the behavior-analysis approach loses its status as an objective account of behavior. It becomes at least as unempirical and as unobjective as it claims the theoretical viewpoints counter to it are.

In other words, adherents of the behavior-analysis approach may often criticize organismic approaches to psychological development as being unobjective (e.g., Bijou 1976; Bijou and Baer 1961), since the latter approaches use such concepts as cognition, reasoning, personality structure, and individual traits. Yet our analysis of the behavior-analysis approach position indicates that its reliance on the stimulus situation does not make it any more objective than these other approaches. As long as the "situational stimulus source of all human behavior" remains as just another elusive, unverified assumption, it seems that all people may continue to have the freedom to believe that they have dignity.

Conclusions

Our analysis of the behavior-analysis approach, as the exemplar of a nurture-behavioral view of human development, leads us to conclude that while this viewpoint does indeed offer a simple formula for the understanding of behavior and development, it is also characterized by rather severe limitations of an empirical and logical nature. Although adherents of this approach contend that all human behavior is merely situation specific—that is, completely controlled by the stimuli present in a specific environmental situation (e.g., Baer 1976; Bijou 1976, 1977)—we have seen that it is just as reasonable to infer that in many cases a human possesses traits, or individual characteristics, that lead to behavioral consistency across different situations. As such, the issue for understanding development may be more a matter of learning how situational *and* personological processes relate to provide a basis for behavior and development (Brim and Kagan 1980; Magnusson and Allen 1983; Mischel 1977; Mischel and Peake 1983), than one of determining if situation or person is more important.

For instance, it is clear that most of us behave differently when we are studying in a library than when we are rooting for our favorite football team. Those developmentalists taking a behavior-analysis approach would point to such instances as evidence for the situational control of behavior. On the other hand, we may also observe that when a person is characterized by the trait of hostility or high intensity of reaction, such a trait may be manifested in various situations in which the person interacts (e.g., in school, at play, waiting on a line, at a party). Trait theorists would take such evidence as supportive of the notion of cross-situational consistency (i.e., situational independency) of behavior. Accordingly, instances may be found where either situation or person seems more potent in explaining behavior. This means that at times the person may be "in control" of the situation, while at other times the situation may override any attempts by the person to control his or her setting. The task for developmentalists, then, should be to discern when—under what conditions—person factors or situational factors seem most important. Through such an analysis the parametric relation between people and their settings can begin to be understood (Lerner 1984).

Put in other words, we may ask, "What is the source of variations among people in their behaviors?" and we may begin to study how people and situations interact to provide a source of behavior and development. That is, it may be useful to treat situations and persons as interdependent phenomena. It is always the case that a person exists in specific situations. A person, with presumably individual characteristics, is continually entering into situations, which have their own presumably special characteristics. From our discussions in previous chapters (especially Chapter 10) we know that people with different individual characteristics may be expected to interact differently in the same stimulus situation and that people with even very dissimilar characteristics may be led to similar behaviors as a consequence of their interactions in different situations. Thus the interaction of a person in a situation may account for behavioral variation.

This possibility is, of course, consistent with the probabilistic-epigenetic organismic notions I have been emphasizing throughout this book. Behavior is not merely a function of either intrinsic or extrinsic factors but is an outcome of an interaction between such influences. Hence, while from the perspective of the behavior-analysis approach one would expect the situation to be the major source of this variation, we might expect the *person × situation interaction* to provide the major source of behavioral variation. Bowers (1973) analyzed and reviewed studies done in an attempt to determine whether situation, person, or the interaction between the two accounts for the major percentage of variation in human behavior. His findings are supportive of our ideas regarding the presence of person-situation interactions and are consistent with the conclusions drawn in subsequent analyses (Magnusson and Allen 1983; Mischel and Peake 1983) as well. Thus they are useful to note here.

Bowers (1973) reviewed several (i.e., eleven) studies in the psychological literature that could be used to address the issue of whether situations, persons, or interactions between the two contribute the major percentage of variation in human behavior. Since some of these had more than one set of measurements, Bowers was able to address this issue through reference to nineteen sets of measurements, ranging in form from actual behavioral observation measurements to self-rating measurements made by subjects.

It was found that the percentage of variation due to the situation was greater than the percentage of variation due to the person in eight of the nineteen measurement sets. Thus the percentage of variation due to the person was greater than the percentage of variation due to the situation in the other eleven measurement sets. However, in all sets the percentage of variation for either the situation or person sources was relatively small. The average percentage of variation due to the person in these measurements was 12.7 percent, while the average percentage of variation due to the situation in these measurements was only 10.2 percent.

What, then, accounted for the most variation in behavior in most of these measurement sets? Consistent with our probabilistic-epigenetic-based expectations, the interaction of persons and situations accounted for a higher percentage of variation than either situation or person alone in fourteen of the eighteen measurement sets (in one measurement set it was not possible to calculate the interaction percentage). Moreover, in eight of these eighteen sets the percentage of variation due to the person × situation interaction was greater than the sum total of the percentage of variation due to situation alone and person alone; and the average percentage variation due to this interaction, 20.8 percent, was greater than the average percentage for either the situation alone or the person alone.

Of course, had Bowers (1973) reviewed other studies, his findings—the percentages of variation associated with person, situation, or the interaction between the two—might, and probably would, have been different. But the major point to take from Bowers's review (1973) or from later analyses of this issue (e.g., Epstein 1983; Magnusson and Allen 1983; Mischel 1973, 1983; Mischel and Peake 1983) is not whether a particular study finds that persons, situations, or interactions account for most variance. As I noted above, settings—ranging from experimental to naturalistic ones—can be found and studied in a way to provide support for any of these outcomes. The point is that both people *and* situations matter, and to advance beyond debates focused merely on whether one or the other is more potent—debates for which *both* sides can find evidence—we must turn our attention to understanding when, under what conditions, person variables, situational variables, and interactions seem most important.

In sum, we see that neither the situation nor the person alone always suffices in accounting for behavioral functioning. We may conclude that, in general, variation in human behavior and development is not a function of just the external stimulus-environment *or* just the person's intrinsic characteristics. Indeed, in many cases behavior and development may be found to be a product of the interaction between such intrinsic and extrinsic variables. In such cases, then, a person may be identified as playing an active participatory role in his or her own development; this means that just as much as environment has served actively to shape the person, the person in turn has acted to shape his or her environment (Lerner 1982; Lerner and Busch-Rossnagel 1981).

12 | Implications for Research

Up to this point in the text, concepts and theories about development rather than "facts" about development have been emphasized. However, once understood, any theory must be related to facts in order for it to have use. As noted in previous chapters, a scientific theory is a statement of the way in which variables are related to each other and from which hypotheses can be drawn. Stated differently, a theory is simply an idea that leads to the generation of additional facts (Hempel 1966; Lerner 1976; Winch and Spanier 1974). Theory must be tied to the examination of data in order for it to have a use in science.

However, it is a complex task to obtain data useful in the study of human development across the life span. Obviously, observation at multiple times of life are needed. But how are such observations to be made in ways that will be of use to scientists studying human development? This key question raises the issue of what scientific methods of investigation are available to human developmentalists.

But why must the study of development involve scientific methods of research? What is wrong with people just sitting back in their armchairs and telling others what people are like, and never actually studying if what they say corresponds to actual behavior? Why would a scientist be more likely to believe a statement about development based on the observation of people as opposed to a view that is in no way backed up by observations?

The answers to all these questions rest on the commitment to the *scientific method,* an approach used by researchers to study the phenomena of the world. The basic attribute of the scientific enterprise is empiricism, a view that knowledge is achieved through systematic, purposeful *observations,* observations that are then communicated, corrected (if necessary), and finally added to the "archive" of scientific knowledge (Kaufmann 1968). This focus on empiricism and on scientific methodology is the major difference between philosophy and science. Those who are not scientists may find knowledge in ways independent of empirical research (e.g., through chiefly speculative rather than observational means). However, for a scientist to know something about the development of humans, people must be examined, questioned, interviewed, or in some way observed. One cannot rely *just* on what one believes or wants to believe about behavior. Rather, one's beliefs must be tested by determining whether they are supported when actual behavior is studied. The set of specific procedures by which a science makes observations and collects and examines data may be termed its *research methods.*

However, there are several problems typically encountered in applying the scientific methods available for research on human development. Preceding discussions have suggested that many factors contribute to development and that, as a consequence, development may take many forms and directions. To observe such plasticity, it is unlikely that any one means of observing development would be appropriate for all contexts, times, or people. Indeed, there are many research methods that may be used to study development. And although each method has its special advantages, each also has limitations.

In order to understand the range of methods that may be used in the study of development, and to become sensitive to the problems in existing data and the dangers such problems present for future data, this discussion will be organized in two parts. First, the variety of research methods that can be used to study development will be discussed. Second, general problems in research, and especially those in human developmental research, will be considered. Ways to avoid such problems are suggested. A general theme throughout this presentation will be that the method one uses depends on the issues of theoretical interest. In other words, it will be argued that the questions one asks about development determine what methods one ought to use; the questions one asks should not be determined by the particular method one likes to use. Theory should determine method and not the other way around.

Finally, however, we shall note that theory and its related research do not exist in a social vacuum. A developmental psychologist clearly exists in a specific society at a specific point in time. Thus research must be conducted in accordance with the strictest ethical standards available. Accordingly, as a conclusion to this chapter we shall consider the ethical standards for developmental research.

We shall see, then, that as much as research needs theory (to organize and understand knowledge and to lead to the generation of new knowledge), theory needs research (to provide tests, substantiations, and revisions of theory). Because of its importance, the student of developmental psychology should be familiar with the dimensions of developmental research, the problems and issues of such research, and in turn, the problems that may exist in attempting to interrelate these empirical concerns with theoretical issues. As I have noted, these facets of the research endeavor are complex. Yet their understanding is nec-

essary for a complete appreciation of the discipline, as well as for an elucidation of some of the theoretical issues we have considered in our previous chapters. Because of their complexity, we will attempt to present the dimensions of developmental research within a framework that may facilitate their comprehension—the developmental research dimensions described by McCandless (1967, 1970).

DIMENSIONS OF RESEARCH METHODS IN HUMAN DEVELOPMENT

For many years Boyd McCandless (1915–75) was an active contributor to the literature of developmental psychology; he contributed both theoretical and research papers and also spoke to the issues, problems, and aspects of developmental research per se. It is this last portion of McCandless's writings that concerns us here.

Boyd R. McCandless

McCandless described (1967, 1970) four dimensions of developmental research. That is, it is possible to place any developmental study on a particular location along each of four continua. In Chapters 7 and 9 we saw that the differential approach to developmental psychology defines individuality as a person's location in multidimensional space. As will be recalled, this definition means that any particular person occupies his or her own individual space on each of a number of bipolar attribute dimensions. Similarly, a given developmental study possesses its own location along each of four dimensions. These four dimensions—or attributes—of developmental research describe the various continua along which any developmental study may vary. Thus, by describing and understanding the characteristics of each of these research attribute dimensions, one will be able to see where any given developmental study fits into the total scheme of possible developmental research. That is, any developmental study has characteristics that allow it to be located along some point of four dimensions of research. Location at one point on one dimension does not necessarily imply a similar location on the other dimensions. The fact that any one study could fall along different points of each dimension means that an almost limitless array of strategies of research is available to the developmental researcher. To see this variety let us turn to the first dimension of developmental research methods.

The Normative-Explanatory Dimension

McCandless (1967, 1970) typically presented the four dimensions of developmental research he discussed in a particular order. However, there is no necessary sequence. All are equally important to consider. The normative-explanatory dimension is presented first for historical reasons. As discussed in Chapter 1, human development was until the 1950s a largely *descriptive* discipline aimed at finding norms of behavior. Increasingly since that time, however, there has been a shift to a focus on theoretical issues, and hence a concern with research aimed at *explaining* behavior change. Because this dimension pertains to a major historical shift in science, it is considered first.

Normative studies are those that describe the typical (mean, median, or modal) behavior of people of particular age levels and specific populations. Such work *describes* some typical characteristics associated with certain groups of people. For example, normative research might be aimed at describing the average height or weight for white, middle-class, thirteen-year-old males and females from the midwestern United States. Indeed, norms such as these have been obtained. Barnett and Einhorn (1972) report that the average height for thirteen-year-old males is 61.3 inches and for thirteen-year-old females 62.2 inches. Similarly, the average weight for these two groups is 98.6 pounds and 105.5 pounds, respectively. In both height and weight, the average early-adolescent female has higher scores that the average early-adolescent male.

By providing typical descriptions of characteristics, norms are useful in indicating what may be expected to occur in groups of people at particular points in their development. Thus, if we look at the height and weight norms for eighteen-year-old males and females, we see that the average male height is 70.2 inches and the average weight is 144.8 pounds. The corresponding measures for eighteen-year-old females are 64.4 inches and 126.2 pounds. Thus for eighteen-year-olds there is a reversal of what was seen at age thirteen. By looking at the growth norms for these two age levels, we can expect that the average late-adolescent male will be taller and heavier than the average late-adolescent female.

The above height and weight norms were published in 1972. Corresponding norms, collected earlier and later in history, would be likely to reveal that what was average for a particular group of adolescents at a particular age has changed across history (Garn 1980). Accordingly, not only does normative research give the researcher an appreciation of the developmental characteristics of people over the course of their life, but also as norms are repeatedly collected over history, they allow the researcher to see the interrelation of individual development with sociocultural change.

But why do norms change over either individual or historical time? Why do height and weight typically change from early to late adolescence? Why have adolescents tended to be taller across history? Why do some researchers believe that such trends are ending? Answers to these questions require discussions we need not enter into here (but see Lerner and Spanier, 1980). But, raising such questions allows me to make the point that descriptions of behaviors are not explanations. Normative research does not explain why behavior changes in the typical manner that it does.

Such explanation is the goal of studies that lie toward the explanatory end of this first dimension. *Explanatory* studies attempt to account for the "why" of social and behavioral development. Such studies, however, clearly depend on the identification of norms. After all, if researchers do not have any ideas about how to describe the typical occurrence of the behavior under study, they will have difficulty explaining it. Thus, norms are necessary for explanatory research. However, norms are not sufficient in and of themselves; they just present a catalog of descriptions, a collection of unaccounted-for facts.

Then where do explanations come from? As emphasized in preceding chapters, explanations come from theory. Researchers attempt to integrate the norms of development within a particular theoretical formulation. They devise an empirical test of their theory, carry out this test, and in this way determine if their explanation is valid. Thus theory is useful in that it provides a basis for doing the type of research that will allow for an accounting of the facts of the discipline. In this regard McCandless has stated:

Norms, while essential and of interest to all, are concerns for the pragmatist. Develop-

mental psychologists . . . are likely to be pragmatists and empiricists. This may be why there are so many facts—and of them there are many about which thoughtful scholars are skeptical—and so few explanations. It is for this reason that . . . an attempt is made to maintain a conceptual orientation. It seems more promising to depend on theory for explanation than on mere collection of facts. (1970, 42)

To illustrate McCandless's view it is useful to note again a point made in Chapter 4 in regard to normative differences in the IQ scores of black and white children and adolescents (Loehlin, Lindzey, and Spuhler 1975). White samples have higher average scores than black samples. Various theories have been advanced to explain this difference (Burt 1966; Gould, 1981; Hirsch 1970; Jensen 1969, 1973), and one such interpretation rests on social-class and cultural differences between the groups. To simplify for purposes of illustration, the gist of this explanation is that variables that exist in different sociocultural settings account for the difference in IQ. For instance, differences in health, nutrition, and education explain why the average black youth—who is more likely than the average white to be in a sociocultural setting having lower levels of these variables—scores lower on IQ tests. The average black youth is not as well-educated, well-fed, or healthy as the average white youth. If it were found that normative IQ differences disappeared for particular samples of blacks and whites who were equated on such variables, then the explanation above of the basis of the norms would find support. Indeed, evidence supporting this explanation has been presented (Kagan 1969).

In sum, the first dimension of research sorts studies on the basis of relative emphasis on either description or explanation. When the latter type of study is done, the researcher attempts to relate one set of observations (the normative ones, the descriptions) to another set of observations in particular ways. That is, the researcher will argue that if the descriptions are to be explained by a particular theory, then certain relations between the described behaviors and other, independently observed behaviors should be seen. If social-class differences explain IQ differences, then particular changes in social-class-related variables (for example, increased quality of education) should be related to certain changes (that is, increases) in IQ scores.

In essence, in explanatory studies the researcher makes a prediction, or forms a *hypothesis,* about how the variables are related to each other. Many different types of data collection techniques are available to the researcher testing such hypotheses. The range of techniques is associated with the second dimension of research.

The Naturalistic-Manipulative Dimension

Although it has been noted that all scientific inquiry rests on the collection and analysis of data, I have suggested there are many different, useful ways in which scientists may obtain these data. Our choice of a data collection technique is determined partly by our interest in avoiding *reactivity*—an unwanted influence on a subject's responses. Reactivity exists when a subject's behavior or responses are influenced by the fact that he or she is participating in a research study. One useful way of avoiding reactivity while studying development is to go into the real world to observe behavior. Observation of behavior as it occurs in its natural setting is termed *naturalistic* observation. In such observation, the researcher avoids manipulation of the ongoing behavior. Rather, after deciding what to observe, the researcher attempts to find such behavior as it naturally exists.

There are two general types of naturalistic observation. *Participant observation* is a technique mostly used by sociologists and anthropologists to discover the nature of social relationships in real-life settings. In this type of research, the researcher becomes a part of the setting for weeks, months, or even a year or two, and systematically observes

what he or she sees and hears. The participant observer may also do some informal interviewing and may supplement his or her observations with other data available in the setting. The researcher usually writes up very comprehensive notes each day about what was said and about what happened in the setting. These notes are carefully analyzed later. Many important social science studies have used this technique, since it allows the researcher to observe social phenomena firsthand. This technique, however, has not been used widely in developmental psychology.

The second type of naturalistic observation is more structured. Psychologists in particular often wish to examine the relationship between a very small number of variables in a given study. Thus it might be necessary to isolate the specific behaviors of interest and systematically observe only those behaviors of interest in a more structured naturalistic study. Although it is clear that such an observational technique gives the researcher an excellent chance of discovering how behavior really develops, it also has some limitations. The behavior of interest may occur at infrequent or irregular intervals, and the researcher may not be able to attend to everything that is possible to observe—even with the help of such apparatus as cameras. Such observations are sometimes difficult to use as a basis for explanations.

For example, suppose a researcher is interested in how adolescents form heterosexual dating relationships and wants to know if people of similar levels of physical attractiveness tend to form relationships with each other (Berscheid and Walster 1974; Huston and Levinger 1978). If the researcher chooses to study such development with the use of structured naturalistic observations, he or she might go out and find an appropriate sample of adolescents and then watch them, for example, at a high-school dance. Of course, a good deal of behavior might be occurring at a very rapid pace. To try to cope with such an enormous input of information, the researcher might look at the adolescents for only thirty seconds at a time, at five-minute intervals. Moreover, a wide-angle-lens camera might be used to record these observations. However, despite these techniques, the researcher avoids manipulating the behavior of the subjects. Thus, if too few adolescents are forming new relationships—for example, by dancing repeatedly with one another or by leaving the dance together—the researcher does not intervene to increase the frequency of the behavior of interest.

Indeed, because no planned intervention in behavior occurs in naturalistic observation, the researcher cannot cancel out or control for the influences of other variables that might relate to the formation of relationships. For example, things other than the physical attractiveness of a potential partner might influence relationship formation in adolescence. Such things as prior acquaintance, mutual friends, or even dancing ability could determine if one person repeatedly dances with or leaves with another. Since the researcher cannot control the role of such other potentially influential variables, it is sometimes difficult to use structured naturalistic observations to support explanations. For example, it would be difficult to assert that people of similar physical attractiveness levels formed relationships in adolescence, because even if sufficient observations of relationship formations occurred, and even if comparable physical attractiveness levels did seem to link people together, the research would not be able to tell if attractiveness (or another possible but uncontrolled-for influence) was the key determinant.

As another example, suppose a psychologist is interested in the development of aggression in five-, six-, and seven-year-olds. If the psychologist chooses to study such development with the use of naturalistic observations, he or she would simply go out and find an appropriate sample of children and then sit down and watch them, for example, at play in a schoolyard. It is possible, however, that after days of such observations the researcher could have few, if any, observations relevant to the behavior of interest. Although this instance is unlikely in the case of aggressive responses, one may easily think of behaviors that do not occur frequently or regularly. For instance, to use a somewhat unusual topic for developmental inquiry but nonetheless a legitimate one, suppose the researcher is interested in observing masturbatory behaviors among these children. Even after days of intense naturalistic observation, the occurrences of such behaviors among this age group of children—and within the free-play situation—would be expected to be extremely low.

In any event, the researcher using this technique would not necessarily be able to make any statements about the variables in the children's development that provided a source of whatever behavior he or she was attempting to observe. Rather the researcher might be able only to describe a particular sequence of events. Although such a description has the virtue of having ecological validity, because of the lack of control over the observations, the data obtained by the researcher may be unsystematic, of a frequency limiting the potential generalizability of any findings, and of a sort that militates against other than descriptive appraisals of the developing behavior.

In sum, the lack of control over behavior—in terms of its frequency and its influence by other variables—is one reason why naturalistic observation cannot be the only observational technique in developmental research. Another reason is that there are some behaviors that are not readily available for naturalistic observation.

Controlled and experimental observations

Some changes in behavior that are of interest require more controlled observational techniques. The child might be put into a situation that maximizes the likelihood that the researcher will see the relevant behavior. Variables that could potentially influence the relevant behavior, but that are not of current interest, would be controlled in the research, or excluded altogether.

Researchers who opt for techniques that allow more control over their observations are conducting research toward the *manipulative* end of the dimension. When the research situation is controlled by the researcher, but the behavior of the person is not directly manipulated, we label this *controlled observation.* In *experimental observation,* on the other hand, maximum control over observations and direct manipulation of behaviors are involved.

To illustrate controlled observation, again suppose that a researcher is interested in seeing if adolescents form heterosexual relationships in school on the basis of similar levels of physical attractiveness. Now using controlled observation to address this interest, the researcher might place a group of male and female adolescents unacquainted with each other in a classroom in order to form two-person study groups to examine a topic about which they have little background. The researcher could have observers rate the physical attractiveness of the people and see who paired up with whom. In this study, then, the researcher has exerted greater control over his or her observations. Although no attempt has been made to manipulate (that is, change) the adolescents' behaviors *directly,* the situation within which the adolescents interact has been controlled, and even some characteristics of adolescents within the situation have been arranged.

In the controlled experiment, one exercises as much control over the situation as possible. One manipulates conditions such that only the variables whose effects on behavior one wants to ascertain would vary, and this variation itself is also controlled. Everything else that could possibly affect the behavior of interest would be either held constant in all conditions or balanced across the research conditions. In other words, one would (ideally) control any variation in the situation that could influence the behavior of interest.

For example, suppose one wants to know the extent to which each of three types of instructional techniques influences learning in ten-year-old children. Since variables such as the sex, age, social class, IQ, race, religion, and type of school could all be related to any effects the instructional techniques might have on learning, one would want to control these variables. Thus, subjects might be all ten-year-old, white, middle-class, Protestant males of average IQ, attending a public elementary school in the South. The only variables that would be different would be the type of instruction to which the children were exposed. Thus the precise effects of instructional techniques on learning could be determined.

However, this information would be known only under the conditions of the study. The effects of such instructional techniques on males or females of different racial and social class backgrounds, attending schools in different sections of the country, for example, would be unknown. Moreover, the known effects of instructional technique even on the subjects assessed would be limited. In the real world, the variables the researcher was able to control in the study would vary naturally. The reason such variables are controlled in the first place is that they are expected to affect learning. Thus how the results of a controlled, manipulative experiment reflect what actually happens in the real world could not be fully determined from this one study. One would have to see if the results could be generalized. The researcher might have to return to a real classroom situation to see how the instructional techniques of interest affect learning in children of the age of interest when such children are actually learning in real-life settings.

It may be concluded that observational techniques always involve a trade-off. One trades precise control over behavior for real-life validity when one uses the naturalistic observation method; on the other hand, one loses such validity when one gains control through manipulation in controlled or experimental observations. However, both types of observational techniques are needed. The researcher who begins with manipulated, controlled observations may recognize the necessity of seeing if and how the results may actually occur in the natural world. The naturalistic observer, on the other hand, may find it necessary to move into the laboratory and make controlled observations in order to verify the impressions of behavior gained in the field setting and to attempt to understand the independent effects of particular variables on specific behaviors.

Questionnaires and interviews

Observational techniques are most useful when social interaction or behavior is of interest, and when such behavior is ethically open to scientific scrutiny. However, different techniques may be needed if (1) there is no overt social interaction or behavior to observe; (2) the behavior is not one that may readily or ethically be seen through observation; or (3) the presence of a researcher when the behavior of interest is occurring would influence that behavior in a way that would not have occurred had the researcher not been present.

An example of the first problem would be if the researcher was interested primarily in feelings, attitudes, values, or recollections of earlier events. In regard to the second problem, researchers may not study behaviors that harm or embarrass their subjects. Thus trying to observe certain behaviors directly—for example, sexual acts—might be prohibited. In addition, some behaviors (for example, those associated with adolescent car accidents) are not often readily available to naturalistic observation, and for obvious ethical reasons cannot be "controlled" by the researcher. Furthermore, other events occur only once in life (such as menarche or the loss of virginity) and at times and in situations making them unavailable for direct observation. Indeed, if a researcher went beyond the bounds of ethics and tried to be present at such an event, it is assured that the person's reactions would differ from what they would have been had the researcher been absent.

The presence of the researcher is the third

problem with making direct observations. Often, there are issues and behaviors of interest to the researcher of human development that cannot be directly observed by him or her because doing so would distort the behavior. Sexual interactions among people are obvious examples of the sort of behavior that would be distorted if a researcher were present. However, drug use and alcohol consumption, voting behavior, and certain types of parent-child interaction (e.g., such as may occur in child-abusing or child-neglectful homes) are other examples of social interaction and behavior that could be influenced by the presence of an outside observer.

Thus, because of the difficulties involved in direct observation, other methods are sometimes used. These take the form of questionnaires and interviews. These techniques involve written or verbal responses to questions. A questionnaire is usually self-administered but may be completed in a group setting with the questions read out loud. Interviews may be conducted in face-to-face settings, by telephone, or by other means. Both questionnaires and interviews can have fixed-choice questions, in which the possible answers are specified, or open-ended ones, in which any answer is possible and the precise response given by the respondent is recorded. Questionnaires and interviews are the techniques of *survey research*.

There are numerous issues in development that can only be studied through the use of survey research methods. However, responses to questionnaires and interviews are not expected to reflect perfectly behavior as it would occur if directly observed. Without a direct assessment of the correspondence between actual behavior and reported behavior, one cannot be certain of how well reports of behavior agree with actual behavior. People might forget, distort, or really not know the answers to various items in these instruments. Although it is possible to take steps to assess how much distortion takes place in people's answers, this is difficult. For example, one could compare people's answers to questions about their behavior with their actual behavior. However, often the unavailability of such direct observation of behavior is, as noted, the reason that indirect-assessment devices were used in the first place.

Survey research, however, is most valuable when one is interested in people's reports or recollections, values, attitudes, or other unobservable information. Furthermore, it allows the researcher to study large numbers of people in a shorter time than is often permitted by direct behavioral observation and to collect data on a large number of variables in a short time span. In addition, since anonymity can be assured, questionnaires may often be answered very honestly and accurately. Interviews allow the respondent and researcher to get better acquainted, and the technique allows the researcher to probe issues or change directions in the midst of data collection.

As with all other research techniques, questionnaires and interviews have assets and limitations. Again there is a trade-off. One is able to investigate behaviors not readily available for observation, but one has to use techniques whose correspondence with the actual behaviors of interest is often uncertain. Yet because of their assets such methods tend to be among the most frequently used by social scientists (Cattell 1973). Finally, one additional value that these techniques have is their ability to be combined with other (for example, behavioral observation) techniques (Parke 1978). For instance, one could see if a person's attitudes or values, as measured by a questionnaire, changed as a consequence of various experimental manipulations.

Nonobtrusive measures
Much research can be done without directly observing, testing, or talking to people. There are data all around us, waiting to be collected, and we often do not even know it. Whenever we use data that already exist in our environment, we are using *nonobtrusive* measures.

There are numerous examples of such re-search studies (Webb et al. 1966). Reading habits on campus could be studied by examining wear and tear on library books; sexual attitudes could be examined by reading the grafitti on bathroom walls; divorce could be researched by analyzing records available at the county courthouse. We could study radio-listening preferences by having auto mechanics find out how car radios are set. And popular versus unpopular magazines in libraries or waiting rooms could be determined by looking at which ones collected the most dust.

In sum, a good researcher is creative and takes advantage of whatever evidence is available to study the research problem best. With the various forms of data-collection techniques open to a researcher, a variety of potential strategies are available for observing people. Although every method has specific strengths and weaknesses, any method may be used depending on the nature of the research question being investigated. But what determines the issue addressed in a given research effort? There is some rationale for every research effort, and this question is addressed by the third dimension of developmental research.

The Atheoretical-Theoretical Dimension

This dimension of developmental research identifies studies on the basis of their relative emphasis on theory as the basis of the research. There may be various reasons that lead a researcher to conduct a particular study. Some research may be done simply on the basis of interest in some particular phenomenon. The researchers may be curious about the way something develops. They may have a hunch about some aspect of development. Or they may simply want to see what happens when a variable is manipulated or assessed. In addition, research may be used as a way of solving a practical problem (McCandless 1970). In these cases research is not being conducted from a theoretical perspective. The research is not based on statements drawn from a theory (hypotheses), and the research ideas, when tested, will not necessarily support, clarify, or refute a theory. Rather atheoretical research is by definition carried out on a theory-independent basis. Although such research may be found to have some relevance to theory after it is completed, this is usually not intended. In fact, the data from such an atheoretical study may end up being just a bit of scientific data that has no meaning or relevance to any given theoretical formulation.

Because of such potential limitations for the study of human development, theoretically relevant research is stressed in this book. As indicated in our historical review of the changing emphases in the study of human development, studies based on theoretical conceptions of development may be seen as most useful in advancing the science. The data resulting from such research are expected to have some direct relevance for understanding development. As I have stressed, the purpose of theory is to integrate existing knowledge and to obtain new knowledge. New knowledge results from the test of hypotheses derived from such theories. Thus theory-related research always has the promise of providing information that expands our understanding of development.

The Ahistorical-Historical Dimension

How does one study the effects of several influences on human development across the life span? The issue is how one can design research to measure intraindividual change, or individual development, as that development is influenced by many variables. Although the preceding discussion offered different observational techniques, there was no statement about how these techniques could be used in a study to assess the nature of developmental change. This concern is addressed in the discussion of the fourth dimension of developmental research. It is this dimension that determines whether a research effort is or is not a developmental one. It is this dimension that sorts studies on the basis of their relative concern with change.

Some studies are concerned with behavior at one particular time in a person's development. In such studies there may be no interest whatsoever in how the behavior came to take the form that it does at this point in development or in what form this behavior may take later. Such studies may be termed *ahistorical,* because behavior is studied at only one point in time (McCandless 1970). For instance, a particular study might be concerned with the effects of a certain type of social reinforcement on aggression in ten-year-olds. If the study is ahistorical in its orientation, it will not be concerned about how the child's earlier development contributed to this relation or about the future status of this relation.

However, as research becomes more concerned with the origins and the future course of behavior, it moves closer to the historical end of the continuum. Thus historical research is concerned not only with the status of a relationship between two or more variables at a particular point in development, but also with the basis of that relation as well as the future status of that relation. Historical research wants to know what variables in the ten-year-old's developmental history provided a basis for the relation between reinforcement and aggression, and what implications the relation at age ten has for later adolescent and adult relations between social reinforcement and aggression. In summary, then, historical research is concerned with the change in behavior over time.

Without historical investigation, basic issues of development could not be studied empirically. The developmentalist would be unable to determine either the continuity-discontinuity or the stability-instability of behavior. Thus although an ahistorical study allows us to know the relations among the variables of sex, social class, race, and IQ at a given age, for example, it in no way allows us to know anything about the previous or eventual interrelations among these variables. A historical research study is thus the most appropriate for developmental inquiry. However, though there are several ways to design historical research, not all such research designs are in fact equally useful for developmental research.

Indeed, although there are three types of historical designs typically noted by developmentalists, none of these conventional methods is completely adequate for developmental research. These three conventional research designs—termed the longitudinal, cross-sectional, and time-lag designs—each have important uses but also some limitations when applied to developmental research. Because of the need to understand the uses and limits of conventional research designs for studying change, the next section focuses on the nature of design in developmental research. Here, however, let us make some final statements about the ideas presented in this section of the chapter.

Conclusions

McCandless's framework for describing the possible dimensions of developmental research allows us to see the ways in which such research may vary. Developmental re-

search is thus multifaceted; there are several dimensions along which a given study may vary, and hence the developmental researcher has available a large array of techniques and approaches with which to obtain information about psychological development. The usefulness of these dimensions of research, then, is to allow us to appreciate the many forms that developmental research may take, the many research emphases that may be stressed in such research, and the assets and limitations of each of these approaches to the study of psychological development. As a summary of these dimensions Table 12.1 presents the end points of each of these four dimensions of developmental research, along with some brief descriptions of their meaning.

DESIGNS OF DEVELOPMENTAL RESEARCH

Many people who attempt to understand an individual's development do so by specifying age-related developmental progressions. An example is attributing storm and stress to

TABLE 12.1
Four Dimensions of Studies in Human Development Research

1. Normative Studies ————————— (Descriptions of averages, frequencies, and norms of behavior.)	Explanatory Studies (Assessment of the causes or bases of behaviors.)
2. Naturalistic Studies ————————— (Studies of people in their actual "real life" [ecologically valid] settings.)	Manipulative Studies (Conditions of the setting are controlled—e.g., as in a laboratory setting. The design of such research is often experimental.)
3. Atheoretical ————————————— (Studies designed to answer practical problems, verify casual observations, or satisfy curiosity.)	Theoretical (Studies designed to test ideas—hypotheses— derived from a theory.)
4. Ahistorical ——————————————— (Studies of relations among variables that have been measured at the same time. No assessment of the antecedents and/or the consequences of the relations that exist at one point in time.)	Historical (Studies of the antecedents and/or consequences of behavior; a focus on the history of the behavior.)

Source: *Based on McCandless (1967, 60).*

the adolescent stage of life. Although age-related, or "stage," progressions may be one source of a person's change, they are not the only processes that provide a basis for change. For example, if a major event occurred in society at a particular time—for instance the Watergate political crisis of the 1970s, the assassination of President John F. Kennedy in 1963, or the 1929 Stock Market crash—behaviors of people might be affected despite the stage or age of development they were in. If one were measuring attitudes toward government during Watergate, the events in society at this time of measurement may have influenced children, adolescents, and adults. As such, it is possible that time of measurement, as well as age-related phenomena, can influence development.

In addition, not only may age and time affect change, but so too may history. Again imagine that attitudes toward government were being measured and that the subjects of the study were people born during the Great Depression in the United States. During this historical era many of the institutions that provided economic security to American citizens (banks, for example) failed, and existing governmental policies were not able to deal with this situation. Accordingly, it may be expected that people born in the 1920s who experienced the effects of the depression during childhood might have developed differently than people born well before or well after this historical era. Indeed, research has found this to be true (Elder 1974).

As mentioned in an earlier chapter, a *cohort* is a group of persons experiencing some event in common. People born in a given year are members of a particular *birth cohort*. By virtue of being in a particular birth cohort, one may have specific experiences that might not be part of the experiences of people born in other historical eras. Such birth-cohort-related influences can affect the character of behavior that people show across their lives. People who were children during the Great Depression may continue to be more wary about the stability of the economy and about the ability of the government to safeguard citizens than may people who were children during eras of affluence and prosperity (the late 1950s in the United States, for example). Because of membership in a certain birth cohort, people may continue to differ from those of other cohorts, no matter at what age they are measured or what exists in the sociocultural setting at a particular time of measurement.

It may be seen, then, that there are at least three components of developmental change. *Birth-cohort-related events,* as well as *time of measurement* and *age-related phenomena,* can contribute to developmental changes. Recognizing that reference is always made to phenomena that change in relation to these components, we label these components *age, time,* and *cohort* for convenience. Thus, when intraindividual change is seen from one point in the life span to another, one must be able to determine how processes associated with each of these three components may influence change.

Until relatively recently (Baltes 1968; Schaie 1965), the three most popular designs of developmental research did not allow for an adequate determination of the contributions of these three components. The three designs—the longitudinal, cross-sectional, and time-lag methods—typically involve a *confounding* of two of the three components of change. When a variable is confounded, its influence on behavior cannot be separated from that of another variable that could be influencing behavior at the same time.

For instance, if one wanted to know if males or females could score higher on a test of reading comprehension, one would not want all the males to be college-educated and all the females to be only grade-school-educated. It is known that education level can influence reading comprehension as well as sex-related variables. If one did not equate the two sex groups on education level (if one did not "control" for the contributions of education), then one would not know if differences between the groups were influenced by their sex or by their educational disparities (or some combination of the two).

Thus sex would be confounded with education. In other words, one could not separate the effects of the two variables. As noted, when the separate influences of two variables cannot be determined, these variables may be confounded, and any study that involves such a confounding has a potential methodological flaw.

Unfortunately, the three commonly used designs for developmental research confound two of the three above-noted components of developmental change and, as a consequence, their utility is limited. Table 12.2 presents the particular confounding factors in each of these designs. Reference to this table will be useful as the discussion turns to an explanation of the characteristics of each of these designs and to an explanation of why they confound what they do.

The Longitudinal Design

The *longitudinal design* (also known as a *panel design*) involves observing the same group of people at more than one point in time. The main asset of this approach is that since the same people are studied over time, the similarities or changes in behavior (i.e., intraindividual change) across their development can be seen directly. However, this method, particularly as it involves repeated observations of the same people over an extended period of time, has some limitations.

It obviously takes a relatively long time to do some longitudinal studies. If researchers wanted, for instance, to do a longitudinal study of personality development from birth through late adolescence, they would have to devote about twenty years of their own lives to such a research endeavor. Such a commitment would be expensive as well as time-consuming, and thus it may easily be seen why relatively few long-term longitudinal studies have been done.

Other limitations of longitudinal studies pertain to the nature of the people studied and to problems with the measurements that may be used. Not everyone would be willing to be a subject in a study that required their being continually observed over the course of many months or years of their lives. Hence samples in such studies tend to be small. Those people who are willing to take part may not be representative of most people. Thus longitudinal studies often involve unrepresentative, or "biased," samples. Results of such studies may not be easily applied, or "generalized," to a broader population. In addition, longitudinal samples typically become increasingly biased as the study continues. Some people drop out of participation, and one should not assume that those people that do remain are identical to the former group. After all, the group that stays may be different just by virtue of the fact that they continue to participate.

Another problem with longitudinal studies is that after some time people may become used to the tests of their behavior. They may learn "how to respond," or they may respond differently than they would have if they had never been exposed to the test. Hence the meaning of a particular test to the subjects may be altered over time through its repeated use with the same sample. Such an occurrence would make it difficult to say

TABLE 12.2
Some Characteristics of Longitudinal, Cross-Sectional, and Time-Lag Designs of Developmental Research

Design	Study involves:	Confounded Components of developmental change
Longitudinal	One birth cohort	Age with time
Cross-sectional	One time of measurement	Age with birth cohort
Time-lag	One age	Time with birth cohort

that the same variable was actually being measured at different times in the subjects' lives.

Often the purpose of using this design is to determine the developmental time course for a particular type of behavior or psychological function. One also wants information that may be applied to understanding development about future generations of people. Yet with a longitudinal study, one is only studying people who are born in one historical era and who are measured at certain points in time. One does not know if findings about this one cohort can be generalized to people in other cohorts.

A confounding of age and time exists when one cohort is studied. Since a longitudinal study involves assessing one particular cohort of people (for example, a group of males and females born in 1965), such people can be fifteen at only one time of measurement (1980 in this case). Thus their behavior at fifteen may be due to age-related phenomena or to phenomena present at the time of measurement (or to both). Similarly, members of one birth cohort can only be twenty at one time of measurement. Thus, as noted in Table 12.2, age and time are confounded in a longitudinal study. One does not know if the results of a longitudinal study can be applied to other fifteen- or twenty-year-olds who are measured at other times.

Hence, the findings about development that one gains from a longitudinal study may reflect age-related changes *or,* alternatively, they may reflect only characteristics of people born and studied at particular points in time. In a longitudinal study one does not know whether the findings are due to universal rules, or "laws," of development (that is, rules that describe a person's development no matter when it occurs), *or* to particular historical events that may have influenced the research subjects, *or* to the particular times the subjects are measured, *or* to some combination of all these influences.

To summarize, although longitudinal studies are useful for describing development as it occurs in a group of people, such studies have expense, sampling, and mea-surement problems; and they may present results not applicable to similarly aged people who grew up in different historical eras or who were measured at different points in time. Because of such problems, alternatives to the longitudinal method are often used.

The Cross-Sectional Design

The most widely used developmental research design is the *cross-sectional design.* Here different groups of people are studied at one point in time, and hence all observations can be completed relatively quickly. The design is less expensive than longitudinal research and requires less time. Because of these characteristics, some have argued that the method allows for a very efficiently derived description of development. However, there are important limitations of cross-sectional research.

If one wanted to study the development of aggression in individuals who range in age from two to twenty years, one could use the cross-sectional method. For example, instead of observing one group of people every year for eighteen years, groups of individuals at each age between two and twenty could be observed at one point in time.

However, it is difficult fully and adequately to control for all variables that may affect behavior differences. One may not be certain if differences between the various age groups are reflections of real age changes or merely reflections of the groups not being really identical to begin with.

Sometimes, to ensure some degree of comparability, the researcher attempts to match the individuals on a number of important variables other than age. However, such comparability is difficult to achieve. Moreover, although it is possible to get less biased, more representative samples for cross-sectional research than for longitudinal studies (people may cooperate more readily since they are only committed to being observed or interviewed once), this better sampling may still not lead to a useful description of the components of developmental change. This failure occurs because of a flaw in the rationale for the use of a cross-sectional method instead of a longitudinal one.

The expectation for some cross-sectional studies is that they will yield results comparable to those obtained from studying the same group of people over time—and that they will do so more efficiently—so long as the only differences among cross-sectional groups are their ages. However, despite how adequately subjects are matched, it is rarely true that the results of cross-sectional and longitudinal studies are consistent (Schaie and Strother 1968).

For example, when studying intellectual development with a cross-sectional design, most researchers report that highest performance occurs in the early twenties or thirties and considerable decreases in performance levels occur after this period (for example, Horn and Cattell 1966). With longitudinal studies of these same variables, however, often no decrease in performance is seen at all. In fact, some studies (for example, Bayley and Oden 1955) have found some increases in performance levels into the fifties. As has been pointed out, it may be suggested that the nature of the subjects typically used in a longitudinal design is considerably different from that of subjects used in a cross-sectional study.

Longitudinal studies, as has also been noted, may be composed of a select sample to begin with, and as the study proceeds, some people will drop out. Such attrition may not be random. Rather it may be due to the fact that subjects of lower intellectual ability leave the study. Hence, in the example of research on intellectual development, this bias could account for lack of decreases in performance levels. In addition, as Schaie and Strother (1968) point out, these longitudinal studies have not assessed intellectual development in the sixties and seventies—the age periods during which the greatest performance decreases have been seen in cross-sectional studies (for example, Jones 1959). Thus comparisons of age-associated changes found with the two methods are not appropriate.

On the other hand, cross-sectional samples have not escaped criticism. Schaie (1959) has argued that such samples do not give the researcher a good indication of age-associated changes because it is difficult to control for extraneous variables in the samples used to represent people of widely different age ranges.

Although these arguments may appropriately be used to reconcile the differences (or perhaps to explain them away), Schaie (1965) suggests that these arguments miss an essential point: They do not show a recognition of an essential methodological problem involved in the consideration of longitudinal and cross-sectional designs. Just as longitudinal studies are confounded (between age and time), cross-sectional studies also are confounded. As seen in Table 12.2, the confounding is between age and cohort. Because the two types of studies involve different confounding, it is unlikely that they will reveal the same results.

The confounding of age and cohort that exists in cross-sectional studies occurs because at any one time of measurement (for example, 1980) people who are of different ages can only be so because they were born in different years. To be twenty in 1980, one has to have been born in 1960, while to be twenty-five at this time of measurement one has to be a member of the 1955 birth cohort. Consequently, because cross-sectional studies focus only on one time of measurement, there is no way of telling whether differences between age groups are due to age-related changes or to differences associated with being born in historically different eras.

To summarize, like the longitudinal method, the cross-sectional method has important limitations. Because of these shortcomings it is difficult to decide whether longitudinal or cross-sectional designs give a more useful depiction of developmental changes. Both designs may potentially introduce serious, but different, distortions into measures of developmental changes. This is perhaps the major reason why information from the two techniques is often not consistent (Schaie and Strother 1968). Similarly, data derived from a third type of design for developmental research, the time-lag design, are not necessarily consistent with those of the former two. This is because yet another type of confounding is involved.

The Time-Lag Design

Although not so frequently used in research as the cross-sectional or longitudinal designs, the *time-lag design* allows a researcher to see differences in behavior associated with particular ages at various times in history. That is, in contrast to focusing on one cohort or one time of measurement, the time-lag design considers only one age level and looks at characteristics associated with being a particular age at different times in history.

For example, earlier in this chapter, when differences between the 1970s and earlier decades in the normative height and weight of thirteen-year-olds were discussed, a time-lag design was actually being indicated. When the focus of research is to determine the characteristics associated with being a particular age (for example, fifteen years old) at different times of measurement (for example, 1950, 1960, 1970, and 1980), a time-lag design is implied.

Of course, such a design involves cross-sections of people and has all the problems of control, matching, and sampling associated with such designs. But there are also additional problems. As indicated in Table 12.2, because only one age is studied at different times, the different groups are members of different birth cohorts. Thus, in a time-lag design, time and birth cohort are confounded, and one does not know, for example, if the behaviors of fifteen-year-olds studied at two points in time are associated with events acting on all people—no matter what their age—at a particular test time or with historical events associated with membership in a specific cohort.

In sum, the three types of conventional developmental research designs do not allow for unconfounded assessment of the contributions of the age, time, and cohort components of developmental change. Because of these shortcomings, it is difficult to decide

which method gives a more useful depiction of developmental changes. Each method may potentially introduce different distortions into measures of developmental changes. This is perhaps the major reason why information about developmental changes derived from these techniques often is not consistent (Schaie and Strother 1968). Although each design has some advantages, the problems of each limit the ability of developmental researchers to describe adequately how individual, sociocultural, or historical variables can influence change. This might lead some to conclude that a bleak picture exists for the study of human development, since the three conventional designs of developmental research have some methodological problems. But of course *no* research method is without its limitations—a point I have noted before and will return to again later in this chapter. As such, my view is that *all* the conventional designs of developmental research may be used to enhance understanding *if* they are employed with a recognition of their limitations. These limitations, however, can be transcended by the use of still other designs, designs that are described in the following section. While these designs also have their limitations (e.g., they typically require large samples of people and are quite expensive to implement), they offer a useful alternative to traditional approaches.

The use of these designs has been made clear through the work of K. Warner Schaie (1965), Paul B. Baltes, and John R. Nesselroade (Baltes 1968; Nesselroade and Baltes 1974). Schaie (1965) demonstrated how the conventional methods were part of a more *general developmental model* for developmental research design. Presentation of this model allowed him to offer a new type of approach to designing developmental research. These are the sequential methods of developmental research.

Sequential Strategies of Design

The problems of confounding involved in the cross-sectional, longitudinal, and time-lag designs may be resolved, Schaie (1965) argues, through use of *sequential methods.* By combining features of longitudinal and cross-sectional designs, the researcher may assess the relative contributions of age, cohort, and time in one study, to know what differences (or portion of the differences) between groups are due to age differences, to cohort (historical) differences, or to time-of-testing differences. In addition, a sequential design allows these sources of differences to be determined in a relatively short period of time.

Research based on sequential designs is complex, due in part to the usual involvement of *multivariate* (many variable) statistical analyses and the numerous measurements that have to be taken of different groups. But a simplified example of such a design may be offered. It will suggest how use of such a design allows the developmental researcher to avoid the potential confounding involved with traditional cross-sectional and longitudinal approaches.

Basically, a sequential design involves the measurement of a cross-sectional sample of people after a given fixed interval of time has passed. A researcher selects a cross-sectional sample composed of various cohorts and measures each cohort longitudinally (with the provision that each set of measurements occurs at about the same point in time for each cohort). In addition, if, for example, three times of testing are included (as the longitudinal component of the design), then control cohort groups, assessed, for instance, at the second and the third testing times, may be used to control for (to assess) any retesting effects. Hence this design calls for obtaining repeated measures from each of the different cohort groups included in a given cross-sectional sample, and for obtaining data from retest control groups to assess effects of retesting. The researcher is thus in a position to make statements about the relative influences of age, cohort, and times of measurement on any observed developmental functions in the results.

Cross-sectional and longitudinal sequential designs consist of sequences of either simple cross-sectional or longitudinal designs. The successive application of these

K. Warner Schaie

Paul B. Baltes

John R. Nesselroade

strategies permits us to describe the extent to which behavior change is associated with age-related or history-related influences. Figure 12.1 provides a contrast between the simple and sequential strategies. The top portion of the figure shows the simple cross-sectional and longitudinal designs described earlier, while the bottom portion of the figure shows the two sequential strategies. Cross-sectional sequences involve successions of two or more cross-sectional studies completed at different times of measurement. Longitudinal sequences involve successions of longitudinal studies begun at different times of measurement. The strategies differ in that cross-sectional sequences involve independent measures on different individuals, while longitudinal sequences involve repeated measures of the same individuals. In practice, one can apply both strategies simultaneously. In any event, the application of sequential strategies permits the discrimination of within- and between-

cohort sources of change, thus increasing the scope of one's descriptive efforts.

To see how this works, it is useful to consider a sample design of such a sequential study. Such a design is presented in Table 12.3 and recast in the form of a matrix in Figure 12.2. Different cohort levels are composed of different groups of people born at different historical periods (1954, 1955, 1956, or 1957). Thus, at the time of the first testing (1970 for this design), the study has the attributes of a cross-sectional study. Indeed, there are three such cross-sectional studies in this particular design—one for each time of measurement (see Figure 12.2). However, the sequential feature is introduced when these same subjects are again measured in 1971 and 1972. Thus for each cohort there is now a longitudinal study. As seen in Figure 12.2, each cohort in a sequential design of this sort is involved in its own short-term longitudinal study (there are four of these in the design shown in Figure 12.2). Additionally, it should be noted that the diagonals of the design matrix of Figure 12.2 represent time-lag studies; people of the same age are studied at different times. Thus a sequential study involves all combinations of observations of other designs in one integrated matrix of observations.

With such a matrix, the researcher can answer a number of questions involving the potentially interrelated influences of cohort, age, and time. Referring to Table 12.3 and Figure 12.2, for example, if the cohort composed of people born in 1955 underwent changes between times of measurement 1 and 2, and were found to be different at age sixteen from the people in the 1954 cohort group when they were sixteen, then there must be some historical difference between these two cohort levels. In other words, if differences are due simply to age-related changes, then people of the same age should perform the same no matter what cohort they are from or when they are measured. A younger cohort group should perform similarly to an older cohort group as members of each group age, *if* there are no historical differences between cohorts and if time of test-

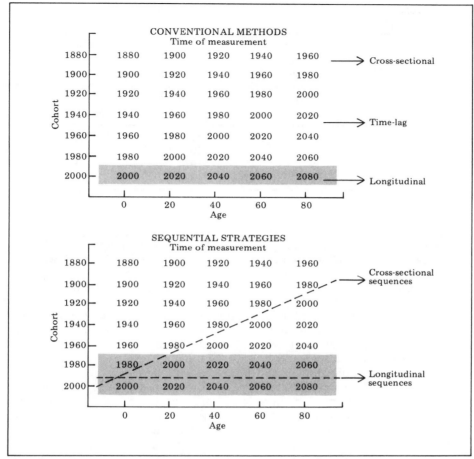

FIGURE 12.1
Illustration of simple cross-sectional, longitudinal, and time-lag designs (*top*) and cross-sectional and longitudinal sequences (*bottom*).
Source: Baltes, Reese, and Nesselroade 1977.

ing does not matter. Again from Table 12.3 and Figure 12.2, the 1957 cohort should show a level of performance on its second measurement comparable to that of the first measurement for the 1956 cohort *if* there are no historical differences between the generations.

In turn, if time of testing were a source of change, then people should respond the same despite their age or cohort. If events in 1972 were the strongest influence on behavior, then one should see that people of all co-

horts represented in Table 12.3 and Figure 12.2 respond the same way.

Finally, of course, if birth cohorts were of most importance, then people of a particular cohort should respond in a given way no matter what age they are and no matter at what time they are measured. As illustrated by the example of children born in the Great Depression (Elder 1974), membership in a particular cohort would override influences due to age or time of measurement.

Additionally, it should be mentioned that

TABLE 12.3
The Design of a Sequential Study

Birth cohort	Time of measurement 1	Age at time 1	Time of measurement 2	Age at time 2	Time of measurement 3	Age at time 3	Time of measurement of retest control group	Age of control group
1957	1970	13	1971	14	1972	15	1972	15
1956	1970	14	1971	15	1972	16	1972	16
1955	1970	15	1971	16	1972	17	1972	17
1954	1970	16	1971	17	1972	18	1972	18

by including groups of subjects to be tested for the first time at the end of the study (see Table 12.3), sequential researchers provide a way to judge the effects of repeated use of the measuring instruments, noted earlier. If subjects in the core sample did not respond differently as a consequence of their having been repeatedly measured (for example, by the same personality or IQ tests), then their behavior at the end of the study should be comparable to a group of subjects matched with them in every way except for the fact that no repeated testing was given. If there are differences, however, between the core sample and these "retest" controls, then there are statistical techniques available to researchers to measure the effects of retesting (Nesselroade and Baltes 1974).

Despite the complexity of data analysis, and the more complex research design and reasoning process associated with it, the sequential approach has advantages not associated with other techniques. It allows for the unconfounding of the age, time, and cohort components of developmental change in one descriptive effort. As such, it allows the contributions of variables associated with multiple levels of influence to be evaluated adequately.

In fact, although sequential research studies are relatively few in number, one such study may be presented here in order to illustrate the use of sequential designs for assessments of development. Indeed, the design illustrated in Table 12.3 and Figure 12.2 was used because it corresponds to the

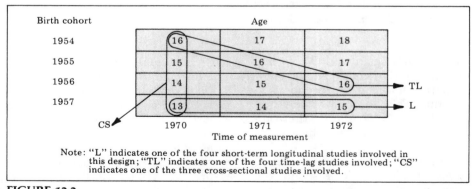

Note: "L" indicates one of the four short-term longitudinal studies involved in this design; "TL" indicates one of the four time-lag studies involved; "CS" indicates one of the three cross-sectional studies involved.

FIGURE 12.2
The design of a sequential study put into the form of a matrix. (The same design as that shown in Table 12.3 is presented.)

one used by Nesselroade and Baltes (1974) in their sequential study of adolescent personality development.

A Sequential Study of Adolescent Personality Development

Noting that most conceptions of adolescent personality development suggest that age-related progressions are influential in this period of life, Nesselroade and Baltes (1974) argued that historical (cohort) and specific sociocultural (time) influences may also be involved. As such, they applied longitudinal sequential methodology to see how these three components contributed to changes in personality in the period from 1970 to 1972.

About 1,800 West Virginia male and female adolescents were measured in 1970, 1971, and 1972. These adolescents were from birth cohorts 1954 to 1957, and thus—as in Table 12.3 and Figure 12.2—ranged in age at the time of first measurement from thirteen to sixteen. Personality questionnaires and measures of intelligence were administered to these subjects.

Contrary to what is stressed by those theorists who focus on personological components of adolescent development (for example, Anna Freud 1969), Nesselroade and Baltes found that change at this time of life was quite responsive to sociocultural-historical influences. In fact, age by itself was not found to be a very influential contributor to change. Rather, for these groups of adolescents, developmental change was influenced more by cultural changes over the two-year historical period than by age-related sequences.

For instance, adolescents as a whole, despite their age or birth cohort, decreased in "superego strength," "social-emotional anxiety," and achievement during the 1970–72 period. Moreover, most adolescents, regardless of age or cohort, increased in independence during this period.

Accordingly, the Nesselroade and Baltes (1974) data show that it was the time at which all these differently aged adolescents were measured that was most influential in their changes. Perhaps due to the events in society of that time—for example, events associated with the Vietnam War—all adolescents performed similarly in regard to these personality characteristics. Despite where they were upon "entering" the 1970–72 historical era, members of different cohorts changed in similar directions, due presumably to events surrounding them at the times they were tested.

Without sequential methodology, the importance of the specific sociocultural setting at that time could not have been suggested. This implication is supported by data obtained from other sequential studies that have shown the influence of birth cohort on intellectual development in children (Baltes, Baltes, and Reinert 1970) and adults (Schaie, Labouvie, and Buech 1973). These data suggest that to understand developmental change, one should consider the interactions among individual and sociocultural-historical processes.

Conclusions

We have seen that there are several ways in which to design developmental research and that each type of design has both methodological assets and limitations. Indeed, I have made a similar point in regard to any study of development, located at any point along each of the four dimensions of developmental research we have discussed in this chapter; that is, any particular method has both some uses *and* some limitations.

However, in addition to such method-specific problems, we should note that all developmental studies have the danger of being biased or faulty if certain general issues of method are not confronted and dealt with. Methodological problems of research are those problems involved in how the actual data of the study are obtained. While certain data-collection procedures may be appropriate, others may yield data with serious problems of interpretation. If one collects data in wrong or biased ways, little confidence may be placed in such data, and thus such data will be of little use to science. Hence, although all research has methodological problems that must be recognized and dealt with, there are some methodological issues of particular relevance to developmental psychological research.

These methodological problems of developmental research—also reviewed by McCandless (1970)—caution us about the many safeguards that must be taken to ensure that the data give as accurate a representation as possible of the facts of development. If these potential methodological problems are recognized and successfully dealt with, the researcher will have confidence not only in the accuracy of the data but also in the interpretations drawn from them. Let us turn, then, to some of the important methodological problems of developmental research.

SOME GENERAL METHODOLOGICAL PROBLEMS OF DEVELOPMENTAL RESEARCH

McCandless (1970) has detailed several of the prominent methodological problems of developmental research. The first one he notes is contamination.

Contamination

When data are contaminated, they are influenced by variables other than those being studied. That is, the results of the study may be due not only to the actual relations among the variables investigated. Contamination may occur in several ways.

In some studies, subjects are tested successively, one after the other. If one subject reveals the intent of the study to a succeeding subject, or in some way tells the later subject what to expect, this revelation might influence the second subject's responses. If the second subject's behavior is influenced by this information, then his or her responses would be due not only to the variables being studied.

Researchers also may contaminate their own data. Suppose a researcher believes that there is a relationship between an adolescent's body type and his or her personality or temperament. To test this belief, the researcher might develop a method to rate body type and temperament. However, it is possible that if the researcher him- or herself does both of these ratings for all the subjects, any relation discovered between body type and temperament might be contaminated by the researcher's hypothesis about this relationship. To illustrate this possibility, the work of William Sheldon (1940, 1942) may be noted. Sheldon developed a theory relating a person's type of physique to the person's temperament. He specified that there are three essential components of body build and that it is possible to characterize the body in terms of their relative contributions. Thus some people are predominantly fat—their bodies are composed essentially of adipose (fat) tissue. Other people's bodies are composed mainly of muscle and bone tissue—they have athletic-looking bodies. Finally, still other people's bodies are essentially composed of neither fat nor muscle tissue but of nervous-system tissue; such a body build would appear thin and linear.

Sheldon also specified that certain types of temperament go along with each of these three body types. He then devised ways to measure the body builds and temperaments of his subjects (4,000 Harvard University male undergraduates). However, Sheldon himself performed both of these sets of measurements. He rated body build and then, even though he knew the hypothesized relation between body build and temperament, he rated temperament. Thus there is the strong possibility that the high relation Sheldon found between these two sets of ratings was contaminated. Of course, Sheldon did not set out to contaminate his ratings intentionally. Such errors may often occur among well-trained but perhaps unvigilant researchers. Hence researchers must take precautions to ensure that their subjects' responses are not affected by anything extraneous to the research situation.

Furthermore, the relations found among their data should not be influenced by their own hypotheses. In science, a question should not determine the answer.

Researcher Effects on Subject Responses

Another related type of methodological problem involving the researcher occurs when the investigator unintentionallly affects the responses of his or her subjects. These researcher effects have been investigated by Rosenthal (1966), who suggests that such errors may play an important part in much research.

Suppose one wants to conduct a study of the attitudes of white adolescents toward black people and chooses to use the interview method. Each adolescent sits alone with the researcher in a small cubicle to conduct the interview. If the interviewer were black, he or she might get verbal responses from the respondents that are different from what might be obtained if he or she were white. White adolescents may be more candid about expressing any hostile or negative racial attitudes when interviewed by a white person than when interviewed by a black person. Thus in this example the researcher's race might affect the answers of the respondent.

Another, perhaps more subtle, example of the researcher affecting subjects' responses may be seen in the following illustration. Suppose a researcher wants to study the differential effects of a particular type of instructional technique on students who do below-average work and students who do above-average work. Obviously, the researcher would want to control everything in the research situation that might conceivably affect the subjects' responses. Thus, beside the fact that one group is slow-learning and the other fast-learning, all other between-group factors should be equivalent. Yet it is possible that the researcher may unknowingly interact with the two groups in different ways. For instance, the researcher may spend more time presenting the in-structional technique to one group than the other, or he or she might be warmer with one group than with the other. Such actions would mean that the conditions between the two groups are not in fact identical and that if differences between the groups are found, they might reasonably be due to the differential effects of the researcher's different behaviors toward the two groups.

Although it is difficult to determine when such researcher effects enter into the subjects' responses, the developmental researcher should always be aware of the potential of such bias and design the method of the study with safeguards. For instance, in the example of the racial attitude study, the researcher might want to use two interviewers, one black and one white, in order to control and test for any possible biasing effects introduced by the race of the researcher. In the second example, a standardized presentation of the instructional techniques might be given, perhaps through the use of a videotape device.

Reconstruction Through Retrospection

There are many ways to obtain information about the events that characterize people's development. In Chapter 8, the method used by Freud (1949) was discussed. By asking his adult neurotic patients to recall the events of their early childhood, Freud reconstructed their developmental histories. However, it was noted that such a method has a strong potential for introducing serious problems into one's data. Events may be recalled incorrectly, partially forgotten, distorted, or even lied about. However, there is usually no way to check on these distortions. With the retrospective method the actual events and interactions are not being observed empirically but are merely being reconstructed through use of a subjective verbal account.

Thus, when one reconstructs the past developmental history of a person through retrospection—by having the respondent look back upon his or her life and recall previous events—one is using a subjective, and perhaps distorted, account of developmental history. Hence the reconstruction-through-retrospection method is a limited way of obtaining information about the events that characterize people's development. Because the data collected through this method may be inaccurate, and because it is difficult to determine the level of inaccuracy, theories and inferences drawn on the basis of such information may have limitations.

However, in Chapter 10 we saw an example of another way of obtaining information about the events that characterize people's development—the prospective construction method used by Thomas et al. (1963) in their longitudinal study of the development of temperament. In this method, behavior is measured at or about the very time it occurs. Hence any constructions or representations of the course of development are based on reports of behavior as it is currently developing. This prospecptive method thus offers more useful, empirical data whose accuracy may be objectively verified; for example, the correspondence between the verbal reports and behavioral observations can be examined.

Faulty Logic

Another important problem in developmental research is presented when the investigator uses faulty reasoning techniques in interpreting data. In fact, such faulty reasoning may actually influence the design of the study itself and the method used to collect data.

Although faulty logic is by no means unique to developmental research it does play an all-too-prominent role in such investigations. The potential problem may be illustrated by offering the following syllogism:

1. Boats float on water.
2. X is floating on water.
3. X is a boat.

Obviously, this is an example of faulty logic. On the basis of the initial premise, one cannot exclude the possibility that things other than boats float on water; thus it is not logical to conclude that just because X floats on water, X is a boat. However, if one asserts that boats *and only* boats float on water, then it *would* follow from this premise that X is a boat.

Although it is clear that the first syllogism is not logical, it is possible just to alter the words of the syllogism (the content) and leave the structure of the logic (or lack of logic) intact. Thus a second syllogism might be:

1. Infants deprived of their mother's breast milk in the first year of life overeat at age fifteen.
2. John, a fifteen-year-old, overeats.
3. Therefore John was deprived of his mother's breast milk during the first year of his life.

Clearly, this conclusion also does not follow from the premise. There may be sources of overeating among fifteen-year-olds other than breast-milk deprivation. Yet, when this logically faulty syllogism is cast in terms of developmental events between mother and child, it somehow all too often acquires an air of believability. Yet the assertion that John's overeating is due to (unseen) breast-milk deprivation in the first year of life is as lacking in logic as the syllogism concerning X being a boat.

Perhaps one reason for such faulty logic in developmental research is that development per se deals with sequential or time-ordered events. There may be the belief that *post hoc, ergo propter hoc,* "after the fact, therefore because of the fact." That is, when events occur sequentially there may be a tendency to infer that if B happens after A, then A must be a source of B. However, such inferences also rest on faulty logic. If a traumatic event occurs early in a person's development, and years later some neurotic disorder emerges, it is simply not logical to assert that the trauma was *the* source—or even *a* source—of the later neuroticism. Although such a relation might actually exist, the mere fact that the trauma was followed by the neuroticism does not represent a logically necessary reason for the conclusion that the trauma is a source of the neuroticism. The neuroticism's emergence might have occurred in any event, and so in general it is merely an instance of faulty logic to assert that when one event follows another in development, the former is a source of the latter. Clearly, no one would assert that if one rises at 4:00 A.M. every day, and then with astonishing predictability the sun rises just a few hours later, that one's personal rising is the source of the sunrise. Yet when similar faulty reasoning is couched in terms of sequential events that occur over the course of development, such lack of logic may all too often slip by unnoticed.

As noted above, such faulty logic in interpretation of results may find its way into the methodological design of developmental research. A researcher may wish to ascertain the developmental source of a particular behavior. Thus the researcher might collect data about events that occurred during the first few years of a child's life and relate this information to data collected at a later time in the child's life. If a relation between these early and later measures is found—perhaps expressed in terms of a correlation coefficient—the researcher might infer that the early behavior provided a source of the later behavior. Yet we have seen that sufficient information was not obtained to make this inference logically necessary.

Throughout this book we have pointed out instances of faulty logic used in relation to the concepts and theories of development we have been discussing. Our discussions of the concept of heritability (in Chapter 3), the notion of instinct (in Chapter 5), and the continuity-discontinuity issue (in Chapter 6) indicated how some psychologists often use faulty logic in their discussions of these concepts and issues. Moreover, in Chapter 11 we saw how the notion that reinforcement may account for all behavior may be based upon faulty, circular reasoning. Thus it is apparent that faulty logic often finds its way

into the developmental literature. Accordingly, the reader must be aware of this problem and be ready to recognize such faulty logic when it occurs.

Inadequate Definition of Concepts

This problem pertains to how researchers define and measure the concepts they are investigating. A *concept* is a term used to represent some aspect of the physical or social world. Concepts, of course, may be more or less abstract. Thus a concept used to represent such things as cars, wagons, and trains—that is, the concept of vehicle—might be considered relatively concrete. The empirical referents of the concept (whatever is being referred to) are generally understood. Other relatively concrete concepts might be animal, body, or height. Yet not all concepts are similarly concrete. Some concepts do not have commonly understood empirical referents. Thus when psychologists use concepts such as aggression, learning, or personality, it is absolutely necessary that they specify precisely what they mean. Then anyone interested in the researcher's work will know exactly what is meant by the use of a term. If such operational definitions are not used, however, considerable communication problems may result. Two different researchers may be studying the same phenomenon, but if they define and measure it differently, their results may not be comparable. If they do not communicate these different meanings clearly, this lack of comparability may never be recognized.

For example, suppose a researcher is interested in studying the "generation gap." What exactly does the term mean? On a simple level one may suppose that it refers to a set of differences that allegedly exist between young people and their parents. But this definition is not sufficient because it does not specify what the differences are. Are the differences referred to by this term differences in the physical appearances of the generational groups—for example, in their respective styles of dress and hair lengths? Or does one mean divisions between the generations in their support for radical political causes? Or does one mean differences between the generations in attitudes about such issues as drug use, sexual behavior, and racism?

If researchers anchor their concepts in precise, empirical terms, considerable confusion may be avoided. For example, some studies (for example, Lerner, et al. 1975; Lerner and Knapp 1975) have defined the generation gap in terms of attitude differences between adolescents and their parents occurring on a list of thirty-six statements dealing with contemporary issues such as sexual mores, war, and drugs. Specifically, members of each of these generational groups were given a list of thirty-six statements dealing with such issues as sex, war, and drugs. Subjects were asked to indicate their agreement or disagreement with each statement through use of a seven-point rating scale, with 1 indicating strong agreement and 7 indicating strong disagreement. Thus a generation gap could be said to have occurred on any item wherein the average responses of each group were located at statistically significantly different points along the rating scale continuum. In most of these studies it was found that an attitudinal generation gap did exist between the sampled adolescents and their parents. But the authors attempted to be precise about limiting their interpretation to the specific definition they employed (Lerner and Knapp 1975). Thus conclusions were limited to the particular samples of people tested, to the specific measure of the generation gap used (i.e., attitude measures), and even more, to the specific instances of attitude statements assessed (Lerner et al. 1975)—for example, the specific statements regarding drug use. These authors recognized the fact that if other attitudes were sampled, if another type of attitude scale had been used, or if other possible domains of intergenerational divisions had been evaluated (e.g., the physical appearance or the behavioral domains), their findings might not have been relevant. In other words, if someone else used a differ-

ent definition of the generation gap, the comparability of findings between this other study and those noted above would not be direct.

However, so long as researchers take pains to define clearly what they mean by their use of any concept, and design their study with such clear definitions in mind, any confusion about the use of the same term to represent different things may be eliminated. To a great extent researchers may define things as they wish, so long as they anchor their definitions in understandable, empirical referents. Once this is done, any possible differences in what is meant by a particular concept may be recognized and understood.

Sampling

Another methodological problem deals with obtaining subjects for developmental research and making inferences about development based on results from a particular sample. If one wants to do a study of the racial attitudes of white and black five-year-olds, one obviously needs groups of white and black five-year-olds to study. The procedures used to obtain such samples will affect the conclusions one can appropriately make from the data.

Ideally one might like to measure the attitudes of all such children. However, this is clearly an economic and practical impossibility. Therefore the researcher must often draw a sample from the larger population— that is, a group of persons from the population that may feasibly be studied. Through the study of this sample, the researcher hopes to obtain results that can be generalized to the entire population.

Thus the researcher must be sure that the sample used is representative of the entire population. If the sample is not representative, if it is *biased,* then he or she may not appropriately infer that results obtained with the sample are characteristic of the entire population. For example, if the researcher conducting a study of racial attitudes among five-year-old blacks and whites chooses as his or her sample white and black children from a small Southern city, then it would be inappropriate to infer that such children are representative of all white or black children living elsewhere.

Standard procedures are available for obtaining unbiased samples. With *probability sampling*, all persons in the population have a known, nonzero chance of falling in the sample. In *nonprobability sampling*, not everyone in the population of interest may have a chance of being sampled.

There are three types of probability sampling. In *simple random sampling*, everyone in the population has an equal chance of being selected. Drawing names from a hat and using a computer to generate random selections are examples of simple random sampling.

Stratified sampling involves proportionately dividing the population according to the categories of a variable of interest, and then randomly sampling from within those categories. For example, if race is an important variable in the study, and only 10 percent of the population is black, then one would obtain only one black respondent for every nine white respondents, using simple random sampling techniques. By using stratified sampling, one could choose equal numbers of blacks and whites for comparison, even though their numbers in the population were different.

The third type of probability sampling is *cluster* (or *area*) *sampling*. This technique involves dividing a state, for example, into areas. First, areas (for example, counties) are sampled, then areas within these areas (towns, for example) are sampled again. Then after a specified number of towns have been sampled, individuals or households within the towns may be sampled further. Thus a statewide study could be conducted by sending observers or interviewers to only a few communities.

There are also three types of nonprobability sampling. *Availability* samples are often used in research in human development, and unfortunately they do not necessarily allow for great generalization. Availability sampling involves using whoever is available for the research—whoever is around and voluteers.

Judgmental (or *purposive*) *sampling* is similar, except that the researcher chooses subjects who fit a specific definition for the study. If, for example, the researcher wanted to study contraceptive use among adolescent females, he or she might look specifically for sexually active females between the ages of fourteen and eighteen. But there would be no guarantee that the girls found would be representative of others.

Quota sampling, the third type of nonprobability sampling, involves the selection of individuals on the basis of whether they can be used to fill a predetermined quota that is set up to represent the population in question. For example, the researcher might want to do a national study without the great expense associated with probability samples. He or she might try to construct a sample that appears to be representative of the nation as a whole by establishing quotas of certain numbers of blacks and whites; Jews, Protestants, and Roman Catholics; males and females; the college-educated and those with high-school educations or less; and married and unmarried adults. Any person can be selected for the sample so long as he or she fills the quota. The sampling ends when all the quotas have been met, and those selected are then studied. This method is often used by national polling organizations and can be quite accurate, even though it is a nonprobability method.

However, although such procedures are well known to all researchers, it is still often the case that studies are done with knowingly biased, unrepresentative samples. Why? To answer this question we must recognize that there are often ethical, economic, and practical problems that interfere with the researcher's desire to obtain a truly representative, unbiased sample. For example, it should be obvious that not all five-year-old black and white children are available for the researcher to sample from. The researcher is located in a particular part of the country, and only children living in that area are usually potentially available for study. Even then, however, not all these children may be available. School authorities may not want or be able to allow a researcher to enter the school to study the children there. And even if a school does cooperate, all the appropriately aged children in that school may not be available for study.

In any psychological study, the researcher is ethically bound to obtain the informed consent of those responsible for the child to study the child. Usually, then, the parents will have to be fully informed of the intent of the study in terms that they are capable of understanding (i.e., the psychologist may not relate the purpose of the study in highly technical and complex terms, incomprehensible to the average layman); the parents must then give their consent for their child's participation. In this way the researcher is taking one necessary step to ensure that the rights and safety of the subjects are not being violated. Of course, while other such steps must be taken (e.g., the researcher may not do a study that he or she even *suspects* will in any way harm the child), the fact that only volunteer subjects may be used limits the representativeness of any sample. In other words, only some population strata will be even potentially available for any researcher to study; only some groups of children will be potentially available within those strata; and only some children will be available within those groups.

Of course, a good researcher will still apply appropriate sampling techniques even within such an unrepresentative sample. Yet because of the seemingly inescapable sampling problems involved in developmental research, any researcher must be aware that any inferences made on the basis of results obtained with such samples are limited. We saw that there were important sampling problems in the Kagan and Moss (1962) longitudinal study (Chapter 9), in the Thomas et al. (1963) New York Longitudinal Study (Chapter 10), and in the research reported by Block (1971) in the *Lives Through Time*

monograph (Chapter 10), which limited the generalizations that could be made from the respective data sets.

Thus sampling is always a problem in developmental research. The investigator must always be aware of these problems of sampling, and in fact, because of absolutely necessary ethical restrictions (imposed on developmental researchers by themselves), more sampling problems are introduced. Hence the results of any developmental study are limited to the extent that biased sampling procedures interfere with obtaining a representative sample. Accordingly, the results of any such study may be generalized to such broader populations only with extreme caution. Thus, because of methodological problems of sampling, the researcher always encounters a related problem—that of generalization.

Overgeneralization

It may be concluded that if limitations imposed on developmental research by sampling are not recognized, the researcher may try to interpret the study's results as being more representative than they actually are. As noted by McCandless (1970), there are other types of overgeneralization. The results of a particular study might indicate that there exist small but reliable differences between two groups. Yet the researcher may speak of these differences as if they reflected wide disparities between the groups. If such statements occur, one may also term this overgeneralization. For instance, suppose that a particular researcher is interested in the attitudes that adolescent males and females maintain about their own bodies. To study such body concepts, the researcher might ask a large group of adolescent males and females to rate several body characteristics (for example, arms, legs, face, body build, height, general appearance) in terms of how important each is in determining the person's satisfaction with his or her body's appearance (Lerner, Karabenick, and Stuart 1973). Now suppose that female adolescents have a mean importance rating for the face of 4.20 (on a 5-point scale, with 5.0 being extremely important), and the corresponding rating for the male adolescents is 3.95. Because of the fact that many adolescent reponses went into the calculation of these means, and thus only small differences are needed for statistically significant differences to occur, the researcher might find that such a small difference between males and females is noteworthy. However, such *statistical* significance may not correspond to *psychological* significance. Can one say that on the basis of only a 0.25 point difference (out of a possible 4-point difference) this one aspect of adolescent females' body concept is considerably different from adolescent males' body concept? Probably not, and in fact, if such an assertion were made, it might be seen as an instance of overgeneralization.

Other types of overgeneralization exist too. Suppose that in the above study, the researcher is also interested in learning what parts of the male body are most important to females in deciding that a male is attractive, and what parts of the female body are most important to males in deciding that a female is attractive. The researcher can again ask the adolescent males and females to rate each of the body parts, but this time in terms of its importance for establishing the attractiveness of the opposite sex. Suppose that it is found that females rate general appearance as the most important characteristic of the male's body in determining male attractiveness, while males rate the face as the most important part of the female's body in determining a female's attractiveness. Would the researcher be justified in concluding that when adolescent males go about choosing a female for a dating partner they make their judgments on the basis of the female's face, and that when females choose a male dating partner they make their judgments on the basis of the male's general appearance? May these ratings be generalized to choice of partners in dating situations? Since the findings of the study pertain to ratings obtained about females and males in general, not about choices of

dating partners, such a generalization would appear unwarranted.

As McCandless had indicated, "applying findings gathered in one situation to circumstances different in essential characteristics" is an instance of unsound generalization (1970, 55). Whenever one applies specific results to situations that may be different in important ways, one is guilty of overgeneralization.

Over the course of this book we have seen several instances of such overgeneralization. In Chapter 6 we saw that Skinner (1956) generalized findings involving some responses of some animals in some situations to all responses of all animals in all situations. Similarly, in Chapter 11 we saw that other nurture mechanistic developmental psychologists also overgeneralize in reference to their use of the concept of reinforcement. Whenever one applies one's specific results found with particular measures in particular situations to situations that may be considered to be different in important ways, one is guilty of overgeneralization.

To avoid unsound overgeneralization, researchers must be wary of attempting to (1) extend their results to situations different from those their data actually bear on; (2) attribute more meaning, clarity, or significance to their results than are actually indicated; and (3) apply their findings to groups of people not actually represented in their sample (McCandless 1970). The developmental psychologist must also recognize that because of sampling, situational, and thus interpretational problems, the body of existing knowledge in the discipline may not be applicable to many groups of people. The "facts" of development, obtained through considerable research work, may in any event not be reflective of the "facts" for all people.

For example, due both to an intense interest in studying child development and the difficulty of readily obtaining samples of children to study, many university and other research institutions set up laboratory schools in earlier decades of this century. Many of the "facts" of development (at that time mostly "normative facts") were obtained through the study of children at these schools. Yet these children were often the children of the university or institute people. Hence they were primarily white, middle-class children of highly educated parents. Certainly, while the "facts" of development of such children are important, these "facts" may not be generalizable to all other children. Most children do not have parents who are professors or researchers. Many children are not white, and many children do not come from middle-class backgrounds. Thus the "facts" of development derived from such samples may be highly biased and unrepresentative. Bronfenbrenner (1977, 1979) has made a similar point (e.g., see Chapter 1 of this book).

In recognition of this problem, research in developmental psychology over the last several years has focused on other populations. Hence developmental psychology today is moving away from being a psychology of the development of only white, middle-class children of highly educated parents. Studies of the poor, of blacks, of chicanos, and of minority groups in general are being conducted in an attempt to broaden the basis of our knowledge of development in all strata of society. Moreover, the increase of scope has not been limited to disenfranchised, culturally deprived, or minority groups within our own country; there has been the recognition of the need for study of other societal and cultural settings (e.g., see Super and Harkness 1980). The facts of development found in this country may not be generalizable to the development of people in all countries, and hence there is a need for and a growing concern with cross-cultural studies of development.

Finally, but by no means least importantly, there has been the recognition that some people—even though they may be white and middle-class—possess characteristics that may make their development considerably different from other people's. These people are women, and until relatively recently there has not been much concern with the possibly unique phenomena

that might be encountered by growing up as a woman in our society. Thus a major recent extension of developmental research and theory has been the concern with women's psychological development (e.g., see Bardwick 1971; Block 1973; Brooks-Gunn and Petersen 1983; Maccoby and Jacklin 1974; Mednick and Tangri 1972; O'Leary 1977; Sarason 1973). In sum, as research broadens, developmental psychology will move toward providing a body of knowledge about the development of all people.

Conclusions

Up to this point we have considered some of the dimensions and problems of developmental research, using the ideas of McCandless (1970) as a framework for much of our presentation. We have seen that a theory is useful if it fulfills its function as an integrator of facts *and* serves as a basis for the generation of new facts. Thus this chapter has considered the problems of doing developmental research in a manner that will allow theory to fulfill its second role. If these problems are not dealt with correctly in developmental research, then such research will not provide an appropriate test of any given theoretical formulation. Yet, we have seen too that issues of ethics and not only of method and design must be considered by the developmental researcher when planning and conducting any study. Among developmental psychologists there is a commitment to an agreed-on set of ethical standards. Let us conclude this chapter by considering them.

ETHICAL ISSUES IN RESEARCH

The major focus of this chapter has been on methods of human development research—techniques involved in the observation and manipulation of variables and the validity of these techniques. However, such research obviously involves an interaction between people—the investigator and the participants. In recent years, researchers, government officials, and the public have become increasingly concerned with the ethics of research. In particular, concern has been directed toward protecting the rights of the individuals who serve as the subjects of research. This concern has been formalized in a variety of ways. For example, the U.S. Department of Health and Human Services, a major source of funds for research, has developed a set of regulations that all recipients of federal research grants and contracts must follow. Similarly, many scientific societies, such as the American Psychological Association, have developed codes of ethics for the conduct of research. Much of this concern evolved out of past abuses. Medical research has been particularly problematic; however, abuses occur in behavioral research as well. Below is a list of ethically questionable practices.

1. Involving individuals in research without their knowledge or consent.

2. Failing to inform participants about the true nature of the research.

3. Misinforming participants about the true nature of the research.

4. Coercing individuals to participate in research.

5. Failing to honor promises or commitments to participants.

6. Exposing participants to undue physical or mental stress.

7. Causing physical or psychologicial harm to participants.

8. Invading the participants' privacy.

9. Failing to maintain confidentiality of information received.

10. Withholding benefits from participants in control groups.

These problems may arise not because the investigator is evil or uncaring. Rather the nature of the problems, variables, and people themselves may cause problems. For example, it may be very difficult to study a significant event, such as the death of a spouse, without exposing the individual to mental stress. Yet knowledge of such an event is important both for its own value and for attempts to help individuals cope with such events. A critical issue, then, is the cost of research versus its benefits. All research has a cost, in other than monetary terms, to the individual involved—time, stress, and so forth. Research may also produce benefits—knowlege. Obviously benefits should exceed cost, but ethical practice requires more than this. At some point, the cost may be too great no matter what the benefit. In other words, the end does not justify the means. During World War II the Nazis allowed the end to justify the means when they immersed concentration camp victims in frigid water until they died to determine how better to protect German flyers who had to parachute into the sea.

Such extreme examples are relatively easy to judge as unethical. However, for most research on behavior there are no absolute answers. One justifiable approach appears to take the form of seeking the advice of others concerning the ethical acceptability of research. This may take place at two levels—internal consultation with colleagues and representatives from potential participant groups (e.g., parents, students) and formal consultation with institutional committees set up for this purpose. The latter is required for research studies conducted on campuses where there is any research funded by the Department of Health and Human Services. However, none of these practices changes the fact that the ultimate responsibility for the ethical nature of the research rests with the investigator. To aid the individual scientist in meeting this responsibility the Division of Developmental Psychology (Division 7) of the American Psychological Association has issued a statement of ethical standards for developmental psychologists to follow when testing children. The major and key portions of this statement are presented in Table 12.4.

TABLE 12.4
Ethical Standards for Developmental Psychologists

Children as research subjects present problems for the investigator different from those of adult subjects. Our culture is marked by a tenderness of concern for the young. The young are viewed as more vulnerable to distress (even though evidence may suggest that they are actually more resilient in recovery from stress). Because the young have less knowledge and less experience, they also may be less able to evaluate what participation in research means. And, consent of the parent for the study of his or her child is the prerequisite to obtaining consent from the child. These characteristics outline the major differences between research with children and research with adults.

1. No matter how young the subject, he or she has rights that supersede the rights of the investigator of his or her behavior. In the conduct of his or her research the investigator measures each question he or she proposes against this principle and is prepared to justify his or her decision.

2. The investigator uses no research operation that may harm the child either physically or psychologically. Psychological harm, to be sure, is difficult to define; nevertheless, its definition remains a responsibility of the investigator.

3. The informed consent of parents or of those legally designated to act *in loco parentis* is obtained, preferably in writing. Informed consent requires that the parent be given accurate information on the profession and institutional affiliation of the investigator, and on the purpose and operations of the research, albeit in layman's terms. The consent of parents is not solicited by any claims of benefit to the child. Not only is the right of parents to refuse consent respected, but parents must be given the opportunity to refuse.

4. The investigator does not coerce a child into participating in a study. The child has the right to refuse and he or she, too, should be given the opportunity to refuse.

5. When the investigator is in doubt about possible harmful effects of his or her efforts or when he or she decides that the nature of his or her research requires deception, the investigator submits his or her plan to an *ad hoc* group of colleagues for review. It is the group's responsibility to suggest other feasible means of obtaining the information. Every psychologist has a responsibility to maintain not only his or her own ethical standards but also those of his or her colleagues.

6. The child's identity is concealed in written and verbal reports of the results, as well as in informal discussions with students and colleagues.

7. The investigator does not assume the role of diagnostician or counselor in reporting his or her observations to parents or those *in loco parentis*. He or she does not report test scores of information given by a child in confidence, although he or she recognizes a duty to report general findings to parents and others.

8. The investigator respects the ethical standards of those who act *in loco parentis* (e.g., teachers, superintendents of institutions).

9. The same ethical standards apply to children who are control subjects, and to their parents, as to those who are experimental subjects. When the experimental treatment is believed to benefit the child, the investigator considers an alternative treatment for the control group instead of no treatment.

10. Payment in money, gifts, or services for the child's participation does not annul any of the above principles.

11. Teachers of developmental psychology present the ethical standards of conducting research on human beings to both their undergraduate and graduate students. Like the university committees on the use of human subjects, professors share responsibility for the study of children on their campuses.

12. Editors of psychological journals reporting investigations of children have certain responsibilities to the authors of studies they review: they provide space for the investigator to justify his or her procedures where necessary and to report the precautions he or she has taken. When the procedures seem questionable, editors ask for such information.

13. The Division and its members have a continuing responsibility to question, amend, and revise the standards.

Source: Newsletter, *American Psychological Association, Division on Developmental Psychology, 1968, pp. 1–3.*

REFERENCES

Abravanel, E. 1968. The development of intersensory patterning with regard to selected, spatial dimensions. *Monographs of the Society for Research in Child Development* 33 (2, no. 118).

Allport, G. W. 1937. *Personality: A psychological interpretation.* New York: Holt.

Allport, G. W. 1954. *The nature of prejudice.* Reading, Mass.: Addison-Wesley.

Anastasi, A. 1958. Heredity, environment, and the question "how?" *Psychological Review* 65: 197–208.

Anderson, P. W. 1972. More is different. *Science* 177: 393–96.

Anderson, W. F., and J. C. Fletcher. 1980. Gene therapy in human beings: When is it ethical to begin? *The New England Journal of Medicine* 303: 1293–97.

Anthony, J. 1969. The reaction of adults to adolescents and their behavior. In G. Caplan and S. Lebovici (Eds.), *Adolescence.* New York: Basic Books.

Arbuthnot, J. 1975. Modification of moral judgment through role play. *Developmental Psychology* 11: 319–24.

Bachrach, R., L. R. Huesmann, and R. A. Peterson. 1977. The relation between locus of control and the development of moral judgment. *Child Development* 48: 1340–52.

Bacon, C., and R. M. Lerner. 1975. Effects of maternal employment status on the development of vocational-role perception in females. *Journal of Genetic Psychology* 126: 187–93.

Baer, D. M. 1970. An age-irrelevant concept of development. *Merrill Palmer Quarterly of Behavior and Development* 16: 238–45.

Baer, D. M. 1976. The organism as host. *Human Development* 19: 87–98.

Baer, D. M. 1982. Behavior analysis and developmental psychology: Discussant comments. *Human Development* 25: 357–61.

Bakan, D. 1966. *The duality of human existence.* Chicago: Rand McNally.

Baldwin, J. M. 1897. *Mental development in the child and the race.* New York: Macmillan.

Baltes, P. B. 1968. Longitudinal and cross-sectional sequences in the study of age and generation effects. *Human Development* 11; 145–71.

Baltes, P. B. 1979a. Life-span developmental psychology: Some converging observations on history and theory. In *Life-span development and behavior,* vol. 2, ed. P. B. Baltes and O. G. Brim, Jr. New York: Academic Press.

Baltes, P. B. 1979b. On the potential and limits of child development: Life-span developmental perspectives. *Newsletter of the Society for Research in Child Development* 1–4.

Baltes, P. B. 1983. Life-span developmental psychology: Observations on history and theory revisited. In *Developmental psychology: Historical and philosophical perspectives,* ed. R. M. Lerner. Hillsdale, N.J.: Erlbaum.

Baltes, P. B., and M. M. Baltes. 1980. Plasticity and variability in psychological aging: Methodological and theoretical issues. In *Determining the effects of aging on the central nervous system,* ed. G. E. Gurski. Berlin: Schering AG (Oraniendruck).

Baltes, P. B., M. M. Baltes, and G. Reinert. 1970. The relationship between time of measurement and age in cognitive development of children: An application of cross-sectional sequences. *Human Development* 13: 258–68.

Baltes, P. B., S. W. Cornelius and J. R. Nesselroade. 1977. Cohort effects in behavioral development: Theoretical and methodological perspectives. In *Minnesota symposia on child psychology,* vol. 2, ed. W. A. Collins. New York: Thomas Crowell.

Baltes, P. B., and S. J. Danish. 1980. Intervention in life-span development and aging: Issues and concepts. In *Life-span developmental psychology: Intervention,* ed. R. R. Turner and H. W. Reese. New York: Academic Press.

Baltes, P. B., F. Dittmann-Kohli, and R. A. Dixon. 1984. New perspectives on the development of intelligence in adulthood: Toward a dual-process conception and a model of selective optimization with compensation. In P. B. Baltes and O. G. Brim, Jr. (Eds.), *Life-span development and behavior* (Vol. 6). New York: Academic Press.

Baltes, P. B., and J. R. Nesselroade. 1973. The developmental analysis of individual differences on multiple measures. In *Life-span developmental psychology: Methodological issues,* ed. J. R. Nesselroade and H. W. Reese. New York: Academic Press.

Baltes, P. B., and H. W. Reese. 1984. The life-span perspective in developmental psychology. In *Developmental psychology: An advanced textbook,* ed. M. H. Bornstein and M. E. Lamb. Hillsdale, N.J.: Erlbaum.

Baltes, P. B., H. W. Reese, and L. P. Lipsitt. 1980. Life-span developmental psychology. *Annual Review of Psychology* 31: 65–110.

Baltes, P. B., H. W. Reese, and J. R. Nesselroade. 1977. *Life-span developmental psychology: Introduction to research methods.* Monterey, Calif.: Brooks/Cole.

Baltes, P. B., and K. W. Schaie. 1973. On life-span developmental research paradigms: Retrospects and prospects. In *Life-span developmental psychology: Personality and socialization,* ed. P. B. Baltes and K. W. Schaie. New York: Academic Press.

Baltes, P. B., and K. W. Schaie. 1974. Aging and IQ: The myth of the twilight years. *Psychology Today* 7: 35–40.

Baltes, P. B., and K. W. Schaie. 1976. On the plasticity of intelligence in adulthood and old age: Where Horn and Donaldson fail. *American Psychologist* 31: 720–25.

Baltes, P. B., and S. L. Willis. 1982. Enhancement (plasticity) of intellectual functioning in old age: Penn State's Adult Development and Enrichment Project (ADEPT). In *Aging and cognitive processes,* ed. F. I. M. Craik and S. E. Trehub. New York: Plenum.

Bandura, A. 1964. The stormy decade: Fact or fiction? *Psychology in the School* 1: 224–31.

Bandura, A. 1965. Influence of models' reinforcement contingencies on the acquisition of imitative responses. *Journal of Personality and Social Psychology* 1: 589–95.

Bandura, A. 1971. *Social learning theory.* Morristown, N.J.: General Learning Press.

Bandura, A. 1974. Behavior theory and the models of man. *American Psychologist* 29: 859–69.

Bandura, A. 1977. *Social learning theory.* Englewood Cliffs. N.J.: Prentice-Hall.

Bandura, A. 1978. The self system in reciprocal determinism. *American Psychologist* 33: 344–58.

Bandura, A. 1980a. Self-referent thought: A developmental analysis of self-efficacy. In *Cognitive social development: Frontiers and possible futures,* ed. J. H. Flavell and L. D. Ross. New York: Cambridge University Press.

Bandura, A. 1980b. The self and mechanisms of agency. In *Social psychological perspectives on the self,* ed. J. Suls. Hillsdale, N.J.: Erlbaum.

Bandura, A., and A. C. Huston. 1961. Identification as a process of incidental learning. *Journal of Abnormal and Social Psychology* 63: 311–18.

Bandura, A., and F. McDonald. 1963. The influence of social reinforcement and the behavior of models in shaping children's moral judgment. *Journal of Abnormal and Social Psychology* 67: 274–81.

Bandura, A., and R. H. Walters. 1959. *Adolescent aggression*. New York: Ronald Press.

Bandura, A., and R. H. Walters. 1963. *Social learning and personality development*. New York: Holt, Rinehart & Winston.

Bardwick, J. M. 1971. *Psychology of women*. New York: Harper & Row.

Barraclough, C. A. 1966. Modifications of CNS regulation of reproduction after exposure of prepubertal rats to steroid hormones. *Recent Progress in Hormone Research* 22: 503–39.

Barry, H., M. K. Bacon, and I. L. Child. 1957. A cross-cultural survey of some sex differences in socialization. *Journal of Abnormal and Social Psychology* 55: 527–34.

Basser, L. S. 1962. Hemiplegia of early onset and the faculty of speech with special reference to the effects of hemispherectomy. *Brain* 85: 427–60.

Bates, J. E. 1980. The concept of difficult temperament. *Merrill-Palmer Quarterly* 26: 299–319.

Bateson, P. P. G. 1964. Effects of similarity between rearing and testing conditions on chicks' following and avoiding responses. *Journal of Comparative and Physiological Psychology* 57: 100–103.

Bateson, P. P. G. 1966. The characteristics and context of imprinting. *Biological Reviews* 41: 177–220.

Bateson, P. P. G. 1979. How do sensitive periods arise and what are they for? *Animal Behavior* 27: 470–86.

Bateson, P. P. G. 1983. The interpretation of sensitive periods. In *The behavior of human infants,* ed. A. Oliverio and M. Zapella. New York: Plenum.

Baumrind, D. 1971. Current patterns of parental authority. *Developmental Psychology Monographs* 4 (no. 1, part 2).

Baumrind, D. 1972. Some thoughts about child rearing. In *Influences on human development,* ed. U. Bronfenbrenner. Hinsdale, Ill.: Dryden.

Baxter, B. 1966. Effect of visual deprivation during postnatal maturation of the electroencephalogram of the cat. *Experimental Neurology* 14: 224–37.

Bayley, N. 1949. Consistency and variability in the growth of intelligence from birth to eighteen years. *Journal of Genetic Psychology* 75: 165–96.

Bayley, N., and M. H. Oden. 1955. The maintenance of intellectual ability in gifted adults. *Journal of Gerontology* 10: 91–107.

Beach, F. A. 1950. The Snark was a Boojum. *American Psychologist* 5: 115–24.

deBeer, G. R. 1959. Paedomorphosis. *Proceedings of the XV International Congress of Zoology* 15: 927–30.

Bell, R. Q. 1968. A reinterpretation of the direction of effects in studies of socialization. *Psychological Review* 75: 81–95.

Bell, R. Q. 1974. Contributions of human infants to caregiving and social interaction. In *The effect of the infant on its caregiver,* ed. M. Lewis and L. A. Rosenblum. New York: Wiley.

Bell, R. Q., and L. V. Harper. 1977. *Child effects on adults*. Hillsdale, N.J.: Erlbaum.

Belsky, J. 1980. Child maltreatment: An ecological integration. *American Psychologist* 35: 320–35.

Belsky, J. 1981. Early human experience: A family perspective. *Developmental Psychology* 17: 3–23.

Belsky, J. 1984. The determinants of parenting: A process model. *Child Development* 55: 83–96.

Belsky, J., and W. J. Tolan. 1981. Infants as producers of their own development: An ecological analysis. In *Individuals as producers of their development: A life-span perspective,* ed. R. M. Lerner and N. A. Busch-Rossnagel. New York: Academic Press.

Bem, S. L. 1974. The measurement of psychological androgyny. *Journal of Consulting and Clinical Psychology* 47: 155–62.

Bem, S. L. 1975. Sex-role adaptability: One consequence of psychological androgyny. *Journal of Personality and Social Psychology* 31: 634–43.

Bem, S. L. 1977. On the utility of alternative procedures for assessing psychological androgyny. *Journal of Consulting and Clinical Psychology* 45: 196–205.

Bengtson, V. L., and L. Troll. 1978. Youth and their parents: Feedback and intergenerational influence in socialization. In *Child influences on marital and family interaction: A life-span perspective,* ed. R. M. Lerner and G. B. Spanier. New York: Academic Press.

Berg, P. 1981. Dissections and reconstructions of genes and chromosomes. *Science* 213: 296–303.

Berndt, T. J. 1977. The effect of reciprocity norms on moral judgment and causal attribution. *Child Development* 48: 1322–30.

Berndt, T. J. 1978. Stages as descriptions, explanations, and testable constructs. *The Behavioral and Brain Sciences* 2: 183–84.

Berscheid, E., and E. Walster. 1974. Physical attractiveness. In *Advances in experimental social psychology* vol. 7, ed. L. Berkowitz. New York: Academic Press.

Bertalanffy, L. von. 1933. *Modern theories of development.* London: Oxford University Press.

Bijou, S. W. 1976. *Child development: The basic stage of early childhood.* Englewood Cliffs, N.J.: Prentice-Hall.

Bijou, S. W. 1977. *Some clarifications on the meaning of a behavior analysis of child development.* Paper presented at the Third Annual Midwestern Association of Behavior Analysis, May, Chicago.

Bijou, S. W., and D. M. Baer. 1961. *Child development: A systematic and empirical theory,* vol. 1. New York: Appleton-Century-Crofts.

Bijou, W. S., and D. M. Baer. 1965. *Child development: Universal stage of infancy,* vol. 2. Englewood Cliffs, N.J.: Prentice-Hall.

Bijou, S. W., and D. M. Baer, eds. 1967. *Child development: Readings in experimental analysis.* New York: Appleton-Century-Crofts.

Binet, A., and T. Simon. 1905a. Sur la necéssité d'établir un diagnostic scientific des états inférieurs de l'intelligence. *L'Année Psychologique* 11: 162–90.

Binet, A., and T. Simon. 1905b. Méthodes nouvelles pour le diagnostic du niveau intellectuel des anormaux. *L'Année Psychologique* 11: 191–244.

Birch, H. G. and A. Lefford. 1963. Intersensory development in children. *Monographs of the Society for Research in Child Development* 28 (5, no. 89).

Birch, H. G. and A. Lefford. 1967. Visual differentiation, intersensory integration, and voluntary motor control. *Monographs of the Society for Research in Child Development* 32 (2, no. 110).

Birnbaum, J. A. 1975. Life patterns and self-esteem in gifted family oriented and career committed women. In *Women and achievement,* ed. M. T. S. Mednick, S. S. Tangri, and L. W. Hoffman. New York: Wiley.

Bitterman, M. E. 1960. Toward a comparative psychology of learning. *American Psychologist* 15: 704–12.

Bitterman, M. E. 1965. Phyletic differences in learning. *American Psychologist* 20: 396–410.

Bitterman, M. E. 1975. The comparative analysis of learning. *Science* 188: 699–709.

Blakemore, C., and Van Sluyters, R. C. 1974. Reversal of the physiological effects of monocular deprivation in kittens: Further evidence for a sensitive period. *Journal of Physiology,* 248: 663–716.

Block, J. 1961. *The Q-sort method in personality assessment and psychiatric research.* Springfield, Ill.: Charles C Thomas.

Block, J. 1971. *Lives through time.* Berkeley, Calif.: Bancroft.

Block, J. 1982. Assimilation, accommodation, and the dynamics of personality development. *Child Development* 53: 281–95.

Block, J. H. 1973. Conceptions of sex roles: Some cross-cultural and longitudinal perspectives. *American Psychologist* 28: 512–26.

Block, J. H. 1976. Issues, problems and pitfalls in assessing sex differences: A critical review of the psychology of sex differences. *Merrill-Palmer Quarterly* 22: 283–308.

Block, J. H. and J. Block. 1980. The role of ego-control and ego-resiliency in the organization of behavior. In *Minnesota Symposia on Child Psychology,* vol. 13, ed. W. A. Collins. Hillsdale, N.J.: Erlbaum.

Bloom, B. S. 1964. *Stability and change in human characteristics.* New York: Wiley.

Bodmer, W. F., and L. L. Cavalli-Sforza. 1976. *Genetics, evolution and man.* San Francisco: Freeman.

Bolles, R. C. 1967. *Theory of motivation.* New York: Harper & Row.

Bolles, R. C. 1972. Reinforcement, expectancy, and learning. *Psychological Review* 79: 394–409.

Boring, E. G. 1950. *A history of experimental psychology.* 2d ed. New York: Appleton-Century-Crofts.

Bouchard, T. J., Jr. 1982. Identical twins reared apart: Reanalysis or pseudoanalysis. *Contemporary Psychology* 27: 190–91.

Bouchard, T. J., Jr., and M. McGue. 1981. Familial studies of intelligence: A review. *Science* 212: 1055–59.

Bower, T. G. R. 1966. Slant perception and shape constancy in infants. *Science* 151: 832–34.

Bowers, K. S. 1973. Situationalism in psychology. *Psychological Review* 80: 307–36.

Brainerd, C. J. 1977. Learning research and Piagetian theory. In *Alternatives to Piaget: Critical essays on the theory,* ed. L. Siegel and C. Brainerd. New York: Academic Press.

Brainerd, C. J. 1978. The stage question in cognitive-developmental theory. *The Behavioral and Brain Sciences* 2: 173–82.

Brainerd, C. J. 1979. Further replies on invariant sequences, explanation and other stage criteria. *The Behavioral and Brain Sciences* 2: 149–52.

Brazelton, T. B., B. Koslowski, and M. Main. 1974. The origins of reciprocity: The early mother-infant interaction. In *The effect of the infant on its caregivers,* ed. M. Lewis and L. A. Rosenblum. New York: Wiley.

Breland, K., and Breland, M. 1961. The misbehavior of organisms. *American Psychologist* 16: 681–84.

Brent, S. B. 1984. *Psychological and social structure: Their organization, activity, and development.* Hillsdale, N.J.: Erlbaum.

Brickman, P., and J. H. Bryan. 1976. Equity versus equality as factors in children's moral judgments of thefts, charity, and 3rd-party transfers. *Journal of Personality and Social Psychology* 34(5): 757–61.

Brim, O. G., Jr., and J. Kagan. 1980. Constancy and change: A view of the issues. In *Constancy and change in human development,* ed. O. G. Brim, Jr., and J. Kagan. Cambridge, Mass.: Harvard University Press.

Brim, O. G., Jr., and C. D. Ryff. 1980. On the properties of life events. In *Life-span development and behavior,* vol. 3, ed. P. B. Baltes and O. G. Brim, Jr. New York: Academic Press.

Brody, G. H., and R. W. Henderson. 1977. Effects of multiple model variations and rationale provision on moral judgments and explanations of young children. *Child Development* 48: 1117–20.

Bronfenbrenner, U. 1960. Freudian theories of identification and their derivatives. *Child Development* 31: 15–40.

Bronfenbrenner, U. 1963. Developmental

theory in transition. In *Child psychology*. Sixty-second yearbook of the National Society for the Study of Education, part 1, ed. H. W. Stevenson. Chicago: University of Chicago Press.

Bronfenbrenner, U. 1977. Toward an experimental ecology of human development. *American Psychologist* 32: 513–31.

Bronfenbrenner, U. 1979. *The ecology of human development*. Cambridge, Mass.: Harvard University Press.

Bronfenbrenner, U. 1983. The context of development and the development of context. In R. M. Lerner (ed.), *Developmental Psychology: Historical and Philosophical Perspectives*. Hillsdale, N.J.: Erlbaum.

Bronfenbrenner, U., and A. C. Crouter. 1983. The evolution of environmental models in developmental research. In *History, theories and methods,* ed. W. Kessen, vol. 1 of *Handbook of child psychology,* 4th ed., ed. P. H. Mussen. New York: Wiley.

Bronson, F. H., and C. Desjardins. 1970. Neonatal androgen and adult aggressiveness in female mice. *General and Comparative Endocrinology* 15: 320–25.

Brooks-Gunn, J., and A. C. Petersen, eds. 1983. *Girls at puberty: Biological, psychological and social perspectives.* New York: Plenum.

Broverman, I. K., S. R. Vogel, D. M. Broverman, F. E. Clarkson, and P. S. Rosenkrantz. 1972. Sex-role stereotypes: A current appraisal. *Journal of Social Issues* 28: 59–78.

Brown, D. D. 1981. Gene expression in eukaryotes. *Science* 211: 667–74.

Brown, R. T. 1974. Following and visual imprinting in ducklings across a wide age range. *Developmental Psychobiology* 8: 27–33.

Brun-Gulbrandsen, S. 1958. Kjonnsrolle og ungdomskriminalitet. Oslo: Institue of Social Research (mimeographed).

Bruner, J. 1964. The course of cognitive growth. *American Psychologist* 19: 1–15.

Bühler, C. 1928. *Kindheit und jugend.* Leipzig: Hirzel.

Bühler, C. 1933. Der menschliche Lebenslauf als psychologisches Problem. Leipzig: Hirzel.

Bureau of Labor Statistics. 1978. *Handbook of labor statistics, 1978.* U.S. Department of Labor, Washington: U.S. Government Printing Office.

Burt, C. L. 1943. Ability and income. *British Journal of Educational Psychology* 13: 83–98.

Burt, C. 1955. The evidence of the concept of intelligence. *British Journal of Educational Psychology* 25: 159–77.

Burt, C. L. 1958. The inheritance of mental ability. *American Psychologist,* 13: 1–15.

Burt, C. 1966. The genetic determination of differences in intelligence: A study of monozygotic twins reared together and apart. *British Journal of Psychology* 57: 137–53.

Burt, C. L., and M. Howard. 1956. The multifactorial theory of inheritance and its application to intelligence. *British Journal of Statistical Psychology* 9: 95–131.

Burt, C., and M. Howard. 1957. The relative influence of heredity and environment on assessments of intelligence. *British Journal of Statistical Psychology* 10: 103.

Buss, A. R. 1979. On the four kinds of causality. *The Behavioral and Brain Sciences* 2: 139.

Cairns, R. B., and K. E. Hood. 1983. Continuity in social development: A comparative perspective on individual difference prediction. In *Life-span development and behavior,* vol. 5, ed. P. B. Baltes and O. G Brim, Jr. New York: Academic Press.

Campbell, R. L., and D. M. Richie. 1983. Problems in the theory of developmental sequences. *Human Development* 26: 156–72.

Capitanio, J. P., and D. W. Leger. 1979. Evolutionary scales lack utility: A reply to Yarczower and Hazlett. *Psychological Bulletin* 86: 876–79.

Caplan, A. L., ed. 1978. *The sociobiology debate.* New York: Harper & Row.

Carlson, R. 1972. Understanding women: Implications for personality theory and research. *Journal of Social Issues* 28: 17–32.

Carter, C. O. 1976. The heritability of intelligence (letter to the editor). *The Times,* November 3, 17.

Cattell, R. B. 1957. *Personality and motivation: Structure and measurement.* New York: World.

Cattell, R. B. 1966. Psychological theory and scientific method. In *Handbook of multivariate experimental psychology,* ed. R. B. Cattell. Chicago: Rand McNally.

Cattell, R. B. 1973. *Personality and mood by questionnaire.* San Francisco: Jossey-Bass.

Cauble, M. A. 1976. Formal operations, ego identity and principled morality: Are they related? *Developmental Psychology* 12: 363–64.

Chandler, M. J., S. Greenspan, and C. Barenboim. 1973. Judgments of intentionality in response to videotaped and verbally presented moral dilemmas: The medium is the message. *Child Development* 44: 315–20.

Chess, S., and A. Thomas. 1984. *Origins and evolution of behavior disorders.* New York: Brunner/Mazel.

Chess, S., A. Thomas, and H. G. Birch. 1965. *Your child is a person.* New York: Viking.

Chess, S., A. Thomas, and H. G. Birch. 1966. Distortions in developmental reporting made by parents of behaviorally disturbed children. *Journal of Child Psychiatry* 5: 226–34.

Chomsky, N. A. 1965. *Aspects of the theory of syntax.* Cambridge: MIT Press.

Chomsky, N. A. 1966. *Cartesian linguistics.* New York: Harper & Row.

Chow, K. L., and D. L. Stewart. 1972. Reversal of structural and functional effects of long-term visual deprivation in the cat. *Experimental Neurology* 34: 409–33.

Ciaccio, N. V. 1971. A test of Erikson's theory of ego epigenesis. *Developmental Psychology* 4; 306–11.

Clark, G. H. 1957. *Thales to Dewey.* Boston: Houghton Mifflin.

Clarke, A. M. 1982. Developmental discontinuities: An approach to assessing their nature. In *Facilitating infant and early childhood development,* ed. L. A. Bond and J. M. Joffe. Hanover, N.H.: University Press of New England.

Clarke, A. M., and A. D. B. Clarke, eds. 1976. *Early experience: Myth and evidence.* New York: Free Press.

Clausen, J. A. 1972. The life-course of individuals. In *Aging and society,* vol. 3. *A sociology of age stratification,* ed. M. W. Riley, M. Johnson, and A. Foner. New York: Russell Sage Foundation.

Colby, A. 1978. Evolution of a moral-developmental theory. *New Directions for Child Development* 2: 89–104.

Colby, A. 1979. Presentation at the Center for Advanced Study in the Behavioral Sciences Summer Institute, July, on "Morality and Moral Development."

Colby, A., L. Kohlberg, J. Gibbs, and M. Lieberman. 1983. A longitudinal study of moral judgment. *Monographs of the Society for Research in Child Development* 48, no. 200.

Collins, J. K., and N. T. Thomas. 1972. Age and susceptibility to same-sex peer pressure. *British Journal of Eduational Psychology* 42: 83–85.

Collins, W. A., ed. 1982. *The concept of development: The Minnesota Symposia on Child Psychology,* vol. 15. Hillsdale, N.J.: Erlbaum.

Colombo, J. 1982. The critical period concept: Research, methodology and theoretical issues. *Psychological Bulletin* 91: 260–75.

Conger, J. J., and A. C. Petersen. 1984. *Adolescence and youth: Psychological development in a changing world.* 3d ed. New York: Harper & Row.

Connolly, K. 1972. Learning and the concept of critical periods in infancy. *Developmental Medicine and Child Neurology* 14: 705–14.

Constantinople, A. 1969. An Eriksonian measure of personality development in college students. *Developmental Psychology* 1: 357–72.

Conway, J. 1958. The inheritance of intelligence and its social implications. *British Journal of Statistical Psychology* 11: 171–90.

Costanzo, P. R., J. D. Coie, J. F. Grumet, and D. Farnill. 1973. A re-examination of the effects of intent and consequence on children's moral judgments. *Child Development,* 44: 154–61.

Crawford, M. L., R. Blake, S. J. Cool, and G. K. von Noorden. 1975. Physiological consequences of unilateral and bilateral eye closure in macaque monkeys: Some further observations. *Brain Research* 84: 150–54.

Cronbach, L. J. 1975. Beyond the two disciplines of scientific psychology. *American Psychologist* 30: 116–27.

Cumming, E., and W. E. Henry. 1961. *Growing old: The process of disengagement.* New York: Basic Books.

Curtiss, S. 1977. *Genie: A psycholinguistic study of a modern day "wild child."* New York: Academic Press.

Curtiss, S., V. Fromkin, M. Rigler, D. Rigler, and S. Krashen. 1975. An update on the linguistic development of Genie. In *Developmental psycholinguistics: Theory and applications,* ed. D. Dato. Washington: Georgetown University Press.

Cynader, M., N. Berman, and A. Hein. 1976. Recovery of function in cat visual cortex following prolonged deprivation. *Experimental Brain Research* 25: 139–56.

Dale, L. G. 1970. The growth of systematic thinking: Replication and analysis of Piaget's first chemical experiment. *Australian Journal of Psychology* 22: 277–86.

Darley, J. M., Klossen, E. C., and Zanna, M. P. 1978. Intentions and their contexts in moral judgments of children and adults. *Child Development,* 49: 66–74.

Darwin, C. (1859). *The origin of species by means of natural selection or the preservation of favoured races in the struggle for life.* London: J. Murray.

Darwin, C. (1872). *The expression of emotions in man and animals.* London: J. Murray.

Davis, A. (1944). Socialization and the adolescent personality. *Forty-third yearbook of the national society for the study of education* (Vol. 43, Part 1). Chicago: University of Chicago Press.

Davison, M. L., P. M. King, K. S. Kitchener, and C. A. Parker. 1980. The stage sequence concept in cognitive and social development. *Developmental Psychology* 16: 121–31.

Davison, M. L., S. Robbins, and D. B. Swanson. 1978. Stage structure in objective moral judgments. *Developmental Psychology* 14: 137–46.

Dewey, J., and A. F. Bentley. 1949. *Knowing and the known.* Boston: Beacon.

Dobzhansky, T., F. J. Ayala, G. L. Stebbings, and J. W. Valentine. 1977. *Evolution.* San Francisco: Freeman.

Dollard, J., L. W. Doob, N. E. Miller, O. H. Mowrer, and R. R. Sears. 1939. *Frustration and aggression.* New Haven: Yale University Press.

Dollard, J., and N. E. Miller. 1950. *Personality and psychotherapy.* New York: McGraw-Hill.

Dorfman, D. D. 1978. The Cyril Burt question: New findings. *Science* 201: 1177–86.

Dorfman, D. D. 1980. Intelligence for beginners? (Review of Hans J. Eysenck's *The Structure and Measurement of Intelligence*). *Nature* 284: 645.

Douglas, J. D., and A. C. Wong. 1977. Formal operations: Age and sex differences in Chinese and American children. *Child Development* 48: 689–92.

Douvan, E., and J. Adelson. 1966. *The adolescent experience.* New York: Wiley.

DuBois, C. 1944. *The people of Alor.* Minneapolis: University of Minnesota Press.

Duncan, C. P. 1982. Book reviews: The intelligence controversy. *American Journal of Psychology* 95: 346–49.

Dunn, L. C. 1965. *A short history of genetics.* New York: McGraw-Hill.

Eacker, J. N. 1972. On some elementary philosophical problems of psychology. *American Psychologist* 27: 553–65.

Edwards, C. P. 1975. Society complexity and moral development: A Kenyan study. *Ethos* 3: 505–27.

Edwards, D. A. 1970. Postnatal androgenization and adult aggressive behavior in female mice. *Physiology and Behavior* 5: 1115–19.

Edwards, J. B. 1974. A developmental study of the acquisition of some moral concepts in children aged 7 to 15. *Educational Research* 16: 83–93.

Eichorn, D. H., J. A. Clausen, N. Haan, M. P. Honzik, and P. H. Mussen. 1981. *Present and past in middle life.* New York: Academic Press.

Einhorn, D., J. B. Young, and L. Landesberg. 1982. Hypotensive effect of fasting: Possible involvement of the sympathetic nervous system and endogenous opiates. *Science* 218: 727–29.

Eisdorfer, C. 1968. Arousal and performance: Experiments in verbal learning and a tentative theory. In *Human aging and behavior,* ed. G. A. Talland. New York: Academic Press.

Eisenberg, L. 1972. The *human* nature of human nature. *Science* 176: 123–28.

Eisenberg-Berg, N. 1976. The relation of political attitudes to constraint-oriented and prosocial moral reasoning. *Developmental Psychology* 12: 552–53.

Eisenberg-Berg, N. 1979. The development of children's prosocial moral judgment. *Developmental Psychology* 15: 128–37.

Eisenberg-Berg, N., and E. Geisheker. 1979. Content of preachings and power of the model-preacher: Effect on children's generosity. *Developmental Psychology* 15(2): 168–75.

Eisenberg-Berg, N., and P. Mussen. 1978. Empathy and moral development in adolescence. *Developmental Psychology* 14: 185–86.

Eisenberg-Berg, N., and C. Neal. 1979. Children's moral reasoning about their own spontaneous prosocial behavior. *Developmental Psychology* 15(2): 228–29.

Elder, G. H., Jr. 1974. *Children of the Great Depression.* Chicago: University of Chicago Press.

Elder, G. H., Jr. 1975. Age differentiation and the life course. In *Annual review of sociology,* vol. 1, ed. A. Inkeles, J. Coleman, and N. Smelser. Palo Alto, Calif.: Annual Review.

Elder, G. H., Jr. 1977. Family history and the life course. *Journal of Family History* 2: 279–304.

Elder, G. H., Jr. 1979. Historical change in life patterns and personality. In *Lifespan development and behavior,* vol. 2, ed. P. B. Baltes and O. G. Brim, Jr. New York: Academic Press.

Elder, G. H., Jr. 1980. Adolescence in historical perspective. In *Handbook of adolescent psychology,* ed. J. Adelson. New York: Wiley.

Elkind, D. 1962. Quantity conceptions in college students. *Journal of Social Psychology* 57: 459–65.

Elkind, D. 1967. Egocentrism in adolescence. *Child Development* 4: 1025–34.

Elkind, D., and R. F. Dabek. 1977. Personal injury and property damage in moral judgments of children. *Child Development* 48(2): 518–22.

Emmerich, W. 1968. Personality development and concepts of structure. *Child Development* 39: 671–90.

Emmerich, W. 1977. Structure and development of personal-social behaviors in economically disadvantaged preschool children. *Genetic Psychology Monographs* 95: 125–245.

Entwisle, D. R., and E. Greenberger. 1972. Adolescents' views of women's work role. *American Journal of Orthopsychiatry* 42: 648–56.

Epstein, S. 1983. The stability of confusion: A reply to Mischel and Peake. *Psychological Review* 90: 179–84.

Erikson, E. H. 1950. *Childhood and society.* New York: Norton.

Erikson, E. H. 1959. Identity and the life cycle. *Psychological Issues* 1: 50–100.

Erikson, E. H. 1963. *Childhood and society.* 2nd ed. New York: Norton.

Erikson, E. H. 1964. Inner and outer space: Reflections on womanhood. In *The woman in America,* ed. R. J. Lifton. Boston: Beacon.

Erikson, E. H. 1968. *Identity, youth and crisis.* New York: Norton.

Erlenmeyer-Kimling, L., and L. F. Jarvik. 1963. Genetics and intelligence. *Science* 142: 1477–79.

Esposito, N. J. 1975. Review of discrimination shift learning in young chidlren. *Psychological Bulletin* 82: 432–55.

Eysenck, H. J. 1976. After Burt. *New Scientist* 25: 488.

Eysenck, H. J. 1976. The heritability of intelligence (letter to the editor). *The Times,* November 8, 13.

Eysenck, H. J. 1976. The heritability of intelligence (letter to the editor). *The Times,* November 12, 15.

Eysenck, H. J. 1976. Twin approach (letter). *New Society* 38 (no. 736, November 11): 323.

Eysenck, H. J. 1977. Sir Cyril Burt. *Bulletin of the British Psychological Society* 30: 257–60.

Eysenck, H. J. 1977. The case of Sir Cyril Burt—on fraud and prejudice in a scientific controversy. *Encounter* 48, January, 19–24.

Eysenck, H. J. 1977. Sir Cyril Burt. *Bulletin of the British Psychological Society* 30: 22.

Eysenck, H. J. 1979. Genetic models, theory of personality and the unification of psychology. In *Theoretical advances in behavior genetics,* ed. J. R. Royce and L. P. Mos. Rockville, Md. Sijthoff and Noordhoff.

Eysenck, H. J. 1980. Jensen and bias: An exchange. *The New York Review of Books* 27, 52.

Eysenck, H. J., and L. Kamin. 1981. *The intelligence controversy.* New York: Wiley. (a)

Eysenck, H. J., and L. Kamin. 1981. *Intelligence: The battle for the mind.* New York: Macmillan. (b)

Falconer, D. S. 1960. *Quantitative genetics.* Edinburgh: Oliver & Boyd.

Fantz, R. L. 1958. Pattern vision in young infants. *Psychological Record* 8: 43–47.

Fantz, R. L., J. M. Ordy, and M. S. Udelf. 1962. Maturation of pattern vision in infants during the first six months. *Journal of Comparative and Physiological Psychology* 55: 907–17.

Farber, S. L. 1981. *Identical twins reared apart: A reanalysis.* New York: Basic Books.

Faust, D., and J. Arbuthnot. 1978. Relationship between moral and Piagetian reasoning and the effectiveness of moral education. *Developmental Psychology* 14: 435–36.

Featherman, D. L. 1985. Individual development and aging as a population process. In *Individual development and social change: Explanatory analysis,* ed. J. R. Nesselroade and A. von Eye. New York: Academic Press.

Feldman, M. W., and R. C. Lewontin. 1975. The heritability hang-up. *Science* 190: 1163–68.

Feldman, M. W., and R. C. Lewontin. 1976. Letters: Heritability of IQ. *Science* 194: 12–14.

Feldman, N. S., E. C. Klosson, J. E. Parsons, W. S. Rholes, and D. N. Ruble. 1976. Order of information presentation and children's moral judgments. *Child Development* 47: 556–59.

Field, T. M., Woodson, R., Greenberg, R., and Cohen, D. Discrimination and imitation of facial expression by neonates. *Science,* 218: 179–81.

Fischer, K. W. 1980. A theory of cognitive development: The control and construction of hierarchies of skills. *Psychological Review* 87: 477–531.

Fisher, H. E. 1982a. Of human bonding. *The Sciences* 22: 18–23, 31.

Fisher, H. E. 1982b. Is it sex? Helen E. Fisher replies. *The Sciences* 22: 2–3.

Flavell, J. H. 1963. *The developmental psy-*

chology of Jean Piaget. New York: Van Nostrand.

Flavell, J. H. 1970. Cognitive changes in adulthood. In *Life-span developmental psychology: Research and theory,* ed. L. R. Goulet and P. B. Baltes. New York: Academic Press.

Flavell, J. H. 1971. Stage related properties of cognitive development. *Cognitive Psychology* 2: 421–53.

Flavell, J. H. 1972. An analysis of cognitive developmental sequences. *Genetic Psychology Monographs* 86: 279–350.

Flavell, J. 1980. Structures, stages and sequences in cognitive development. Paper presented at the 1980 Minnesota Symposium on Child Psychology, October.

Flavell, J. H., and J. F. Wohlwill. 1969. Formal and functional aspects of cognitive development. In *Studies in cognitive development,* ed. D. Elkind and J. H. Flavell. New York: Oxford University Press.

Flint, B. M. 1978. *New hope for deprived children.* Toronto: Toronto University Press.

Fraiberg, S. 1977. *Every child's birthright: In defense of mothering.* New York: Basic Books.

Frankel, J. 1976. Controversial areas of research. *Science* 190: 12.

French, V. 1977. History of the child's influence: Ancient Mediterranean civilizations. In *Child effects on adults,* R. Q. Bell and L. V. Harper. Hillsdale, N.J.: Erlbaum.

Freud, A. 1969. Adolescence as a developmental disturbance. In *Adolescence,* ed. G. Caplan and S. Lebovici. New York: Basic Books.

Freud, S. 1923. *The ego and the id.* London: Hogarth Press.

Freud, S. 1949. *Outline of psychoanalysis.* New York: Norton.

Freud, S. 1954. *Collected works, standard edition.* London: Hogarth.

Friedrich, W., and J. Boriskin. 1976. The role of the child in abuse: A review of the literature. *American Journal of Orthopsychiatry* 7: 306–13.

Fromkin, V., S. Krashen, S. Curtiss, D. Rigler, and M. Rigler. 1974. The development of language in Genie: A case of linguistic isolation beyond the "critical period." *Brain and Language* 1: 81–107.

Gagné, R. M. 1968. Contributions of learning to human development. *Psychological Review* 75: 177–91.

Gallatin, J. E. 1975. *Adolescence and individuality.* New York: Harper & Row.

Garcia-Coll, C., J. Kagan, and S. J. Resnick. 1984. Behavioral inhibition in young children. *Child Development* 55: 1005–19.

Garn, S. M. (1980). Continuities and change in maturational timing. In O. G. Brim, Jr., and J. Kagan, ed., *Constancy and change in human development.* Cambridge, Mass.: Harvard University Press.

Gengerelli, J. A. 1976. Graduate school reminiscence: Hull and Koffka. *American Psychologist* 31: 685–88.

Gergen, K. J. 1973. Social psychology and history. *Journal of Personality and Social Psychology* 26: 309–20.

Gerson, R. P., and W. Damon. 1978. Moral understanding and children's conduct. *New Directions for Child Development* 2: 41–59.

Gesell, A. L. 1929. Maturation and infant behavior pattern. *Psychological Review* 36: 307–19.

Gesell, A. L. 1931. The individual in infancy. In *Handbook of child psychology,* ed. C. Murchison. Worcester, Mass.: Clark University Press.

Gesell, A. L. 1934. *An atlas of infant behavior.* New Haven: Yale University Press.

Gesell, A. L. 1946. The ontogenesis of infant behavior. In *Manual of child psychology,* ed. L. Carmichael. New York: Wiley.

Gesell, A. L. 1954. The ontogenesis of infant behavior. In *Manual of child psychology,* 2d ed., ed. L. Carmichael. New York: Wiley.

Gesell, A. L., and H. Thompson. 1941. Twins T and C from infancy to adolescence: A biogenetic study of individual differences by the method of co-twin control. *Genetic Psychology Monographs* 24: 3–121.

Gewirtz, J. L. 1961. A learning analysis of the effects of normal stimulation, privation and deprivation on the acquisition of social motivation and attachment. In *Determinants of infant behavior,* ed. B. M. Foss. New York: Wiley.

Gewirtz, J. L., and K. G. Stingle. 1968. Learning of generalized imitation as the basis for identification. *Psychological Review* 75: 374–97.

Ghiselli, E. E. 1974. Some perspectives for industrial psychology. *American Psychologist* 29: 80–87.

Gibson, E. J. 1969. *Principles of perceptual learning and development.* New York: Appleton-Century-Crofts.

Gibson, H. 1969. Early delinquency in relation to broken homes. *Journal of Abnormal Psychology* 74: 33–41.

Gillie, O. 1976. Crucial data was faked by eminent psychologist. *The Sunday Times* (London) October 24, 1–2.

Gillie, O. 1979. Burt's missing ladies. *Science* 204: 1035–37.

Gillie, O. 1980. Burt: The scandal and the cover-up. *Supplement to the Bulletin of the British Psychological Society* 33: 9–16.

Glasersfeld, E. von, and M. F. Kelley. 1982. On the concepts of period, phase, stage and level. *Human Development* 25: 152–60.

Goddard, H. H. 1912. *The Kallikak family: A study in the heredity of feeble-mindedness.* New York: Macmillan.

Goddard, H. H. 1914. *Feeble-mindedness: Its causes and consequences.* New York: Macmillan.

Goldberg, S. 1979. Premature birth: Consequences for the parent-infant relationship. *American Scientist* 67: 214–70.

Goldberger, A. S. 1979. Heritability. *Economica* 46: 327–47.

Goldberger, A. S. 1980. Review of "Cyril Burt, Psychologist." *Challenge: The Magazine of Economic Affairs* 23: 61–62.

Gollin, E. S. 1965. A developmental approach to learning and cognition. In *Advances in child development and behavior* vol. 2, ed. L. P. Lipsitt and C. C. Spiker. New York: Academic Press.

Gollin, E. S. 1981. Development and plasticity. In *Developmental plasticity: Behavioral and biological aspects of variations in development,* ed. E. S. Gollin. New York: Academic Press.

Gollin, E. S. In press. Developmental malfunctions: Issues and problems. In *Malformations of development: Biological and psychological sources and consequences,* ed. E. S. Gollin. New York: Academic Press.

Goodnow, J. J. 1962. A test of milieu differences with some of Piaget's tasks. *Psychological Monographs* 76 (36, whole no. 555).

Goodnow, J. J., and G. Bethon. 1966. Piaget's tasks: The effects of schooling and intelligence. *Child Development* 57: 573–82.

Gordon, E. M., and A. Thomas. 1967. Children's behavioral style and the teacher's appraisal of their intelligence. *Journal of School Psychology* 5: 292–300.

Gorsuch, R., and M. Barnes. 1973. Stages of ethical reasoning and moral norms of Carib youths. *Journal of Cross-Cultural Psychology* 4: 283–301.

Gottlieb, G. 1970. Conceptions of prenatal behavior. In *Development and evolution of behavior: Essays in memory of T. C. Schneirla,* ed. L. R. Aronson, E. Tobach, D. S. Lehrman, and J. S. Rosenblatt. San Francisco: Freeman.

Gottlieb, G. 1976a. Conceptions of prenatal development: Behavioral embryology. *Psychological Review* 83: 215–34.

Gottlieb, G. 1976b. The roles of experience in the development of behavior and the nervous system. In *Neural and behavioral specificity: Studies on the development of behavior and the nervous system,* vol. 3, ed. G. Gottlieb. New York: Academic Press.

Gottlieb, G. 1983. The psychobiological approach to developmental issues. In *Handbook of child psychology: Infancy and biological bases,* 4th ed., vol. 2, ed. M. M. Haith and J. J. Campos. New York: Wiley.

Gould, S. J. 1976. Grades and clades revisited. In *Evolution, brain, and behavior: Persistent problems,* ed. R. B. Masterton, W. Hodos, and H. Jerison. Hillsdale, N.J.: Erlbaum.

Gould, S. J. 1977. *Ontogeny and phylogeny.* Cambridge, Mass.: Belknap Press of Harvard University Press.

Gould, S. J. 1980a. Jensen's last stand. *New York Review of Books* 27, 38–44.

Gould, S. J. 1980b. Jensen and bias: An exchange. *New York Review of Books* 27, 52–53.

Gould, S. J. 1981. *The mismeasure of man.* New York: Norton.

Gove, W. R., and J. F. Tudor. 1973. Adult sex roles and mental illness. *American Journal of Sociology* 78: 812–35.

Greenough, W. T., and E. J. Green. 1981. Experience and the changing brain. In *Aging: Biology and behavior,* ed. J. L. McGaugh, J. G. March, and S. B. Kiesler. New York: Academic Press.

Grouse, L. D., B. K. Schrier, E. L. Bennett, M. R. Rosenzweig, and P. G. Nelson. 1978. Sequence diversity studies of rat brain RNA: Effects of environmental complexity and rat brain RNA diversity. *Journal of Neurochemistry* 30: 191–203.

Grouse, L. D., B. K. Schrier, and P. G. Nelson. 1979. Effect of visual experience on gene expression during the development of stimulus specificity in cat brain. *Experimental Neurology* 64: 354–64.

Grove, W. R., and J. F. Tudor. 1973. Adult sex roles and mental illness. *American Journal of Sociology* 78: 812–35.

Gruber, H. E. 1981. Nature versus nurture: A natural experiment. *The New York Times Book Review* March 1, 7, 8, 22–23.

Gump, P. V. 1975. Ecological psychology and children. In *Review of child development research,* ed. E. M. Hetherington. Chicago: University of Chicago Press.

Haan, N. 1974. The adolescent antecedents of an ego model of coping and defense and comparisons with Q-sorted ideal personalities. *Genetic Psychology Monographs* 89: 273–306.

Haan, N. 1977. *Coping and defending.* New York: Academic Press.

Haan, N. 1978. Two moralities in action contexts: Relationship to thought, ego regulation, and development. *Journal of Personality and Social Psychology* 36: 286–305.

Haan, N., J. Langer, and L. Kohlberg. 1976. Family patterns in moral reasoning. *Child Development* 47: 1204–6.

Haan, N., M. B. Smith, and J. Block. 1968. Moral reasoning of young adults: Political-social behavior, family background, and personality correlates. *Journal of Personality and Social Psychology* 10: 183–201.

Haeckel, E. 1868. *Natürliche Schöpfungsgeschichte.* Berlin: Georg Reimer.

Hakstian, A. R., and R. B. Cattell. 1975. An examination of adolescent sex differences in some ability and personality traits. *Canadian Journal of Behavioral Science* 7: 295–312.

Hall, C. S. 1954. *A primer of Freudian psychology.* New York: World Publishing Co.

Hall, G. S. 1904. *Adolescence: Its psychology and its relations to physiology, anthropology, sociology, sex, crime, religion, and education.* Vols. 1 and 2. New York: Appleton.

Hall, G. S. 1922. *Senescence: The last half of life.* New York: Appleton.

Hamburger, V. 1957. The concept of development in biology. In *The concept of development,* ed. D. B. Harris. Minneapolis: University of Minnesota Press.

Harley, D. 1982. Models of human evolution. *Science* 217: 296.

Harlow, H. F. 1959. Love in infant monkeys. *Scientific American* 200: 68–74.

Harlow, H. F. 1965. Total isolation: Effects on macaque monkey behavior. *Science* 148: 666.

Harré, R., and P. F. Secord. 1972. *The explanation of social behavior.* Oxford: Basil Blackwell & Mott.

Harris, D. B., ed. 1957. *The concept of development.* Minneapolis: University of Minnesota Press.

Harris, S., P. Mussen, and E. Rutherford. 1976. Some cognitive, behavioral, and personality correlates of maturity of moral judgments. *Journal of Genetic Psychology* 128: 123–35.

Hartup, W. W. 1978. Perspectives on child and family interaction: Past, present, and future. In *Child influences on marital and family interaction: A life-span perspective,* ed. R. M. Lerner and G. B. Spanier. New York: Academic Press.

Havender, W. R. 1976. Heritability of IQ. *Science* 194: 8–9.

Havighurst, R. J. 1951. *Developmental tasks and education.* New York: Longmans.

Havighurst, R. J. 1953. *Human development and education.* London: Longmans.

Havighurst, R. J. 1956. Research on the developmental task concept. *School Review* 64: 214–23.

Havighurst, R. J. 1973. Social roles, work, leisure, and education. In *The psychology of adult development and aging,* ed. C. Eisdorfer and M. P. Lawton. Washington: American Psychological Association.

Hearnshaw, L. S. 1979. *Cyril Burt, Psychologist.* New York: Cornell University Press.

Hebb, D. O. 1949. *The organization of behavior.* New York: Wiley.

Hebb, D. O. 1970. A return to Jensen and his social critics. *American Psychologist* 25: 568.

Held, R., and A. V. Hein. 1963. Movement-produced stimulation in the development of visually guided behavior. *Journal of Comparative and Physiological Psychology* 56: 872–76.

Hempel, C. G. 1966. *Philosophy of natural science.* Englewood Cliffs, N.J.: Prentice-Hall.

Herrnstein, R. J. 1971. I.Q. *Atlantic Monthly* 228: 43–64.

Herrnstein, R. J. 1977. The evolution of behaviorism. *American Psychologist* 32: 593–603.

Hess, E. H. 1973. *Imprinting.* New York: Van Nostrand Reinhold.

Hewitt, L. S. 1975. The effects of provocation, intentions, and consequences on children's moral judgments. *Child Development* 46: 540–44.

Hiatt, S. W., J. J. Campos, and R. N. Emde. 1979. Facial patterning and infant emotional expression: Happiness, surprise, and fear. *Child Development* 50: 1020–35.

Hilgard, E. R., and G. H. Bower. 1966. *Theories of learning.* 3d ed. New York: Appleton-Century-Crofts.

Hill, K., and M. Enzle. 1977. Interactive effects of training domain and age on children's moral judgments. *Canadian Journal of Behavior Science* 9: 371–81.

Hinde, R. A. 1962. Sensitive periods and the development of behavior. In *Lessons from animal behavior for the clinician,* ed. S. A. Barnett. London: National Spastics Society.

Hirsch, J. 1963. Behavior genetics and individuality understood. *Science* 142: 1436–42.

Hirsch, J. 1970. Behavior-genetic analysis and its biosocial consequences. *Seminars in Psychiatry* 2: 89–105.

Hirsch, J. 1981. To "unfrock the charlatans." *Sage Race Relations Abstracts* 6: 1–65.

Hodos, W., and C. B. G. Campbell. 1969. Scala Naturae: Why there is no theory in comparative psychology. *Psychological Review* 76: 337–50.

Hoffman, H., and A. Rattner. 1973. A reinforcement model of imprinting. *Psychological Review* 80: 527–44.

Hoffman, L. W. (1985, April) *Maternal employment and social change.* Paper presented at The Pennsylvania State University, Department of Individual and Family Studies, University Park, Pa.

Hoffman, L. W., and F. I. Nye. 1974. *Working mothers.* San Francisco: Jossey-Bass.

Hoffman, M. L. 1975. Sex differences in moral internalization and values. *Journal of Personality and Social Psychology* 32: 720–29.

Hogan, R., and R. H. Emler. 1978. Moral development. In *Social and personality development,* ed. M. E. Lamb. New York: Holt, Rinehart & Winston.

Hogan, R., J. A. Johnson, and N. P. Emler. 1978. A socioanalytic theory of moral development. *New Directions for Child Development* 2: 1–18.

Hollingworth, H. L. 1927. *Mental growth and decline: A survey of developmental psychology.* New York: Appleton.

Holstein, C. B. 1976. Irreversible, step-wise sequence in the development of moral judgment: A longitudinal study of males and females. *Child Development* 47: 57–61.

Homans, G. C. 1961. *Social behavior: Its elementary forms.* New York: Harcourt, Brace & World.

Horn, J. L. 1970. Organization of data on life-span development of human abilities. In *Life-span developmental psychology: Theory and research,* ed. L. R. Goulet and P. B. Baltes. New York: Academic Press.

Horn, J. L., and R. B. Cattell. 1966. Age differences in primary mental ability factors. *Journal of Gerontology* 21: 210–20.

Horton, D. L., and C. B. Mills. 1984. Human learning and memory. *Annual Review of Psychology* 35: 361–94.

Hubel, D. H., and T. N. Wiesel. 1970. The period of susceptibility to the physiological effects of unilateral eye closure in kittens. *Journal of Physiology* 206: 419–36.

Hull, C. L. 1929. A functional interpretation of the conditioned reflex. *Psychological Review* 36: 498–511.

Hull, C. L. 1952. *A behavior system.* New Haven: Yale University Press.

Hultsch, D. F., and T. Hickey. 1978. External validity in the study of human development: Theoretical and methodological issues. *Human Development* 21: 76–91.

Hunt, J. McV. 1961. *Intelligence and experience.* New York: Ronald Press.

Huston, T. L., and G. Levinger. 1978. Interpersonal attraction and relationships. *Annual Review of Psychology* 29: 115–56.

Huston-Stein, A., and A. Higgins-Trenk. 1978. Development of females from childhood through adulthood: Career and feminine orientations. In *Life-span development and behavior,* vol. 1, ed. P. B. Baltes. New York: Academic Press.

Immelmann, K., and S. Suomi. 1981. Sensitive phases in development. In *Behavioral development,* ed. K. Immelmann, G. Barlow, L. Petrinovich, and M. Main. New York: Cambridge University Press.

Inhelder, B., and J. Piaget, 1958. *The growth of logical thinking from childhood to adolescence.* New York: Basic Books.

Isaac, G. L. 1982. Models of human evolution. *Science* 217: 295.

Izard, C. E., R. R. Huebner, D. Risser, G. C. McGinnes, and L. M. Dougherty. 1980. The young infant's ability to produce discrete emotion expressions. *Developmental Psychology* 16: 132–40.

Jackson, S. 1965. The growth of logical thinking in normal and subnormal children. *British Journal of Educational Psychology* 35: 255–58.

Jacob, F., and J. Monod. 1961. On the regulation of gene activity. *Cold Spring Harbor Symposia on Quantitaive Biology* 26: 193–209.

Jacobson. S. W. 1979. Matching behavior in the young infant. *Child Development* 50: 425–30.

Jenkins, J. J. 1974. Remember that old theory of memory: Well forget it. *American Psychologist* 29: 785–95.

Jensen, A. R. 1969. How much can we boost

IQ and scholastic achievement? *Harvard Educational Review* 39: 1–123.

Jensen, A. R. 1970. IQ's of identical twins reared apart. *Behavior Genetics* 1: 133–48.

Jensen, A. R. 1973. *Educability and group differences.* New York: Harper & Row.

Jensen, A. R. 1974. How biased are culture-loaded tests? *Genetic Psychology Monographs* 90: 185–244.

Jensen, A. R. 1976. Did Sir Cyril Burt fake his research on heritability of intelligence? *The Times* December 9, 11.

Jensen, A. R. 1976. Letters: Heritability of IQ. *Science* 194: 6–14.

Jensen, A. R. 1980. *Bias in mental testing.* New York: Free Press.

Jerison, H. J. 1978. Smart dinosaurs and comparative psychology. Paper presented at the meeting of the American Psychological Association, August, Toronto, Canada.

Jinks, J. L., and D. W. Fulker. 1970. Comparison of the biometrical genetical, MAVA and classical approaches to the analysis of human behavior. *Psychological Bulletin* 73: 311–49.

Johanson, D. C., and M. A. Edey. 1981. *Lucy: The beginings of humankind.* New York: Simon & Schuster.

Jones, H. E. 1938. The California Adolescent Growth Study. *Journal of Educational Research* 31: 561–67.

Jones, H. E. 1939a. The Adolescent Growth Study. I. Principles and methods. *Journal of Consulting Psychology* 3: 157–59.

Jones, H. E. 1939b. The Adolescent Growth Study. II. Procedures. *Journal of Consulting Psychology* 3: 177–80.

Jones, H. E. 1958. Problems of method in longitudinal research. *Vita Humana* 1: 93–99.

Jones, H. E. 1959. Intelligence and problem solving. In *Handbook of aging and the individual,* ed. J. E. Birren. Chicago: University of Chicago Press.

Jones, J. G. and R. W. Strowig. 1968. Adolescent identity and self-perception as predictors of scholastic achievement.

Journal of Educational Research 62: 78–82.

Jones, M. C., and N. Bayley. 1950. Physical maturing among boys as related to behavior. *Journal of Educational Psychology* 41: 129–48.

Jones, W. H., M. E. O. Chernovetz, and R. O. Hansson. 1978. The enigma of androgyny: Differential implications for males and females. *Journal of Consulting and Clinical Psychology,* 46: 298–313.

Juel-Nielsen, N. 1965. Individual and environment: A psychiatric-psychological investigation of monozygotic twins reared apart. *Acta Psychiatrica et Neurologica Scandinavica,* Monograph Supplement 183.

Kacerguis, M. A., and G. R. Adams. 1980. Erikson stage resolution: The relationship between identity and intimacy. *Journal of Youth and Adolescence* 9: 117–26.

Kagan, J. 1966. Reflection-impulsivity: The generality and dynamics of conceptual tempo. *Journal of Abnormal Psychology* 71: 17–24.

Kagan, J. 1969. Inadequate evidence and illogical conclusions. *Harvard Educational Review* 39: 274–77.

Kagan, J. 1980. Perspectives on continuity. In *Constancy and change in human development,* ed. O. G. Brim, Jr., and J. Kagan. Cambridge, Mass.: Harvard University Press.

Kagan, J. 1983. Developmental categories and the premise of connectivity. In *Developmental psychology: Historical and philosophical perspectives,* ed. R. M. Lerner. Hillsdale, N.J.: Erlbaum.

Kagan, J., and H. Moss. 1962. *Birth to maturity.* New York: Wiley.

Kamin, L. J. 1974. *The science and politics of IQ.* Potomac, Md.: Erlbaum.

Kamin, L. J. 1980. Jensen's last stand. A review of Arthur Jensen *Bias in Mental Testing. Psychology Today,* February, 117–118, 120, 123.

Kaplan, B. 1966. The comparative-developmental approach and its application to symbolization and language in psychopathology. In *American handbook of psychiatry,* vol. 3, ed. T. Arieti. New York: Basic Books.

Kaplan, B. 1983. A trio of trials. In *Developmental psychology: Historical and philosophical perspectives,* ed. R. M. Lerner. Hillsdale, N.J.: Erlbaum.

Karniol, R. 1978. Children's use of intention cues in evaluating behavior. *Psychological Bulletin,* 85: 76–85.

Kaufmann, H. 1968. *Introduction to the study of human behavior.* Philadelphia: Saunders.

Keasey, C. B. 1974. The influence of opinion agreement and quality of supportive reasoning in the evaluation of moral judgments. *Journal of Personality and Social Psychology* 30: 477–82.

Kellogg, W. N., and L. A. Kellogg. 1933. *The ape and the child.* New York: McGraw-Hill.

Kendall, P. C., R. M. Lerner and W. E. Craighead. 1984. Human development intervention in childhood psychopathology. *Child Development,* 55: 71–82.

Kendler, H. H., and T. S. Kendler. 1962. Vertical and horizontal processes in human concept learning. *Psychological Review* 69: 1–16.

Kessen, W. 1962. "Stage" and "structure" in the study of children. In *Thought in the young child,* ed. W. Kessen and C. Kuhlman. *Monographs of the Society for Research in Child Development* 27: 65–82.

Kimble, G. A. 1961. *Hilgard and Marguis' conditioning and learning.* New York: Appleton-Century-Crofts.

Klaus, M., and J. Kennell. 1976. *Maternal-infant bonding.* St. Louis: C. V. Mosby.

Kluckhohn, C., and H. Murray. 1948. Personality formation: The determinants. In *Personality in nature, society, and culture,* ed. C. Kluckhohn and H. Murray. New York: Knopf.

Kohlberg, L. 1958. The development of modes of moral thinking and choice in the years ten to sixteen. Unpublished doctoral dissertation, University of Chicago.

Kohlberg, L. 1963a. The development of children's orientations toward a moral order: I. Sequence in the development of moral thought. *Vita Humana* 6: 11–33.

Kohlberg, L. 1963b. Moral development and identification. In *Child psychology. 62nd Yearbook of the National Society for the Study of Education,* ed. H. Stevenson. Chicago: University of Chicago Press.

Kohlberg, L. 1968. Early education: A cognitive-developmental view. *Child Development* 39: 1014–62.

Kohlberg, L. 1971. From is to ought: How to commit the naturalistic fallacy and get away with it in the study of moral development. In *Cognitive development and epistemology,* ed. T. Mischel. New York: Academic Press.

Kohlberg, L. 1973. Continuities in childhood and adult moral development revisited. In *Life-span developmental psychology: Personality and socialization,* ed. P. B. Baltes and K. W. Schaie. New York: Academic Press.

Kohlberg, L. 1976. Moral stages and moralization: The cognitive-developmental approach. In *Moral development and behavior: Theory, research, and social issues,* ed. T. Lickona. New York: Holt, Rinehart & Winston.

Kohlberg, L. 1978. Revisions in the theory and practice of moral development. *New Directions for Child Development* 2: 83–88.

Kohlberg, L., and R. B. Kramer. 1969. Continuities and discontinuities in childhood and adult moral development. *Human Development* 12: 93–120.

Korn, S. J. 1978. Temperament, vulnerability, and behavior. Paper presented at the Louisville Temperament Conference, September. Louisville, Kentucky.

Krashen, S. D. 1975. The critical period for language and its possible bases. *Annals of the New York Academy of Sciences* 263: 211–24.

Kreps, J. M., ed. 1976. *Women and the American economy: A look to the 1980's.* Englewood Cliffs, N.J.: Prentice-Hall.

Kuhn, T. S. 1962. *The structure of scientific revolutions.* Chicago: University of Chicago Press.

Kuhn, T. S. 1970. *The structure of scientific revolutions.* 2d ed. Chicago: University of Chicago Press.

Kuhn, D. 1976. Short-term longitudinal evidence for the sequentiality of Kohlberg's early stages of moral development. *Developmental Psychology* 12: 162–66.

Kuhn, D., and J. Angelev. 1976. An experimental study of the development of formal operational thought. *Child Development* 47: 697–706.

Kuo, Z. Y. 1967. *The dynamics of behavior development.* New York: Random House.

Kurtines, W., and Greif, E. B. 1974. The development of moral thought: Review and evaluation of Kohlberg's approach. *Psychological Bulletin,* 81: 453–69.

Landsbaum, J. B., and R. H. Willis. 1971. Conformity in early and late adolescence. *Developmental Psychology* 4: 334–37.

Landsell, H. 1969. Verbal and nonverbal factors in right-hemisphere speech: Relation to early neurological history. *Journal of Comparative and Physiological Psychology* 69: 734–38.

Langer, J. 1969. *Theories of development.* New York: Holt, Rinehart & Winston.

Langer, J. 1970. Werner's comparative organismic theory. In *Carmichael's manual of child psychology,* vol. 1, ed. P. H. Mussen. New York: Wiley.

Langford, P. E., and S. George. 1975. Intellectual and moral development in adolescence. *British Journal of Educational Psychology,* 45: 330–32.

Langlois, J. H., and A. C. Downs. 1979. Peer relations as a function of physical attractiveness: The eye of the beholder or behavioral reality? *Child Development* 50: 409–18.

Langlois, J. H., and C. W. Stephan. 1981. Beauty and the beast: The role of physical attraction in peer relationships and social behavior. In *Developmental social psychology: Theory and research,* ed. S. S. Brehm, S. M. Kassin, and S. X. Gibbons. New York: Oxford University Press.

Lathey, J. W. 1970. Training effects and conservation of volume. *Child Study Center Bulletin.* Buffalo, N.Y.: State University College.

LaVoie, J. C. 1976. Ego identity formation in middle adolescence. *Journal of Youth and Adolescence* 5: 371–85.

Layzer, D. 1974. Heritability analyses of IQ scores: Science or numerology? *Science* 183: 1259–66.

Lazorowitz, R., W. G. Stephen, and S. J. Friedman. 1976. Effects of moral justifications and moral reasoning on altruism. *Developmental Psychology* 12: 353–54.

Lehrman, D. S. 1953. A critique of Konrad Lorenz's theory of instinctive behavior. *Quarterly Review of Biology* 28: 337–63.

Lehrman, D. S. 1970. Semantic and conceptual issues in the nature-nurture problem. In *Development and evolution of behavior: Essays in memory of T. C. Schneirla,* ed. L. R. Aronson, E. Tobach, D. S. Lehrman, and J. S. Rosenblatt. San Francisco: Freeman.

Lenneberg, E., I. Nichols, and E. Rosenberger. 1964. Primitive stages of language development in Mongolism. In *Disorders of communication* (vol. 42): *Research publications.* Baltimore, Md.: Williams & Wilkins.

Lenneberg, E. 1967. *The biological basis of language.* New York: Academic Press.

Lenneberg, E. 1969. On explaining language. *Science, 165,* 635–43.

Lerner, J. V., and R. M. Lerner. 1983. Temperament and adaptation across life: Theoretical and empirical issues. In *Life-span development and behavior,* vol. 5, ed. P. B. Baltes & O. G. Brim, Jr. New York: Academic Press.

Lerner, R. M. 1969a. The development of stereotyped expectancies of body build-behavior relations. *Child Development* 40: 137–41.

Lerner, R. M. 1969b. Some female stereotypes of male body build–behavior relations. *Perceptual and Motor Skills* 28: 363–66.

Lerner, R. M. 1972. "Richness" analyses of body build stereotype development. *Developmental Psychology* 7: 219.

Lerner, R. M. 1973. The development of personal space schemata toward body build. *Journal of Psychology* 84: 229–35.

Lerner, R. 1976. *Concepts and theories of human development*. Reading, Mass.: Addison-Wesley.

Lerner, R. M. 1978. Nature, nurture, and dynamic interactionism. *Human Development* 21: 1–20.

Lerner, R. M. 1979. A dynamic interactional concept of individual and social relationship development. In *Social exchange in developing relationships,* ed. R. L. Burgess and T. L. Huston. New York: Academic Press.

Lerner, R. M. 1980. Concepts of epigenesis: Descriptive and explanatory issues. A critique of Kitchener's comments. *Human Development* 23: 63–72.

Lerner, R. M. 1981. Adolescent development: Scientific study in the 1980s. *Youth and Society* 12: 251–75.

Lerner, R. M. 1982. Children and adolescents as producers of their own development. *Developmental Review* 2: 342–70.

Lerner, R. M. 1984. *On the nature of human plasticity*. New York: Cambridge University Press.

Lerner, R. M. 1985. Individual and context in developmental psychology: Conceptual and theoretical issues. In *Individual development and social change: Explanatory analysis,* ed. J. R. Nesselroade and A. von Eye. New York: Academic Press.

Lerner, R. M., P. Benson, and S. Vincent. 1976. Development of societal and personal vocational role perception in males and females. *Journal of Genetic Psychology* 129: 167–68.

Lerner, R. M., and B. Brackney. 1978. The importance of inner and outer body parts attitudes in the self-concept of late adolescents. *Sex Roles* 4: 225–38.

Lerner, R. M. and N. A. Busch-Rossnagel, eds. 1981. *Individuals as producers of their development: A life-span perspective.* New York: Academic Press.

Lerner, R. M., and N. A. Busch-Rossnagel. 1981. Individuals as producers of their development: Conceptual and empirical bases. In *Individuals as producers of their development: A life-span perspective,* ed. R. M. Lerner and N. A. Busch-Rossnagel. New York: Academic Press.

Lerner, R. M. and E. Gellert. 1969. Body build identification, preference, and aversion in children. *Developmental Psychology* 1: 456–62.

Lerner, R. M., D. F. Hultsch, and R. A. Dixon. 1983. Contextualism and the character of developmental psychology in the 1970s. *Annals of the New York Academy of Sciences* 412: 101–28.

Lerner, R. M., S. Iwawaki, and T. Chihara. 1976. Development of personal space schemata among Japanese children. *Developmental Psychology* 12: 466–67.

Lerner, R. M., S. Iwawaki, T. Chihara, and G. T. Sorell. 1980. Self-concept, self-esteem, and body attitudes among Japanese male and female adolescents. *Child Development* 51: 847–55.

Lerner, R. M., and S. A. Karabenick. 1974. Physical attractiveness, body attitudes, and self-concept in late adolescents. *Journal of Youth and Adolescence* 3: 307–16.

Lerner, R. M., S. A. Karabenick, and M. Meisels. 1975a. Effects of age and sex on the development of personal space schemata towards body build. *Journal of Genetic Psychology* 127: 91–101.

Lerner, R. M., S. A. Karabenick, and M. Meisels. 1975b. One-year stability of children's personal space schemata towards body build. *Journal of Genetic Psychology* 127: 151–52.

Lerner R. M., S. A. Karabenick and J. L. Stuart. 1973. Relations among physical attractiveness, body attitudes, and self-concept in male and female college students. *Journal of Psychology* 85: 119–29.

Lerner R. M., M. Karson, M. Meisels, and J. R. Knapp. 1975. Actual and perceived attitudes of late adolescents and their parents: The phenomenon of the generation gaps. *Journal of Genetic Psychology* 126: 195–207.

Lerner R. M., and M. B. Kauffman. In press. The concept of development in contextualism. *Developmental Review*.

Lerner R. M., and J. R. Knapp. 1975. Actual and perceived intrafamilial attitudes of late adolescents and their parents. *Journal of Youth and Adolescence* 4: 17–36.

Lerner R. M., and J. R. Knapp. 1976. Structure of racial attitudes in white middle adolescents. *Journal of Youth and Adolescence* 5: 283–300.

Lerner, R. M., J. R. Knapp, and K. B. Pool. 1974. The structure of body build stereotypes: A methodological analysis. *Perceptual and Motor Skills* 39: 19–29.

Lerner R. M., and S. J. Korn, 1972. The development of body build stereotypes in males. *Child Development* 43: 912–20.

Lerner R. M., and J. V. Lerner. 1977. The effects of age, sex, and physical attractiveness on child-peer relations, academic performance, and elementary school adjustment. *Developmental Psychology* 13: 585–90.

Lerner R. M., J. B. Orlos, and J. R. Knapp. 1976. Physical attractiveness, physical effectiveness, and self-concept in late adolescents. *Adolescence* 11: 313–26.

Lerner R. M., and C. D. Ryff. 1978. Implementation of the life-span view of human development: The sample case of attachment. In *Life-span development and behavior,* vol. 1, ed. P. B. Baltes. New York: Academic Press.

Lerner R. M., and C. Schroeder. 1971a. Kindergarten children's active vocabulary about body build. *Developmental Psychology* 5: 179.

Lerner R. M., and C. Schroeder. 1971b. Physique identification, preference, and aversion in kindergarten children. *Developmental Psychology* 5: 538.

Lerner R. M., E. A. Skinner, and G. T. Sorell. 1980. Methodological implications of contextual/dialectic theories of development. *Human Development* 23: 225–35.

Lerner R. M., G. T. Sorell, and B. E. Brackney. 1981. Sex differences in self-concept and self-esteem in late adolescents: A time-lag analysis. *Sex Roles* 7: 709–22.

Lerner R. M., and G. B. Spanier. 1978. A dynamic interactional view of child and family development. In *Child influences on marital and family interaction: A life-span perspective,* ed. R. M. Lerner and G. B. Spanier. New York: Academic Press.

Lerner R. M., and G. B. Spanier. 1980. *Adolescent development: A life-span perspective.* New York: McGraw-Hill.

Lerner R. M., S. Vincent, and P. Benson. 1976. One-year stability of societal and personal vocational role perceptions of females. *Journal of Genetic Psychology* 129: 173–74.

Levinson, D. J., C. N. Darrow, E. B. Klein, M. H. Levinson, and B. McKee. 1978. *Seasons of a man's life.* New York: Knopf.

Lewis, M., and L. A. Rosenblum, eds. 1974. *The effect of the infant on its caregiver.* New York: Wiley.

Lewontin, R. C. 1970. Race and intelligence. *Bulletin of the Atomic Scientists,* March, 2–8.

Lewontin, R. C. 1973. The apportionment of human diversity. *Evolutionary Biology* 6: 381–98.

Lewontin, R. C. 1976. The fallacy of biological determinism. *The Sciences* 16: 6–10.

Lewontin, R. C. 1981. On constraints and adaptation. *The Behavioral and Brain Sciences* 4: 244–45.

Lewontin, R. C., and R. Levins. 1978. Evolution. *Encyclopedia Einaudi,* vol. 5, Turin: Einaudi.

Liben, L. S., ed. 1983. *Piaget and the foundations of knowledge.* Hillsdale, N.J.: Erlbaum.

Liebert, R. M., and R. Wicks-Nelson. 1981. *Developmental psychology.* 3d ed. Englewood Cliffs, N.J.: Prentice-Hall.

Livson, N., and H. Peskin. 1967. Prediction of adult psychological health in a longitudinal study. *Journal of Abnormal Psychology* 72: 509–18.

Livson, N., and H. Peskin. 1980. Perspectives on adolescence from longitudinal research. In J. Adelson (ed.), *Handbook of adolescent psychology.* New York: Wiley.

Loehlin, J. C., G. Lindzey, and J. N. Spuhler. 1975. *Race differences in intelligence.* San Francisco: Freeman.

Loevinger, J. 1966. The meaning and measurement of ego development. *American Psychologist* 21: 195–206.

Loevinger, J. 1976. *Ego development.* San Francisco: Jossey-Bass.

Loevinger, J., and R. Wessler. 1970. *Measuring ego development,* vol. 1. San Francisco: Jossey-Bass.

Long, B. H., E. H. Henderson, and L. Platt. 1973. Self-other orientations of Israeli adolescents reared in kibbutzim and moshavim. *Developmental Psychology* 8: 300–308.

Looft, W. R. 1971. Egocentrism and social interaction in adolescence. *Adolescence* 6: 487–94.

Looft, W. R. 1972. The evolution of developmental psychology. *Human Development* 15: 187–201.

Looft, W. R. 1973. Socialization and personality throughout the life-span: An examination of contemporary psychological approaches. In *Life-span developmental psychology: Personality and socialization,* ed. P. B. Baltes and K. W. Schaie. New York: Academic Press.

Lorenz, K. 1937. The companion in the bird's world. *Auk* 54: 245–73.

Lorenz, K. 1940. Durch Domestikation verursachte Störungen arteigenen Verhaltens. *Zeitschrift für angewandte Psychologie und Charakterkunde* 59: 2–81.

Lorenz, K. 1965. *Evolution and modification of behavior.* Chicago: University of Chicago Press.

Lorenz, K. 1966. *On aggression.* New York: Harcourt, Brace & World.

Lovell, K. 1961. A follow-up study of Inhelder and Piaget's "The growth of logical thinking." *British Journal of Psychology* 52: 143–53.

Lovejoy, C. O. 1981. The origin of man. *Science* 211: 341–50.

Lowenthal, M. F., M. Thurnher, and D. Chiriboga. 1975. *Four stages of life: A comparative study of women and men facing transitions.* San Francisco: Jossey-Bass.

Lykken, D. T. 1982. Research with twins: The concept of emergenesis. *Psychophysiology* 19: 361–73.

Maccoby, E. E., and C. N. Jacklin. 1974. *The psychology of sex differences.* Stanford, Calif.: Stanford University Press.

Mac Donald, K. 1985. Early experience, relative plasticity, and social development. *Developmental Review* 5:99–121.

MacDonald, N. E., and I. W. Silverman. 1978. Smiling and laughter in infants as a function of level of arousal and cognitive evaluation. *Developmental Psychology* 14: 235–41.

Macfarlane, J. W. 1938a. Some findings from a ten-year guidance research program. *Progressive Education* 7: 529–35.

Macfarlane, J. W. 1938b. Studies in child guidance. I. Methodology of data collection and organization. *Monographs of the Society for Research in Child Development* 3 (6, whole no. 19).

Magnusson, D., and V. L. Allen, eds. 1983. *Human development: An interactional perspective.* New York: Academic Press.

Marcia, J. E. 1964. Determination and construct validity of ego identity status. Ph.D. diss., Ohio State University.

Marcia, J. E. 1966. Development and validations of ego-identity states. *Journal of Personality and Social Psychology* 5: 551–58.

Marcia, J. E. 1967. Ego identity status: Relationship to change in self-esteem, "general maladjustment," and authoritarianism. *Journal of Personality* 1: 118–33.

Marcia, J. E. 1976. Identity six years after: A follow-up study. *Journal of Youth and Adolescence* 5: 145–60.

Marcia, J. E., and M. L. Friedman. 1970. Ego identity status in college women. *Journal of Personality* 38: 249–63.

Martin, J., and C. Redmore. 1978. A longitudinal study of ego development. *Developmental Psychology* 14: 189–90.

Martorano, S. C. 1977. A developmental analysis of performance on Piaget's formal operations tasks. *Developmental Psychology* 13: 666–72.

Mason, W. A., and M. Kenney. 1974. Redirection of filial attachments in rhesus monkeys: Dogs as surrogate mothers. *Science* 183: 1209–11.

Masters, R. D. 1978. Jean-Jacques is alive and well: Rousseau and contemporary sociobiology. *Daedalus* 107: 93–105.

Matteson, R. 1974. Adolescent self-esteem, family communication, and marital satisfaction. *Journal of Psychology* 86: 35–47.

Matteson, D. R. 1977. Exploration and commitment: Sex differences and methodological problems in the use of identity status categories. *Journal of Youth and Adolescence* 6: 353–74.

McCall, R. B. 1981. Nature-nurture and the two realms of development: A proposed integration with respect to mental development. *Child Development* 52: 1–12.

McCall, R. B., R. D. Parke, and R. Kavanaugh. 1977. Imitation of live and televised models by children one to three years of age. *Monographs of the Society for Research in Child Development* 42 (no. 173).

McCandless, B. R. 1967. *Children.* New York: Holt, Rinehart & Winston.

McCandless, B. R. 1970. *Adolescents.* Hinsdale, Ill.: Dryden Press.

McClearn, G. E. 1970. Genetic influences on behavior and development. In *Carmichael's manual of child psychology,* vol. 1, ed. P. Mussen. New York: Wiley.

McClearn, G. E. 1981. Evolution and genetic variability. In *Developmental plasticity: Behavioral and biological aspects of variations in development,* ed. E. S. Gollin. New York: Academic Press.

McGeorge, C. 1974. Situational variation in level of moral judgment. *British Journal of Educational Psychology* 44: 116–22.

McHale, S. M., and R. M. Lerner. 1985. Stages of development. In *International encyclopedia of education: Research and studies,* ed. T. Husen & T. N. Postlethwaite. Oxford, England: Pergamon Press.

McKay, H., L. Sinisterra, A. McKay, H. Gomez, and P. Lloreda. 1978. Improving cognitive ability in chronically deprived children. *Science* 200: 270–78.

McKusick, V. A. 1981. The anatomy of the human genome. *Hospital Practice,* 16: 82–100.

McLaughlin, B. 1977. Second language learning in children. *Psychological Bulletin* 84: 438–59.

McNeill, D. 1966. Developmental psycholinguistics. In F. Smith and G. A. Miller, eds. *The genesis of language: A psycholinguistic approach.* Cambridge: MIT Press.

Mednick, M. S., and S. S. Tangri. 1972. New social psychological perspectives on women. *Social Issues* 28: 1–16.

Meltzoff, A. N., and M. K. Moore. 1977. Imitation of facial and manual gestures by human neonates. *Science* 198: 75–78.

Miller, D. R., and G. E. Swanson. 1958. *The changing American parent.* New York: Wiley.

Miller, N. E., and J. Dollard. 1941. *Social learning and imitation.* New Haven: Yale University Press.

Mischel, W. 1973. Toward a cognitive social learning reconceptualization of personality. *Psychological Review* 80: 252–83.

Mischel, W. 1977. On the future of personality measurement. *American Psychologist* 32: 246–54.

Mischel, W. 1983. Alternatives in the pursuit

of the predictability and consistency of persons: Stable data that yield unstable interpretations. *Journal of Personality* 51: 578–604.

Mischel, W., and H. N. Mischel. 1976. A cognitive social-learning approach to morality and self-regulation. In *Moral development and behavior,* ed. T. Lickona. New York: Holt, Rinehart & Winston.

Mischel, W., and P. K. Peake. 1982. Beyond déjà vu in the search for cross-situational consistency. *Psychological Review* 89: 730–55.

Mischel, W., and P. K. Peake. 1983. Some facets of consistency: Replies to Epstein, Funder, and Bem. *Psychological Review* 90: 394–402.

Misiak, H., and V. S. Sexton. 1966. *History of psychology in overview.* New York: Grune & Stratton.

Misiak, H., and V. M. Staudt. 1954. *Catholics in psychology: A historical survey.* New York: McGraw-Hill.

Mitchell, D. E. 1978. *Recovery of vision in monocularly and binocularly deprived kittens.* Paper presented at the Eleventh Symposium of the Center for Visual Science, June, N.Y.: Rochester.

Mitchell, D. E., M. Cynader, and J. A. Movshon. 1977. Recovery from the effects of monocular deprivation in kittens. *Journal of Comparative Neurology* 176: 53–64.

Moir, D. J. 1974. Egocentrism and the emergence of conventional morality in adolescent girls. *Child Development* 45: 299–304.

Moltz, H. 1973. Some implications of the critical period hypothesis. *Annals of the New York Academy of Sciences* 223: 144–46.

Moltz, H., and L. J. Stettner. 1961. The influence of patterned-light deprivation on the critical period for imprinting. *Journal of Comparative and Physiological Psychology* 54: 279–83.

Money, J., and A. E. Ehrhardt. 1972. *Man and woman, boy and girl.* Baltimore: Johns Hopkins University Press.

Montemayor, R., and M. Eisen. 1977. The development of self-conceptions from childhood to adolescence. *Developmental Psychology* 13: 314–19.

Moran, P. A. P. 1973. A note on heritability and the correlation between relatives. *Annals of Human Genetics* 37: 217.

Morris, E. K., D. E. Hursh, A. S. Winston, D. M. Gelfand, D. P. Hartmann, H. W. Reese, and D. M. Baer. 1982. Behavior analysis and developmental psychology. *Human Development* 25: 340–64.

Morton, N. E. 1976. Heritability of IQ. *Science* 194: 9–10.

Moshman, D. 1977. Consolidation and stage formation in the emergence of formal operations. *Developmental Psychology* 13: 95–100.

Murchison, C., ed. 1931. *Handbook of child psychology.* Worcester, Mass.: Clark University Press.

Murray, H. A., et al. 1938. *Explorations in personality.* New York: Oxford.

Murray, H. A. 1959. Preparations for the scaffold of a comprehensive system. In *Psychology: A study of a science,* vol. 3, ed. S. Koch. New York: McGraw-Hill.

Mussen, P. H., ed. 1970. *Carmichael's manual of child psychology,* 3d ed. New York: Wiley.

Mussen, P. H., S. Harris, E. Rutherford, and C. B. Keasey. 1970. Honesty and altruism among preadolescents. *Developmental Psychology* 3: 169–94.

Mussen, P. H., and M. C. Jones. 1957. Self-conceptions, motivations, and interpersonal attitudes of late- and early-maturing boys. *Child Development* 28: 249–56.

Muuss, R. E. 1975a. The philosophical and historical roots of theories of adolescence. In *Adolescent behavior and society: A book of readings,* 2d ed., ed. R. E. Muuss. New York: Random House.

Muuss, R. E., ed. 1975b. *Adolescent behavior and society: A book of readings,* 2d ed. New York: Random House.

Muuss, R. E. 1975c. *Theories of adolescence,* 3d ed. New York: Random House.

Nagel, E. 1957. Determinism in development. In *The concept of development,* ed. D. B. Harris. Minneapolis: University of Minnesota Press.

Nash, J. 1978. *Developmental psychology: A psychobiological approach.* Englewood Cliffs, N.J.: Prentice-Hall.

Neimark, E. D. 1975. Intellectual development during adolescence. In *Review of child development research,* vol. 4, ed. F. D. Horowitz. Chicago: University of Chicago Press.

Neimark, E. D. 1978. Improper questions cannot be properly answered. *The Behavioral and Brain Sciences* 2: 195–96.

Neimark, E. D. 1979. Current status of formal operations research. *Human Development* 22: 60–67.

Nelson, D. D. 1971. A study of personality adjustment among adolescent children with working and non-working mothers. *Journal of Educational Research* 64: 328–30.

Nesselroade, J. R. 1983. Implications of the trait-state distinction for the study of aging: Still labile after all these years. Presidential address to Division 20, Ninety-first Annual Convention of the American Psychological Association, August, Anaheim, California.

Nesselroade, J. R., and D. H. Ford. In press. P-technique comes of age: Multivariate, replicated, single-subject designs for research on older adults. *Research on Aging.*

Nesselroade, J. R., and P. B. Baltes. 1974. Adolescent personality development and historical changes: 1970–72. *Monographs of the Society for Research in Child Development* 39 (154).

Nesselroade, J. R., and P. B. Baltes, eds. 1979. *Longitudinal research in the study of behavior and development.* New York: Academic Press.

Nesselroade, J. R., K. W. Schaie, and P. B. Baltes. 1972. Ontogenetic and generational components of structural and quantitative change in adult cognitive behavior. *Journal of Gerontology* 27: 222–28.

Neugarten, B. L., and N. Datan, 1973. Sociological perspectives on the life cycle. In *Life-span developmental psychology: Personality and socialization,* ed. P. B. Baltes and K. W. Schaie. New York: Academic Press.

Newman, H. H., F. N. Freeman, and K. J. Holzinger. 1937. *Twins: A study of heredity and environment.* Chicago: University of Chicago Press.

Novak, M. A., and H. F. Harlow. 1975. Social recovery of monkeys isolated for the first year of life: I. Rehabilitation and therapy. *Developmental Psychology* 11: 453–65.

Novikoff, A. B. 1945a. The concept of integrative levels and biology. *Science* 101: 209–15.

Novikoff, A. B. 1945b. Continuity and discontinuity in evolution. *Science* 101: 405–6.

Nye, F. I. 1974. Effects on mother. In *Working mothers,* ed. L. W. Hoffman and F. I. Nye. San Francisco: Jossey-Bass.

O'Donnell, W. J. 1976. Adolescent self-esteem related to feelings toward parents and friends. *Journal of Youth and Adolescence* 5: 179–85.

Offer, D. 1969. *The psychological world of the teen-ager.* New York: Basic Books.

Offer, D., and K. I. Howard. 1972. An empirical analysis of the Offer self-image questionnaire for adolescents. *Archives of General Psychiatry* 27: 529–33.

Offer, D., E. Ostrov, and K. I. Howard. 1977. The self-image of adolescence: A study of four cultures. *Journal of Youth and Adolescence* 6: 265–80.

O'Leary, V. E. 1974. Some attitudinal barriers to occupational aspirations in women. *Psychological Bulletin* 81: 809–26.

O'Leary, V. E. 1977. *Toward understanding women.* Belmont, Calif.: Brooks/Cole.

Olson, D. R. 1978. A structuralist view of explanation: A critique of Brainerd. *The Behavioral and Brain Sciences,* 2: 197–199.

Orlofsky, J. L., J. E. Marcia, and I. M.

Lesser. 1973. Ego identity status and the intimacy versus isolation crisis of young adulthood. *Journal of Personality and Social Psychology* 27: 211–19.

Overton, W. F. 1973. On the assumptive base of the nature-nurture controversy: Additive versus interactive conceptions. *Human Development* 16: 74–89.

Overton, W. F. 1976. The active organism in structuralism. *Human Development* 19: 71–86.

Overton, W. F. 1978. Klaus Riegel: Theoretical contribution to concepts of stability and change. *Human Development* 21: 360–63.

Overton, W. F. 1984. World views and their influence on psychological theory and research: Kuhn—Lakatos—Lauden. In *Advances in child development and behavior,* vol. 18, ed. H. W. Reese. New York: Academic Press.

Overton, W. F., and H. W. Reese. 1973. Models of development: Methodological implications. In *Life-span developmental psychology: Methodological issues,* ed. J. R. Nesselroade and H. W. Reese. New York: Academic Press.

Overton, W., and H. Reese. 1981. Conceptual prerequisites for an understanding of stability-change and continuity-discontinuity. *International Journal of Behavioral Development* 4: 99–123.

Padin, M. A., R. M. Lerner, and A. Spiro III. 1981. The role of physical education interventions in the stability of body attitudes and self-esteem in late adolescents. *Adolescence* 16: 371–84.

Papalia, D. E. 1972. The status of several conservation abilities across the life span. *Human Development* 15: 229–43.

Parke, R. D. 1978. Parent-infant interaction: Progress, paradigms and problems. In *Observing behavior. Vol. 1: Theory and applications in mental retardation,* ed. G. P. Sackett. Baltimore: University Park Press.

Peluffo, N. 1962. The notions of conservation and causality in children of different physical and sociocultural environ-ments. *Archives de Psychologie* 38: 275–91.

Peluffo, N. 1967. Culture and cognitive problems. *International Journal of Psychology,* 2: 187–98.

Penfield, W., and L. Roberts. 1959. *Speech and brain mechanisms.* Princeton: Princeton University Press.

Pepper, S. C. 1942. *World hypotheses: A study in evidence.* Berkeley: University of California Press.

Pervin, L. A. 1968. Performance and satisfaction as a function of individual-environment fit. *Psychological Bulletin* 69: 56–68.

Peterson, L., D. P. Hartmann, and D. M. Gelfand. 1977. Developmental changes in the effects of dependency and reciprocity cues on children's moral judgments and donation rates. *Child Development* 48: 1331–39.

Petrinovich, L. 1979. Probabilistic functionalism: A conception of research method. *American Psychologist* 34: 373–90.

Piaget, J. 1923. La pensée l'enfant. *Archives of Psychology,* Geneva, 18: 273–304.

Piaget, J. 1950. *The psychology of intelligence.* London: Routledge & Kegan Paul.

Piaget, J. 1952. *The origins of intelligence in children.* New York: International Universities Press.

Piaget, J. 1954. *The construction of reality in the child,* trans. M. Cook. New York: Basic Books.

Piaget, J. 1955. Les stades du développement intellectuel de l'enfant et de l'adolescent. In *Le problème des stades en psychologie de l'enfant,* ed. P. Osterrieth et al. Paris: Presses Universitaires de France.

Piaget, J. 1961. *Les mécanismes perceptifs.* Paris: Presses Universitaires de France.

Piaget, J. 1965. *The moral judgment of the child.* New York: The Free Press.

Piaget, J. 1968. *Six psychological studies.* New York: Random House.

Piaget, J. 1969. The intellectual development of the adolescent. In G. Caplan and S. Lebovici (Eds.), *Adolescence:*

Psychosocial perspectives. New York: Basic Books.

Piaget, J. 1970. Piaget's theory. In *Carmichael's manual of child psychology,* vol. 1, ed. P. H. Mussen. New York: Wiley.

Piaget, J. 1972. Intellectual evolution from adolescence to adulthood. *Human Development* 15: 1–12.

Piaget, J., and B. Inhelder. 1956. *The child's conception of space.* London: Routledge & Kegan Paul.

Piaget, J., and B. Inhelder. 1969. *The psychology of the child.* New York: Basic Books.

Pinard, A., and M. Laurendeau. 1969. 'Stage' in Piaget's cognitive-developmental theory: Exegesis of a concept. In *Studies in cognitive development: Essays in honor of Jean Piaget,* ed. D. Elkind and J. Flavell. New York: Oxford University Press.

Plomin, R., and J. C. DeFries. 1976. Heritability of IQ. *Science* 194: 9–12.

Plomin, R., and J. C. DeFries. 1980. Genetics and intelligence: Recent data. *Intelligence* 4: 15–24.

Podd, M. H. 1972. Ego identity status and morality: The relationship between two developmental constructs. *Developmental Psychology* 6: 497–507.

Pressey, S. L., J. E. Janney, and R. G. Kuhlen. 1939. *Life: A psychological survey.* New York: Harper.

Prigogine, I. 1978. Time, structure, and fluctuation. *Science* 201: 777–85.

Prigogine, I. 1980. *From being to becoming.* San Francisco: W. H. Freeman.

Pullis, M., and J. Caldwell. 1982. The influence of children's temperament characteristics on teachers' decision strategies. *American Educational Research Journal* 19: 165–81.

Ratner, A. M., and H. S. Hoffman. 1974. Evidence for a critical period for imprinting in khaki campbell ducklings (*anas platyrhynchos domesticus*). *Animal Behavior* 22: 249–55.

Reese, H. W. 1976. Conceptions of the Active Organism (introduction). *Human Development* 19: 69–70.

Reese, H. W. 1982. Behavior analysis and developmental psychology: Discussant comments. *Human Development* 35: 352–57.

Reese, H. W., and L. P. Lipsitt, eds. 1970. *Experimental child psychology.* New York: Academic Press.

Reese, H. W., and W. F. Overton. 1970. Models of development and theories of development. In *Life-span developmental psychology: Research and theory,* ed. L. R. Goulet and P. B. Baltes. New York: Academic Press.

Rest, J. R. 1975. Longitudinal study of the defining issues test of moral judgment: A strategy for analyzing developmental change. *Developmental Psychology* 11: 738–43.

Rest, J. R., D. Cooper, R. Coder, J. Masanz, and D. Anderson. 1974. Judging the important issues in moral dilemmas—an objective measure of development. *Developmental Psychology* 10: 491–501.

Riegel, K. F. 1973. Dialectical operations: The final period of cognitive development. *Human Development* 16: 346–70.

Riegel, K. F. 1975. Toward a dialectical theory of development. *Human Development* 18: 50–64.

Riegel, K. F. 1967a. The dialectics of human development. *American Psychologist* 31: 689–700.

Riegel, K. F. 1967b. From traits and equilibrium toward developmental dialectics. In *Nebraska symposium on motivation,* ed. W. Arnold. Lincoln: University of Nebraska Press.

Riegel, K. F. 1977a. The dialectics of time. In *Life-span developmental psychology: Dialectical perspectives on experimental research,* ed. N. Datan and H. W. Reese. New York: Academic Press.

Riegel, K. F. 1977b. History of psychological gerontology. In *Handbook of the psychology of aging,* ed. J. E. Birren and K. W. Schaie. New York: Van Nostrand Reinhold.

Riley, M. W., M. E. Johnson, and A. Foner, eds. 1972. *Aging and society: A sociology of age stratification.* New York: Russell Sage Foundation.

Roberge, J. J. 1976. Developmental analyses of two formal operational structures: Combinatorial thinking and conditional reasoning. *Developmental Psychology* 12: 563–64.

Rosenberg, F. R., and R. G. Simmons. 1975. Sex differences in the self-concept in adolescence. *Sex Roles* 1: 147–59.

Rosenthal, P. 1966. *Experimenter effects in behavioral research.* New York: Appleton-Century-Crofts.

Roubertoux, P., and M. Carlier. 1978. Intelligence: Individual differences, genetic factors, environmental factors and interaction between genotype and environment. *Annales de Biologie Clinique* 36: 101.

Rubin, K. H., and K. T. Trotter. 1977. Kohlberg's moral judgment scale: Some methodological considerations. *Developmental Psychology* 13: 535–36.

Runyan, W. M. 1978. The life course as a theoretical orientation: Sequences of person-situation interaction. *Journal of Personality* 46: 569–93.

Runyan, W. M. 1980. A stage-state analysis of the life course. *Journal of Personality and Social Psychology* 38: 951–62.

Russo, N. F. 1976. The motherhood mandate. *Journal of Social Issues* 32: 143–53.

Salili, F., M. L. Maehr, and G. Gillmore. 1976. Achievement and morality: A cross-cultural analysis of causal attribution and evaluation. *Journal of Personality and Social Psychology* 33: 327–37.

Salzen, E., and C. C. Meyer. 1968. Reversibility of imprinting. *Journal of Comparative and Physiological Psychology* 66: 269–75.

Sameroff, A. 1975. Transactional models in early social relations. *Human Development,* 18: 65–79.

Sampson, E. E. 1977. Psychology and the American ideal. *Journal of Personality and Social Psychology* 35: 767–82.

Sanford, E. C. 1902. Mental growth and decay. *American Journal of Psychology* 13: 426–49.

Sanford, N. 1962. Developmental status of the entering freshman. In *The American College,* ed. N. Sanford. New York: Wiley.

Santrock, J. W. 1970. Influence of onset and type of paternal absence on the first four Eriksonian developmental crises. *Developmental Psychology* 3: 273–74.

Santrock, J. W. 1975. Father absence, perceived maternal behavior, and moral development in boys. *Child Development* 46: 753–57.

Sarason, S. B. 1973. Jewishness, Blackishness, and the nature-nurture controvesy. *American Psychologist* 28: 962–71.

Sarbin, T. R. 1977. Contextualism: A world view for modern psychology. In *Nebraska Symposium on motivation, 1976,* ed. J. K. Cole. Lincoln, Nebr.: University of Nebraska Press.

Scarr, S. 1982. Development is internally guided, not determined. *Contemporary Psychology* 27: 852–53.

Scarr, S., and K. McCartney. 1983. How people make their own environments: A theory of genotype → environment effects. *Child Development* 54: 424–35.

S. Scarr-Salapatek. 1971a. Unknowns in the IQ equation. *Science* 174: 1223–28.

S. Scarr-Salapatek. 1971b. Race, social class, and IQ. *Science* 174: 1285–95.

Schacter, B. 1968. Identity crisis and occupational processes: An intensive exploratory study of emotionally disturbed male adolescents. *Child Welfare* 47: 26–37.

Schaefer, E. S., and R. Q. Bell. 1958. Development of a parental attitude research instrument. *Child Development* 29: 339–61.

Schaie, K. W. 1959. Cross-sectional methods in the study of psychological aspects of aging. *Journal of Gerontology* 14: 208–15.

Schaie, K. W. 1965. A general model for the study of developmental problems. *Psychological Bulletin* 64: 92–107.

Schaie, K. W. 1979. The primary mental abilities in adulthood: An exploration in the development of psychometric intelligence. In *Life-span development and behavior,* vol. 2, ed. P. B. Baltes and O. G. Brim, Jr. New York: Academic Press.

Schaie, K. W., V. E. Anderson, G. E. McClearn, and J. Money, eds. 1975. *Developmental human behavior genetics.* Lexington, Mass.: Heath.

Schaie, K. W., G. V. Labouvie, and B. V. Buech. 1973. Generational and cohort-specific differences in adult cognitive functioning: A fourteen-year study of independent samples. *Developmental Psychology* 9: 151–66.

Schaie, K. W., and C. R. Strother. 1968. A cross-sequential study of age changes in cognitive behavior. *Psychological Bulletin* 70: 671–80.

Scheck, D. C., R. Emerick, and M. M. El-Assal. 1974. Adolescents' perceptions of parent-child external control orientation. *Journal of Marriage and the Family* 35: 643–54.

Schenkel, S. 1975. Relationship among ego identity status, field-independence, and traditional femininity. *Journal of Youth and Adolescence* 4: 73–82.

Schneirla, T. C. 1956. Interrelationships of the innate and the acquired in instinctive behavior. In *L'instinct dans le comportement des animaux et de l'homme,* ed. P. P. Grassé. Paris: Masson et Cie.

Schneirla, T. C. 1957. The concept of development in comparative psychology. In *The concept of development,* ed. D. B. Harris. Minneapolis: University of Minnesota Press.

Schneirla, T. C. 1959. An evolutionary and developmental theory of biphasic processes underlying approach and withdrawal. In *Nebraska Symposium on Motivation,* ed. M. R. Jones. Lincoln: University of Nebraska Press.

Schneirla, T. C. 1966. Instinct and aggression: Reviews of Konrad Lorenz, *Evolution and modification of behavior* (Chicago: The University of Chicago Press, 1965), and *On aggression* (New York: Harcourt, Brace & World, 1966). *Natural History* 75: 16.

Schneirla, T. C., and J. S. Rosenblatt. 1961.

Behavioral organization and genesis of the social bond in insects and mammals. *American Journal of Orthopsychiatry* 3: 223–53.

Schneirla, T. C., and J. S. Rosenblatt. 1963. Critical periods in behavioral development. *Science, 139,* 1110–14.

Schwebel, M. 1972. April. Logical thinking in college freshmen. Final report, Project No. O-B-105, Grant No. OEG-2-7-0039(509). Washington, D.C.: U.S. Office of Education.

Scott, J. P. 1962. Critical periods in behavioral development. *Science* 138: 949–58.

Sears, R. R. 1957. Identification as a form of behavioral development. In *The concept of development,* ed. D. B. Harris. Minneapolis: University of Minnesota Press.

Sears, R. R. 1975. Your ancients revisited. In *Review of child development research,* vol. 5, ed. E. M. Hetherington, J. W. Hagen, R. Kron, and A. H. Stein. Chicago: University of Chicago Press.

Secord, P. F., and C. W. Backman. 1964. *Social psychology.* New York: McGraw-Hill.

Self, P. A. 1975. The further evolution of the parental imperative. In *Life-span developmental psychology: Normative life crises,* ed. N. Datan and L. H. Ginsberg. New York: Academic Press.

Selman, R. L. 1976. Social cognitive understanding: A guide to educational and clinical practice. In *Moral development and behavior,* ed. T. Lickona. New York: Holt, Rinehart & Winston.

Shaffer, D. R. 1979. *Social and personality development.* Monterey, Calif.: Brooks/Cole.

Shappell, D. L., L. G. Hall, and R. B. Tarrier. 1971. Perceptions of the world of work: Inner-city versus suburbia. *Journal of Counseling Psychology* 18: 55–59.

Sheldon, W. H. 1940. *The varieties of human physique.* New York: Harper & Row.

Sheldon, W. H. 1942. *The varieties of temperament.* New York: Harper & Row.

Sherrington, C. S. 1951. *Man on his nature.* Cambridge: Cambridge University Press.

Shields, J. 1962. *Monozygotic twins brought*

up apart and brought up together. London: Oxford University Press.

Shirley, M. M. 1933. *The first two years.* Minneapolis: University of Minnesota Press.

Siegel, A. W., J. Bisanz, and G. L. Bisanz. 1983. Developmental analysis: A strategy for the study of psychological change. *Contributions to Human Development.* 8: 53–80.

Siegel, L. S., and C. J. Brainerd, eds. 1977. *Alternatives to Piaget: Critical essays on the theory.* New York: Academic Press.

Siegler, R. S., ed. 1978. *The origins of scientific reasoning. Children's thinking: What develops?* Hillsdale, N.J.: Erlbaum.

Siegler, R. 1981. Developmental sequences within and between concepts. *Monographs of the Society for Research in Child Development* 46 (189).

Sigel, I. E. 1979. A structuralist response to a skeptic. *The Behavioral and Brain Sciences* 2: 137–54.

Simmons, R. G., F. R. Rosenberg, and M. Rosenberg. 1973. Disturbances in the self-image in adolescence. *American Sociological Review* 38: 553–68.

Simmons, R. G., and F. Rosenberg. 1975. Sex, sex roles, and self-image. *Journal of Youth and Adolescence* 4: 229–58.

Simpson, E. L. 1974. Moral development research: A case study of scientific cultural bias. *Human Development* 17: 81–106.

Skinner, B. F. 1938. *The behavior of organisms.* New York: Appleton.

Skinner, B. F. 1950. Are theories of learning necessary? *Psychological Review* 57: 211–20.

Skinner, B. F. 1953. *Science and human behavior.* New York: Macmillan.

Skinner, B. F. 1956. A case history in scientific method. *American Psychologist* 11: 221–33.

Skinner, B. F. 1966. The phylogeny and ontogeny of behavior. *Science* 153: 1205–1213.

Slaby, R. G., and A. R. Hollenbeck. 1977. *Television influences on visual and vocal behavior of infants.* Paper presented at the Biennial Meeting of the Society for Research in Child Development, March, New Orleans.

Snyder, M. 1981. On the influence of individuals on situations. In *Cognition, social interaction, and personality,* ed. N. Cantor and J. F. Kihlstrom. Hillsdale, N.J.: Erlbaum.

Sorell, G. T., and C. A. Nowak. 1981. The role of physical attractiveness as a contributor to individual development. In *Individuals as producers of their development: A life-span perspective,* ed. R. M. Lerner and N. A. Busch-Rossnagel. New York: Academic Press.

Spanier, G. B., and P. C. Glick. 1979. The life cycle of American families: An expanded analysis. *Journal of Family History* 4: 97–111.

Spence, J. T., and R. Helmreich. 1978. *Masculinity and femininity: Their psychological dimensions, correlates and antecedents.* Austin: University of Texas Press.

Sroufe, L. A. 1979. The coherence of individual development. *American Psychologist* 34: 834–41.

Sroufe, L. A., and E. Waters. 1977. Attachment as an organizational construct. *Child Development* 48: 1184–99.

Stern, C. 1973. *Principles of human genetics.* 3d ed. San Francisco: Freeman.

Stevens, S. S. 1946. On the theory of scales of measurement. *Science* 103: 677–80.

Strauss, S., J. Danziger, and T. Ramati. 1977. University students' understanding of nonconservation: Implications for structural reversion. *Developmental Psychology* 13: 359–63.

Streissguth, A. P., S. Landesman-Dwyer, J. C. Martin, and D. W. Smith. 1980. Teratogenic effects of alcohol in humans and laboratory animals. *Science* 209: 353–61.

Suomi, S. J., and H. F. Harlow. 1972. Social rehabilitation of isolate-reared monkeys. *Developmental Psychology* 6: 487–96.

Super, C. M., and S. Harkness, eds. 1980. Anthropological perspectives on child development. *New Directions for Child Development*, 8.

Super, C. M., and S. Harkness. 1981. Figure, ground, and Gestalt: The cultural context of the active individual. In *Individuals as producers of their development: A life-span perspective*, ed. R. M. Lerner and N. A. Busch-Rossnagel. New York: Academic Press.

Surber, C. F. 1977. Developmental processes in social inference: Averaging of intentions and consequences in moral judgment. *Developmental Psychology* 13: 654–65.

Sutton-Smith, B. 1973. *Child psychology.* New York: Appleton-Century-Crofts.

Swartz, D. 1982. Is it sex? *The Sciences* 22: 2.

Terman, L. M. 1916. *The measurement of intelligence.* Boston: Houghton.

Terman, L. M., ed. 1925. *Genetic studies of genius, I: Mental and physical traits of a thousand gifted children.* Stanford, Calif.: Stanford University Press.

Terman, L. M., and M. H. Oden. 1959. *Genetic studies of genius, V: The gifted group at mid-life.* Palo Alto, Calif.: Stanford University Press.

Terman, L. M., and L. E. Tyler. 1954. Psychological sex differences. In *Manual of child psychology,* ed. L. Carmichael. New York: Wiley.

Thomas, A., and S. Chess. 1970. Behavioral individuality in childhood. In *Development and evolution of behavior,* ed. L. R. Aronson, E. Tobach, D. Lehrman, and J. S. Rosenblatt. San Francisco: W. H. Freeman and Co.

Thomas, A., and S. Chess. 1977. *Temperament and development.* New York: Brunner/Mazel.

Thomas, A., and S. Chess. 1980. *The dynamics of psychological development.* New York: Brunner/Mazel.

Thomas, A., and S. Chess. 1981. The role of temperament in the contributions of individuals to their development. In *Individuals as producers of their development: A life-span perspective,* ed.

R. M. Lerner and N. A. Busch-Rossnagel. New York: Academic Press.

Thomas, A., S. Chess, and H. G. Birch. 1968. *Temperament and behavior disorders in children.* New York: New York University Press.

Thomas, A., S. Chess, and H. G. Birch. 1970. The origin of personality. *Scientific American* 223: 102–9.

Thomas, A., S. Chess, H. G. Birch, M. E. Hertzig, and S. Korn. 1963. *Behavioral individuality in early childhood.* New York: New York University Press.

Thomas, A., S. Chess, and S. J. Korn. 1982. The reality of difficult temperament. *Merrill-Palmer Quarterly* 28: 1–20.

Thomas, A., S. Chess, J. Sillen, and O. Mendez. 1974. Cross-cultural study of behavior in children with special vulnerabilities to stress. In *Life history research in psychopathology,* ed. D. F. Ricks, A. Thomas, and M. Roff. Minneapolis: University of Minnesota Press.

Thorndike, E. L. 1904. The newest psychology. *Educational Review* 28: 217–27.

Thorndike, E. L. 1905. *The elements of psychology.* New York: Seiler.

Thorpe, W. 1961. Sensitive periods in the learning of animals and man: A study of imprinting. In *Current problems in animal behavior,* ed. W. Thorpe and O. Zangwill. Cambridge, England: Cambridge University Press.

Timney, B., D. E. Mitchell, and F. Griffin. 1978. The development of vision in cats after extended periods of dark-rearing. *Experimental Brain Research* 31: 547–60.

Tobach, E. 1978. The methodology of sociobiology from the viewpoint of a comparative psychologist. In *The sociobiology debate,* ed. A. L. Caplan. New York: Harper & Row.

Tobach, E. 1981. Evolutionary aspects of the activity of the organism and its development. In *Individuals as producers of their development: A life-span perspective,* ed. R. M. Lerner and N. A. Busch-Rossnagel. New York: Academic Press.

Tobach, E., J. Gianutsos, H. R. Topoff, and C. G. Gross. 1974. *The four horses: Racism, sexism, militarism, and social Darwinism.* New York: Behavioral Publications.

Tobach, E., and G. Greenberg. 1984. The significance of T. C. Schneirla's contribution to the concept of levels of integration. In *Behavioral evolution and integrative levels,* ed. G. Greenberg and E. Tobach. Hillsdale, N.J.: Erlbaum.

Tobach, E., and T. C. Schneirla. 1968. The biopsychology of social behavior of animals. In R. E. Cooke and S. Levin, eds., *Biologic basis of pediatric practice.* New York: McGraw-Hill.

Toder, N. L., and J. E. Marcia. 1973. Ego identity status and response to conformity pressure in college women. *Journal of Personality and Social Psychology* 26: 287–94.

Tomlinson-Keasey, C. 1972. Formal operation in females from eleven to fifty-four years of age. *Developmental Psychology* 6: 364.

Tomlinson-Keasey, C., and C. B. Keasey. 1974. The mediating role of cognitive development in moral judgment. *Child Development* 45: 291–98.

Toulmin, S. 1981. Epistemology and developmental psychology. In *Developmental plasticity: Behavioral and biological aspects of variations in development,* ed. E. S. Gollin. New York: Academic Press.

Towler, J. O., and G. Wheatley. 1971. Conservation concepts in college students: A replication and critique. *Journal of Genetic Psychology* 118: 265–70.

Traeldal, A., 1973, August. The work role and life satisfaction over the life-span. Paper presented at the Biennial Meeting of the International Society for the Study of Behavioral Development, Ann Arbor, Mich.

Trivers, R. L. 1971. The evolution of reciprocal altruism. *The Quarterly Review of Biology* 46: 35–39, 45–47.

Tuddenham, R. D. 1959. The constancy of personality ratings over two decades. *Genetic Psychology Monographs* 60: 3–29.

Turiel, E. 1969. Developmental processes in the child's moral thinking. In *Trends and issues in developmental psychology,* ed. P. H. Mussen, J. Langer, and M. Covington. New York: Holt, Rinehart & Winston.

Turiel, E. 1974. Conflict and transition in adolescent moral development. *Child Development* 45: 14–29.

Turiel, E. 1978. The development of concepts of social structure: Social convention. In *The development of social understanding,* ed. J. Glick and A. Clarke-Stewart. New York: Gardner Press.

Turiel, E., and G. Rothman. 1972. The influence of reasoning on behavioral choices at different stages of moral development. *Child Development* 43: 741–56.

Uphouse, L. L., and J. Bonner. 1975. Preliminary evidence for the effects of environmental complexity on hybridization of rat brain RNA to rat unique DNA. *Developmental Psychobiology* 8: 171–78.

U.S. Bureau of the Census. 1978. *Statistical Abstract of the United States: 1978.* 99th ed. Washington: U.S. Government Printing Office.

U.S. Bureau of the Census. 1978a. Characteristics of American children and youth: 1976. *Current Population Reports,* ser. P-23, no. 66. Washington: U.S. Government Printing Office, January.

U.S. Bureau of the Census. 1978b. School enrollment—social and economic characteristics of students: October, 1976. *Current Population Reports,* ser. P-20, no. 319. Washington: U.S. Government Printing Office, February.

U.S. Bureau of the Census. 1978c. Perspectives on American husbands and wives. *Current Population Reports,* ser. P-23, no. 77. Washington: U.S. Government Printing Office, December.

U.S. Bureau of the Census. 1980. *Statistical Abstract of the United States.*

U.S. Department of Health, Education and Welfare. 1978. *Vital statistics of the United States, 1976.* Hyattsville, Md.: National Center for Health Statistics.

van den Daele, L. D. 1969. Qualitative models in developmental analysis. *Developmental Psychology* 1: 303–10.

van den Daele, L. D. 1974. Infrastructure and transition in developmental analysis. *Human Development* 17: 1–23.

van den Daele, L. D. 1975. Ego development and preferential judgment in lifespan perspective. In *Lifespan developmental psychology: Normative life crises,* ed. N. Datan and L. H. Ginsburg. New York: Academic Press.

Veevers, J. E. 1973. Voluntarily childless wives: An exploratory study. *Sociology and Social Research* 57: 356–66.

von Noorden, G. K., Dowling, J. E., and Ferguson, D. C. 1970. Experimental amblyopia in monkeys: I. Behavioral studies of stimulus deprivation amblyopia. *Archives of Ophthalmology,* 84: 206–14.

von Noorden, G. K., and A. E. Maumenee. 1968. Clinical observations on stimulus deprivation amblyopia (*amblyopia ex anopsia*). *Journal of Ophthalmology* 64: 220–24.

Waddington, C. H. 1957. *The strategy of genes.* London: George Allen and Unwin.

Waddington, C. H. 1966. *Principles of development and differentiation.* New York: Macmillan.

Wadsworth, B. J. 1971. *Piaget's theory of cognitive develoment.* New York: McKay.

Wahler, R. G. 1980. Parent insularity as a determinant of generalization success in family treatment. In *The ecosystem of the "sick" child, implications for classification and intervention for disturbed and mentally retarded children,* ed. S. Salzinger, J. Antrobus, and J. Glich. New York: Academic Press.

Walker, L. J., and B. S. Richards. 1976. The effects of a narrative model on children's moral judgments. *Canadian Journal of Behavioral Science* 8: 169–77.

Washburn, S. L., ed. 1961. *Social life of early man.* New York: Wenner-Gren Foundation for Anthropological Research.

Washburn, S. L. 1982. Is it sex? *The Sciences* 22:2.

Waterman, A. S. 1982. Identity development from adolescence to adulthood: An extension of theory and a review of research. *Developmental Psychology* 18: 341–58.

Waterman, C. K., M. E. Beubel, and A. S. Waterman. 1970. Relationship between resolution of the identity crisis and outcomes of previous psychosocial crises. *Proceedings of the 78th Annual Convention of the American Psychological Association* 5: 467–68.

Waterman, G., P. Geary, and C. Waterman. 1974. Longitudinal study of changes in ego identity status from the freshman to the senior year at college. *Development Psychology* 10: 387–92.

Waterman, A. S., and J. A. Goldman. 1976. A longitudinal study of ego identity development of a liberal arts college. *Journal of Youth and Adolescence* 5: 361–70.

Waterman, A. S., E. Kohutis, and J. Pulone. 1977. The role of expressive writing in ego identity formation. *Developmental Psychology* 13: 286–87.

Waterman, A. S., and C. K. Waterman. 1971. A longitudinal study of changes in ego identity status during the freshman year at college. *Developmental Psychology* 5: 167–73.

Watson, J. B. 1913. Psychology as the behaviorist views it. *Psychological Review* 20: 158–77.

Watson, J. B. 1914. *Behavior: An introduction to comparative psychology.* New York: Holt.

Watson, J. B. 1918. *Psychology from the standpoint of a behaviorist.* Philadelphia: Lippincott.

Watson, J. B. 1928. *Psychological care of infant and child.* New York: Norton.

Watson, J. B., and R. Raynor. 1920. Conditional emotional reactions. *Journal of Experimental Psychology* 3: 1–14.

Watson, R. I. 1977. Psychology: A prescriptive science. In *R. I. Watson's selected papers on the history of psychology,* ed. J. Brozek and R. B. Evans. Hanover, N.H.: University of New Hampshire Press.

Webb, E. J., D. T., Campbell, R. D. Schwartz, and L. Sechrest. 1966. *Unobtrusive measures: Nonreactive research in the social sciences.* Chicago: Rand McNally.

Weiner, B., and N. Peter. 1973. A cognitive-developmental analysis of achievement and moral judgment. *Developmental Psychology* 9: 290–309.

Werner, H. 1948. *Comparative psychology of mental development.* New York: International Universities Press.

Werner, H. 1957. The concept of development from a comparative and organismic point of view. In *The concept of development,* ed. D. B. Harris. Minneapolis: University of Minnesota Press.

Werner, H., and B. Kaplan. 1956. The developmental approach to cognition: Its relevance to the psychological interpretation of anthropological and ethnolinguistic data. *American Anthropologist* 58: 866–80.

Werner, H., and B. Kaplan. 1963. *Symbol formation: An organismic-developmental approach to language and the expression of thought.* New York: Wiley.

White, C. B. 1975. Moral development in Bahamian school children: A cross-cultural examination of Kohlberg's stages of moral reasoning. *Developmental Psychology* 11: 535–36.

White, C. B., N. Bushnell, and J. L. Regnemer. 1978. Moral development in Bahamian school children: A 3-year examination of Kohlberg's stages of moral development. *Developmental Psychology* 14: 58–65.

White, S. H. 1968. The learning-maturation controversy: Hall to Hull. *Merrill-Palmer Quarterly* 14: 187–96.

White, S. H. 1970. The learning theory tradition and child psychology. In *Carmichael's manual of child psychology,* 3d ed., ed. P. H. Mussen. New York: Wiley.

White, S. H. 1976. The active organism in theoretical behaviorism. *Human Development* 19: 99–107.

Wiesel, T. N., and D. H. Hubel. 1965. Extent of recovery from the effects of visual deprivation in kittens. *Journal of Neurophysiology* 28: 1060–72.

Willems, E. P. 1973. Behavioral ecology and experimental analysis: Courtship is not enough. In *Life-span developmental psychology: Methodological issues,* ed. J. R. Nesselroade and H. W. Reese. New York: Academic Press.

Willis, S. L. 1982. Concepts from life span developmental psychology: Implications for programming. In *New directions for continuing education: Programs for older adults* (no. 14), ed. M. Okun. San Francisco: Jossey-Bass.

Willis, S. L., and P. B. Baltes. 1980. Intelligence in adulthood and aging: Contemporary issues. In *Aging in the 1980s: Psychological issues,* ed. L. W. Poon. Washington: American Psychological Association.

Wilson, E. O. 1975. *Sociobiology: The new synthesis.* Cambridge, Mass.: Harvard University Press.

Winch, R. F. 1971. *The modern family.* 3d ed. New York: Holt, Rinehart & Winston.

Winch, R. F., and G. B. Spanier. 1974. Scientific method in the study of the family. In *Selected studies in marriage and the family,* 4th ed., ed. R. F. Winch and G. B. Spanier. New York: Holt, Rinehart & Winston.

Wohlwill, J. F. 1963. Piaget's system as a source of empirical research. *Merrill-Palmer Quarterly* 9: 253–62.

Wohlwill, J. F. 1973. *The study of behavioral development.* New York: Academic Press.

Wohlwill, J. 1980. Cognitive development in childhood. In *Constancy and change in human development,* ed. O. G. Brim, Jr., and J. Kagan. Cambridge: Harvard University Press.

Worell, J. 1978. Sex roles and psychological well-being: Perspectives on methodology. *Journal of Consulting and Clinical Psychology* 46: 777–91.

Wylie, R. C. 1974. *The self-concept.* Vol. 1. Lincoln: University of Nebraska Press.

Yarczower, M., and L. Hazlett. 1977. Evolutionary scales and anagenesis. *Psychological Bulletin* 84: 1088–97.

Yarczower, M., and B. S. Yarczower. 1979. In defense of anagenesis, grades, and evolutionary scales. *Psychological Bulletin* 86: 880–84.

Youniss, J., and A. Dean. 1974. Judgment and imagery aspects of operations: A Piagetian study with Korean and Costa Rican children. *Child Development* 45: 1020–31.

Yussen, S. R. 1976. Moral reasoning from the perspective of others. *Child Development* 47: 551–55.

Zukav, G. 1979. *The dancing Wu Li Masters.* New York: Bantam Books.

NAME INDEX

SUBJECT INDEX

PHOTO CREDITS

P. 14 New York Public Library Collection. **16** National Library of Medicine. **21** Culver Pictures. **24** Courtesy of the University of Chicago. **26** Courtesy of the University of Michigan, photo by Bob Kalmbach. **27** Courtesy of the New York State College of Human Ecology at Cornell University. **92** Courtesy of Fordham University, photo by Tommy Weber. **152** Ralph Buchsbaum. **170** Thomas McAvoy, Life Magazine © Time Inc. **193** Courtesy of International Universities Press. **245** AP/Wide World Photos. **253** Courtesy of University of Rochester Medical Center. **268** Courtesy of Harvard University News Office. **293** National Library of Medicine. **417** K. Bendo.

TEXT AND ILLUSTRATION CREDITS

P. 2 Figure 1.1 copyright 1973 by the American Psychological Association. Used by permission of the publisher and the author, K. W. Schaie. **P. 3** Figure 1.2 used by permission of Academic Press. **P. 37** Figure 1.4 copyright © 1966 by Rand McNally & Company, Chicago. Reprinted by permission of Rand McNally College Publishing Company.

P. 74 Figure 2.3 copyright 1962 by the American Psychological Association. Used by permission of the publisher and the author, Howard H. Kendler.

Pp. 110–112, 114–115 quotations and Tables 4.1, 4.2, and 4.3 copyright 1974 by the American Psychological Association. Reprinted by permission of the publisher and the author, L. Kamin. **Pp. 114, 137** quotations copyright © 1981 and reprinted by permission of Sage Publications, Inc., and Jerry Hirsch. **Pp. 116–117, 130** quotations reprinted with permission of Stephen J. Gould and *The New York Review of Books*. Copyright © 1980 Nyrev, Inc. **P. 118** Table 4.4 copyright © 1981 by the American Association for the Advancement of Science. Reprinted by permission of the publisher and the author, T. Bouchard, Jr. **Pp. 125–126, 127–128, 130, 137–138** quotations copyright © 1975 by the American Society for the Advancement of Science. Reprinted by permission of the publisher and the author, Marcus W. Feldman. **Pp. 125–127, 136** Figure 4.1 and quotations copyright © 1974 by the American Society for the Advancement of Science. Reprinted by permission of the publisher and the author, David Layzer. **Pp. 127, 130** Figures 4.2 and 4.3 copyright © 1975 by the American Association for the Advancement of Science. Used by permission of the publisher and the author, Marcus W. Feldman. **Pp. 133, 134** Tables 4.5 and 4.6 reprinted by permission of Tieto Ltd.

P. 151 Figure 5.1 used by permission of Donald C. Johanson. **P. 160** Figure 5.4 copyright 1963 by the Society for Research in Child Development, Inc. **P. 176** Figure 5.6 used by permission of Academic Press. **P. 177** Figure 5.7 used by permission of Cambridge University Press.

About the Author

Richard M. Lerner is professor of child and adolescent development and professor in charge of the graduate program in human development and family studies at Pennsylvania State University. He received his Ph.D. in psychology from the City University of New York in 1971. He is the author or editor of fifteen books and more than a hundred journal articles and book chapters. He is on the editorial boards of *Child Development* and *Developmental Psychology,* is the Associate Editor of the *International Journal of Behavioral Development,* and is co-editor of the annual series *Life-Span Development and Behavior.* He was a 1980–81 fellow at the Center for Advanced Study in the Behavioral Sciences, a visiting scientist in 1983 at the Max-Planck Institute for Human Development and Education in Berlin, and a co-director of the Center for Advanced Study in the Behavioral Sciences' Summer Institute on "Individual Development and Social Change." He is a fellow of the American Psychological Association and the American Association for the Advancement of Science. He has written extensively about philosophical and theoretical issues in human development and is noted for his research on children's and adolescents' personality and social development. His current research involves a longitudinal study of early adolescent development.